In My Father's House
Are Many Mansions

The Fred W. Morrison Series
in Southern Studies

In My Father's House
Are Many Mansions

Family and Community in Edgefield, South Carolina

ORVILLE VERNON BURTON

The University of North Carolina Press

Chapel Hill and London

Library of Congress Cataloging in Publication Data

Burton, Orville Vernon.

In my Father's house are many mansions.

(The Fred W. Morrison series in Southern studies)

Bibliography: p.

Includes Index

1. Edgefield (S.C.)—Social conditions.   2. Edgefield
(S.C.)—Rural conditions.   3. Family—South Carolina—
Edgefield—History—19th century.   4. Edgefield (S.C.)—
Race relations—History—19th century.   I. Title.

II. Series.

HN79.S62E343   1985   306'.09757'37   84-25830

ISBN 0-8078-1619-1

For Vera Beatrice and
Vera Joanna Burton

Contents

List of Tables

List of Figures and Maps

MAPS

List of Illustrations

Preface

The Bible taught black and white Southerners long ago what historians are now asserting: that the family is a crucial determinant of human behavior. Because many questions of southern history have reached a stage of debate where we now need to investigate the issues in the most concrete surroundings possible, I am engaged in an ongoing study of life in one rural county, Edgefield, South Carolina. There family and community mesh together in the kind of setting where most nineteenth-century Southerners played out their roles.

I have tried to construct as much as possible a total, almost encyclopedic, history of nineteenth-century Edgefield families and their communities. On most subjects, I have let the people of nineteenth-century Edgefield speak for themselves. For example, as interpreted in their churches and homes, the religious views of nineteenth-century Edgefieldians, for most, evangelical Protestantism, explained the meaning of their existence.

The history of the South was and is the history of both blacks and whites. I have tried to explore how all Southerners lived before and after the Civil War in an agrarian society. With this project completed, I see that I have just begun that exploration, and I plan in other works to examine the interaction of Edgefield blacks and whites in more detail.

One reason why I selected Edgefield as a case study is that it affords an abundance of excellent scholarship. Edgefield's local history association has been most active in acquiring information over the years, and my debt is great to a number of local genealogists and historians. I greatly benefited from Richard Maxwell Brown's works, especially his essay that focused on Edgefield for a national audience. Edgefieldian Francis Butler Simkins's books and articles are invaluable guides to understanding Edgefield. Published biographies exist for Louis Wigfall, William Gregg, George McDuffie, Daniel Augustus Tompkins, and Thomas Green Clemson. James Henry Hammond has attracted four biographers, three of whom have had their works published: Elizabeth Merritt, Robert C. Tucker, Drew Gilpin Faust, and Carol Bleser. Dissertations have treated Francis W. Pickens, Daniel Augustus Tompkins, Benjamin Ryan Tillman, John Gary Evans, and J. Strom Thurmond. Recent dissertations of a more social science character have also focused on Edgefield as part of the Augusta hinterlands. Randolph Werner applied central place theory to the Edgefield area, and J. William Harris, in a model of regional study, compared antebellum Edgefield to Georgia counties. Lewis Chartock included Edgefield as one of the counties in his pioneering analysis of Freedmen's Bureau labor contracts. In addition, Douglas Deal shared his careful quantitative study of Edgefield district from 1850 to 1860. Tom Terrill's articles on Graniteville also contain useful quantitative and qualitative material. I have also benefited immensely from a number of published and unpublished articles and master's theses on various people and events in Edgefield. In every instance where I have quoted or cited the same primary source material as any of these other scholars, I have gone to the original sources (sometimes using other scholars' notes as guides). No one else should be liable for my interpretations. This book owes much to the work of many other historians; I hope in turn my work will benefit others.

The works of these historians on Edgefield and Edgefieldians tend to reinforce Richard Maxwell Brown's belief that in its impact on South Carolina history and in South Carolina's impact on national history, Edgefield County, although little known outside the state, is one of the most historically significant local communities in America. I am proud for my work to be a part of a growing body of Edgefield studies.

I have been studying Edgefield for more years than I would like to remember, and I have benefited from the support, advice, and criticism of innumerable scholars. In addition, more than two hundred nonacademicians have provided me with food and lodging in the course of my research. To recount all who made this possible would require its own book; I can only hope that this book in itself repays the kindnesses and generosity shown me. Mention in this acknowledgment does not begin to express the extent of my gratitude for the contributions of so many.

To support my research, I was fortunate to receive a Rockefeller Foundation Humanities Fellowship and an American Council of Learned Societies Grant in Aid for Recent Recipients of the Ph.D. Although not given for this specific project, these grants contributed toward it.

Sections of this book draw upon earlier published articles, and permission to reprint portions is gratefully acknowledged. Town and country differences discussed to some extent in this book are elaborated on in "The Rise and Fall of Afro-American Town Life" (published in *Toward a New South?* edited by Orville Vernon Burton and Robert McMath, Jr. [Westport: Greenwood Press, 1982]). My discussion of antebellum free blacks in chapter five is an elaboration of "Anatomy of an Antebellum Rural Free Black Community" (*Southern Studies* 21 [Fall 1982]: 294–325).

The Research Board of the University of Illinois made possible keypunching, computer time, some typing costs, and support for graduate research assistants. I appreciate all and especially the research assistants, who helped with various tasks. From the history department, a special thanks to James

Ducker and Charles Moss, who labored long hours with me coding, entering, and checking data. The same is true for Tony Fahey from the Sociology Department, who worked through not only years of data errors but sociological theory as well. Thomas B. Watkins of the Educational Policy Studies Department spent many late hours with me as we worked on data management schemes, the merging of huge data files, and appropriate statistical tests for historical data. David Davenport of the Geography Department labored over statistics and maps to trace people, locate where Edgefieldians lived, retrace census enumerators' routes, and determine the reliability of census records.

Because quantitative techniques and computers have been important tools in this study of Edgefield, the Computing Services Office of the University of Illinois has been invaluable. The people there have spent endless hours of consulting time with me, allowed me to run huge computer jobs across tielines that stopped everything else for a day, and provided keypunching, graphics capabilities, and terminals. From top to bottom, I have never dealt with a finer group of people. The Social Science Quantitative Laboratory, the Social Science Research Survey Laboratory, and the Mathematical and Statistical Consulting Committee have all aided me at various times, answering my questions and helping me with computer programs and applications. Special thanks to Mrs. Francis Sykes for keypunching, Kevin Barnes for special computer consultation, and Gregory A. German for help with graphs.

I am indebted to several of my former students at the University of Illinois: Tracy Childs, Scott Fiducci, Bill Link, Albert Madden, Carl Phillips, Volie Pyles, Maria Richter, Jeff Rubin, Tom Taylor, Susan Westbury, and Bob Winters. Barbara Feltes read and made suggestions on the book manuscript as well as worked with the Edgefield Data Set. Barry Mehler, who shares my interest in the computer, quantitative techniques, and their applications for historians and social scientists, has made useful suggestions about statistical presentations in this book. Stephen Preskill is the kind of graduate student who makes teaching a rewarding profession. His suggestions were excellent, and exchanging ideas with Steve has been an intellectually exciting experience.

Donna Reed graciously loaned me her typewriter. Irene Blenker, Diana Burtch, Carol Luckenbill, Joyce McFarlane, Nadine Rutledge, and Gwen Varnell all typed portions of the manuscript.

The people of Edgefield County, South Carolina—librarians, county officials, and all with whom I dealt—were eager to help. Among local historians several have been especially helpful to me. David Richardson Parker has been an invaluable supplier of new manuscript sources. Hortense Woodson is the unchallenged authority for Edgefield's history. Her personal library and archives are perhaps the best source for Edgefield history. Mr. and Mrs. Charles Bruce Bailey, Sr., Mrs. Janie Harrison, Benjamin E. Mays, and Catherine and Pat Williams were invaluable in providing me with an appreciation of the Afro-American perspective on Edgefield's history. Hendrik Booraem, Bruce

Ezell, Augustus Graydon, June Henderson, J. Hilton Lewis, Carlee McClendon, Mrs. Billy R. McKinney, Mrs. Julian Mims, Sr., W. W. Mims, Bettis Cantelou Rainsford, and Motte J. Yarbrough all shared knowledge of Edgefieldians or sources with me.

The staffs of all research libraries listed in the bibliography, as well as of the University of Illinois, were always courteous, supportive, and helpful. The South Carolina Department of Archives and History and the South Caroliniana Library deserve special recognition. Wylma Wates, Julian Mims (who also shared his own research with me), and a host of others, especially the night staff, guided me through the archives. While she worked at the Caroliniana, for a time I lived with Mrs. Ollie and the Reverend Owens. As any researcher in South Carolina knows, Allen Stokes and his staff have created an excellent research atmosphere at the Caroliniana. My debt to Allen in helping me locate manuscripts and sources, as well as for his friendship, which I cherish, is greater than can be expressed here.

This book began as a thirty-page chapter of my dissertation. I presented that chapter to the Shelby Cullum Davis Center for Historical Studies at Princeton University in 1976. As I began rewriting the chapter as an article, I needed some advice, and several persons read that extended article and made comments. The gist of that article is now in chapter 7, thanks to the comments of Ira Berlin, David Carlton, Janet Cornelius, Eric Foner, Myron Guttman, Leslie Moch, John Pierson, Demitri Shimkin, Dan Scott Smith, and Scott Strickland.

As a student of communities, I have come to appreciate our special community of scholars. For moral support when we write, particularly these first-book efforts, most of us need the encouragement and advice of others. Especially supportive and helpful to me on this book were Stanley Engerman, Drew Gilpin Faust, J. William Harris, J. Morgan Kousser, Robert C. McMath, and John Modell.

My teachers at Furman University, the Harvard-Yale-Columbia Intensive Summer Studies Program (ISSP), and Princeton University continue to be sources of inspiration. James McPherson has continued to read my manuscript and offer wise counsel; my admiration for him as a scholar, teacher, and friend has continued to grow since my first course with him. My colleagues at the University of Illinois have also extended personal courtesies and encouragement. Frederic Cople Jaher has read most of this manuscript and made especially sarcastic but useful suggestions.

A special debt of thanks goes to Jeremy Tennenbaum. No greater love hath any man than to drive a dilapidated Chevrolet from New York to Urbana to work day and night through a friend's murky quagmire of words and ideas. This book has benefited greatly by the efforts of all mentioned above.

I am fortunate to have the best editor in the United States as my friend. Lewis Bateman recognized the potential of this book manuscript when it was

130 pages of text and 227 tables. Lewis's skills as an editor are surpassed only by his loyalty to friends. My respect for Lewis's judgment saved readers of this book twice the text and more tables than most could imagine. He has left me with a lifetime of work turning deleted material into articles. David Perry, my manuscript editor at the University of North Carolina Press, has also helped to make this a better book. He has calmly accepted rewrites, additions, deletions, recalculations, and missed deadlines.

In My Father's House, which studied the family, was also a family affair. My children, Joanna, Maya, Morgan, Beatrice, and Ali helped by entering data into the computer, copying tombstone inscriptions, and reminding me of the really important things in life. I have the best family in the world.

Finally, there is Georganne, my northern urban wife, who enjoys the world and ways of a rural Southerner and Baptist. From her I derive my strength, my confidence, and my inspiration. This book could never have been completed without her. Like my love, my thanks to her knows no bounds.

I dedicate this book to the wisest and kindest person I know, my mother, Vera Beatrice Human Burton, who exemplifies the best in the South—the beauty, grace, and goodness—and who reared me in a female-headed household, and to Vera Joanna Burton, my eldest daughter, who, along with my mother, has been with me on this project the longest, and who, but for the grace of God, the prayers of my church and friends, and the skill of attorney Burt Greaves (who will dispute this order of importance), would have been reared in a single parent female-headed household.

In My Father's House
Are Many Mansions

Introduction

*By the grace of God, my kinfolk and I are Carolinians. . . . We are
interested in our ancestors—they were us in another age.*

Ben Robertson, *Red Hills and Cotton*

The importance of family in the South, while long noted, has been little
studied.[1] This history of family and community in nineteenth-century Edgefield, South Carolina, is intended to convey the enormous richness and complexity of family and community life, a life complicated by the violent strains
of slavery, Civil War, freedom, Reconstruction, and Redemption.[2]

In My Father's House investigates the actual experience of nineteenth-
century Edgefield families by comparing black and white families within a
single large community and by exploring the differences and similarities between the values of southern whites and Afro-Americans.* This study shows
the ties that bound black and white together—ties of exploitation and oppression, of charity and cooperation. It examines the cultural values and standards
of behavior that parents and community leaders taught their children, the
questions of infidelity, illegitimacy, one-person households, and single-parent
families. Finally, it shows how different classes were tied together by life on
the land and a common commitment to the preservation of "southern values."

This book is the product of a thorough study of letters and family histories,
newspapers, former slave narratives, and local government and church records. Works drawing on such traditional sources tend to focus on the elite and
therefore give an incomplete understanding of the agrarian South. This volume, however, tries to merge traditional historical sources with statistical
analyses of census information on every household, family, and farm in the
area.† This comprehensive data base and the great amount of archival material

*Afro-American and *black* are synonymous and can be taken to mean both blacks and mulattoes.
In the analysis of differences between mulatto and nonmulatto Afro-Americans, however, "Afro-
American" still refers to both groups, but "black" signifies nonmulatto. *Mulatto* means a person
of mixed black and white parentage. The mixture was visible to the census enumerator, who
determined the classification on the basis of physical appearance.

†*Household* is used as a term distinct from the word *family*. Household is simply a unit of measure
which refers to the census grouping listed as a household by the census enumerator. The household

which exists for Edgefield offer an outstanding opportunity to test hypotheses regarding family and community life. Social history should mediate between traditional history and social theory.[3] This book is an effort to merge older, time-tested methods with more recent quantitative ones in order to present a "total history" of Edgefield before and after the Civil War. Furthermore, the book's concentration on a rural locale fills a gap: by and large, the new social historians have directed their attention to cities, even though most nineteenth-century Americans lived in rural areas and small towns during the crucial antebellum and postbellum years.[4]

I selected Edgefield for a case study of a southern community for four reasons: representativeness, diversity, leadership, and scholarship (see preface). This study focuses on the nineteenth century, and the primary statistical data base for black and white comparisons is from 1850 to 1880. Robert Swierenga argues persuasively that communities for study should be selected as representative of certain types or regions "based on multivariate analyses of characteristics that vary among communities—such as size, spatial organization, degree of urbanization, rate of growth, economic function, etc. In this way, each community can be identified and located along various continua."[5] In Swierenga's ecological and social system, Edgefield was representative of the large Piedmont section of the up-country that stretched from North Carolina, through South Carolina, to Georgia. Edgefield was rural; the few towns were small. Almost all the people farmed, and farming techniques used in Edgefield were representative of techniques used throughout the Carolina and Georgia Piedmont.[6]

Nineteenth-century Edgefield County was a typical rural area of South Carolina. The majority of the work force, farmers, faced the same adversities—western competition, cotton and slave price fluctuations, and soil exhaustion—and made the same adjustments as farmers elsewhere in the state. Statistical comparisons also suggest that Edgefield County was representative of rural South Carolina in the mid-nineteenth century. As shown in Fig. I-I, Edgefield's black population as a proportion of the total paralleled that of South Carolina for most of the nineteenth century. Edgefield demographic patterns (age and gender structure, death and birth rates) were also remarkably like those of rural South Carolina as a whole. Excluding the city of Charleston, Edgefield's statistical totals (of persons not born in South Carolina, blacks, mulattoes, average farm sizes, proportion of landowners, proportion literate,

---

head is the first individual listed for a given household. Household is the unit of analysis generally used in studying the family, particulary because before 1880 the relationship of household members was not listed. In the nineteenth century the important functions of the family were social welfare, transmission of culture, and economic suppport; thus, household structure is crucial. For a working definition of "family" see Degler, *At Odds*, pp. 3–4.

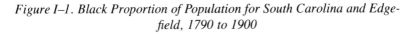

Figure I–1. Black Proportion of Population for South Carolina and Edge-field, 1790 to 1900

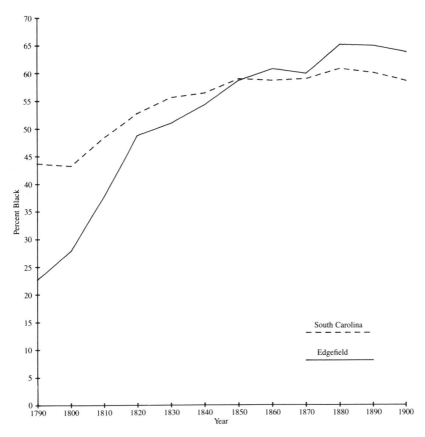

Note: See Table 1–1 for sources and notes.

proportion of improved acreage) were nearly identical to the averages for all rural counties in the state.[7]

Other South Carolinians have remarked on Edgefield's representative character. According to journalist William Watts Ball's *The State That Forgot*, Edgefield's leading families, "gave to their village and county a character that was South Carolinian."[8] Professional historians, too, have looked at Edgefield and Edgefieldians as representative of the South. Clement Eaton in *Mind of the Old South* selected an incident surrounding young Edgefieldian Louis T. Wigfall to typify antebellum southern aristocratic values, especially a sense of honor.[9] In the popular textbook *The American Republic*, Richard Hofstadter,

William Miller, and Daniel Aaron cited the Edgefield Tillman family as representative of the South's violent character.[10] Indeed, Edgefield's reputation for violence is widespread, and although modern historians have shown that Edgefield was typical of up-country South Carolina's lawlessness, Edgefield did lead the state in murders.[11] Edgefield's unsettled frontierlike wooded areas and the nearness of Augusta helped account for this, but as Richard Maxwell Brown showed in "The Edgefield Tradition," violence was very much a part of the region's culture.[12] Within limits, friction between different personalities and groups in Edgefield, instead of disrupting, actually helped to define the boundaries of the community.

Not only was Edgefield known for local troubles, but it was famous for its state and national troublemakers. Although nineteenth-century Edgefieldians were unaware of their statistical similarity to South Carolina, they saw themselves as representative of South Carolina and of the South, and they self-consciously articulated and acted upon what they believed to be southern ideals. One of the ideals was leadership. According to Alvy L. King, the biographer of Louis T. Wigfall, "Charleston and Edgefield contributed most of the famous leaders of the Palmetto State." This was true for pre–Civil War South Carolina, and also for the postbellum nineteenth century. In the late nineteenth century South Carolinians complained of an "Edgefield ring," and Ben Tillman claimed Edgefield had "so many men holding high office that the other counties are complaining and kicking like mules."[13] As South Carolina led the South—first in nullification, then in proslavery and prosouthern arguments, and later in secession—Edgefield led South Carolina. Edgefield was the home of two Civil War governors, Francis W. Pickens and Milledge Luke Bonham.[14] Former Confederate generals Matthew Calbraith Butler and Martin Witherspoon Gary directed the "Edgefield Plan" to redeem the state and return it to the conservative white elite in 1876.[15] Edgefield was the home of Benjamin Ryan Tillman, who spearheaded the farmer protest of the 1880s and 1890s, and of J. Strom Thurmond, who was Dixiecrat candidate in 1948.[16] Edgefield also produced dissenting "other southerners" Benjamin E. Mays and Marion Wright.[17]

Perhaps conscious of their role as spokesmen for the South, these leaders kept thorough records and left rich manuscript collections. Other important sources include a complete Agricultural Club Record and the oldest continuing newspaper in South Carolina.[18] In selecting Edgefield, I also considered work done by other scholars and local historians.[19] In addition, Edgefield area residents have left reflective and descriptive autobiographical accounts of life in the area. William E. Woodward, Benjamin E. Mays, and Louis B. Wright give us accounts of life in the region; if some are basically confined to the twentieth century, they nonetheless speak to the entire postwar period.[20] Although much of family history is statistical by nature, Edgefield County offers this more traditional and time-tested evidence with which to fill out the statistics. Since the primary object of this book is to describe a regional culture, a richly documented Edgefield is even more important than representativeness in any abstract statistical sense.

Edgefield County, clearly defined politically, culturally, and economically, provides an excellent laboratory for gaining a sense of family and community: a microcosm of the wealth groups and institutions in the South, it is small enough for comprehensive study and large enough to reflect diverse social, political, and economic arrangements. Edgefield had plantations and yeoman farmsteads; it had towns and nascent industries that produced many types of goods. Its population from 1850 to 1880 was larger than all southern cities except Charleston and New Orleans.[21]

Although I argue, along with a number of other scholars, that Edgefield is representative of South Carolina and the South, I believe that the issue of "typicality" for local studies can be overemphasized. A focus on the particular, on how people lived and felt, enables an understanding of larger human concerns, of the development of systems and institutions.[22] This local study tells not just of Edgefield but of family, community, slavery, tenantry, racism, and capitalism in a particular locale.

Local historical study has the potential to be enormously illuminating, especially in a community representative of southern life.[23] As Eudora Welty suggests in *The Eye of the Story*, "One place comprehended can make us understand other places better. Sense of place gives equilibrium; extended, it is sense of direction."[24] I will be satisfied if this study can furnish new insight into the nature of nineteenth-century southern rural life, and thereby provide a new perspective, and perhaps a new "sense of direction."

Historians of the southern family enter both a scholarly and a popular battlefield strewn with prejudices about plantation owners, poor whites, and blacks. Although studies have not explicitly investigated the white southern family,[25] assumptions about the family influence interpretations of southern society. At the risk of oversimplification we may group interpretations of the antebellum South into four categories. These interpretations are particularly important because the literature on the postbellum South emphasizes the question of continuity from Old to New South.[26] Thus the interpretation one accepts of the New South depends upon one's view of the antebellum South.

Perhaps the most popular school focuses on the planters as capitalists and views the southern family and values perpetuated by the southern family in terms similar to the capitalistic North. This view, presented in various forms by Lewis C. Gray, Kenneth Stampp, and Robert Fogel and Stanley Engerman, characterizes the southern economy as essentially capitalistic and the planters as rational economic men who responded, above all, to market forces.[27]

A second school is represented by Eugene D. Genovese, now the foremost critic of "planter capitalism" as an interpretive framework for analyzing the Old South. Writing from a Marxist perspective, Genovese emphasizes the sources of irrationality internal to any slave system, including the one which developed in the American South. His early work came close to characterizing the southern social system as "flawed feudalism." Like U. B. Phillips, Genovese puts the relations between master and slave, rather than relations between planters and the market, at center stage. Genovese's development of ideas on paternalism and reciprocity as the standards of human relationships adds further to his influential interpretation of the antebellum South. This view of southern society assumes a strong male-dominated elite family and further-more implies the subservience of nonplanter and black families. Planters' values are the only ideas accepted by all classes and races in the society.[28] Historian Paul Escott has caught both the main thrust and the complexity of Genovese's argument in his observation that Genovese "asserted the moral independence and cultural unity of the slaves, yet always emphasized more strongly the pervasive and controlling influence of the masters."[29] However, Genovese's emphasis on planter hegemony need not preclude slaves nor poorer whites from being patriarchal in their own family arrangements and beliefs. For instance, in Edgefield, while the hegemonic society demanded the subjugation of slaves, patriarchal tradition also pervaded the black family. Consequently, the Afro-American male was always viewed as the dominant figure in the black family. Furthermore, with emancipation the Afro-American male's desire to control and provide for his family impelled him to elect a tenant arrangement as a compromise labor system.

A third interpretation deemphasizes both planters and slaves and views southern society as being shaped by the democratic frontier experience of yeomen. This emphasis on the "plain people" has been most commonly asso-ciated with the work of Frank and Harriet Owsley and Owsley's graduate students, who, beginning in the 1930s, conducted pioneering community studies of the late antebellum South. Owsley turned to manuscript federal census returns to recreate the lives of the plain folk, the "anonymous southern-ers" of the nineteenth century. These studies have been rightly criticized for understating the significance of slavery in the region's political economy, but until quite recently they have stood virtually alone as studies of the social structure of nonplanter southern whites.[30]

Owsley's interpretation denied any class conflict among antebellum whites,[31] and few historians have since challenged the Owsley notion of class harmony. Owsley laid the foundation for eminent historians like the late Clement Eaton and Francis Butler Simkins and southern journalist W. J. Cash to argue that before the Civil War there was no class consciousness among nonplanter whites.[32] In their ongoing reinterpretation of southern herdsmen, Forrest McDonald and Grady McWhiney reinforce Owsley's conviction of the importance of the southern plain folk. Arguing that Celtic ancestry bequeathed a spirit of independence, clanishness, and racism, McDonald and McWhiney believe that white Southerners were not class conscious.[33] Although different in fundamental interpretation, Owsley, Eaton, Cash, Simkins, and McDonald and McWhiney are consistent with Genovese's argument that local aristocrats' paternalism muted class friction.[34]

David M. Potter advanced yet another interpretation of the Old South when he categorized the region as a "folk culture." Potter noted the persistence of cultural patterns in the South in which "relations between the land and the people remained more direct and more primal" than in industrial cultures and patterns that "retained a personalism in the relationships between man and man which industrial culture lacks."[35]

Potter's emphasis on family and community suggests the ideal typology which Bertram Wyatt-Brown used to explain antebellum southern society as a "family-centered, particularistic, ascriptive culture." Much of what Wyatt-Brown's ideal typology suggests about southern culture was true for Edgefield, exaltation of husband and father, masculinity and bravado as social mores applied to males. Important to Wyatt-Brown's typology is slavery's role in the patriarchal system, which bound masters to slaves as thoroughly as it bound slaves to masters. Within the slave system itself, paternalistic relationships grew and reinforced the emphasis on husband and father in white society. As stated above, in Edgefield paternalistic values also permeated the Afro-American slave family.[36] This study of Edgefield tries to do what Wyatt-Brown calls for, "to show how all parts of southern society functioned to form a social whole." Wyatt-Brown has furthermore determined that "the main thrust of southern life was the preservation of its traditions."[37] This study attempts to use the structuralist approach that Wyatt-Brown and Potter have suggested to determine what were the traditions that whites and blacks attempted to preserve both before and after the Civil War in Edgefield.

In contrast to the paucity of scholarship about the southern white family, an enormous literature refers to the southern black family. Indeed, the study of the Afro-American family has been the great exception to the long neglect of family studies in American history. A steady succession of major studies on the black family over the last century testifies to the persistent interest in this area. However, much of this interest focuses narrowly, if not negatively, upon the "distinctiveness" of the black family as measured by the deviation from the assumed typical white family pattern. This negative focus has been evident from the pejorative contrasts drawn between the black family as pathological and the white family as the normative model.

Once again, to simplify a complex situation, I divide scholarly explanations of the origins and evolution of the black family into four groups, each with its own model to explain perceived and imagined problems with the Afro-American family. The first is the anthropological and African origins model, initially proposed by a group of black scholars and forcefully argued by Melville Herskovits.[38] Demitri B. Shimkin and his associates, who studied the ethnography of Holmes County, Mississippi, have been, with these Afro-American scholars and Herskovits, the major proponents of the theory that an African heritage most influenced the black family.[39] The anthropological school minimized the importance of slavery and, in particular, the impact of whites on blacks in order to deny any "mimicry" on the part of Afro-American culture.

The second and third models are both sociological. The older one, represented by Howard Odum, W. E. B. DuBois, E. Franklin Frazier, and, more recently, Daniel Moynihan, blamed slavery for disrupting the development of black family life.[40] This model has generally been associated with the literature on matriarchy. This school theorized that because of the restrictions of slavery the Afro-American family was ill-adapted for modern society. Slavery destroyed most of African culture and offered little to replace that heritage, and it undermined the authority of the black male and thus fostered matriarchy. These scholars viewed blacks as reasoning that they could overcome their southern rural and slave handicaps by migrating to northern cities.

Some opponents of the matriarchy thesis, such as Robert Fogel and Stanley Engerman, John Blassingame, and Eugene Genovese, have also argued that the slave experience was the decisive factor in shaping the black family. Unlike the believers in the matriarchy theory, though, they claim that slaves were able to synthesize elements from white culture; this synthesis created black community, religious, and family life. Yet even the opponents of the matriarchy thesis accepted the basic tenet of the sociological school: that slavery was the greatest source of problems for the black family.[41]

The more recent sociological model sees modern urban life, and not necessarily the legacy of slavery, as the great obstacle to the black family. The abandonment of the slavery origins of the matriarchy/weak family thesis led scholars to associate present-day indices of family disorganization (illegitimacy, female-headed households, father-absent families, poverty, and low level of education) with conditions that arose from black internal migration within the United States. These sociologists and historians identified the northern industrial city, with its anomie, its destruction of community and tradition, and its impoverishment and oppression of blacks as the setting responsible for the decline of the Afro-American family. This model has linked the problems of the American black family to the general modern phenomenon of rural adaptation to city life, with the attendant alienation, and destruction of rural norms and folkways in the context of an urban industrial economy.

Theodore Hershberg and his Philadelphia Social History Project, Frank Furstenberg, Jr., and John Modell argue that the excessive male mortality rate in the city, and not the rural origins of black families, caused the higher proportion of female-headed urban households.[42] Elizabeth Hafkin Pleck's monograph on blacks in Boston disputed both the rural origins and the high male mortality theses. Instead, she asserted that "the combined effects of poverty, sterility, and declining community regulation of family life" produced greater marital instability among black urban families.[43]

Finally, a number of scholars have arrived at their interpretations primarily from findings grouped as a "Family Economy Model." Generally these writers took a market approach to the workings of the family. All the work has been quantitative, and involved complex neoclassical economic theory and model building far beyond the descriptive and analytical devices common to historians. The decisive issue for historian Crandall Shifflett and econometricians Roger Ransom and Richard Sutch is the extent to which economics influenced and was influenced by the family. For this school of interpretation, matriarchy or family disorganization has never been an issue.[44]

Economist Gary Becker and his associates at the University of Chicago represent an extreme of this "new home economics" approach. Becker's interest centered on the construction of a model of marriage and the family. A basic feature of this model is the assertion that income can be maximized by marriage. Becker's model assumes that economics can explain human behavior since economics is basically concerned with rational behavior under constraints. Thus, economics can even explain such subjective decision-making processes as marriage and divorce.[45] Although most historians have rejected such utilitarian ideas out of hand, the work along these economic lines has been impressive. For example, cliometrician Warren C. Sanderson, drawing on Gary Becker's economic theory of marriage, argued that marital breakup related positively to equalization of the market income for husband and wife. Sanderson argued that as a legacy of slavery, black male and female wage rates were more nearly equal than white gender wage rates. Thus, there was less economic incentive for marriage, and this explained the historical origins of the currently observed racial differentials in marital stability rates. Indeed, a subtle implication of some of this family economy literature (such as that of Becker and Sanderson) is that the black family pioneered a transformation that eventually affected white American families: as women gained equality in the market economy, marital relationships became more unstable.[46]

Econometrician Claudia Goldin has found support for revisionist conclusions that black and white female-headed households and families existed in about equal proportion in urban areas in 1870 and 1880. She agreed with Sanderson that slavery's legacy was a difference between black and white women in participation in the labor force. Goldin felt black women had successfully worked during the antebellum period and valued working but because of the stigma of slavery, white women, especially in the South, denigrated working.[47]

While all these models are useful and add to the understanding of the black family, Herbert Gutman has shown how a social historian, by using a "thick description" approach, can demolish many misconceptions. Gutman, an eclectic and complex scholar, absorbed elements from many sources to refute the idea of a black matriarchy. He presented two basic arguments: first, that a male-headed, two-parent family was the typical domestic arrangement for blacks before and after slavery and, second, that Afro-American family traditions developed out of black historical environments and from freely chosen elements rather than through imitation of white culture or from owner-imposed arrangements.[48]

Gutman opposed the simplistic view that blacks chose either African or white culture by stressing the emergence of an independent Afro-American culture. He asserted that blacks created an autonomous culture (composed of African, white American, and accommodation to slavery elements) which was reflected in the families of both slaves and freedmen.[49]

The Black Family in Slavery and Freedom left some important questions unanswered. One is the issue of adaptability—what difference did black family forms have on the circumstances in which Afro-Americans found themselves in the years following emancipation? Except for naming patterns and social mores against endogomy, Gutman does not thoroughly analyze the influence of the community, the family, or religion on black culture or values.[50] Yet one cannot deal with the South without considering the role of the church in the formulation of values and attitudes, and without a recognition of the centrality of the church in community and family life for whites and for blacks both before and after the Civil War. Nor can the inevitable daily interaction between blacks and whites be ignored. Gutman also did not look at mulattoes or antebellum free blacks, and he maintained near silence on the economic contexts in which the black family developed, both before and after emancipation. Demographic samples in *The Black Family in Slavery and Freedom* were drawn primarily from areas with a proportionally high black population, and did not include the piedmont situations.

Gutman was most critical of Moynihan's matriarchy thesis. Because Gutman discredited Moynihan and matriarchy, one must explain why it remains important to study the Afro-American family, especially the question of black matriarchy. Many unsettled issues persist in the post-Gutman era. Moynihan found 21 percent of New York City black families headed by females in 1960 and concluded that there was a matriarchy. In 1976 Gutman looked back at New York City black families of 1925 and found 23.3 percent female headed and denounced black matriarchy as a misconception. These contradictory conclusions suggest that expectations, not data, have shaped scholarly analysis and that the statistical basis for the matriarchy legend was never strong. An even more significant point than the Moynihan-Gutman dispute is the subtle academic question of whether one emphasizes universal similarities or certain major differences between black and white families.

No matter what ideological, political, and social contexts are used to explain the changes in interpretations revealed in the statistically similar, but radically different, studies of Gutman and Moynihan, one still has to explain the post-Moynihan trends. Since scholars began attacking Moynihan and the matriarchal literature, a drastic rise has occurred in female-headed black households, children living with one parent, and illegitimacy. While increases in these same measures also appeared in the white population, the developments are clearly more dramatic for Afro-Americans. Unless we assert that the present has no roots in the past, how do historians explain these trends?[51]

In My Father's House shows how scholars distorted real problems by viewing them from prejudiced perspectives and reexplores older themes of the studies of the black family to explain how prejudice and scholars' personal experiences led to denials of the patriarchal reality of the black family. The scholars who initiated the discussion of the matriarchy thesis were not simple racists; indeed, most were reasonable people whose ideas came from the sources they used, supplemented by their experiences. However, most of them lived in cities and used urban sources. Subsequent literature has successfully attacked the matriarchy thesis and other misconceptions but has failed to yield a full explanation of the origins and durability of the myth of the black matriarchy. More recent students of the black family still tend to come from cities and tend to form their ideas from their own urban experiences.[52] Yet knowledge of agrarian society is the key to understanding the matriarchy misconception and demonstrates why rural southern society was patriarchal.

Patriarchy is only one issue illuminated by a total history perspective. Fuller understanding of religious, social status, and economic factors in family and community life in Edgefield also emerge through extensive examination of census statistics and literary sources. Investigation of the complex webs of interactions in Edgefield and analysis of such concepts as patriarchy in concrete contextual terms correct previous misunderstandings about the history of black-white relations in the South.

Precise definitions of sociological terms may be of interest to some social scientists, but a detailed portrait of a single community over time provides scholars with an opportunity to explore sociological theories in terms of historical experience. Most Edgefieldians could not have satisfactorily defined patriarchy, matriarchy, or family, but residents of Edgefield tacitly understood their meaning because they experienced them daily as values and as institutions.

By examining variations in family culture and structure, both black and white, free and slave, this study attempts to specify which elements in those variations are race specific and which derive from the general social and cultural environment that affected whites and Afro-Americans equally. *In My Father's House* searches for the origins of the prejudices and stereotypes of southern black and white families and explores what difference family and community made in the course of events in nineteenth-century Edgefield.

1. Edgefield, South Carolina

*There is nothing that distinguishes the settlement of Edgefield from that of
other districts in the upper and middle country.*

Robert Mills, *Statistics of South Carolina*

Midway between the Blue Ridge Mountains and the Atlantic Ocean, Edgefield
County (a "district" until 1868) was on the western border of South Carolina,
separated from Georgia by the Savannah River (see Map 1).[1] To the north lay
Abbeville District, and to the east, separated from Edgefield by the Saluda
River, Newberry. In the northeast corner, where it joined Newberry and Abbe-
ville, Edgefield intersected the southeast tip of Laurens. To the south were
Barnwell, Orangeburg, and Lexington. Edgefield itself, 1,702 square miles,
was more a region than a county. In 1860 Edgefield, with 951,451 acres of
land, was the second largest district in the state after the Charleston Coastal
District.

After the Civil War new counties were formed from old Edgefield County
(see Map 2). In 1871 the southernmost section of Edgefield County (along
with areas from the northern parts of Orangeburg, Barnwell, and Lexington
counties) was detached to form Aiken County. This area of old Edgefield
County included the town of Hamburg, the Horse Creek area where William
Gregg built his famed antebellum textile mill, the town of Aiken, and the rich
land of Beech Island, where antebellum governor and U.S. senator James
Henry Hammond had his home, Redcliffe. During the 1895 constitutional
convention the county of Saluda was created entirely from Edgefield County.
This section was the home of the prominent Butler family, which included
Pierce Mason Butler, governor of South Carolina, as well as two heroes of the
Alamo, Commander William Barret Travis and James Butler Bonham.

In 1897 Greenwood County was formed from Edgefield and Abbeville; this
northern part of the section was the home of Congressman Preston Brooks,
famed for his attack on Senator Charles Sumner, and the home of Benjamin E.
Mays, a well-known twentieth-century educator. Finally, in 1917 part of the
area that had been taken from Edgefield County to form Greenwood County
was combined with a part of Abbeville County to form McCormick County.
This northwestern section of the Edgefield District was the home of postbel-

lum governor John Sheppard and of the Tillmans: George D., congressman, and his younger brother, the colorful Benjamin Ryan, more popularly known as "Pitchfork Ben," postbellum agrarian protest leader, governor, and senator.[2]

Although boundaries have shifted, all of these various counties and areas may be regarded as a single economic, geographical, and social entity. Neither black nor white people of Edgefield recognized rigid boundaries. Social, political, and economic concerns overlapped county and even state boundaries. For example, James Henry Hammond's main plantation was in Barnwell District, but his home was in Edgefield. Edgefield blacks and whites traveled to Chappells in Newberry County to have their cases heard by a local trial justice. During Reconstruction crises, white militia companies rode from neighboring counties to the aid of other white paramilitary groups.[3] Nevertheless, statistical sources for family life in South Carolina were collected by county; therefore the quantitative data for the period prior to 1871 comes from within the defined geographical limits of pre-1871 Edgefield County and, subsequent to 1871, from all the area of the antebellum district except for that which was lost to Aiken County.

South Carolina was traditionally divided into up-country and low-country sections, each section having its own geography and culture. The low country was emblematic of the plantation aristocracy of the South; it comprised generally the tidewater and sand-hill regions of the state. The up-country coincided very nearly with what is called the Piedmont region of the state. The land in the up-country had a heavy red clay soil and lower temperatures and a shorter growing season owing to the proximity of the Blue Ridge Mountains. Although Edgefield District was considered part of the up-country, the lower section of the district had the sand hills more commonly associated with the low country. Since the aristocratic elements of the state imputed unattractive connotations to the designation "up-country," many in Edgefield preferred to call part of the district the "midlands," identifying "culturally" with districts like Camden and Cheraw and the state capital, Columbia.[4]

The Savannah River, Edgefield District's western border, one of South Carolina and Georgia's most important avenues of commerce, linked coastal ports with inland areas. Reaching from the mountains to the sea, the river obstructed westward movement; Augusta and Hamburg developed at the site of one of the few natural fords. Buffalo, deer, and other wild game had long used this crossing, and Indians and then eighteenth- and nineteenth-century pioneers followed. Augusta, on the Georgia banks of the Savannah River, was established in the 1730s as a frontier outpost. It was sited at the fall line, above which waterfalls and rapids made navigation upriver difficult.[5]

Opposite Augusta, a twenty-mile-wide belt of steep rolling hills stretched across South Carolina in a northeasterly direction from the bottom lands of the Savannah River. These sand hills were the vestiges of an ancient ocean shoreline, a region of porous sandy soil that supported little indigenous vegeta-

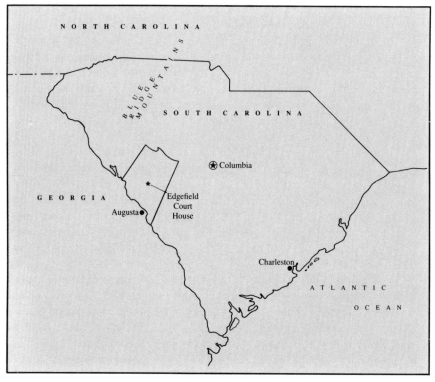

Map 1.

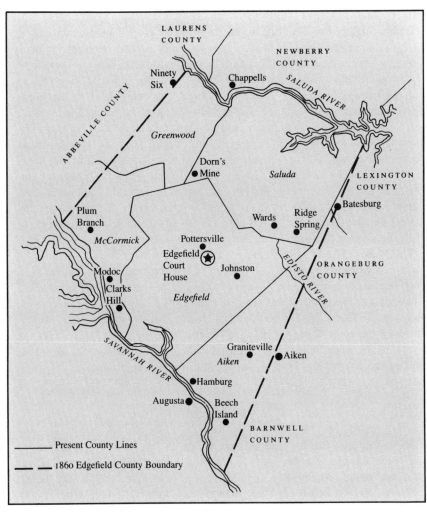

Map 2.

tion beyond thick pine stands and scrub brush. Undulating gently, these hills climbed slightly for about fifteen miles in from the river, then rose abruptly to a six-hundred-foot-high plateau. The sand hills plateau was nearly level, running toward the southeast before it blended into the hills of the upper pine belt region below Edgefield District. In the east this ten-mile-wide plateau descended rapidly to the South Edisto River. The bottomlands of the South Edisto and North Edisto in the southeastern section of Edgefield District were swampy and densely overgrown, and an eight-mile-wide sandy plateau obstructed east-west travel by wagon or horseback. Thus the Edisto plateau communities were drawn more toward Columbia and the low country for travel and trade than were the other sections of the district. From the northern limits of this plateau, near where the Reconstruction settlement of Johnston grew around the Charlotte-Columbia-Augusta Railroad, a ridge of steep granite and clay hills six hundred feet high ran west to the Savannah River valley north of Edgefield Court House and then northwestward up the Savannah toward Abbeville District. This ridge–fall line zone, with an elevation of over five hundred feet, ran westward from Edgefield Court House, crossed the Savannah River, and passed north of Augusta. North of the ridge the terrain descended slightly. To the South, however, it was steep and undulating, marked by large streams, such as the Horse, Turkey and Stevens creeks, that carved numerous valleys through the land. These fast-flowing streams severely limited travel between settlements, so the topography funneled trade and travel toward Augusta and, for a time, toward Hamburg on the South Carolina side of the river.

Settlement

David Ramsay's history reported that as late as "the year 1755 the country from the Waxhaws on the Catawba across to Augusta on the Savannah River did not contain twenty-five families."[6] But permanent settlers had begun moving into the area about 1748, after treaties with the Indians were signed. Soon after the Revolution the same area was sufficiently populated to contain twelve political units. Edgefield County was one of these twelve, the largest and most southern of the six (Abbeville, Newberry, Laurens, Union, and Spartanburg) created from the Ninety Six District, most of the entire northwestern portion of South Carolina. With the encouragement of bounties from the Carolina colonial government, European immigrants settled in and around areas that would become Edgefield County. The government especially encouraged the English and Irish, and in 1737 a group of Swiss located in New Windsor in what is now Aiken County; in 1764 more than one hundred French Huguenots settled at New Bordeaux in what is now McCormick County; in 1765 more than two hundred German Palatines moved south of Ninety Six, where they felt more secure from Indian attacks than in the area originally designated for them near New Bordeaux. Despite these groups of bounty immigrants from Europe, though, most settlers in Edgfield had emigrated from Pennsylvania and Virginia into North Carolina and then into the Piedmont of South Carolina and thence into Edgefield. They came into Edgefield District through two peripheral communities, an eastern outpost (Ninety Six) or up the Savannah to a western outpost (Augusta).[7]

Blacks and whites entered the area at about the same time. In addition to a few free black families, Afro-American slaves came into Edgefield with the early migrants and helped settle the frontier. As early as 1736 slaves rowed boats laden with a thousand pounds sterling worth of furs down the Savannah river from the Carolina frontier outpost at Fort Moore to the coast. Many of the blacks in Edgefield were reputed to be of the Gullah African tribe, defiant and unruly as slaves. Afro-Americans were not the only unfree persons, however. In the mid-eighteenth century Edgefield had both white indentured servants and Indian slaves. Then too Indians made slaves of white captives. During the frontier years race was probably less an issue than status.[8]

Blacks came to outnumber whites in the first decade of the nineteenth century (Table 1-1 shows how their numbers increased from 1790 to 1900). Important black leaders emerged from the old Edgefield district. Afro-American leaders established the first independent black church in America in Edgefield District between 1773 and 1775. David George, a slave exhorter who preached at the Silver Bluff Baptist Church, took advantage of the British offer of freedom for slaves and emigrated first to Nova Scotia in 1782 and then to Sierra Leone in 1792, establishing Baptist churches wherever he went. David George's childhood friend and fellow Edgefield slave George Liele left the Edgefield Silver Bluff Church and established a Baptist ministry in Jamaica. Alexander H. Bettis founded more than forty churches, two Baptist associations, and an educational academy. Baptist preacher and educator Dr. Benjamin E. Mays became president of Morehouse College and the spiritual and intellectual mentor to several generations of local and national black leaders, including Martin Luther King, Jr.[9]

During Reconstruction a number of former Edgefield slaves served as state representatives. Lawrence Cain was a state senator, and among the state representatives were Paris Simkins, David Graham, and Augustus Simkins. Black leaders also held local offices. Civil War hero Prince Rivers, the "Black Prince," called Edgefield his home, as did the famous militia leader Ned Tennant.[10]

The ratio of black to white persons changed over time. In 1800 the population of whites was 13,063, but by 1820 had decreased to 12,864. Slaves, 5,006 in 1800, numbered 19,198 by 1820. This nearly fourfold increase in the number of slaves and a decrease in the number of whites signified the development of an increasingly wealthy white planter class in Edgefield.[11]

Many of these large planters came from the coastal plains of South Carolina.

Table 1-1. Population of Edgefield County, 1790–1900

Year	Edgefield Aggregate Population	Number White	Number Black
1790	13,289	9,605	3,684
1800	18,130	13,063	5,067
1810	23,160	14,433	8,727
1820	25,119	12,864	12,255
1830	30,509	14,957	15,522
1840	32,852	15,020	17,832
1850	39,262	16,252	23,010
1860	39,887[b]	15,653	24,233
1870	42,486[b]	17,040	25,417
1880[a]	45,844	16,018	29,826
1890[a]	45,259[b]	17,340	31,916
1900	44,444	16,166	28,278

a. Parts of Edgefield County were lost to form new counties: in 1871, Aiken; in 1896, Saluda; in 1897, Greenwood. However, Saluda County, created entirely from Edgefield, is included in the 1900 figures above.

b. When the total exceeds the sum of blacks and whites, American Indians and Chinese have been added. In 1860, there was one Indian; in 1870, twenty-nine Indians; in 1890, two Indians and one Chinese. The censuses aggregated Chinese and Indians as white population.

Source: U.S., Bureau of the Census, *8th* (1860) *Census*, vol. 1, *Population*, pp. 449–52; U.S., Bureau of the Census, *9th* (1870) *Census*, vol. 1, *Population*, pp. 60–61; U.S., Bureau of the Census, *11th* (1890) *Census*, vol. 1, pp. 38, 427, 440, 448; U.S., Bureau of the Census, *12th* (1900) *Census*, vol. 1, *Population*, pt. 1, p. 37; S.C., Dept. of Agriculture, Commerce, and Immigration, *Handbook of South Carolina*, pp. 524, 527–28; Wallace, *History South Carolina*, 3:504.

They were Episcopalians and closely linked to the Charleston elite. These low-country migrants, accustomed to command, considered themselves more refined and more noble than their rustic neighbors, even when those neighbors owned large numbers of slaves.[12]

Still, the great majority of whites were usually Baptists and Methodists (Presbyterians were prominent elsewhere, but not in Edgefield). In contrast to the aristocratic settlers from the seaboard areas, these whites were fiercely independent and democratic; early settlers were noted for disobeying officers and officials and for arguing with authorities. This area became the home of the regulator movement in South Carolina, and the Revolutionary War was here a civil war as well, marked by extreme violence and vengeance.[13]

Perhaps this mixture of seaboard aristocracy and heterogeneous backcountry elements in Edgefield helped to account for the distinguished white political leadership that emerged. For from among whites alone Edgefield has produced ten governors and five lieutenant governors. From George McDuffie's election to the Senate in 1842 (to replace William Preston) until the Civil War, Edgefield supplied one of South Carolina's national senators (McDuffie, A. P. Butler, James Henry Hammond). As soon as the Democrats regained control of the state in 1877, Edgefield again supplied a senator, Matthew Calbraith Butler until 1894, followed by Benjamin Ryan "Pitchfork Ben" Tillman. Edgefield's representatives in the Senate had national as well as statewide influence.[14]

One clue to the number of prominent politicians was the high quality of lawyers in the county. Leaders at antebellum Edgefield Court House were celebrated by Judge J. Belton O'Neall as a "brilliant galaxy." In his 1859 history of the South Carolina bar, O'Neall wrote that "from 1820 to 1832 no interior Bar of South Carolina presented abler counsellors than there appeared often in the Edgefield Courts." George McDuffie came to Edgefield as a young lawyer in 1815 because he was attracted by the large law practice and extensive library of Col. Eldred Simkins, a congressman and South Carolina lieutenant governor. Francis Pickens, too, came to read law at the firm of his father-in-law, Eldred Simkins, and George McDuffie. Martin Witherspoon Gary, reared in Abbeville, came to Edgefield after graduating with honors from Harvard to study in the law office of Chancellor James P. Carroll. William Preston wrote, "The object of a Southern man's life is *politics* and subsidiary to this end we all practice law."[15]

These lawyers were also important in the spreading of ideas. They rode circuit with judges and traveled from one small district seat to another, as well as to the state capital. They made friendships and alliances in the process. Thus, along with the local newspapers and the church associations, lawyers linked Edgefield with the other South Carolina districts.[16]

Religion

Neighborhoods within the various areas of Edgefield were often centered around church buildings, and the boundaries of these settlements, or communities within the larger community, were areas served by the church. The Johnston Baptist Church explicitly acknowledged the connection in a resolution thanking their departing pastor "for the kind and zealous interest he has always shown towards us as a church and community." Religion was central to the family and society in Edgefield. Throughout the nineteenth century both blacks and whites lived in a narrow world of kin, neighbors, and fellow church members, and religion helped shape the world view of this agrarian community. The members of one's Sunday school class or prayer group were likely to be one's relatives. In 1860 there was one church building for every 252 white people in Edgefield. By 1890 there was one church for every 240 whites and one church for every 404 blacks.[17]

Of course church buildings did not signify attendance, and a dispersed rural population had difficulty getting to church. In 1854 the editor of the Edgefield *Advertiser* mentioned the sparse attendance at churches within the town and confessed that since he lived four miles out into the country, he rarely made it to services. A New England schoolteacher living in Edgefield complained that her preacher serviced several churches, and this practice, combined with bad roads, meant she could "attend church very seldom." The following notice by an Edgefield minister in the weekly paper was typical of "Religious Notices": "I will by divine permission, preach at the following places: October 15th, at Graniteville, at night; Mt. Pleasant the 16th; at Mt. Ebal 17th; at Bethel 18th; at Dry Creek the 19th; at Philipi 20th; at Rocky Creek 21st; at Mt. Tabor 22nd; at Stephen's Creek 23d; at Good Hope 24th; at Red Bank 25th; Salem at eleven o'clock in the morning and Sardia at 2 o'clock."[18]

Limited preaching meant that when a preacher was available, people of different denominations would attend the same church; hence the values of different denominations were mingled. So men like Joseph Abney could be a deacon in the Baptist church and an elder in the Episcopal church in Edgefield. The elite were generally Episcopalians, but when Episcopal priest John Cornish preached in Aiken he recorded in his diary that "all sorts from Romanists to the most radical Presbyterians" attended. One church tradition which dates back to the antebellum period and is indicative of Edgefield's communal spirit is the Fifth Sunday Union Meeting. In any month in which a fifth Sunday occurred, church representatives of various denominations congregated to worship, and afterwards to air concerns about religious and secular issues affecting the churches. These meetings provided an important forum for individuals of different classes and creeds to mingle and to learn of one another's problems. Moreover, these meetings suggest that at least some of the churches exhibited a degree of tolerance necessary to foster a larger sense of community.[19]

In the summer months particularly, week-long and two-week-long revivals also helped Edgefieldians reestablish their common values. James Rainsford, recently emigrated from England to Edgefield, was an astute observer of religious customs. After attending a two-week "protracted meeting" for blacks and whites conducted by ten preachers of different denominations during August 1833, Rainsford recorded in his diary that, nearly every night during the revival, "most of the congregation were affected to tears, from very old men to young men and boys. From 20 to 30 or 40 left their seats at the close of each days service and went to the ministrating brethren, requesting them to pray for their salvation and very many others, saying, pray for my son or daughter or father or relatives and before the meeting broke up (today) 2 of the preachers shook hands with every person in the congregation requesting all to join in one united prayer."[20]

Popular historian William E. Woodward wrote about revivals he remembered in the mill village of Graniteville in the 1880s, some fifty years after Rainsford's description. Of course by that time segregation in religious services had been instituted, so that only whites attended, and Woodward himself was a religious skeptic. Nevertheless, the descriptions are remarkably similar. Religion and revivals continued to play important roles in the lives of Edgefieldians throughout the nineteenth century.[21]

Generally the churches were community affairs, built and paid for by members and nonmembers. When wagons were needed to haul material from Hamburg and help needed to place the stones in the tower of St. Mary of the Immaculate Conception, equal numbers of Catholics and non-Catholics, slaveowners and nonslaveowners assisted. Father Bermingham remarked in his diary that the completion of the tower was "truly a community project" and publicly thanked "the generous people of Edgefield, of all classes and religious denominations." Elitist Trinity Episcopal Church, however, was built by hired carpenters, and for several years the rector's salary was paid by one man, Francis W. Pickens.[22]

As Figure 1-1 shows, Edgefield was most heavily influenced by Baptists. Traveling through Edgefield in 1809, Bishop Francis Asbury observed that "the Baptists are carrying all before them; they are indebted to Methodist camp meetings for this." A Presbyterian minister who came to Edgefield in 1882 more ruefully (and mistakenly) noted, "Edgefield County . . . enjoyed the distinction of being the one county in South Carolina without a Presbyterian church. . . . Growing a crop of Presbyterians from seed corn of four members was a man's job. The county had been pre-empted by the Baptists for one hundred years."[23]

Of those four who formed the Presbyterian church, three were women, and the only man was elected the ruling elder. Similarly, it was a woman who spoke up confessing her sins who began the establishment of Bethany Baptist Church. While women were often influential in establishing churches, in general they did not receive leadership roles. Still, religion was critical for black and white women. A conversion experience placed women and slaves in God's kingdom, an ultimate authority that outweighed even that of a husband or owner. In the patriarchal rural society conversion especially gave women an escape from male oppression. White and black women (as well as male slaves) spoke out about their liberating religious experiences, sometimes even in church; white women also confided their thoughts to diaries and prayer books.[24]

For all denominations the relationship of slavery and religion was ambiguous. In 1851, C. B. Walker, the superintendent of the Episcopal Sunday

Figure 1–1. Churches by Denomination, 1850–1870 and 1890

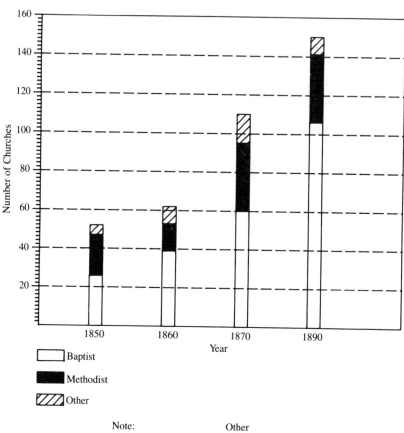

Note: Other

	1850	1860	1870	1890
Catholic		1	1	2
Episcopalian	1	3	2	3
Lutheran	3	4	8	4
Presbyterian		1	4	1
Universalist			1	

In 1870, fifteen Baptist, ten Methodist, three Presbyterian, and the Universalist congregations did not have church buildings. Comparable information on churches was not available for 1880.

Source: Edgefield Data Base; U.S., Bureau of the Census, *7th* (1850) *Census*, pp. 349–51; *8th* (1860) *Census*, vol. 4, *Statistics*, pp. 462–64; *9th* (1870) *Census*, vol. 1, *Population*, p. 553; *11th* (1890) *Census*, vol. 9, *Report on Statistics of Churches*, pp. 38, 79, 164, 175, 204, 245, 445, 549, 565, 588, 609, 694, 717.

school, proudly reported that two of the seventy-seven "colored scholars have applied to be received as candidates for baptism and are inquiring 'What must I do to be saved?'" Superintendent Walker felt the need to reassure the community, however: "I need scarcely inform you, that the instruction of the colored scholars is *altogether oral*, and our Teachers wholly trustworthy. The Catechism used is one prepared by the Rev. C. C. Jones . . . a Presbyterian Clergyman, a native Georgian."[25]

Edgefield's predominant religious group and culture had grown out of the New Light or Separate Baptists. The coastal aristocrats had been suspicious of these early churches owing to the Baptists' misgivings about slavery and their more open attitudes about women. Asked to help in the ordination of Daniel Marshall, a zealous Separatist Baptist, a Regular Baptist minister ruefully refused because he believed Newlights to be a "disorderly set . . . permitting every ignorant man to preach that chose, and that they encouraged noise and confusion in their meetings."[26]

An observer in 1772 described what would be the first Baptist Church in Edgefield District: "The families are about 150, whereof 130 persons are baptised. Communion is here celebrated at no set time. No established salary. . . . In the Church the love feast, washing feet are used, also ruling elders, imposition of hands, deaconesses, etc." Believing that a person walked behind the plow for six days and God inspired his sermon on the Sabbath, these early Baptists saw no need for either a regular or a trained clergy. Sometimes the thoughts "sent by God," however, ran counter to the interests of the planter class and threatened its dominance. One reason that the Furman Academy, later Furman University, was founded in Edgefield in 1826 was to indoctrinate the Separatist Baptists in up-country South Carolina and across the river in Georgia.[27]

Although the Regular Baptists were firmly established in Edgefield after the Revolutionary War, the influence of the questioning, open attitudes and the egalitarian nature of the early Separatist Baptists was evident even as late as the 1840s. The formation of the Bethel Baptist Association in the up-country (Edgefield churches participated in this association) allowed people formally to pose moral questions. One of the first issues brought before the association was whether it was even right for Christians to own slaves. The association sidestepped the issue, as it would most other matters regarding slavery. One reason the issue was so sensitive was that some preachers owned slaves. The association also asked, "Is it justifiable in correcting the servants with stripes?" The Baptist organization answered that masters could "use the rod if needs be," but that slaveowners were subject to church discipline if they administered lashes cruelly or if they oppressed their slaves unduly and in an un-Christian manner. The basic principle upon which the association based its decision was patriarchal: that both masters and parents had the right to govern their households and that heads of households sometimes had to resort to force to control children, wives, and slaves.[28]

Besides inquiries concerning slavery and disciplining, the Bethel Baptist Association asked other sensitive questions. In 1845 the question arose, "What is regarded as valid matrimony among our colored brethren?" The chairman of the committee that decided this issue was the famed Reverend William Bullein Johnson, pastor of the Edgefield Village Church and first president of the Southern Baptist Association. His committee reported that "Colored Brethren are not known to law as citizens . . . not subject to regulation as to matrimony. . . . Valid matrimony with them, must be determined by God's law. Their co-habitation should be made known—having witnesses that they have agreed to marry and it is desirable that ministers perform some ceremony over the parties." Because the association sanctioned slave marriages, the committee recommended that "Christian masters use utmost care to prevent . . . separation" of slave families.[29]

Circumstances in Edgefield suggest that the developing slavocracy had good reasons to fear the New Light Baptists. Separatist minister Daniel Marshall established several churches in the section that later became Edgefield District. After establishing Stevens Creek Church, Marshall and his associates founded in 1768 Horn's Creek Church a few miles from Big Stevens. In 1824, when the church clerk traced the history of Horn's Creek, he recorded that the "first fruits of his [Marshall's] labor were Benjamin Ryan and his wife." Government records show that this same Benjamin Ryan tried unsuccessfully to manumit several slaves. After his death his brother and fellow Baptist John Ryan, as executor of Benjamin's will, again unsuccessfully petitioned the legislature in 1815, 1820, and 1824 to free the slaves. In 1815 another Marshall New Light Baptist convert who had become the pastor of Stevens Creek Church attempted to free his slaves, as did his wife after his death.[30]

Perhaps the influence of Separatist backcountry Baptists influenced Basil Manly, a young North Carolinian studying at the South Carolina College when in 1821 he wrote a theme on the emancipation of slaves. Already an ordained Baptist preacher he argued: "Slavery seems to be repugnant to the spirit of our republican institutions. While the framers of our constitution recognize most distinctly the principle that all men are naturally free and equal; with the very hand that subscribed it, and fought to maintain it, they held the chain that bound a portion of their fellow men to perpetual servitude." That same year, 1821, he became the preacher in Edgefield Village and at Little Stevens Creek. Although Manly's views on slavery changed (forty years later as president of the University of Alabama he delivered the invocation at Jefferson Davis's inauguration), his passionate antislavery theme suggests that religion and proslavery feelings in the first quarter of the nineteenth century were not synonymous. The attempts by Separatist Baptists to manumit their slaves amplified this diversity.[31]

The combining of the Regular Baptists from the coastal areas with the backcountry Separate Baptists eliminated radical or even moderate stances on the issue of slavery. Slaveowners overcame possible compunctions about owning, whipping, or separating slave families. By the mid-1830s, Edgefield's George McDuffie could exclaim without misgiving that "no human institution . . . is more manifestly consistent with the will of God, than domestic slavery." Baptist minister Iveson L. Brookes used his Edgefield pulpit to defend slavery in the 1850s as "an Institution of heaven and intended for the mutual benefit of master and slave, as proved by the Bible" and to proclaim "that slave holders are Bible reading, and God fearing men."[32]

The other sensitive issue that had to be overcome was the role of women in the church. The Regular Baptists around Charleston and the seaboard disdained the up-country Separate Baptists, who allowed women to pray in public and had women officers—deaconesses and elderesses. After Separate and Regular Baptists combined, however, the importance of women in the church was not reflected in the elected leadership. Indeed, few women were on any church committees until fifteen years after the Civil War. In 1880 five women were appointed as a committee to study repairs for an Edgefield church. As early as 1830, though, women *were* involved as Sunday school teachers and in missionary societies, and after the Civil War the Baptist Missionary Society became almost exclusively a women's organization, perhaps in compensation for their exclusion from leadership roles in their own churches.[33]

Edgefield whites relied on the Old Testament patriarchs for a religious justification of slavery. According to Julien and Milling, they "worshipped the warrior God of the old Testament and believed that scalping an Indian for bounty was just as praise-worthy as the sack of Jericho or the destruction of the Amalkemites." With severity as its philosophy and a stern God its deity, the church tried to control social mores. Before the Civil War churches were biracial, but church leadership and most discipline committees were white.[34]

Slaveowners recognized the danger religion posed to whites as well. John Bauskett, who owned 221 slaves in Edgefield in 1850, worried that "there was some danger of the fanaticism of the north spreading among and infecting the consciences of the weak minded good Christian people of the South, upon the question of *Right* in the whites to maintain the existing relation with the Africans amongst us." That year the wealthy Edgefield planter arranged for the publication of several of Edgefield minister Iveson L. Brookes's defenses of slavery in pamphlet format.[35]

Thus, the attempt to use religion as a means to manipulate a group of people was not restricted to blacks. As William Gregg himself explained to the South Carolina Manufacturing Company in one of his earliest annual reports on the Graniteville mill in Edgefield District: "To get a steady supply of workmen, a population must be collected *which will regard themselves as a community.*" Gregg elaborated that the church was essential to promoting the stability and moral uplifting necessary for a community of industrial workers. As late as 1907 industrialist Daniel Augustus Tompkins conferred with Edgefield preachers about ways religion could be used to improve the "general mill situation" and promote better relations between white mill workers at the Edgefield Manufacturing Company and the townspeople.[36]

Although some planters and industrialists used religion as a tool for social control, religion also served as a buffer. For slaves it was a buffer against the oppression of slavery, and in the postbellum period it helped some blacks to sever ties of dependency with paternalistic whites. Black efforts to control towns politically, to build schools, and to establish economic independence during Reconstruction were often initiated by churches and religious leaders.

Whereas whites emphasized the Old Testament, blacks looked to the loving God of the New Testament and were especially partial to the writings of John (although there was also quite an identity with the Israelites and the Exodus of the Old Testament). John 14 provides the title of this book, and like so many of the cryptic messages in the Bible, it has several meanings. One of the meanings Afro-Americans took to heart was the open and forgiving nature of God; there was room in God the Father's House for both blacks and whites of Edgefield. A significant theme of John's gospel is to love one another—your neighbors and your enemies—and one finds in the black Christianity of Edgefield a loving and forgiving community.[37]

Towns

Like most of nineteenth-century America and especially the South, Edgefield was rural. A Yankee observer on a trip down the Mississippi was typical of other outsiders when he exclaimed, "But where are the towns?" Compared to the Northeast and Midwest, with their emphasis on towns and urban developments, the South was a land of farms and plantations. The county or district, not the town, was the unit of government.[38]

But towns did exist, and townlike centers dotted the rural countryside. Towns and villages provided economic and political focus for the countryside. Different social structures developed in the towns in response to economic arrangements. Important differences emerged in the politics, life-styles, and culture of country people and townfolk. Backcountry towns became microcosms of large cities with merchants who, according to Harold Woodman, were "urban-oriented even when they were not urban dwellers."[39]

Made the county seat in 1791 and incorporated in 1830, Edgefield was the most important town in the district. It was referred to as either Edgefield Village, Edgefield Court House, or just "the Court House." Although never large, it was the political, judicial, social, and, to a more limited extent, commercial hub of a predominantly rural area. In 1826 the village had forty to fifty houses "scattered" and thirty-eight families with a total population of about three hundred. According to the local newspaper, in 1851 Edgefield Village had "four preachers, twelve lawyers, . . . four doctors, one dentist, four teachers, three instructors in music, . . . six regular dry goods stores in full operation, two merchant tailor establishments, with a full assortment of cloths, one apothecary shop, one family grocery, three anti-family groceries, each with a billiard table, . . . one silversmith's shop, one coach factory, two boot and shoe factories, two tin establishments, two cabinet rooms, three blacksmith's shops, one tanyard and one saddlery, three churches, four hotels, one restaurant or cellar, one barber shop, one engine house and engine, one steam mill and one printing press."[40]

Built near the geographical center of the district, the courthouse symbolized Edgefield's role as the local seat of power. The courthouse was the center for display of rank, dignity, and local authority, and Edgefield Village's physical layout exemplified this, with the courthouse building as its topographical focal point. Built on two and one-fourth acres deeded to the judges of Edgefield County Court for public ground, the courthouse was constructed at the highest point. Noted architect Robert Mills designed the courthouse so that the front was at the very crest, with the building extending down the hill. This perfected a square, so that the courthouse reigned supreme over a sort of amphitheater. The editor of the Edgefield *Advertiser* exclaimed in 1839, "The new Court House is . . . a large and noble looking building. . . . As the visitor enters the village by either of the great thoroughfares, the Court House presents a commanding appearance, and immediately attracts his attention." In the splendor of the courthouse and the "public square," Edgefield's antebellum white elite presided over communal affairs. Religious services, Masonic meetings, intellectual gatherings, musical recitals, educational examinations, and all legal and political meetings were held at the courthouse. Here the Philosophical Society, the Bar Association, the Debating Society, and the Literary Club were organized. Militia troops drilled on the square and from there marched off to Florida, Mexico, and the Civil War. In 1854, "Harper" explained that the Edgefield courthouse functioned as an "Oral System" of education: "It is our only college in which the rich and otherwise educated, as well as the poor and illiterate can learn . . . the rights and practical duties of a citizen."[41]

Although important commercially, Edgefield Court House was not the principal marketplace of the district. Because the town was not on any railroad until the 1880s, when a line was established between Edgefield and Trenton that linked the two towns with Aiken, farmers and planters traveled with wagons loaded with cotton bales to Hamburg and Augusta on the Savannah River to market their crops and purchase supplies.

The only other incorporated town in antebellum Edgefield District was Hamburg, twenty-five miles away on the Savannah River. Hamburg was the brainchild of an eccentric German, Henry Shultz, who was buried standing up on Shultz's hill with his back to Augusta. In 1813, Shultz and Lewis Cooper had built a toll bridge from Hamburg across the Savannah River to the prospering hinterland city of Augusta. Before 1 July 1821, not a house stood in Hamburg, but by 1826, two hundred houses and fifty to sixty stores served twelve hundred inhabitants. For a brief period, owing to the energies of Shultz, antebellum Hamburg rivaled Augusta. Trade down the Savannah River from Augusta to the seaport at Savannah became so profitable during the 1820s that Charleston merchants financed construction of a railroad from Charleston to Hamburg to tap the rich trade of the central Savannah River valley. At the time the South Carolina Railroad was the longest in the world.[42]

In the 1830s and 1840s Hamburg handled much of the marketing of cotton and the distribution of the trade of northwestern South Carolina. The Savannah River market centers were so important that the community built a twenty-six-mile-long plank road from Edgefield Court House to Hamburg to overcome the mud and floods that hindered travel to market. During the months of November and December this road was crowded with wagons loaded with bales of cotton. The roads as far as six miles from Hamburg would be so jammed with wagons that travel would slow to about one mile an hour. On the outskirts of the town the wagoneers would pitch camp, with as many as five or six hundred people waiting for morning in order to take their cotton to market in Hamburg. The streets of Hamburg itself were so lined with the wagons of country folks from Georgia, Tennessee, and the Carolinas that pedestrians sometimes had to walk four to five blocks before finding a place to cross the bustling streets. The planters and cotton producers usually purchased the goods and services they would use for the year, or for at least half the year, at the same time that they brought their crops to market. This was normally the only trip that country people made to markets like Hamburg, Augusta, and Columbia; it was a lively and spectacular time.[43]

After the loss of trade following the Panic of 1837, when reduced cotton production combined with economic depression, Augusta's merchants became more determined to undo Hamburg, their east-bank South Carolina rival. The Augusta canal was built to take trade from Hamburg, as well as to provide support for manufacturing and smaller industries, therefore reducing Augusta's total dependence on cotton production. The canal was completed in 1847, and both economic diversification and industry followed along its route. It brought new trade to the Georgia hinterland city and effectively cut Hamburg off from upriver trade.

The Greenville-Columbia Railroad was built in the western portion of the state and stretched from Anderson, through Abbeville County, the northeast tip of Edgefield, Newberry, and Lexington, to Columbia. By the 1850s farmers in western South Carolina shipped their cotton by this rail line. Soon after Hamburg's decline in the 1850s, the South Carolina Railroad, which had terminated at Hamburg, purchased a site for a depot in Augusta and built a trestle across the Savannah to Augusta. The Charlotte-Columbia-Augusta Railroad was originally to terminate in Hamburg, but the Civil War delayed construction, and the Georgia General Assembly voted to extend the railroad to Augusta. Hamburg continued to do a small cotton market business, but the town became best known as a bastion of Republicanism, a town controlled by Afro-Americans during Reconstruction. This once-thriving community is best remembered as the scene of the "Hamburg Massacre." After this 1876 massacre of six black men, Hamburg became a ghost town. It eventually reemerged as North Augusta, South Carolina.[44]

Augusta thus remained for most of the nineteenth century the only urban center in the area around Edgefield County. By the beginning of the nineteenth century, cotton had become a major market crop, and a number of steamship lines ran from Augusta to Savannah to carry cotton for shipment to New England or to Europe for manufacture. By the 1820s Augusta was the central cotton market for upper South Carolina and Georgia. Even when Hamburg challenged Augusta's position as the up-country cotton capital during the 1840s, over seventy thousand bales a year were transported through Augusta. Local lore held that at market time one could walk a mile over bales of cotton and never touch the ground.

In the 1850s Augusta began to prosper as more than just a cotton marketplace. New manufacturing concerns located on the canal. The Civil War served as a spur toward economic specialization and differentiation. Augusta, a major producer of manufactured goods for the Confederate Army, escaped damage in the Civil War and continued to grow afterward. The canal was expanded to provide additional power for new industry. Begun in 1872, this three-year project used 400 Chinese and Afro-American workers for arduous and dangerous jobs. Three textile mills had survived the war, and three additional ones had been built by 1883. New enterprises, ranging from boiler repair shops to chemical companies, appeared. Augusta was a leading Georgia banking center and had rail links to Charleston, Columbia, Atlanta, Savannah, and Charlotte. In the 1870s a railroad was built which connected Augusta to Port Royal harbor in South Carolina. The railroad ran southeast and passed through the Beech Island Section of Old Edgefield District, by then part of Aiken County. In the 1880s another railroad connected Augusta with Greenwood, South Carolina. Despite efforts to bring the Knoxville and Augusta Railroad through the town of Edgefield, the railroad ran twenty miles to the northwest, through the Savannah River valley. The railroads tied Edgefield County even more closely to Augusta.[45]

Before Reconstruction, besides Edgefield Court House and Hamburg, which were the only incorporated towns in antebellum Edgefield District, only two mill villages around the Graniteville and Vaucluse textile plants resembled anything like a town. Even without urban centers, however, an area as large as Edgefield enjoyed neighborhoods, communities, and social networks tied together through economic activities, churches, voluntary organizations, and friendships. A neighborhood generally had its own church and agricultural clubs, police clubs, or Masons. Many small neighborhoods in the district had inhabitants who identified themselves with a specific locale, but no census or history ever recorded these locales as towns or villages. They were demarcated by a church, a post office, or even a store. Places like Ridge Spring, Ward, Liberty Hill, Beech Island, and Red Bank were identifying areas within the community. In 1854, Campbell's *Southern Business Director and General Commercial Advertiser* listed, in addition to Edgefield Court House and Hamburg, twenty-one other post office locations with businesses.[46]

Within these neighborhoods whites knew each other and each other's business, whether first-hand or through gossip, to a greater extent than most of us today can imagine. Militia companies mixed various elements of society on the local level. Excluding that in Augusta and Hamburg (at its height), society in Edgefield District and the small communities within it was characterized by personal interaction and friendship. Black and white communities were geographically one, but psychologically as well as racially distinct. Whites generally knew all the other whites through contacts in local churches and civic groups, but knew few, if any, blacks other than those they owned or hired. Whites kept in touch with others throughout the district through the local newspapers: the Edgefield *Advertiser*, the *Informer*, the *Chronicle*, the Pottersville *Hive*, and the Johnston *Daily*. For those in the western Savannah River areas, the Hamburg *Republic*, the *Valley Pioneer*, the *Courier*, and Augusta papers served a similar function. The editors of these small-town papers were gifted gabbers. People from other sections of the district were not strangers; they were known from marriages, various meetings, market time, sale day, political campaigns, and the Monday when the district court met.[47]

Slaves knew some of the whites, at least by reputation, and certainly knew neighboring slaves, whom they met at churches and more clandestine activities. Slaves who were hired or loaned out relayed news from outside the plantation. After emancipation blacks knew other blacks through their community institutions, just as whites did (except only a few blacks used the newspaper).[48]

Railroads brought little southern towns into existence all along the lines— Clarks Hill, Modoc, Parksville, Plum Branch, McCormick, Troy. The railroads built depots where county roads crossed or where a small settlement already existed—usually no more than a few houses, a store, and a church. At the border of Edgefield and Lexington counties where the Columbia-Augusta Stage Coach Road and the Charleston–Orangeburg–Mt. Willing road crossed, Batesburg grew up on the Charlotte-Columbia-Augusta Railroad. Aiken began as a railroad station some seventeen miles from Hamburg. This antebellum town on the line between Barnwell and Edgefield districts survived largely because of the 3,800-foot inclined plane that lowered trains over the steep plateau slope at the western edge of the settlement. Because of the railroad, Aiken prospered and became a small marketplace. As early as 1836 Edgefield planters quoted Aiken prices. During the late nineteenth century Aiken became a nationally famous resort town. The opening of the large and fashionable Highland Park Hotel in 1870 made Aiken a haven for prosperous Yankees during the winter. By 1872 Aiken was singled out by the Edgefield *Advertiser* as one of the South's "most progressive places."[49]

To the northeast, some twenty-seven miles from Edgefield Court House, was the old district judicial center of Ninety Six, renamed Cambridge by the South Carolina General Assembly in 1787. With the construction of the Greenville-Columbia Railroad in 1851, the little village shifted two miles eastward to the railroad line. Greenwood prospered on the same line, some nine miles north of Ninety Six. The railroad reached northward to both Anderson and Abbeville by 1852. Right across the Saluda River in Newberry County was Chappels, which grew as a depot on the same railroad. First a ferry and then a bridge linked Edgefield to Newberry at Chappels.

During Reconstruction at least four other towns emerged from places like those listed above where the railroad passed through the district. The Pine House was an area landmark dating from the Revolutionary War, located on the Edgefield Village–Aiken wagon road. Trenton grew up around the Pine House, seven miles south of Edgefield Village and twenty-six miles from Augusta and Hamburg, owing to the Charlotte-Columbia-Augusta Railroad. Ward, named after Clinton Ward, who owned a plantation through which the Charlotte-Columbia-Augusta Railroad ran, was chartered when the railroad was built during the Civil War. For five years Ward was the terminus of the railroad. A Baptist church built around a small stream of clear water in the ridge area of eastern Edgefield gave the name of Ridge Spring to the town that grew up there on the Charlotte-Columbia-Augusta Railroad. Johnston was only a small settlement some seven miles from Edgefield Court House until the building of the Charlotte-Columbia-Augusta Railroad through it in 1869. Almost immediately, Johnston became the leading commercial center north of Augusta and the envy of Edgefield Court House. By 1873 Johnston shipped about ten thousand cotton bales a season and had nine dry goods stores, a drug store, plus several other stores and service establishments.[50]

Industry

Antebellum Edgefield District had modest manufacturing establishments. In 1860 the census listed seventy-four "factories." These included a paper mill at Bath and two famed cotton textile plants, Graniteville and Vaucluse, which employed 169 men and 230 women. Vaucluse was older; Graniteville was established in 1849 under the direction of William Gregg, one of the antebellum South's most celebrated industrialists. These textile factories employed whites only; they were two of the oldest and most successful in the South. They were located about twenty and twenty-five miles from Hamburg and Augusta up the stream known as Horse Creek, which fed into the Savannah River near the two towns. In 1860 South Carolina had only seventeen cotton goods manufacturing establishments, with a total of 891 employees. Edgefield's two mills accounted for over half the capital, purchased over half the raw material, recorded over half the annual cost of labor, and had nearly half of the employees in the whole state. In addition, the lumber-sawing industry, which had twenty-six businesses and employed 113 men and one woman, had great economic significance. Most of the other factories in Edgefield District were small businesses with few workers, such as the three blacksmith shops, which averaged two employees per shop.[51]

Edgefield contained a goldmine, which produced small quantities of ore and was eventually bought by Cyrus McCormick. Edgefield also contained deposits of high-quality clay; in fact, Josiah Wedgewood, the famed eighteenth-century potter, recognized the quality of Edgefield's kaolin clay and shipped three tons of it home to England. With the availability of this fine clay, Abner Landrum built the first pottery establishment between 1810 and 1820 using free and slave labor, and the artisan town of Pottersville developed around it. About one and one-half miles north of Edgefield Court House, this village consisted mostly of potters and skilled workers in the stoneware establishments. A contemporary described Pottersville: "The village is altogether supported by the manufacture of stoneware." But the village also had blacksmiths, wagon makers, wagon drivers, millers, and wheelwrights. By 1826 sixteen houses contained sixteen families, and a few stores had grown up there. This village even had its own newspaper, the Unionist *South Carolina Republican*.

A number of other pottery factories sprang up in Edgefield. In 1834, Lewis Miles, Landrum's son-in-law, established Miles Mill. In 1840, Collin Rhodes and Robert W. Mathis (with managerial skills of Landrum's brother Amos) founded the Phoenix factory. In 1847, Thomas Chandler, a potter artisan in the Phoenix factory, started his own business at Kirksey's Crossroads. In 1862, Col. Thomas Jones Davies established a pottery at Bath, twenty-two miles south of Edgefield Court House. During the Civil War, Davies hired Anson Peeler from Bennington, Vermont, a noted pottery center, to direct his slave potters. Edgefield pottery works used slave labor, yet also employed four-fifths of the state's free pottery workers. Two-thirds of the state's pottery works were located in Edgefield District.[52]

By 1860 Edgefield District's capital invested in manufacturing ($989,175) and annual cost of labor ($162,761) were second only to Charleston's. Annual value of products ($761,155) and number of males employed in industry (486) were third in the state; the number of females employed (253) was the highest in the state.[53]

Agriculture

Most of the wealth of Edgefield derived from agriculture. The first settlers in the area—hunters, trappers, and traders—were soon followed by others who devoted their time to herding or collecting cattle and driving them to Charleston, Savannah, or other distant markets. Along with these cattle drovers, however, came the first permanent settlements, and farming became the settlers' livelihood. Small farmers and landless cattle drovers continued to allow their stock to pasture in the timberlands and open fields. For the landless and small yeoman farmers this was a distinct advantage, but planters and farmers had to fence their crops to keep out cattle and hogs, which roamed wild. For the large planter, the open range laws were a major barrier to agricultural reform. Only if stock were fenced or penned could manure be collected for fertilizer, and although the plantations had large numbers of hogs, cattle, oxen, mules, sheep, and horses in the antebellum period, planters, concerned about the quality of stock and breeding, began to build pens and fences to keep their cattle separated from stock that roamed wild.

Open grazing of cattle and hogs allowed a continuation of the early stock drover's way of life, which involved hunting, fishing, some subsistence farming, and living off the land. This way of life was as much a part of the up-country culture as was that of the more celebrated plantation. After the Civil War the open range also provided opportunities for former slaves. This ended with the enactment of the fence laws in the early 1880s, a triumph for large plantation owners, who no longer had to fence their vast crop acreages.[54]

Antebellum plantations in up-country Edgefield were more rustic than the typical low-country plantations. The up-country plantation economy was also more diversified, producing timber and more corn, oats, wheat, rye, barley, and other grains than those in the low country. Edgefield farmers even grew some tobacco and rice, and in 1850 and 1860 Edgefield led the state in animal and crop production. The value of Edgefield's livestock, the number of horses, mules, asses, and swine, and the value of animals slaughtered were greater than those of other districts. Edgefield was high in butter and cheese production. With the largest improved farm acreage in the state in 1850 and 1860, Edgefield was either first or second in cotton, orchard, oat, Irish potato, and corn production. In 1850 Edgefield was third in the value of produce from market gardens and led the state in the value of homemade manufactures, an index of self-sufficiency.[55]

In 1860, whether small farmer, cattle drover, or planter, two-thirds of the gainfully employed white population were directly engaged in agriculture, either as farmers or farm laborers. With the addition of those listed in the census as "laborers," which meant essentially farm laborers, household heads employed directly in agricultural production constituted seven out of every ten free household heads in the district.

The slaves in Edgefield were nearly all agrarian laborers. Before the Civil War, most plantation slaves worked under the "gang" labor system, where slaves were divided into specific groups and each group was responsible for a certain amount of work. (An alternative system was the more individualistic "task" system, where each slave was assigned a specific chore.) The gangs were generally organized into plow gangs, which consisted of strong young males (some women plowed, but they were exceptions and usually used shallow one-horse plows), and hoe gangs, which consisted of elderly slaves and women. Planters wanted to maintain the gang labor system after the Civil War, but former slaves refused to work in gangs and the family-oriented tenant system predominated. Plantation owners, however, continued to find Afro-American laborers in the towns who would work gang-style on those acres not allotted to tenants.

A few slaves were skilled artisans, but most of these employed their skills as blacksmiths or carpenters on farms. Rare indeed was the skilled slave who had not performed some sort of farm labor, at least in the peak work seasons. An Edgefield slaveowner claimed that although slaves could "become efficient and profitable operatives" in factories in the South, they had to remain in the "appropriate sphere" of agricultural labor. The use of slaves in "manufactures and mechanic arts" was not a safe or sound policy, because "whenever a slave is made a mechanic, he is more than half freed, and soon . . . the most corrupt and turbulent of his class."[56]

Cotton Production

Edgefield life was regulated by the agricultural economy and especially, after the 1840s, by the cultivation of cotton. Although Edgefield, free and slave, worked at a diversity of agricultural and industrial pursuits, by 1850 the routine of taking care of the white-blossomed and white-bolled short-staple cotton plants increasingly typified rural Edgefield existence. The labor system changed dramatically, but the actual cultivation procedure changed little throughout the nineteenth century. A bed for the cotton had to be prepared by clearing out the old stalks from the previous crop. Sometimes these stalks were beaten down with clubs; if they were large (four to five feet), they had to be pulled by hand. Generally manure or commercial fertilizer was placed as deeply as possible in the furrow. The cotton bed was built up in February and March. The actual planting of the cotton seed was in April; early planters risked frost, late planters risked dry spells. Most planting was done by hand, but some postbellum farmers used mechanical planters drawn by horses. Within a month to a month and a half, the plants were thinned. From July through August, the crop was cultivated with a sweep plowed between the rows four or five times and hoed by hand three or four times. In the middle of

June, when they were anywhere from six inches to a foot high, the cotton plants bloomed. Around the last of July or first of August, forty-two to forty-five days after they had blossomed, the cotton bolls opened. Picking began as early as 12 August, but usually began about 20 August.

Cotton, harvested as soon as it opened, was picked by the middle of December. Most of the crop was ginned immediately. The average amount of seed cotton used to make a 400-pound bale of lint was about 1,225 pounds (it ranged from about 1,200 to 1,400). Cotton was shipped to market continuously in the fall and winter, from September through January. The bales had to be transported from the gins to a local market and then on to larger markets. By 1880 the charge for shipment from Augusta down the Savannah River to Savannah was seventy-five cents per bale of cotton, and the charge down the Pee Dee River to Charleston was a dollar. The cost of the Port Royal Railroad to Charleston or Savannah was two dollars for a 450-pound bale of cotton with a surcharge of twenty cents for every hundred pounds over. From Augusta and the stations along the South Carolina Railroad, the cost was a dollar and a half for a bale weighing up to 500 pounds and 35 cents for each hundred pounds over. The demanding cultivation and transportation of cotton required the labor of the majority of men, women and children in Edgefield.[57]

Edgefield proslavery writers justified the southern agrarian life for planters, yeomen, and even slaves as the most virtuous and manly of occupations and coupled it with republican government for whites. According to the editor of the Edgefield *Advertiser*, Arthur Simkins, agriculture was not only a means to wealth and power, recommending it to the "cold utilitarian," but it also appealed to those "who love virtue for its own sake." The day was approaching when the "rich blessings we have inherited from a virtuous ancestry" would move southern agriculturalists to stand as the "immoveable bulwark" of America's republican democracy against the violence of the "mobocratic tendencies in American society," emerging from the "larger cities and more populous manufacturing towns" of the Northeast.[58]

James Henry Hammond cherished agriculture as "the very Foster-Dame of Freedom." He expounded the virtues of the "ancient and illustrious calling of agriculture, which . . . cherishes and promotes a generous hospitality, a high and perfect courtesy, a lofty spirit of independence, an uncalculating love of country, and all the nobler virtues and heroic traits of man." Hammond believed that "in cities and factories, the vices of our nature are more fully displayed, while the purest morals are fostered by rural life." While calling for industrialization and for factories like that at Graniteville near his Edgefield home, Hammond still maintained that it was "of utmost importance in all governments, especially in one so democratic as our own and in all social systems, especially where, as in ours, so much equality prevails, that the preponderating influence should be agricultural."[59]

The Edgefield planter class defended its power base. The cultivation of cotton by a large slave labor force had, according to Hammond, "created a large class elevated above the necessity of any kind of labor, many of whom have devoted themselves to letters, to travel, and to public affairs. Even those who . . . superintend in person their own concerns, are accustomed to take enlarged and manly views of every thing; to govern masses; to sway, comparatively, a broad expanse of territory; to control and scorn to be controlled, except by kind affection, sound reason, and just laws. Such characters are essential elements of a high state of civilization." Reverend Iveson Brookes claimed, "No Republican government can long exist without the institution of slavery incorporated into it." Even the northern-bred son-in-law of John C. Calhoun, Thomas Green Clemson, when pondering the sale of his slaves and his Edgefield plantation, "Canebreak," acknowledged the inextricable connection between slavery and southern society: "Slaves are the most valuable property in the South, being the basis of the whole southern fabric."

In 1851, at Edgefield Court House, Francis Pickens outlined the alternative to slavery: "The terrible effects of abolition when brought to our homes and to our fire-sides? Three millions of black slaves, turned lose upon the community . . . would work for little or nothing—a bottle of rum and twist of tobacco; what would become of the free artisans, enterprising mechanics, and industrious laborers of our country?" Joseph Abney proclaimed that without slavery "a Democratic Republic cannot exist." Slavery "is the safeguard and very bulwark of Republicanism."[60]

Housing

In Edgefield District most houses were simple and functional, essentially cabins. Even the owner of eighteen slaves and twelve to thirteen thousand dollars of real estate might live in a one-story, four-room, ceiling-exposed house built of rough-sawed lumber. These houses were as conservative and straightforward as their owners. Rooms often led straight into other rooms, for walls inhibited the multiple uses of rooms. A single room might serve as office, parlor, dining room, workshop, kitchen, or bedroom, as needed. In most cases, the houses did not have much ornamentation and only details that served a purpose were included. House and furnishings reflected the use of materials from the locale. Sometimes a second story was added to these plain homes. A family lived close together, and there was little privacy; husband and wife were with one another almost every day and night, working together in the field or artisan shop during the day and sleeping together at night.[61]

Slave houses were constructed simply, generally with one open room. Houses stood near one another, fostering homogeneity and community. A number of former slaves from Edgefield described slave homes. A former Edgefield slave, born in 1852, explained that they "had houses of weather-boards, big enough for chicken coop—man, wife and chillun life dere." The slave house was too small for more than one family. Another former slave, however, remembered that "our house wuz made outter logs. We didn't have nuthin much nohow, but my mammy, she had plenty o'room for her chillun. Us didn't sleep on de flo'—we had a bed. De people in de plantation all had beds. . . . De houses wuz in rows." Rachel Sullivan, former slave of Governor Francis W. Pickens, the area's largest slaveowner, also commented upon the houses: "Des like dis street—two rows facin' each odder, only dey was log houses." Although they had only one room, "dey drap a shed room down if dare was a heap o'chillun." Postbellum Afro-American housing developed along the same lines as the other housing in Edgefield.[62]

In contrast, financed by the success of commercialized cotton production (made possible by slavery, the cotton gin, and improved transportation), the wealthy Edgefield plantation owners built elaborate and impressive mansions for themselves after 1830. The mansions, which were definitely the exception rather than the rule for both antebellum and postbellum whites, became beautiful artifacts, large and grand, as imposing as the people who built them. Two or three stories with broad front porches, these buildings reflected the symmetrical theories of Georgian styles. Open piazzas greeted those of equal social status.

Southern elite families began to feel a need for increased privacy. The houses provided privacy through controlled access, and unlike the inhabitants of common houses, husbands and wives on the great plantations had their own bedrooms and apartments. The rooms, which served specialized functions, were connected by a system of broad halls.

The occupants of these mansions felt that they were set apart, and their homes served to strengthen this belief. In contrast to the rough boards and logs of other homes, the exteriors were whitewashed, and the great houses stood apart from the slave quarters and at a distance from any road, even in the towns. The Edgefield Village home where Preston Brooks was born and reared had four acres of flower gardens in the front. Places of refuge and seclusion, they were visible reminders of the status and position of their owners. Sited to advantage, they dominated their environments.[63]

The mansions were more than merely places to live. Passed down through generations, they came to symbolize the families themselves. It was not unusual for children to be born, live, marry, die, and be mourned by their own children, who would then repeat the process, all in the same home. The southern aristocracy was based only on the acquisition of land and slaves; it had no conferred legitimacy. Thus the Southerner's mansion, built on real foundations, was the symbolic foundation for his claim of membership in an upper order. Each of these Edgefield family homes was given a name: Center Springs House, Roath Wood, Forest Hill, Cedar Grove. In choosing a name for his estates, the Edgefield aristocrat sought immortality for his dynasty by tying the name of his house to a permanent, immortal feature of the geography. The silver bluffs and red cliffs that provided the names for Hammond's plantation and his Edgefield home were features noted by De Soto in his 1540 American exploration.[64]

These houses served as social centers. The bigger the home, the more splendid the party it could contain, and dances would begin early in the evening and last far into the night. Women would stay over for several days, and men would leave and return again for the next night's festivities. Parties of this sort attracted people from all over the state and Georgia.

These vast homes symbolized patriarchy as well; they protected the women and children and served as castles and refuges from the world. Harry Hammond made this point when he complained to his wife in Edgefield of the Confederate leader Jubal Early's attacks in the North. In 1864, Hammond stated that Early should be sent to Georgia, where he "might be better employed . . . than in imitating the barbarity of our enemies in burning down the homes of women and children." Symbolism aside, these mansions were also homes. After being away with his family, Francis Pickens noted with relief as he arrived at his house in Edgefield that he was back at "sweet home."[65]

Economy

Slavery and cotton production were not always the rule in early nineteenth-century Edgefield and the Piedmont South.[66] With the perfection of the cotton gin in 1793, the area was the locus of the first great cotton boom. After the "bust" of 1819 slashed cotton prices, the area went through a considerable decline through the 1840s, as erosion, soil exhaustion, and the lure of fresh land in the West reduced both population and productivity. In Edgefield, however, vigorous agricultural reform led by local agricultural societies renewed vitality. The prewar decade found cotton prices stabilized at about twelve cents a pound, which farmers found profitable. Both large and small farms followed the same planting and production patterns; almost all farms raised cotton as a cash crop, but the smaller farms grew more corn and less cotton than larger enterprises. By 1860, with the state's fourth largest population, most of whom were engaged in farming, antebellum Edgefield District led South Carolina in the number of bales of cotton produced. The large cotton crop was due primarily to the presence of large plantations and large numbers of slaves; in the total values of real ($11,025,269) and personal ($27,442,589) property the area was second only to Charlestown.[67]

The decade preceding the Civil War saw a decrease in concentration of land ownership as well as a decrease in both the free black and white population. In 1850, 1,839 Edgefieldians owned land and by 1860, 2,007 did. However, great economic disparity persisted among the free population. Although from the agricultural census it appears that the number of farms increased from 1850 to 1860 (see Figure 1-2), the number of farms that are recorded in the census with no acreage increased from three in 1850 to 240 in 1860 (see Figure 1-3). These farms without acreage were tenant farms; tenants operated 14 percent of all 1860 Edgefield farms. Thus, average size and number of farms is deceiving. The number of farms operated by landowners actually decreased and when one excludes farms with no reported acreage, the average farm size increased from 1850 to 1860. By 1860, there was a total of 310,768 improved acres. (The Civil War and Reconstruction account for the drastic increase in small farms in 1880; this is discussed in chapters 6 and 7.) Nevertheless, whereas in 1850 nearly three of every ten farms had been five hundred acres or more and only one of ten had been less than fifty acres, in 1860 nearly a tenth of all farms were five hundred acres or more in size, while more than a third were less than fifty acres. In 1850 the mean value of landholdings for households had been $2,038 and a median value of landholdings had been five hundred dollars, with the top 10 percent of landowning household heads controlling 62 percent of the total wealth, while 41.6 percent of all household heads had no land. In a detailed breakdown of the total real estate wealth for Edgefield District's free population in 1860, the mean value for household heads was $2,370, but the median value was nine hundred dollars. The top 10 percent of landowning household heads held 61 percent of the total land of the district, while 38.1 percent of all household heads owned no land.[68]

The 1860 manuscript census for Edgefield revealed great disparities in the personal estate of individuals and household heads. Although the mean value was $8,656 and the median personal wealth for all household heads was one thousand dollars, the wealthiest 10 percent accounted for 73 percent of the wealth, while the poorest quarter of household heads all together owned less than $200 personal estate. Part of this great discrepancy can be accounted for by the practice of counting slaves as personal wealth. Twenty-two individuals had more than $100,000 invested in personal property. Among non–household heads, 280 owned personal property of more than one thousand dollars (at least 147 of these owned slaves); half of the household heads in 1860 had less than a thousand dollars in personal estate. Of the total wealth (real and personal) in 1860, the 10 percent of wealthiest households owned 57 percent of the total. The top 1 percent of household heads controlled 18.8 percent of the total wealth.

About half of all households headed by farmers in 1850 owned no slaves, and half of those households owned no land either. From 1850 to 1860 only a few farmers who had previously lacked land and slaves acquired both. However, only a very few of those who stayed in Edgefield lost land or slaves. For some of the wealthiest people in 1850, the gains were extraordinary. Still in 1860, two of every five households headed by farmers owned no slaves, and again, nearly half of those households owned no land either. The increased

Figure 1–2. Average Acreage per Farm, 1850 to 1880

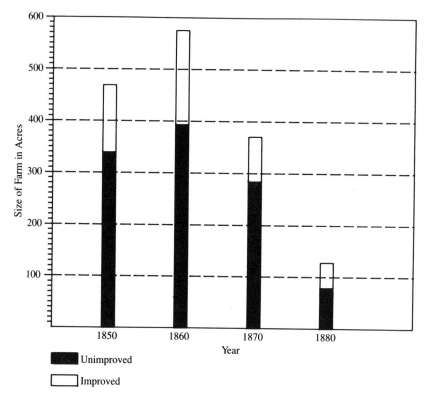

Note: Excludes farms reporting no acreage; see Figure 1–3.

Source: Edgefield Data Base; see also U.S., Bureau of the Census, *7th* (1850) *Census*, p. 345, *8th* (1860) *Census*, vol. 2, *Agriculture*, pp. 128, 244, *9th* (1870) *Census*, vol. 3, *Statistics of Wealth*, pp. 239–41, *10th* (1880) *Census*, vol. 3, *Report of Production of Agriculture*, pp. 25, 84–85, 132; Smith, *Economic Readjustment*, p. 81.

wealth of Edgefield District was not shared proportionately by all whites, but most of those who stayed made some material gains.[69]

Edgefield leaders worried about the migration that carried so many whites and their slaves to the southwestern states of Georgia, Alabama, Mississippi, Louisiana, Arkansas, and Texas. In 1852 the editor of the Edgefield *Advertiser* "grieved to see the spirit of emigration so rife among our friends." Slightly more than 40 percent of white household heads who lived in Edgefield in 1850 were still there in 1860. Almost all of those who stayed the decade made economic progress, measured in accumulation both of land and of slaves. For all persisters, the mean number of slaves owned increased 14 percent. The

Figure 1–3. Farms by Size, 1850 to 1880

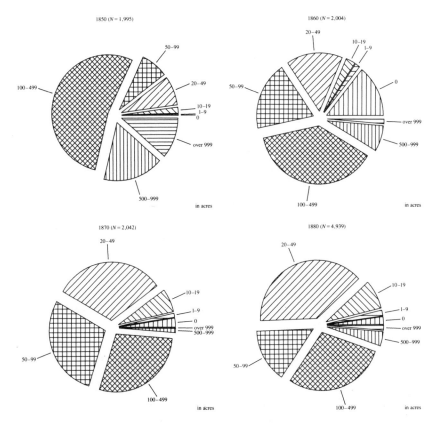

Note: Generally, acreages of zero indicated that the farm operator was a tenant.

Source: Edgefield Data Base; see also U.S., Bureau of the Census, *8th* (1860) *Census*, vol. 2, *Agriculture*, pp. 128, 214, 244, *9th* (1870) *Census*, vol. 3, *Statistics of Wealth*, pp. 140, 362, *10th* (1880) *Census*, vol. 3, *Report of Production of Agriculture*, pp. 25, 84–85, 132; Smith, *Economic Readjustment*, p. 81.

wealthier the individual in 1850, the greater the proportionate increase in wealth for 1860.[70]

Age was a factor in the accumulation of wealth. Some of the "poor" were really the children of well-to-do parents. In 1850, Noah D. Timmerman was listed in the household of his father, a large landowner. In 1860 and 1870 he headed his own household and was landless. By 1880 he had inherited his father's lands. Other younger household heads, however, like Jonathan C. Harris, son of poor antebellum tenant farmer Andrew Harris, did not inherit land and probably would have remained poor and landless if not for the political opportunities offered by the Republican party during Reconstruction.[71]

In Edgefield District slaveowners paid most of the taxes. In 1857 slaves were assessed $.70, and real estate twenty mills per hundred dollars value. Free blacks paid a tax of three dollars on themselves. By the Civil War the tax on slaves had reached one dollar for each slave.[72]

Slavery was the basis of economic prosperity in Edgefield; those with slaves prospered. Between 1850 and 1860 upward mobility depended upon increased slaveownership. With slaves as collateral, planters obtained credit from cotton factors, and they could rent or sell slaves if the need arose. Taxes levied upon slaves provided the antebellum district with its revenue to pay salaries, care for indigents, and repair roads. In 1860 62.8 percent of white households owned land, and 65.6 percent of landowners owned slaves.

Slaveownership

Scholars have generally been misled by the statement in the 1860 census that "it would probably be a safe rule to consider the number of slaveholders to represent the number of families directly interested in the slave population." In Edgefield, at least 158 non–family heads owned slaves.

From 1850 to 1860, the actual number of individuals owning slaves in Edgefield decreased by 97, while overall the white population decreased by 599. The tendency of a few proprietors was toward owning more slaves (see Figure 1-4a). Yet in 1850 and 1860, respectively, 57.9 and 55.1 percent of slaveowners owned fewer than ten slaves, and 20.8 and 23.6 percent owned twenty or more slaves (twenty slaves was considered enough to constitute a plantation). Edgefield had twelve individuals who owned a hundred or more slaves in 1860, which made them a part of the group often referred to as the "great planters." In 1850 the census enumerator listed 3,032 households and in 1860, 3,007, which would suggest that in 1850 about 57 percent and in 1860 about 54 percent of household heads were slaveowners. However, the above figures for percentage of households owning slaves include in their numbers some households and families in which different members owned slaves. In 1860, 46.1 percent of household heads owned slaves in Edgefield.[73]

From the perspective of the average white slaveowner, Edgefield could be seen as something of a slaveholder's herrenvolk democracy. But the Afro-American perspective was the opposite. Figure 1-4b compares the distribution of slaves to the distribution of slaveownership (Figure 1-4a) and illustrates different perspectives for southern whites and for Afro-Americans. While only between a fifth and a fourth of white slaveowners had twenty or more slaves in 1850 and 1860, respectively, three-fifths and two-thirds of all slaves lived on

Figure 1–4. Distribution of Slaves and Slaveownership, 1850 and 1860

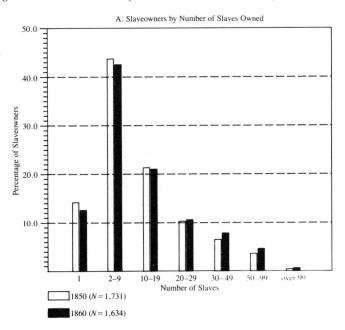

A. Slaveowners by Number of Slaves Owned

□ 1850 (*N* = 1,731)

■ 1860 (*N* = 1,634)

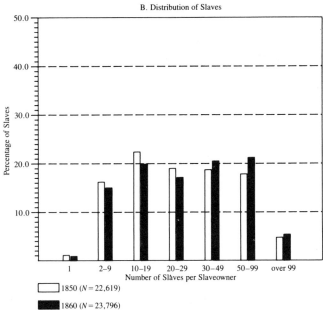

B. Distribution of Slaves

□ 1850 (*N* = 22,619)

■ 1860 (*N* = 23,796)

Source: Edgefield Data Base; see also, U.S., Bureau of the Census, *8th* (1860) *Census*, vol. 2, *Agriculture*, p. 237.

plantations of twenty or more slaves in those census years. Increasingly the average slave was from the plantation, not the small farm.

Summary

The varied geography of Edgefield District allowed for different types of farms and levels of wealth. While largely agricultural, Edgefield had substantial trade and nascent industry; professional and nonprofessional occupations were represented. By the Civil War, Edgefield, while it lacked a railroad to Edgefield Court House, had a well-developed transportation system.

Edgefield District was coherent in its socioeconomic outlook—not only did large and small farmers plant the same, but they were in much agreement on values, goals, and modes of interaction, all of which proceeded from a society based on complex kinship, religious, and social ties. There were, however, important differences between rich and poor whites, as well as between blacks and whites. Slavery made possible a particular kind of culture and society. The large slaveowners composed a unique class, a class reared to command and manage large agricultural enterprises and inculcated from birth with notions of honor, duty, manliness, and paternalism.

2. Edgefield from the White Perspective

What then were these regional mores that set the South apart from the more plastic North . . . (1) an exaggerated sense of honor, based on the cult of the gentleman; (2) a profound religious orthodoxy; (3) an intense local attachment or patriotism that was supported by a strong feeling for family (including blacks and whites)—Calhoun said that the North was an aggregate of individuals, the South of communities.

Clement Eaton, *The Mind of the Old South*[1]

The poor, yeoman middle class, and elite held many values in common. Notions of honor and virtue, of paternal priority in the family, of the importance of religion—all were shaped and shared by the different groups.[2] Mores are long-lived, and despite the effects of the Civil War on white society, most of the values of the antebellum community survived the war. While this chapter considers white society before the Civil War, much of the discussion of culture is also applicable to the postbellum period. Change over time will be discussed primarily in later chapters where postbellum blacks and whites are compared.

Poor Whites

The South has been viewed as a land of extremes, of Tara and Tobacco Road, of cavalier aristocrats and poor white trash. On the one hand, popular literature depicted a paternalistic and aristocratic South devoted to tradition, with family as the cornerstone of that tradition. On the other hand, we have images of Snopeses and of the Erskine Caldwell characters who starved a grandmother to death.[3]

In rural Edgefield almost everyone, poor or rich, black or white, did the same thing in basically the same way: they farmed (see Table 2-1). Most, of course, had agricultural jobs. Even those with special skills were usually involved in agriculture-related activities, such as blacksmithing. Almost four-fifths of those whites gainfully employed in 1850 (excluding women, since the

1850 census did not list their occupations) and more than two-thirds in 1860 worked in farming as laborers, farmers, planters, or overseers.

In Edgefield poor, yeoman middle class, and rich were tied to each other in a multifaceted social economy consisting of networks of obligations, trade, and exchanges of labor, services, and products. Different wealth groups made various arrangements for payment. Most paid cash. Sometimes slaveowners loaned merchants a slave for a day or two in payment for goods. A carpenter and a blacksmith worked on drayman James Mitchell's wagons in exchange for services. Some produce was exchanged as pay. These sorts of informal payments were possible in a rural community where people knew one another and one's word was one's bond. People trusted one another. Most labor exchange was done after merchants had delivered goods to their customers, neighbors, and friends.[4]

No matter what their occupations or wealth, whites were not segregated, even in the towns. In Edgefield the landless whites and landowning elites lived next to each other and had reciprocal community obligations. The poor often worked for the rich. Small farmers often depended upon the help of large planters in getting their cotton ginned and to market. Yeomen and the less affluent often depended on more affluent neighbors and relatives to act as agents. The 1860 manuscript census showed that the very wealthy Francis W. Pickens had neighbors of varying economic status. At fifty-five years of age, Pickens reported $45,000 worth of real estate and $244,206 worth of personal estate. His next-door neighbors in one direction were a middle-class farmer and his wife, the Gallmans, who owned land valued at $1,200 and a personal estate of $4,000. Next to them were David and Susan Kissie and their five children. Kissie, a mechanic with $150 of personal property, was fifty years old, landless, and illiterate. Two of his sons were laborers living at home. Pickens's neighbors in the other direction were a wealthy farmer and his family; the Nicholsons owned $30,000 worth of land and $80,000 worth of personal estate. Next to them lived Pickens's daughter Maria and son-in-law Matthew Calbraith Butler with their two-year-old son, Francis Pickens Butler. Butler, twenty-four years old, owned $7,000 of real estate and $17,000 of personal estate. Next to them lived Mr. and Mrs. Crawford with their three children. Crawford, twenty-eight years old, was a literate mechanic with $150 in personal estate and no land.

Diversity in economic status created differences in life-styles. In December 1850, Pickens spent fifty dollars for five tickets so that his family could hear Jenny Lind (the Swedish Nightingale) sing in Charleston. In addition, the entry in his diary recorded the costs of the round trip to Charleston, dinners at expensive restaurants, and a visit to the family dentist. By comparison, one-eighth of the white households in Edgefield had less than fifty dollars in personal estate in 1860.[5]

A small group of indigents in Edgefield always depended on the local

Table 2-1. Occupations of Whites, 1850 and 1860

	1850[a]				1860			
	Employed		Household Heads		Employed		Household Heads	
Occupation	Male (N=3,931)	Female (N=24)	Male (N=2,485)	Female (N=487)	Male (N=3,600)	Female (N=751)	Male (N=2,520)	Female (N=432)
Farmer	73.2	37.5	72.6	0.4	63.2	33.0	69.2	53.5
Laborer	6.7	0	4.6	0	17.6	23.6	11.4	0.7
Artisan and semiskilled	9.2	0	9.6	0	8.5	0.4	8.7	0.5
Professional, business, low white collar	10.6	62.5	9.0	0.8	10.2	4.5	8.8	1.9
Domestic	0.4	0	0.3	0	0.5	38.5	0.4	27.3
Other			3.9	98.8			1.5	16.2

a. In 1850 the census enumerator was instructed not to record the occupations of females. He did record that of twenty-four women who were teaching and farming, however.

Note: For occupational groupings see appendix 2.

Source: Edgefield Data Base.

government for support. In 1826 about fifty "unfortunate persons" lived in Edgefield District. Robert Mills explained that in Edgefield "the poor . . . are put to work under a superintendant. The tax to support them, formerly amounting to thirty percent of the general tax, has been considerably reduced under the present regulation. This is a subject of deep concern to the community." Much earlier, colonial South Carolina had established a vagrancy act against those wanderers and "all persons (not following some handicraft, trade or profession, or not having some known or visible means of livelihood,) who shall be able to work, and occupying or being in possession of some piece of land, shall not cultivate such quantity thereof as shall be . . . necessary for the maintenance of himself and his family." In addition, in 1778 the state legislature added to the vagrancy list "any person convicted of fire hunting," that is, hunting deer by night, blinding them with torchlight to shorten the hunt. In 1830 the Edgefield Village Bible Society reported fifty-five families "destitute of a Bible" and voted Bibles to those families too poor to buy one. In 1835 the Edgefield free school commissioners reported, "There are a great many poor children in our District, and they scattered over" the countryside. One of these school commissioners was Press Bland, an Edgefield planter who was especially influential during the Nullification Crisis. He regularly visited the small railroad town of Aiken on the border of Edgefield and Barnwell districts during the 1840s. Overindulging in the liquid entertainment available there, he would mount his horse and head for home singing at the top of his lungs: "Barnwell District, Aiken Town; O Lord in mercy do look down! The land is poor, the people too; If they don't steal, what will they do?"[6]

In 1850 and 1860 some of the destitute lived in the Edgefield County poorhouse. They usually listed their occupation as pauper or indigent. (For household heads in 1850 and 1860, these occupations were included with "other" in Table 2-1.) In 1851, W. C. Prater, superintendent of the poorhouse, defended his and his wife's management against accusation that the house was not properly maintained. The local newspaper praised the care given to the paupers in the poorhouse and agreed that "the white paupers of our District were . . . the most comfortably sustained paupers in the world." Each year the board of commissioners of the poor presented a report. In 1860 the poor tax amounted to $1,767.13, and funds from two bastardy cases involving female inmates brought in $47. At the time of the report nineteen people resided in the poorhouse, including five adult men and ten adult women. The only destitute inmates were three young women and their children; most of the residents were blind, idiotic, deformed, afflicted, epileptic, or crippled. The poorhouse had 202 acres, of which 60 acres were cleared and cultivated "by a hired negro man, and each of the Paupers that are able . . . [produced] nearly a sufficiency of corn to support the place."[7]

In Edgefield, where land was the key to wealth, 40 and 37 percent, respectively, of white household heads owned no land in 1850 and 1860. Households headed by women were more likely to be landless than those headed by men. Generally, the more land a household had, the greater the likelihood of its being male-headed. When we consider total wealth in 1860, only the two poorest deciles had fewer than 80 percent of their households headed by males. Of the remaining deciles, 84 to 90 percent of the households were headed by males.

Wealth helped determine a widow's chance for remarriage. Whereas widows of rich planters and even women who inherited only modest amounts of property remarried with relative ease, poorer widows with families had a difficult time remarrying. George Tillman, who had killed a mechanic, Henry Christian, in an argument over a card game, supported Christian's widow because she had no sons, only daughters, and thus had no way to make a living and little chance of obtaining another husband. Wealthier widows, on the other hand, had no trouble remarrying if they so chose; Hester Smallwood (of the Bonham family) was left a widow by four husbands in fifty years.[8]

Widowed women with children had few options if they did not remarry. Tutoring or teaching was a possibility, but most women in the poorest classes did not have the schooling needed to teach. Seamstress, nurse, knitter, governess, or domestic employee were possibilities, but before and after the Civil War white women competed with black women for these jobs. Augusta's houses of ill repute were a sordid option; one white woman in Augusta in 1860 lived with a free black man and listed "lady of pleasure" as her occupation.[9]

Especially disturbing was the plight of elderly widows. Those left without family, such as Rachel Temple or Esther McGraw (for whose support Edgefield neighbors petitioned the state legislature), were "in a distressed situation." Even an older widow who owned land and had children nearby could need financial assistance. In 1839 neighbor James Yeldell wrote for seventy-three-year-old Mary Robertson, "praying" the legislature for a Revolutionary War pension. Yeldell described her as in "moderate circumstances." Robertson "resided on a small tract of 150 acres, a life estate which, with a little house, furniture, and a small stock is her whole property." She had two children by her first husband, a Revolutionary War veteran in North Carolina, and four more by her second husband. Although her youngest son lived with her, "being poor and obliged to devote much attention to . . . [his mother] he cannot do much for himself or for her. Some of her other children are in somewhat better circumstances but all are quite moderate circumstances."[10]

Thus the line between poor and yeoman was never very distinct, especially when women headed the household. The dividing line between destitution and "respectable" poverty was drawn by different people in Edgefield at different levels. Edgefield preachers Godfrey Drehrer, Abiah Morgan Cartledge, and John Cornish visited many in the countryside who were destitute and others who, like John Barton, his wife, and five children, "tho' poor . . . seem[ed] to be in comfortable circumstances, cleanly, neat & tidy & industrious."[11]

In 1847 the Episcopal priest John Cornish visited Mrs. Lowe, a widow with five daughters near Aiken. Mrs. Lowe owned a small farm, and she lived in a "neat & Tidy" log house. Cornish wrote that she hired "a 'cropper' in summer, & usually raised provisions on her farm enough for her family." In 1860, Margaret Lowe's occupation was "farming," an occupation used in 1860, 1870, and 1880 to describe women who owned small to medium parcels of land and who rented or hired tenants to work the land. Men who actually worked on the land of others, such as Mrs. Lowe's "cropper," also sometimes listed their occupation as "farming" to distinguish them from the more prestigious occupation of "farmer." In 1860, 675 whites listed their occupation as "farming." Some, like Mrs. Lowe's landless "cropper," worked as tenants (more than forty whites in the agricultural manuscript census had the word *tenant* on their agricultural record). Between 10 and 15 percent of all farms in 1850 and 1860 were operated by families who had no land.[12]

Most of the really poor whites worked as "laborers" on the farms and plantations of other Edgefield whites. Most often these laborers were young white men; sometimes their parents (especially widowed mothers) placed them on the farm of a landowner who had no or only a few slaves. The landowning farmer could use the extra help, and the young men learned how to farm.[13]

Another occupation open to the poor was that of overseer of a plantation. Planters and politicians, who were often away from the farm for long periods, and widows with large numbers of slaves depended on overseers. In three years, Thomas Green Clemson had four overseers for his Edgefield plantation. The popular stereotype pictures an overseer as a nasty bully, but quite a few overseers were actually the sons of plantation owners getting first-hand experience. Sons of yeomen also could work as overseers until they inherited a farm or were able to buy their own land. A substantial group of men in Edgefield chose the position of overseer as their life's work. The job was difficult and often exasperating. Their ability to compel slaves to work and obey was restricted because planters strictly limited the power of overseers. Thomas Green Clemson's instructions to one of his Edgefield overseers detailed the management of the plantation so meticulously that Francis Pickens believed "if attended to strictly [they] would prevent a crop almost." When the Reverend Mr. Brookes chastised the overseer of his Georgia plantation for cruelty and "barbarity," the overseer responded, "Do you not remember what you told me the time you employed me that I faild to make you good crops I would have to leave." The overriding concern of employers was that the overseer turn a profit.[14]

Nonagricultural laborers constituted only 8 percent of the work force. Such laborers as railroad or sawmill workers or factory operatives were listed with agricultural laborers in Table 2-1. In 1850 and 1860 the two textile mills employed fewer than a tenth of the labor force and only 2 percent of all household heads. Textile workers were only a small proportion of the Edge-field poor. One must be careful not to let mill workers symbolize poor whites. Because they lived near one another in their own "villages" and came to symbolize the "New South," observers have paid more attention to these poorer whites than to those dispersed throughout the countryside. In both the antebellum and postbellum periods, many families who worked for Granite-ville and for the Edgefield Manufacturing Company (built in 1895, began operation in 1898) moved back and forth from farm to mill village.[15]

Textile pioneer William Gregg remarked in 1845 that thousands of whites in the state "lived in comparative nakedness and starvation." In 1837, Gregg successfully used both white and slave labor in the Vaucluse cotton mill. He decided white labor was abundant and cheaper than slave labor. With the goal of providing employment for "a large class of miserable poor white people among us, without any employment to render them producers to the State," Gregg and his Edgefield brother-in-law, General James Jones, built a model mill village. Graniteville Manufacturing Company began operation in 1849.[16]

The coming of mills to the South was generally heralded as the salvation of the poor whites. A visiting newspaper editor gushed over Graniteville and equated the new mill with a religious mission. "There is in this State as impoverished and as ignorant a white population as can be found in any other in the Union and the Graniteville factory is the first missionary in the work of ameliorating their condition; we hope its example may be followed by others, until the entire class be provided with the means of employment."[17]

But others were not so quick to lavish praise on these symbols of a new South. In 1850 a correspondent to the Edgefield *Advertiser* interviewed some Graniteville workers, several "old Neighbors . . . whose children worked in the Factory." He found that eight and nine year olds toiled the same long hours as adults, from 4:45 A.M. to 7:00 P.M. in summer (with two forty-minute meal breaks) and from 6:15 A.M. to 7:30 P.M. in winter (with a thirty-five-minute dinner break). The "evil must eventually outweigh all the benefits that we shall reap from its manufactory and inflict an incalculable injury on the physical, moral and intellectual character of our state and will do much towards destroy-ing that dignity and independence of character so peculiar to our beloved State. . . . Such is the condition to which the sons and daughters of proud South Carolina have already been reduced by the manufacturing system im-properly conducted. . . . There is indeed a condition of slavery."[18]

The turnover of personnel in the mills was large. The persistence rate of household heads was significantly lower for Graniteville (ranging from 14 to 23 for the decades from 1850 to 1880) than for all white household heads in Edgefield for the same thirty years and for Afro-Americans from 1870 to 1880 (for blacks and whites the persistence rate was usually greater than 40 per-cent). But among households and families in Graniteville who did persist, the majority were church members. The workers who moved up in the textile hierarchy to become weavers, spinners, and loom fixers were generally churchgoers. Most among the few workers who became second hands and foremen were deacons or elders. Other church leaders were salaried workers at the apex of the mill workers' class system. A Graniteville native explained: "The social distinctions were sharply defined. . . . Even among the mill hands there were upper and lower classes. . . . They were not the bosses, or department managers, nor did they belong to the white-collar office contingent, but they were capable and skilled mechanics, such as loom fixers and engineers and machine repair men." Along with the merchants, mill superintendents, and department managers (who were all church leaders), these skilled workers also joined the Masonic and Odd Fellows lodges in Graniteville.[19]

Mill families, like the country people from whom they came, looked to religion as a way of life. In 1848, the Reverend Cornish visited Graniteville and, preaching in a warehouse, drew a crowd of fifty to one hundred. In 1850, the treasurer of the Graniteville Manufacturing Company claimed that, within the village, "the Sabbath is regarded with reverence. The worship of God is strictly attended." In 1883, when Hamilton Hickman, president of the Graniteville Manufacturing Company, testified before a Senate committee, he asserted that every Sunday in Graniteville one saw "our operatives, the men and the women, at church, dressed up very nicely and looking very respectable." Historian W. E. Woodward recounted from his own experiences in Graniteville that no matter how disreputable one's life had been, subsequent church attendance, biblical knowledge, and proper conduct rectified one's character in the mill community.[20]

Baptists and Methodists established churches when the village was created, Lutherans constructed a church during the Civil War, and Episcopalians started a mission during Reconstruction. The Graniteville company actually built the Baptist and Methodist churches, a custom which became standard practice for southern mills. These churches segregated mill workers from townspeople. Even the superintendent was expected to set an example by actively participating in a church leadership role.[21]

Religion also helped the workers cope with the trials of life. A resident of Graniteville who was hanged was recorded as he ended his life as being "cool and unterrified, yet softened by religion. . . . His will which sustained him so long in life, left not him in the hour of facing his fate."[22]

Mill villages had no black residents, and the only jobs open to Afro-American males were in ground maintenance, freight handling, and privy cleaning. This pattern did not change after the Civil War, although black women did find work as domestics in the homes of the merchants who operated the dozen stores in the town and in the homes of the mill executives. After the Civil War more of the white men who headed households in the mill village's cottages worked in the factory. By 1880 many of the wives of the mill operatives worked as well, and during the late 1880s even the mill workers hired black domestics to work in their homes.[23]

From 1840 to 1880 the mills more than doubled the number of their employees (to 646 factory operatives). In 1850, Gregg boasted to northern industrialist Amos A. Lawrence, "From the day we commenced we never had the slightest difficulty in procuring hands who our overseers (Eastern men) pronounce to be equal to any in the Eastern states." Through 1900 there was never a shortage of labor (except for some skilled workers), and after 1860 the applications for work far exceeded the demand. The board of directors commented in 1876, "The supply of labor is abundant and cheap." After the Civil War, W. E. Woodward's father confronted a former sharecropper who worked in Graniteville about the arduous twelve-hour-day mill toil. The mill hand replied that he enjoyed his comfortable mill-supplied home and his neighbors as opposed to the rural isolation and, according to Woodward, explained, "I worked jes' as long when I lived in the country . . . and it was harder work, too. Anyway, I dont know what to do with myself when I ain't at work." Moreover, as a struggling tenant farmer he had had nothing at the end of each year, but with him and his three daughters working in the mill while his wife cared for the home, as he exclaimed proudly, "I get money every Saturday."[24]

From eight to nine hundred people lived in the hundred cottages and twelve boarding houses that Gregg built and rented to employees and their families. According to James H. Taylor, a cotton manufacturer in Charleston who served briefly as treasurer of the Graniteville Manufacturing Company soon after operation began, the houses "filled with respectable tenants who paid a fair interest on this part of the capital; and, while the sons and daughters worked in the mill, the father would engage in cultivating his land, hauling wood, &c., and the mother would attend to the housekeeping department. Thus each found employment suited to their age and capacity." Graniteville residents were allowed to farm the large lots that came with each house and even to keep stock if the animals were properly fenced. Mill hands worked in family units and were paid what the textile industry termed a "family wage."[25]

In antebellum Edgefield a substantial number of the fathers heading Graniteville households did not work in the mills, and most of their wives did not work in the mills, but many of their children did. By 1880, 60 percent of the factory laborers were female. But Gregg's attempt to establish a boarding system for the single daughters of the poor, similar to that of New England's Waltham mills, failed. Although each boardinghouse was entrusted to a respected matron who assured "a most exemplary state of morals" to ensure unmarried southern women would "not lose caste," the boardinghouses did not survive the Civil War. The poor white family was too proud and patriarchal to allow its daughters to leave the family for boardinghouses.[26]

Mills shaped the lives of white families, not just the individuals within the families. Mills used methods of social control such as eviction, the credit system in a company store, scrip compensation, and segregated schools and churches. Southern textile mills used the South's patriarchal values to recruit families for labor and to socialize and stabilize the work force.

As head of the mill household, the father received all the wages his children earned. He was also responsible to the mill officials for his children's work. In 1850, praising the Graniteville system for "its safety to the morals of the people," Taylor explained that "the youth of the place are under the watchful eyes of their parents." These nineteenth-century patriarchal customs persisted into the twentieth century. At the turn of the century, two attorneys, James H. Tillman (George Tillman's son) and J. William Thurmond (father of Senator J. Strom Thurmond), challenged the white laboring patriarch's responsibility and ability to speak, act, and be held accountable for his family. In 1906 a mill employee, J. N. Wilson, went to Augusta, got drunk, caused some disturbance, and was arrested and fined one hundred dollars. The Edgefield Manufacturing Company interceded, negotiated the fine to fifty dollars, and paid it. In return, Wilson bound himself and four children to work in the mill for one year. According to a mill executive, that "slime of the serpent Jim Tillman" convinced Wilson to take his case to court, and the mill lost this peonage case. Edgefield County mill executive A. S. Tompkins fumed, "If it is illegal to make a contract with the head of a family to bind him and his family of children to work to pay off money for their necessary support . . . to keep the father off the chain gang, then all the mills might as well shut down." While this type of peonage might appear extreme today, it was not regarded as such in the South at the time and was a legacy of the nineteenth-century patriarchal South.[27]

With or without mills, jobs were scarce. James Henry Hammond, whose daughter married Gregg's son, proclaimed in 1850 that a sixth of South Carolina's white population could not make an adequate living. Hammond himself, son of a Yankee schoolteacher and Edgefield mother, came from a yeoman middle class background. He complained about poor whites who maintained "a precarious subsistence by occasional jobs, by what is in its effects, far worse—trading with slaves, and seducing them to plunder for their benefit." Hammond realized that because slavery made agricultural employment unproductive for whites, South Carolina's abundant and cheap white labor worked "evil to both our social and political system." He believed that, because of slavery, these poor whites were not compensated in agricultural labor "as every white person in this country is, and feels himself entitled to." Those who worked infrequently did so "not more from inclination, than from the want of due encouragement." He argued that the poor white had shown "no serious prejudice" against textile labor and that "they [had] been prompt to avail themselves, at moderate wages, of the opportunity it affords of making an honest and comfortable support, and decent provision for the future." He called for factories, like Graniteville near his home, to convert the "unemployed or insufficiently compensated population into active and intelligent workmen, buying and paying for the products of her soil, which their families consume."[28]

Although Gregg described South Carolina poor whites as "poor, ignorant, degraded" and suggested they were "too lazy to work themselves," and Frederick Law Olmsted gave an even harsher assessment of the "wretched starvlings and wild men of the pine woods," the antebellum poor were closely tied to the Edgefield community. They attended the same churches and shared and shaped many of the community's values. Some poor households were headed by widows; some poor were related to yeomen, and a few to the wealthy; some actually moved up the rural social ladder into the ranks of the more prosperous; and some of the more affluent slid from prosperity into the ranks of the poor.[29]

Yeoman Middle Class

What divided the poor from the respectable and the respectable from the prosperous? If the criteria included ownership of a slave, then less than half of Edgefield white households were prosperous in 1850 or 1860. The bottom wealth quartile of the 1860 white population owned only $270 in total wealth. There are no easy answers, but the summation of a local historian of the area rings true. "Taken as a whole, it was a self-supporting and self-respecting people" which lived in the area, even though "now and then a family disabled by sickness, needed help to keep the wolf from the door. Some were not ambitious to abound in resources and even a black sheep appeared here or there." Although a few families had reputations for raiding neighbors for food, or for living off the land, Edgefield's population resembled the self-sufficient yeomen that Frank L. Owsley called the plain folk of the South.[30]

Notwithstanding dramatic extremes of wealth, basic problems of rural living crossed class lines: poor roads, isolation, bad weather, and insects as well as the problem of "demon liquor." Drinking had terrible effects on the fortunes of poorer white families who did not have the means to survive lost work days or the erosion of their small holdings.[31]

Edgefield yeomen shared values as well as problems with other classes. Religion was important for all classes. The values of the churches shaped the mores of the society. The death notices and the gravestones of antebellum and postbellum Edgefield illustrated the premium placed on living, or at least on dying, a righteous and Christian life. In addition, in rural neighborhoods where everyone knew everyone else, one's ability to obtain credit or work sometimes depended on one's spiritual reputation.

The Baptists and the Methodists were stricter than the Episcopalians, and since many in the elite were Episcopalians, and most of the poor and yeomen middle class were Baptists and Methodists, there were differences between the culture of the rich and that of the common white man. Almost every church had some members who were large slaveowners, however, so differences may have been minimal.

Ministers made it a practice to call on families in the communities. In both antebellum and postbellum Edgefield, Cornish visited rich and poor alike. In Cornish's social as well as business circles, the closely-knit, well-adjusted family seemed to be a constant. Whether calling on households in his capacity as Episcopal priest or being, as he wrote in the spring of 1867, "hospitably entertained," by virtue of his prominent position in the community, his experience was that family gatherings offered a most congenial and friendly atmosphere. The same is true for the experiences recorded by the Baptist preacher Abiah Morgan Cartledge in antebellum Edgefield. A new Methodist pastor at McKendree church, H. A. Roggins, informed his congregation in 1880 that he already "had visited about ⅛ of the members of the church," and expected to call on the rest soon. Although his visitations had been very pleasant, he warned those not yet called upon and admonished those he had visited to be better prepared next time. He had been "alarmed to find so few family alters."[32]

Baptist and Methodist churches were especially involved in the lives of their congregations, and members of Edgefield churches understood that church membership carried responsibilities. In 1833 the pastor of the Bethany Baptist Church resisted his church's desire to adopt rules of decorum and advised his flock to read the New Testament and use it for their rule book. In 1840, however, the church adopted a constitution with a set of rules for its membership. All members had to agree to obey the "councel of the church" and to accept any church disciplinary action. All members of Bethany were to exercise "forbearrance and love" toward each other and pray for all fellow members, "simpathising with each other in the various circumstances of life." The rules also made certain that every member who was charged for wrongs before the church was first given a chance privately to change his ways. Rule number two stated, "No member shall be at liberty to bring a charge against another member before the church until he shall have proceeded with him according to the direction of the word of God Mathew 18:15-17."

The constitution of the Johnston Baptist Church, written in 1875, was very similar to the Bethany rules of 1840. Rules twelve and thirteen stated: "We promise as believers in Christ to watch over each other in the love and fear of God for the benefit of each other and of the Church . . . and to submit ourselves to the discipline of the church as it may be guided by the word and spirit of God." The constitutions of both Bethany and Johnston insisted that the churches were democratic; a majority vote decided all issues.[33]

Baptist and Methodist churches had standing committees on discipline, and refractory members were dismissed if they did not mend their ways. A committee of fellow church members counseled and "cited" communicants. Church committees cited members absent from church as many as three times, those reported for dancing, gambling, or drinking, and members having misunderstandings with a spouse or a neighbor. Generally churches excommunicated "sinners," but readmitted members who promised to do better. Most Baptist and Methodist church records proclaimed dancing to be a sin, yet dancing was a favorite pastime in Edgefield, and members were constantly being expelled for going to dances. One Baptist church debated whether fiddles were sinful and decided that at least they would no longer be used at their church service. After discussion in 1839 a Baptist church agreed that races and chicken fights were "altogether against the religion of Jesus" and that it was wrong to attend.[34]

Churches took a special interest in domestic matters. Family relations of all sorts were carefully observed. Single members were expelled for fornication; married members, for adultery. In June 1838 a church heard "a charge against Bro. Stiron for neglect of his family, &c. Bro. Mims & Bro. McDaniel appointed to cite him to the Church." Men were excommunicated for beating wives, and wives for striking their husbands. Women were even excommunicated for not keeping neat, orderly houses. Members were chastised for unfair business practices. Cheating another person was grounds for excommunication, as was lying. Sometimes the repenter confessed, as did E. S. Mays, who "disciplined himself for selling damaged cotton (damaged by water)" in Hamburg. Especially before the Civil War and even during it (this occurred less often after the war), many churches acted as citizens' courts in civil disagreements between neighbors. Most of the main business between November 1863 and January 1864 of the Sweetwater Baptist Church's meeting was devoted to trying to settle a dispute between brethren Stephen Mays and William Howard. Mays accused Howard of killing his bull without his consent [35]

Another case of confession involved murder. "Brother William Colclazur having accidentally killed one of his own Negro boys by striking him on the head with a stick, disciplined himself." After some debating, Brother Colclazur was "restored to full fellowship." Relations with other members of the community had to be regulated. Elizabeth Limbaker was excommunicated for "unchristian conduct." A Mr. Rhodes was charged with beating drums for slaves to dance. A committee investigated and the church discussed a Mr. Roper's saying unkind things about a Mr. Cooper, and a Mr. Thorn was cited for swearing at a neighbor. Equality before God meant that all whites in the churches of the Baptists and the Methodists were judged as equal. One Baptist church, for example, disciplined a planter for having a fight with his overseer. The same church was very sensitive about slavery and reported, "Brother Whatley for saying that there would be War soon and the Negroes would be all free, as he expressed at different times, is excommunicated."[36]

Churches were also concerned about less fortunate white families in their neighborhoods. Episcopalians generally left this responsibility to their priests. The membership of the Baptist and Methodist churches, however, involved themselves in ministering to their less fortunate white neighbors. Baptist churches regularly received reports from domestic missions committees. Each year Bethany Baptist Church devoted a service to the "Anniversary Meeting of the Bethany Benevolent Society" at which a contribution was applied to the domestic missions in the community. Particularly in the decades after the Civil War Baptist and Methodist churches concerned themselves with the poorer whites in their neighborhood. McKendree Methodist Church regularly inquired as to the poor and suffering and queried, "What is the church doing for the relief of the poor?"[37]

The practices, if not the religious convictions, of yeomen were stricter in many respects than those of the wealthier. Although reared in the traditional strict Presbyterian tradition of his up-country grandfather and father, Francis Pickens espoused the more moderate theology of the Episcopal church. With the establishment of the Trinity Episcopal Church certain of Edgefield's elites publicly declared themselves aristocrats. In 1833, Pickens was a founding vestryman of Trinity, spearheaded the raising of money for a church building in 1836, and for a time paid the rector's salary. In 1834, Pickens teased his sister-in-law Maria Calhoun about the "derangement" of her brother Arthur Simkins, a Baptist who had recently claimed to have been converted during a revival. Pickens expressed disdain for the fundamentalist religion of the Edgefield plain people, a people very similar to his father and grandfather. He concluded, however: "There is mad temporal derangement on the subject at present. I suppose every person must have some matter on which they are deranged—I *know* I *have*."[38]

On a Sunday in 1839 when the rest of his family had "all gone to church" and Pickens had "remained at home alone, because there is no preaching in 'our church' and it is at the Methodist (you know I cannot take interest in that church, as I am a great man for my own church only)," he wrote another informative letter to Maria about the dances and parties in Edgefield the past week. Referring to his wife's Baptist background, he told her sister, "By the by I ought to have mentioned that your sister did not go to the dances of course." Tongue-in-cheek, Pickens continued, "I propose to build a house outside of our gates on the other hill, our purpose to give dances in as our children grow, so that the church shall not say 'Ah! Mrs. Pickens had a dance in her home eh! eh!' 'I said so didn't I'?"[39]

At a huge dinner party given annually for the neighbors of planter James Henry Hammond, the country folks were shocked by an impromptu dance performed by another guest, Senator Clement C. Clay of Alabama. Mrs. Clay observed, "I am sure, those good people felt themselves to be a little nearer to the burning pit than they had ever been before. . . . I felt sure it would be a difficult task to try to convince my husband's audience that his own religious feelings and convictions were of the deepest and most spiritual quality." Mrs. Clay wrote of these people: "The majority were stiff and prim and of the quaint, simple, religious class often to be found in back districts. They seemed ill at ease, if not consciously out of place, in Senator Hammond's parlours."[40]

For poor and yeoman middle-class whites life revolved around the family and church. Since all family members contributed to work on the farm, church get-togethers were as much retreats from the toil of farming as they were escapes from the factory for the artisan or the textile worker. Membership in churches brought families together with their neighbors, and church activities also provided opportunities for courtship. James T. Ouzts kept a diary of his experiences as an overseer and yeoman farmer, and he began and ended his entries every year with his thanks and praise to God. Throughout this diary, except for reports of the weather, religious themes predominated. A devout Methodist, this yeoman regularly traveled at his own expense to conference meetings, even when they were in other districts.[41]

The Ouzts family was typical of the yeoman middle-class families that populated Edgefield. Peter Ouzts (1757–1829) and Elizabeth Harling Ouzts (1770–1847) had thirteen sons and two daughters. By 1880 they had 940 descendants, most living in Edgefield. Ouzts bequeathed land, slaves, and equipment to his surviving children, the one daughter faring about as well as the sons. "I will and bequeath unto my beloved son-in-law and his wife, my beloved daughter, Elizabeth, one negro boy named April valued at two hundred and fifteen dollars." Most of the sons received land assessed between $250 and $300, but some received land, equipment, or animals worth less than $215. Real or personal estate was bequeathed directly to the sons with no mention made of their spouses, but the gift to the daughter, Elizabeth, was given to her and her husband because of legal requirements.

Peter and Elizabeth Ouzts's son George Ouzts (1801–80) married Frances Timmerman (1804–89), and they had five children. By 1860, George and Frances lived alone, but their children lived close by. Daughter Permelia married William Still, a farmer who had $1,500 in real estate and $5,945 in personal estate (eight slaves). Son Jacob Brantley was a landless overseer with a $3,000 personal estate (two slaves). Twin boys James T. and Shemuel had been landless overseers, but by this time owned farms. James had a farm worth $2,500 and personal estate worth $5,465 (six slaves); Shemuel had a farm worth $1,560 and personal estate worth $3,715 (four slaves). Daughter Elizabeth married Elijah Dorn, owner of two slaves.

Although almost all received land from father Peter, the members of the Ouzts family had various occupations and degrees of wealth. George's brother Jacob Ouzts, a shoemaker, at age fifty-five had no land and only twenty-five dollars in personal property. His wife, Dicie, was illiterate. Jacob obviously headed a poor white household. Another brother, Martin, who lived near George and Jacob, owned real estate worth $5,000 and personal estate worth

$13,990 (fifteen slaves). At sixty-one, Martin was among the wealthy. Martin and his wife, Mary, had three children living at home; their oldest son was a landless overseer. The next-door neighbor to Martin was Elizabeth Ouzts, widow of another brother, Abraham. In 1860 she had no land and her personal estate was worth $460. Elizabeth had four sons and one daughter living at home. Two sons farmed. Elizabeth and her daughter were also employed; Elizabeth wove and sewed, and Mary sewed and knitted. A female "stranger" lived in the household, L. Friday, who was employed as a seamstress. At fifty-two years of age, Elizabeth obviously had gone through a hard time providing for her family after Abraham died. Although she and the members of her immediate family were not wealthy, they were nevertheless solid citizens of the area. They attended church regularly and supported the community just as their wealthier neighbors did. Elizabeth's son James was killed in the Civil War, along with several of his wealthier cousins; her son Peter became a prominent Mason, and her grandson Jesse a prominent minister.

George Ouzts, with real estate valued at $4,000 and personal estate at $14,000 (ten slaves), made special provisions for his oldest daughter, Permelia. On 30 March 1867 he executed a deed of trust for $800 "for Permelia during her life and her children afterwards." Less than a month later, George left a tract of 175 acres for the benefit of his daughter Permelia, thus helping to establish his oldest child.

Much affection between brothers and sisters was shown by naming patterns. The twins James and Shemuel each named a son after the other. When Shemuel died and his widow, Mary E. Herrin Ouzts, was left with four children, Dr. J. M. Rushton (who was married to Mary Ouzts's sister Maggie) applied for letters of guardianship for his four nephews on his wife's side. This example of intermixed and extended families was a theme of family life in Edgefield.

When Shemuel died from a wound received during the Civil War, the Edgefield *Advertiser* wrote: "He has left a stricken widow to whom he was most tenderly attached, and four little boys, but he has left to them the priceless legacy of a pure and spotless memory. To his father and mother he was a most devoted son, and he most affectionately regarded his twin brother. . . . His last words to his bereaved wife were, 'Remember that you are mortal. . . . Meet me in Heaven.' The church to which he belonged will long miss in its choir the beautiful voice of him who now occupies the Soldier's grave."

The yeoman middle-class white family believed that patriotism and religion were components of family honor. In 1939, when the Ouzts family built a monument to their pioneer ancestors, they inscribed it with the following: "A Loyal and Patriotic Family. Served in every war from Revolutionary War to present day. Peter I served in Revolutionary War. He willed a sum of money to McKendree Methodist and Little Stevens Creek Baptist Churches."[42]

William O. Howard headed another Edgefield yeoman middle-class family. Like many yeomen, Howard had several occupations: farmer, brick and stone mason, sawmill and gristmill owner. In 1850 he owned seven slaves and had cattle, sheep, hogs, and horses. Typical of many yeomen, Howard believed in the work ethic. According to his son, Thomas Jefferson Howard, "My father was opposed to idleness. . . . We were taught and required to do every kind of farmwork the slaves did and consider it an honor instead of disgrace."[43]

Another Edgefield yeoman family was that of nonslaveowner John Kreps. Kreps also had several occupations, including farmer, teacher, and jeweler. A letter written in 1849 told of this patriarch's worries about his children. It also gives some indication of life in a yeoman family. One of Kreps's primary concerns was that his small landholdings were not sufficient to induce his family to stay with him. His two daughters were married and lived close by, but not on his land. Daughter Ann lived eleven miles away with her husband, Elisha Jones. Daughter Elizabeth lived three miles away, where she and her husband were tenant farmers. His five sons lived on the father's property; son States and wife (sister of Ann's husband, Elisha) lived in his household. Three of his sons were planning to move; Kreps wrote that his children were "too independent to be confined to this one place and I cannot blame them,—the land is an excellent tract,—but it is too small." Son Andrew was a wagon maker, and the youngest, Barnabas, quit school to help him. Andrew had already purchased two tracts of land on which to build a home. Son Robert was moving also, and although Kreps hoped he would move near to Andrew, Robert did not like that settlement and chose to move closer to his church. Barnabas, who presently lived with Andrew, would stay in Andrew's old house, and Kreps was trying to decide whether to give Robert's home to Elizabeth and her husband or to use it as a school. He must have worried about Elizabeth, whose husband, Hesley Clay, was a salesman, "going about with a carriage, selling Botanic Medicine, and sometimes absent a month or more." The worst for Kreps was that his son Elias planned to migrate west with Edgefield friends. (Andrew and Barnabas were building his wagon, and States planned to move into his house.) The elder Kreps worried that the West was yet too wild. "I regret that my son Elias is going Westardly," where people were "desperate in their dealings between Man and Man." His son's "going hurts my feelings, and grieves me not a little." The elder Kreps died within the year; son-in-law Clay and family moved into the home with Kreps's widow.[44]

Families like Hesley and Elizabeth Clay, who did not have a farm and who tried to maintain a middle-class status, often had to separate. Elisha Hammond, an accomplished schoolteacher, continually struggled to maintain his family on his teacher's salary. Near the end of his life, the family separated, Elisha taking the sons to Macon, Georgia, where he established a school, while his wife took the daughter to Hamburg. The school failed, and Elisha despaired that he might once again have to become a butcher, but was able to buy on credit "156 acres of River land 20 acres cleared which will raise 500 bushels of corn next year & other things enough to support the family." He wrote his son James Henry that "if your Mama does not feel disposed to come here now all that I can make over our support here I will send her."[45]

Like Elisha Hammond and Kreps, many men in Edgefield combined teaching or the ministry with farming and other trades in order to make enough money to be part of the respectable yeomanry. Most preachers were not members of the elite: Baptist and Methodist circuit-riding men of God came from yeoman middle-class and sometimes poorer backgrounds. John Trapp, a Baptist minister for twenty-eight years, also worked as a potter. Another preacher, Abiah Morgan Cartledge, also worked as a teacher and farmer. Teaching and the ministry were the two professions in which white yeomen and poor might achieve social mobility in Edgefield.[46]

Typical of the career of the country schoolteacher was that of Elijah Timmerman, born into a yeoman family around 1818. Timmerman got an elementary education in the "field schools" of Edgefield, but never went to college. The 1841 Free School Reports for Edgefield District listed Elijah Timmerman as a teacher at three schools: one during May, another during August, and yet another during November. Teachers did not teach in one location for the year, but moved each quarter as necessary. An undated contract (probably for some period between 1842 and 1845) for Timmerman to teach English five days a week for 240 days at $12 per scholar (5 cents per day) at Summer Hill suggests that Timmerman moved again. In 1846, Timmerman taught at East Hill and at Mountain Creek, and in 1849 he signed a contract to teach English beginning 1 January 1850 for one year, five days a week, and received $5 per scholar.

He married in 1844, and in 1846 he bought 150 acres on Sleepy Creek from Anthony Ouzts for $745. Timmerman had been teaching the Ouzts children for a number of years, and they must have decided that he would make a good neighbor. In the 1850 census returns, Timmerman was listed as a teacher with his wife, two daughters, and an infant son. In 1860, he was no longer listed in the census as a teacher (although he still taught school), but as a farmer along with his wife, three daughters, and two sons. Twenty-one-year-old William Timmerman, a "farmer," also lived with Elijah. Elijah owned land worth $1,000, and most of his personal property was tied up in the fifty-five-year-old female slave he had purchased. Elijah Timmerman had become a slaveowner.

Timmerman was also very active in the Methodist church. He was the church clerk, and he raised money to build McKendree Church at Sleepy Creek. In 1865 a new church clerk listed members who had gone to the Civil War and not returned; Elijah Timmerman was included. Private Elijah Timmerman, who rose from an itinerant schoolteacher to become a propertied slaveowning farmer and neighborhood teacher, was a member of Company K,

Fourteenth Regiment, and was fatally wounded in the Battle of Gettysburg, 1 July 1863.[47]

A teacher was even able to enter the upper levels of Edgefield society, as Elijah Keese did. In 1848, Keese came to Edgefield District from the mountains of South Carolina to teach school. He was employed by a wealthy planter, Benjamin Landrum, and while teaching, lived in the Landrum home. He married Landrum's daughter Sally and moved to Edgefield, where he taught at the Edgefield Academy. Married into Edgefield's planter class, he could now buy a home and farm on the outskirts of Edgefield. With the help of his wife's inheritance, Keese bought a half interest in the Edgefield *Advertiser* in 1856 and entered the ranks of the elite.[48]

The Elite

The elite was as difficult to define in 1850 as it is today; it was something which one "felt" rather than articulated. The "aristocrats" of the backcountry Edgefield elite claimed descent from two groups. First were those early backcountry settlers who had moved from Pennsylvania, Virginia, and North Carolina into inland South Carolina during the mid-eighteenth century. Many had participated in the Regulator Movement of 1767–69 and had been committed to commercial farming for a living, acquiring slaves and land even before cotton planting spread to the up-country. Most began amassing their early fortunes, however, through trading with Indians, merchandising, and surveying. Patrick Calhoun, Andrew Pickens, and LeRoy Hammond (not related to James Henry Hammond) were all merchants and surveyors, but they referred to themselves as having been planters and farmers, not merchants or tradesmen. Their ancestors fought as Whigs in the Revolution. Within one generation, this group of backcountry planters rose to wealth and prominence and established the basis of their descendants' claims to aristocracy. They generally married women with similar up-country backgrounds and became the magistrates, sheriffs, and, later, legislative representatives. It was the second generation which aligned itself with the South Carolina coast and Charleston aristocracy.[49]

Another group of Edgefield aristocrats had even closer ties to the tidewater section of South Carolina. After 1790 and the spread of cotton farming to the up-country, wealthy low-country families purchased up-country plantations. Levi Durand Wigfall, a Charleston merchant who married Eliza Trezevant of the tidewater patriciate, bought a plantation in Edgefield and moved his family there. His oldest son, Arthur, was born in Charleston, but his third child, Lewis Trezevant Wigfall, was born in Edgefield in 1816. By 1830 it was common for prominent tidewater families to have summer residences in the backcountry or for their sons and daughters to have plantations there. Generally these aristocrats were Episcopalians.[50]

These aristocrats composed, with other groups, the Edgefield elite in the nineteenth century. The members of the elite were wealthy in land and slaves. Their ranks included attorneys, doctors and officeholders who attained and maintained wealth, status, and influence through their professional and political positions.

Patriciate clans formed interlocking relationships through marriage just as middle-class families did. The elite's leadership of the community and the state made the family linkings of this group significant. Marriages were important factors in political alliances and allegiances, as well as in individual success. By the time of the Civil War, first families of Edgefield—the Butlers, Bonhams, Brookses, Simkinses, and Pickenses—had intermarried.[51]

Francis Pickens, a southern aristocrat by birth, was a congressman, minister to Russia, and South Carolina's secession governor. He was a grandson of Gen. Andrew Pickens (who had married John C. Calhoun's cousin) of Revolutionary War fame and son of Andrew Pickens, governor of South Carolina in 1817. After attending the University of South Carolina, Francis read law at Edgefield Court House and entered the law firm of Eldred Simkins and George McDuffie (both served as congressmen). He married his childhood sweetheart, Simkins's eldest daughter, and thus joined the patrician Pickens family to one of Edgefield's oldest, wealthiest, most illustrious, and most influential families. John C. Calhoun remembered Simkins as "my earliest and best friend." Simkins's second oldest daughter married Andrew Pickens Butler, the senator from Edgefield for whom kinsman Preston Brooks struck Charles Sumner. Another daughter married James Edward Calhoun, brother-in-law and intimate of John C. Calhoun.[52]

Matthew Calbraith Butler married Francis Pickens's daughter Maria Calhoun Pickens. Butler was a grandson of Gen. William Butler, who fought in the Revolution, served as a congressman and was a militia general in the War of 1812. His sons became congressmen, senators, governors, and judges. Preston Brooks's grandmother was Gen. Butler's sister. The Brookses were an old Edgefield family, and they were related to the Bonhams, who, in turn, were related by marriage to the Butlers and the Simkinses. Families commonly gave their sons and daughters surnames from the maternal side of the family, as in the cases of Whitfield Butler Brooks, a hero of the Mexican War, and James Butler Bonham, a hero of the Alamo.[53]

The wealthiest families formed an elite group, but this may or may not have been the same as the "aristocratic" elite or the "political" elite. An index of the 136 wealthiest people in 1860 Edgefield District shows that all headed households and only nine were women. All but twenty listed themselves as planters or farmers, the latter being by far the more common designation. The twenty nonfarming occupations included four merchants and three lawyers who were officeholders. The wealthiest was "miner" W. B. Dorn, whose goldmine alone was valued at over a million dollars. Only one widow did not give an occupation. The eight doctors tended to give more attention to planting than medicine. Most doctors in the nineteenth century studied a few years with another doctor or, as did many sons of Edgefield planters, attended the medical college in Augusta for a year or so. Some, however, were well-trained for their day.[54]

Even children from wealthy families felt great apprehension about success in the class-conscious Edgefield of the 1850s. Benjamin Nicholson, the son of a wealthy slaveowner who ranked seventy-third of the 136 wealthiest people in Edgefield, read law with Milledge Luke Bonham at the courthouse in the mid-1850s and pondered moving west. "In this state a greater regard is paid to family & wealth, & consequently without either a young man must possess great ability to succeed."[55]

With great ability and luck, one could move into the elite class. George McDuffie, James Henry Hammond, and Joseph Abney became successful members of the Edgefield elite. McDuffie's father was a blacksmith. The other two were from solid middle-class backgrounds. Contrary to popular myth, it was unusual for a man to go from extreme poverty to wealth in one generation in Edgefield. What distinguished McDuffie, Hammond, and Abney from the vast majority of their yeomen middle-class brethren was their intellectual brilliance, sincere belief in slavery, and willingness to express those beliefs convincingly enough to convert others.

Education was crucial to the people who entered the elite from below. They generally distinguished themselves at local academies and hence received the sponsorship of elites. The Calhouns sponsored McDuffie at John C. Calhoun's brother-in-law Moses Waddel's school, where he excelled. Later, Governor McDuffie attended the public exercises of the Greenwood Academy and heard Abney, whom he sponsored, deliver a commencement address. Attendance at South Carolina College was important if one wished to make the connections for a successful professional and political career which could open the door to elite status. Moreover, an education at the academies and colleges included instruction in the social graces, important for those who wanted to become part of South Carolina's chivalric society. Election to the state legislature marked one's becoming part of the local elite. Election to state office, particularly to the governorship or the lieutenant governorship, or to the Congress meant one had arrived in state society. An orator or writer could also build a political base, and the communication of ideas was one way to establish oneself as a member of the elite. Thus, it is not surprising that McDuffie, Hammond, and Abney taught school and that Hammond and Abney owned and edited newspapers at one time in their careers.[56]

Control of newspapers was important; the Edgefield *Advertiser* generally served the community as the voice of the rich, the well-born, and the powerful. Editors, owners, and publishers were accepted into elite circles even if they had humble origins. For example, William Francis Durisoe, orphaned at an early age, ran away from a printer's apprenticeship to Edgefield, where he worked as a typesetter on the Pottersville *Hive*. In 1839 he became editor and owner of the Edgefield *Advertiser*. He also published the *Ploughboy* for the Edgefield Agricultural Society. He became a local officeholder and saw those of his fourteen children who survived merge easily into Edgefield's elite.[57]

Editors were generally backwoods intellectuals who wielded mighty influence among town and country subscribers, and they were well aware of their power and importance. Maximilian LaBorde, the Edgefield *Advertiser's* first editor, warned readers, "Few men can take a newspaper for any length of time without being generally impressed in some way or other, by the editor's notions." The editor of the Hamburg *Republic* explained, "The duty of an editor is a distinct and lofty profession, exercising great influence over society. It is a power that has never been measured." John Edmund Bacon graduated from South Carolina College, married Governor Pierce Mason Butler's daughter, and became associate editor of the Edgefield *Advertiser* all in the same year. In his first editorial he wrote, "Believing then, as I do, that the Press is the very great paladium of our domestic liberty, the very fount from which we are to expect the waters of our salvation . . . I shall follow where honor and conscience dictate." During the Civil War, editor Arthur Simkins revealed the importance of his profession when he lauded those who went to fight, but paid an equal tribute to the "workers at home . . . the pulpit, the bar, the medical profession, merchants, bankers, civil officers, and last but not least the *Press*—all these have their peculiar privileges of doing the state service in their respective avocations—a service too that is none the less beneficial from being discharged without a flourish of trumpets or implied professions of superior loyalty."[58]

The paper advised on politics, agriculture, domestic relations, and local society. Generally newspaper editors were civic boosters and leaders of the community. Embroiled in a good-natured controversy with the editor of neighboring Newberry's paper, Arthur Simkins of the Edgefield *Advertiser* proudly proclaimed: "Before yet the Dutch had begun to develop the name of Newberry, Edgefield was a community known and esteemed for the spirit of her sons and the loveliness of her daughters. The elegant hospitalities of life were cultivated among her children when yet a Newberrian would have run away affrighted from a parlor assemblage of ladies and gentlemen, dreaming that he has tumbled upon beings of supernatural endowments."[59]

One of the Edgefield elite's most important sources for interpreting the world, exploring the meaning of life, and defending its interests was the church. A few exceptional Baptist preachers, like Dr. William Bullein Johnson, pastor of the Edgefield Village Baptist Church and for many years headmaster of the Edgefield Female Academy, became powerful individuals in the community and region. Johnson pastored the Edgefield church when he was elected the first president of the newly formed Southern Baptist Association in 1849. Unlike churches scattered across the countryside, the Village Baptist Church held services every Sunday. As the church clerk noted, the congregation sometimes revealed its aristocratic pretensions and the awe in which it regarded Johnson by occasionally referring to the Baptist divine as "the Bishop." Preachers from wealthy and influential families, such as the Baptist minister Iveson Brookes, could be extremely useful spokesmen for the planter interests.[60]

Elite or wealthy ministers like Johnson and Brookes were rarely Baptists or Methodists; Episcopalian ministers, however, like Arthur Wigfall, were generally from aristocratic families. Holders of high office (governors, congressmen, and senators) were generally Episcopalian. Even local officeholders from Methodist, Baptist, or Presbyterian backgrounds joined the Episcopal church after reaching elite status. It was not unusual for members of the elite to be associated with two denominations, belonging to the Baptist Association as well as to Trinity Episcopal. Symbolic perhaps of the establishment of a permanent elite, the Edgefield *Advertiser* was founded by Maximilian LaBorde and Gen. James Jones in 1836, the same year Episcopalians built the brick Trinity Church on a hill overlooking the simple, wood-frame Village Baptist Church.[61]

The Reverend Edward Reed was the priest at antebellum Trinity Episcopal Church. In 1850 he officiated at the wedding of Mr. and Mrs. David Richardson Strother. The bride was the minister's wife's youngest sister. The groom was much older, a widower with children and a planter who owned more than one hundred slaves on plantations in South Carolina, Georgia, and Mississippi. Strother had a reputation as a stern master. His new brother-in-law addressed the couple as "brother and friend." "Will my dear friends allow me to make them so sober a gift on their wedding day as a Bible? . . . It contains the only secret of happiness in our social and domestic relations. It's faithful study, and an honest effort to practice its sacred precepts with prayer . . . will bless you with peace and mutual love in your new connections as husband and wife—will make you tender and faithful parents and masters."[62]

The Edgefield elite was not a unified community, but one composed of economic, denominational, and old- and new-rich factions. Whereas a self-made man like James Henry Hammond saw the established Edgefield aristocracy as weak, indecisive, and effeminate, a member of the Old Guard felt only scorn for the crass behavior and low origins of the newer members of the elite. Following Hammond's election to the Senate after Andrew Pickens Butler's death, Francis Pickens wrote Lucy Holcombe: "The line was drawn distinctly between virtue and honor on one side, and open vulgar blagarddism [*sic*] on the other." The Carolina aristocrats wanted to defeat Hammond, "who had no family of distinction, but was the son of a Massachusetts adventurer." Pickens made no mention of the Spann family, Hammond's maternal ancestors, who had come from Wales to Virginia and migrated to the South Carolina back-country in 1756 at the same time as the Pickens and Calhoun families. Pickens believed that he should have been elected instead of this man who had committed "crimes of the deepest dire . . . but it was necessary to put down aristocracy in the state, and raise a persecuted man up."[63]

Nevertheless, Pickens felt no compunction, when cotton prices were at a low 6.2 cents per pound in 1842, in asking Hammond to relieve his financial difficulties. Debt was a never-ending threat to the elite. Pickens complained constantly of the inability of his overseers to make enough money. Lucy, his third wife, married him for his money, and when his crops failed in 1859, she complained to her mother, "One plantation with 50 hands does not make 50 bales of cotton—on another with 25 hands, 30 bales." Pickens complained of his slaves, "I have remaining about 300, and many are children and they, like anxious hounds will devour me unless I attend to them with care & economy."[64]

Debt was a fact of life in Edgefield. Not only the poor but also the wealthy and powerful were in debt. But while bankrupt yeomen became tenants and mill workers, members of the elite seemed to reemerge, even after bankruptcy, among the wealthy and powerful. This was possible because rich relatives and friends could be counted on for support and loans and because a man with a profession always had a source of income. With the proper educational background, particularly college training, one could also use speaking and writing abilities to maintain high status. Louis Wigfall could not pay his debts because of the huge medical expenses his son had incurred: suffering from a rare and painful skin disease, John Manning Wigfall died at age three. Wigfall tried to borrow from friends, to whom he was already heavily indebted, and he attempted to get a mortgage on his Edgefield property. William Yancey came to his rescue once, but this only forestalled the inevitable. Three sheriff's sales of Wigfall's possessions, from his slaves to the baby's crib, could not prevent his bankruptcy. Although he loved South Carolina passionately, Wigfall left for Texas. Unlike the small farmers who lost their lands in sheriff's sales, however, Wigfall had the help of his Texas cousin James Hamilton. Hamilton, who had been South Carolina's governor during the Nullification Crisis, arranged a law partnership for Wigfall, who was able to start over again as a professional.[65]

John Blocker, Jr., second son of Julianny Johnston and John Blocker, Sr., also survived with help from relatives. The senior Blocker, a private in the South Carolina militia during the Revolution, had acquired thousands of acres in Edgefield, much of it through land grants between 1787 and 1790. Two of his sons, including John, Jr., were surveyors, a sure way of acquiring more land. John, Jr., married Mary Talbot Johnson, also of Edgefield, in 1807, when he was almost thirty and she was only fifteen. For his bride he built a mansion, Cedar Grove, which is still a showcase today. The spacious and beautiful home fulfilled his dream, but also helped bankrupt him. In 1825 he advertised "a large and valuable plantation containing 2,000 acres on which there is one of the best dwelling houses in the up country, with all the necessary outbuildings: good water . . . excellent saw and grist mill and about 300 acres of cleared land under good fence. . . . Twenty likely negroes can be sold at the same time." But the home was not sold until four years later and then at a forced sheriff's sale. "Said land was struck off to John Bones for the sum of eighteen hundred and fifty dollars, he, being the highest and last bidder." A year later, the buyer, Augusta merchant John Bones, evidently believed his title was not clear because of the wife's dower rights, and consequently paid another five hundred dollars to Mary Talbot Blocker so that she "relinquish[ed] all my right title and interest of Dower which I have or might have."[66]

John, Jr., was bankrupt, but two of his brothers, Jesse and Abner, gave his wife "in consideration of the sum of one dollar [which was paid by brother-in-law Jesse to Abner] the negroes who are slaves for life with the future increase of the females thereof, to wit, Peter and Hannah, and their ten children." The trust was established so that Mrs. Blocker had them for life and "yet so that those slaves, nor either of them shall in any wise be liable to any debts which her husband John Blocker has heretofore contracted." When both John and Mary died, the slaves and their increase would be given to the Blocker children.[67]

In 1828, staked by two of his brothers, John, age fifty, took his family, his brother Abner, then forty-two, Abner's wife and three children, and Abner's seven children by his first wife and headed west for Alabama. Abner and his family stayed in Alabama, but John moved on to Florida, where he again established himself as a wealthy planter. All the land he acquired was in his brother Jesse's name. Jesse deeded the land in trust to John's wife, Mary.[68]

Occasionally, children and grandchildren of sworn enemies within the elite community married, perhaps ending political rivalries or other long-standing feuds. The elite disagreed violently over many issues, although they all agreed that Afro-Americans were inferior and that slavery should be perpetuated. Local political contests were generally hotly debated. At election times tempers flared, accusations flew, and behind-the-scenes politicking and back-stabbing were common practices.[69]

Although interlinking family networks served as political alliances and contemporaries assumed as much, it was not always the case. In 1860 a resident wrote from Edgefield, "The minutemen have held several *secret* meetings of the sensational kind. Many and very inflamatory speeches were made. Champagne flowed freely. . . . I suspect that Gen. Adams, Col. P as well perhaps Mr. Rhett are at the bottom of it. At all event the kinsman & friends of Adams & Pickens are leaders of the movement here." In reality, Francis Pickens knew nothing of the minutemen group. To give another example, Pickens had been sponsored in his early career by his kinsman John C.

Calhoun, and aspiring politicians often tried to influence Calhoun through Pickens. But when Pickens took an independent stance on the question of war with Mexico, Calhoun disassociated himself from Pickens, and Pickens's political career floundered until after Calhoun's death in 1850.[70]

The machinations of the 1840 gubernatorial campaign in Edgefield reveal how the members of the Edgefield elite were aligned along family lines, and the limitations of those alignments. Louis Wigfall's best friend, college classmate John L. Manning, was the nephew and campaign manager of 1840 gubernatorial candidate John P. Richardson. James Henry Hammond, Richardson's principal rival, was aligned with Congressman Francis W. Pickens and Col. Whitfield Brooks, Sr. Since newspapers nominated candidates for major offices, the Edgefield *Advertiser* wielded influence in the election. The *Advertiser*'s editor, Maximilian LaBorde, Brooks's brother-in-law, initially pledged the newspaper to Hammond. Since Hammond had Edgefield roots and relatives and because Pickens, trusted lieutenant of kinsman Calhoun, supported Hammond, it appeared that Hammond had Edgefield.

Out of devotion to Manning and contempt for the Brookses (he blamed the Brookses for keeping his older brother Arthur, an Episcopal preacher, from getting a church in Edgefield), Wigfall worked behind the scenes for Richardson. At the same time Wigfall was courting the same woman as Preston Brooks, and he wrote to Manning: "We must not be cut out of *our* Governor— if we have been out of our church & I'll try not to be out of wife either. If I go to Augusta, . . . make love to la belle Anna—shoot two [Brookses] in the morning—return to Edgefield & gain all my cases do you think she could say No? Would not that be brilliant? Damn me!"

Wigfall concentrated on the major owner of the newspaper, William Francis Durisoe. With the help of Dr. John Harwood Burt of Edgefield, whose cousin was one of Calhoun's intimates, Wigfall convinced Durisoe that Calhoun wanted the state united behind Richardson, and the paper gave Richardson a mild endorsement. When, however, Hammond brought influence to bear on LaBorde and Durisoe, through Brooks and Pickens, the *Advertiser* retracted its endorsement of Richardson. Finally, though, Wigfall used campaign money to purchase subscriptions to the paper and wrote countless articles for the *Advertiser*, always linking Calhoun's magical name with Richardson.

In the end Richardson got the newspaper's endorsement. LaBorde resigned as editor and sold his interest in the paper to his brother Pierre, who resigned within a few weeks and sold all interest in the *Advertiser* to Durisoe. In his brief stint as editor, Pierre LaBorde summed up some of his frustrations. "When we hear a man boast of his love for the dear people we are strongly inclined to suspect him of a love for the peoples' offices." Thus Durisoe became both editor and publisher, and Wigfall gloated over his control of

Durisoe. "I can now say to him 'go' and he goeth—'come' and he cometh." Wigfall became the secret editor during the campaign and wrote editorials endorsing Richardson, who won the election.[71]

This election had great consequences. Pickens's lack of influence on Calhoun was obvious to all, and this was the beginning of the end of Pickens's and Hammond's friendship (Hammond would later describe Pickens as a "treacherous friend"). Within the next five months, Wigfall engaged in a fistfight, three near duels, a shooting (in which Whitfield Brooks's nephew Thomas Bird was killed), a duel with James Parsons Carroll (Brooks's brother-in-law), and a duel in which both he and Preston Brooks were shot. In addition, a board of honor had been conducted earlier to prevent a duel between Preston Brooks and Wigfall. Some of Brooks's relatives had tried to get the dispute settled without bloodshed because they thought Edgefield could not afford to lose either talented young man. Wigfall himself remained friends with a cousin who had supported Hammond; he even interceded with Governor Richardson on behalf of a member of the hated Brooks family, proclaiming Maximilian LaBorde "is a good creature—he has no sense & a large family & nothing to feed them on."[72]

Two years later Hammond was elected governor. In less than a decade, Preston Brooks defeated Francis Pickens for the congressional seat. Political alliances shifted quickly among the elite, and politics yielded estranged kin as well as strange bedfellows.[73]

While family ties were important in forging political alliances, other issues also entered in. Even brothers like Ben and George Tillman could disagree over issues. In Edgefield some brothers differed on the Civil War. James Henry Hammond's brother, John Fox Hammond, became a surgeon with the Union army. Episcopal minister Edward Reed cast his lot with the Confederacy, while his brother fought with the Union. No animosity, however, appears to have ensued. During Reconstruction, Reed sent a son to New York to be educated by this same brother.[74]

During Reconstruction, when the world no longer belonged to the Edgefield white elite, families would not tolerate members who challenged racial barriers. One such incident divided Truman Root and his daughter. In total wealth in 1860, Root was just below the wealthiest fourth of all white household heads. Born in Massachusetts, this Edgefieldian was a devout Episcopalian who served with the elite as a vestryman of Trinity Church, yet was sympathetic to black political rights. In 1868 his home was attacked by whites. According to the sworn testimony of several Afro-American witnesses, his wife went "to the door of the hall to beg the men to desist from mashing in the outer door." The mob threatened to kill him, and "called him a G-d d--n Radical son of a b----h, and was nothing but a G-d d--n scalawag." They felt that his daughter, however, was a lady; she would not stay with him "because he was a Radical, and they were going to pay her a great deal of money for not staying with him." Root sold his store and home "at a sacrifice" and left Edgefield.[75]

Another split separated Phillip Eichelberger and his kin. Eichelberger was a man on the way to the top of his society before the Civil War. He and his family had come to Edgefield from a neighboring Laurens District planter family only a few years before the Civil War. He was a young attorney who had attended South Carolina College with Martin Witherspoon Gary. In 1860, at twenty-six, he owned land valued at $35,000 and personal estate valued at $47,500 (which included twenty-nine slaves). Eichelberger served as a captain in the Confederacy, but upon his return home to Edgefield he accepted the new order. Supporting black political rights and eventually becoming a partner in business with a former slave, Eichelberger became Edgefield's leading white Republican. Under oath he told the following story. In October 1868 a mob "rode into my yard with their pistols cocked and fingers on the triggers, and cursed me for a d--n Radical, and ordered me out of my house; said they intended to kill me. . . . My wife threw herself between us, and said they would have to kill her first; after which one Captain, ordered the men to leave the yard." Eichelberger's kin in Laurens disowned him.[76]

Even with the turmoil of Reconstruction, South Carolinians continued to admire the stereotypes of plantation life in Edgefield County. It seemed that Edgefield families personified southern ideals and values. The varied amalgamation of individuals who became the Edgefield elite came for many to symbolize the very essence of the South Carolinian. The influential editor of the Charleston *News and Courier* applauded Edgefield as having

had more dashing, brilliant, romantic figures, statesmen, orators, soldiers, adventurers, daredevils, than any county of South Carolina, if not of any rural county in America. James Bonham and William Barrett Travis, leaders of the Texan defenders of the Alamo, the American Thermopylae that "had no messenger to tell its story," were born on its soil. Edmund Bacon, the "Ned Brace" of Judge A. B. Longstreet's *Georgia Scenes*, was one of the earliest of a family of brilliant Edgefieldians. The Brookses, Simkinses, Pickenses, Butlers were Edgefield families. All of these were kin, by blood or marriage, and they and other related families gave to their village and county a character that was South Carolinian, more intense, more fiery, than was found elsewhere. Not less cultivated and courtly than the men of Camden or the "Old Cheraws," they seemed to be, if they were not, harder riders, bolder hunters, more enterprising and masterly politicians. Their virtues were shining, their vices flamed. They were not careful reckoners of the future, sometimes they spoke too quickly, and so acted, yet in crises an audacity that might have been called imprudence by milder men made them indispensable to the state. Martin Witherspoon Gary, stormiest leader of the Hampton campaign, born in Abbeville, "belonged" in Edgefield, where his life as a lawyer was spent. The Tillmans also were of Edgefield, established as planters and slaveholders, but were not of the accepted tribal chiefs—wherein is one of the keys to the political revolution that Benjamin R. Tillman engineered in 1890.

So from town to town and county to county one might go . . . to find each with its savor, however they be of one blood. They seemed tied together with an affection like that among grown-up sons and daughters having families of their own, and the state was the mother.[77]

Class and Conflict

Many ties of cooperation and charity bound whites, but consciousness of class lines, differences, and conflicts also shaped community life in Edgefield. A linking of conflict and community was acknowledged in the Edgefield *Advertiser* in 1861 under the heading of "General News Items": "Good dinners have a harmonizing influence. Few disputes are so large that they cannot be covered by a table-cloth." Louis Wigfall revealed the bonds of community when he wrote to Langdon Cheves of an Edgefield barbecue held for his political enemy Francis Pickens. "In addition to seeing fifteen hundred of the sovereign people devour meat enough to fill five thousand hungry dragoons—In addition to the pleasure Col. P's speech will offer you (if you survive it) which will not be less than two hours long . . . you will have the pleasure of seeing . . . 'the Belle of Augusta.' "[78]

Conflict was nearly as important as harmony in defining community among whites. Whether it was Preston Brooks fighting a duel with Louis T. Wigfall or George Tillman haranguing against an Edgefield aristocracy, the people of Edgefield identified with those controversies. Historian of American communities Thomas Bender suggests that "community, by providing an arena for conflict, can strengthen the sense of local boundedness."[79]

In rural communities farming folks often resented those who made their livings other than by the sweat of their brows. A planter warned neighbors, "It is not well to be too near doctors or lawyers," observing that "in the neighborhood of doctors there is always sickness and in the neighborhood of lawyers always quarreling." At times feelings of frustration found their way into the letters in the local paper. A correspondent who signed himself "Many Farmers" denounced the legal guild as "a profession that had reduced lying and immorality to a perfect science and who derive a regular and splendid subsistence by the indiscriminate defense of right and wrong," and added in tones of class consciousness that Edgefield attorneys were held in such low esteem "by honest yeomen our language has no term of reproach, the mind no idea of detestation, which has not been applied to them."[80]

Animosity was not directed only at lawyers or doctors. In answer to a newspaper's query, "What has caused the decline of sociality in our community?" a number of letters revealed community tensions. A commentator felt that with mechanization farmers no longer depended on neighbors for help. The acquisition of wealth "tempted men to be unsocial." Finally, wealth brought selfishness and distrust that poorer neighbors wanted something from their wealthier neighbors. Furthermore, "there has been added to wealth . . . aristocracy, and sometimes they *would be* something which they are not, and turn out to be crab apple aristocracy." He complained that "by throwing society into castes on social occasions, there is made a number of societies where there should be but one. And this produced jealousy, recrimination, and retaliation amoung the castes in society."[81]

The division was not always one of wealth. Both George D. Tillman, scion of a wealthy landowning and slaveowning Edgefield family, and Martin Witherspoon Gary, son of an Abbeville planter, inveighed against Edgefield's "aristocracy." Tillman argued against the legislature's power to elect presidential electors, senators, and the governor. Speaking about the government in South Carolina, he declared, "By its peculiar organization, an oligarchy of five hundred men are permitted to rule the State with iron will." Edgefield state senator William C. Moragne defended South Carolina against Tillman's charges of "aristocracy." At Edgefield Court House he proclaimed, "We live in a REPUBLIC, where the people are the legitimate source of all power—in which only one class is known to the law—where all are politically free and equal, enjoying the same rights and privileges."[82]

Rhetoric about "the people" abounded and became even stronger after the Civil War. During a heated state senate campaign in 1865, Tillman's opponent, R. G. M. Dunovant, a former Confederate general who married into the wealthy Brooks family, accused Tillman, a former artillery private, of "ignoring the people in their greatest hour of trial . . . clutching convulsively at Federal honors." Most offensive of all to Dunovant, Tillman rallied Edgefieldians to "band together and drive away the sheriff who came to collect taxes." Dunovant labeled Tillman a "lawmaker turned lawbreaker." The people, however, cast their lot with Tillman, 885 to 400; the Civil War private won thirty-two of thirty-six election boxes in triumphing over the former Confederate commander of Charleston harbor.[83]

Ben Tillman, George's younger brother, made successful use of class conflict in his rise to power as leader of the South Carolina agrarians. In 1894, when Governor Benjamin Tillman replaced fellow Edgefieldian Matthew Calbraith Butler as Senator, Tillman told an audience composed primarily of farmers that the aristocratic Butler "doesn't realize your needs as one who sprung from you."[84]

The upper classes could pretend no conflict existed as long as "the people" agreed with them. Yet, even in very subtle areas, class was an issue. For example, men divided women according to wealth. The census enumerators in 1850 and 1860 differentiated among women by use of the term "Mrs." This designation often meant a widow, but it was much more common for wealthier women to be listed as "Mrs." and for poorer women and working women household heads to be listed by given name. This custom persisted into the twentieth century.[85]

Then again, remarks from the wealthy about certain elements of the white population at times sounded very unflattering. When in 1859 members of the Beech Island Farmers Club (generally well-to-do planters) were discussing how to make the slave patrol more effective, a Mr. Mills turned the discussion to poor whites. "There is a class of white men about here that a patrole would do good in katching those Hunting Fishing & Steeling rascals; the patrole could not chastise them, but they could take them up & prosecute them & this should be done."[86]

Disgusted with the "worthlessness and obstinacy" of a wagoner from Edge-field, young Edward Spann Hammond complained that "white laborers are the hardest to get on with." He confined those remarks to his diary, however. Like many sons of planters and upper class, he had political ambitions, and since almost every white man in Edgefield, poor or rich, voted, no politician could afford publicly to offend the poor or yeoman.[87]

Although a candidate in antebellum South Carolina had to own five hundred dollars in property to run for state office, there was no poll tax and after 1810 every white man could vote. Planters were aware of the differing interests of their less wealthy neighbors and had to take those interests into account. For example, when the Beech Island Farmers Club debated whether to impose a "dog tax" to cut down on the number of dogs, which often killed farmers' livestock, particularly sheep, the argument was made that if half the dogs in Edgefield District were done away with, "we would . . . save seventy-two thousand dollars annually, which amount if applied to the Education of poor children the benefit would be incalculable." J. M. Clarke explained why the plan would not work: "Every poor man will oppose such a law." The poor needed their dogs for guarding their property and for hunting.[88]

Early in his career, Martin Witherspoon Gary, who would later earn the title "The Hotspur of Democracy in South Carolina," learned the lesson of offend-ing the white southern working class. When Gary defended George Tillman for the murder of an Edgefield mechanic, local artisans interpreted some of Gary's remarks at the trial as insults. As a candidate for the state legislature in 1858, Gary tried to defend himself against charges that he had disparaged mechanics. Gary claimed that some of his best friends were mechanics and that his opinions of people were based on their characters, not their occupations. "I am not conscious of having said anything that can wound the feelings of mechanics as individuals or as a class. . . . In forming my friendships, I never look to the calling but to the man." Claiming identity with the working man, he tried to portray himself as a victim of the "vulgar" and "purse-proud rich." Gary was hardly a poor man at all, but, like many sons of the wealthy, was awaiting his inheritance as he built his lucrative law practice. He stated, "I am but a poor man myself, and it would be but natural that I should hope for their support." Gary lost that election, but won in 1860.[89]

Class antagonism appeared during political campaigns. In 1844, Francis Pickens's Whig opponent was Hugh L. Wardlaw. The aristocratic Pickens described the campaign to his kinsman and sponsor John C. Calhoun. "They rode day and night and made the low appeal of rich *against* poor. They even brought Whigs over from Augusta to vote in Hamburg *against* me . . . & locked men up & made them drunk to get a vote, and not withstanding all I beat Wardlaw 996 votes."[90]

The temperance movement of the early 1850s had class overtones; one aim was to control poorer whites, whom prohibitionists believed too susceptible to tavern demagogues. The temperance advocates saw liquor as the cause not only of poverty but also of crime and violence. In 1852 a slate of prohibitionist candidates won Edgefield Court House's municipal elections and closed the "grog-shops." At the annual Fourth of July volunteer toasts, yeoman H. C. Turner proclaimed: "To the members of the legislature—Cease to dictate to the people what they shall drink. Remember who constituted you agents, and be not puffed up in the pride of power." In 1856 one class-conscious taxpayer wanted property and slave taxes reduced and a poll tax implemented so that the "*loafing vagabond* and *idle drone*," that is, the poor and those not working, would help with the costs of operating Edgefield District. He challenged candidates to "defy" the "*Pauper Vote*." Throughout the nineteenth century, Edgefield's wealthier residents complained about local politicos' appeals to poorer citizens.[91]

The patriciate complained of their poorer white neighbors, but less wealthy whites objected to their aristocratic neighbors. Thomas Jefferson Howard, son of a yeoman, stated that the upper class did not mingle with others. "They considered themselves and families above the former classes socially. . . . There was not such distinction at churches as was manifest at other gatherings." One Edgefield resident, writing under the pseudonym "Sweet Home," decried the propensity of large planters to buy up more land in the belief that "even poor land is a good neighbor." He felt they were "driving our small land owners from the country" and "negro mechanics" were "expelling the non-slaveholding artisan. . . . Luxury, ignorance and degeneracy" flourish in societies of large slaveholders, he warned, and pride fosters "ignorance among the masters of a slave community."[92]

In 1849 a more pointed attack appeared in a pamphlet distributed throughout the state and discussed in the Edgefield *Advertiser*. According to "Brutus," those whites who "have to work with their own hands" were basically powerless; "the great mass of the people are virtually disfranchised." Brutus asked, "What can the poor man do here? He can make nothing to lay up for his family. He cannot get his children educated. He and his family are doomed to poverty and ignorance, and to the contempt of the favored aristocrat." Calling for a political movement such as Ben Tillman would initiate nearly half a century later, and using rhetoric similar to that used by the agrarian protest movement which led to a new state constitution, Brutus exhorted the people to "teach the masters of overgrown plantations that we cannot always endure this state of things." He called for a new South Carolina constitution "in which the interests of the *free* laborer shall be provided for." The editor of the *Advertiser* denounced Brutus's "abolitionist mind," declaring, "There are no doubt, men working . . . in our midst" who desired to "excite political discord and social enmity." He warned the residents of the community to keep "an eye upon them."[93]

During the Civil War James Henry Hammond wrote: "The poor hate the rich & make war on them every where & here especially with universal suffrage & therefore they demand that rich men shall not put in substitutes. This war is based on the principle & *fact* of the inequality of mankind—for policy we say *races*, in reality, as all history shows it, the *truth* is *classes*. . . . *Here* under our Institutions it is so easy to rise from the lowest to the highest class by merit that this thing of forever grinding at wealth & place should be stopped." In another instance Hammond feared his family would lose the home, plantation, and aristocratic status he had built. "All are Epicurean philosophers. . . . Without means, your Epicurean philosophers female, drop right down to the wash tub, and male to billiard markers or porters. This . . . can only be staved off by some one *else* doing the work. . . . What will become of them when I die? In twenty years not a vestige. I am building and improving here for some Tom Foster or Trowbridge." Tom Foster, a forty-four-year-old Edgefield wheelwright in 1850, worked for Hammond. John and William Trowbridge were carpenters in Augusta in 1860. Hammond worried that hard-working artisans would be socially mobile, much as he had been, and that the children of the wealthy, without hard work, would move down the social ladder. Yeomen believed that social mobility was possible, but very difficult. Thomas Jefferson Howard remembered that it "was a slow process. Money was scarce and all kinds of farm produce very low. And the interest on borrowed money while only 7 percent, hard to pay."[94]

Education

Education in a rural farming community was more than schooling. One could learn how to plow, plant, and harvest from family, elders, and one's own experience. Wanting their sons to learn how to farm, widows sometimes apprenticed them to successful farmers. Artisans such as blacksmiths, carpenters, and potters also passed on their skills through first-hand experience, and a strong oral cultural tradition developed among the rural people, black and white, of Edgefield.[95]

Nevertheless, the people of Edgefield wanted proper schooling for their children. In 1843, B. R. Tillman, a fairly wealthy landowner who had fifty slaves, bemoaned the ignorance of four of his children owing to his inability to find a teacher. "I appreciate education as paramount to any thing but Religion & I regret the ignorance of my children for want of schools near me." Work and school were important parts of growing up white in antebellum Edgefield, but they meant different things to rich and poor children. The celebrated "little red schoolhouses" of America were not part of the tradition of the rural South. Schools that existed were unpainted and made of log or, at best, weatherboard. The southern aristocrat's sense of noblesse oblige did not extend to the education of the common people; in fact the planters thwarted public education and used public education funds for the benefit of their own children to the exclusion of others.[96]

In a letter published in the Edgefield *Advertiser* in May 1852, a critic cited the trend toward ever-enlarging plantations and still greater concentrations of slaves as one cause for the failure of public education in Edgefield. But more significantly this correspondent proclaimed that "the lordly pride and haughty disdain" of these up-country patricians induced them to oppose compromise and eschew discourse with the less privileged groups in the community. He ventured to suggest that this was merely "a local application of a general principle." He maintained that, in general, "the excessive pride of the southern people prevents them from having associative action, in any measure of public, or private importance." Indeed, in Edgefield, when some initiative led to the establishment of a free school, he maintained that the "self-willed Bell Cows" were able to curtail severely the salubrious influences of education for all. They did this by appropriating insufficient funds to build decent school-houses or attract competent teachers or by extending free education exclusively to the indigent.[97]

The yeomen, artisans, and middle class in Edgefield wanted their children schooled. On 25 January 1811 a group of Edgefield yeomen and craftsmen sent to the state legislature a petition for education infused with Jeffersonian principles. First, the petitioners acknowledged the importance of higher education, which elites readily supported, but then explained: "The children of the poorer and by far the most numerous of our citizens, are, by their situation and circumstances, precluded from the advantages of collegiate education, and doomed to regret that fortune has imposed upon them the hard lot of entering upon the world with all the disadvantages attendant on the unenlightened and uncultivated mind." Believing that education is absolutely essential to produce a wise and independent citizenry, the petitioners went on to proclaim:

> Where the minds of the great mass of the citizens are enlightened by science and literature, freedom and independence will remain secure, but where learning and science is bounded in a narrow circle and ignorance pervades the great body of the people, despotism will rear her head and oppression grasp the scepter of unlimited power. Believing then that the general diffusion of knowledge is essential to the existence of freedom and the best means of securing to posterity all the blessings resulting from a free and independent government, blessings which we at this moment enjoy, and feel anxious to hand down unimpaired to posterity.[98]

In response to petitions like this, the General Assembly introduced the "Bill to Establish Free Schools throughout the State." Through a series of legislative compromises, however, the final bill provided that the area with the greatest demand for white public education received the smallest appropriations.[99]

Although the bill had been significantly weakened in the legislature, Edgefield nabobs still objected. Seventy-seven of the wealthiest Edgefield slaveowners, several of whom, like leading citizen Arthur Simkins, were local government officials, unsuccessfully petitioned for the repeal of the Free School Act. Nevertheless, the act only partly met up-country demands for public education and actually reinforced the plantation social order. Funds from the free school system were used to establish elite academies. To get into one of these academies, primary levels of schooling were required, and the tutored children of the wealthy qualified.[100]

For most Edgefield children schools were not public; they were private institutions, often sponsored by a community, neighborhood, or church. T. J. Howard, the son of a yeoman farmer and grist and saw mill owner, explained that "they were all supported by neighbors. There was no free schools in the country then." Neighbors got together and hired a teacher and sometimes built a one-room log or frame structure. Parents usually took turns providing the teacher's board and paid fees for their children to attend the school. Sometimes even the children of the wealthy, who, like the poor, lived dispersed throughout the countryside, attended these "field schools." Ben Tillman's mother was one of Edgefield's wealthiest slaveowners, but Ben attended just such a school along with his neighbors, many of whom were the children of small farmers. Tillman's mother supplied the schoolhouse on her plantation.[101]

In response to a government questionnaire, Howard wrote of his school experiences. He attended "neighborhood schools supported by the farmers who boarded the teachers and paid his sallary from their own purses. The teachers were well qualified and the progress of the students satisfactory. . . . I went to school very irregular . . . three years altogether." He attended four different schools at different places, "but not regular as my help was required in harvest on the farm." He felt that neighborhood children attended school pretty regularly "considering the ability of their parents financially." Seven years later on a similar government questionnaire, he said he attended school "about 4 years all told, but there were intermitions of from 6 months to a year between school terms, we did not get the benefit we might have gotten had we gone regular untill our education was finished."[102]

In his autobiography Abiah Morgan Cartledge tells of his career from part-time student to full-time teacher in Edgefield. Abiah Cartledge's father was a farmer who "gave his children such educational advantages as were available at the time." Until he was twelve, Cartledge attended a school, "mostly in an Academy conducted by my uncle Evan Morgan." He explained, however, that "on account of reverses with which my father met, he was unable to keep me at school. . . . It was necessary for me to do something to help him along." The next two years Cartledge lived with and assisted his grandfather on a farm, "working on the farm about ten months and going to school some two months each year." The next two years he lived with his uncle Drury Morgan and worked on his uncle's two farms and "did not go to school any, these last two years." Thus, at seventeen, with only about six years' total of school, Cartledge believed he "had an education equal to most of the school teachers of those times. But as I had decided to engage in teaching, as an occupation, I wished to prepare myself more fully for the work." He returned to his father's and for the next six months attended school again. Then in July he conducted his own school with "some thirty students." The school was twelve miles from his father's home, and so Cartledge boarded with an aunt for five dollars a month and cleared two hundred dollars. The next year, 1835, at nineteen years of age, Cartledge took over a larger school, some twenty miles away but still in Edgefield. He boarded for forty-five dollars a year with an uncle and "cleared six or seven hundred dollars for teaching the two years."[103]

A contract in 1841 between twenty-three-year-old schoolteacher Elijah Timmerman and a group of farmers who had from one to five slaves each shows something of the operation of these one-teacher field schools. The contract called for him to teach 260 days, five days per week, in Edgefield District 6 and included the rules and regulations of the school for that year.

> No scholar shall be permitted to nor quarling nor restleing no cursing no swearing no telling lyes no telling tales in or out of school no talking in or out of doors in time of Books. The boys and girles are not to play together neither are they to be seen at the spring together. The boys are to play on one side of the house and girles on the other. No scholar shall be

permited to be roming over the fields around the schoolhouse you are not
to tarry longer at the spring than you get water no laughing in or out of
doores in time of Books. NO playing going from or to school and when
you meet any person going from or coming to school you are to speak to
them and make you obediance and go on about your business and when
any person talks to you you are to say yes sir and no sir yes mam and no
mam all large scholars has to com under the same rule as the small ones
no scholar shall be permited to leave the schoolhouse that is to go to any
persons house without permission.[104]

Poor children seldom got an education. In 1835 the free school commissioners (appointed by the legislature and members of the elite class) explained that,
as usual, they had not expended all the money appropriated to them because of
their "rigid system": "They suffer no children to enjoy the benefits of the
Public Schools, but orphans, illegitimates, or those who have poor parents,
disabled in body or entirely unable to pay for their education. No one is
allowed to classify the poor scholars but a Commissioner, even the classification of a former Commissioner is not received."[105]
    In 1847 the Edgefield commissioners announced that they would pay for
education for poor children only according to three "classes" of need. The first
class included children who were indigent, fatherless, or had parents unable to
work. The second included children whose parents owned no more than a cow
and the children of widows whose estate was not worth more than five hundred
dollars. The third comprised children whose fathers were not worth more than
five hundred dollars; the commissioners paid for one child from each family in
this last class. In Edgefield in 1850 more than 40 percent of all white household heads owned no land; in 1860 that proportion was 37 percent. The poor
were poor indeed, and except for the few at Graniteville (after 1849), where
the company had a school for the children of the operatives, it was most
difficult for the poor to find the money and the establishment to educate their
children. Some indigent pupils were sponsored by trustees and commissioners
of the public school fund, but many of the neediest children preferred to avoid
free schooling and its attendant stigma of poverty. The great bulk of children,
those of middling wealth, had no access to free education because they were
not poor enough. Since only the very poorest were allowed free schooling,
public education in the South came to be equated with pauper education.[106]
    Although started with monies from the Free School Fund and receiving
some public money, most Edgefield academies were private institutions. The
district had no academies before the act of 1811. The Edgefield commissioners
took the money from the Free School Act and established the Edgefield Male
Academy in 1814 at Edgefield Court House, where most of the commissioners
lived. A few years later, the same commissioners used the public funds to

establish Long Cane Academy. They were the first schools to offer more than one teacher; besides reading, writing, and arithmetic, their curriculum usually included music and the sciences.[107]

The free school commissioners also used public funds to establish an academy for girls at Edgefield Court House. The academy could provide girls with enough education to become teachers. Teaching was the only profession open to women, and wealthy Southerners always needed tutors and governesses to teach their children. In 1839 the editor of the Edgefield *Advertiser* warned that the lack of physical training at the Edgefield Female Academy caused "false fashion for ladies." Heeding this advice, the Edgefield Village Female Academy "added Ornamental branches, with Callisthenicks."[108]

Women's education was debated in the South. Many felt that young girls should not be sent away from home and parental authority, and some believed that men should not be allowed to instruct girls. Moreover, many held to traditional notions that women's education should be restricted to domestic arts and entertainment. Aware that some Southerners worried that education could prevent young girls from pursuing their proper role, an 1850 Edgefield Female Institute circular added, "Utmost attention will be paid to their moral, without any interference with their religious tenets, and a system will be adopted which will have for its aim the development of the understanding and powers of thought, rather than burdening the memory with unexplained and unprofitable incongruities." For most Southerners the notion of women's education continued to be like that advertised on a card that Isaac William Hayne mailed to James Parsons Carroll concerning Mrs. Hayne's arrangements for taking young ladies to board "who desire to spend a month . . . in the city [Charleston] either for the assistance of finishing Masters in accomplishments, or the advantages of Society."[109]

Not all Southerners saw southern women as only mothers and wives. In 1844, B. R. Tillman was inquiring about possible academies for his daughter. She and a friend, the daughter of a planter named Jones, had been together in school for a number of years and Tillman hoped that he could persuade this "most affectionate of fathers," for whom "money was no object," to send his daughter to the Reverend Iveson Brookes's school at Pennfield. Tillman said Brookes should get Jones's "daughter there and converse with her and exemplify the advantages of the philosophical and chemical apparatus or theory in teaching other sciences to her by a *lecture* . . . so as not to doubt your school to be equal to any other." Cordelia Strother of Edgefield attended the South Carolina Female Collegiate Institute at Barhamville near Columbia. Her commencement essay extolled the advantages of "mental culture" for women. After the Civil War, Harry Hammond encouraged his daughters to pursue advanced studies at the Harvard Annex and in Baltimore.[110]

Edgefield and adjoining areas were famous for such academies as Moses Waddel's, Cambridge College at Ninety Six, and George Galphin's school at

Liberty Hill. Unlike the field schools, the best academies often had as teachers members of the elite. Academies were training grounds for colleges, especially South Carolina College, attendance at which was one means of entry into the upper orders. The Edgefield Male Academy advertised, "The object of the school is to prepare thoroughly, for the higher classes, such young men as may wish to enter any Southern College, and to afford to such as do not intend to prosecute a Collegiate course of study, facilities for acquiring a thorough and practical business education."[111]

Academies offered foreign languages, arts, mathematics, classics, and other subjects. Students were taught the republican theory of government, with an emphasis on the legal justification of slavery. In classroom recitation they learned oration and the ability to think on one's feet. An important part of the curriculum was the inculcating of moral obligation. Moses Waddel wanted his students to learn "equity, sympathy and veracity toward men, with due regard to the government of passions and employment of time; a regard for the social virtue of temperance, industry and modesty of manners." The Edgefield Male Academy purported in a circular to stress both the mental and "morale culture" and to inculcate "the habit of investigation and independent thought." Religious values too, played a role. Another Edgefield academy advertised in a brochure: "Religion and morality form the basis, as far as the subject will admit, of every branch of education taught within the Institute. The Bible is one of the textbooks of the school."[112]

Many of the academies were denominational schools. At some of the best schools, a noted minister, like Iveson Brookes at Pennfield or William Bullein Johnson, was in charge. Even in the field schools, many of the teachers were closely tied with churches. Some were young men like Abiah Cartledge who would later become ministers. Cartledge remembered that, when teaching, "it was my custom to open the school with the reading of a passage of Scripture, and prayer. I also frequently made some remarks to the pupils, in connection with the passage of Scripture read." A field-school teacher's religious reputation made a difference in whether the rural Edgefieldians entrusted their children to that teacher's care.[113]

While children who could only go to field schools had to take what they could get in the area, schools calling themselves "academies" proliferated in the late 1830s. For Edgefield parents, choosing an academy was not easy. In 1842, when George Galphin closed his school at Liberty Hill, B. R. Tillman had to find alternatives for his four children, who had traveled more than ten miles each way to attend the academy. Two of Tillman's children, Martha and George, were far enough along to attend academies in preparation for higher education; the other two were still at the elementary level. Many parents in the neighborhood planned to send children to academies in Georgia and in contiguous districts; some even suggested schools in Washington and further north. Tillman was most interested in Rev. Iveson L. Brookes's school near

Hamburg. In three long letters Tillman discussed with Brookes the concerns that an up-country rural parent had about sending his children to an academy. "How many students is under your charge & Is their a large class of girls advanced their—how many *male* students is in the institute & how far is a student to be advanced to be receive their. What Branches are taught in both schools & prices of Tuition. how do you like the labor with study & what proportion. and does the boys all bord with a stuard or where they please. What will the expense of a *son* be there a *year*."[114]

In a slave system that required order, discipline was often violent, even in the school system. Maximilian LaBorde attended the Edgefield Academy, and he remembered the teacher as a good one. Yet LaBorde, an educator, criticized the severity as "extreme. He appeared to think that the lash was everything. He whipped without mercy. One hundred lashes with a tough hickory were often inflicted. I have seen the blood run down the legs of many a poor boy to the floor. Every day the system of flagellation was regularly going on, but Monday was peculiarly appropriated to this purpose. . . . It was a standing rule that the length of the composition should be at least twenty lines . . . and that a single mistake then was good for thirty or fifty lashes, well laid on, as he never failed to do."[115]

Long Cane Academy never reached the prestige of the academy at the village. It stressed elementary education with some attention to college preparation for older students. A woman who attended the academy in the late antebellum period remembered that teacher Mack McCants began classes with the youngest students and allowed them to go out and play afterwards while he worked with the older students, who had longer concentration spans. "We did not do much studying then at home. The teachers were put there to teach and they taught, and often to the tune of a hickory stick." Both D. A. Tompkins and his younger brother Arthur remembered this antebellum academy. They rode there together on the same horse, Arthur behind D. A., five miles each way; D. A. recalled McCants as "a keen smart teacher who whipped with a stout hickory switch."[116]

There was at least one attempt to provide an "academy" for the working class. The Manual Labor School was organized in December 1839 at Solomon Dorn's residence seventeen miles from Edgefield Court House. In this school a "scholastic year" was eleven months of spelling, reading, writing, arithmetic, English, grammar, geography, natural philosophy, Latin, and Greek. According to the prospectus, students who "enter as laborers will be required to rise before the sun, and labor until 8 o'clock; school will commence half after 8, and continue until 12, one hour will be given for recreation, after which school will commence and continue until half after 4 o'clock, then labor until night. After supper studies will be resumed till nine o'clock." This school lacked the support needed and did not last the year.[117]

Students who attended academies, seminaries, or finishing schools often had to leave home and find a place near the school to board. This added expense discouraged not only the poor but also the middle classes from sending children to academies. Sometimes, as was the case with young Benjamin Tillman, the students boarded with the teacher. A daughter of John C. Calhoun lived in his friend Eldred Simkins's home while attending school in Edgefield. Some academies provided room and board; another, however, advertised "good board can be had nearby at $5 to $8 per month."[118]

Location was also a factor. The area still suffered from a number of epidemics, and some places were believed to be healthier than others. One Edgefield Academy claimed, "Not surpassed for health." Another noted that it was "a newly erected and neatly furnished Academy situated in a healthy portion of Edgefield District." Inquiring about a certain school, a parent wrote, "Is the health of Pennfield good?" Parents also wanted a location without immoral influences. Thus one school assured parents, "Removed from the haunts of vice and dissipation which too frequently destroy the youthful mind."[119]

Because most academy students boarded away from home, end of session examinations were a special occasion when families traveled to see what the children had learned. It was also an opportunity for the aristocracy to appraise the values being taught. As the editor of the Edgefield *Advertiser* explained on one such occasion: "They were examined orally by the trustees for two days. . . . There were exercises in speaking." The slavocracy could appreciate the topics usually chosen for speeches—defenses of slavery, the advocacy of self-sacrifice, and the duties of citizenship. The community, family, and friends enjoyed these events; as the newspaper editor added on this July occasion, "In these dull, hot times this dramatic entertainment came in good season—To the students therefore we return our thanks." On another occasion the editor was very pleased to hear an Edgefield Academy graduate give the first address of the South Carolina College senior class spring exhibition. The student had learned his lessons well, as his address on the patriotism of the South Carolinian showed; according to the editor, "he enlarged on the importance of this noble sentiment of self-sacrifice to common good, scorned the sordid and selfish view which opposed patriotism. He reviewed very happily the striking illustrations of patriotism that history affords from Leonidas down to our Washington."[120]

Examinations were really not necessary for the slaveowning aristocracy to insure that students were inculcated with the proper values. The principal of an academy at Edgefield Court House assured, "Particular care will be had in the introduction of the works of Southern authors, as soon as such appear fitted to the purpose of solid and correct instruction." In an addendum to the school's catalog, the trustees of the academy and the free school commissioners vouched for the principal's "true Southern principles and feelings, and for the care which he has taken in the selection of his assistants in this and every other respect."[121]

Although Edgefield produced a cultured and educated elite, it was the private resources of the planters as well as their control over public funds that made this possible. More to the point, the planters resisted public education and limited its impact. Although in a few cases rural backcountry children would use the South Carolina school system to improve themselves and move up in the world, they would be exceptions.[122]

The situation in the mill town of Graniteville was somewhat different. Antebellum textile pioneer William Gregg recognized the desire of poor whites to be educated and capitalized on this by building a school in Graniteville. The objectives of his school differed from those of upper-class education, however. Gregg wished to produce good workers.

In the labor contract all mill workers signed, they agreed that all children between the ages of six and twelve would attend the Graniteville Mill school. The school was not free; working parents were responsible for their children's education and were required to pay a small fee. Interestingly, the free school records indicate that the largest amount of the district's public school money went to the teachers at Graniteville, who were supposedly supported entirely by the mill company. Parents of children who did not attend school were fined five cents for each day of school missed. Only the president of Graniteville Mills could decide if a parent's excuse for a child's absence was a "good and sufficient excuse."[123]

The institutionalized training at Graniteville was designed to produce a corps of orderly, obedient workers. At the last stockholder's meeting he presided over before his death, Gregg explained that the school was "one of the prominent means of keeping up a steady working force at Graniteville." In addition, the school was "a nursery for the best class of factory operatives. Aside from a charitable point of view, it is most assuredly a source of profit to our company." From the start of Graniteville Mills production in 1849, the stockholders annually inspected the school, quizzed the students, and gave company funds for the school's support.[124]

In 1883, Hamilton H. Hickman, the president of Graniteville Mills, expressed his beliefs on educating the poor and working classes. Taxes should not be used to give paupers or laborers a high school education. He felt that if they were not satisfied with elementary education only, "they ought to be made to be satisfied with it, whether they are black or white. . . . The poor class of white people, get very little advantage of any school above the elementary grade." Hickman maintained that the mill workers "cannot let their children go to school longer than the time that is required to give them a mere elementary education. After that they have to take them away and put them to work to get a living."[125]

Hickman claimed to have risen from the southern masses and when questioned as to why he would give children an elementary education and not more, he explained, "All children should know how to read and write. It makes them better qualified to take care of themselves; not so liable to be swindled by other people, and then everybody ought to know how to read the Bible, if he has got sense enough." When he explained why it was bad for the working classes to go beyond, Hickman revealed his interest as an industrialist. "A great many of our aspiring people in this country become worse citizens when they get above that; you cannot get them to work any more; they are willing to teach school, or to be politicians, or to hold a Government office, or to preach, but they are not willing to do anything else."[126]

D. A. Tompkins supported his reformist sister Grace when she complained that the Edgefield Manufacturing Company managers forced children younger than twelve to work in the mill, thus keeping them from school. He advised her to "go as far as you can without antagonizing the mill to keep the children out of the mill."[127]

Mill executives argued for enough education to teach children the habits and attitudes necessary to make them reliable workers. Beyond that they believed education would only frustrate them and make them dissatisfied with their work.

Although impressionistic evidence suggests that most of the poor and mid-dling classes could not afford to send their children to school, defenders of the antebellum school maintained that more than 90 percent of South Carolinians who fought for the Confederacy could read and write. This is somewhat misleading, since female household heads (at least in Edgefield), who had a lower rate of literacy, were excluded, as were males who were unable or unwilling to fight.[128]

The census statistics on literacy for Edgefield, however, also suggest that most white Southerners were literate, though a striking correlation existed between illiteracy and poverty on the eve of the Civil War. Among the wealthiest Edgefield white households, less than 2 percent of household heads were illiterate and only 1 percent of their wives could not read and write. In contrast, more than a fifth of the poorest white household heads and their wives were illiterate, and the functional literacy of the four-fifths who, ostensibly, could read and write is open to question. The poor had neither the money to buy nor the leisure time to read books and newspapers; so their often rudimentary knowledge of reading and writing was seldom exercised. The Reverend John Cornish distinguished between levels of literacy. He noted that in the farm family of "poor" Joshua Barton, which included Barton, his wife, and their five children, none could read or write "distinctly." Regarding the Blalock family, he said, "All of them are totally ignorant." The census enumerator agreed that the Blalocks were illiterate; the Barton family, however, was recorded as literate in the census.[129]

Poor children who attended school did not go much further than their parents in gaining the basics of literacy. Parents could not spare them from the work force. Nevertheless, poor and middle-class families may have tried to enable different children to attend school at different stages in their growing up at least long enough to learn to read and write.

Statistics of the federal population census show that Edgefield school attendance was closely related to wealth. The children of the antebellum poor were not as likely to go to school as were the children of the wealthy. For example, 61 percent of the wealthiest households in 1850 with children of school age had children attending school, 42 percent of the next wealthiest, and 32 percent of the third wealthiest, while only 26 percent of the landless households with children of school age had children attending school that year. The proportion of the children of school age who attended also varied correspondingly with wealth, from two-thirds of the wealthiest to less than a fifth of the landless school-age children attending school. In 1860 the same distinctions were true: four-fifths of the wealthiest quartile of households with children of school age sent their children to school in 1860, while only a third of the poor households did; two-thirds of rich school-age children attended school that year, and only one-third of poor school-age children did.[130]

Most striking was the difference among the boys from fifteen to twenty; less than a fifth of the poor households had any boys from this age group attending school, while nearly four-fifths of the rich households had older boys in school. This group was going beyond the elementary education available in field schools and attending academies. In this age group rich households had proportionately fewer girls in school than boys; interestingly, for the poorer households the opposite was true. Girls fifteen to twenty were slightly more likely to be in school than were the poor boys of that age. The labor of boys was valued more highly than that of girls, so more of the girls remained in school.[131]

Southern Honor

Notions of honor and virtue were characteristic of the southern family, and the families of Edgefield were no different. Edgefield youths heard of their virtuous ancestors and were taught that they also should live by a moral code. Ideas of individual, family, and community honor were instilled from youth. Honor generally connoted personal rectitude, independence of spirit, and the courage to maintain these characteristics against challenges. It meant living by one's word, no matter what the consequences. Finally, honor meant having to seek redress for grievances and defending perceived "rights."

Clement Eaton, in *Mind of the Old South*, selected an incident involving a young Edgefieldian "to depict the typical sense of honor and values of the upper class of the Old South." While away at the University of Virginia for a year, Louis Wigfall was at a dance given by a professor where a Southern Belle refused to dance with him. Feeling insulted, Wigfall challenged the girl's escort. When the university administration stopped the duel, students at the university conducted a "court of honor." The student court decided after testimony, including that of the girl, in which she acknowledged that she had been mistaken in thinking Wigfall drunk, that the incident had arisen from a misunderstanding and a "delicate sensibility" of all concerned. Honor was not involved; Wigfall had not been under the influence of alcohol, but he was a young man of "natural impetuosity."[132]

On many occasions the idea of honor led to personal and violent resolution of conflicts. Wigfall believed that the *code duello* improved a community's morals and manners, encouraging more courteous speech. Preston Brooks and Wigfall quickly challenged to a duel anyone who sullied their own or any relative's honor. Ben Tillman, Sr., wrote that although his son George had been taught good manners, he "was not of a disposition to submit to imposition or insult." George fought duels with Brig. Gen. John R. Wever, a man named Wells, and Preston Brooks. Passions often arose over politics within Edgefield District, especially between Wigfall and the Brooks family. George McDuffie fought two duels with his political enemy William Cumming. To the delight of his supporters, McDuffie, spotting a placard where Cumming had posted him, slowly approached the placard, carefully read the words impugning his honor, stepped back and covered it with a wad of tobacco and juice. But duels were so common that even the young intellectual James Henry Hammond accepted challenges on the field of honor.[133]

Best friends and members of the Seventh Regiment of the Confederate army Emmett Seibels and Elbert Bland became involved in a dispute over chess. Captain Bland from Edgefield criticized a chess move by Major Seibels, and two moves later Seibels questioned Bland's criticism. Bland perceived the exchange as a matter of honor and challenged Seibels to a duel. Despite military rules prohibiting personal feuds, they met on the field of honor a few days after the Battle of Bull Run. Seibels was struck in the chest by Bland's bullet but was not seriously wounded.[134]

Many in Edgefield opposed dueling, but sometimes the repercussions of refusing a challenge to a duel were great. When Col. Whitfield Brooks refused to meet Louis Wigfall on the field of honor, Wigfall "posted" Brooks, placing an announcement in the Edgefield Court House square proclaiming Brooks a coward. Brooks's brother-in-law, James Parsons Carroll, and nephew, Thomas Butler Bird, intended to convince Wigfall not to post Brooks. When they arrived at the town square, they found Wigfall guarding his placard. A scuffle ensued, pistol shots were exchanged, and young Bird was killed. Carroll and Wigfall met on Goat Island in the Savannah River for a duel. Both shot quickly and missed, and after negotiations the duel was stopped. The showdown between Carroll's second, nephew Preston Brooks, and Wigfall could not be averted, however. After missing their first volleys, Wigfall shot Brooks through the hip and Brooks shot Wigfall in the thigh.[135]

South Carolina was the last state in the Union to outlaw dueling. In 1812 a law was passed which required heavy fines for dueling and a year in jail for all participants, including the seconds. If a duelist were killed, the survivor could be prosecuted for homicide. Legal technicalities involving self-incrimination of witnesses and later laws weakened legal prohibitions, however. Although a few duelists were found guilty of manslaughter, none in South Carolina was ever convicted of murder, and most never even went to court. A law prohibited duelists from holding public office, but many of the state legislators and jurists had been involved in duels. Some believed that dueling was a prerequisite for holding office or for being part of the upper order. Indeed, defenders argued that the duel was necessary because the law provided no other means for gentlemen to avenge insults. To duel was a mark of class.

Dueling was also a ritual. Duelists followed closely a set of rules, *The Code of Honor*, written in 1838 by John Lyle Wilson, a former South Carolina governor and Charleston minister. He claimed that the object of his rule book was to have the seconds prevent the duel once the initial insult and challenge had been made, but the offended party was not to "turn the other cheek" at the cost of honor. Participants in duels used the words, the number of paces, and even the angle of the pistol prescribed by the book.[136]

The duel pointed up differences between the culture of the aristocrat and the common folks. Of thirty-seven people murdered between 1844 and 1859, twenty-seven were killed by means other than guns, including knives, rocks, clubs, axes, poison, a sharpened stick, a horse's skull, a metal-bound Bible, and the "tip of a umbrellar." Most of these killers did go to court, and some were found guilty of murder. This prompted Arthur Wigfall, the older brother of the more famed Edgefield combatant Louis, to point out the hypocrisy of the duel in his denunciation of the code. In the widely publicized *Sermon upon Dueling* he argued that the immunity of the duelist showed that the legal system existed "for but one class of citizens and those are the weak . . . the ignorant and the defenseless." Whereas the common folk were tried in court for murder, the members of the patriciate established for themselves only a law above the court, where "they may and do commit murder with impunity." According to the English observer James Buckingham, South Carolina excused even duels in which participants were killed as simply "manifestations of manly spirit."[137]

More than personal pride was at stake in the concept of honor. Politicians explained their actions by appealing to notions of "honor" and defense of "rights" and "manliness." Francis Pickens told Congress that "before a free people can be dragged into a war, it must be in defense of great national right as well as national honor." In another instance a correspondent wrote James Henry Hammond that South Carolina had declared her "intention to resist" so many times that "she can not back down without dishonor." In trying to mend his relations with his patron, Pickens explained to Calhoun, "I have never for one moment felt a single aspiration separate from the honor and the interests of South Carolina." Pickens wrote to Arthur Simkins, who reprinted the letters in the Edgefield *Advertiser*, "I only desired to discharge all my duties under the compact so long as we could do so consistently with our rights and *honor*." South Carolina should stay in the Union "as honor and safety permitted," suggested Hammond, and only if "rights and honor did not perish," claimed the editor of the Edgefield *Advertiser*. The *Advertiser* later believed South Carolina's "honor" had been violated and the state had "to redress her wrongs." During the crisis of 1850, *Advertiser* editor William Moragne defended "a high minded people . . . in defense of their liberties against the encroachments of a reckless and deluded majority." Northerners attacking the South were "degenerate offsprings from the noble spirits who achieved our Revolution," and those within the South who opposed the "Southern Movement" had left "the path of duty and honor."[138]

Pickens claimed that it was with "honor" that "I am discharging manfully all our duties under the federal compact to the last." Courting the legendary and fickle beauty Lucy Petaway Holcombe, Pickens proclaimed: "I believe I would turn now from any political office in the World, and be by your side in your mother's garden . . . if it were not for the obligation of honor that I . . . incurred *before* I *knew* you."[139]

The Edgefield elite was hypersensitive about what it perceived to be matters of honor. When his kinsman Milledge Luke Bonham was accidentally wounded in the Mexican War, Preston Brooks remarked in a letter to him that his courage and honor were being questioned because of his delay in returning to the war. When Brooks himself became ill during the same war, he returned home, where he had his "feelings wounded" because "even worthy citizens reproached" him in "consequence of my absence." Brooks wrote to the regimental physician requesting a letter explaining that kinsman Col. Pierce Mason Butler and the doctor had insisted that Brooks return home to recover. But Brooks wasted no time, quickly returning to the battlefield, where his fellow officers presented a resolution of support regretting that, because of orders, Brooks had been "deprived of the honor of participating in the glorious achievements of our army in the valley of Mexico." Nevertheless, Brooks felt his honor stained, and his father interceded to request a regular army commission "for an opportunity for doing something to repair, what he conceives, he has lost."[140]

Brooks figured in a notorious incident as a result of his hypersensitivity about honor. In 1856 the honor of his family and his South were motives for his attack on Charles Sumner, the senator from Massachusetts. On 22 May, Brooks caned Sumner in the Senate chambers to avenge unfavorable comments Sumner had made about Brooks's Edgefield relative Senator Andrew Pickens Butler, who was not present in the Senate at the time and thus could not defend himself or seek his own retribution. Although condemned by the

North, the assault committed by Brooks, Edgefield's congressman, was applauded throughout the South.[141]

On 28 May 1856, Brooks wrote an account of the assault. "I deem it proper to add that the assault . . . was not because of his [Sumner's] political principles, but because of the insulting language used in reference to my State and absent relative." To his younger brother he explained:

As you will learn by Telegraph that I have given Senator Sumner a caning and lest Mother should feel unnecessary alarm I write to give a more detailed statement of the occurrence. Sumner made a violent speech in which he insulted South Carolina and Judge Butler grossly. The Judge was & is absent and his friends all concurred in the opinion that the Judge would be compelled to flog him. This Butler is unable to do as Sumner is a very powerful man and weighs 30 pounds more than myself. Under the circumstances I felt it to be my duty to relieve Butler & avenge the insult to my State. I waited an hour and a half in the grounds on the day before yesterday for S when he escaped me by taking a carriage. Did the same thing yesterday & with the same result.

I then went to the Senate and waited until it adjourned. There were some ladies in the Hall and I had to wait a full hour until they left. I then went to S's seat and said, "Mr. Sumner, I have read your Speech with care and as much impartiality as was possible and I feel it my duty to tell you that you have libeled my State and slandered a relative who is aged and absent and I am come to punish you for it." At the concluding words I struck him with my cane and gave him about 30 first rate stripes with a gutta percha cane which had been given me a few months before by a friend from N. Carolina named Vick. Every lick went where I intended. For about the first five or six licks he offered to make fight but I plied him so rapidly that he did not touch me. Towards the last he bellowed like a calf. I wore my cane out completely but saved the Head which is gold. The fragments of the stick are begged for as sacred relics. Every Southern man is delighted and the Abolitionists are like a hive of disturbed bees. I expected to be attacked this morning but no one came near me. They are making all sorts of threats. It would not take much to have the throats of every Abolitionist cut. I have been arrested of course & there is now a resolution before the House the object of which is to result in my expulsion. This they can't do. It requires two-thirds to do it and they can't get a half. Every Southern man sustains me. The debate is now very animated on the subject. Don't be alarmed it will all work right. The only danger that I am in is from assassination, but this you must not intimate to Mother.

Love to all. I am glad you have all paid our Brother James a visit.

Your affectionate brother

Brooks's sense of honor required that he protect his mother from the truth if it might worry her and that he be forthright with a male relative and share his feelings in detail.[142]

In a subsequent letter to his constituents, Brooks explained his actions. "I felt that you had committed your honor to my care, together with your interests . . . and I . . . vowed . . . I would be a sentinel to her [South Carolina's] honor." Although the House of Representatives could not get the required two-thirds vote needed to expel him, Brooks resigned and then ran for his vacated seat, appealing to the voters of the Fourth South Carolina District: "If in aught I have failed to represent you as you are, then in God's name send some man whose blood is more sluggish than mine." He was overwhelmingly reelected; one newspaper joked, "We observe in the Washington Star a statement that Colonel Brooks had 6 votes against him. This is a mistake. A single vote in Newberry was blank and is supposed to have been given by a 5th cousin of a friend of Sumner's."[143]

Brooks died shortly thereafter in Washington. Editorials and obituaries especially praised "his manly qualities and chivalric character." The homeward journey of Brooks's body was that of a hero. This man, so concerned with honor, was given a very honorable funeral by his supporters. Crowds paid tribute along the way, at points meeting the train, then following the procession on foot. In Augusta the casket was placed upon a caisson under the military guard and pulled by six black horses. Next morning the cortege continued to Edgefield Court House, where throngs passed before the bier and civic and military leaders eulogized the hero. His mother, Mary Carroll Brooks, his own widow and children, and the village of Edgefield laid Preston Brooks to rest in the Brooks square with his father, Whitfield Brooks, Sr., and his younger brother, Whitfield Brooks, Jr. Following the burial ritual, the crowd departed. His tombstone proclaims Preston Brooks as "one in whom the virtues loved to dwell" and twice reminds of his masculinity: he was "manly" and prepared heaven "to receive a manlier spirit."[144]

The Military

Most men and women felt the honor of family, community, and country was at stake in military endeavors and translated these feelings into nationalism. Before marching off to war with Mexico, the "Old 96" volunteers marched out to the public square in front of the Edgefield courthouse to the strains of the "Star Spangled Banner," and there awaited the presentation of the colors. According to an account in the local newspaper, Capt. Preston S. Brooks stated their object in "a manly address," followed in the same strain by Lieutenant Moragne, Sergeant Simkins, Joseph Abney, and Whitfield Brooks, Jr. Then came Susan Pickens, daughter of Francis W. Pickens, mounted on a dappled grey steed and wearing a black riding habit with a white plume flowing from her black cap. She addressed the volunteers and presented the banner to Preston Brooks, who pledged to bear the colors honorably, to "bear it aloft in triumph, or perish beneath it in glory." Governor and Regimental Commander Pierce Mason Butler wrote kinsman Brooks, "I am much gratified at the spirit & Patriotism evinced by yourself & other officers. From old Edgefield nothing less was expected."[145]

When the survivors of the Mexican campaign returned, they brought their standard to Edgefield Court House on 16 October 1848 with a message regarding the " 'Battle Flag' presented to our corps by one of our own fair country-women and baptized in the purest of Carolina's best blood. We present it to the people of Edgefield District, as a voucher of the patriotism and gallantry of her children." Family and community, male and female, were all bound by the values of their society. In 1850 a fair maiden urged: "Men of the South, it is your duty to yourselves—to your gallant ancestors—to the cause of humanity, to strike all together." Another woman, Rebecca Bland, "embroidered by her own lovely hands" a flag for her husband Colonel Elbert Bland's Civil War regiment. Inscribed on this flag were the words "Give Us a Place Near the Flashing Guns."[146]

Ideas of honor, loyalty, and bravery were transmitted by southern white families. When Sergeant William Butler Blocker's leg was shot off close to his body, he turned to his comrades, handed the nearest one his Bible (a gift from his mother), and asked that it be sent to his father with the message that he had died like a man at the head of his company. The dying words of young Whitfield Butler Brooks on the field of battle in Mexico explicitly connected the family and manly virtues: "Have I discharged my duty?" The reply from his commander and kinsman was, "Yes, like a man; you are an honor to yourself, your family and your country." These last words were chosen for his tombstone in Edgefield.[147]

Southerners killed in military actions were remembered by their families as particularly honorable, noble, and virtuous. After having copied in his diary the letter from his son's commanding officer which praised young Whitfield Brooks's courage, the elder Brooks noted, with characteristic southern stoicism: "Thus is fallen one of my dearest of sons. Mysterious are the ways of God." Never again did the father mention the incident in his diaries. In a letter to a friend, the elder Brooks listed his family's contributions to the Mexican War and included the killing of "the noblest son that father ever raised." Ben Tillman wrote of one older brother who died from wounds received in the Civil War that he was "loved by his men" and his "record as a soldier is one of which the family has every right to be very proud." Noted southern historian and Edgefield native Francis Butler Simkins wrote, "The most precious heritage of that branch of the Simkins family to which I belong is the following about my grandfather taken from the principal history of the Confederate Army: 'Lt.

Col. Simkins, standing on the rampart and cheering his artillery, fell in the heat of battle, a noble type living or dying, of the gentleman and the brave soldier.'" The last words of Colonel Simkins, a member of the Edgefield aristocracy, were not unlike those of Shemuel Ouzts, a yeoman, reported above. The officer with Simkins when he died wrote his widow that "upon being informed that he was wounded through the right lung, with small chance of recovery, he . . . said, 'Bid my sweet wife farewell . . . I desire to live, but if I must die I fall in a just cause.' His last words were 'Dear girl.'" Grandson Francis wrote, "We were preoccupied with the reading and rereading of the prize relic of the family." He explained, "This was to us a perfect death. It was as it should have been."[148]

Edgefield youth learned about the glories of the military from watching those around them as well. An important group of youths witnessed the Nullification Crisis of 1831–32 in Edgefield. Matthew Calbraith Butler, George Tillman, Milledge Luke Bonham, Preston Brooks, and Louis Wigfall had watched South Carolina go to the brink over nullification. Wigfall's cousin, Governor James Hamilton, Jr., personally commanded the troops called to defend Edgefield from the invasion of federal troops who stood armed and waiting in Augusta, anticipating orders from President Andrew Jackson. Bonham remembered that "though but a boy at the time of that . . . struggle for the constitutional rights of a whole Section, I learned my first political lesson in that school." The military glory, the honor, and the successful aversion of armed conflict by the Compromise Tariff of 1833 had a tremendous impact on the youth of the area. And it was a nonslaveholder who at the annual Fourth of July barbecue in Edgefield toasted: "May the people of the state teach their children the value of 'liberty of conscience,' and swear them upon the alter of our country *never* to submit."[149]

Feelings of honor, patriotism, and nationalism were shared across class boundaries, though it would be interesting to know to what extent the rough democratic patriotism of the backcountry yeomen and poor was influenced by the notions of chivalric honor and gallantry that motivated the sons of the wealthy planters. David Adams, however, young son of an Edgefield middle-class farmer, grabbed the company banner and held it aloft at Churubasco, where he died. His last words were, "Tell my father I died fighting for my country."[150]

Values of honor and patriotism were thus not solely the property of the planters. Middle class, yeomen, and poor marched to war defending home, community, and country, even though they had no great stake in the conflict, especially in the contest over slavery. Minutemen and those who enlisted for the Mexican and Civil wars came from all levels of society. The rich and the poor fought, were injured, and died together.[151]

Young attorneys, most of whom were aspiring politicians, were always the first to volunteer. Military service was a means to become a hero, obtain political office, and move into the Edgefield elite. At election times newspapers regularly reminded voters of their obligations to the men who had fought for them in various conflicts, often linking the ideals of the Revolutionary War to later military encounters.

Politically, South Carolina was divided into "military" districts; subdivisions were called "regiments." A military ethos pervaded South Carolina's culture. Governor James Henry Hammond helped establish a state military college, the Citadel in Charleston. Elite military academies emphasizing military science in their curricula flourished in antebellum Edgefield. All white males were required to be members of the state militia. Drills, parades, and even week-long bivouacs and manuevers regularly occupied militia troops in Edgefield. Local militia officers always made public speeches at celebrations, such as Fourth of July gatherings.

The less wealthy felt the pull of the culture and the glorification of military honor; yet they also received financial rewards for answering the call to military service in salaries, enlistment bonuses, and sometimes land grants. Moreover, pensions brought real money to the retired soldier in an economy where cash was scarce, and cash money received regularly could be invested to improve one's financial status. Families in Ninety Six District, including what would become Edgefield District, had been ravaged by the Revolution. Reportedly, the district contained fourteen hundred widows and orphans following the war. Over the years this violent frontier society experienced Indian massacres, regulator movements, the Revolutionary War, the War of 1812, the Seminole Indian War, the Mexican War, and the Civil War. Again and again, South Carolina called upon men to leave their women and children behind and to face death. Life was particularly difficult for widows and orphans in the backcountry, and military pensions could make the difference between indigence and respectability.[152]

Despite the glorification of the military and war, some Edgefield families found war and the military less praiseworthy. Francis Pickens noted in his diary in 1846, "Volunteers for Mexico Started—never before saw such excitement—tears and weeping—War is dreadful—when it comes home to our firesides." Despite the initial enthusiasm, Preston S. Brooks, in responding in the summer of 1847 to the adjutant general's request for more troops for the Mexican War, noted that Edgefield District had furnished its quota of soldiers with the initial summons. Edgefield did not have many more potential recruits remaining; moreover, "the reports of discharged soldiers as to the disasters of the climate . . . have quite destroyed the spirit of volunteering." Julia Bryan Cumming wrote to her daughter Emily Cumming Hammond that she was "feeling very badly in mind and body" following her son Julien's withdrawal from service in the Civil War. Of a younger son, however, Mrs. Cumming wrote her daughter that Mr. Cumming was annoyed with Tom's desire to be in the army. "Your father . . . [says] there will probably be fighting enough to wait until his time comes." George Tillman expressed a similar sentiment about the Tillmans' avoidance of army service when he advised fourteen-year-old Ben and nineteen-year-old James Adams to stay in school; there would be time later to "fight and act like men, patriots, citizens, and soldiers." George had experienced the horrors of battle first-hand and he reminded his brothers that "three of our family have been food for bullets. Let us try at least to avoid a similar fate."[153]

Early in the Civil War, Edward Spann Hammond, like many of the sons of the elite, secured an appointment as a major on the medical staff of a general. In 1861 he served with Edgefield's General M. L. Bonham. However, in December of that same year, his father James Henry wrote close friend William Gilmore Simms that Spann had purchased a Mississippi plantation and had gone "with negroes to work it." In November 1862, James Henry reported that Spann had hired substitutes for the Civil War. Paul Hammond, too, with the encouragement of his father, hired a substitute for part of the war. A family friend and neighbor believed these actions caused many in Edgefield to resent the Hammonds. "For every man who does not go into this rebellion . . . will not soon be forgotten." However, those rich and powerful like the Hammonds were less vulnerable to social pressures than others in the community.[154]

Patriarchy

Male dominance characterized southern society. Rich and poor shared the patriarchal values of Edgefield culture. Slaveowners thought of themselves as patriarchs and of their plantations as kingdoms where each planter "exercise[d] in his own person, all the high functions of an unlimited monarch." Proslavery theorist George McDuffie wrote, "The government of our slaves is strictly patriarchal." In 1878 the Charleston *News and Courier* characterized Edgefield society as "somewhat feudal, somewhat patriarchal."[155]

In its laws South Carolina exemplified a patriarchal society. The state had a law in force from the eighteenth to the early twentieth century allowing a father to deed his children. In the early twentieth century this law was the basis of an Edgefield County father's conveying his children to their paternal grandfather, Senator Benjamin Ryan Tillman, in order to keep the mother, granddaughter of Civil War governor Francis W. Pickens, from obtaining custody of the children. A notorious custody trial resulted. Although this was an unusual incident, it showed that in South Carolina the father was the supreme power in the family and possessed considerable legal authority for his power. And, although writing in a humorous manner, Anna Calhoun Clemson mentioned the legal basis of the husband's "rule." Writing to her best friend, the daughter of Edgefield's Eldred Simkins and the wife of James Edward Calhoun, whose plantation lay just north of Edgefield, Anna pleaded with Maria to come to

Fort Hill for a visit. If the husband refused, Anna teased, "do if you get a chance come without him. You see I invite you to rebellion against the lawful authority."[156]

Nineteenth-century Edgefieldians thought of male politicians as South Carolina's patriarchs and referred to South Carolina as their mother. Having coveted Andrew Pickens Butler's Senate seat, which James Henry Hammond won, a rejected Francis Pickens wrote, "She is my mother, and although repelled and repudiated by her; yet I will proudly lay my head upon her bosom, even though her heart never beat for me." The paper wrote of Pickens's "dutiful devotion to his Mother State and deep concern for her welfare and honor." Gen. R. G. M. Dunovant declared at a rally at Edgefield Village that the state was a "pious mother in weal or woe, to the preservation and safety of her loving children."[157]

If South Carolina was mother, in the antebellum years John C. Calhoun was father. Historians refer to Calhoun as the antebellum "Carolina patriarch," and in 1846 Joseph Abney wrote from Edgefield that "South Carolina belongs to Calhoun." Calhoun was a stern father to younger politicians from Edgefield, such as Francis Pickens and James Henry Hammond—dishing out rewards to favored children or punishing prodigal ones. It is no wonder that, following Calhoun's death in 1850, no son came forward to replace the father; the sons had for too long feared offending the patriarch to step in and guide and control the state.[158]

Recently a historian has written of the postbellum period, "In South Carolina's patriarchal society, Hampton reigned as almighty father." At the end of the nineteenth century, the South Carolina state senate had to choose between the patriarch Hampton and John L. M. Irby, protégé of the Edgefield horny-handed farmer "Pitchfork" Ben Tillman, for a seat in the Senate. Irby was quite a contrast to the aristocratic Hampton. At times, Irby went on drunken binges, whipping his Laurens County neighbors, and once he allowed his black servant to beat a white man. On one occasion when charged with murder he hid in a remote area of Edgefield County. But Tillman was determined to "slay" the "father" Hampton, and he mustered his forces behind Irby. The other senator, Edgefield's Matthew Calbraith Butler, like Hampton an ex-Confederate general, begged the state senate to act "honorably" and "manly" and to reelect Hampton. But backed by Tillman, Irby defeated Hampton. Four years later Tillman replaced Butler as senator.[159]

Historians' condemnation of Tillman's displacement of Hampton as senator reveals something of the patriarchal stature that Hampton enjoyed, even among later generations. Francis Simkins believed that "Tillman's act was a ruthless violation of cherished traditions of which Hampton was a living symbol. For his services and tragic losses he had been given the people's highest award, the emoluments and honors of what was expected to be a lifetime career in the national Senate." The verdict of South Carolina's state historian, David Duncan Wallace, was that Tillman and his agrarian upstarts could have "better honored themselves" by reelecting South Carolina's aristocratic leader. Instead, "no single act of ruthless power by the greedy victors was more discernable . . . than turning out the leader of 1876."[160]

The home was as much of a patriarchal domain as was the political arena. Whereas women were highly praised and remembered for their gentleness, Christian character, and love for husband and family, testimonials to men emphasized their leadership and contributions to the community. Men's roles in society, not their places in the family, were remembered on family tombstones. Few antebellum tombstones even mentioned the deceased as father or son; rarer still were references to the role of husband. Thomas Wainwright Blease, ancestor of Governor and Senator Coleman Livingston Blease, died leaving a wife and seven children. His tombstone celebrates "his integrity of purpose, independence of character, and pure moral worth [which] won for him the confidence and esteem of all who knew him."[161]

Other inscriptions memorialized citizenship and offices of trust and honor. Not until the twentieth century does one find tombstones celebrating men as husbands, and even then it is only part of the inscription: "John William Thurmond, L.D.D. . . . Devoted Husband and Father A Friend of the People and Loved by Them Rendered distinguished service to his country as Lawyer, Statesman, Legislator, Solicitor, U. S. District Attorney, Special Circuit and Supreme Court Judge. As a lawyer, able and profound. As a man, kind, courageous, and true."[162]

Widows whose husbands had been in public life often dutifully tried to preserve their memories and secure their places in history. Preston Brooks's widow copied and bound a volume for the years 1849–56 and entitled it "Extracts from My Beloved Husband's Diary." Although Catherine Fitzsimons Hammond had borne much as the wife of James Henry Hammond, she and her children found ways, such as publishing Hammond's letters and speeches, to preserve his place in history. In the patriarchal world of nineteenth-century Edgefield the man's place was in society, supported by a loving wife and family. Women generally accepted this role dutifully and took pride in their husbands' accomplishments.[163]

This patriarchal system placed a premium upon sons. They continued the family name and were sources of economic help. Following the Civil War, former governor Francis W. Pickens, who had led South Carolina out of the Union, wrote to his wife concerning their financial hardships. He lamented that "I have no sons to work & to help me or I might be independent." On the death of Pickens, his eulogizer noted that he had died "but lately amid the endearments of domestic life, and with children's faces around his bed, but leaving no heir male to transmit to after generations the name which has been so long and so much honored in South Carolina. . . . He has left 'no son of his succeeding' to perpetuate his name." Charles Martin, the son of a poor white who had been a soldier in the Mexican War, regretted that his children were mostly girls "and not of much use" to help him financially.[164]

Dreams of young men about their future families and their posterity show the desirability of sons; none ever mentioned a daughter. An example is a Louis Wigfall letter to John Manning in 1839, in which he discussed his "ideal" family: "I'll build a comfortable little house & get me a pretty wife. . . . And then I'll have a spare room for my friend & his lady & when they come I'll . . . introduce them to *my* lady & show them a pretty little boy . . . & when they ask him what his name is he shall answer 'John Manning Wigfall, Sr.' Ma foi! I'll be a happy fellow yet!" The Civil War did not change the importance Edgefield men placed on having sons. In 1874, D. A. Tompkins wrote his fiancée of his hopes for their future family: "Should any of our posterity, however, become a Shakespeare or a Milton, or anyone else of sufficient consequence to make some publisher believe his biography would be a profitable book, it would begin,—he was descended from a respectable family living in Edgefield, South Carolina."[165]

In the patriarchal system independence was an important part of the white man's conception of himself as a household head; in a sense it differentiated adult from child, man from woman, and citizen from slave. This was especially true if the whites were members of the landowning elite. The prosperous planter-aristocrat represented the virtues of the patriarchal independent farmer writ large. The emphasis on the importance of individualism and independence in the antebellum South must be viewed with some skepticism since so much of southern life has been based on fairly restrictive hierarchical and patriarchal patterns. Yet these elements are reconcilable when they are considered in a family and community context. Thus independence in rural Edgefield was an independence of white male family heads from one another, and certainly in no way included autonomy for women, slaves, or free blacks. Their ideal of independence and autonomy was only understandable as part of a local community dominated by a highly complex network of kin and neighborhood relationships.

In 1855 Edgefield *Advertiser* editor Arthur Simkins explained that the kinship of yeoman and planter resulted from their common zeal for independence. Simkins condemned the "feeling of dependence, if not inferiority . . . where the relationship of landlord and tenant subsists," causing agriculture to be less attractive to the "manly and independent spirit" in other countries (he made no mention of the nearly four out of every ten landless white Edgefield households and the substantial number of antebellum tenants):

> In free America agriculture is among the most honorable as it is everywhere the most useful of human pursuits. . . . The commonest cottager, on his hundred acres of pine land, looks upon his little possession around him as his own . . . in the enjoyment of which he is safe from intrusion

so long as he discharges his obligations to the community in which he lives; while many a Southern planter, as he surveys his broad acres and passes in review of his hundreds of slaves [only twelve persons in Edgefield had a hundred slaves when Simkins wrote], feels the pride of a baron of the olden times. . . . Each man is master within his own domain and has no rival there. Especially with us, where landed possessions are reckoned by hundreds and very often, thousands of acres, the farmer or planter is in most instances literally 'lord of all he surveys.' . . . Alone and unfettered, he directs his household, prepares his land, plants his crop and cultivates it, all according to his own ideas of propriety and expediency. In doing this he jostles no one and no one jostles him.[166]

3. The White Family and Antebellum Social Structure

Wide reading, supplemented by a constructive faith in history, has taught me that, at least among Southerners, an exalted life must be built upon the exaltation of forebears.

Francis Butler Simkins,
Edgefieldian and southern historian

Our view of white family life in Edgefield and the rest of the South has been obscured by the passage of time, the influence of stereotypes and received ideas, and the complexity of free society (as opposed to the cruel "simplicity" of slavery). Edgefield was an agrarian community, with farms and families of different sizes and configurations. One-mule farms were worked next to plantations that utilized hundreds of slaves. Families consisting of parents and children had as neighbors households in which no one was related. Edgefield embraced out-of-state relatives of wealthy families, who came to learn plantation management, and maintained links with families who migrated to the West.

Family Relations

White Southerners were an especially family-centered people. Attacks upon Yankee civilization frequently included charges that Northerners tended to sexual excess, that is, free love, marital instability, and divorce. After the Civil War, when social relations with blacks were painfully unsure, the family took on special significance because it was the most enduring and stable institution.

White Edgefield glorified the home and the family. Poems such as Thomas H. Shreeve's "The Bliss of Home" praised "the joy which gleans around / The hearth where pure affections dwell / Where love, enrobed in Smiles, is found." In 1832 Augusta attorney Henry Cumming told his wife, Julia, of his wish to withdraw from the world into his family. "But you have always said &

perhaps, rightly, that this contact with the world, notwithstanding the many annoyances, was necessary to domestic happiness." By the time Louis Wigfall was a teenager, both his parents had died, which gives added poignancy to his lonely lament as a young bachelor: "I have no 'blooming wife' nor 'child to cheer my hope.'" After caning Massachusetts Senator Charles Sumner, Preston Brooks was heartened by a letter from his brother John Hampden in Edgefield. Preston explained that "while entire strangers from nearly every State in the Union have expressed a word of kindness or sympathy," his greatest "comfort" were those words of support from "*home*."[1]

In 1859, Harry Hammond expressed the importance of his family in a letter to his father. "And after all I can't help feeling that I am one of the happiest and most fortunate men that ever lived. Whether I think of you and Mother or of my two brothers and two sisters, or of the excellent person who has consented to share with me . . . the future. Such are the sources of my pride and enjoyment. They are above position, or wealth or fortune, they are in God's hands as they were his gifts."[2]

During the Civil War, Matthew Calbraith Butler, notorious as something of a lady's man, wrote to his wife, Maria Calhoun Pickens Butler, from the battlefield, "I know you do not think that I like the quiet of home, but how much mistaken you are." The letter was signed, "Your affectionate and devoted husband."[3]

Amidst the turmoil of Reconstruction, Paul Hammond "made enough by planting to keep my wife and five children comfortable." He felt his life was satisfactory, reading newspapers, novels, poetry, and theology, "occasional sports," and "plenty of work in the fields." This, combined with "my wife and five children to love and provide for," made a nice, comfortable life. In 1881, Harry and Emily Hammond's daughter, Julia, wrote her sister from school in Boston that "while Redcliffe stands and you all are there to have me with you, to love me and to be loved by me, I could never tarry away, there is never a land as fair as our dear home." Home and family were synonymous, both symbolized escape and retreat into serenity.[4]

Relations between children and parents in the typical Edgefield family were often close and affectionate. While fathers demanded to be the undisputed heads of their families, they also wanted to be loved. James Henry Hammond and his eldest son Harry depended upon each other for admiration and approval. Harry had squandered his money while at college in 1851, and James Henry gave him a lecture on character: "My experience is that . . . men who are incapable of living within their income, whatever it may be, are the very worst men in the community," and while he scolded him, he also praised him for his candor in admitting his errors. By 1856, James Henry valued Harry's advice so much that he sent him a thesis he was composing. Pointing out that he had not even shown the material to William Gilmore Simms, his close friend and the critic to whom he usually showed drafts of his writings, he claimed that Simms "would not comprehend or fully appreciate it . . . & *I will not allow it to go to press* until you look over it again."[5]

Matthew Calbraith Butler also spoke of his parents with great admiration. His mother "was a woman of remarkable force of character. She raised twelve children, eight boys, and impressed her strong personality on all of them." Butler described his father as a "stern, but very just man of the highest and most exalted character." Although his father owned slaves, Butler's life was far from soft; he began plowing fields at the age of thirteen. When the family moved from Edgefield to Arkansas (he was thirteen), he had to drive a wagon, attend to his mule, and grease the wagon every other day. His father never let any of the boys "order a servant to saddle or hitch up a horse," his purpose being to teach his children self-reliance. Butler concluded, "Whatever I have achieved in life; whether anything worthy of record, I owe it to the training, example and character of my much revered father and mother." Yeoman Thomas Jefferson Howard expressed similar sentiments. "My father was opposed to idleness. . . . We were taught and required to do every kind of farmwork the slaves did and considered it an honor instead of disgrace."[6]

In the aftermath of the Civil War, Francis Pickens replied to a letter from his wife, Lucy, who asked for help for her sister and mother. Pickens teased Lucy a little about her sister: "You know she almost had my love." Although he would have liked to help her financially, Pickens admitted that he was "far too poor" to provide money. He was able to provide a house in Augusta and wrote, "I shall always be ready to divide with her." Others expected Pickens's support as well: "Aunt Emily & Minnie will always look to us for support entirely." But Pickens assured his wife regarding her mother: "But our precious dear mother say to her I will always give her a welcome home as long as I can be able to plough a corn patch."[7]

Brothers were also supportive of each other. John Hampden Brooks wanted to rush to older brother Preston, to stand with him against possible attack after the caning of Sumner in Washington. In turn, Preston was especially concerned about John. On the death of the father, older brothers often became acting heads of families. They dutifully guided younger brothers, especially when there was great disparity between their ages. Thus Ben Tillman related that his older brother George was like a "second father to us all." Sometimes brothers sponsored younger brothers when a father died, giving them financial support and sending lengthy discourses on professions, habits, matrimony, duty, and honor.[8]

Southern men revered their mothers, exalted them almost to sainthood, and were concerned that they worried too much about their sons. Many of the Edgefield women deserved the praise they received. Sophia Tillman, for example, braved the fighting to bring home her injured son during the Civil War.[9]

Two other women who stayed with their husbands and sons during wartime became Edgefield folk heroes. Victoria Gary Evans followed her husband, Gen. N. G. Evans, to every battlefield, where she helped with the wounded. Lucinda Horne, the wife of a private, drew the attention of the Edgefield United Daughters of the Confederacy, who compared her with Mrs. Evans: "The other woman, more lowly, but none the less noble, lived among the men of the ranks. She followed her husband and son and worked with her hands, doing the humble tasks of cooking and washing and patching in the camps, so that her husband and son and others might have comforts."[10]

After the Civil War, Jane Z. Perry Butler was presented to the United States Army commander in South Carolina, General Sickles, as the sister of Commodore Oliver Perry, of Lake Erie fame, and of Commodore Matthew Calbraith Perry, who opened American commercial relations with Japan. This Rhode Island Southerner replied defiantly: "I had rather be known as the mother of Calbraith Butler!" referring to the Civil War general, one of five sons who had served in the Confederacy.[11]

A newspaper editor described the community's feeling about relationships between sons and mothers. Following the death of the controversial Martin Witherspoon Gary, he wrote, "He had one trait of character that proved him to be at the core, a good man. He was the best of brothers and most affectionate of sons. Beyond even the devotion to his country were his love and care for his mother, and we hold it eternally true that no son that loves his mother can be other than a good man, despite any other unfortunate environment."[12]

Patterns of inheritance demonstrate the love and esteem of parents for their children. Virtually every parent in Edgefield, rich or poor, attempted to divide estates equally among all children, both sons and daughters, although the home was usually passed on to one family member. If daughters did not inherit land as often as their brothers, parents did try to equalize the dollar value of each child's inheritance through distribution of slaves and other properties. Yeoman Levy Lamb in 1825 insisted "that all my household and kitchen furniture and plantation tools should be equally divided between my daughter Lelia Lamb and son John Dunken Lamb." A family lawyer for farmer Bailey Corley wrote to Corley's son: "Your Father Bailey Corley died in Year 1863 leaving a will bequeathing you $500 out of his estate and an equal share of the Estate with your Brothers & Sisters at the death of your Mother Barbery Corley." Joseph L. Talbert insisted emphatically three different times in his will that every child, son or daughter, "share and share alike."[13]

On those rare occasions when some children were favored in wills, the parents attempted to make it clear to all concerned why they had done so. James Henry Hammond's grandmother, Elizabeth Fox, explained why one daughter's children were not included. Fox had been married three times, to Capt. Sterling Turner, Capt. James Spann, and Ellington Clark, and in her will she listed her four children. To Hammond's mother, Catherine Fox Spann

Hammond, she left four slaves and half the land she owned in Edgefield District on Red Bank Creek. To her one son, James, she willed one slave, her house and lot in Columbia, and the other half of the Edgefield lands on Red Bank Creek. To her daughter Eliza Ann and husband, who had already migrated to Florida, she left a slave, household and kitchen furniture, and other personal property. Her daughter Rebecca Francis, married to Abraham Giles Dozier, a notable Edgefield attorney, had died before Hammond's grandmother had passed out bequests in her will. The will simply states, "I make no provisions for my beloved grandchildren, orphans of my late daughter Rebecca Frances; not for any want of affection, but they are already better provided for than any of the rest."[14]

In 1862, Baptist minister William Bullein Johnson wrote to his son in the Confederate army explaining in meticulous detail why he left the bulk of his property to his Edgefield daughter, Elizabeth.

> I have left the largest portion to Elizabeth, for the following reasons: 1st. For sometime before your Mother's death, the care of the family rested upon Elizabeth, & since that event, *altogether*, notwithstanding her feeble health.
> 2. [Her illness will require major expenses.] I am sure that none of my children would wish to know that she was dependent upon other resources than her own.
> 3. I have another reason. None of my children have done well as to this world. And I have confidence in Elizabeth's principles to believe, that if any of her brothers or sister, or their descendants should be in distress, she would relieve them. These reasons, my dear Son, have determined me to give the largest portion of my small estate to your sister, Elizabeth. . . . p. s. I assure you that, in the bequest of the larger portion to Elizabeth, I have acted from a conviction of duty, without the slightest suggestion from her.[15]

The tendency of parents to bequeath equal shares of wealth to their children meant that the children's landholdings would generally be smaller than those of their parents. These inheritance patterns were one motivation for Southerners to move west and seek the extension of slavery. Of course, in a single generation sons of the wealthy could become bankrupt, while the sons of industrious middle-class families could acquire land and slaves.

The inheritances, affections, indulgence, and time that wealthy parents gave their children were one aspect of the relationship. They also expected their children to succeed and to bring honor to the family. Family members who took pride in the accomplishments of their kin pushed their children and siblings to be the very best. While young Ben Tillman was away from home in school, a sister wrote to him, "Don't relax in your efforts to gain an education. . . . I want you to be an ornament to your family." Two years later another sister encouraged him, "Do Bud, study hard and make good use of your time. . . . I want you to do something for the Tillman name." After the Civil War, the children of the elite were held to even higher standards, not only by parents but by Southerners in general, who saw these young people who left the South to go to school and compete with non-Southerners as representatives of southern culture and traditions. In 1893, for example, Katharine Hammond wrote from the North to her mother that she had been admonished by a friend to do well in her nursing studies, "as I was a southern woman."[16]

Sometimes the pressures to perform at the highest levels were too much. Put in charge of his father's plantation, Harry Hammond failed miserably.

> I have for nearly 27 years enjoyed every advantage . . . wealth, education, the love, counsel, indulgence and support of [my] parents. . . . I have dreamt of doing a great many things, I have tried faithfully to do some, and I have accomplished nothing—a few words from you opened my eyes and I saw how wretchedly incompetent I had been to trusts which ordinary men, overseers, and even negroes may execute successfully. . . . Some men have cut their throats when they were disappointed in love, others because they have failed in business—I had failed in everything. I was the living, walking realization of utter incompetency, patent to every eye.

Harry left Redcliffe and went to Harvard, where he prepared to become a college professor.[17]

Much less serious was Ben Tillman's "failure." In 1864, Tillman was in his last year at Bethany Academy and had achieved the acclaim his family desired by placing first in his class. He was to give the main address at graduation. So sure was he of his recitation that he mailed his copy of the speech home. The pressure was so great, however, that when in front of the class and those who had gathered for the eventful day he forgot his speech, ran out the door of the academy, mounted his horse, and galloped home, mortified and disgraced.[18]

Household Size

Wealthier households tended to be larger households. Relatives and nonrelated persons swelled the household beyond the dimensions of the nuclear family. In 1850 at least a fifth of households in each wealth decile contained persons with a surname different from that of the household head. However, the wealthier households were nearly twice as likely as the poorer households to contain individuals with surnames different from that of the household head.

Throughout this book households are divided into three basic types— nuclear, non-nuclear, and irregular (see Figure 3-1). Non-nuclear families are then subdivided into those which were extended and those which were augmented, although the information for this distinction was not available from the manuscript census until 1880. The first, the nuclear family, contained elements of the basic family unit of husband (father), wife (mother), and children. In 1850 and 1860 the majority of all wealth groups except for the 1850 wealthiest group consisted of nuclear families.

The second, non-nuclear households, included members of a nuclear family and someone else residing in the household. In 1850 and in 1860, even when age of household head is held constant, the more wealthy a household head, the more likely persons other than the nuclear family lived in the household. For example, in 1860, among the poorest quartile of household heads under thirty years of age, only 18 percent headed non-nuclear households, while the wealthiest quartile of household heads had 48 percent.[19] Among the non-nuclear households, the extended families were those which included relatives living together, generally three generations.[20] Only a small proportion (between 8.2 and 11.8 percent) of any wealth group in 1850 or 1860 could be positively identified as households comprised of relatives (for the most part until 1880, extended households were in reality households including people with the same surname as nuclear family members).

Augmented households included individuals in the household who could not be identified as relatives of the household head. In the few cases in which both relatives and "strangers" were present, the household was considered to be extended. Augmented households included nuclear families with boarders and servants and no identifiable relatives. For 1850 and 1860 about one-third of the wealthiest group, nearly a quarter of the second wealthiest group, and about one-fifth of each of the two poorest groups (except for the 1860 poorest, with only 18.7 percent) were augmented. Richer families sometimes had tutors or lifelong companions living with them. When James Blocker died in 1831, his will provided for the support of family friend Mary Spratt, who continued to live with Blocker's widow, Isabella M. Blocker, at the Blocker home, Belle Grove, until the latter died in 1873. The seventy-year-old Miss Spratt then moved to Oakwood, the home of Mrs. Blocker's daughter Elizabeth and her husband, Felix Lake. Families with relatives with different surnames were in this group, since they could not be identified as relatives until the 1880 census. The Lakes and Blockers, for example, often had relatives counted as nonkin household residents. Felix and John Lake had no children of their own, but they reared the children of three different relatives. When Emma Perrin died in Abbeville, the Lakes took her youngest child, Catherine Emma Perrin, and Isabella M. Blocker took another granddaughter, Julia Elizabeth Perrin, to live at Belle Grove.

Finally, irregular households were those in which no family identifications could be ascertained. Most irregular households consisted of solitary persons or of a single individual listed as the head of a household containing boarders and servants. Institutions such as boarding houses, poorhouses, jails, or rock

Figure 3–1. White Household Structure by Wealth, 1850 and 1860

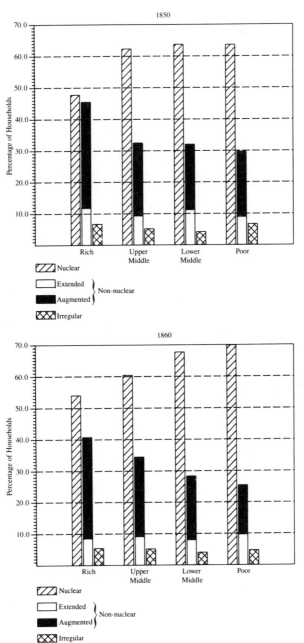

Note: See Table 3–1 for *N*s, notes, and source.

quarries were also counted as irregular households. Only a few households in any wealth group were irregular and differences in proportion among wealth quartiles were insignificant.

What should be emphasized are the differences in life-styles in single-person households. Richer household heads owned slaves, who worked for them. The poor were really alone.

The remarkably strong correlation of family composition to wealth of the household head can be seen in Table 3-1 where one can determine the proportion of households for nuclear and non-nuclear (extended plus augmented) family type and the presence of other people in the households of the rich, yeoman, and poor for 1850 and 1860. Only when there was a single-parent family were the poor, much more than the rich, likely to have additional members in their household. By contrast, the wealthy often added to a full nuclear household. House size accounts for some of this difference: houses of the rich had room for kin, friend, and boarders; houses of the poor did not. Wealthier families, for the most part, added people with jobs. The poor were generally unable to increase their households with people who could supplement family income. Although the poorer whites of Edgefield had very little, they shared what they had with others in need. A poor white woman whose husband was in jail wrote that she had problems finding work since she had four small children and "it takes all I can work for to get them something to eat." The family was "living arount" her brother. "My dear Brother helps me all he can but that is not much for he has my Mother and sister and too young brothers to support. When my husband was home he supported my Mother or at least hope to do so." The extended supportive family was part of an existing welfare system in rural societies, where primarily families and churches provided assistance to the needy.[21]

Although the greater number of extended and augmented households among the wealthy accounted somewhat for their larger household size, other factors also affected the variations in the size of the households of rich and poor antebellum white Southerners. As mentioned in chapter 2, more women headed less wealthy households in 1850 and 1860. Households headed by women generally tended to be smaller because of the absence of a husband-father; furthermore, without a husband there was less chance of continued childbearing.

Differences in the number of children also affected household size. Rich households contained more children in 1850 and 1860. In households with both parents present, the wealthy had more children than the poor. In most age cohorts, the children of the rich numbered substantially more than the children of the poor. Nutrition and infant mortality varied with wealth; the rich could also afford to have more children.[22]

The children of older couples, both rich and poor, lived at home. For two-parent families, most children were at home when the fathers were in their

Table 3-1. Selected Characteristics of White Households by Wealth Quartiles and Household Structure, 1850 and 1860
(percentages shown with selected characteristics)

	Rich (N=644)		Upper Middle (N=794)		Lower Middle (N=331)		Poor (N=1,203 landless)	
	Nuclear	Non-nuclear	Nuclear	Non-nuclear	Nuclear	Non-nuclear	Nuclear	Non-nuclear
1850								
Male-headed	91.2	87.4	88.5	87.6	83.9	75.5	82.7	78.4
Spouse present	83.4	72.0	84.2	75.6	79.6	68.9	81.0	67.5
Children present	91.2	79.5	91.7	83.3	93.8	77.4	87.8	77.6
Children and both parents present	74.4	61.1	75.2	65.9	72.5	60.4	68.6	57.7
1860	(N=745)		(N=734)		(N=733)		(N=740)	
Male-headed	93.0	83.2	88.9	84.2	90.5	83.7	84.5	71.8
Spouse present	84.1	72.6	82.8	72.3	85.5	74.5	78.5	56.4
Children present	89.8	89.8	89.4	89.7	89.1	90.9	89.6	84.6
Children and both parents present	74.2	72.8	72.3	70.6	76.0	72.7	68.2	52.9

Note: Non-nuclear includes extended and augmented; irregular and solitary households are excluded. Quartiles are approximate, especially for 1850, when 40.5 percent of all households had no land.
Source: Edgefield Data Base.

forties, and the average number of children of all wealth groups for this age cohort was almost identical. Children were born to couples well into middle age in antebellum Edgefield, and this had two results. First, few couples had any time alone together. Second, many young children witnessed the death of a parent. Almost all white women who died after the age of twenty-five had been married. About four-fifths of all white men who died after reaching the age of twenty-five had been married. In 1860 the mean age of death for married whites twenty years and older was 52 for husbands and 39 for wives; most men and women who were married and died left single-parent families. The death of siblings was also common.[23]

Youth

Strictly enjoined to respect parental authority, Edgefield children nevertheless had a youth filled with games and toys that are still enjoyed today, as well as with pastimes no longer in fashion. Despite church opposition, racing horses was a favorite pastime. Horsemanship was prized, and the children of the wealthy treasured fancy horses. Boys and girls rode both as a means of transportation and for enjoyment. A northern teacher in Edgefield who had returned to Philadelphia for school wrote to her former employers in Edgefield about the pleasant rides she had had on the horse they had provided. In 1826, Robert Mills reported that "dancing is the principal amusement in this district." This was in spite of church opposition; every Baptist and Methodist church regularly dismissed members for dancing, and even parents like Mrs. B. R. Tillman in 1853, who allowed her children to go dancing, were dismissed.[24]

There were other, less controversial pastimes. Robert Mills explained, "There is one custom, that has for many years existed in the village, which though trivial, is an evidence that the primitive simplicity of former days is not entirely passed away; namely, a general turn out of all the villagers on a whortleberry expedition once or twice a year." Cornshuckings, birthday parties, revivals, fairs, fish fries, school days, and one-to-three-week revivals and prayer meetings brought the young together. Among these forms of entertainment was singing taught by William Miller in 1838 for one dollar a student. Men with musical ability were especially praised in Edgefield. Children played with dolls and toy soldiers, tops, hoops, and other toys. They played games such as marbles and baseball—a game where the players were hit by a rubber ball. Hunting was part of growing up male in rural Edgefield for every boy, whether rich or poor. Swimming, fishing, boxing, wrestling, and other active sports were enjoyed, at least by boys, while their sisters embroidered, played musical instruments, sewed, or learned to cook and run a household.[25]

In the more affluent families able to afford books, boys and girls were sometimes voracious readers. Probate records indicate that libraries were common in the homes of the wealthy; they usually included novels, poetry, history, biography, sermons, and especially Sir Walter Scott's Waverly Novels, romantic stories of English chivalry. For the rich, the yeomen, and even the poor, a Bible was among the possessions listed in probate.

Other pastimes for boys and young men were not as healthy. Smoking and tobacco chewing were common. Drinking and gambling could become serious problems and often resulted in fights. For the daring who could afford the cost, Augusta offered many sins, including houses of prostitution, which some young Edgefield men, such as Louis Wigfall, frequented.[26]

Learning the responsibilities of work was also part of the wealthy young Southerner's upbringing. D. A. Tompkins remembered that the "Southern planter before the war trained his sons to the responsibilities of life." M. C. Butler recounted, "As soon as we were able to work my father required all of his sons to go to the field and work." When they were in school, they had to work on Saturday. At the time, Butler noted, he could not understand it, since they had slaves, but later in life he admired his father's "wisdom in inculcating habits of self-reliance in his sons." It was not unusual for teenage sons of the wealthy to work as managers and overseers or even to farm on shares with their fathers. B. R. Tillman wrote that his son George was accustomed to work, having been an overseer for a plantation when he was only fifteen years old. Sons of yeomen also worked in the fields alongside slaves.[27]

Although rich men often referred in their diaries to their "working" childhoods, their situations were different from those of the poor. Interestingly, in 1850 the sons of the second wealthiest quartile were more often employed than those of the other wealth groups. In two-thirds of all poor households sons between the ages of fifteen and nineteen were employed; only a third of the wealthier households had sons employed. An even greater disparity existed between the rich and poor where daughters were concerned. The daughter of only one rich household head worked; she was a teacher. Among the poor, 28 percent of those households with daughters twenty or older had daughters in the work force, and approximately a fourth of the poor households with daughters between the ages of fifteen and nineteen had their daughters gainfully employed. These young women worked as domestics, textile workers, laborers, and seamstresses. Poor children experienced work at an early age—work to help families make ends meet, not labor to learn what work was about.[28]

D. A. Tompkins, a youth from an elite Edgefield family, worried about working in the factories with coarse laboring men when he went to Rensselaer Polytechnic School in Troy, New York, during Reconstruction. He was concerned that working with them might cause him to lose his feelings of being a gentleman and that he did not display the dignity that Northerners did in the company of the other youth at the school and at social occasions. He discovered that among northern people of "refinement," the "emotional parts of one's nature is not expected to be shown." Tompkins blamed his shortcomings in society on his Edgefield upbringing, where the country people did not restrain themselves. The white men of the community tended to wear their hearts on their sleeves; the Civil War did little to change their romanticism or their openness.[29]

Courtship was one of the most keenly anticipated experiences of growing up. Among the upper classes passion and intimacy were often intensified by an increasingly loving and voluminous correspondence. Letters of lovers show them to be modest about their achievements and open about their perceived shortcomings. The lovers saw their relationship as a source of new growth, maturity, and even humaneness; the relationship itself provided the lovers with an identity. Often a young man would write to a woman of his being unworthy to be her husband. Lovers persistently equated theirs with higher, spiritual love. "My love for you is a true love. True love comes from God, and it never will change." Christopher Poppenheim wrote several letters to his Edgefield fiancée expressing how important she was in forming the nobler aspects of his character. Letters often contained gentle teasing. Matthew Calbraith Butler, a dashing cavalry general who lost a leg at Brandy Station, was still celebrated by William Watts Ball as "the handsomest man in South Carolina, if not in the country. Whatever one might think of him as a politician, one could not be with him without loving him, for he was the most gracious gentleman." Notorious as a lady's man, Butler wrote to his wife from the battlefield about the numbers of beautiful women he had been with, but added that none compared to her. Scores of letters written by Harry Hammond to his fiancée and future wife, Emily Cumming, survive. Many were similar in tone to courting letters written thirty years earlier by Emily's father, Henry Cumming, to his future wife, Maria Bryan. Some letters expressed concern about not having heard from the other person. There were often expressions of the joy and the happiness that wives and fiancées brought into the man's life. In 1859, Harry Hammond wrote Emily that she should not be worried by the serious tone of his letters, for "they are the random expressions of a man entirely unused to this happiness he is enjoying now." "I have been a stone, a block, and now . . . you have told this stone to live and move."[30]

One has to wonder, however, about the hypocrisy of Martin Witherspoon Gary's drafted poem, which was written "for only you," but sent to many different women by the man whom the local paper called the South's most eligible bachelor. Perhaps he remained a bachelor because women perceived his lack of sincerity.[31]

Although most parents did not interfere with their children's courting, there were exceptions. At fifty-five, Francis Pickens was worried when he courted his third wife, the twenty-six-year-old titian-haired beauty Lucy Holcombe, because "your mother and father are so bitterly opposed to your marrying me. That they will not consent for you to receive me, except to give me a 'public refusal.' " Then six months later he wrote desperately, "It is now 56 days since you wrote me your last letter & yet I have written you twice a week & sometimes oftener. Your two last letters were ominous, in one you said you could never be my wife if your mother opposed it. You also wrote all your family were bitterly opposed to me." Catherine Fitzsimon's family opposed her marriage to James Henry Hammond, but Hammond persevered. Hammond, however, successfully opposed his son Spann's marriage to a second cousin, Clara Kirkpatrick. Generally, children married into families of comparable wealth and status. Sometimes a daughter from a wealthy family married a young man from a less privileged background, but in those cases the man was usually a professional who was obviously gaining in social status. Parents' objections usually did not need to be along class lines.[32]

Extended Communities

White kinship ties influenced the concept of community and extended that concept beyond geographical boundaries. Not only did relatives help one another, but Edgefield residents, rich and poor, kept close track of each other even when separated by considerable distances, as when family members or acquaintances moved to another state. Neighbors and relatives sometimes moved together from Edgefield. Liberty Church was founded by a group of Edgefield migrants in Bullock County, Alabama, around 1853.[33]

By means of letters and visits, Edgefieldians retained ties over distances small and great. If they lived within the state, many returned regularly to Edgefield. In 1854, the *Advertiser* commented: "We are glad to find our respected friend and former fellow-townsman, Professor M. LaBorde, had not forgotten to pay his annual visit to the spot of his nativity. . . . The people of Edgefield are always delighted to see the Doctor come again and sit for awhile amongst them." Those who traveled out of state also maintained links to Edgefield. Francis Pickens's father, who had been governor of South Carolina, migrated to Alabama, yet maintained ties with kin and friends. His influential kinsman John C. Calhoun sponsored young Pickens when he returned to South Carolina. William Butler was born in Edgefield, but, a navy surgeon, he traveled extensively. After leaving the service, he returned to Edgefield for a while before moving on. His son Matthew Calbraith Butler was born near Greenville in 1836, and moved with the family to Arkansas when he was thirteen. Shortly thereafter his father died, and at age fifteen Matthew returned to Edgefield to live with his paternal uncle, Senator Andrew Pickens Butler, whose plantation, Stoneland, was four miles from Edgefield Court House. For these men, family transcended spatial boundaries.[34]

Residents and Edgefield migrants corresponded regularly, and when the railways came, they visited each other. White Edgefieldians in Georgia,

Texas, Mississippi, Alabama, Arkansas, and elsewhere subscribed to the Edgefield *Advertiser*, the Hamburg *Republic*, or one of the other local newspapers of the period. Letters and visits allowed former residents to continue to feel part of the community. On 13 December 1833, James Beale Rainsford wrote in his diary, "Many families are leaving this state and district for the states of Alabama, Georgia, Mississippi, and Florida." Rainsford corresponded with these friends, and less than a decade later made a trip to the Deep South to visit some of the people who left. He wrote that he and his wife "paid a visit to N. G. Christmas and friends one week near Columbia, Georgia and to Mr. L. C. Cantelou for near 2 weeks near Montgomery, Alabama."[35]

These contacts were not limited to the planter class. During the Civil War the son of a nonslaveowning Edgefield farmer regularly corresponded with his father and two sisters. In 1864 he wrote, "Pa I saw an Edgefield paper a few days ago which give an account of the casualties in the 7th Regt. I saw in it where Poor Joseph Whitlock was killed. I saw where Lovelit was severely wounded in the shoulder. Elbert Wells informs me that Martin Whitlock is at home. . . . I would write to Sister Hannah but the most of my Envelopes are directed to you. I think it ought to satisfy all for any of you to hear from me. Write to me once per week without fail." Robert Irwin came from Belfast and settled in the Hard Labor area around 1771. Of his five children, two married and moved to Illinois. They then persuaded their youngest sister to join them. Irwin's son Francis and daughter Mary stayed in Edgefield. One of Francis Irwin's sons moved west, as did seven of Mary's sons. None returned except for Francis's son, and three of *his* children followed relatives who had settled in Georgia, Alabama, Mississippi, Louisiana, and Texas. Other small farmers, like the Lewis and Smith clans of Edgefield, corresponded from antebellum years down to the 1930s with long-departed relatives they had never seen, exchanging news of births and family. These long-distance relatives were important to rich and poor. Nephews sometimes made long trips to the homes of aunts and uncles and got their initial start in a community by living with their relatives. In addition, the travel that the more well-to-do families undertook gave additional opportunities for the sons and daughters of Edgefield families to meet other young people and establish courtships. While on one of his usual summer visits to his maternal grandparents in Elberton, Georgia, Benjamin Tillman began the courtship of his future wife.[36]

Age at Marriage

Women married at a younger age than men. In 1860 the average age for brides marrying for the first time was twenty; for grooms it was twenty-five. Wealth significantly influenced Edgefield household arrangements. In 1850 and 1860 there was a clear pattern in the ages of husband and wife: the older the age of the household head, the greater the age difference. Young men tended to marry someone of the same age; the community frowned on a young man's marrying someone not yet of marriageable age or marrying an older woman. For Edgefield women, marrying a younger man went against their "scruples." As one Edgefield woman who loved a man two years younger wrote to him, "It was a serious thing to me to know that you were *younger* than myself. . . . Then of all the detestable things . . . none was more so than a young lady encouraging one younger than herself." Older men, either marrying late or remarrying, tended to wed younger women. In 1860, fifty-five-year-old Francis Pickens took as his third wife Lucy, who was twenty-six, about the same age as two of Pickens's married daughters.[37]

This tendency was more pronounced among the poor (see Table 3-2 for details). Poor older husbands (over forty) had a greater age separation from their wives than did rich older husbands. Perhaps in Edgefield society older, poorer white men, who had little wealth to bolster a patriarchal position, could more easily assume a dominant stance in a home with younger women. On the other hand, it may have been that some poorer men took longer to establish themselves financially and therefore married later, when they could select from unmarried women their own age as well as from those who were younger. Marrying a woman because she was pretty or a virgin may also have been a factor, for those were values prized in patriarchal society.[38]

Cousin Marriages

Cousin marriage, although assumed to be common in southern culture, especially among the elite, rarely occurred in Edgefield, and was even more unusual after the Civil War.[39] Among all wealth groups, however, brothers of one family often married sisters of another family. For example, eighteen double-cousins lived in a one-mile radius of one Edgefield plantation house in the nineteenth century. In addition, following the death of a spouse, the widow or widower sometimes married the relative of the deceased mate. Maximilian LaBorde's second wife was the sister of the deceased wife. Thus, it was not unusual for a stepmother or stepfather to also be an aunt or uncle. Preston Brooks's second wife was the first cousin of his deceased spouse. Daniel Augustus Tompkins's mother, Virginia Smyly, a relative of John C. Calhoun, died in 1867, and his father later married his wife's cousin Ella Smyly. Tompkins had great affection for his stepmother, whom he called Cousin Ella, and she in turn gave motherly affection to Tompkins and his brother and sister.[40]

Even more confusing for genealogists were intermarriages like that of the Reed and Strother families. Mary Caroline Blocker's older sister, Julia, married the Episcopal minister Edward Reed. Mary Caroline married the wealthy

Table 3-2. *Average Age Differences of White Husbands and Wives by Wealth Quartile, 1850 and 1860*

Age of Husband	1850				1860			
	Rich N=468	Upper Middle N=613	Lower Middle N=241	Poor (Landless) N=861	Rich N=558	Upper Middle N=550	Lower Middle N=579	Poor N=512
Less than 30	4.1	3.9	3.5	4.4	3.2	4.7	3.5	3.4
30 to 39	6.4	5.7	5.3	5.9	6.3	5.7	4.9	6.0
40 to 49	7.1	6.7	8.2	8.0	7.9	6.4	7.6	6.9
50+	8.7	7.9	10.2	10.9	9.8	8.2	9.6	11.6

Note: Quartiles are approximate, especially for 1850 where 40.5 percent of all households had no land.
Source: Edgefield Data Base.

Edgefield widower David Richardson Strother. Her two stepsons by Strother's first wife adored their vivacious stepmother, and they married two of her nieces, daughters of the Reverend Edward and Julia Blocker Reed. Hence what appeared to be two marriages between first cousins (marriage to the child of one parent's sibling) were not intermarriages of blood relatives at all. The intermarrying of the various families produced "kissing cousins," but that was something quite different from the pattern of endogamous marriages ascribed to the South without regard for class, regional, or chronological differences. As Lila Carroll explained about living with her aunt, Mrs. Whitfield Brooks, near Ninety Six in Edgefield District, "We were a family of congenial cousins." Blood-first-cousin marriages were rare and not a preferred pattern among nineteenth-century Edgefieldians.[41]

While consanguine marriages occurred among Edgefieldians, they were rare, and almost nonexistent among the less wealthy; the common folk frowned on such unions. Such marriages that did occur generally involved people from other locales. Two cases of cousin marriage occurred among the Cheatham family, who had moved into the Abbeville and Edgefield districts from Virginia. A grandson of one brother wedded the daughter of another, and a great-grandson and granddaughter of these same two brothers also intermarried. James Beale Rainsford came from England to claim his share of his grandfather's estate in Edgefield. While there, he fell in love with his Edgefield cousin Esther Rainsford. They married, and he settled in Edgefield. Rainsford was English and his cousin Esther's father was also English, and among the English upper orders, endogamous marriages may have been more common.[42]

Most Edgefield families who practiced endogamous marriages, however, were from Charleston and low-country South Carolina. Perhaps this pattern resulted from the difference in white population density between up-country and low-country South Carolina. From the time of the great migration in the mid-eighteenth century, the white population density in the Piedmont was so great that there was little need for endogamous marriage. In the low country, however, the white population was sparse and distributed among a large black population so that the choice of local white marriage partners was much more restricted. Louis Wigfall's family was from Charleston, and he married a second cousin. Her grandmother was the younger sister of Wigfall's maternal grandmother. A telling note, however, is added by Wigfall's biographer. "It was not at all unusual in antebellum Tidewater society for cousins to marry."[43]

Hints of this pattern lace the letters and actions of Edgefield residents. While serving in the Confederate army, Harry Hammond was disappointed by the conduct of individuals from the coast. James Henry Hammond advised his son not to be hard on the tidewater inhabitants because inbreeding had resulted in "genius & imbecility[;] chivalry and poltroonery & meanness were always strangely mixed up among the salt water people—not in each one—but in classes."[44]

Further insights into cousin marriage are found in a marvelous collection of letters between Mary Elinor Bouknight of Edgefield and her second cousin Christopher Pritchard Poppenheim of Charleston. William Bouknight farmed substantial land with more than sixty slaves in Edgefield and was the first cousin of Dr. John F. Poppenheim, a rice planter of Goose Creek, near Charleston. The Edgefield Bouknights were Baptist; the Charleston Poppenheims were Episcopalian. Cousins Mary E. and Christopher met first in 1859 or 1860, and the letters of their romance reflect the ups and downs of most love affairs. They were finally married at the Edgefield plantation, Bouknight's Ferry, 24 November 1864. Mary had requested that her cousin destroy all letters she mailed him because of their intimate nature. In the fall of 1863, however, away at war, Christopher decided to save the rest of his beloved's missives as an inspiration. In the first letter he saved from her, Mary bared her soul. In a letter addressed "Confessions to 'one' dearer than Life!" she wrote:

> There are two other things I must tell you my beloved Christie, that have caused me many, many sleepless nights of tears. I struggled against my fate and tears were only my relief. It was a serious thing to me to know that you were *younger* than myself, and a "*cousin*". Two things I had bitterly opposed all my life and thought that there was not a cousin on the globe even without being younger than myself, who could cause me to overcome my great scruples enough to think of marriage with. But my heart bid defiance to all calculation, and let what come that would against you, it would stand even singly and alone in your defense. When I thought of these two things I almost thought it sinful to encourage you in the least, if it was God's will we should ever be united, He would guide us and unite us in His own good time.

Although these two cousins married, the reference to scruples points out the stigma attached to cousin marriages; it was not common.[45]

Cousin marriages occurred considerably more frequently in Episcopalian than in Baptist and Methodist-Evangelical families, but religious persuasion did not appear to be the most influential factor against cousin marriage. The argument against cousin marriage was made not on moral or religious grounds but on eugenic grounds when Dr. Thomas Jefferson McKie, an Edgefield planter, wrote another physician, Thomas P. Baily, who resided in tidewater Georgetown. Although the letter McKie wrote has not been found, Baily's reply provided insight into the Edgefield planter's views on endogamy. Baily illustrated his points with examples from Georgetown:

> What you say about family traits & marital relations and affirmities, should in this age of progress in the arts & sciences command attentive

consideration, but I believe there is improvement in almost everything except in the true social status and ties of consanguinity. So far civilization as it advances, has rather encouraged incongruities in *natural selection* than not. Now how frequently we hear of *first* cousin marrying & the result mental & physical deformities with idiocy have resulted. Where there has been unusual intellectual brilliance (and I know of such) there is consumption scrofola etc.—from this circumstance the appellation *Kings'* Evil has been made use of I *suppose*. Only lately I attended the nuptials of one of the sweetest young ladies of our town. . . . But Alas! much of the romance fled, when I called to mind that her Benedict was Consumptive and her *first* Cousin. Well! alls well that Ends well & one will hope for the best but don't you think the future looks critical?

Thus, Baily, a low-country Episcopalian, and McKie, an up-country Baptist, agreed that cousin marriages were to be shunned.[46]

Southern Womanhood

In Edgefield the roles of southern women, like those of southern men, were in some ways similar among all classes and in other ways very different. Women were primarily the perpetuators of the family. Before and after the Civil War women of all social classes had children with remarkable frequency. After giving birth to Alfred Cumming Hammond, her fifth child, Emily Hammond wrote her mother a letter about the suffering and horror of childbirth. Her mother replied:

You spoke of the restraints mental and bodily you had borne to save Maria and myself from a feeling of "disgust." . . . My prevailing feeling is one of consideration at the bodily suffering which characterizes, more than is common I think, your troubles of this sort, but apart from that I cannot even regret it. You are the very person to multiply your offspring, especially, if they get most of your nature (and not the slightest disparagement to the paternal one is here indicated), and besides this, the profound, intense enjoyment you have in loving and cherishing your children much more than repays whatever of disturbances they may have cost you. I hope . . . that each one . . . may be to you and Harry loving and bright, and causing that delight and pride which it seems to me would be ingratitude to their Maker not to feel.[47]

More typical of the feelings expressed about the birth of children was that of Emma Blocker Perrin, who wrote to her mother two weeks after the birth of her third child, Julia Elizabeth. "You never saw a little creature grow so rapidly as my dear little babe. . . . I haven't the least trouble with her except to wash and keep her and supply her wants when she is hungry. I thought some time past that I did not have love enough to divide with another; but . . . she is such a dear good little creature that I believe I love her more than I ever loved a little baby before."[48]

Whether charwoman or chatelaine, the woman was first of all mother, homemaker, and partner in family economics. She was responsible for all domestic chores. When she was not confined to bed in pregnancy or child-birth, environmental, social, and economic conditions dictated her day-to-day routines: gardening, canning, preserving, cooking; spinning, weaving, sew-ing, knitting; washing, ironing, cleaning; nursing and caring for husband, children, friends, and animals. Just keeping the animals involved a multitude of chores—feeding, pasturing, milking, birthing, and so forth. In 1830 the Potterville *Hive* proclaimed, "There is no female accomplishment more valu-able than housewifery."[49]

Women in wealthy families had more leisure time, more formal social duties, and more managerial responsibilities. Yet, even the daughter of the Carolina patriarch John C. Calhoun found moving into her Edgefield planta-tion home with her family demanding. Anna Clemson wrote to Maria Simkins Calhoun in spring 1844: "Here we are at last & have been for the last four days & I am sure I have done more hard & dirty work in that time than in all the rest of my life put together but now that I have got to be near about as comfortable as we can be in this house I am determined to go on by degrees in the rest of my fixing and such a fixing as it is."[50]

Women who possessed more than the minimum of real and personal prop-erty commonly owned maidservants and other domestic slaves. Yeoman Anna Thorne Howard had one slave to help her in the house, yet her son recorded, "In a family of 8, it took my mother's whole time to eat, sew, and keep the house." He mentioned also that his mother did not have to spin and weave; "as there was a large cotton factory nearby, we could buy our cotton good at the factory cheaper than we could make it at home." Women from elite families had more slaves to do daily chores.[51]

Not all women were full-time homemakers; some white women were ac-tively engaged in the antebellum work force. In 1850, because the census enumeration did not include the occupations of women, the number listed was too small to be of much help in determining just how many white women were part of the daily population laboring for wages in Edgefield. Nine women in 1850 were "farmers." One was described as a "milliner and mantua maker."

In 1850, seven teachers and six "tutorisses" (one of each was a household head) were among the "professional" women in Edgefield (refer to Table 2-1). In 1860, when women were listed with occupations, twenty-two were teach-ers, of whom twenty-one were living in the household of someone else.

Although it has been commonly believed that the teaching profession in the South was first feminized during the Civil War and after, there is evidence in

Edgefield that this process began before the war in the late 1850s. In the 1830s and 1840s, when women began to enter the common schools of the Northeast in large numbers, almost no females were recorded on the Edgefield Free School Reports, although women had been working for some time as tutors for the children of the wealthy. As late as 1856, out of some eighty teachers in the Edgefield Free School Reports only two or three were women. Yet in the three years before the Civil War, the number of female teachers increased some fivefold to about fifteen out of eighty, and this increase was then further accelerated with the absence of male teachers during the Civil War.[52]

Circumstantial evidence suggests that the New England pattern largely instituted by Horace Mann and Henry Barnard in the late 1830s to hire more female teachers was only beginning to make its way to the South and South Carolina particularly in the 1850s. It is worth noting that Christopher G. Memminger, the first commissioner of education in Charleston in 1856 and later the secretary of the treasury to the Confederacy, corresponded frequently with education leaders in the North—especially Barnard. He praised female teachers for their sweet and loving temperaments, and spoke of them, much as Mann and Barnard did, as most fit to be teachers of elementary school children.[53]

This development also paralleled the gradual emergence of the separate male and female spheres, which scholars have claimed accompanied movement toward a more industrialized and urbanized society. The female teacher was thus widely regarded as a sort of surrogate mother in the schoolroom who eased the transition of the young child from the home to the community and furthermore prepared the child to take his or her place in the rapidly emerging society.

In Edgefield these changes were taking place much more slowly than in New England, which in part explains the fifteen-year time lag. Yet even in the late 1850s up-country South Carolina was still far behind the North's industrial and urban development. The fact that the feminization of teaching predated industrialization in the South suggests that ideological shifts may have preceded the changes in the economic base ostensibly required to bring them about. A final point to be made on this question is that although these developments were observable in the late antebellum period, the Civil War and its aftermath further accelerated and solidified these changes.

In 1860 most working women, however, were not teachers; they were domestics. A significant number were also listed as "farmers" or as "farming." Eleven women were employed in businesses, and more than half of all the 1860 factory workers were women. Only two of these female factory operatives headed households. Nonagricultural laborers constituted 26 percent of women employed, but only 2.6 percent of the women who headed households. Only two wives, both from the poorest quartile of household heads in 1860, listed occupations (seamstress and domestic). Still, in 1860 women constituted

17 percent of all employed whites, and they also headed 15 percent of all white-headed households in both 1850 and 1860. Graniteville Mills hired only children twelve and older and preferred hiring women fourteen and older (although in 1883, Hamilton Hickman, president of the Graniteville Mills, and in 1907, D. A. Tompkins, of the Edgefield Manufacturing Company, implied that in their mills children as young as ten were working).[54] Even among white women over twenty in 1860, only 13 percent were employed.

Although few wives were employed, significant numbers of white household heads worked outside the home well before the Civil War (when 1,500 seamstresses worked for the Confederacy in Augusta). Other women were a critical part of the farm work force and contributed toward the family income along with their husbands, not only carrying on housework and child care but also helping with the planting, harvesting, and improving of their farms. One woman in 1850 was listed as a "farmeress," a term in the rural South for a woman who was managing a farm of modest size. In 1860 one woman was a postmistress; others were employed as teachers, milliners, landlords, and domestics. Some women even owned and operated business enterprises; working was not limited to the lower classes.[55]

Although the 1850 manuscript census returns for population did not list women who were employed, the industry census provided an idea both of the variety of paid nonagricultural jobs available for working-class white women (and men) before the Civil War and the wages paid. In 1850 sixteen different establishments reported hiring a total of 283 women. Almost all of these were employed in the two textile mills, 63 at Vaucluse and 190 at Graniteville. The next largest employers were two merchants who had each hired four women.

The 1860 manuscript census for industry listed substantially fewer establishments that employed women, primarily because it excluded the mercantile establishments and milliners. Nevertheless, nine industries employed 253 women. Although they employed fewer women than in the previous decade, the two textile plants were again the chief employers, with Vaucluse hiring 44 women and Graniteville employing 186.

Male workers earned far more than their female counterparts. For example, in 1850 the male employees of Graniteville Mills received an average of $16.52 a month, while the women were paid only $5.04. There were occasional exceptions, such as William McEnoy's shoe and boot factory, where men and women received equal pay, but more typical was merchant John Lyon Colgan, who paid his four male employees an average of $35 per month while he paid his four female employees an average of $15 per month. Differentials in pay were precise at Graniteville in 1860; men earned $24 and women $12 per month. Both made less at the Vaucluse mills, but the difference in pay between men and women was also smaller. Men made $9.81 and women $6.14 per month. At a pottery factory four women made a total of $48 and ten men made a total of $200 per month. Whereas the wages of male textile industry employees rose by half during the decade of the 1850s, women's wages rose only a fifth. Women were consistently paid from 33 percent to 50 percent less than men, but were not involved in the heavy manual labor; nor did women get the training for specialized skills. Male bosses and managers gave orders to women and reinforced the ideal of male authority in a patriarchal society.

If there seemed to be no complaints about the pay differentials in the working world, a local paper complained about the lack of cost differentials for wives. In 1830, after reading a biography of George Washington which noted that wives were purchased for 150 pounds of tobacco in 1620, the editor wrote, "It surely does not comport with our notions of justice and equity, to exact the same price for a bad wife that is paid for a good one."[56]

Most women hoped to become wives, and Edgefield men had definite images of the women they wanted to marry. In 1841, Louis Wigfall outlined the characteristics of his "ideal" wife. He wanted to marry someone reared in "the same circle," someone intelligent, well educated, who could "feel poetry." This remarkable woman must also "admire" her husband. Writing in 1844 to J. Edward Calhoun, his brother-in-law by his first marriage, Francis Pickens described his second wife: "The lady I have selected has been educated & raised in the best manner by worthy & pious parents, & she has all the diffidence & retiring softness to which I have been so accustomed in life."[57]

Not all reports of women were glowing. Swearing devotion only to the law, young Louis Wigfall vowed to never marry, for women "ruined the first man—the wisest—the best man—the strongest man—(Adam, Solomon, David, Sampson) & I expect she will ruin the last man. They have come damned near ruining me." In a letter that shows an interesting view of the tariffs on manufactured items which the agricultural South opposed and which led to the nullification crisis in the early 1830s, Elisha Hammond warned James Henry, "Never marry, unless a rich, or a poor woman raised to hard work. The idleness, economical ignorance, extravagance & pride of Woman are beggaring the Southern States. . . . Did women properly know & discharge their duties, spin & weave and cloath their families—whom would the tariff effect? The riches and happiness of every married man depend on his wife. She can wear out, ride out & eat out more than any profession can bring in—it is considered despotism here to oppose, no matter how extravigant, the wishes of a woman." Believing that "when you get a Scorpion in your bosom you feel the sting," Elisha thought the South Carolina Legislature should pass resolutions against extravagant wives and daughters, not against the tariff. James Henry continued the tradition of warning younger brothers and sons about the dangers of "southern womanhood," but complimented his own wife when advising younger brother Marcellus: "Unless you can marry a rich woman & an angel do not think of it. I have been lucky myself."[58]

Most Edgefield men had only the highest praise for southern women and for marriage. The testimonials husbands left wives reveal something of what they felt for their spouses. Several of the epitaphs in the Edgefield Village Cemetery paid tribute to women from families of middling and extreme wealth, and while the monuments of the middle class were not as majestic, the praise was no different from that found on the wealthiest family tombstone.

> She had in no ordinary degree the virtues and attractions of her sex, but her modest, meek and affectionate spirit gave peculiar interest to her character. Throughout life she manifested the most delicate religious responsibility and beautifully illustrated the sweet influences of practical Christianity. Her death was calm and tranquil, and humbly trusting in the love and mercy of her Saviour, she departed with the cheering hope of happy immortality. This marble is placed over her mortal remains by her bereaved husband as a testimony of his affection.

> This lady was endowed by nature with the virtues and graces which peculiarly become and adorn a woman. Her mind was quick and sprightly. Her disposition frank and cheerful, and her principles, naturally elevated, were purified by the most ardent piety. As a wife she loved her husband with a sincere attachment, and as a mother she was devoted to her children, for whose welfare and honor she felt the liveliest interest. This piece of marble was placed over her remains as a tribute of love and respect by her affectionate husband.[59]

Letters also carried reminders of how important wives were to husbands. In 1865, Francis W. Pickens gave a pecuniary evaluation of his wife's worth to him: "Gov. Perry has sent on & affirmed my pardon, for a supposed value of over $20,000, but I know I am not worth it except in *your Jewelry*, if it be I am legal owner of that [which he was]. I know I own my wife and that she is worth over one million in hard money, but then the U.S. Gov. will not value her that high." This high appraisal of his wife came only four years after she had informed Pickens "that he would make any human being miserable."[60]

Wives were valuable to their husbands, particularly in handling the various responsibilities and duties of the household. For mistresses of large plantations, this was quite a job. Young Emily Hammond wrote her mother that "my servants are so young, & flighty that company in the house, and kitchen, upsets them completely, and much of the time I should like to devote to my guests, is spent seeing that one little job after another is performed without an interval of more than an hour between each." When husbands were away from the plantations for extended periods, as many Edgefield planters and politicians were, women often had to make important decisions.[61]

Although these wealthy southern women had definite responsibilities, it is difficult to assess their power in a patriarchal society. When women married, they traded their autonomy for the protection and support of their husbands. If they earned incomes, their wages belonged to their husbands. Although wives could act for husbands in certain circumstances, they were not independent economic agents. They could not make contracts, sue or be sued, or execute a valid will. Prior to the 1868 Reconstruction constitution only single women and widows in South Carolina could own real property in their own names. With legal assistance wealthy women could set up separate estates in trust, but there were no guarantees these would be upheld in court.[62]

The complicated inheritance patterns whereby daughters were left property jointly with husbands make it difficult to generalize about the amount of wealth controlled by women. Even when married, daughters generally received an equal share of the parents' legacy, although daughters did not get land as often as sons. In their own names, white women constituted 12 percent of all white owners of real estate in 1850 and owned 8.6 percent of all land owned by whites. In 1860 women constituted 15 percent of all white persons who owned real estate and 17 percent of all white persons who owned personal estate. They owned 12 percent of the land and 12 percent of the personal wealth.[63]

Hints about the influence of women lace diaries, letters, and memoirs. For example, James Rainsford recorded in his diary that he chose to reside in Edgefield because of his wife's desire to do so. Senator Andrew Pickens Butler wrote of his father, William Butler, and mother, Mary Bethehald Foot Moore. The pair had met when the dashing Butler had spied her during the Revolutionary War, but his intended's stepfather refused permission for him to court Mary Moore. The couple eloped and married when she was nineteen and he thirty. William Butler's lifelong companion, "a woman of strong . . . traits of character, always exercised great influence with her husband and he relied much upon her judgment and advice." It was to his wife that the high-spirited Butler gave "a positive pledge, which he kept, never to run another race or to play another card." Butler "considered it a defect in his sons not to ride well," so he had the sons break the horses. His wife ended that practice when two sons, Pierce Mason and Andrew Pickens, drew lots to see who would ride a particularly fierce "Dare Devil" colt. According to the memoir, Mrs. Butler "interposed, telling her husband that they were her children as well as his" and to have the slaves break any future colts. Although he did not like it, General Butler gave in to his "devoted" wife.[64]

Butler's interesting tale supports the contention that the nineteenth-century woman played a definite role in running the family unit and that she was not a mere adjunct to her husband's life and wishes. "Devoted" did not mean subservient, as some literary stereotypes indicate.[65]

To assert themselves, women, especially among the elite, could leave their husbands and take the children with them. Prolonged separations were common for married couples among the elite, and perhaps even among the more struggling middle wealth groups.

Since the wives of the well-to-do often visited relatives, one cannot but wonder if they did not wish to be away from home. Often, too, husbands wrote letters pleading for their return. It seems that, to a large extent, wives determined when they would be at home, which indicates an exercise of power by some women in the patriarchal society. Maria Calhoun Pickens Butler traveled so often to visit her sisters that her husband, Matthew Calbraith, offered to fix a room up for one sister, Eliza, if Maria would return home instead of visiting with the sister continuously.[66]

When James Henry Hammond refused to break off the relationship with his slave mistress Louisa, Catherine Hammond, who had stood by him during the revelations of his misconduct with her deceased sister's daughters, left him. She took the children and returned to her family's home. For more than two years Catherine and the children stayed away, until James Henry finally agreed to Louisa's becoming the personal maid of his wife's sister. A few months after his family returned, Hammond brought Louisa and her family home again to the plantation. With strong-willed patriarchs, wives had difficulty enforcing agreements.[67]

Sometimes, even for strong-willed women whose husbands adored them, circumstances could prevent their exercising their power to leave. Lucy Pickens hated Russia and wanted her husband, Francis Pickens, the American ambassador, to take her home. She believed that she had made, in her words, "a sacrifice" when she married him, twenty-eight years her senior, and that he should placate her by letting her take "her child" and return to her mother in Texas. Lucy wrote her mother that she had admitted to Pickens that the only reason she had married him was so that he would pay off her father's debts and obtain a plantation for Lucy in Texas. She had wanted to leave so desperately that she had "begged him on her knees to let her go." The usually doting Pickens stood firm, however. Nevertheless, he and Lucy continued to present a gay façade.[68]

Elisha Hammond's wife, Catherine Fox Spann, perhaps expressed discontent with her marriage when she requested to be buried, not with her husband, but at the foot of her mother's grave in Augusta, a lasting protest to her situation in a patriarchal world. Her tombstone explains, "She lies here by request in filial humility at the feet of her mother."[69]

Former slaves often recalled white women as influential in plantation decision making. They were, in general, favorably disposed to their white mistresses; yet there were exceptions. The various temperaments and personalities of individual owners often determined the treatment of slaves. Peggy Grisby remembered that her Edgefield owner "was a fair master, but his wife was awful mean to us."[70]

Often the plantation mistress had the final word, and sometimes she single-handedly ran the plantation. Susannah Wyman recalled that her master had been drinking and "tried to sell two boys, my brudder and another youngster for a pair o' young mules." The white mistress, Elizabeth Robertson, whom the former slave remembered as a good mistress, interceded, declaring to her husband, " 'No! you don't sell *my chillun* for no mules!' And he didn't sell 'em neider."[71]

Former slave Isiah Solbert Butler thought his master had been a good man. "But de ole lady, ole 'miss Jenny,' she wuz very rough. She hired all de overseers, and she do all." She also kept the slaves from seeing the master about their grievances.[72]

Another former Edgefield slave told her story about a mistress's influence. "I was a girl in slavery, worked in the fields from the time I could work at all, and was whipped if I didn't work. I worked hard. I was born on John Bedenbaugh's place; I was put up on the block and sold when a girl, but I cried and held tight to my mistress's dress, who felt sorry for me and took me back with her."[73]

Although women had no official role in the church structure, they were a powerful force in insuring the participation of their families, both immediate and extended, black and white. A typical monthly Edgefield Episcopal Sunday school report complimented the local teachers. "In the occasional absence of one or more of our regular Teachers, their places have been kindly supplied by other Ladies. To those who statedly or occasionally have here engaged in this labor of love, I tender my hearty thanks, and pray that while blessing others they may be blessed of the Lord, and 'turning many to righteousness,' may hereafter shine as stars for ever and ever." Plantation mistresses were given credit (whether deserved or not) for teaching Christian beliefs to the slave population. Although at institutionalized churches women sometimes taught slaves in Sunday schools, no available manuscripts give any indication that southern women gave religious instruction to slaves on their plantations. What Du Bois and Frazier suggested may have been the case: houseservants who had contact with the whites may have benefited. Alexander Bettis's mother, for example, was a houseservant of Mrs. Jones, who was credited with Bettis's religious instruction.[74]

It would be an overstatement to claim that antebellum southern women were inhibited in their churches. The philosophy of the evangelical churches, at least, allowed for the equality of every person before the Lord. The ideal of evangelical womanhood stressed piety, purity, domesticity, and submission. This ideal allowed women to be active outside the home, while it taught submission to men as a traditional and familial duty derived from a religiously invoked paternalism that stressed mutual responsibilities of husbands and wives. Although still repressive, it suggested a spiritual egalitarianism and strength of character tempered by religious strictures on female roles. Taken a bit further, evangelical womanhood also inspired some women and men with the belief in the moral superiority of women. Thus armed, some Edgefield women were able to reject the restriction of women's influence to the home and to go out into the community to remake the world in the image of the Christian home.[75]

Both before and after the Civil War, Baptist women went before congregations, their immediate family, other relatives, and black and white neighbors of varying status and wealth and gave testimony. Horn's Creek Baptist Church kept fairly detailed records. In May 1851, following the invocation, "Miss Mary Whitlock came forward and related her experience and was received into full fellowship with this Church." In September eight women "came forward and related briefly what the Lord had done for their souls." Speaking in front of all the church and relating something as personal as one's conversion to Jesus took courage, and the ritual of sharing with other church members helped bond members to the community. The roots of the strong, self-assured evangelical woman were deep in rural Edgefield.[76]

Although before 1880 the active role of church women seemed limited, one found exceptions. In 1813 Big Stevens Creek appointed a committee composed entirely of women to investigate and advise another woman. In 1827, although Eliza Johnston Drysdale lay buried in Edgefield Village Cemetery with only a plain slab marker, minutes of the Edgefield Baptist Church reported, "Notice was then taken of the death of our dearly beloved sister, Eliza J. Drysdale, one of the constitutional members of this church." A marginal note read, "The founder of the first Sunday School in Edgefield County at Edgefield Village." In the 1830s Female Benevolent Societies and Home Mission Societies proliferated in Edgefield, as did Temperance Societies. The male Edgefield Domestic Missions Society was supported by three "respectable Female Societies, auxiliaries to it." In 1876 three women were among the seven members of a committee whose charge was to develop a systematic plan of collecting church tithes for the Johnston Baptist Church.[77] Early in the twentieth century, Senator Ben Tillman inserted the article "The Mission of Woman," a strong statement of the model of evangelical womanhood, into the *Congressional Record*. In addition to the lengthy essay, Tillman added his own assessment under the subhead "Inferior Animals but Superior Beings": "In brute force, in all that constitutes the mere animal frame and nature, women are inferior to men; but in purity of mind, in refinement of sentiment, in all that most nearly assimilates our race to the good angels above, they are superior to men."[78]

When Francis Pickens compared the nature of men and women, he described men as "miserable, selfish, contracted little creatures . . . with none of the nobleness and dignity of human nature." On the other hand, he lauded southern women who "indulge in the softer sympathies of nature—who observe what they see and take interest in all around them, who indulge in the feelings and affections of the heart—who utter refined and delicate sentiments . . . who are mild and modest—whose eyes kindle with hope . . . whose bosom heaves with the most elevated and refined affections of the human heart." He urged Anna Calhoun to prepare herself for the world by reading "well-written books particularly on taste, such as Burke on the sublime and beautiful—Addison in the Spectator—Cicero's letters—the best novels of Scott . . . study Milton, Pope, and Shakespeare. (Byron is corrupt although splendid)—read Virgil and Homer—read in History, the Bible, Rollin . . . Plutarch Gibbon . . . Robertson's Chrles 5th. Robertson's Scotland, Homer . . . Ramsay's U.S. Ramsay's South Carolina."[79]

Women fostered the belief that they were the guardians of purity and refined civilization. Using the ideas of patriarchy and honor to their own advantage, they undertook a mission to transform their spouses into better persons. This conception affected the outlook of women in all literate groups, and was shared by the poorer classes. Letters between lovers, romantic literature of the day, and the local newspaper all contained examples of this "civilizing" role. Henry H. Cumming wrote from Augusta in 1823 to his betrothed, Julia A. Bryan, that she should "amuse [herself] . . . in devising means for making me more the ideal personage." In 1841, while visiting with her sister in Edgefield, Maria Calhoun advised her older husband, "I hope you are a good man, and read your Bible on Sunday anyhow—if you could only know what was for your good you would study it at all times, and abide by its precepts—but I will not give you what you are not deserving of—a sermon." Christopher Poppenheim wrote Mary Bouknight in Edgefield, *"Every good I possess I owe to you My darling one."* Time and again, Edgefield male Southerners indicated that it was the woman's responsibility to make a better person out of the man, even inscribing this role on their epitaphs.[80]

By the Civil War, Edgefield men saw women as the saviors of society, not just of their husbands. Cumming's son-in-law Harry Hammond wrote, "The only solution of this country is in the hands of women not only now in all that they inspire men to do and bear and to believe in, or in the present help and aid they render to the country—but if ever this war does end it will be their part to restore order and to reform society."[81]

In the 1840s, Benjamin Tillman, Sr., attributed his joining a temperance movement to the encouragement of one of his daughters. By the 1880s women had become active in reform groups. They established schools and Sunday schools among the mill children at the Edgefield Manufacturing Company, and progressive women social reformers worked among the mill families encouraging everything from the planting of kitchen gardens and shrubbery to the organizing of temperance societies. At the turn of the century the editor of the Edgefield *Chronicle*, in a long article "The Baptist Women's Great Convention a High, Mighty and Noble Thing," acknowledged tongue-in-cheek the extremely active role of southern women in the Baptist Missionary Conference. "From Tuesday . . . until Friday morning Edgefield was one vast, strenuous, tumultuous, happy bee hive in which male drones found neither place nor toleration. . . . And gradually the bee-hive became a flaming Vesuvius in active eruption, sending forth red streams rolling to the far and mighty East, streams helping the women of South Carolina to take the dark and beckoning East for Christ."[82]

Except for church functions, women had few opportunities to gather, beyond visits, quilting parties, and the like. From the 1820s the Edgefield Female Library Society offered some privileged women a fortnightly gathering. The Daughters of Edgefield, whose slogan was "Equality and Independence," was formed at the time of secession. Even before South Carolina adopted the Ordinance of Secession, this group spurred the men on to fight. Symbolizing the community nature of the call to the Civil War, on 5 November 1860, when Edgefield men assembled in answer to the call for volunteers, hundreds of women were also present for the festive occasion.[83]

During the Civil War women found many ways to contribute to the war effort. While one member of the Edgefield Female Library Society read aloud, others rolled bandages, sewed uniforms, knitted, prepared provisions, and packed supplies for soldiers at the front. Mrs. Milledge Luke Bonham was the president of the Edgefield Soldiers Relief Association, which prepared boxes of clothes and other provisions to send to the front. Officers of the association included both men and women, as did its board of directors.[84]

Yet many besides the wives of the traditional upper orders found that the exigencies of the Civil War enabled them to make a more substantial and active contribution to community life than they had previously had the opportunity to make. Throughout the summer and early fall of 1861 a spate of women's aid associations were founded to raise funds for purchasing and producing clothing and supplies for Edgefield's earliest volunteers. During the subsequent months the local newspaper often carried articles on the important contributions being made by these women's associations. Initially, they were largely formed in specific settlements or in neighborhood churches within Edgefield to sponsor the volunteers from those particular settlements. Soon nearly every church and neighborhood had one—the Gilgal Church Relief Association, the Ridge Spring Church Relief Association, the Red Oak Grove Soldiers Aid Association. As opposed to the better-known societies of the elite, these local, mostly rural settlement associations were composed exclusively of women. The leaders of these associations were almost always married women.[85]

Both the more exclusive and the rural inclusive organizations formed by women during the Civil War were the precursors of the later nineteenth- and twentieth-century women's clubs so prominent in the South. Later in the nineteenth century, Rebecca Pickens Bacon, daughter of Francis W. Pickens, was president of South Carolina's first chapter of the United Daughters of the Confederacy. Organizations such as these and the Baptist Home Mission societies offered southern women opportunities to engage in club work and social feminism in support of traditional values within a conservative and respected setting.[86]

Besides their femininity, southern women were also praised for teaching traits that were important to the patriarchal values of southern culture. One of the duties of women in the South was to insist on certain kinds of behavior from the males. The gender of black and white household heads was not crucial to the instilling of patriarchal values. A case in point was the Tillman family of Edgefield. No one questioned the "masculine" traits of the salty and fiery agrarian Benjamin Tillman. But Sophia Hancock Tillman was the one who taught her son those masculine values as well as "habits of thrift and industry; to be ambitious; to despise shams, hypocrisy, and untruthfulness; to bear trouble and sorrow with resolution." Tillman recalled "the frequency with which she would hover me to her bosom and tell me she would rather see me a good man that a great man. She always taught me to tell the truth and whipped me if she caught me story-telling. Another one of her teachings was to do things well. I have repeatedly heard her say that 'anything worth doing at all was worth doing well,' and she lived up to that motto for she was very thorough in her work." Tillman was absolutely devoted to his mother and wrote, "To *her* I owe whatever of ability and judgment I have."

Sophia Tillman bore eleven children, four daughters (one died in infancy) and seven sons. She survived her husband by twenty-seven years; he died in 1849 leaving her fifty slaves and 1,800 acres of land. By 1860 this woman had amassed eighty-six slaves and 3,500 acres, valued at $71,620 in personal and $36,000 in real estate. Despite financial success, her life was filled with tragedies. By 1866 she had lost five of her seven sons. Another, George, fled after murdering an innocent man in a fit of rage; he finally returned to serve a jail term for manslaughter after wandering the world as a fugitive. Historian Francis Butler Simkins praised Mrs. Tillman as "energetic and ambitious, accomplishing everything expected of the men. She nursed ill slaves, super-vised the education of her children, taught her daughters to sew, and person-ally managed extensive planting and lumbering operations." She was a thrifty and shrewd businesswoman. Although one of Edgefield's wealthiest citizens, when she went to Augusta on business trips, Sophia Tillman hitched her horse in Hamburg and walked across the bridge to keep from paying the toll for a wagon. She spoke her mind to others, often bluntly.[87]

Further evidence of women's ability to instill patriarchal values was the rearing of aristocrat Maj. Andrew J. Hammond, celebrated throughout the Edgefield and Georgia region for his "manly qualities." Captain of the Hus-sars, elected a major in the Civil War, and serving on the Confederate gen-eral staff as well as representing Edgefield District in the state legislature, Hammond inherited, according to local historian John Chapman, "courage, strength of character, and noble attributes." Hammond's father, Charles, a merchant in Hamburg, died when the boy was an infant. Charles's widow survived her husband by fifty-four years and reared their son at the old homestead. This venerable Edgefield matriarch was "noted throughout Edgefield for her fine business habits, strong intellect, great charity, and goodness of heart. All these fine traits of character were transmitted to her son, Andrew J. Hammond." These examples from antebellum Edgefield show that southern matriarchs instilled masculine virtues, yet tempered them with the gentler traits ascribed to white southern women.[88]

Women showed business ability in a man's world. Most women were intelligent, capable, and active partners in the running of plantation, farm, or business. They were administrators and supervisors of complex and busy households. Dr. Johnathan O. Nicholson died in 1851, leaving his wife, Elizabeth Julia Nicholson, heavily in debt. A remarkable business person, Mrs. Nicholson was able to pay off her debts, turn a profit, and leave each of three children a plantation and slaves. To give another example, during the Civil War, while his father was at the front, Daniel Augustus Tompkins's mother managed their two thousand acres and forty slaves with the aid of an elderly overseer. When the father returned in 1862, he practiced medicine in Edgefield while the mother continued managing the plantation. Mrs. Tompkins hid thirty to thirty-five bales of cotton and later sold them for thirty cents a pound in gold, thus enabling the Tompkins family to enter the postwar period already well-to-do, with twenty thousand dollars in hard cash. Tributes to a woman's business acumen and shrewdness were often sandwiched in between traditional acclamations of femininity. One finds among the qualities attributed (on her tombstone) to a businesswoman who died in 1851 "a masculine intellect, an admirable judgment, and extraordinary energy and dignity of character, and withal a Christian humility, a winning countenance, a cordial affability, a generous sympathy, a kindly charity."[89]

When, forced by circumstances to become tough, businesslike women, widows succeeded in those spheres of life that were generally considered male domains, they were not condemned; instead, they were celebrated. The virtues of George Tillman's spouse were touted: "Margaret Jones, an heiress of the masculine type as capable as George's mother of managing her broad acres." The appraisal of white matriarchy has been complimentary whereas the appraisal of black matriarchy has tended to be negative.[90]

Divorce, Premarital Sexuality, and Adultery

Family relationships were not always tranquil. Parson Mason L. Weems, the creator of the George Washington cherry tree legend, was at one time an Episcopal priest in Edgefield. In *The Devil in Petticoats or God's Revenge Against Husband Killing* he celebrated the notoriety of one Edgefield wife, writing the "awful history of the most beautiful but depraved Mrs. Rebecca

Cotton, who most inhumanely murdered her husband John Cotton." (She murdered three husbands.) Domestic unrest was as real as the patriarchal image of the lordly husband. On 3 October 1849, at a widely publicized trial at Edgefield Court House, Martin Posey was convicted for the murder of his wife, Matilda H. Posey.[91]

Throughout the nineteenth century, churches, particularly the Baptists and Methodists, had standing committees on discipline to help with family problems. Frances De Laughter was under censure from her church for threatening to stab her husband and attempting to leave him. Churches at times accused men at church meetings of whipping or abusing wives. Often families were counseled by committees of other members. Single men and women were excommunicated for fornication and married men and women for adultery. Upon admission of their sins and on promises not to repeat the offenses, churches readmitted the dismissed members to fellowship. An Edgefield Baptist church sent the following inquiry to the Baptist association: "If a man puts away his wife for fornication, can he still join the church or remain a member?"[92]

Except for a brief period during Reconstruction divorce was not a viable legal alternative to a troubled marriage. Even divorces obtained in other states were not recognized in South Carolina. Prohibition of divorce was supposedly for the protection of women, who, in the words of a South Carolina jurist, "have their charms destroyed and their constitutions wrecked in childbearing . . . the justification for which agony and bloody sweat is the security of the attentions of the one man for whom all was borne." But the impossibility of divorce also reinforced male dominance and sometimes left women in precarious circumstances. Elizabeth Hamilton petitioned the General Assembly to have her marriage to John Yeargin annulled and to be freed from any obligation for debts owed by Yeargin. In the words of her petition, Hamilton "gave herself in marriage to a Mr. John Yeargin of Virginia." After she had lived with Yeargin about four months, he "purchased some slaves with the intention of speculating." He left his wife with Edgefield relatives, and she had not heard from him since. She hired two agents, who found Yeargin living in Savannah under an alias. He had married again and even admitted that he had been married in Virginia when he married Hamilton. He left Hamilton "nearly destitute of a support," yet Yeargin's creditors had law suits pending against her.[93]

In 1878 at McKendree Methodist Church, M. J. Collins had to face charges of adultery for marrying another man without obtaining a divorce from her former husband. She was found guilty and expelled. Poor whites who could not obtain a legal divorce simply separated. The Reverend John Cornish described the pathetic situation of a "destitute woman" and explained in a knowing way that her husband was "among the missing." At times the wealthy resorted to the same tactic when a marriage was not working out. After Edward

Spann Hammond returned home in 1870, his wife, Marcella, remained with him only six weeks. She decided she despised the Edgefield country life, so "Spann took her to the depot and she never returned." Spann continued to live in the Beech Island area, where he was both a planter and practicing attorney; his wife died in Virginia at her parents' home in 1878.[94]

Throughout history the wealthier classes have complained about the morals of the working classes. Condemnation of the licentiousness of early settlers anticipated the later white complaints about Afro-Americans. Indeed the descendants of these very people who were condemned by the upper orders for their life-styles would make the same charges against blacks and their religion. Before the Revolution, Anglican minister Charles Woodmason raved against the pernicious influence of the "New Light" religious movement in the backcountry. In the up-country of which Edgefield was a part, Woodmason maintained, many whites who came under the influence of the New Lights, or Separatists, as they were sometimes called, survived close to the land; "many live by Hunting and killing of deer." Because of the lack of churches many had been married by civil authorities who "ask no Questions, but couple Persons of all Ages, and ev'ry Complexion, to the Ruin and Grief of many families." The traveling preachers of the New Lights followed the example of the magistrates and thus, "the sacred Bond of Marriage is greatly slighted. . . . For many loose Wretches are fond of such Marriages; On Supposition, that they are . . . Dissoluble, whenever their Interests or Passions incite them to Separate. Thus they live *Ad Libitum*; quitting each other at Pleasure, Inter-Marrying Year after Year with others; Changing from Hand to Hand as they remove from Place to Place, and swapping away their Wives and Children, as they would Horses or Cattle. Great Scandal arises herefrom to the Back Country, and Loss to the Community. . . Concubinage establish'd (as it were) *by Law*: The most sacred Obligations are hereby trampled on, and Bastardy, Adultery" become common. Without education the children of the backcountry "lead Idle and Immoral lives. . . . Their Lives are only one continual Scene of Depravity of Manners, and Reproach to the Country; being more abandoned to Sensuality." Woodmason claimed that 94 percent of the brides he married were pregnant. And since the spread of the New Light religion, he maintained, there were "more Bastards, more Mullatoes born than before."[95]

Similarly, upper-class whites misunderstood the living arrangements and attitudes of the emerging South Carolina textile operative class. In the early twentieth century, Grace Tompkins, a social reformer from a wealthy Edgefield family, complained about the low morals of the Edgefield Manufacturing Company mill workers. Two-thirds of the operatives, she believed, had two or more living spouses. In addition, she worried about the large number of marriages between boys and girls who were only thirteen or fourteen years old.[96]

Sexuality was no respecter of wealth, of course. Upper-class southern men, particularly the young "bloods," considered "low-born" women fair game for their passions. Slave women were automatically fair game; so, apparently, were Indian women. While stationed at Fort Gibson in Arkansas, Marcellus Hammond developed a liaison with a woman and fathered at least one child, whom they named "Redbird." Marcellus bought the woman a house and sent her money. He also wrote to her over the years in warm and intimate letters that included news about his legitimate family. In 1875 he closed his letter, "Good-bye—it may be forever. Whatever may happen I have had some good times."[97] In 1839, Francis Pickens had been the subject of Washington gossip when, supposedly upset over his wife Eliza's serious illness, he was seen in the company of the famous beauty Ellen Bevine. Pickens's friend and boarding house colleague Congressman R. M. T. Hunter wrote his wife that while his Eliza lay on her deathbed, Pickens was the "first man to call upon Ellen Bevine who flitted through town last week."[98]

Francis Pickens wrote to his young protégé Milledge Bonham insisting a man's character should not be judged by what women of low order said about him. James Henry Hammond was taking the part of a woman who claimed that Pickens was the father of her illegitimate son. Pickens claimed: "If a man's character depends upon maids or low women, he would indeed be damned in this world as well as the next. None can know this better than the General [Hammond]. The first year of my offense I paid to the old mother by way of house rent, room rent, etc, etc, several hundrd dollars—besides every single year since I have regularly at different times paid my full share." Indeed, Pickens did support the illegitimate child, although he expressed some doubts as to whether the child was really his. He mailed a hundred-dollar draft to Bonham to give to the boy, not to the mother. Leaving to Bonham's discretion the manner in which to give him the money, he added, "If you think sending him to school if he will go, best for him he could go at least three or four months. I once told you *confidentially* why I had reason to believe he was not mine, but perhaps in this I may be mistaken, and this the reason why I have given money for him ever since 1843." Pickens explained to Bonham that he had "got into a scrape" with this woman, but claimed she had "acted much more *imprudently* than I did." This unnamed white woman of supposedly low character had succeeded in the patriarchal southern society of Edgefield in getting support for herself and her son from one of South Carolina's aristo-cratic political leaders.[99]

Pickens tried to place the circumstances in perspective for his young pro-tégé. "Of course all of this is between us. I am sorry to trouble you in this matter at all, but when I succeeded McDuffie I did the same and more for him & perhaps your successor may have to do it for you, if he is a gentleman in the true sense of the term."[100]

When James Henry Hammond was a law student, Elisha Hammond ex-plained to his disappointed son why his mother's well-to-do uncle John Fox rejected James Henry's request for patronage: Elisha had threatened Fox "for attempting to destroy the chastity of your Sisters—a thing I never intended to have related to you; but he did it more than one, twice or thrice." Fox, therefore, maintained a "splight" against Elisha and refused to support the younger Hammond's career.[101]

As the student president of a South Carolina College debating club, the Euphradian Society, Hammond's last speech took the negative side of the question, "Should seduction be punished by death?" This very issue of seduction was one which later plagued Hammond. From the descriptions in his diary in 1840, a young lady of Charleston with whom James Henry Hammond became involved was from the upper orders. She was a "dear sweet girl" and after Valentine's Day Hammond had "more free & frequent intercourse with the beloved."[102]

Hammond always maintained silence about his reputed affairs with the daughters of his wife's sister and brother-in-law Wade Hampton II. He argued that to do otherwise was to compromise the honor of his four nieces, and charged that that was precisely what their father did in exposing the incident. None of the four Hampton sisters involved ever married, lending some credence to Hammond's claims of the danger of the story to the girls' honor. (Their never marrying, however, could also be seen as supporting the truth of the affair.) Hammond never even revealed the cause of his dispute with Hampton, but rumors reached Hammond's brother, Marcellus, who wrote to Hammond about them. Hammond refused to confirm or deny any charges, but replied to his brother that rumors as unsavory as those concerning his seduction of Hampton's daughters "have been told of most of the leading men in the State. . . . And charges as bad *are known* of nearly all the parties moving against me . . . [and they would] do all I am charged with if they could with impunity." Hammond believed that the people of South Carolina would side with him. "They would not mind it a pins worth if it was known I had seduced all Hampton's daughters."[103]

Indeed, fathering black, red, or white illegitimate children or participating in extramarital affairs was apparently not an impediment to being elected to office. Marcellus was elected to the state legislature from Edgefield District, and James Henry believed his brother could be governor if he could control his drinking problem. The influential politicians who elected McDuffie and Pickens governors were probably familiar with their dalliances. And James Henry Hammond's notoriety did not prevent the state legislature's electing him to the Senate. Sins of the flesh were easily forgiven or overlooked among the elite.

No great number of children were born out of wedlock, but the fathers named in Edgefield bastardy cases were from all classes. In 1826 the Edgefield Village Baptist Church threatened excommunication of Mrs. Harriet Caldwell if she could not provide a satisfactory explanation of the "supposed guilt inferred from the shortage of the time between her marriage and the birth of her child." In 1836 her church excluded Sarah Hancock for having an illegitimate child, and in 1876, at another church, Winfield Scott reported Pauline Ripley for bastardy and Ripley was expelled. Preachers sometimes baptized illegitimate children. Generally a single woman who became pregnant married. James Henry Hammond complained about his son Paul's courtship of "I fear truly a 'fast woman.' " Paul married the woman, and Hammond wrote that "he got married in November 1858 and in less than 9 months presented us with a fine grandson."[104]

In one unusual case, which involved the son of an antebellum tenant farmer and the daughter of a prosperous merchant, the father of the pregnant girl threatened to shoot the boy, young Marvin Harris, if he should come near their home. Harris wrote with great sincerity but to no avail: "I am verry sorry that Elizabeth has happened the misfortune and I am willing to marry hir and always have bin."[105]

The family of the bride could face embarrassment. While in Russia as the United States Ambassador, Francis Pickens had to arrange a quick marriage between his daughter Rebecca and the legation's secretary, Rebecca's close Edgefield friend, widower John Bacon. Stepmother Lucy expressed her husband's feelings toward his daughter's predicament: "Then came Rebecca's marriage full of pain & mortification to her father." While parents may have felt great mortification, the subsequent lives of the couple involved suffered no apparent stigma.[106]

South Carolina law punished bastardy not on grounds of immorality but because illegitimate children might become state wards. Fathers of illegitimate children were prosecuted, but not mothers. There were no legal proscriptions against fornication, and adultery was not punished. According to legal historian Michael Hindus, the enforcement of laws concerning moral behavior was "consistent with the southern sanctification of family and womanhood, and illustrative of the sexual and legal double standard in this planter-dominated state. . . . The planter's wife had her security, the planter his freedom, and everyone else had religion!"[107]

In calling for laws against adultery, an 1805 Edgefield grand jury presentment typified attitudes in up-country districts in the early antebellum period. The grand jury believed adultery not only destroyed marriages and families but also hurt the community: "A strict observance of the rule of morality is indispensable and necessary for the good order, peace, and harmony of any community." The low-country-dominated legislature, however, failed to act and in 1822, 1844, and 1856 voted down bills against adultery. The state senate committee on religion explained that morality was not something to be legislated but a practice to be "restrained by the silent admonitions of religion . . . and the indignations and contempt . . . of the community."[108]

That sense of indignation, combined with notions of honor, could give rise to violence and family revenge. Two of the wealthy Sophia Tillman's sons, John and Oliver, were killed because of allegations that they had insulted a southern woman's honor. Two landless brothers, twenty-two-year-old John C. Mays and forty-seven-year-old George R. Mays, killed John Miller Tillman on 6 May 1860. On 29 December 1860, Oliver Hancock Tillman was killed in Florida in a domestic quarrel. Poorer whites demanded retribution in cases of honor even when it meant crossing class lines. In 1878, Robert McEvoy, the son of an Irish Catholic immigrant who had lived and worked in Graniteville since 1856 both as a gardener for William Gregg and as a textile laborer, was hanged for the murder of James J. Gregg, son of William Gregg and son-in-law of James Henry Hammond. McEvoy's motive was the defense of the virtue of his sisters, who worked in the Graniteville Mills. According to Francis W. Dawson, friend to the Gregg and Hammond families and editor of the state's most influential newspaper, the Charleston *News and Courier*, if McEvoy had killed Gregg to protect the honor of his sisters, then he should not be hanged "for having done what any white man in South Carolina would feel justified in doing."[109]

Death

Like marriages and births, deaths occurred in the home. Whether in a grand mansion or a log cabin, Edgefieldians had intimate experience of death of family members. Religion was a bulwark to wealthy and poor, a way of explaining life and death in the agrarian community. At time of death family and neighbor support brought the community together. Funerals functioned as family and community rituals, a proclamation of the worth of the deceased in the eyes of God and the community as well as a reaffirmation of life for those remaining. Religion, kin, friends, neighbors, churches—all helped a family to accept death. The wakes, the food brought by neighbors and churches for the family, and the sharing of that food at the home during the mourning period, as well as the religious service preached over the departed, all reinforced actual bonds of community and aided the family, whether rich or poor.

In 1833 transported Englishman James Rainsford observed his first funeral among Edgefield yeomen. The community's preacher had just finished a sermon and the baptizing of blacks and whites at the river by the church. Then the minister and most of the congregation "went 3 miles to attend the funeral of Mrs. Addisson (she died at the age of 25 and left 5 small children)." A hundred people attended. "The coffin was carried on three sticks, by 6 farmers (neighbours) and entered a corner of the field adjoining the house. She was bureied within 22 hours of the time she died." Rainsford was surprised at the simplicity of the event. "Everyone appeared in his or her usual self." He remarked that there was no "show." The preacher then "went home a distance of about 18 miles," since he had to continue the revival the next day.[110]

In Edgefield preachers played key roles at times of death; many kept regular records of the deaths in the families they visited. Lutheran minister Godfrey Dreher in one week in 1843 noted he preached from 2 Timothy 10, "it being a funeral service for a child." The next day he buried Michael Lawless's child and preached from "St. John 14: 3. Friday the 13 buried Michael Lawless wife and P[reached] from Col. 3.4." One man lost four successive wives within a year of childbirth, and only one child survived. Two families had lost all of their children; one family lost five children, the other three. During a yellow fever epidemic, the Reverend John Cornish consoled Mr. and Mrs. James Black, who lost three children in three weeks.[111]

Cornish preached at the funeral of a miller in 1857 and remarked that more than fifty people shared pork, beef, pot pie, peach pie, turnips, corn, wheat bread, coffee, and persimmon beer, "a feast in its way." Cornish also visited families with "a bad reputation. The Mother loves the Bottle." When one daughter of this poor white family was dying in 1854, he visited her regularly. He baptized her when she accepted Christ, and the week she died he gave her communion and recorded a moving scene: "Many very poor people were gathered around the head of that poor sick girl in the hovel where she is lying. The scene was awfully solemn."[112]

The wealthy often recorded their own feelings about death and its effects. Isabella Morrison Blocker, daughter of the minister of the First Presbyterian Church of Charleston, married Edgefield District native John Blocker, the first man to enter into the mercantile business at Edgefield Court House. John Blocker and his wife grew wealthy in land and slaves, but affluence could not protect them from the tragedy of children dying. Isabella's first child was born in 1813, when she was twenty. She had eleven children before her husband died in 1831. Of the eleven, she saw eight die; four of her children died in infancy or childhood. Following the death of a seven-month-old son, her mother wrote with stoic Presbyterian predestination and aristocratic restraint: "My beloved child, I . . . hope you are quite reconciled to the loss of your darling babe. As it was the will of God to take him, we must obey, and He will be angry at us if we go past moderate grief." All six (two married Lake brothers) surviving daughters married young and at Belle Grove. Two daughters married at age seventeen; one died at age twenty-seven, the other at thirty-one. Two daughters married at age fifteen, and both outlived their mother. Two daughters married at age sixteen; one died that same year, and the other outlived her mother. George Miller, the only son to reach maturity, married Margaret C. Perrin in 1845 at her home in Abbeville when he was twenty-three; he died ten years later. Daughter Emma married Samuel Perrin, brother of Margaret, in 1846. She died 7 June 1860, shortly after her own child passed away.[113]

On 10 June, three days after her daughter Emma's death, Isabella Blocker began a prayer book, which she continued until her death. Religion gave her the strength that enabled her to bury so many of her children and grandchildren who unnaturally preceded her to the grave. She wrote, "This day forty-seven years ago, I gave birth to my first child, my Georgianna. Bless the Lord, O my soul, that I have been honored to be the mother of eleven children for my precious Master's kingdom." On 26 June she wrote: "This day one month ago, the precious babe was conveyed to heaven; since then the mother, my Emma, my darling, precious daughter. O, thanks . . . to my heavenly Father, for His kind Providence." Five years later, her thoughts once again turned to her daughter and granddaughter. "Truth my beloved Emma is where no tears are shed. O precious one, I trust ere long I shall meet thee and thy dear little babe in glory." Throughout the Civil War (in which she witnessed grandsons die) and into Reconstruction, her prayer book reveals her concerns for her family, friends, community, and religion; she did not involve herself in the great events surrounding her. Those who had passed away often came to her in dreams and reinforced her faith in God.[114]

Following the death of his son Eldred and then his wife Eliza only two days later, Francis Pickens wrote, "In my prosperity and unbounded happiness heretofore, I had almost forgot there was a God, and now I stand the scattered . . . and blasted monument of his just wrath." Having loved his wife since they were both children in Edgefield, he despaired, "Oh God! I am now left alone with no human being to commune with and to breathe out the inmost secrets of my soul to."[115]

Young children sometimes witnessed the deaths of both parents. Children of the wealthy were generally provided for; they received inheritances that assured that relatives would want them. Louis Wigfall's father died when he was two, his mother when he was thirteen; his inheritance was thirteen thousand dollars. This enabled his guardian to fulfill Mrs. Wigfall's wish to rear Louis "carefully and handsomely . . . according to his degree."[116]

Most orphans, however, were not as fortunate as Wigfall. The welfare of orphans not taken into homes was mainly left to individual benefactors. John de la Howe settled on the Savannah River after the revocation of the Edict of Nantes. In 1797 he left instructions in his will for his estate to provide for the education and support of twelve poor boys and twelve poor girls, preference to be given to orphans, so that they might be educated in a manner similar to that of an independent French peasant. Another benefactor was Alexander Downer, whose will of 1818 provided for the establishment of a school in the Beech Island section of Edgefield District for the maintenance and education of orphans from Edgefield District and the adjacent county of Richmond, Georgia. "Having been myself an orphan and having received a partial education at the Orphan House in Georgia by which I have learned how to estimate the value of an education, and by which I have been able to obtain a sufficiency to support myself, my wife and Seven Orphan children which I have raised—I dispose of the balance of my estate for the benefit of the Orphans of Edgefield District."[117]

Altruism rarely occurred on the scale of de la Howe or Downer. Sentiments stimulating private benevolence, however, also inclined the aristocratically controlled South Carolina state legislature to support the education of orphans. The legislature believed that orphans were entitled to some benefits and also worried that they might grow up unattached to the social system.[118]

Death also affected nonfamily members. White laborers and artisans who depended on planters or farmers for jobs might lose their source of income. Also, the death of a slaveowner meant the division of slaves.

Impact of Slavery on the White Family

Wealthy whites had black slaves to cook, serve, clean, and do their bidding. Freed from many of the drudgeries of housework, the wealthy white woman had time to spend with her children. Wealth enabled women to influence the events in their lives, to achieve some power. Freed from working in the fields or outside the home, they could, if they wished, rear their children and not delegate child care to others. Wealthy white men hired overseers or used slave drivers to manage plantations and could spend more free time with their children if they wanted. Slavery helped make possible an extremely cultured group in Edgefield. Time was available for leisure, politics, and travel.[119]

Although many whites were especially fond of certain bondsmen and saw their slaves as part of the "extended family," all white children learned racism. Belief in the supremacy of whites was strong and ingrained, and whites closed their minds to any other viewpoint. Their racism was inspired, in part, by fear of the violence that loss of freedom could breed in the slaves. In this frontier-like region, violence was common. Whites fought whites; blacks fought blacks; whites and blacks attacked one another. Between 1844 and 1859 the Edgefield coroners recorded sixty-five murders. Whites killed sixteen slaves—fourteen men and two women. Sometimes white Edgefieldians forced or hired slaves to kill other whites.[120]

Given the almost absolute power of the male family head, sexual liaisons between master and slave were not uncommon, and this was a source of distrust on the part of the mistress of the house. Meanwhile, the white woman was thought to need constant protection from the black man's barbarism. An Englishman reported that the slave insurrectionists in 1819 in Augusta, in which the revolutionaries' leader, Coco, expected assistance from Edgefield slaves, planned to kill the white children and old women and take the young women as their wives. Dr. Edward B. Hibbler's slave Hampton was executed after a trial by a court of justices and officeholders convened at Mrs. Stalmaker's for "committing a rape on the body of Dolly Stalmaker."[121]

Slavery produced anxiety in the minds of the dominant class, but it also brought a strange kind of security and status. The Edgefield *Advertiser* exhibited this paradox when it noted that "African slavery . . . makes every white man in some sense a lord. . . . Here the division is between white free men and black slaves, and every white is, and feels that he is a MAN." The Edgefield editor added his own fears of emancipation. "Insolent free negroes would thrust themselves into society and make proposals of marriage with their [whites', especially poor whites'] sons and daughters." The concern reached new heights during the Civil War. The editor of the *Advertiser* in 1864 announced: "Yankee white men, taking odoriferous sable wenches to share their bed and board, and white women, Yankee white women, taking big black, reeking Sambos and Pompeys and Bucks to become the fathers of their children. My God! Doesn't the remotest contemplation of such a thing make you fearfully sick? But why should it, if the thing is confined to Yankee men and women, as it most certainly will be?"[122]

Nervous proponents of slavery were quick to suppress opinions different from those of the dominant culture. Residents near Liberty Hill met in 1859 to censure Tom Burch, Irish bricklayer and plasterer. Proclaiming themselves "a law-abiding people, and allow[-ing] to others the privilege which we claim to ourselves; ie., the free expression of opinion, provided such expression . . . does not conflict with the interests of the community generally," they resolved to drive the "good workman" from Edgefield for his "seditious" language, which threatened "very great injury among our negroes," and to alert other communities about Burch. Hamburg's minutemen first whipped and then shaved one side of the head of a man "whose tongue had been running too freely with the colored population." The Reverend Robert C. Grier, president of Erskine College in neighboring Abbeville District, felt compelled to write to the local newspapers and to publish a broadside circulated in Edgefield to defend himself of charges that he was inciting slaves because his slave George had been overheard telling other bondsmen to pray for freedom. In 1849 the five-member Committee of Safety for South Carolina, which included Francis Pickens, addressed an "Open Letter" to the citizens: "We urge your caution against everyone who, under the pretense of religion or humanity, could use that sacred good to cover his mischievous designs."[123]

Tension increased as the Civil War approached. Worried Edgefield planters felt the need to broaden the base of slave ownership. Among several schemes discussed during the decade preceding the war were proposals to reopen the slave trade and to sell on credit one of every ten slaves to a poor white. As South Carolina prepared for secession, minutemen associations formed in Edgefield; one of their purposes was to put down internal opposition to slavery. One minuteman explained, "I have seen it mentioned in Abolition journals that they have allies among the non-slave owners, of which class I am sorry to say I am for reasons that I very much regret, I never was able to own one."[124]

After the Civil War whites remained ambivalent about blacks and their influence on white families and communities. In 1866, in a series of three letters on behalf of Edgefield planters, former governor Francis Pickens corresponded with his antebellum political ally, the current governor James L. Orr, about rumors that Gen. Daniel E. Sickles, the military governor of the state, planned to remove all the freedmen from Edgefield District because of the violence of the whites toward the erstwhile slaves (designed to keep them in servitude) and also because of the low wages offered the freedmen there. Pickens protested that the removal of the black community would ruin the planters, his neighbors, in Edgefield.[125]

Despite the class differences and racial antagonisms, whites and blacks did occasionally interact in a more egalitarian fashion. Even before the war there were a few cases of intermarriage between free blacks and Edgefield whites. Edgefield planters also complained of the illegal traffic between poorer whites and slaves. The local paper blamed "wicked white men" for luring slaves into crime. After the Civil War this contact between whites and blacks was a constant worry for textile executives and temperance reformers, who noted that blacks supplied white mill operatives with liquor. For a brief time during Reconstruction some whites and Edgefield blacks allied politically to gain control of local government for the Republicans. These political alignments led to joint economic enterprises and even some social interaction between those whites and former slaves.[126]

But before Appomattox no one could have imagined such a situation. After all, antebellum Edgefield was a slave society in which the white community endeavored to control black lives and to squelch black efforts to assert their independence. Yet against this almost insurmountable domination Edgefield blacks created a unified and highly developed culture that drew on both their African and slave roots. Central to perpetuating and enriching this black culture and enabling Afro-Americans to survive bondage was the slave family.

4. The Slave Family

I wonder where is all my relation. . . .
Friendship to all—and every nation.
L. M. Aug. 16, 1857, Dave

Written around the top of a storage jar
by the Edgefield slave potter, Dave

Afro-Americans were the majority in Edgefield. In the antebellum period they were the property of white people. After the war, though free, they lived in a culture heavily influenced by the experience and memories of slavery.[1]

A remarkable fact in demographic history, with implications for comparative history that are only beginning to be explored, is that the black population in the United States increased under slavery as well as in freedom. The slave population grew by an average of 27.3 percent in each decade after 1810; this growth was almost entirely the result of natural increase. In comparison, the natural expansion of the white population during the same period (1810–60) was 29 percent per decade. By contrast, the decennial natural decrease of the slave population in Barbadoes between 1712 and 1762 was 43 percent. Except for that of the United States, all slave populations in the Western Hemisphere, and in Africa before the twentieth century, failed to reproduce themselves and depended on the importation of other slaves for continued growth.[2]

While the integration of southern plantation production into the capitalist economy provided the economic base for this increase, the unique demographic vitality of the slave population of the southern United States also required a social base—stable families that provided physical, emotional, and cultural support for childbirth and child rearing. Traditional historical analysis has regarded the essential element in this framework to be the relationship of mother and child. Yet, despite the most difficult circumstances, the slave family in the South was typically a male-dominated nuclear family (father, mother, children), the prevailing form the world over. More recent literature has emphasized the autonomy of the slave family, but in so doing has often minimized the impact of slavery. Afro-Americans themselves never minimized the tragedies of slavery. In 1883 the black clergy of the Protestant Episcopal church were concerned about the "moral disasters which have come to the colored race through the existence of slavery and that family life paternal authority and marriage integrity have been broken down almost beyond repair by the system."[3]

Families as Social Control

The idea that the slave family did not exist in the South originated with abolitionist attacks on the institution of slavery. Northern abolitionists, middle- and upper-class elites imbued with nineteenth-century ideas concerning the sanctity of the family, castigated the southern states for denying slave marriages legal sanction and protection. This lack of de jure family rights was one of the aspects of slavery that most troubled northern critics.[4]

In 1839 Francis Pickens noted, "My negroes are nearly all of them family negroes of the very *best kind*." In 1850 James Henry Hammond insisted his slaves "Live[d] . . . in families." Slaveowning economics went hand in hand with slaves' desire for families. After the slave trade was prohibited in 1808, the family became of paramount importance in increasing the slave population. For the slaveowners, slaves represented capital investment, and each slave birth meant an increase in wealth. Hammond wrote that "marriage is to be encouraged as it adds to the comfort, happiness and health of those who enter upon it, besides insuring a greater increase."[5]

Slaves understood the need to reproduce for owners. Asked why slaves were sold, Susannah Wyman, born 15 May 1833 in Edgefield, explained: "But people did sell women, old like I am now, or say they didn't have no chillun—the fus' speclator come along and want to buy, he kin have you. De marster say—'bring me hans in. I want hans.' "[6]

Slave families were also a means of social control for the slaveowner. For example, family ties and responsibilities deterred slaves from running away. From 1831 to 1835 slaves on Hammond's plantation made fifty-three unsuccessful attempts to escape. Those without kinship ties on the Hammond plantation were the ones most likely to run away; perhaps slaves acquired from other plantations were running away to restore prior family ties. Thirty-five percent tried to run away more than once. Married slaves were sometimes runaways, but much less frequently than single persons. Male slaves who were married often took their wives in escape attempts, and the women, 16 percent of the runaways, tried to escape only with their husbands. The average runaway was thirty-three years old and had been owned for only two years. The correlation between family ties and a reduction in escape attempts did not go unnoticed by slaveowners.[7]

Slave Marriage

Planters encouraged marriage between slaves because slaves themselves chose to live as couples and in families. Marriages were important to the slave community and attracted much attention. Slaveowners sometimes commented upon slaves' marriages: "Leven and Branch married last night—Alfred and Little Rose to-night." "Marriages at the Bluff Place today."[8]

Some planters ritualized slave marriage as a way of controlling the slave community, while on other plantations marriages and families were recognized, but the ceremonies were not elaborate. The Reverend Allen Dozier, a Baptist minister, had a large Edgefield plantation, and a former slave remembered that the master officiated at the marriage of his father and mother. Because both slaves were houseservants, they were intimately involved with their master and his family. Another slave, Cora Sheppard, had come across the Savannah River after emancipation to live in Edgefield County. On the plantation where she had lived, she recalled later, weddings were not special occasions. "When niggers marry, white boss marry 'em. He would go to de court house and get a commit from de head man and come back. Dey ju' go up to de house and he marry 'em, give you a house, and you start living together."[9]

A former slave of Francis Pickens, from one of his plantations in the northeast corner of Edgefield District near Ninety Six, remembered that "in dem days all dey hadder do to git married was step ober de broom." The preacher did not perform the ceremony. "De broom wus de law! . . . Jus' say you wanner be married and da couple git together 'fore witnesses and step ober de broom." Although different from the rites that some white owners thought important, this ceremony nonetheless had special significance for the participants. Pickens did not reside on the plantation near Ninety Six; overseers were in charge. On plantations with resident masters, whites often took a more active part. For example, former slave Susannah Wyman remembered that "when cullud people wuz married, white people give supper, colored man whut lives on place marries 'em."[10]

Former slave Annette Milledge presented an interpretation of marriage that differed from those of other slaves. "Folks didn' marry—dey wouldn't let you marry but dey let you live together. Dey say if you marry you would belong to your husban' and go off." Her memories may have differed from other accounts because she lived in Hamburg and was the slave of a storekeeper; slave marriage customs may have been influenced by the "urban" environment.[11]

Slaves on small farms and houseservants, who were more intimately associated with whites, often had more formalized wedding ceremonies involving whites. Molly Brown and her family had belonged to the Harrises and the Joneses, who owned only a few slaves in Edgefield District. "I was born at Edgefield County, South Carolina, and lived there till after I married. I married at home, at night, had a supper, had a nice dance." A slave preacher, Jim Woods, had performed the ceremony; he had read the ceremony out of a little book; she "wore three or four starched underskirts trimmed in ruffles and a white dress over em . . . [and] a long lacy veil of net." The ceremony was followed by a "nice supper." "White folks helped fix my weddin' supper. Had turkey, chickens, baked shoat, pies and cake—a table piled up full. Mama helped cook it. It was all cooked on fireplace."[12]

Whether they lived on large plantations or on small farms, slaves had marriages and families recognized by the community if not by the law. The marriage ceremony may have varied, but it was always a meaningful event shared with others in the community.

Community

Slaves on a plantation forged for themselves a community. When Thomas Green Clemson considered selling his Edgefield plantation, his father-in-law, John C. Calhoun, noted that "the negroes all appear to be much attached to the place and were much alarmed at the idea of its being sold." The plantation was home, where friends and kin formed a community. The decision of Bill Lawrence's family illustrates the strong commitment slaves of a plantation had to each other. A gift from John C. Calhoun to Anna Calhoun and Thomas Green Clemson, Daphney Lawrence had nursed the Clemson children. Thus, when Clemson wrote Francis Pickens, who served as his agent for the Edgefield plantation, he insisted, because of Anna, "that she [Daphney], her husband, (Bill Lawrence,) and their son Benjamin, should be permitted to choose their master." However, the Clemsons were informed that Daphney and her family wanted to stay with the other slaves on the plantation. Thus, the community of Edgefield Cane Break slaves were sold together. The sense of attachment to place, the importance of a particular plantation, was so strong that Nancy Fryer said, "I got married to General Butler's place where my mother was."[13]

The plantation slave community appears to have been an interplantation or intraarea community that included both small farm slaves and town slaves. Family social life was centered around the church, but there were also dances, which many saw as evil and contrary to religion. Fiddles and banjos were regarded as instruments of the devil. The musicians were always men, and the narratives of former slaves repeated the stereotype that men were "wilder" and "badder," just as white males were expected to sow their wild oats. Former slaves mentioned dances away from the master's house, quiltings, dinners, corn shuckings, hunting, and even raids on the master's storehouse; these activities usually involved families. A former Edgefield slave remembered that "de slaves from all de plantations 'round come to our corn shuckin's. Us had 'em down in de orchard. Lots of white folks comed too. Dey kilt hogs and us had a big supper and den us danced." Another former slave recalled the corn shuckings and cotton pickings that the whites sponsored for blacks "in slavery and after freedom, too." There would be a big supper and "some neighbors walk ten mile, like. walking to church or to school." A sense of family and community and a consensus on values among slaves were forged from this camaraderie.[14]

Whites in Edgefield complained constantly about slaves' traveling between plantations. According to one planter, "There is not 2 negroes in this neighborhood but thinks they have purfict liberty to walk any mans plantation & no negro will fear his master finding him out for being from Home, for as soon as the master goes to sleep he is off & Back again before day." In 1857, a planter proclaimed, "We may talk about keeping them home at night—It cant be done." The editor of the local paper blamed slave "corruption and disobedience on the outragious habit of leaving their homes at night. At the hour of midnight . . . they are ever visiting and visited."[15]

Folktales also contributed to a sense of family and community. Slave tales usually infused the hearer with a moral message of proper conduct and righteous living, often focusing on family values and on obligations between members of the family. Often cryptic, they were also filled with strategies for survival.[16]

The poetic verses of the slave potter Dave also carried cryptic themes and messages. For example, one particularly poignant verse about the family introduces this chapter. Another, "this jar is made cross / if you don't repent you may be lost," may have reflected his feelings about slavery, religion, or both. On his enslavement he wrote, "Dave belongs to Mr. Miles / where the oven bakes the pot biles." Another pot holds an oblique reference to the biblical sanction allowing early Christians to eat pork (Acts 10): "Good for lard or holding / fresh meat / Blest we were when / Peter saw the folded / sheet." Dave probably was reflecting on freedom when he wrote, "The Fourth of July is surely come / to sound the fife and beat the drum." (Blacks were prohibited from beating drums after the Stono Rebellion of 1739.)[17]

Religion

Brief History of Edgefield's Independent Black Churches

The Afro-American community was also reinforced by religion. Religious fervor in the black community dated back to colonial times and helped to give the new Reconstruction independent black churches a solid foundation. The first independent Afro-American church in the United States was founded in old Edgefield District at Silver Bluff, around 1773, on a plantation owned by George Galphin. The minister was a white Baptist named Palmer, but all the officers of the new church were black men, and women were active participants.

During the Revolutionary War white ministers were not allowed to preach to blacks, for fear they might inform the slaves of the British proclamation of freedom for slaves in exchange for support of the British cause, and church elder David George assumed ministerial duties. When the British occupied the city of Savannah, some 175 miles downriver from Silver Bluff, and George Galphin, who was both slaveowner and patriot, fled the area, Galphin's slaves took refuge in Savannah until the rebels retook the area. In 1782, David George took much of his congregation with him to Nova Scotia and freedom. Ten years later he migrated to Sierra Leone with a group of black colonists and established another black Baptist church. Former slave Liza Mention was a proud member of Silver Bluff Church: "I'se a member of de Silver Bluff Church, and I been goin' to Sunday School dar nearly ever since I can 'member. You know dey say dat's de oldest Nigger church in de country."

A childhood friend of David George, George Liele, had been converted to Christianity by another white Baptist minister, Mathew Moore, at about the time of the founding of the Silver Bluff Church. Liele preached in the area around Silver Bluff until the British left, and then he took some of his fellow Edgefield area slaves with him in 1784 to Jamaica, where he founded a Baptist church.

Jesse Peter (or Galphin), old-time activist in Silver Bluff Church, stayed on for a while after the Revolutionary War and reformed the Silver Bluff Baptist Church; he was a free man who preached at three or four other places throughout the area. "His countenance is grave, his voice charming, his delivery good, nor is he a novice in the mysteries of the kingdom." With a membership of about sixty in 1793, his congregation moved from Galphin's plantation to Augusta, Georgia, some twelve miles away, and formed the First Baptist Church of Augusta.[18]

Early in the settlement of the Edgefield area, blacks and whites had noted the independent black church and its revolutionary capability to lead slaves toward freedom. Black churches and preachers survived in the area. When James Rainsford stayed overnight in Augusta before moving to his new home in Edgefield, the first people he heard singing hymns were four slave women and "the first preacher I heard was a black man." On 18 June 1833 he toured Augusta and found six to eight places of worship. He went to a Baptist and a Methodist chapel, where he "saw the blacks sitting in the galleys. The lower part or body of the chapel was used for whites exclusively. The men and women sitting apart as in the Quaker chapels in England. I was told that . . . there are no Quakers in Augusta."

The Reverend Iveson Brookes complimented independent black churches in his defense of slavery. "I invite you to visit me and I promise to conduct you on the Sabbath to houses of worship, neat and commodious, erected by themselves in the neighboring city, where you may see full congregations of 'black Nancies and Scipiones Africani,' whose dress, order and general appearance come perhaps as near to what the Bible requires of christian worshipers, as many congregations in Boston or London exhibit; and you shall hear a 'Scipio Africanus' speaking forth the orthodox truths of God to his attentive audience, many of whom rejoining in the truth, as it is Jesus."[19]

Religion as a Means of Social Control

Planters sought to use religion and churches as devices for social control; they hoped that their slaves would be more manageable if they attended church and heard white preachers reciting such passages as Ephesians 6:5, "Servants be obedient to them that are your masters according to the flesh, with fear and trembling, in singleness of your heart, as unto Christ."[20]

In a debate on the "best method of managing negroes" sponsored by Edgefield District's agricultural club, J. J. Boyd argued that the surest technique "was that which rendered them contented." Different slaveowners viewed matters of control differently, but Boyd debated for "just and liberal treatment." In reply to another Edgefield planter, who argued for corporal punishment, Boyd said that slaves "must have moral and religious training." This training included instructing slaves on the duties of Christian marriage and the need to work better for the master. Another planter agreed with Boyd and argued that "every slaveholder is bound to the religious instruction of his slaves. Religion does not make a servant insubordinate, the religion of christ does not make him proud, but humble and submissive. When the master has made his servant a christian he has accomplished much."[21]

Black Christian slaves interacted with whites while developing a unique theology and religious structure that evolved from their position as a recipient culture and from their Afro-American world view. Afro-Americans believed that the Bible spoke to them in a special way, and they resented the slaveowners' abuse of God's word. Former slaves from the Edgefield area recalled the various messages of social control. A former slave who came to Beech Island after the war remembered that her Georgia owner allowed prayer meeting every Saturday night and that a "colored man preach. Better not 'sturb his (her owner's) niggers when old carriage driver John Johnson preach! I 'member his tex'—'Love yo' marster, love yo' Miss. Obey! Be subdued to yo' marster and yo' Misses.' " Joe McCormick remembered a harsh slave life with "no frolics or celebrations," relieved only on Sundays, when they were allowed to go to the "bush arbor" and hear a sermon preached by a white pastor. The pastor always cautioned them "to be good Negroes and mind their master."[22]

According to another former slave, born in 1842, "Sometimes we go to Chu'ch—to de white folks chu'ch. We didn't hab no colored preacher den, but all dey talk 'bout was obeying Massah and obeying Missus." A prayer taught to former slave Sylvia Cannon combined respect for her black family with respect for her white owners. Cannon had been sold from her mother and father, slaves belonging to William Gregg, to small slaveowners. The whites in whose house she lived "taught me to say a prayer dat go like dis: 'De angels in Heaven love us, Bless mamma an bless papa, Bless our Missus, Bless de man dat feedin us, For Christ sake.' " Often these messages carried the idea of reciprocity. As another former Edgefield slave remembered, "The better you be to your master the better he treat you. The white preachers teach that in the church."[23]

Church discipline committees also helped control slaves. The records of antebellum Edgefield churches were filled with cases of slaveowners' bringing their bondspeople who were church members before the board for lying, theft, drunkenness, and refusing to live with husbands. In every case the preacher and deacons (black and white) visited and counseled the slaves brought before the church for corrective measures. In their disciplining they were generally stern but whenever slaves were dismissed from church, they almost inevitably asked to be restored to church membership, and were usually successful.[24]

Some slaveowners built churches for their slaves, a generous and practical maneuver, but one which contributed mightily to their ability to control their slaves. When James Hammond came to Edgefield in 1831, one of his first actions on his plantation was to order that night meetings be discontinued. Hammond recognized the revolutionary potential of religion, particularly of an unsupervised religion. The Bible contained elements of an ideology for black revolution, and Hammond would have none of it. As he wrote in his diary, "Intend to break up negro preaching & negro churches." When a slave requested permission to join the Afro-American church, Hammond denied the request and arranged instead for him to join the congregation of the white church that Hammond had attended the previous week. He insisted on white-supervised religious services. Caucasian clergymen knew to emphasize the compensatory function of religion; they stressed obedience and suppressed the revolutionary messages. Hammond thought that the control of religion was so important that he paid itinerant white ministers to conduct Sunday afternoon services, and he visited each of his neighbors soon after his arrival to ask them to follow his example.

When Spann Hammond addressed the local agricultural club concerning the principles of slave management that his father had formulated over the years, he stated, "Their religious training must be of the moderate sort, avoiding all excitements." To Hammond and others outside the slave community, it appeared at the time that he had succeeded. On the eve of the Civil War a visitor who attended a service at James Hammond's slave church found during worship at St. Catherine's none of the usual "mixture of hysteria and superstition" or "religious excesses" that whites generally described as characteristic of slaves. "I can recall no Church service at once more thrilling and reverential."

But as James Hammond knew, despite his best efforts the slaves continued to hold private services. Finally, the planter even agreed to allow his slaves to hold four prayer meetings in the slave quarters each week. His inability to stop independent black worship was revealed in an entry in his diary some twenty years after he first resolved to destroy the independent black worship services. He once again felt threatened by the slaves, feared that the black church "allowed too much organization—too much power to the head man & too much praying & Church meeting on the plantation," and thought it was once again time to "break up negro preaching."

Hammond was never successful in preventing independent black religious meetings. Although he may have received concessions from his slaves that satisfied his own need for mastery and gave the impression that slave religion was under control, as the rules he set down for his overseer and others made clear, slaves in their quarters, the area most out of reach of the master and whites, continued to worship in ways that they wanted. For example, Hammond modified the rules prohibiting slave religious meetings to permit singing and praying, but a great deal of subtle meaning could be conveyed in song and prayer.[25]

During a Farmers Club discussion, Hammond raved about the revolutionary aspects of black religion: "No very extencive inserection can take place except through their churches. It is very easy to convert a religious organization into a military one & these negro churches we must put down." Other Edgefield planters disagreed. W. E. Eve had an independent black church on his plantation and was "sorry to see General Hammond run down the negro churches." As long as a white man was present, Eve believed, the planters should allow them to have churches.[26]

Independent black churches existed, but whites sent patrollers to watch over them. Annette Milledge from Hamburg remembered, "We had a patteroler in de cullud people's church, too. You know we had our own church wid a cullud preacher. It was Providence Baptis' Church."[27]

The use of religion as a mechanism for social control did not end with emancipation. As a slave exhorter during the Civil War, Alexander Bettis, who founded forty Baptist churches and continually served four of them, preached humility and submissiveness. As a postbellum accommodationist, he preached peace on earth and good will to all men. Bettis did not want blacks to retaliate against whites and attempted to analyze the postbellum situation from a white perspective. His biographer credited his "common sense and good will towards the white people" at the Ned Tennant Riot, where he forestalled bloodshed by demanding that members of his churches come out of the companies.[28]

Religion as a Buffer

Social control worked both ways. Masters wanted their slaves to be Christians so that the slaves would heed biblical teachings, but once the slaves were converted, the masters themselves were obliged to obey biblical injunctions. The religious dilemma in which many white slaveowners found themselves served as a protection against some of the worst oppressions of bondage.

The problem for white slaveowners was how to live according to their Christian beliefs in a society in which those beliefs conflicted with the demands of slavery. Sensitive Christian planters found themselves increasingly unable to reconcile a world view that urged a strong Christian family with the civil law's lack of sanction for slave marriages and their progeny.

Slaves seem to have gotten around some of the strictures of the patriarchal church tradition. Every church had to deal with involuntary separation of slave spouses. As early as 1819, Big Stevens Creek Baptist Church answered the query "Does a slave's removal because of his master moving, void his marriage?" by agreeing that "the slaves are at liberty to take other mates." Slaves were able to obtain church-sanctioned separations, whereas whites could not divorce.[29]

Slaves were also able to gather other "earthly" privileges from the Christian culture that they and their white owners shared, notably those concerning the observance of the Sabbath and the religious holidays. Christmas was the major holiday period. James Hammond once planned to shorten the Christmas season because of his slaves' poor performance, but he was "persuaded out of my decision by the Negroes." The Sunday rest day was a rule in both Pickens's and Hammond's plantation manuals; slaves were required to be on their way to the fields before daylight every day except Sunday. Sunday meant additional freedoms. Only when they went to church could more than six slaves together leave Hammond's plantation. The only time slaves were able to leave Pickens's plantations without a pass was on Sunday when they went to church. W. E. Eve told other planters that his "Negroes are allowed to go where they please on Sunday." Another Edgefield planter complained that the slaves "think they are independent on Sundays."

Former slaves from Edgefield remembered that Sundays and holidays were special days for them, a relief from the general toil and routine. A former slave reared on a plantation near Edgefield Court House remembered that "we used to wake up at sun-up and work till sundown," but "on Sunday we went to church and talked to neighbors. On Christmas we celebrated by having a big dinner which the master give us. We had three days holiday or sometimes a week." Another former Edgefield slave, Junius Quattlebaum, remembered that "when Christmas come, all de slaves on de plantation had three days give to them, to rest and enjoy themselves." He went on to describe a ritualized

Christmas service around a Christmas tree where the white family gave gifts to every slave.[30]

Revolutionary Aspects of Religion

Some teachings of Christianity pointed to a radically different egalitarian society. Couching their words in these teachings, blacks, who lacked access to political power and had no elaborate ideology, were able to pass judgment on society and to express dissatisfaction within the social order.[31]

Religion was central to the slaves as a means of establishing their own self-worth. A former slave from South Carolina spoke of Genesis from a black perspective. Charity Moore's father told black and white children "tales 'bout de fox and de rabbit, de squirrel, brer tarrapin, and sich lak, long befo' they come out in a book."

> White folks, my pa had Bible tales he never told de white chillun. . . .
> He 'low dat de fust man, Adam, was a black man. Eve was ginger cake color, wid long black hair down to her ankles. Dat Adam had just one worriment in de garden and dat was his kinky hair. Eve hate to see him sad, 'cause her love her husband as all wives ought to do, if they don't. . . . [Eve and the devil meet and talk. The devil said,] "Just git Adam to eat one bit out dat apple 'bove your head and in a night his hair will grow as long, be as black, and as straight as your'n." [The devil confused and convinced Eve, who said to Adam,] "Husband eat quick and your hair will be as long, as black, and straight as mine, in de mornin'." While he was eatin' it, and takin' de last swallow of de apple, he was 'minded of de disobedience and choked twice. Ever since then, a man have a "Adam's Apple" to mind him of de sin of disobedience. Twasn't long befo' de Lord come alookin' for them. Adam got so scared his face turned white, right then, and next mornin' he was a white man wid long hair but worse off than when he was a nigger.[32]

Within Baptist churches, black members came before the entire congregation and, as did the three slaves of Gen. M. L. Bonham, "related what the Lord had done" for their lives. Whether whites acknowledged it or not, when they listened to their slaves' conversion experiences, voted them members of the congregation, and baptized them, they were admitting to an equality before God of bond and free, slave and master. Slaves identified with the Jewish people, whom God delivered from bondage; through their stories, sermons, and songs, slaves expressed a concept of themselves as the children of God, a God more powerful than any earthly white master.[33]

Male-headed Slave Families

The great majority of plantation slaves in Edgefield lived in families with two parents and permanent marriages. Planters' records often listed slaves in family units. Francis W. Pickens, James Henry Hammond, Col. Whitfield Brooks all listed their slaves in this way. Some slaves changed partners, but only to enter into other stable relationships. A slave might live with a woman for ten years and then form another alliance for the rest of his life.[34]

If slave cabin listings are considered to be similar to census households, then slave households most often contained a male-headed nuclear family plus other relatives (and sometimes unrelated single individuals or children). In addition, on every plantation there were extended kin networks and the recurrence of certain slave surnames that differed from the name of the owner. A substantial minority of women, however, had children with unidentified fathers. (Proportions ranged from a fifth to nearly a third of all slave mothers at various times on different plantations.) Having children out of wedlock was not a cause for social stigma, but rather showed fertility and attested to one's worth as a marriage partner.[35]

A diary of Colonel Brooks's contained, "a catalogue of negroes owned by me in 1843 at home and at the plantation." The 118 slaves included were divided into fourteen different groups; all but one contained from three to nine persons. All but one grouping comprised two-parent households, although a few contained several families, and three units listed the female before the male slave. The largest group consisted of fourteen slaves in three separate families; they were the slaves at Brooks's home in the town of Edgefield. The others were slaves at his plantation near old Ninety Six, in the northeast section of the district. Some of the male-headed slave cabins also housed women with children with no identified father. In 1852, when Brooks's will was probated, an inventory of slaves was drawn up, and slaves were again listed in family units. Slaves whose names appeared on both lists were still with the same spouse or, in the case of older slaves, with other members of their families. Many of the Brooks slaves had long-lasting relations similar to marriage commitments.[36]

Francis Pickens maintained careful plantation records; lists of slaves' names for 1839–44, 1847–50, 1852–53, 1857, 1860, and 1864 survive. In 1839 the names were compiled in family groupings. In 1842, Pickens simply listed, in three adjacent columns, "men and boys" as one group of 76, "women and girls" as a second group of 60, and "children" as a third group of 83. In most cases the columns of men, women, and children were joined in horizontal groups. He also recorded eight births for that year. For the first four, he gave names of mother and child; for the last four he listed the mother along with the father and the child. The next year, Pickens headed his compilation of slaves "Negroes in families" and listed them according to family. The aggregate figures—85 men and boys, 80 women and girls, and 69 children—suggest a stable family life and a more even sex ratio than in 1842. In 1847, Pickens listed slaves from three different Edgefield plantations. At his new plantation he listed a total of 89 slaves: 33 men, 20 women, and 36 children. On the other two plantations, his records were again by "families": 79 people composed 14 families on one and 123 composed 28 families on the other. In 1852, Pickens again arranged his slaves as "Negroes by families" and grouped husbands, wives, children in three adjacent columns and employed horizontal arrows to link husbands to wives to children. The "List of negroes" in 1864 repeated the 1852 method; both depicted a concrete family structure which was generally two parent, male headed, and recognized by slave and master. The slave families remained the same from list to list, an indication of the continuity of marriages and kinship networks. Again, however, within these stable cabin units made up of a father and mother and children, there were sometimes women with children and no father or husband identified.[37]

James Henry Hammond, who acquired plantations and 147 slaves through a fortuitous marriage in 1831, had increased that number to 213 by 1846. In 1860, Hammond was one of the South's largest slaveowners with 333 slaves.

Like Brooks and Pickens, Hammond listed and inventoried his slaves by family groups when he arrived in 1831, and he continued to list his slaves by families throughout the years that he managed the plantation. In 1851, for example, Hammond entitled his slave inventory, "The Number of Negroes and Each Family, January 1, 1856." Like Pickens also, he kept careful records.[38]

From Hammond's acquisition of the plantation through the Civil War (his sons assumed management of the plantation in the late 1850s), two-parent families predominated and a minority of slaves lived in other sorts of arrangements. Some family patterns suggested polygamy (a male slave who sired families by two women during the same period of time) or concubinage (slave women who never named the father of their children for Hammond's plantation records). The general pattern, however, was one of long-term affiliation between two partners. Couples who were living together when Hammond took over the plantation were separated only by death. Many had children and grandchildren grow up on the plantation.

Exceptions to the two-parent families existed; a quarter of the "marriages" ended in "divorce." Premarital pregnancy was sometimes followed by permanent alliances. More than a fifth of the women who bore illegitimate children formally and permanently associated with one man and had children by him.[39]

Incentives to Marry

Because slaveowners saw slave families as a means not only to increase the labor force but also to enhance social control and plantation stability, they often offered incentives for slaves to marry. Some formalized marriage cere-monies and made them festive occasions for the plantation, usually coinciding with the holidays. Hammond's plantation manual stated that slaves were to be "encouraged" to marry. He gave newlyweds five dollars ($3.50 for subsequent marriages), a generous sum, especially for slaves, for whom cash was scarce. Hammond and Pickens provided men with trousers and shirts for the year; women were given cloth, needles, and thread.[40]

Slave men and women often married to pool their resources by setting up a household in a slave cabin. All large plantation owners in Edgefield provided slaves with "cabins" for homes, each of which had a garden patch. Residents of cabins were allowed time off from plantation chores in order to tend gardens. Allotments of food were made on an individual basis; each slave laborer generally received three pounds of bacon or pork and a peck of meal for the week. Pickens gave men more than women, and children received about a third of an adult's share, plus additional vegetables.

Plantation owners generally had special diets for slave children. Pickens wrote out an elaborate diet routine and insisted to his overseers "that no child shall want food for a moment. See that the woman who cooks for them does justice to all." Casper Rumple, a former slave from that area, remembered a difference between adults' eating routines and those of children. The adult slaves were responsible for "their own cooking. They got for the grown ups 3 pounds meat, 1 pk. meal a week. They fed the young chaps plenty so they wouldn't get stunted. They keep em chunky till they get old nough to grow up tall and that make big women and big men."[41]

Husband and wife, as well as their progeny, worked in the family garden. On most plantations each couple, regardless of the number of children, got an equal-sized garden plot. Individual plots, as opposed to a plantation-wide communal arrangement, gave the family a special incentive to cultivate its own garden. The practice of allowing separate family gardens for slaves exemplifies the flexibility of plantation slavery and foreshadows the share-renting and sharecropping systems that succeeded slavery. Former Edgefield slaves testified to the custom. One remembered that "each fam'ly had a garden patch. . . . What we raised we et." Another, whose master lived at Edgefield Court House, remembered that "in slavery time we had extra patches of ground to work for ourselves which we sometimes worked on Saturday after-noons as we had dat time off." Still another reported, "Our master gave us a small patch of land to work for ourselves and plant anything we wanted."[42]

In this region a garden patch was not simply a summer affair. Turnip greens and collards, both vitamin-rich green vegetables, withstood the cold (collards tasted better after the first frost); they were planted as fall crops and harvested throughout January, February, and March, when the spring gardens were planted. Other vegetables and fruits harvested during the fall months were dried and preserved for the winter months.

The slave narratives consistently reported adequate amounts of food. Matilda Brooks, former slave of Governor Pickens, described a diet that "consisted largely of potatoes, corn bread, syrup, greens, peas, and occasionally ham, fowl and other meats or poultry. Their chief beverage was coffee made from parched corn." A former slave from Berry Cochran's plantation explained the attitude that forged a sense of community among the plantation slaves concerning the sharing of rations. Slaves had enough to eat, for "Marster put out a side uv meat and a barrul o'meal and all ub us would go and git our rations for de week," but they did not abuse this situation, and the supply did not run short. They "knowed better'n to do dat kinder thing. Eve'ybody, had er garden patch an' had plenty greens and taters and all dat kinder thing."[43]

Better and larger meals combined individual allotments with food from the cabin gardens. In addition, men hunted and trapped game; many slaves owned hunting dogs. Both sexes fished in the numerous rivers, creeks, and streams for food as well as for recreation. Men and women fished with poles, but setting baskets and running lines of hooks was generally men's work. A former Edgefield slave told how her slave father hunted "and bring in possum and coon. He sho could get 'em a plenty." Two others remembered that "we hunted wild game." Another former slave, who had belonged to Judge Andrew Pickens Butler, remembered specifically that "we used to hunt 'possums, rabbits, squirrels, wild turkeys, doves, partridges, and set traps for partridges and set box gums for rabbits." Peggy Grigsby recalled, "The men folks hunted much; doves, partridges, wild turkeys, deer, squirrels, and rabbits. Sometimes dey caught rabbits in wooden boxes, called 'rabbit-gums.' "[44]

Slaveowners continually accused slaves of "stealing" (especially chickens, swine, and potatoes), either to use for themselves or to sell. These activities were carried out by the male slaves in order to supplement diets and obtain goods to trade with whites for liquor or cash for the cabin "economy." Wives provided the husbands with alibis and doctored them if they were caught. Julia Henderson described one such incident: "My grandmother said my grandfather uster slip off widout askin for no pass. Sometimes de young bucks would bus' in de smokehouse and steal rossin' potatoes and broilin' meat. De overseer come lookin' and grandfather tore out to git home, but dey whip de res' whatever dey caught. Yes, dey whip 'em bad."[45]

Besides providing economic benefits, the family, to some extent, shielded its members from the negative effects of slavery. Edgefield slaveowners appear to have tried to avoid selling slaves who had families on their plantations. Having a spouse to love, to accompany, and to grow old with was important in the difficult circumstances of slavery. While wives prepared meals and mended clothes, husbands chopped wood, hunted, fished, and worked the garden. Finally, slave women who were married were probably less vulnerable to sexual harassment.[46]

Parental Authority

A stable family, where mother and father shared parental responsibility, made the rearing, nurturing, and disciplining of children easier. Slave parents disciplined children and passed on family and community values. Sylvia Cannon remembered that "my mammy tell me don never tell nothin but de truth." A former slave from Edgefield living in Augusta explained, "De parents teach manners. And when a boy got in devilment, if his mammy waz't dere, anybody standing 'round would whup him. If he tole his mammy about it, and that he was bad, she whup him all over again." Her story was much like the story told by a Virginia former slave. "In my time if I done wrong most any grown person whoop me. Then mama find it out, she give me another one. I got a double whooping."[47]

In the above cases, the mother disciplined and imparted moral instruction to the children, but several former Edgefield slaves emphasized the male authority in their homes, and indicated that the father had some influence with the white master. The slave of a Baptist preacher wanted to join the church "when religion got to me, but my pappy say ter marster: 'Doan let her jine, she too little.' " Another, Nancy Settles, had a father on another plantation, and he was the final authority. She explained, "Evy time I heayd a fiddle, my feets jus' got to dance and dancin' is devilment. . . . When I was a gal I sure wuz into plenty devilment." But, she added, she was not "'lowed to dance nothin' but de six-handed reel," indicating that her parents restricted her to the proper kind of dance for a young lady. Asked if she got out at night and if she was ever caught by the patrollers, Settles answered, "No, ma'am, I never wuz caught by de patterol; my Pa wuz the one I was scart uv."[48]

White slaveowners perceived and even prescribed the male-father responsibility pattern. In 1843, Col. Whitfield Brooks marked "expected advancement" by the names of several slaves; in every case it was a male heading a family to whom the advanced allotment was owed. Even when the slave father lived on a different plantation, he often assumed responsibility for his family. Settles's father spent Saturday afternoons cutting firewood for his wife and family, and on Wednesdays he brought game to supplement their diet—game he had caught while hunting at night.[49]

Men obtained passes to go visit their wives, families, or girlfriends. Women did not generally get passes. Asked whether they had "dances and frolics," Francis Pickens's former slave Rachel Sullivan explained, "Yassum, on Sadday night. But boys had to git a pass when dey go out or de Padderola git em." Hammond wrote in his plantation manual that "negroes living at one plantation and having wives at the other can visit them only between Saturday night and Monday morning."[50]

A former slave described the role his father played both as the final authority and dispenser of wisdom:

Niggers went to white peoples church in dat day en time. Miss Lissie
. . . good teacher. . . . I recollect it well she told me one Sunday dat if I
didn' change my chat, dey were gwine to whip me. . . . She say,
"Charlie, who made you?" I tell her papa made me. She ax me another
time who made me and I tell her de same thing another time. I thought I
was right. I sho thought I was right. She took de Bible en told me God
made me. I sho thought papa made me en I go home en tell papa Miss
Lissie say she gwine beat me Monday mornin. He ax me what I been
doin cuttin up in church. I say, "I won' doin nothin, She ax me who
made me en I tell her you made me." He told me dat God made me. Say
he made Miss Lissie en he made everybody. Ain' nobody tell me dat fore
den, but I saved my beaten cause I changed my chat.[51]

The patriarchal nature of the slave family mirrored that of the patriarchal
society. Edgefield planters referred to slave leaders as "head men," and many
slaveowners and overseers recognized specific black men as leaders (drivers).
James Henry Hammond made certain that the slave driver was "the most
important negro on the plantation." Still, severe limits on the slave man's
patriarchy, as discussed later, complicated the slave legacy.[52]

Youth

Planters made their power known by devising elaborate rules on family matters, including child rearing. Rule 5 of Hammond's plantation manual required
that "all children be brought in in entirely clean clothes twice a week. It is the
duty of their mothers to do it and of the nurse to see that it is done or
immediately report it."[53]

Passively resisting efforts to control their families, slaves demonstrated that
their owners were not adequate to the job. Hammond acknowledged failure: "I
am satisfied that I have endeavored to take too much care of the negro
children. It has made parents careless. They rely entirely on my management
and will not learn to manage themselves. I should do better to feign perfect
indifference and force them to scuffle for themselves, taking care to give
them opportunity without their being aware of it. I cannot do worse by any
system."[54]

It was common to have a nursery on large plantations. An elderly slave,
sometimes aided by older children, was in charge of slave youngsters. Plantation owners' records and former slave reminiscences confirm that slaves were
supervised in a day-care arrangement until they reached the age of ten. Slave
children were placed in nurseries at from one to three months after birth, while
their mothers went back to work. During the work day, breast-feeding mothers

returned at least three times a day. A former slave remembered, "All the pickaninnies of the plantation were cared for by one woman in a nursery and the women came in from the fields at certain times to nurse them." Warren McKinney was a slave until he was eleven years old on the smaller Edgefield plantation of George Strauter, which had twenty-five to thirty slaves. He remembered, "All the children that couldn't work stayed at one house. Aunt Mat kept the babies and small children that couldn't go to the field." Susannah Wyman remembered that, while all working hands drew rations and cooked their own meals, "de smaller chillun eat in teams in de yard, de cook-woman take care o' dem while the mudder fadder in de fiel'—at dinner time de teams of chilluns eat and some good sized chaps take care o' the chullun while the parents wukked." Several of the Edgefield former slaves remembered "nursing" younger slave children while the parents worked.[55]

There was work even for the slave children. Matilda Brooks, former slave of Francis Pickens, remembered that "when cotton crops were large children spent their evenings picking out seeds from the cotton bolls, in order that their parents might work uninterruptedly in the fields during the day." At about eleven and sometimes as early as ten years of age, slave children left the daycare arrangement and began limited tasks in the fields, such as carrying water or actually working alongside adults as "quarter" hands—that is, their labor was considered one-fourth the labor of an adult. A former slave remembered, "When I wus 'bout ten years old day started me totin' water—you know ca'in water to de hands in de field. 'Bout two years later I got my first field job, tending sheep." Nancy Settles remembered, "I started choppin' cotton when I wuz twelve years old."[56]

Matilda Brooks also recalled that in seasons other than cotton-picking time, the children were usually allowed to play in the evenings. Former slaves from Edgefield remembered playing marbles and various kinds of rope games from jumping rope to high jumping. Other childhood games included "hide-&-seek" and "Old Dan Tucker," in which children circled, singing chants, until the round ended, when another child would then be "it." Some remembered "fishing" in little holes in the earth and reciting a special rhyme to entice doodlebugs out of their holes. A former slave from the section of Edgefield County that became Greenwood County remembered that "us chaps didn't play many games 'cept marbles, rope-skipping, and jumping high rope. We didn't git to go to school."[57]

Naming Patterns

Another family concern was naming children. Slaveowners exercised their prerogative to give names to their slaves and sometimes named slaves after places, friends, or heroes. They sometimes changed the names of slaves they purchased, but some slaves found surreptitious ways to reaffirm their original names and identities.[58]

The recurrence of surnames in slave lists also suggested elaborate kinship networks that included not only parents and grandparents but also lateral relations, such as uncles, aunts, and cousins. A namesake could not be determined for the vast majority of slaves, but from Edgefield plantation compilations, narratives of former slaves, biographies and genealogies, 177 Afro-Americans have been identified for whom a relative can be determined as a namesake and who were named while slaves. It is not clear whether the slaves or the masters were doing the naming, but these naming patterns reveal the importance that someone—either slave or master—attached to preserving family names and the memory of family members. The names of relatives linked slaves to their ancestors and contemporaries and honored the person for whom the slave was named. More than a third of all slave children were named for their fathers, as against less than a tenth named for mothers.[59]

Grandparents accounted for almost as many names as mothers and fathers. After fathers, grandmothers were the most likely namesakes: a little more than a fifth of all slaves were named after their grandmothers, as against less than a fifth named for grandfathers. Slave children named for grandmothers were more often given the maternal grandmother's name.[60]

Obviously there was a patriarchal naming pattern. Slaves (or their owners) on both small farms and large plantations named their children after the fathers. More than half the slaves identified with a namesake were named after fathers, grandfathers, or uncles, while only about a third were named after mothers, grandmothers, or aunts.

By comparing the names of slaveowners with the names of free postbellum Afro-Americans, one can theorize about naming patterns. Among slaveowners in 1860 there were 615 different surnames, but among the blacks in Edgefield in 1870 there were 1254 surnames. There were twice as many surnames of blacks than there had been slaveowners. Blacks had created and maintained their own family identities through their surnames.[61]

Divorce

Some slaveowners tried to assert their dominion over slaves even in the selection and abandonment of mates. James Henry Hammond punished slaves who he thought disregarded marriage vows and thereby disrupted plantation order. Slaves could only separate with his approval. Hammond originally prohibited "divorce," but there was an accepted pattern of divorce among the slaves: long periods of relations between two slaves were replaced by alliances with others.

Hammond finally standardized the ending of slave alliances. In his plantation rules Hammond wrote that divorce was possible, but carried a penalty of a hundred lashes. Even the rule-prone Hammond made exceptions for circumstances and individuals. An excerpt from Hammond's diary illustrated his approach. "Fine day. Had a trial of Divorce and Adultry cases. Flogged Joe Goodwyn and ordered him to go back to his wife. Ditto Gabriel and Molly and ordered them to come together again. Separated Moses and Amy finally—and flogged Tom Kollock. He had never been flogged before—Gave him 39 with my own hand [for] interfering with Maggy Campbell, Sullivan's wife. Did not break him of his Driver ship." Hammond attempted to control slave marriages and tried to keep peace within slave unions, while he preserved a facade of total dominion over the Afro-American community. Slaves manipulated his control in order to obtain sanction for choosing and discarding marriage partners. Thus, in what was established practice before emancipation, slaves were able to obtain a "legalized" divorce in an era when it was impossible for whites to do so.[62]

Edgefield churches endorsed the remarriages of slaves who had been separated from mates. After his wife had been sold out of state, slave Charles received a sympathetic hearing from the Horn's Creek Baptist Church on whether he could remarry. Other slaves used this sort of precedent to sanction ending unsatisfactory marriages even when their spouses had not been sold. In June 1835, Mrs. Quarles's slave Jim, a respected black leader in the church, was cited for leaving his wife and "taking up with another woman." Refusing to return to his former wife, he was excommunicated. Two years later he was restored to membership with his new wife. Soon he was again assuming leadership positions among the slave members of the church.

When Betsy, like her master J. Hollings, a member of the Edgefield Village Baptist Church, refused to live with her husband, the owner took her before the church, which tried to persuade the slave woman to return to her husband. According to church records, "It appeared that she had separated herself from her husband without assigning any good cause for so doing—And that she was resolved on continuing to stay in that state—That her conduct in all its connection with that matter was that of a disorderly member of society, and worthy of excommunication which the church proceeded to announce." Finally, however, the church gave in and accepted the "divorce" of their black church member; Betsy was reinstated. The concept of companionate marriage had a special meaning because mismatched couples could sometimes dissolve the union. Most whites had to tolerate unhappy marriages.[63]

Family and Household Structure

Although literary evidence exists for both slave marriage and family, generalizations about slave families or households are difficult. No definite evidence about slave families was found in the slave schedules of the manuscript census returns for 1850 and 1860 because individual slaves were listed only by age and sex (not by name), under the name of the owner. Nevertheless, some groupings within the census resembled families. Information on male and female slaves of comparable age was frequently followed by that for several younger slaves, who were probably the couple's children. The census did not consistently use this sort of listing, however; slaves were often arranged in groups from eldest to youngest.

Distribution of slave ownership as listed in the Edgefield District manuscript census returns for 1850 and 1860 is summarized in Figure 1-4. In 1860 the number of houses where slaves lived was also recorded with the number of slaves a person owned. Thus, it is possible to estimate the average number of slaves in a slave dwelling. Some slaveowners, however, listed no slave dwellings. If the number of slaves was large, the omission of the number of slave dwellings was probably an oversight. If the number of slaves owned was small, the slaves probably lived in the same house as the owner. Three-fourths of those who listed no slave houses had no more than five slaves. A number of former slaves remembered sleeping in the master's house, even on large Edgefield plantations. One former slave reported that as a youth he slept in the room with the elderly white husband. "I slept on a bed—little bed—homemade bed . . . and my mother slept in the kitchen a whole heap so she be there to get breakfast early." Another former Edgefield slave who "nussed" the master's children "slep' on a couch in their bedroom 'til I was 12 years old, den 'mancipation come."[64]

For this analysis, all 1860 cases that reported no slave houses were omitted. The average number of slaves per slave house was 4.2, a figure smaller than the average household size among the total free population between 1850 and 1880. Thus, slaves lived in families and were probably living in nuclear-family housing units.[65]

The use of the average size of the slave cabin households to indicate cabin nuclear families is sometimes difficult, however, because slaves often married off the plantation, notwithstanding their owners' desires.

Marriage off the Plantation

Former slaves explained the difficulties experienced in courting and selecting mates, particularly if they wanted to marry off the plantation. A man who had been one of seventy-two slaves on a plantation recalled "dat a nigger had a hell of a time gittin' a wife during slavery. If you didn't see one on de place to suit you and chances was you didn't suit them, why what could you do? Couldn't spring up, grab a mule and ride to de next plantation widout a written pass. S'pose you gits your master's consent to go? Look here, de gal's marster got to consent, de gal got to consent, de gal's daddy got to consent, de gal's mammy got to consent. It was a hell of a way!" Verifying the former slave's complaint was a letter that gave permission for "my boy Isaac" to marry one of your "black women" and recommended his male slave "as a boy of very good Character . . . very honest." Another former slave told of problems even when slaves succeeded in marrying off the plantation. "A man dat had a wife off de place, see little peace or happiness. He could see de wife once a week, on a pass, and jealosy kep' him 'stracted de balance of de week, if he love her very much."[66]

Nancy Settles, who was born on a plantation about fifteen miles from Edgefield Court House and whose first child was born while she was a slave, reported, "Me and my husband lived on diffunt plantashuns till after Freedom come."[67]

On smaller farms it was more common for the father and mother to belong to different owners, since these smaller places provided fewer choices of mates, but marriages also occurred between the slaves of larger slaveowners. Alexander Bettis's father belonged to a large plantation owner of that name, whereas his mother was a houseservant on another large plantation owned by the Joneses. A number of marriages between slaves of different plantations have been documented for Edgefield District and the Augusta hinterland.[68]

Love and marriage between slaves of different plantations could pose a problem for planters. The newspaper warned slaveowners not to allow marriage off the plantation. Rule 9 for Pickens's plantations stated: "No negro man is to have a wife off of the plantation and no strange negro is to have a wife on the plantation." Hammond proclaimed that "no marriage will be allowed with negroes not belonging to the master." In a discussion at a local agricultural society on 7 August 1847, another Edgefield landowner, Dr. Cook, agreed with Hammond and Pickens that "allowing negroes to have a wife off the plantation is injurious to owner and negro." Yet despite rules, some of Pickens's and Hammond's slaves had spouses on other plantations, and some of the unnamed fathers of slave children may well have been men from other plantations. Hammond recorded in his rule book that chances for visits were to be allowed for slaves "living at one plantation and having wives at another." Another version of Hammond's rules read, "at the other . . . plantation." These other plantations probably referred to farms owned by Hammond, but Hammond might have made exceptions to his rule prohibiting outside slave marriage.[69]

Even when slaves were allowed to have spouses from other plantations, one has to question what the arrangement meant for the homelife of the family.

Amelia Dorsey's father, Rufus Simkins, for example, was allowed to visit his wife and children only on Saturday night and then only with a pass from the slave master.

The slave narratives show great devotion to spouse and family in the face of such obstacles and reveal something of the desire of Afro-Americans for autonomous families. Charlie Davis's mother lived on a large plantation and his father on another in Richland County, near southeast Edgefield. Davis said, "Mammy said dat de patrollers was as thick as flies 'round deses plantations all de time, and my daddy sho' had to slip 'round to see mammy. Sometime they would ketch him and whip him good, pass or no pass. . . . My mammy and daddy got marrid after freedom, 'cause they didn't git de time for a weddin befo'. They called derselves man and wife a long time befo' they was really married, and dat is de reason dat I's old as I is now. I reckon they was right, in de fust place, 'cause they never did want nobody else 'cept each other, nohow." Perhaps prompted by his parents' devotion, Davis added, "Here I is, I had been married one time and at no time has I even seen another woman I wanted. My wife been dead a long time and I is still living alone."[70]

Samuel Boulware told a similar story of the devotion of separated spouses. He lived with his mother on the plantation of a Dr. Hunter. "My daddy was a slave on Reuben Boulware's plantation, 'bout two miles from Marster Hunter's place. He would git a pass to come to see mammy once every week. If he come more than dat he would have to skeedaddle through de woods and fields from de patrollers. If they ketched him widout a pass, he was 'sho in for a skin crackin' whippin'. He knowed all dat he would slip to see mammy anyhow, whippin' or not." Former slaves had truly heroic love stories about the devotion of their parents to each other, convincing evidence of the importance of marriage among slaves.[71]

Several narratives chronicled the problems of slaves who could not marry or who, although "married," suffered in various ways at the hands of whites. Cora Sheppard remembered that a fellow slave had a family on another plantation. One of the couple's children was sick, and the slave tried to get to his family without having obtained a pass from his master. Sheppard recalled the injustice: "Dey whipped de man when he went to see his wife."[72]

Ellen Campbell, a slave on a plantation right outside Augusta, was a grown woman when freedom came. She knew slaves from across the Savannah River in Edgefield and reminisced about the problems of separated loved ones.

"Old Mr. Miller had a man name Jolly and he wanner marry a woman off annuder plantachun, but Jolly's Marster wanna buy de woman to come to de plantachun. He say, 'What's fair fer de goose is fair fer de gander.' When dey couldn't come to no 'greement de man he run away to de woods. Den de sot de bloodhounds on 'im. Dey let down de rail fence so de hounds could git fur. Dey search de woods and de swamps fer Jolly but dey neber find him. De slaves dey know whar he is, and de woman she visit him. He had a den down dere and plenty o' grub dey take 'im, but de white folks neber find him. Five hundred dollars that what Miller put out for whomsover git him."

[Interviewer:]
"And you say the woman went to visit him?"

"Yes, Ma'am. De woman would go dere in de woods wid him. Finally one night when he was outer de swamp he had to lie hidin' in de ditch all night, cross from de nigger hospital. Den somebody crep' up and shot him. . . . He die three days later."

This passage reveals the cohesion of the slave community; the other slaves hid Jolly even when there was a reward for his discovery.[73]

Marriage across plantation or farm boundaries kept families apart. In 1850, 14.2 percent and in 1860, 12.6 percent of Edgefield slaveowners owned only one slave. Consequently, unless the master was part of a larger slaveowning family, at least 246 slaves in 1850 and 208 slaves in 1860 were probably not living with a black family (Figure 1-4).

Other Separations

Even within the same plantation, slave couples and families were sometimes separated for the convenience of the owners. Squire Harris, a slave on an Edgefield plantation, had a father who tended to the stock and a mother who was a spinner. His mother also looked after the slave children while their parents worked in the fields. The mother lived apart from the family; "My mother lived in de [master's] house." So firm was the connection between the master's house and where his mother lived that he said that on Monday nights, when each family was given its food allotment, the slaves went up to "our mother's house and de boss man's house." Slave units with only one female (of appropriate age) and children probably indicated separated marriages (or a widowed family).[74]

Separations occurred, too, if the master took a vacation or extended visit; Pickens took his personal servants when he went to Russia. Another former Edgefield slave remembered, "My own Mammy took long trips with ole Mistis, to de Blue Ridge Mountains and sometimes over de big water." Some slaves accompanied their masters during the Civil War. When Harry Hammond's servant was injured in Virginia, Hammond asked his wife to send another from Edgefield.[75]

When choices were made whether to break up families, slaveowners usually overcame moral or religious convictions against separation. Consider the twisted logic with which one area slave mistress, an in-law of Harry Hammond, equated religious and paternalistic values with her self-interest:

> Mr. Bryan who has always been determined to have Dinah, when he found that there was no longer any reason or excuse for detaining her, sent her to Mr. Parker, who has written to ask me as he says at the request of Dinah to beg that she might be permitted to stay as she has married and did not like to leave her husband. Mr. Bryan I suppose thought that this plea would be effectual, and that touching me upon my religious scrupples was assailing me at my weak points, and would complete his purpose . . . but Dinah has a husband every few months, and I conceive it is far more good to bring her back than to leave her to the uncertainty she would always be in there from changing owners.[76]

Slave rental exacerbated the problem of family separation. Renting a slave was often a prelude to buying. (The rental period could be a time of "testing" by both white and slave.) In 1860, 235 slaves were listed as employed in the slave manuscript census returns. They were hired out as individuals and separated from their families. Renting could be profitable; an estate sale claimed that four of the slaves to be sold were carpenters who rented out at twenty dollars per month. Teenage slave children were sometimes rented out as nurses who tended children or helped some elderly white. The members of H. K. Miller's family were the only slaves a widow owned; the owner rented Miller's brother to a widow some thirty miles away.[77]

Besides the misery of separation itself, whites who rented slaves could be cruel. The mistress of fifteen-year-old Ellen Campbell took her to Augusta, where she "rented me out to a lady runnin' a boarding house. De rent was paid to my missus." This lady hit Ellen in the head with a butcher knife. A former Edgefield slave told how her father was rented out: "Pa was hired out and they was goner whoop him and he run off and got back to the marster." When one of Hammond's slaves, Henderson, believed to be Hammond's son, was rented out to Charles Axt, Hammond received an anonymous letter describing cruelty to Henderson.

> Dear Sir:
>
> We think it our duty—not only from the highest regard and esteem to your excellency, but from pure humanity—to inform you of the condition of one of your Negroes.
>
> The said Negro is hired to a man by the name of Chas. Axt in Crawfordville . . . —By his brutal treatment as he was knocked and dragged over the whole yard, dogs set on him threatened to be shot he was forced to run away. He was taken here in Augusta and lodged in jail—Chas. Axt took him out the jail tied hands behind his back and feet together and brought or dragged him in the roughest manner to Mr.

Rappold's Bar Room where he knocked him down several times and dragged him by his hair over the whole house—As this brute was tired of this he took the poor Negro in the kitchen . . . his legs still tied together and his hands also behind his back took an other rope wound it round his wrists and hung him on a beam face or head downwards suspended in the air. . . . The cries and agonies of the poor sufferer went to the hearts of the hearers . . . who forced Axt to give up the key and liberated him in a fainting condition. . . .

After checking into the matter, Hammond's response was to write a friend near there, "As you are so near Axt, you would lay me under a great obligation if you would occasionally make an inquiry about the boy." The response satisfied Hammond that the initial letter had been an overreaction.[78]

John C. Calhoun worried that people who rented slaves did not take care of them. He felt that renting slaves was so wrong that when his son-in-law Thomas Clemson was planning to rent out his slave force, Calhoun offered to buy them. Another slaveowner explained what he meant by taking good care of the rented Edgefield slaves: "To feed and cloth them well and make them work and know their places is what I mean by good treatment."[79]

Forced separations of families also took place during the Civil War. Four hundred Edgefield bondsmen (and two free blacks) were conscripted and sent to Georgia to work on Confederate fortifications. James Henry Hammond protested the requisition of his slaves to work on defenses at Charleston. Slaves, too, remembered the breakup of their families because of the war effort. Warren McKinney recalled that "when de war come on my papa went to build forts." Squire Harris stated, "I 'member when my two brothers was on de coast, working for de war." Margaret Green's Edgefield master, Cook McKie, took her father as his body servant and her mother to cook for him when he joined the war. A former slave from Augusta remembered that when Union troops were near Waynesboro, "orders were sent to all the masters of the nearby plantations to send ten of their best men to build breastworks to hold back the northern advance." Ironically a letter to the local newspaper in April 1865 lamented that the Yankee troops had "seduced from their masters, their wives and children and their contented firesides, a portion of our male slaves."[80]

Although most masters sanctioned slave marriages, some, including Pickens and Hammond, even while proclaiming they did not want to, separated families. The vulnerability of slave families to destruction by action of the master received greater criticism from abolitionists than did the physical abuse of slave families. Slaves were rented, willed, given, sold, and purchased according to the needs of owners, and the slave's desire for family autonomy was given short shrift.

Selling Slaves

Slaves could be sold to faraway owners or to persons closer to home; either could be devastating to the family life of those concerned. Whereas white commentators tended to minimize the frequency and effects of slave sales, former slave narratives and oral histories reveal the trauma and horrendous emotional costs of being separated from their loved ones.[81]

Proslavery theorists protested that objections to the selling of slaves were exaggerated. Edgefield minister Iveson Brookes wrote, "Involuntary separation of families among slaves seldom happens in their removal or exchange of owner, as most people feel disposed to keep them together, where they desire it; and, in case of separation, the parties are always assured that their friends or children will fall under the care of masters whose personal interest will not allow their property ever to want the necessaries to preserve health and life."[82]

Malinda Mitchell, former slave of an Edgefield Baptist preacher, claimed that "Marster wouldn't sell none of his slaves, an' when he wanted to buy one, he'd buy de whole fambly to keep fum having them separated." Most often, however, slaves were bought as individuals rather than as part of a family, although sometimes they were bought as part of a work gang. Some of the conflicting feelings that slaveowners felt about the separation of slave families were expressed by Francis Pickens in 1860: "I have ever looked on my negroes as part of my family, for most of them came by inheritance from my father (having sold to Mr. Dearing the $70,000 worth purchased by me) and I feel a personal attachment that makes it my duty to be near them to protect them kindly."

Despite efforts to keep *their* slave families intact, planters did effect separations. According to his diary, Col. Whitfield Brooks gave to one daughter "Gabriel and family, Edmund, Nesbit, Charles, Amanda, Alster"; to another he gave "Lewis and family"; but to another, only the "daughter of Andy and Violet." At one point, Pickens mentioned bringing, without his family, one "Negro man, French" from his Alabama plantation to Edgefield. In an 1839 description of slaves, Pickens listed:

> Harper
> 　his son Mosley
> 　　"　　"　Harper　　10 *Sold*
> 　　"　daughter Caroline.[83]

Planters may have been sensitive about slave families they already owned, but often purchased slaves without their families. At Christmas 1846, Pickens bought Big Allen, age twenty-seven, his wife Sarah, age twenty-eight, and their child Silvey, age three. In addition, he purchased twelve-year-old Frederic, nine-year-old McDuffie, eighteen-year-old Brown, twenty-four-year-old Martha, none of whom were related. Unless they were orphans, slaves purchased as individuals were separated from their families and, even if orphaned, torn from their plantation communities.[84]

Owners placed the family life of faithful servants in jeopardy also. The will of Mary Carroll dispersed "favored" bondspersons to various children and grandchildren: To a daughter she bequeathed "my negro slave Sarah and the youngest two children she may have at the time of my decease"; to a grandchild she willed "my negro slave Jane and her future increase"; to another she gave "my negro girl Fanny and her future increase." In the 1838 account of "Sales of the Estate of Eliza H. Simkins dec'd" the impersonal horror of family separation was recorded between other items of property:[85]

1 Bedstead	James Reynolds	6.25
1 negro man Allen	F. W. Pickens	$ 880
1 " " Henry	Do = Do =	945
1 woman, Nancy and 2 children		
Harriet & Sam	W. M. Butler	1000
1 negro man Gabriel	F. W. Pickens	725
" " girl Julia	Do = Do =	455
45 acres of land on Cambridge		
Road	Do = Do =	869.50

The death of even the kindest master who had the best of intentions left slaves in a predicament. A few slaveowners tried to free some slaves or left provisions for freeing certain slaves, but the legislature denied these requests. One master's will specified that each slave should have the opportunity to select a master "to purchase such Negro at a fair and true valuation." For a special slave and her children, the slaveowner stipulated that they could remain on the plantation in their houses "for the first 12 months succeeding my decease on their paying a reasonable compensation . . . in order that they may have a better opportunity of making such selection of a future owner."[86]

Considerations of age and gender of slaves sold without families made a bad situation even worse. In the above list, prices indicated that the males were of prime age, but the girl Julia was young. The slaves Pickens bought at this estate sale were for speculation. He later sold two mothers with their children, two teenage girls, and, without any accompanying parent, one "child, Nancy, age 3." Brooks, Hammond, and Pickens also sold recalcitrant slaves. Asked if her old owner, Pickens, would "sell any of the slaves off his plantation," Rachel Sullivan replied, "No'm—not 'less dey did wrong."[87]

James Rainsford came to Edgefield from England in 1833 to claim the legacy left him by his grandfather. He married his cousin Esther Rainsford, and although his own inheritance was still disputed by his uncle, he claimed his wife's slaves. Rainsford purchased several tracts of land in Edgefield over the years; by 1844 he owned fifty-four slaves, and in the 1850 census he reported real estate worth eighty-five thousand dollars. He kept a careful record of the prices of male and female slaves sold in Hamburg and Augusta. On 8 January 1834 he attended an auction and recorded the following diary entry:

> I this day attended the auction sale of the late Mr. Coleman's property, about 6 miles from my house. I went in company with Mr. G. Willman and saw Negroes (13 in number) for 33 dollars [sic] and a cow in calf (a young one) for 6 dollars and on the terms of one year's credit or one year allowed for cash, the Negroes sold as follows: Peter, a man about 50 years of age and rather a small man was bought by the widow Coleman for $501 and his wife, a woman about 25 years of age and her infant about 12 months old for $581 and her boy about 2 years old for $100 and her daughter about 4 years old for $148 and one girl about 14 years old for $501 by the widow. One woman and her child a boy about 2 years old were bought by Mr. Reynolds for $705. One young woman was sold for $400. 1 Girl about 15 years old for $520, one girl about 16 years old bought by Mr. Colrazie for (Elij) $501. One woman about 35 years old (not a healthy looking woman) was bought by Mr. Murrell for $344 and 1 boy about 9 years old by Mr. G. Gison for $300. The 13 Negroes bought or sold on 1 year's term $4601, only 2 men amongst them one or both of diminutive size.[88]

Henry Shultz of Hamburg gave notice in 1819 of his intention to sell slaves. He was leaving the country for Europe and advertised sale of his interest in the "Bridge company of Augusta" with a listing of other property to be sold, including "some Shares Steam-Boat & State Bank stock, 8 negroes, men, women & children accustomed to house work."[89]

Grim reminders of the flourishing local slave trade were the regular newspaper advertisements for slaves and the census listing of individuals whose occupation was "Negro Trader," two in 1850 and four in 1860. Like many antebellum attorneys, Augusta attorney Henry Cumming regularly drew up the legal papers for the sale of slaves. He wrote his wife in July 1832 that he had to be at the sale of "50 odd negroes" in one week. Some sales involved complicated legal agreements, such as the shared ownership of George, a horse trainer, by James Henry Hammond and Pierce M. Butler in 1835.[90]

Even in times of prosperity separation might occur. In 1839, Hammond purchased 580 acres in Fairfield District and set up a new plantation he named Green Valley. "On the 28 November eleven Negroes to wit—Jack Smith (foreman), Dick (Waggoner), Henry Fuller, Patrick (Blacksmith), Ben Smith, Nero, Adam, Moses, Dye Fuller, and two children, Ivanna, and Hager, daughter of Joe Shubrick and Nancy, left Silver Bluff with a wagon and four mules for Green Valley."[91]

Slaves were also given away as gifts. Maria Bryan asked about a slave given to her sister in Augusta by the family: "Ma feels anxious to know how you like

Daphne and how she behaves." At the age of eighty-five, former slave Julia Bunch remembered: "I b'longed to Marse Jackie Dorn of Edgefield County, I was gived to him and his wife when dey was married for a weddin' gift." A former slave in Augusta recalled, "When you marry, they give you so many cullud people. My mother, her brother, and her aunt was give to young Missis when she marry de Baptis' preacher and come to Augusta."[92]

Female former slaves remembered being presented to one of the master's children as "their personal maids." Most of the former slaves interviewed for the slave narratives such as Malinda Mitchell and her sister, who were given to the two daughters of an Edgefield minister and plantation owner, were young when the Civil War came and so were not separated from the plantation or from their families. If the war had not interrupted slavery, they would have gone off with the master's children when they moved away.[93]

In the best of times slaves lived at the whim of their owners. Gen. William Butler, grandfather of Col. Whitfield Brooks and Matthew Calbraith Butler, ran out of money in a high-stakes card game. He then bet his loyal manservant Will. Butler won, but was shaken enough at the prospect of losing his slave that he swore off betting for the remainder of his life.[94]

Two other examples of the precarious status of slaves were documented in correspondence between Thomas Green Clemson and his father-in-law, John C. Calhoun. Calhoun was looking after his son-in-law's Edgefield plantation while Clemson was in Belgium. One of Clemson's favorite bondsmen had been taken away from his Edgefield home to Calhoun's plantation and was causing trouble. From Belgium, Clemson explained, "Charles is an excellent cook—takes pride in it. He is stubborn and wants to be kept up to mark. He is a very handy fellow and one of the best hands I have on the plantation. I presume the reason why Mrs. Calhoun did not like him was, that he wished to return to Edgefield to his wife, and did not wish to give satisfaction." Clemson added that he had purchased Charles without a family in Charleston. If Charles gave "any [more] trouble," he added, he "might be sold." Clemson recommended selling this good servant, whom he obviously admired, because the man preferred to be with his family at home on the Edgefield plantation.[95]

Long and faithful service was no guarantee against being sold. One mistake in a lifetime might result in the sale of a slave. Henry Cumming wrote his wife from Augusta regarding "our black family." He wrote about a kinsman's slave Cathy, of whom he and his wife were fond. The relative had decided, because of the slave's recent bad behavior, "to put her out of his family, notwithstanding her long and valuable services." Sometimes circumstances over which a slave had no control led to his or her sale. Maria Bryan Harford wrote her sister Julia Bryan Cumming, in Augusta, that their father could not pay his debts "unless by the sale of property—and of negro property which he is unwilling to engage in." Two years later, in 1841, Maria wrote Julia that "Pa said he disliked selling negroes out of the family, but would part with Cuffee."[96]

During the depression decades of the late 1830s and 1840s, farmers who sold land sometimes sold slaves as well. The slaves sometimes went with the land, but all too often they were sent to the slave markets in Columbia, Augusta, and Hamburg, where they went to the highest bidder. Pickens and Hammond left bills of sale for slaves they bought from neighbors, the court, friends from different states, and slave markets.[97]

In Edgefield District and the surrounding areas, public opinion opposed the selling of one's slaves. Ben Tillman wrote that because his brother John bought land and slaves which he could not afford, "my mother had often to take off his hands, as she would take the negroes herself rather than have them resold." Harry Hammond wrote to his father James Henry that "nothing would be more painful to me than to see you sell a single negroe, or an acre of land." Although Hammond listed thirty purchases of individuals and groups of slaves for the years 1834 to 1851, there were only four records of sales. Nevertheless, his tirades and threats of sale caused concern among his family and slaves. When Hammond assumed management of his plantations, he claimed that slaves were "trying him at every step." Finding one slave particularly difficult to manage, Hammond "flogged him until [he was] tired" and considered returning him to his previous owner. In 1833, a slave named Cudjo ran away so much that Hammond tried without success to sell him. Over the years, however, he tried to avoid selling slaves who had family ties on the plantation, and, according to his biographer Drew Faust, "he often bought old or injured slaves when they came in a package with a family." Yet he had "no place in his regime for a real revolutionary," and he would sell a threatening slave. After repeated escapes Hammond's slave Hudson was jailed in Barnwell for arson. Hammond hired an attorney to protect his investment, and Hudson was acquitted. After the trial, Hammond sold him.[98]

If the separation of families occasioned some regret on the part of the whites, it seldom brought anything but suffering for the slaves. A former Augusta slave "was next to the youngest of six children born to a slave couple in South Carolina." When she was a baby—some time prior to 1860—her mother and five children were sold to an Alabama planter who lived twelve miles west of the Georgia line, while the father-husband and one child, a son, remained in South Carolina. A former slave remembered, "I saw many slaves sold on the block—saw mammy with little infant taken from her body and sent away. I saw families separated from each other, some going to one white master and some to another." Maggie Wright had been a slave of the sheriff of Newberry County. Her plantation had been near Martin's Depot in Edgefield, and she remembered the slave auctions and "old General Kinard—from Edgefield" selling the slaves on the auction block. She also remembered an appropriate song that the slaves in the area of Edgefield and Newberry had sung: "You may never press me to your heart again, mother; Oh, I'll never forget you my mother."

Sylvia Cannon reported: "I see em sell plenty colored peoples away in dem days cause dat de way white folks made heap of dey money. Coase dey ain' never tell us how much dey sell em for. Just stand em up on a block bout three feet high en a speculator bid em off just like dey was horses. Dem what was bid off didn' never say nothin neither. Don' know who bought my brothers, George en Earl. (She cried after this statement). I see em sell some slaves twice fore I was sold en I see de slaves when dey be travelin like hogs to Darlington. Some of dem be women folks lookin like dey gwine to get down dey so heavy."

Augusta and Hamburg were major markets for the purchase of slaves. There were two places to sell slaves in Augusta. The slaves to be sold were kept in a large building in Hamburg known as the slaves' quarters. Former slave Eugene Smith remarked that he "saw 'em selling slaves myself. They put 'em up on something like a table, bid 'em off just like you would do horses or cows. . . . They would sell a mother from her children." Laura Stewart was just as blunt: "I kin 'member slaves being sold at both markets, outside. . . . Dey would line 'em up like horses or cows, and look in de mouf' at dey teef' and den march 'em down together to market in crowds on first Tuesday sale day."[99]

When asked if she was ever sold, Ellen Campbell replied, "No'm, I wa'nt sold, but knows dem what wus. Jedge Robinson he kept de nigger trade office over in Hamburg. . . . Den dey brung 'em over to da market and put 'em up fer sale. Anybody fixin' to buy 'em, 'zamines 'em to see if dey all right. Looks at de teef to tell 'bout de age." There were constant references by former slaves about how whites treated blacks like animals when selling them.[100]

One of the most poignant stories of both slave sale and sexual abuse was told by Mollie Kinney, who had lived in a little town in Georgia across from Edgefield District.

> Dey had slaves in pens, brung in drove and put in dem pens jes' lak dey wus cows. Dey sold dem by auctionin' off to the highest bidder. . . . Dey put girls on the block and auctioned dem off. "What will you give fer dis nigger wench?" Lot of the girls wus being sold by their master who wus their father, taken rat out uv the yards with their white chilluns and sold lak herds uv cattle.
>
> My sister wus given away when she wus a girl. She tole me and ma that they'd make her go out and lay on a table and two or three white men would have in'ercourse with her befo' they'd let her git up. She wus jes' a small girl hone. She died when she wus still a girl. Oh! You . . . don't know the tortures the slaves went through. Honey, slavery wus bad.[101]

Although the records of Edgefield whites indicated that the selling of slaves was, at most, an occasional occurrence, the statements of former Edgefield slaves indicate that it was a constant and potent threat. Prominent in the history of the black Butler family is the story that Easter Butler angered her owner and he retaliated by selling three of her children. Annette Milledge remembered, "Down dere in Hamburg near de bridge, dey had a big house. Dey would sell de mothers fum de babies, and if you cry after dem, dey would w'hoop you. Dey didn't 'low you to cry." Casper Rumple recalled that along the road that divided Laurens and Edgefield districts men came from out of the cities, "tradin' and selling slaves. Nother way they sell em was at public auction."[102]

Slaves tried in various ways to cope with being sold away from families. Some who were sold within the area got passes to go back for visits. A former slave remembered her master allowing her to return and be with her mother and father for a week at Christmas. Others relied on family and kin. Amelia Dorsey's father belonged to the Simkins plantation, and she and her mother belonged to Tom Myers in the Beech Island area of Edgefield. She remembered, "Dey sold my mother. I didn't even know she gone, I so little and ain't know much, ain't got sense to miss her. She put me and my sister with one o' our aunties in Beech Island and we stay dere till freedom declared."[103]

Even when a master did not sell them, slaves were not safe, for outlaws stole slaves and sold them. James Beale Rainsford reported in his diary in Edgefield on 14 February 1838: "On Friday last I saw two men hung for Negroe stealing, one James Reed, an Irishman for stealing 2 Negroes from Col. Key and Thomas Evans for stealing one from Mr. Lamar and one from a neighbour of his." The high prices for slaves encouraged organized thievery.[104]

Many whites left their families or went west, but white family breakups were quite different from those of Afro-Americans, since coercion was seldom, if ever, a factor. While whites could use mail, newspapers, and visits to communicate with friends and family who had left Edgefield, slaves had to resort to other means, which Herbert Gutman has carefully outlined: naming patterns, reliance on kin and friends, use of plantation-based obligations, adoption of orphans and those separated from family, and acceptance of illegitimate children (albeit with strict attitudes about adultery).[105]

Occupations and Work Gangs

Plantations (farms with at least twenty slaves) were the homes of 60.3 percent of Edgefield slaves in 1850 and 64.2 percent in 1860. Although most slaves lived on large units, the varied size of plantations produced varied experiences. Percentages do not really tell us about the slave's life, but an Edgefield absentee landlord, Thomas Green Clemson, gave some sense of what numbers of slaves meant when he wrote to John C. Calhoun, "The gang consists of 37 in all. Of these 24 are workers and 13 children." More than a third of the plantation's slaves were considered too young to be useful in routine farming chores, but children were important because they were the future work force.

Calhoun, who was looking after his son-in-law's Edgefield plantation, commented that for that year "there has been no death, nor birth, but the prospect of a large increase next year."[106]

Although Clemson, Hammond, and Pickens owned different-sized plantations, the number of slaves considered too young for strenuous field labor was generally around a third of all the slaves owned. Of Clemson's 37 slaves, the percentage who were children was 35.1 percent in 1845; of Hammond's 174 slaves it was 31.3 percent in 1831; of Pickens's 219 slaves, it was 17.9 percent in 1842, of 234 slaves it was 29.5 percent in 1843, and on a new plantation with 89 slaves it was a high 40.4 percent in 1847. Age pyramids from the 1850 and 1860 manuscript slave censuses show the same pattern. From 1840 to 1860 the percentage of children under ten years of age for Edgefield whites, free blacks, and slaves ranged from 28.3 (free blacks in 1860) to 35.6 (slaves in 1840). This age-group generally comprised about one-third of the total population for each of the three groups; slaves usually had slightly larger proportions of their population under ten years of age.[107]

Although men and women generally worked at different tasks (except at cotton-picking time), both were expected to perform hard physical labor. One planter warned his club members, "Much injury is done by requiring women to perform improper labor such as rolling logs, building fences, etc." Another argued against a neighbor's use of women to plow; he felt that "females are often improperly used put to work, especially in a pregnant state unsuitable for them." A Major Mills, however, disagreed: he regarded "raising children as a matter of luck" and had his slave women plow and do other heavy jobs. He told other Edgefield planters that slave women would do hard work. Soon after the Civil War, a northern visitor reported on one example of women's work. The process of repacking cotton usually employed a harnessed mule to walk around in a circle turning a central post. This particular place substituted women for the mule. "One would run round once or twice, then another would take her place, and the old planter stood by to superintend."[108]

Edgefield slaves' precise job descriptions are unobtainable. Table 4-1 indicates occupations from the 1860 slave mortality census (skewed by age). Hammond meticulously outlined tasks for his slaves. In 1851, when Hammond had seventy-three male and seventy-four female slaves, he was able to use sixty-one slaves in the field on crops, one to watch the livestock, eight slaves in his sawmill, one slave in the gristmill, and seven slaves on the landing where the steamboats that traveled the Savannah River purchased wood to burn.[109]

One of the skilled trades practiced by slaves was that of pottery. Edgefield used both black and white labor in stoneware manufacture, which was generally an artisanal skill reserved for whites during this period. Although in Africa pottery was, and still is, a woman's craft, only slave men were used in Edgefield, and some, such as Dave Potter, established reputations as skilled

Table 4-1. *Occupations of Slaves Who Died in 1860 (by gender)*

Occupation[a]	N Male	N Female
Farm Laborer	45	36
Domestic Servant	1	14
Carpenter	5	0
Cook	1	4
Blacksmith	4	0
Farmer	1	0
Shoemaker	1	0
Works on Ship	1	0
Fisherman	1	0
Baker	0	1
Nurse	0	1
Cook and Nurse	0	1
Totals	60	57

a. Five slaves twenty years and older had no occupation listed. Four slaves who were younger than fifteen years had an occupation listed. This table includes all slaves for whom an occupation was listed, regardless of age.
Source: Edgefield Data Base.

potters. Manufacturers often exchanged slaves for short periods between potteries, forming a larger, interconnected community of slave potter artisans. In all the sales of slave potters, never was the sale of the potter's family mentioned.

Dave, who lived to be eighty-three years old, became the most accomplished potter in the antebellum South. His pots tended to be very wide at the shoulders, and his forty-gallon jar is the largest piece of stoneware known in the South, a ceramic monument which awes today's folk potters. He threw larger and heavier ware than anyone, sometimes using fifty pounds of clay. Dave's owners and co-workers, black and white, respected the great strength and skill required to turn such pots. Dave's poetry, mentioned above, also shows strength of spirit.[110]

The Master-Slave Relationship

The key variable in the family life of slaves on various plantations or farms was not the number of slaves but the personality and values of the slaveowner.

Hammond was gratified that "my negroes . . . love and appreciate me," but his reputation among blacks did not bear out this assessment. Although not one of Hammond's slaves, Amelia Dorsey, who was born in Edgefield District on Beech Island, remembered, "Dey wouldn't let de chillun see dem whippin de han's—I year de old people tell 'bout how Governor Hammond chastise he han's." Hammond's reputation for punishment left a more enduring legend than did his perception of having been loved by his slaves.[111]

Sometimes the relationships with whites were more tolerable. Molly Brown, whose wedding was discussed above, belonged to the Harrises, and some of her relatives belonged to the Joneses, kinsmen of the Harrises. Together, the Joneses and the Harrises had two or three families of slaves. "They didn't have no big sight of land. They was good to us." Unlike slaves on larger plantations, the Joneses' and the Harrises' slaves were pretty much left alone as long as they did their work. She had no memories of slaves either being sold or whipped.[112]

Paul Escott's analysis of the former slave narratives discovered that slaves on farms with fewer than fifteen slaves reported significantly fewer whippings and less cruelty, more often rated their food as equal to that of their owners (although on the larger plantations the former slaves more often remembered their food as having been good or adequate), and had a more favorable attitude toward their master than did slaves on larger plantations. A former Edgefield slave believed that "when a man had one or two slave families he treated em better an if he had a great big acreage and fifteen or twenty families." Annette Milledge said, "My marster was jus' like a father to me. . . . I might say I was free myself in slavery times, my people treat me so good." Her memories of her master were positive, but they were always juxtaposed with the situations of her neighbors and others she observed. Her master did not sell any slaves, although he bought them. "There were no whippings." Her father was a free black man who bought shoes for his child, and her mother made the child's clothes on a loom. Her mother made daily trips to Augusta to do the shopping for the Ransomes. Milledge claimed that "Marster had a storeroom right next to my mother's room, and anything she wanted to get to cook, she could go dere and get it." She added, "We had anything we wanted to eat." On most plantations planters contracted arrangements with doctors or did their own doctoring on slaves, but Milledge remembered, "When we got sick Marster would send for de doctor."

There was a sadder side to Milledge's memories. Apparently she "feared and hated" her master's second wife. "De las' wife was mean. She wouldn't want you to wear good shoes. She even had all my hair cut off, shaved, almost."[113]

Easter Jones was owned by a small slaveowning family, but she recalled whipping and toil as her lot. Born in 1842, she was the slave of Georgia attorney William Bennett, who owned only two slave families. The white family felt intimate enough toward their slaves to record Jones's birthdate in the Bennett family Bible. Easter's life was concisely summarized by the WPA interviewer: "The old woman is now very bitter about those years during which she was held as a slave. She says there was nothing but hard work and cruel treatment." While generalizations that slaves received better treatment from small farmers than from large planters usually proved true, stories like Easter's showed that much depended on the owners.[114]

While slaves who belonged to whites owning only a few slaves may have had fewer constraints imposed on them than slaves on large plantations with hired overseers, small slaveowners were more susceptible to economic crises that caused them to feel that they had to sell or rent slaves. But it was on small plantations of about 20 slaves that slaves had the worst of it. Whites who had one or two slaves or one slave family might become intimate with their slaves; and the largest plantations, like those of Brooks, Hammond, or Pickens, had large slave communities that served as buffers against white oppression. Slaves on small plantations, though, could look neither to intimately known whites for protection nor to a complex and considerable slave society for succor.

The Slave Family and White Authority

In abolitionist literature bondage was symbolized by the whip. Whites had absolute authority to whip slaves, whether adult or child. Slave parents had to stand aside if whites wanted to whip children. Slave spouses and children had to watch while whites humiliated and whipped fathers and mothers. Violence and the threat of physical punishment underlay all other devices and strategies for the control of slaves. Some masters standardized whipping punishments, generally allowing more for males and less for women and children and limiting the number of lashes given at any one time to twenty or less. One plantation owner advocated whipping slaves every Saturday night. He thought the men should have twenty-five and the women thirty lashes, "for women were worse than the men." The editor of the Edgefield *Advertiser* admonished, "Spare the rod and you spoil your negroes."

Slave memories of whippings were vivid. One Edgefield former slave remembered that "de overseer would whip de slaves when dey couldn't work." Nancy Settles believed that slaves were "whipped mostly cause de marster *could* whip 'em." Annette Milledge "had dreadful recollections of slaves being punished on adjoining plantations. . . . Sometimes dey would w'hoop dem terrible. Dey tied dem acros't a barrel and w'hooped dem until de blood run out. De leas' little thing dey w'hoop de hide off 'em." Casper Rumple said that if slaves stole from someone other than their own master and got caught, then "the sheriff have to whip him. They would have a public whippin." Julia

Henderson remembered that when slaves were punished, "dey whip 'em bad—dey raise a fence and put dey head under de fence and whip 'em." Lydia Calhoun Starks had belonged to James Taggart. "I can remember seeing the old over-seer on the plantation joining ours, jes' whippin' dem po' ole slaves till de couldn't even stan' up," she said. Peggy Grisby remembered that her master's wife had "poked my head in a rail fence once and whipped me hard with a whip."[115]

There were many such stories by former slaves throughout the South; some told of seeing their parents whipped. One such story of a former slave from a neighboring county revealed the impact that watching whites humiliate and whip their parents had upon slave children. Manda Walker's father, who belonged to a different master from his wife and family, had to ford a creek to come to see them. On one occasion the creek was flooded. "I to dis day 'members one time pappy come in all wet and drenched wid water." Her father stayed longer than his pass allowed, and the patrollers came into the slave cabin. "Pappy tried to explain but they pay no 'tention to him. Tied him up, pulled down his breeches, and whupped him right befo' mammy and us chillun. I shudder to dis day, to think of it." Then they forced her father to take his mule and swim the dangerous creek. The former slave complained of the kind of people who were on the slave patrol, "a strippin' de clothes off men, lak pappy, right befo' de wives and chillun and beatin' de blood out of him." Julia Henderson told of her grandmother being whipped because she talked back to the "Bossman." "She give him stiff talk, and he whip her from one end of de road to de udder, and de blood run down in her shoes. . . . I am so glad I ain't slave!" Warren McKinney remembered that when he was little, his Edgefield master "whipped my ma. It hurt me bad as it did her. I hated him. She was crying. I chunked him with rocks. He run after me, but he didn't catch me."[116]

White-Black Sexual Liaisons

Along with whippings, separation, and violence, whites' sexual liaisons with slaves affected slave family life. Such liaisons in Edgefield created radically different oral traditions in the black and white communities. Blacks recalled how their ancestors were coerced into having sex with whites and yielded to conditions beyond an individual's power to resist. In some cases, the slave woman was pictured as a folk hero who resisted the advances of a powerful white slaveowner. One Afro-American told of an ancestor, Charlotte, who was forced to sit naked on a pile of manure until she finally submitted to her lecherous white owner, Arthur Augustus Simkins (editor of the Edgefield *Advertiser*). After he was through with her and she had borne their child, he passed her on to his cousin, by whom she had another child. Whites never told such stories; nor did they admit to the use of force. White tales of master-slave liaisons stressed the sympathy and understanding of the prominent whites involved and emphasized the special privileges bestowed on slave mistresses. The white interpretation of the above story was of course quite different.[117]

Even defenders of slavery, such as Iveson Brookes, did not deny the "charge that the delicate subject of virtue, is desecrated through our institution of slavery. . . . Slaves are multiplied by expedients, criminal and beastly. We admit that this kind of desecration exists to fearful extent, as the result of the fallen state of human nature, not only in low, but in high life, especially among men, and doubtless for the perversion of God's purpose on this point, a fearful reckoning will be had at the eternal judgment." The divine's only defense was an argument that the "crime" did not arise "out of slavery, *per se*, or that it is in any wise peculiar to the South." Houses of ill repute "from Boston to New Orleans" were filled "from the ranks of New England" domestics who, "corrupted at home, and thrown out of business destitute of friends and means, plead the necessity of a resort to the wages of iniquity for their bread. No 'black Nancy' at the South was ever placed, at least, under that sort of necessitous temptation, either as a cause, or as an excuse for her sins."[118]

Slaveowners had their slave consorts, and some slaveowners developed a sense of responsibility to their mistresses and to the offspring of their unions. When he was ambassador to Russia, Francis Pickens asked a young protégé to ensure that a former slave mistress and their child were well cared for. As stout a defender of the slavocracy as E. Merton Coulter suggested that Pickens had fathered black radical Aaron Alpeoria Bradley (a former slave of Pickens), and as late as 1950 a former slave living in Ninety Six claimed to be Francis Pickens's daughter.[119]

James Henry Hammond particularly favored the purchase of light-skinned women. Among Hammond's bills of sale were several mentions of mulatto women being purchased: on 22 April 1835, a "light complexioned negro woman"; on 6 June 1843, a "mulatto girl"; on 18 April 1845, a "Yellow Girl named Lucy." Another entry, that of a "Yellow girl Anne," recorded her consignment to Hammond following the owner's death.

Two of Hammond's mistresses were a mother and her daughter who never named the fathers of their children for plantation records. The two women and their respective children shared a slave cabin, and during slavery neither woman ever formed a permanent relationship with a black man. Hammond's wife discovered the liaisons, but Hammond rejected her demands that he sell the women. To insure that these women and their children received special treatment, Hammond identified his slave mistresses to his legitimate son Harry, who apparently had also had a liaison with the younger slave woman. He wrote:

My Dear Harry,

In the last Will I made I left to you, over & above my other children, Sally Johnson the mother of Louisa and all the children of both. Sally says Henderson is my child. It is possible, but I do not believe it. Yet act on her's rather than my opinion. Louisa's first child *may* be mine. I think not. Her second I believe is mine. Take care of her and her children who are both of *your* blood if not of mine & of Henderson. The services of the rest will I think compensate for indulgence to these. I cannot free these people and send them North. It would be cruelty to them. Nor would I like that any but my own blood should own as slaves my own blood or Louisa. I leave them to your charge, believing that you will best appreciate & most independently carry out my wishes in regard to them. Do not let Louisa or any of my children or possible children be the Slaves of Strangers. Slavery in the family will be their happiest earthly condition.

Ever affectionately
J. H. H.

The slave mistress had some influence over her owner and lover; Hammond insisted that his son take the word of his slave over his own opinion.[120]

These cases put new light on the often-cited remark of Mary Boykin Chesnut in her celebrated *Diary from Dixie*: "Like the patriarchs of old, our men live all in one house with their wives and their concubines; and the mulattoes one sees in every family partly resemble the white children. Any lady is ready to tell you who is the father of all the mulatto children in everybody's household but her own. Those, she seems to think, drop from the clouds."[121]

Benjamin E. Mays wrote of his wife's father and her maternal grandfather, both of whom had been fathered by slave masters. The grandfather was very bitter toward his white father, but Mays's father-in-law spoke with affection about his white father. Mays's wife told him: "My father did not hate his father. He adored him. When I asked my father one day how he could love his father, who left his property to Mercer University to educate white boys, and left him nothing, my father cried. He said, 'Daughter, you do not understand. My father was a good man. I was a slave in the system, and he was a slave to the system.' "[122]

Sexual relationships between white men and slave women were not restricted to the slaveowner and his slave. Indeed, a high proportion of interracial sexual relations was not between the owner and slave. Sexual relations between white men and black women basically depended on the opportunities for contact. In areas where whites were concentrated the proportion of mulatto slave children in the population was higher. Of course, the proportion was high in urban areas.[123]

Church records show that several slave women were excommunicated because they had mulatto children. One church wrote, "James Briggs' Elizas expelled for having a 'molato child.'" Another time it recorded that "Mr. Jones' Molly excluded for having a mulatto." The secretary had first written "white child," which he crossed out to enter "mulatto." On several occasions white members were reported to their churches for having sexual liaisons with slaves. A typical response, however, was, "Nothing could be proved, so he continued in membership."[124]

Sometimes slaveowners added the word *mulatto* beside the name of the mother and infant for whom no father was named, implying that the father was white. In a few instances, the slaveowners identified the white fathers of the slaves. Slaves also identified the white fathers of slave children. Rachel Sullivan remembered that Pickens sold three of his female slaves. "Three of 'em had chillun by de overseer, Mr. Whitefield, and Marster put 'em on de block. No ma'm he wouldn't tolerate dat. He say you keep de race pure." The overseer was sent to another plantation. "He sont him down to de low place" [another plantation owned by Pickens]. Elaborating on why it did not matter that slaves were not allowed to marry, Annette Milledge explained: "Anyway de white men would do things—nex' place to us Mr. Stokes had a brother-in law, he would go back in de yard, make de husban's git out—go in himself and take de woman, and better not say nothing to him. Our marster told his son: 'Don' you never mess with cullud people!' And he tole him what he was goin' to do with him if he did."[125]

Molly Brown had an "auntie" in Edgefield, a "light woman—Julia. Her pa was a white man; her ma a light woman." Molly was a little confused about whether it was her grandfather or great-grandfather who was white, but among her maternal ancestors was a white man. "Remember grandpa. His daddy was a white man. His wife a black woman. Mama was a brown woman like I is. . . . My grandpa was a white man; mama's pa."[126]

Casper Rumple explained that his mother had been a cook on a plantation across the road from Edgefield District. "My father was a Irishman. Course he was a white man—Irishman. Sho I did know him. He didn't own no slaves. I don't guess he have any land. He was a overseer in Edgefield County. His name was Ephraim Rumple. . . . He went off to fight the Yankees and took Malaria fever and died on Red River. I could show you bout where he died." This former slave had taken his white father's surname and kept it throughout Reconstruction, both while he remained in Edgefield County and when he migrated to Arkansas in 1881. Casper named a son for his white father.[127]

As discussed above, Charlotte Simkins's owner, Arthur Augustus Simkins, fathered her first child. His cousin fathered her second child. Charlotte then had more children in a permanent relationship with her husband, fellow slave George Simkins. Paris and Andrew Simkins, the children fathered by the whites, were taken into the new Afro-American family. In this case both the children and their stepfather shared the surname of the white father. Like

Casper Rumple, Paris Simkins named one of his sixteen children, Arthur, after his biological father.

The reputations of Afro-American women caught in liaisons with whites did not necessarily suffer in either the black or white community. Charlotte Simkins's reputation for piety and regular church attendance was emphasized in the black oral history tradition and was acknowledged by Edgefield whites as well. She received praise for "Decorous Christianity" in a white history of the Edgefield Village Baptist Church. [128]

If historians have not greatly explored white male–slave female sexual relations, even less has been said about the other side of black-white sexual relationships. During the turbulent years just prior to the Civil War, Edgefield citizens presented the following grand jury indictment: "All mulattoes hereafter born of a white woman shall be sold at public outcry, by the Commissioners of the poor whenever said mulattoes shall be two years old." A letter written to James Henry Hammond during the Civil War by William Gilmore Simms confirmed Hammond's theory that miscegenation between black men and white women was widespread while the planters were off to war. In 1831, Maria Bryan wrote to her sister, Julia, in Augusta, that their brother had discovered in the woods a white woman who had a black child. [129]

Summary

Edgefield slaves endured cruelty, separation, and sexual abuse from their masters, but both owner and slave wished to maintain stable families in order to promote profit, happiness, comfort, and contentment. Transient conditions on the plantation and white interference in the slave community fragmented slave families, but this conflicted with the basic logic of the slave economy. Still, even if it were sometimes more profitable to break up families by the sale of slaves, avoiding such breakups was part of the ideology of paternalism—as was the sale of some slaves in order to maintain social control by the threat of breaking up families.

Although a case study of Edgefield District has confirmed the existence of patriarchal families for both blacks and whites in the antebellum South, structural differences in household and family between whites and blacks appeared after the Civil War and some of these differences had their roots in the antebellum period. Scholars have perhaps been too quick in attributing the fragmentation of the ghetto family to slavery, however. The slave family existed despite adversity, and under the circumstances their devotion to the family ideal was heroic.

Careful study of the elusive and scarce materials for the slave family provides a background for an understanding of the postbellum Afro-American family. Four implications can be drawn from this study. First, stable Afro-

American families existed, and were highly valued by blacks under slavery. Second, as they struggled for stability and continuity, Afro-American families faced a number of obstacles inherent in their slave condition, obstacles not shared by whites. Third, there are no grounds for assuming that slavery left a lasting legacy of weakness in the Afro-American family. In fact, the persistence of family patterns and ideals in spite of adversity suggests the opposite, that difficult circumstances reinforced the Afro-American commitment to the family ideal. In the historiography of the slave family, scholars have incorrectly deduced that present-day conditions are the results of slavery, but the slave family does not prefigure the twentieth-century family. Fourth, the complex legacy of slavery for the black family can be uncovered, not by making deductions from slave conditions to explain postslavery conditions, but by examining how the Afro-American family evolved after emancipation. Such an examination shows that the antebellum legacy was more complex and elusive than has hitherto been recognized and that, although a critical one, it was only one among a number of factors that shaped the black family in the years after emancipation.

ARTHUR SIMKINS

Born in Virginia in 1742, Arthur Simkins was a founder of Edgefield, a captain in the
American Revolution, member of the Provincial Congress, and county court judge.
(Photograph courtesy of Mr. Augustus T. Graydon.)

STONEWARE JAR BY DAVE THE POTTER
Dave Potter, a slave artisan who lived and worked in Edgefield from 1780 to 1863, created this stoneware jar with an ash glaze. Dave inscribed this jar, "Pretty little girl on the virge / volca[n]ic mountain how they burge" and signed the work, "Lm Aug 24 1857 Dave."
(Photograph courtesy of Dr. George Terry, Director, McKissick Museum, University of South Carolina.)

CHARLOTTE SIMKINS

A former slave of Arthur Simkins (1818–63), Charlotte Simkins bore his son Paris.
She later married another slave, George Simkins, a founder and leader of the black
Baptist church, Macedonia
(Photograph courtesy of Mr. and Mrs. Charles Bruce Bailey, Sr.)

PARIS SIMKINS
*Born a slave in 1849 in Edgefield, Paris Simkins trained as a barber and went with
the Confederate troops to the battlefield. During Reconstruction he was a state
legislator and second in command of the state militia.*
(Photograph courtesy of Mr. and Mrs. Charles Bruce Bailey, Sr.)

MARY ANN SIMKINS AND DAUGHTER MATTIE R.
*Born a slave in 1850 in Edgefield, Mary Ann Noble married Paris Simkins in 1868.
Mattie was the fifth of sixteen children. Mary Ann Simkins died in 1916.
(Photograph courtesy of Mr. and Mrs. Charles Bruce Bailey, Sr.)*

LUCY PETWAY HOLCOMBE PICKENS

*Born in Tennessee in 1832, the legendary Texas beauty Lucy Holcombe was twenty-six
years old when she married the twice-widowed fifty-three-year-old wealthy
Edgefieldian Francis W. Pickens. The beautiful Lucy had a Confederate company
named after her and her picture appeared on the Confederate hundred dollar bill.
(Photograph courtesy of Mrs. Judge Jane Greer.)*

MARIA PICKENS AND MATTHEW CALBRAITH BUTLER

Maria Pickens, born in 1833, was the eldest daughter of Francis W. Pickens and his first wife, Margaret Eliza Simkins. She married Matthew Calbraith Butler, born in 1836, grandson of General William Butler, who had been Maria's grandfather Eldred Simkins's opponent in the congressional election to replace John C. Calhoun. This is their wedding picture of 1858
(Photograph courtesy of Miss Ellen I. Butler.)

EDGEFIELD COURT HOUSE

Erected in 1839 from plans by Robert Mills, the courthouse and the town square have been the scene of cultural, political, and social gatherings significant to the entire state and region. The photograph, which appeared on a postcard, had to be taken after 1902 when the present probate office was constructed next to the courthouse.
(Courtesy of Mr. and Mrs. George Hodges.)

TRINITY EPISCOPAL CHURCH
Edmund B. Bacon deeded property for the church. Prominent families of state and national importance (Pickens, Butler, Brooks, Wigfall) were members.

MACEDONIA BAPTIST CHURCH

When Afro-Americans left the Edgefield Village Baptist Church in 1868, they founded the Macedonia Baptist Church just across a hill. Reconstruction black state legislators Lawrence Cain and Paris Simkins were among the founding members.

ROSELANDS

Roselands, the plantation house of Whitfield Brooks, is located south of Ninety Six in the Cambridge community (originally a cluster of large plantations) on one of the highest elevations of Greenwood County.

ROSELAND TENANT AND SLAVE CABIN

The farm shed in the background is reputed to have been a slave cabin on the Roseland plantation. On the tractor in the foreground is General McDuffie Anthony, a tenant on the farm.

GRANITEVILLE MILL VILLAGE HOUSE

In 1846, pioneer industrialist William Gregg built this house for employees in his model mill village Graniteville. Each single-family home had its own lot for a vegetable garden and flowers. Gregg maintained that he "intended to give to the inhabitants a taste for the beautiful, and to encourage among the operatives a pleasant rivalry in making their homes agreeable."

(Photograph by Carl Julien from Ninety Six: Landmarks of South Carolina's Last Frontier *[copyright © 1950 by the University of South Carolina Press], reproduced by permission of the publisher.)*

SLAVE CABIN
This house, originally used by a slave family on the Blocker plantation in Edgefield, was later used by tenant families.

TENANT HOUSES
These two tenant houses date back to the nineteenth century.

5. The Free Afro-American in Antebellum Edgefield

*In the communities of free Negroes . . . families took on an institutional
character. Economic competency, culture, and achievement gave these
families a special status and became the source of a tradition which has been
transmitted to succeeding generations.*

E. Franklin Frazier,
The Free Negro Family

Most free black families in South Carolina in the early part of the nineteenth
century descended from free ancestors. Some were the descendants of slaves
who gained their freedom during the colonial era. Others had been freed
during a brief period of liberalization inspired by the Revolution. In addition,
many light-skinned "free people of color," like many of their white countrymen, fled Toussaint L'Ouverture's Haitian revolution in 1792 and, despite bans
on the "French Negroes," entered through the ports of Charleston and Savannah. Furthermore, the economic uncertainty between the collapse of the indigo
trade and rise of the cotton culture encouraged a few masters to free slaves.
The majority of the free black population, however, derived from the manumission of mulatto children (usually the result of unions between masters and
their slave mistresses). Some masters acted out of affection; others, to excul-
pate their guilt.

After the prohibition of manumission in 1820, most requests to the state
legislature for a slave's freedom were denied.[1] One of the most fervent appeals
to the state legislature for the manumission of a South Carolina slave was made
during the excitement of the Mexican War. Edgefield legislator B. C. Yancey
brought David L. Adams's petition to free his slave Charles before the General
Assembly in 1847. The petition told how Adams's son Lt. David Adams, one
of the Edgefield Volunteers of the Palmetto Regiment, had been killed in
action in Mexico. Charles stood vigil over his dead master's body day and
night, leaving his side only to help with the wounded on the battlefield. The
petition was rejected, however. After 1820 increase in the free black population came from children born of white mothers and free black women.[2]

Given the increasing hysteria over slavery after 1850, it is perhaps surprising that free blacks stayed in Edgefield, but many had reason to remain. Some lacked the capital or skills necessary to establish themselves in a city, and others preferred to remain with friends and slave members of their families, since after 1830 a decision to leave the state was irrevocable. Free blacks were culturally Southerners; almost all were native South Carolinians, and many were native Edgefieldians. Despite increased tensions in the 1850s, the laws concerning free blacks in South Carolina were still more lenient than those of other southern states. Even after legislation in 1820 and 1840 restricted their civil and political rights, free Afro-Americans were still guaranteed rights of life, liberty, and property. Free blacks owned their labor, could marry and raise families, and could move and live anywhere in the state.

In Edgefield District free blacks made up approximately 1 percent of the black population, but they were more important in the community than their numbers would suggest. Their success in farming and the skilled trades contradicted the contention of some whites that blacks lacked the necessary competence to be free. To the 24,000 slaves and 15,653 whites in Edgefield District at the time of the Civil War, the 173 free blacks were a reminder that an alternative to slavery did exist.[3]

At midcentury Edgefield District's free black population numbered 285, or about 2 percent of South Carolina's free black population. Between 1850 and 1860 the number of free blacks in Edgefield decreased by 112. The editor of the *Advertiser* bragged about Edgefield that "free blacks do not flourish well on her soil."[4] In 1860, when Edgefield stood third in South Carolina in number of whites and fourth in number of slaves, the district ranked fifteenth of thirty in free black population. Since the district harbored such proslavery writers and advocates of secession as George McDuffie, Louis T. Wigfall, Preston Brooks, James Henry Hammond, and Francis W. Pickens, this decline is hardly surprising: free blacks were always weakest in areas of strong proslavery sentiment.[5] Moreover, just across the river lay Augusta, with its greater freedom and opportunity.[6]

Unlike free blacks in large cities, those in the up-country left few records. No free black voluntary association existed comparable to Charleston's Brown Fellowship Society, and no free black newspaper was published comparable to the New Orleans *Tribune*; as far as is known, no free black kept a diary, accumulated letters, or created other manuscript records in Edgefield.[7] Few surviving records even mention this tiny minority. A prolific diarist, James Henry Hammond only briefly acknowledged the free blacks in his own community; a single entry in his extensive diary mentioned riding through a free black settlement located near a swamp.[8] A Catholic priest traveling between neighboring Abbeville and Edgefield noted that he baptized a mulatto free man about to be hung for murdering his wife.[9] And a Barnwell District grand jury petitioning against adultery indicted a free black woman along with several whites and complained of interracial liaisons.[10] But by far the majority of commentators on antebellum Edgefield simply said nothing on the subject. While Iveson Brookes railed against the free blacks of the North, he did not even notice those in his own neighborhood.[11] At times, one wonders if in a society marked by the peculiar institution the existence of the free black was even recognized.

As they did throughout the state of South Carolina (except for the enclave in Charleston), free blacks in Edgefield District lived in rural areas. In 1860 only 3,604 of the 9,914 free blacks in South Carolina lived in the fifteen communities listed in the 1860 census as towns and cities. Moreover, most of the towns listed were rural villages, hubs of agricultural regions like the hamlets of Edgefield and Hamburg. Edgefield, the larger of the two, had a total population of 518 excluding slaves in 1860. Southern planters generally insisted that their towns be off-limits for slaves, and since they believed all blacks should be slaves, towns were off-limits for the free blacks as well.[12] As a result, free blacks could find little work in the rural hamlets, and those who ventured into the isolated villages beat a hasty retreat. Only one free black household, a woman and her three children, resided among the whites of Edgefield Court House. Seven free blacks resided in Hamburg. In Edgefield and Hamburg free black men established not a single independent male-headed household. In 1860 the oldest "urban" free black man was seventeen-year-old mechanic Elvin Boss, who lived in his fifty-five-year-old free mother's household with his two younger sisters. None of the other 162 free blacks in the district lived in communities as large as either of these. In the up-country, free black family life was rural life.[13]

In general, the Edgefield antebellum free black community was composed of rural, light-skinned persons; a large proportion of the households and families were headed by women. The proportion of nuclear, extended, and augmented family types were less for the antebellum free blacks than the whites; proportionately more black individuals lived alone (see Figure 5-1). In addition, the proportions of one-parent families and female heads among free blacks were much higher than for whites. In 1850 most free blacks lived in neighborhoods dominated by landless whites.[14] In 1860 free blacks were integrated more evenly with whites of varying wealth categories.[15] Even more striking was the shift in concentrations of free blacks during the decade. Free blacks were much less likely to live near each other and more likely to live interspersed among the whites in 1860 than in 1850.[16]

Landowners

Work was more plentiful in the countryside, and like most other residents of Edgefield District, free blacks labored on the land. Only a few free blacks

Figure 5–1. Free Black Household Structure, 1850 and 1860

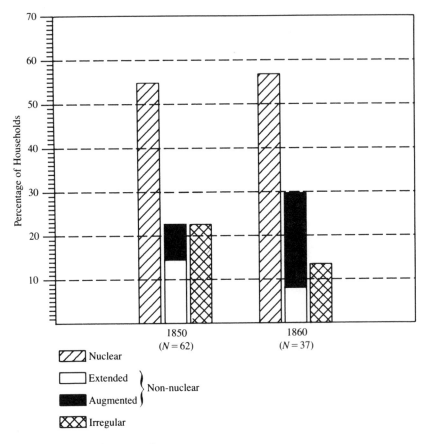

Note: See Table 5–1 for notes and sources.

owned their own land or merited the census designation of "farmer," a term of esteem generally reserved for whites (see Table 5-2).[17] Those blacks who did own land were at the top of the local black social structure.[18] Land ownership and the ideal of the self-sufficient yeoman took on special significance for the antebellum free black. Despite constant reminders of their African lineage and efforts to label them aliens, all Edgefield free blacks had been born in the United States—almost all in South Carolina. Owning land confirmed their nativity and provided a place with which to identify.

Because land was important symbolically as well as economically for the antebellum free black, Edgefield free blacks purchased land as they could. During the decade from 1850 to 1860, the number and proportion of white and

Table 5-1. Selected Characteristics of Free Black Households by Household Structure, 1850 and 1860
(actual numbers shown with selected characteristics)

	1850		1860	
	Nuclear ($N=34$)	Non-nuclear ($N=14$)	Nuclear ($N=21$)	Non-nuclear ($N=11$)
Male-headed	11	5	13	5
Spouse present	11	4	13	5
Children present	31[a]	9[b]	18	8
Children and both parents	10	3	11	5

Note: 22.6 percent (14) of the 1850 and 13.5 percent (5) of the 1860 households were nonfamilies: solitary, irregular, or institutions. Of these 14 in 1850, 3 were male-headed; of the 5 in 1860, 1 was male-headed (1850, $N=62$; 1860, $N=37$).
a. In addition there is one 1850 nuclear family of siblings.
b. In addition 3 extended 1850 families were composed of siblings.
Source: Edgefield Data Base.

free black landowners increased in number, although the free black and white population as a whole declined (see Figure 5-2). In 1850 only three free blacks (5 percent of free black household heads) owned real estate, with a total worth of two thousand dollars. Ten years later, thirteen free blacks (eleven of whom were household heads) owned land, worth a total of nearly nine thousand dollars.[19]

Free blacks moved frequently. Most of the free blacks who lived in Edgefield in 1850 were not there in 1860. But free black landowners, generally more prosperous than their white neighbors, stayed put, and they and their descendants persisted during the decade and transferred land ownership within the family. Free black Harry Todd, a shoemaker, left Augusta with his family in 1819. White citizens of the city gave Todd papers testifying to his good character and recommending Todd's free black family "to the humanity and protection of all persons among whom they may travel or settle."[20] The Todds moved to Edgefield. In 1850, eighty-three-year-old Todd owned land valued at five hundred dollars and two slaves. His wife Peggy and daughter Delia were the only members of his household, and his son-in-law, Benjamin Ardis, a Baptist exhorter, and Martha Todd Ardis, along with Todd's three grandchildren, lived next door on Todd's farm. By 1860, Martha Todd Ardis's parents and her husband had died, and Martha had inherited the family's two-hundred-

Figure 5–2. Heads of Households Owning Land, 1850 and 1860

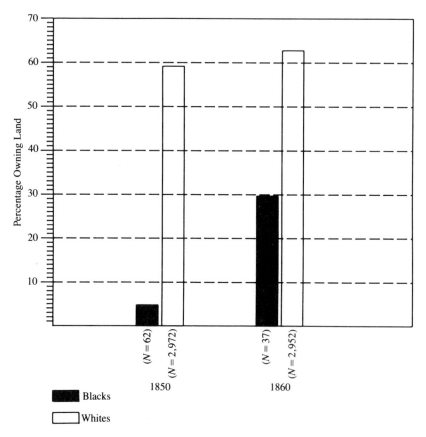

Blacks

Whites

Source: Edgefield Data Base.

acre farm and a thirty-three-year-old male slave, possibly her brother-in-law. She headed a household which contained the persons who had resided in Benjamin's household in 1850 and several additional members, including her children—young Ben, fifteen; Harry, thirteen; William, eleven; Margaret, five—and her sister Delia. Landowners thus provided stability for the free black community. They remained from decade to decade, transferred their land within the family, and perpetuated their names through relatives, just as white landowners did. Two of Martha and Benjamin's children were named for Martha's mother and father and the oldest son for Benjamin himself.

In 1860 all free black landowners listed personal estates. One had only fifty dollars, but the rest had one hundred dollars or more; most had more than three hundred dollars. Martha Ardis had twenty-two hundred dollars (most of these

Table 5-2. *Occupations of Free Blacks, 1850 and 1860*

	N Gainfully Employed			N Household Heads		
	1850[a]	1860		1850[a]	1860	
Occupation		Male	Female		Male	Female
Farmer	4	5		4	4	
Farming		10	5		4	5
Skilled	9	6		3	3	
Laborer	14	19	3	7	6	2
Domestic	0		7			5
No occupation listed				48[b]	2	6
Total	27	40	15	62	19	18

a. Employed for 1850 is identical to males employed since the census did not report the occupations of women in 1850.

b. Includes all forty-three of the 1850 free black women who headed households. Thus, only five who have no occupation listed in the 1850 census are men.

Note: For occupational groupings see appendix 2.

Source: Edgefield Data Base.

assets were invested in her slave), which was nearly twice as much as the next wealthiest free black landowner.

Free black landowners lived in diverse family situations. In 1860, only five landowners had spouses. No landowners lived alone, however. Five had only their immediate family living with them (nuclear families), three had additional relatives (extended families), and five had people in the household who could not be identified as related to the landowner (augmented families).

Free black landowners generally lived scattered among white landowners throughout Edgefield and not near other free blacks. Their white neighbors were a diverse lot: most stood in the middle ranges of wealth, but some came from the poorest group, and a few derived from the wealthiest group. The neighborhoods of free black landowners varied markedly in 1860. For example, of the four "farmers" who were landowners, one had four white neighbors who were wealthy, another had three; two free black "farmers" had only one wealthy white neighbor. One free black had three poor neighbors, while the other three free blacks had only one.[21]

Farm Operators

Less than half of the thirteen free black landowners cultivated their own farms. Meanwhile, six other free blacks, who did not own land, farmed land owned by whites or perhaps the free blacks.[22] These landless farm operators were tenant farmers, since they worked land that belonged to someone else.[23] In addition to the six farm tenants, two landowning farmers worked acreage more valuable than that which they owned. W. N. Smith owned land valued at $40, but operated a seventy-six-acre farm valued at $775. George Quarles owned real estate valued at $1,000, but operated a five-hundred-acre farm valued at $2,500. Tenants' personal property ranged in value from fifty dollars to a respectable four hundred dollars, which compared favorably with white household wealth and was even more favorable for the landowning farm operators than for the tenants.[24]

For the six landless Afro-American farm operators and their families, tenancy was not an institution that emerged after the Civil War. In 1860 almost a fourth of all free blacks in Edgefield District lived in families who either worked as full-time land tenants or rented part of the land that they farmed. Though only a minority of antebellum free blacks engaged in tenantry, blacks, like many whites, were familiar with the practice before the war.

The six landowning farm operators and six tenants made up an elite group of free blacks who assumed the responsibilities and risks of working and managing farms.[25] These twelve free black farm operators, both landowners and tenants, had stock and grew crops, which indicated they were self-sufficient and relatively prosperous. The four "farmers" among them were the most affluent. On the eve of the Civil War, Edgefield's free black farmer produced grain crops, cash crops, and food for his family. His household numbered more people than did the average household. He tended to be about ten years older than the average free black head of household, and, generally, the older he was, the more personal and real property he had.

Although newly arrived in Edgefield, free black Martin Wilson, a fifty-five-year-old farmer, headed a household of five mulattoes in 1860. He held real estate worth about $450 and personal estate worth $365. Martin farmed forty-five improved acres and forty-four unimproved acres.[26] He worked his entire farm with one mule and with tools valued at $35. He had two milk cows, two other head of cattle, and eighteen hogs. In that year, he slaughtered animals valued at $63, churned twenty-five pounds of butter, made two gallons of wine and two gallons of molasses, and harvested orchard products valued at $7. In addition, he produced twenty-one bushels of peas and beans, five bushels of Irish potatoes, and thirty bushels of sweet potatoes for his family and his farm animals and sold extra produce to neighboring plantations and in the villages. Martin Wilson also had cash crops—two bales of cotton and twenty-five pounds of tobacco. His son Barentine, aged sixteen, was employed on the farm that his father owned. For slaves and whites in Edgefield District, Martin Wilson and the other self-sufficient free black yeoman farmers demonstrated the free black's ability to succeed in the rural South.

The family structure of free black landowners who farmed differed from that of tenant farm operators. Whereas only half the tenants had spouses present in their households, among landowning household heads, all but widow Martha Ardis had a spouse present. Generally, the landowning farming households could better afford to support and employ others, as indicated by the larger number of augmented families among landowning than among tenant farm operators.[27]

The more economically secure they were, the more likely free blacks were to reside among men and women of equal economic status. Half the tenants lived near other free black families, but only one landowning farm operator, a woman, resided near any other free blacks.[28] For both tenant and landowning free black farmers, most neighbors were whites. Free black tenants had slightly wealthier neighbors, from whom they could rent land, but they too lived within easy reach of whites of all classes. In contrast, the free black landowner who farmed independently was most likely to live near whites in the middle ranges of wealth (which included landowning husbandmen, whom the free black landowner most resembled).

Agricultural Laborers

If free black farm operators were few, free black farm laborers were many. In 1850 the terms "laborer" and "farm laborer" delineated subservient positions for Edgefield free blacks, although the census taker also labeled 130 whites the same. Yet in 1850 fourteen of the twenty-seven free black men who listed an occupation (52 percent) and in 1860 twenty of the forty-one males who listed an occupation (49 percent) were laborers and farm laborers.[29] (In 1850 only 9 households or 1.7 percent of all white household heads and in 1860 only 4 percent of all white household heads listed "laborer" or "farm laborer" as occupations.)

Free blacks who signed year-long contracts and had a continuing relationship with a single farmer were generally designated in the census as "farm laborer"; others did not hold steady jobs and took odd jobs and helped out during the planting and harvest seasons. These latter were usually distinguished from the former by the simple label of "laborer." Small farmers—slaveholders and nonslaveholders—found these men and women particularly useful to supplement their labor force. A number of free black laborers lived in white households and worked for wages or for room and board.[30] Many free black laborers thus worked and lived in conditions similar to that of slaves. But others used their position in white households to improve their lot. Most of these free blacks were usually young men, literate, light in color, and propertied, while the members of the host white family were often illiterate. Blacks in white households also tended to be younger than black household heads. Employment within a white household appears to have been a step toward earning enough money to set up one's own household.

Free black "laborers"—as opposed to "farm laborers"—who became household heads had remarkably stable families. In 1850 six of the seven had spouses present in their homes. Ten years later all of the "laborers" had spouses, but the two "farm laborers" who had worked independently remained single.[31] In both 1850 and 1860 these younger and poorer families tended to be nuclear; they could ill afford to support more than their immediate family members.

Although none of the household heads who were specifically labeled "farm laborers" resided near any other freed blacks, half the six designated simply as "laborers" lived near three other free black families and yet another lived among four free black families in 1860. Thus, the poorest and least skilled of employed free black household heads were most likely to live in close proximity to one another. "Laborer" household heads were also most likely to live among the poorest whites, whom they most resembled in wealth and status, and least likely to live among the richest whites. Although one free black laborer did own land, in 1860 only two of the seven household heads had more than fifty dollars personal estate and none of them operated a farm.

Skilled Free Blacks

Most of the free blacks worked on the land, but a few found employment as semiskilled and artisans. Only one skilled workman, a seventeen-year-old mechanic residing in his mother's household, lived within the corporate limits of a town; all the other craftsmen—black mechanics, wheelwrights, sawyers, shoemakers, blacksmiths, draymen, and shinglers—lived in rural farming areas. In 1850 two and in 1860 three male heads of households practiced skilled trades. In both censuses all the skilled free blacks were listed as literate.

In 1850 both skilled free black household heads (all three if the Baptist exhorter, Benjamin Ardis, is included among the skilled) had wives and children, and one had other people living in his household as well. In 1860 the mechanic and blacksmith both were married, but only the older of the two, the mechanic, had children. He also had other relatives and whites living in his household, since he operated the most valuable farm that any free black owned and could afford to support, as well as employ, extra people on the farm. The shingler, the least skilled and only black (as opposed to mulatto) artisan, lived alone.

No free black artisan household head lived near other free black families.

Instead, they lived near whites for whom they worked. Their white neighbors tended to be in the middle and especially upper wealth ranges. These white slaveowners, not owning enough slaves to hold slave artisans, hired free black skilled laborers. The shingler and the blacksmith had no poor white neighbors. The landowning mechanic, however, who was married to a white woman and had other whites in his household, had four poor white neighbors. The blacksmith owned personal property valued at twenty-five dollars, while the shingler and the landowning mechanic each held about three-hundred-dollar personal estates. With the probable exception of the blacksmith, free black artisans owned all their tools.

Family and Work

The general poverty of the free black community meant that, like at least a quarter of all antebellum whites, everyone in the family worked, sometimes outside the household. Poverty also prevented many free blacks from establishing their own independent households and prevented free black householders from taking in boarders. Yet despite hardship, in 1850 nearly a third of the households (somewhat fewer in 1860) contained people who were not part of the nuclear family.[32] In 1850 five households included boys aged five to seventeen who were not family members. Four households had extra girls of this age. The youngest of these children did not contribute to the household income. Of households that included people who were not immediate family members, only three had nonfamily members who were employed (two of the three households had two persons working).

When old enough to work, some young free black men and women lived with and labored for whites, especially for the poorer whites and the small slaveholders, who welcomed additional hands at little expense. A white non-slaveowning tenant farmer, R. Carter, lived between another white landless farmer and a white small farmer with one slave. In 1860 Carter's household included seven white members and Hannah Roten, a twenty-year-old mulatto laborer. (Roten does not appear among the 1850 free blacks.) Carter farmed 50 improved acres and 550 unimproved acres with a total value of eighteen hundred dollars. Roten labored in the fields alongside members of the Carter family.

Other whites with little or no land or personal estate sometimes had adult free blacks living in their households. In 1860, free black Thomas Robinson, a twenty-year-old literate wheelwright, lived in the household of R. Turner, a forty-seven-year-old illiterate white man. Turner was landless but listed "farming" as his profession. He valued his personal estate at only fifty dollars. The other eight members of the household were white and much closer in age to Robinson than to Turner—the eldest of the eight was Polly Turner, age twenty-four. A similar case was that of Ezekiel Germen, who in 1850 resided in a household with his free black older brother and mother. In 1860, Ezekiel was eighteen years old, literate, and "farming." He lived with William Grisham, William's wife Martha, their two children, and William's brother John. Grisham was a miller who owned no land and who had a personal estate worth only fifty dollars, and his younger brother John, like Germen, was property-less and "farming."

Free Black Women

Like most women in Edgefield, free black women worked, and like most free black men in the district, most free black women worked the land. Forty-five percent of all free black women household heads in 1860 and about 39 percent of all free black women with an occupation or who headed a family in the household of another person were engaged in agriculture.[33] Free black women participated in the 1860 Edgefield work force in nonagricultural occupations as well. About 30 percent of the women household heads in 1860, and about the same share of all women in the work force, worked in the traditional domestic occupations—governesses, seamstresses, and domestic servants. All the free black women in this category were literate, and all but one, a sixty-five-year-old seamstress, were mulattoes. Once married, free black women worked at home. Whereas young single free black adults lived and worked in white households, wives of only two free black household heads, one a laborer and the other a mechanic, reported occupations in 1860—both were domestic servants. The wife of the landowning mechanic was white. The only free black wife to be employed outside the home lived with her "laborer" husband and five children. In Edgefield the rural free black male household head was employed; his wife worked at home alongside other family members.

Free black women headed a high proportion of all free black households. In 1850 about two-thirds (43) of Edgefield District free black households were headed by women, compared to 15 percent of white Edgefield households. During the last antebellum decade, however, this situation changed. In 1850, 45 percent (19) of all adult free black men (twenty years of age and over) and 49 percent (39) of all adult women were household heads. In 1860, free black men were much more likely to be heads of households than were free black women. In that year 58 percent (19) of all adult free black men and 35 percent (18) of all free black women headed households. In addition, in both decades more free black women than men headed single-member households. As free blacks without family ties were the most likely to leave, the outmigration of free blacks from Edgefield left the district with proportionately more male-headed, two-partner free black households.

By 1860 there was one more male than female household head, but in both

1850 and in 1860 significantly more free black women than men headed families within households headed by other individuals. In 1850 no married free black couples lived in the household of another person. Excluding sibling families, twelve family groupings (a parent and at least one child) lived with other households. Of these, only two were male headed; ten were female-headed families. In 1860 two couples lived in households headed by other persons. Both couples had children. There were three other one-parent, female-headed families, in addition to seven separate sibling families; all resided in households headed by others in 1860.

Because they were more likely to work as domestics for whites, free black female household heads were also more likely than male household heads to live among the wealthiest whites. Although most independent female households lived like other free blacks, dispersed among the white population, they were slightly more likely to have free black neighbors than were male-headed households.

The most distinctive feature about independent free black female household heads was the extraordinary proportion of the free black wealth they controlled. In antebellum Edgefield, where white women owned only a small proportion of the total white wealth, free black women controlled a significant amount. In 1850 and 1860 white women controlled about a tenth of all white-owned land.[34] By comparison, in 1850 black women owned three-fourths of the land held by Afro-Americans, and in 1860, nearly half. In 1860 white women owned only a little more than a tenth of all personal property; of the thirty-nine free blacks who owned $44,096 in personal property, eighteen women owned nearly nine-tenths.[35] Even when Susan Moore, who owned thirty-five thousand dollars in personal estate (nearly 16 times the amount of the next largest share), is excluded from the analysis, the remaining seventeen women still owned nearly half the 1860 personal estate.[36] Women controlled 82 percent of the total free black wealth (real and personal).[37]

Although free black women controlled the largest share of antebellum free black wealth, women still remained the most vulnerable, especially those who had little wealth. The years immediately preceding the Civil War were particularly hard on antebellum free Afro-Americans, especially women household heads. Elizabeth Bug, a free Edgefield black, petitioned the South Carolina legislature in 1859 that for a year she had desired to become the slave of W. P. Hill in Greenwood, just to the northeast of Edgefield District. She asked the legislature to make the necessary arrangements. Lucy Dennis gave the legislature no choice. She simply announced in her petition in 1860 that she and her five children had become the slaves of Dr. Asa Langford of Edgefield.[38]

Color within the Community

As it did throughout the Americas, skin color played a significant role in the structure of the society and the relations between persons in Edgefield's free black community. In 1850, 55 percent of all free blacks were mulatto, and by 1860 that proportion had increased to nearly three-fourths.

In many ways blacks and mulattoes mixed easily in the free black community. In 1850, while a majority of free people were mulatto, all the landowners (three) were black. Studies of cities such as Charleston found the opposite: antebellum mulattoes owned most of the land.[39] In 1860 black and mulatto landownership was more similar than different. Three of the thirteen free Afro-American landowners were black, and these three owned a fourth (the non-mulattoes' proportion of the free Afro-American population) of all free black landed wealth. In addition, black household heads owned nearly a third of the landed value of the eleven free Afro-American household heads.[40]

When the value of personal estate is added to the value of land, it appears at first glance that the economic situations of blacks and mulattoes differed sharply in 1860. Blacks owned only about a tenth of all Afro-American wealth in Edgefield. As with women's wealth, however, when the thirty-five thousand dollars in personal estate that one individual mulatto, Susan Moore, had invested in slaves and slave houses is discounted, the adjusted black proportion was nearly a third. Judged by overall wealth, the darker-skinned free blacks in rural Edgefield were as wealthy as the lighter-skinned free blacks. And except for Susan Moore, free Afro-Americans, whether mulatto or black, were not wealthy either in slaves or land.

Black household heads were slightly more likely to have other free black neighbors than were mulattoes. Moreover, although free people of color lived interspersed with whites throughout the district, black household heads were more likely to live among the very wealthiest whites (which included the largest slaveowners) than were the mulattoes, but less likely to live among the next wealthiest quartile of whites. Mulatto household heads were also slightly more likely to have poor white neighbors.

More striking differences existed in the marriage patterns of the darker-skinned and lighter-skinned free Afro-Americans in Edgefield. Blacks had a difficult time finding marriage partners. Only eight blacks, compared to twenty mulattoes, had free spouses in 1850, and seven blacks, compared to twenty-seven mulattoes, found free wives or husbands in 1860. In 1850, when Edgefield counted fifty-eight blacks and sixty-eight mulattoes over the age of twenty in the free black community, only a small percentage of all free people, black or mulatto, had spouses who were black. Blacks composed 48 percent of the marriageable population, but only 17 percent of the spouses. In 1860, when the free population included twenty-one blacks and fifty-four mulattoes over the age of twenty, the gap was less severe: 38 percent of the marriageable Afro-American population and about a quarter of the spouses were black. Still, in both 1850 and 1860 mulatto free men were more likely to marry white women than they were to marry black women.

Free Blacks and Slaves

The scarcity of free black (black and mulatto) spouses suggests that close ties existed between free blacks and slaves and that perhaps most free blacks married slaves (unions which would not be revealed by census records). Two former slaves, both dark-hued, told of marriages in their families between a slave and an Edgefield free black. Ida Bryant did not clearly remember her grandfather, Hansen Terry, but she noted that he "was a free man," who "molded his own money." Her father, Major Terry, was a slave of Bill Talbot but "slipped off from his master."[41] Annette Milledge, on the other hand, was precise about her free black father. She remembered that he had been born in Virginia, and "did his part by his 21 children." According to the former slave, her "father was free, he didn't belong to none of dem. He work round de depot and different places, run dray and different things, never been in slavery. He bought my shoes."[42]

Free blacks had slave wives, and there may have been free black women who had slave husbands as well. Two free black women in 1860 owned male slaves, who may have been spouses or relatives.[43] In neighboring Newberry District, a woman who had been free before the Civil War reported that her mother had been married to a slave. She and her mother had worked as servants, though they were treated as slaves, for Maj. John P. Kinard, who also owned land and slaves in Edgefield.[44] Prescilla Jessup, a nonmulatto free black woman with several children, owned substantial property in Abbeville District, just north of Edgefield. In 1845 she petitioned the South Carolina Legislature to free her husband, John, whom she had purchased in 1834. She had been married to John for thirty years. Because children followed the mother's status, their children were free. However, Prescilla feared that if she preceded her husband in death, John could be made a slave of another owner and their children would be without protection.[45]

The patterns of free blacks and mulattoes showed that the darker-hued free people were more likely to have intermarried with slaves than were the lighter-skinned ones.[46] Free black Delia Todd and the slave man of the same age owned by Delia's sister, Martha Ardis, fit this pattern. The same was true for the solitary free black shingler who lived by himself among large slaveowners and for James Drayton, a farm laborer and the only nonwhite member of John J. Jennings's household. Drayton was a thirty-year-old free black man. Jennings owned thirteen slaves, including a forty-seven-year-old female, a twenty-seven-year-old female, and a fifteen-year-old female (the oldest male was only thirteen). It is possible that one of the slaves was Drayton's wife.[47]

As family ties suggest, despite the difference in legal status, little distinguished the lives of most rural free blacks from those of slaves. For example, even if free, the rural Afro-American worshiped with his slave brethren. The free black members of the Bethany Baptist Church took their place in the balcony at the back of the church with their slave brethren.[48]

Moreover, white attitudes also pushed slaves and free blacks together. As early as 1835, Edgefield's George McDuffie, while serving as governor, was prepared to reduce free blacks to slaves. As McDuffie argued before the General Assembly, "that the African negro is destined by Providence to occupy this condition of servile dependence is not less manifest. It is marked on the face, stamped on the skin, and evinced by the intellectual inferiority and natural improvidence of this race. They have all the qualities that fit them for slaves, and not one of those that would fit them to be freemen. . . . Emancipation would be a positive curse, depriving them of a guardianship essential to their happiness. . . . Amalgamation is abhorrent to every sentiment of nature; and if they remain as a separate caste, whether endowed with equal privileges or not, they will become our masters or we must resume the mastery over them."[49]

In 1850, anticipating secession, South Carolina Governor Whitemarsh B. Seabrook wanted to rid the state of all free blacks who were not landowners or slaveowners.[50] In 1859, at the fall term of the Edgefield grand jury, the chairman told the judge, "We respectfully present the free-negroes as a common nuisance." Jurors asked that a law be passed that required all free Afro-Americans either to leave the state or become slaves, and that mulatto children of white women be sold as slaves.[51]

During the Civil War the Confederacy also conscripted Edgefield free blacks to work on fortresses with slaves. When Yancy Kennady and Dick Grantt, two Edgefield free blacks, worked for the Confederacy, they were listed with over four hundred slaves conscripted in 1864, and did the same work as the slaves.[52] Even in earlier years, white records generally listed free blacks with slaves. Listed by first name and identified as simply "free," Tom was the only antebellum free black to be included in the membership lists of Big Stevens Baptist Church. Along with other church members he was baptized in the waters of the stream that flowed by the church. Tom's name appears with the four slaves who were identified along with their owners. In the 1811 church register, Tom is listed with the male slaves.[53]

Free Blacks and Whites

Not all relations between free blacks and whites were hostile. Some whites continued to free their slaves, despite legal prohibitions, and maintained friendly relations thereafter. Often these friendly relations smacked of paternalism; sometimes they were literally so, as the large mulatto majority in the free black population indicated continued sexual relationships between whites and blacks in antebellum Edgefield District.[54]

Not all of these matches were between rich planters and poor blacks. Among free blacks and yeomen whites, who were in somewhat the same situation economically, friendly, sometimes egalitarian, relations could be found at the lower end of the social scale. Many blacks lived in racially mixed households (sixty-seven blacks in thirty-three mixed households in 1850 and sixty-six blacks in thirty mixed households in 1860). Whites headed a substantial minority of these racially mixed households; about twenty free blacks resided with whites. Of the households headed by whites in 1850, twenty-seven included one or more of forty-four free blacks; in 1860, twenty-one included one or more of thirty-eight free blacks. In 1850, six households headed by blacks contained ten whites, and in 1860, nine households headed by blacks contained twenty-five white members. Most mixed households were simply the result of whites hiring cheap free black labor, but some derived from family relationships and suggest interracial kinship ties (see Table 5-3).

Such relations could be complex. In 1850, Paten Kerwin, age thirty-eight, was the only free black and the only male in a household with three white women. A mulatto, he listed no occupation and owned no real estate. Margaret Kerwin, sixty-four years of age, headed the household, which also contained her relatives Druscilla, forty-four, and Margaret, twenty-four. The elder Margaret, the only person in the household with land, owned real estate valued at $740. By 1860, Paten Kerwin had become a "farmer" who owned real estate valued at $840 and personal estate valued at $1,158. Aged forty-nine, he was the only other member of a household headed by Druscilla Kerwin, aged fifty-three, who owned real estate valued at $1,910 and personal estate valued at $9,663. She was listed in the agricultural manuscript census returns as the operator of a 275-acre farm valued at $2,750—this figure was the total value of the real estate owned by Paten and Druscilla. Their closest neighbors included another household of Kerwins, a white landless overseer, and Druscilla's seven slaves (one of whom probably belonged to Paten), who lived in her two slave houses.

In 1860 four white households contained free black children who were members of the white family.[55] For example, John Allen was a thirty-year-old miller with a personal estate of $20. Twenty-five-year-old Mary was listed after John in the household order and then the first nonwhite member, fourteen-year-old Franklin Allen. After Franklin came a white boy, six-year-old

Table 5-3. Estimated Relationships of Free Blacks to Whites in Mixed Households, 1850 and 1860

	1850	1860
Black Headed		
White spouse (some with children)	4	6
White grandchildren	1	1
Probably related, different names	0	1
Probably not related	1	0
Laborer	0	1
Total	6	9
White Headed		
Black spouse (some with children)	4	1
Black children	2	1
Sibling	0	1
Name same, undetermined relationship	2	3
Guardian	2	4
Laborer	3	8
Unknown, but probably not related	17	3
Total	30	21

Source: Edgefield Data Base.

Robert Allen, then a four-year-old mulatto girl, Narcissa Allen, and finally a one-year-old white female, Marcilla Allen. Of the four households in this group, the one female head of household was the only illiterate person in any family; of course none of the free black children attended school. All four families were landless and lived in poor neighborhoods.

In 1850 several free blacks headed households containing white children. Free black Rubin Brown's wife and children were white. Jonathan Williams, a forty-five-year-old black laborer, was enumerated with children Samuel, twenty-one, Ansabel, eighteen, and Delila, twelve. In his household, listed after his own children, were a white woman, Sally Walker, aged twenty-eight, and her three daughters, Martha, ten, Lydia, five, and Margaret, two. The two-year-old Margaret was listed as a mulatto, and might possibly have been named for Jonathan's seventy-eight-year-old mother, Margaret Williams, the last person listed in this household.

In 1860 a mulatto governess headed a household with three white members, all children under six years of age, who bore her surname. Elbert Dunn was a mulatto head of household. He and his mulatto wife, Rebecca, had five mulatto children in their household. Also in the household was nine-year-old white Cornelia Robertson. In contrast to the dispersed pattern of other free blacks, the Dunn clan, five related families, lived near each other and included three mixed marriages. Sixty-year-old Martha Dunn, washerwoman and the only non-native South Carolinian, was the only female household head in this family. Three of her sons, all laborers with no real estate, had married white women. Two of the men were illiterate, but all three of the white women they had married could read and write.

Besides the three Dunn couples, four mixed marriages existed in the district in 1860. Young persons headed five of these seven households. Two others were headed by David Chavers and mechanic Jerrot Abney, both free black farm operators. Both of these men had more personal property than anyone in the other mixed marriages. The existence of older, wealthier racially mixed couples may indicate that age brought acceptance by the white community as well as time and opportunity to accumulate capital.

Between 1850 and 1860, while more free black men married white women, the number of white men married to free black women in Edgefield declined from four to one. In 1850 perhaps the best-known white with a free black wife was Henry Shultz, who gave his occupation as "founder of Hamburg." Shultz's eccentricities are still remarked upon. Meriah Shultz was noted as black—not mulatto, as were the other Afro-American wives of white men. In 1856, the Reverend John Cornish baptized the four children of a married couple whom he described in his diary as "the Father white—Mother coloured."[56]

In 1860 one census entry unmistakably indicated a white man with a free black wife. The woman, Iurana Reddy, was twelve years older than her husband, Bazil Reddy, and their two children, both under five, were recorded in the census as white. In three other cases, however, white men lived in households with free Afro-American women.[57] The proportion of men to women in the "marriageable" age group of twenty to sixty years of age for Edgefield District in 1860 favored men in the white, free black, and slave populations. In the rural district of Edgefield, marriageable men were at a premium; this explains, in part, why so many free black women headed households.[58]

Assimilation

The growing number of mixed families contributed to the decline in the free black population from 1840 to 1860. The manuscript census returns show cases of mixed families in which some children were classified as white and some as mulatto. Census enumerators seem to have declared the children white or mulatto on the basis of their physical features.[59] This reinforces the notion that mulattoes passed as whites. In each census from 1840 to 1860 the greatest number of free blacks were under twenty years of age. Many of these children simply "went over" to the white community as they became older. Other free Afro-Americans left Edgefield for the North, Charleston, Savannah, or Augusta.[60] A number of light-skinned postbellum free blacks, including relatives of John Hope from Augusta, moved north and west and passed as white.[61] On the eve of the Civil War, the barriers between whites and free blacks were not as formidable as many have thought.[62]

Many Edgefield District free blacks were classified lighter with time. Men and women recorded as black in 1850 were noted as mulatto in 1860. For example, Fannie Smith, the wealthiest free black landowner in 1850, and her entire household were recorded as black in 1850 but as mulatto in 1860. Benjamin and Martha Ardis and all their children were black in 1850 (Benjamin died before 1860); in 1860 the children were classified as mulatto, while Martha remained black.

This process continued after the war. In 1860 the entire Quarles family claimed to be black, but in 1870 and 1880 most members of this large landowning family claimed to be mulatto. No individual, however, changed classification over the years from mulatto to black. It appears that a black in 1850 had to be quite light to be considered a mulatto, less so in 1860, and even less so after the Civil War.

As Edgefield moved toward the Civil War, it appears light skin carried an increased premium. During this period the proslavery case depended more and more on racial and antiblack arguments. The acceptance of free blacks and their survival in the white-dominated society depended on emphasizing whiteness, no matter how slight.

Some evidence suggests that light-skinned Afro-Americans had some choice in whether they would integrate the white world or be part of the black community in Edgefield. In 1840 militia orders required that "all free male persons of color between the age of eighteen and forty-five" be liable for patrol duty.[63] One does not know to what extent the free blacks participated with the notorious "paddy rollers" before 1840; nor does one know whether, if forced to participate, Edgefield free blacks were sympathetic or hostile to slave brethren. In early spring 1863 the tax collector added a special explanation to Edgefield's tax notice: "Free Negroes not now nor having been in the Confederate service are subject to tax—those from the ages of 15 to 50 years."[64] Most Edgefield free blacks did not elect to fight or work for the Confederacy, however.

After the Civil War some antebellum free Afro-Americans from Edgefield who fought in the Confederate cause were incorporated into the white community. George Tillman, Edgefield representative at the South Carolina constitutional convention, gave evidence of this. Tillman objected to a delegate's proposal to define as "Negro" individuals with "any" African ancestry. The usually negrophobic Tillman stated that there were no pure Caucasians, since every person had ancestors from one of the "colored races," although not necessarily Negroid. Tillman argued that he personally knew families "which had a small degree of Negro ancestry, yet had furnished able soldiers to the Confederacy and were now accepted in white society," and he did not think it necessary to embarrass these families by redefining black. He proposed that an individual with one-fourth or more African ancestry, that is, with one black grandparent, be defined as "Negro."[65]

Harbingers of the Postbellum Rural South

Households headed by free blacks dispersed among all areas populated by whites in 1850 and 1860, but the majority were in areas where middle-class yeoman craftsmen and farmers, landless farmers, and other less affluent whites were located. Free blacks worked the same land as their white neighbors, in the same ways, and with the same success.[66]

Except for color, little distinguished the economic life and standard of living of the antebellum free black in Edgefield from that of yeoman and poor whites. Whites and free blacks ate the same kinds of foods: cornbread, bacon, garden vegetables, and occasional fresh meat. They wore clothes made from the same materials; some free blacks and some whites kept sheep for wool clothing. Blacks and whites wore shoes made by the black cobblers Berryman Kemp and Benjamin Boss. Their homes were made from the same kinds of wood; their roofs, from shingles made by free black Charles Bugg. The more economically secure and occupationally independent of white domination a free black family was, the more likely it was to be a stable two-parent unit. Wealthier free black households were more likely to have other people besides nuclear family members residing in the home.

The social structure and the lives of the antebellum free blacks in rural Edgefield District anticipated the experiences of the masses of freedmen in the immediate postbellum era. In both eras there was a systematic exclusion of males from the small towns. There was significant experience with tenantry, but tenantry was a move up the social ladder from the more widespread experience of laboring on farms owned by whites. General poverty but a stable family and generosity to others in need were evident among the antebellum and postbellum Afro-American population. Although some younger blacks lived in white households, most would live in independent black households and those who did not were working toward that end. The complex variety of race relations in the antebellum free black community recurred in the postbellum world.

Relationships between people sometimes defied racial barriers, and Afro-Americans in Edgefield District were integrated to some extent with both the slave and white communities, although the same free blacks may not have mixed with both slave and white. The 1859 grand jury presentment made it clear that some whites were determined to reduce free Afro-Americans to slave status, while other Edgefield rural folks lived in an integrated world.

Free blacks, who were much less likely to live near other free blacks in 1860 than in 1850, had thus become more spatially integrated with whites in the community. Although they were far fewer in number in 1860 than in 1850, in rural Edgefield free Afro-Americans appear to have prospered in that decade, especially in acquiring land and advancing occupationally. Yet that same decade was a time of growing discrimination against free blacks.

Understanding what happened to free Afro-Americans in the decade 1850–60 helps explain two paradoxes of Reconstruction. Why, when they held political power during Reconstruction, did Afro-Americans not demand more major social reforms, such as redistribution of property? Also, despite the reverses of Reconstruction, why did the black community remain basically optimistic?

In seeking confiscation of the land they had been forced to work or domination in the communities in which they had been subjugated, they would have been demanding not retribution but simple justice. Yet throughout Reconstruction and well into what is now termed the Second Reconstruction, the local Afro-American communities in the South asked simply for the chance to prove themselves acceptable citizens. They asked and expected to be treated just as any other citizen of the community would have been, with an equal chance to earn their way in society.

The answers to these questions may be found partly in the role that free blacks played for slaves and whites before the Civil War. The success of black independent farmers and artisans, who persevered despite white opposition during a hostile decade, was a model for those who had to find new life-styles after emancipation. Some in the antebellum white community had obviously tolerated and even accepted free Afro-Americans in the last decade before the war, and blacks no doubt felt that it could be so for all who were freed from slavery. Edgefield blacks hoped only for their fair share in a democratic political system. Since free blacks after the war were no longer an insignificant numerical minority but made up a majority of the population, however, whites could not afford to tolerate democracy, as events would show.[67]

6. The Culture of Postbellum Afro-American Family Life

"But I don't like it when I hear a man say—be he colored or white—that
we've never had anything, and we've always been so low. We've been without
things, and we've been at the bottom! I agree. But we've been God-fearing.
We've had God; and He's something to have—Someone. And I'll tell you;
we've had each other to turn to."

A rural South Carolina black migrant
to a northern city in Robert Coles, *The South Goes North*

Historians generally treat the Civil War as a major divide in the smooth flow of American history. They study the war as a unique phenomenon, but few scholars have rigorously traced the changes that occurred in southern society because of it.[1]

Before the Civil War, the Edgefield "Minutemen," formed in various Edgefield neighborhoods in fearful anticipation of Lincoln's election, pledged themselves to the defense of Edgefield and "honor, independence, and personal equality." One of these local groups, the Saluda Minutemen, was organized originally on 24 November 1860 with twenty-five members. By their fourth meeting, they had accumulated seventy-four men ready to die for Edgefield. When D. Denny, the group's captain, proposed that the company "offer their services" to the state of South Carolina, he fully expected the entire company to volunteer. Surprisingly, though, only thirty-three members answered that call. Thus, while all were presumably ready to defend Edgefield, less than half were willing to offer their allegiance at that time to the state. The story of how Edgefield changed and gave more allegiance to the Confederacy is an interesting story that must be told elsewhere. The results of the Civil War, however, had an enormous effect on the families of black and white.[2]

The Civil War in Edgefield was not just a rich man's war and a poor man's fight. The sons of the white wealthy, middle class, and poor fought and died. For most Edgefieldians the Civil War was a local affair. From the first call to support a war for southern independence to news of surrender at Appomattox, Edgefieldians interpreted the meaning of the conflict and reacted to its demands from the perspective of their own families, relatives, friends, and the local community. Edgefield's response to the Civil War was an affirmation of community identity. South Carolina perceived grievances, and her men mounted to her defense. For these people the war was not simply to secure slavery or to protect the planters' way of life; it was a matter of honor.

The white plain folk of Edgefield had their own reasons for answering the drums of war. Even if they had no slaves, the nonelite had a stake in the community. Families and kin settled near one another and generally attended the same church in what was termed their "settlement." Generally, at least some relatives owned slaves, and more hoped to someday.

One went to war not to protect slavery or an aristocracy but to protect one's family, home, kin, and community. Under the bold title "Awake! Awake!" an Edgefield citizen called: "Come from the rivers, hills, vallies and plains. Come to the rescue of our country from the dangers that threaten our wives, our children and our domestic peace. Come without prejudice to any man, and let us reason together as patriots and not as partisans." Speaking of a different war, Joseph Abney, editor of the Edgefield *Advertiser*, revealed the primary reason that Edgefieldians volunteered: "But the blow has been struck . . . and whether she be right or wrong, we go for our country with all our mind, and with all our heart. . . . The man that pauses now to ask, who brought about the conflict, is like the man, who, when his neighbor's house is on fire, cries 'stop the incendiary', whilst the devouring flames roll on unrestrained, and wrap the noble tenement in destruction and ashes. . . . We are truly proud to see our countrymen, from all quarters rushing with heroic ardor to the conflict—it does honor to them as Americans,—it does honor to the country they call their own."[3]

Black and white, men and women, left Edgefield during the war, but only for white men can a good approximation of casualties be made. Native Edgefieldian and noted southern historian Francis Butler Simkins wrote that the men of Edgefield "left the Union in 1860 with a shout, and, in the war years which followed, struggled as one man against the northern invaders." Yet further study of census records indicates that although Edgefield was well known for its patriotism and its fighting men, it sent only 59 percent of its eligible men to the front. This suggests, especially in light of the initial enthusiasms for enlistment, that in the latter years of the war Edgefield and perhaps other communities as well were not as fully committed to the Confederate cause as has been commonly believed. Still, of Edgefield's 2,137 enlistments, many were wounded, some maimed for life, and 613 died. This was a heavy toll for one community.[4]

Of the 136 wealthiest Edgefieldians in 1860, only 41 were still listed in the county in 1870. Many, including Francis Pickens, William Gregg, Gen. James Jones, and James Henry Hammond, died between 1860 and 1870. None of the missing 95 individuals who had been among the prewar wealthy had died fighting in the war, however. The 41 wealthy persons who are recorded in both the 1860 and 1870 censuses suffered a decline in mean real estate valuation of 75 percent and in personal estate valuation of 97 percent. In 1860 per capita wealth for whites in the county was $2,457; for the 41 wealthy, it was $47,873. In 1870 the per capita wealth was $497; for the 41 wealthy persons still in Edgefield it was $4,460. Wealth declined sharply for the whole county: although the wealthiest remained wealthy, differences in wealth between whites narrowed.[5]

One of the important changes the Civil War worked on the South was the change in the image of the southern woman. Although women had long been viewed as the conservators of culture, this took on special meaning for white southern womanhood after the surrender of April 1865. Southern women who supported the fight remained the only undefeated whites of the community.

Especially after the end of slavery, "Southern Womanhood" became a battle cry for the repression of southern blacks. After Reconstruction the systematic legal disfranchisement and segregation of blacks were part of white South Carolinians' attempts to reestablish a stable social order similar to that which they believed existed before the Civil War. Many whites saw the Afro-American as a destroyer of social order, and they saw the white family, the basis of social stability, as the most obvious point of defense against imagined or real attacks on the social order. According to this myth, white women, symbolizing the family, needed protection from rape and also from intermarriage with blacks.[6]

The actual number of rapes declined after the Civil War; rape of white women did not increase, and rape of black women by whites decreased. Yet some men, such as Ben Tillman, used rape as a symbol to deny Afro-Americans their civil rights. He raged: "Whenever the Constitution [of the United States] comes between me and the virtue of the white women of the South, I say to hell with the Constitution!" Tillman even argued that burning black men accused of murder was "evidence of the spirit of liberty." In particular, he portrayed the white women of the South at all times vulnerable to rape by Afro-American men. For his Senate colleagues he described the southern maiden who, after being subdued and knocked unconscious, was raped, "her chastity taken from her and a memory branded on her brain as with a red-hot iron to haunt her night and day as long as she lives." He went on to ask if it was any wonder that the whites of her community, "the whole countryside rises as one man and with set, stern faces seek the brute who has wrought this infamy." Vividly portraying the rape scene, Tillman argued that the rapist had "put himself outside the pale of the law, human and divine. . . . Kill! kill! kill!"[7]

Fears expressed on the surface as sexual were actually social in basis. The safety of white women was a concern long before the Civil War, but this concern was magnified after emancipation. In Edgefield the free black population increased from 173 to 25,417, and these free blacks had political rights.

Most disturbing to white notions of racial propriety and symbolic of the worst racial fears of whites was the marriage of white Republican Judge William Ramey to a former Edgefield slave on the courthouse steps in 1872.[8]

Although most family values did not change over the course of the war, important changes occurred in the community. During slavery the slave community had served to soften some of the more oppressive aspects of the peculiar institution. The Civil War and Reconstruction disrupted this community, but it reemerged following the war as a free black community. Common problems, relative homogeneity, kinship ties, developing economic and occupational possibilities, and an open political leadership fostered a sense of "belonging" among blacks and promoted the stability of their situation in Edgefield. From 1867 through 1876 former slaves acquired political power within the Republican party and were elected and appointed to local government positions in Edgefield County. Blacks gained in wealth and social prestige as long as they held political power, and in the community of Edgefield prominent blacks now interacted with whites. In addition to political gains free Afro-Americans sought family autonomy. Whereas in the antebellum period large-scale farming had been done with gang labor, the freedmen resisted this system, wanting their own land and family farms. The tenantry system, based on family labor, was the resulting compromise.[9]

Most antebellum free blacks either could not or chose not to assimilate into the postbellum white community. Those who remained in Edgefield identified with their former slave brethren: together they worked to forge a strong sense of community among free blacks. R. Barrentine Wilson, a mulatto and the son of antebellum free black farmer Martin Wilson, served in the state militia at Edgefield Court House alongside thirteen former Edgefield slaves. Curry Peters, a mulatto free black who had lived with a white family in 1860, served in the Hamburg militia. Because of their extremely radical views, Peters and four other black militiamen were marked for execution by whites at what became known as the Hamburg Massacre of July 1876. The sons and grandsons of antebellum free black landowner and successful farmer George Quarles continued to farm in Edgefield County near Quarles's home, and they all married former slaves from Edgefield. In 1850 and 1860, Elvin Boss, a young skilled free black, lived with his free black mother, a laundress, in the town of Edgefield. After the Civil War he was still in the village of Edgefield, still living with his mother, but married to a former Edgefield slave. He announced that he was going "to enlighten and serve and to teach the freedmen their rights and interests." Weighing his words before a mass audience of freedmen that also included several prominent members of the traditional white planter elite, he cautioned the former slaves against expecting social equality from the whites, but implored them to "stand up for that political equality which is now . . . [theirs] by law." His older sister Martha was married to a harness maker, a former Edgefield slave, and lived next door to her brother and mother in Edgefield. This young antebellum free mulatto woman taught former slaves in the public schools throughout Reconstruction.[10]

In postbellum years mulattoes (about three-fourths of all Edgefield District antebellum free blacks) were proportionately wealthier, more literate, and more likely to have a high-status occupation than were nonmulatto Afro-Americans. But the common problems that blacks and mulattoes faced in the first fifteen years following emancipation and their common condition of being "not white" gave blacks and mulattoes a sense of identity that contributed to stability within the Afro-American community. Mulatto Harrison N. Bouey was born a slave in Edgefield District; at the age of twenty-four he was elected probate judge for Edgefield County. In a letter he described himself as "a colored man or a yellow man." Bouey identified himself with the mass of Afro-Americans in Edgefield by using such terms as "our," "we," "me and my race," and "the masses of our people" eleven times in one paragraph. His feelings of identity with nonmulattoes in Edgefield were evident from his attempts to convince others to migrate with him to Liberia, which he identified as his homeland and where he eventually went as a missionary.[11]

Before the Civil War whites thought they knew blacks. But as blacks got political power, the whites changed their opinions about their former slaves. In 1866 the Edgefield *Advertiser* complimented Lawrence Cain's "genteel manner" and "his good sense and good feeling." After Cain began to organize the former slaves politically and he himself ran successfully in local elections, the editors could hardly find words adequate to defame him. A contemporary chronicler of South Carolina Reconstruction demonstrated this changed attitude: Cain now appeared "offensive to the white people" of Edgefield because of his "swagger and bad character." Ben Tillman remarked that the blacks had been "inoculated with the virus of equality." In 1868, when Democratic candidate W. F. Durisoe, for many years the editor of the Edgefield *Advertiser* and since 1859 an ordinary (probate judge) for Edgefield District, lost the election to the Republican candidate, an Edgefield former slave, the new editor of the paper remarked that the new probate judge was "elected under the new and dark order of things. A dark period in our history." Years later, Thomas Jefferson Howard, son of an Edgefield yeoman, recalled this time when Edgefield whites were "lorded over by Negroes. It makes my blood boil when I think of those times." Whites spoke more and more of the racial elements of their "community." They saw Edgefield as a white person's community, and after the end of Reconstruction whites had few direct contacts with blacks in Edgefield.[12]

Some former slaves internalized the values that Edgefield whites had attempted to inculcate. Junius Quattlebaum, an aged former Edgefield slave, spoke to a white interviewer fondly about his years of bondage. He "had de best folks to live and work wid. . . . Dere is no sich kindness dese days betwixt de boss and them dat does de work. All de slaves worked pretty hard sometimes but never too hard. They worked wid light and happy hearts, cause they knowed dat marster would take good care of them; give them a plenty of good vittles, warm clothes, warm houses to sleep in, when de cold weather come. They sho' had nothin' to worry 'bout and no overseer to drive them to work, lak some slaves on other plantations had."[13]

The records of Reconstruction, however, show that slavery did not produce a population of freedmen who necessarily saw the world or their roles in it from a subservient point of view. Edgefield blacks understood freedom as whites did. After the Civil War and emancipation they sought to achieve that freedom in all its aspects and to shake off the associations of slavehood.

Although the complex and exciting stories of the Civil War and Reconstruction must be told elsewhere, one of the primary expressions of the push by blacks for a new society was an enthusiastic assertion of their commitment to the family and to the church. The black culture of this period was not identical to that of whites; yet in cultural values and in the structure of the family, blacks and whites had much in common. As shown in chapters 2 and 3, white Edgefield families usually embodied the traditional Christian concept of a stable male-headed nuclear family, with additional relatives in the household, as was common in the American rural South. This description applied to black families as well.[14]

The family values of love, respect and support for one another, hard work, education, and political activism were of great import in molding and maintaining the Afro-American family after the war. Families were buttressed in this effort by community values, which were dictated in large part by the independent black churches. The church's affirmation of the Christian life, its support of the needy, and its sponsoring of education all served to reinforce family values. The church stressed patriarchal roles, solidified community spirit, and often focused community activity toward social and political ends.

Postbellum Afro-American Families

During Reconstruction the husband and father was responsible for his family's economic well-being in southern agrarian society, and planters recognized the male as the head of the Afro-American family. For example, in 1866, when a group of Francis Pickens's former slaves wanted to rent land, Pickens agreed to let each family have about forty-five acres "to work their own immediate families under them, the head men being responsible for my share of the crop." In a letter to Pickens, chairman of the Edgefield Democratic Executive Committee in 1868, the local Democratic Club of Liberty Hill wrote that "feeling it to be our duty, a duty which we owe to posterity," the club, while acknowledging the black man's responsibility for every member of his family, had decided, "after the expiration of existing contracts, not to employ any negro or any member of his family" unless the black man brought certification from his former employer that he and each family member were Democratic voters. When Gen. Matthew Calbraith Butler attempted to sell 650 acres of land to the South Carolina Land Commission in 1869, a group of former Edgefield slaves asked the commission to let them buy the land, arguing that they had worked this land with their families since emancipation and now wanted a chance to buy family plots. These eighteen men made their marks above their names under the following: "And the undersigned your petitioners, would further represent that they are each the head of a family and desirous of procuring homesteads on the land above described and hereby agree to purchase the entire tract among themselves upon the terms allowed in such cases." This was dated 1 May 1869.[15]

The Freedmen's Bureau records contained repeated references to former slave families. The 1866 model contract for landowners and former slaves obligated the employer to give a half-acre of land to each head of family where he had "comfortable quarters" (those who were not family heads received only a quarter-acre). If the freedmen were dismissed, "the wages due him or her shall be paid by the employer to the *family*." In the summer of 1867 an agent wrote to the governor that he had distributed corn in his "community" in the northeast section of Edgefield District to nearly four hundred black and white "heads of families." Although Charleston District records reflected a concern about bigamy and Edgefield District records contained some references to women, children, and elderly persons, the vast majority of references in the bureau records were to male-headed black families. In General Order Number 1, issued 1 March 1866, local agent John Devereux pledged fair treatment to freedmen and, in return, insisted that the former slaves "work industriously to support themselves and families." Almost all labor contracts were made between white landowners and black men.[16]

Acknowledging the existence of conventional nuclear families among the freedmen, the Edgefield *Advertiser* commented, after emancipation, that the notorious Black Codes, which were to govern the relations between whites and blacks, allowed Afro-Americans too much freedom. "Freedom from being sold on the block and separated from his wife and children is all the freedom he ought to have."[17]

Despite this recognition of black families, whites were reluctant to admit that blacks had feelings and devotion to their families equal to their own. An 1867 letter from a poor white woman in Edgefield District gave some idea of white attitudes toward the black family. The woman asked the governor to pardon her husband since "I have bin told that you reprieved all the nigroes in Edgefield jail and God knows my poor Husband is more precious to me than they was to their familys."[18]

Black family members were sincerely devoted to each other. Marriage records, public and private genealogies, notes in family Bibles, and oral traditions testified to the strength of black family values in Edgefield. Freedmen had an especially strong sense of family that resulted from the reconstitution of families torn apart during slavery. Amelia Dorsey reported how her family was reunited. "My mother come back to Beech Island after freedom and got me and my sister, and went to Augusta and work with some white people. She went down to Barnwell to my father, and they got together again, and dey had three mo' chillun by that unit."[19]

Genealogies and naming practices used by blacks attested to strong family values. Several Edgefield Afro-American genealogies began before emancipation. One listed the white slaveowner as the father of the patriarch of an influential Afro-American family, but the others, like most of the genealogies recorded in family Bibles or carried in oral tradition, began with two slaves. Alexander Bettis's grandfather, a slave of "unadulterated African extraction" who belonged to an aristocratic planter family named Bettis, married another slave who belonged to Col. John Fair. Their son was called Jack Bettis "during slavery as well as in the after years of freedom: in accordance with his paternal inheritance," even though he belonged to Colonel Fair. Jack Bettis married Annis Jones, who was owned by a widow Jones; they named their son Alexander Bettis. The continuity of the Bettis name, despite several shifts of owners, testified to the importance that these slaves attached to their family.[20]

The Morgan family's genealogy began with two former Edgefield slaves, Alfred (overseer for Francis Pickens) and Rosa Morgan. As late as 1979, the survivors of this family—3 children, 21 grandchildren, 80 great-grandchildren, 108 great-great-grandchildren, and 12 great-great-great-grandchildren still got together for family reunions. The Morgan family's history stressed the importance of education, religious participation and reputation, and hard work. Their ancestors were active in three black churches in Edgefield— Simmon Ridge, Macedonia, and Pleasant Grove. The family was proud that the former slaves accumulated enough money to purchase a small plot of land and leave it "title-free" to their children. To quote the Morgan family commemoration: "So, all-in-all, it seems that our ancestors were law-abiding and God-fearing citizens of this community: lovable family members, friendly and benevolent neighbors, and friends."[21]

Love and Support between Family Members

Blacks revered their mothers and fathers. Former slave Harrison N. Bouey, twelve years old when slavery ended, wrote in 1877: "I am my mother and father's only child. They are both living with me, and are going with me to Liberia. . . . Mother is 46. Has been a cook all her life from 14 years old up to the close of the war." Although his father could neither read nor write, the younger Bouey, a schoolteacher, took special pride in him. "Father is about 54 and is in excellent health. He is a first class house carpenter—and has practical ideas on most any thing. His mental and physical forces having been equally taxed, he shows no signs of a failure."[22]

Husbands and wives in former slave narratives spoke with pride about how long their marriages had lasted. Warren McKinney commented: "That is all the wife I ever had. We lived together 57 years. It is hard for me to keep up with my mind since she died. She has been dead five years nearly now." Another former slave, Squire Harris, stated, "And atter freedom I got me a acre o' land, run away wid my gal and ma'yed her, and settled down to make a living. . . . My old lady and me live togedder fifty-three years."[23]

Family members supported each other in times of need. Mothers helped their daughters give birth to and care for children, and relatives took in children if their parents were ill. One former slave took her sister-in-law's child to wean. Another woman's sister took one of her children to rear after the father died. A young former slave fled a former master she had defied, leaving her infant child with her mother. Another young woman from Edgefield, married to a black soldier who mistreated her, left him and traveled to Charleston, where she found her mother's sister who had been sold away from Edgefield years before but had maintained contact with her family. The aunt arranged for her safe return home.[24]

Young black children played games such as marbles and jump rope and listened to stories. Former slaves from Edgefield reminisced: "My husban' useter tell de chillun stories to make 'em laugh"; "Us chaps played all de time wid white chilluns jus' lak dey had all been Niggers"; "chillun . . . wuz satisfied jus' to play all de time. I 'members on Sundays us used to take leaves and pin 'em together wid thorns to make usselves dresses and hats to play in."[25]

Hard Work as a Family Value

Dr. Benjamin E. Mays, born in 1893, discussed the values of hard work that his sharecropping parents, former Edgefield slaves, had instilled in him.

My parents were industrious. There wasn't a lazy bone in their bodies. They didn't sit back and make the children do it. They did their part on the farm. In addition to cooking, seeing that our clothes were washed and ironed, and keeping the house clean, Mother hoed and picked cotton and Father worked equally hard. I must have caught their spirit of work. To this day, I am impatient with lazy people. Father believed that a man should earn his living by the sweat of his brow, and that, to him, meant working on the farm in the blazing hot sun. And my parents were honest.

I never heard them scheming how they might get something for nothing. I never suspected them of stealing anything from anybody. They taught their children honesty. I believe that not a single child in our family expected to get anything except through honest channels and by his own efforts.[26]

Lucy Gallman reported: "When freedom come, all slaves went to some place to get work. My father give me six cuts a day to work in the house to spin the yarn. . . . I helped at the corn mill, too, always went there and tote a half bushel corn many days. . . . I worked hard, plowed, cut wheat, split cord wood, and other work just like a man." Molly Brown also spoke of hard work: "What ain't I done! Farmin', I told you. Buildin' fences was common. Feedin' hogs, milkin' cows, churnin'. We [she and her husband] raised hogs and cows and kept somethin' to eat at home. I knit sox. I spin. . . . Pieced quilts. Could I sew? Course I did!" And Annette Milledge stated, "I was raised to work." William Ballard explained why he preferred freedom to slavery: "I think anybody who is any count can work and live by himself."[27]

Figure 6-1 presents information on employed members of black and white households. Disregarding children younger than five, Afro-American households in 1870 had 60.4 percent of their members gainfully employed, compared to 43.9 percent of white household members. The figures were similar for 1880. Interesting variations existed between mulatto and black and between rich and poor of all colors; the proportions for mulatto-headed families generally fell between those of black and white (refer to Figure for these details).

Care and Comfort for the Elderly

A life of hard work often went unrewarded, and old age was a time of insecurity if children or relatives did not take care of the elderly. The respect and love of family members was the only welfare provided for the elderly. Former slaves were cared for by relatives. "Fus' one chile and den de udder take care of me, do de bes' dey kin." Some relatives came from far away to do so; Casper Rumple's daughter and son-in-law (who gave up a good job) came from Cincinnati to care for him. Sometimes the care was less personal. "I had fo' daughter and three 'grads', but all gone now but one niece. I deeded de place to her. She live out north now, but she send back de money fer de taxes and insurance and to pay de firemans."[28]

Those with no children or relatives to help were lonely at best, and often in very bad straits. Molly Brown had no relatives to care for her and was too old to work or raise a garden. This proud woman had to beg to live. Even then she admitted, "I know I do get hungry." Aged Liza Mention also regretted that "I

Figure 6–1. Household Members Employed, 1870 and 1880

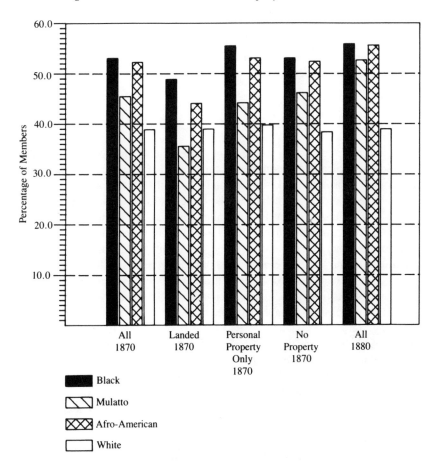

Note: See Table 7–2 for *N*s, note, and source. This figure includes all persons in the household. The text, however, refers to percentages of households, eliminating children under five.

hasn't a chile to my name, nobody to move nothin' when I lays it down and nobody to pick nothin' up."[29]

Malinda Mitchell's children were dead, but she derived comfort from a great-granddaughter. "I worked an' I taught my chillun to work. Dey's all dead now. My grand-daughter bought this little house and gave it to me. She's dead now too, and when she knowed she wouldn't live long she got this child, just a baby then, so I'd have some company wid me. . . . She's been a heap o' comp'ny too."[30]

Not only love and caring but a respect for the elderly was an Afro-American tradition. This oral culture placed special emphasis on older persons, who were links to the past. This respect comes out in Louise Pettis's narrative. Her family was part of the exodus of black people from the area during the Reconstruction lynchings and killings. "Pa was old and they would listen at what he said. He made a speech at Rob Roy and told them Let's come to Briscoe. Eleven families come."[31]

Family Support in Time of Death

Death, more than any other single event, linked family and community in the rural South. Typically, the community came together over the death of one of its members to provide food, support, and fellowship at wakes at which friends and relatives spent all night talking about the deceased. When former slave and radical political leader Paris Simkins died at his home in Edgefield, children and old friends traveled from as far away as Washington and New York for the funeral. They sat up telling stories about Simkins. In the antebellum period too slave funerals were significant affairs, and there is evidence that funerals provided slaves some additional freedom. An Augusta ordinance prohibited blacks from preaching without a license or without white witnesses, "except at funerals or sitting up with the dead."[32]

During the mass violence of Reconstruction, whites left the bodies of murdered blacks where they fell, which enabled them to shoot at those who attempted to retrieve them. Whites were well aware of the terrible effect that their inability to bury the dead had on the Afro-American community. Matilda A. Evans, a black physician, who as a young girl attended school near Edgefield County, later wrote of one such incident. A group of men attempted to bury one of the bodies left on display. Because of white attacks, they had to put the murdered man "in a pine box of cheap manufacture, just as the unhappy man had fallen, without a funeral robe or garment, in everyday old working clothes."[33]

Burial affirmed the social position of everyone, black or white, in the rural society. During Reconstruction and the years following, blacks formed burial societies to help bury members. Death rites were also part of the welfare system in rural communities. When George Tillman proposed during Reconstruction that whites who refused to join the Agricultural and Police Club would be treated by the white community "as a whole nigger should be treated, pass him and his whole family with silent contempt; let him or any of his household get sick, or even die with none to cheer the lonely hours, or to bury these tainted remains but his nigger associates," he threatened something of real import to whites and to blacks.[34]

Tombstone inscriptions in cemeteries, which surrounded black churches, testified to the importance of family ties. The inscriptions linked the dead to their communities by commentaries on their roles as family members. Some of the tombstone inscriptions were verses from Ephesians, chapter 6, cited elsewhere in this chapter. Devoted spouses, revered parents, and loved children were all remembered: "Andrew W. Simkins—He was Fond of The 23rd Psalm"; "In Memory of Our Devoted Mother, Mime Williams—Children Don't Grieve For Me, I Have Made Peace with Jesus, Prepare to Meet Your Mother"; "Johnson, Enlou, Born Sept. 12, 1850 Died Sept. 14, 1872—There is no Death The Stars Go Down, to Rise Upon Some Fairer Shore, and Bright in Heaven, Jewelled Crown, They Shine Forever More"; "Nicholson, A. W.— Thy Life Was Beauty, Truth, Goodness & Love Edna L.—Loving Wife. She Died as she Lived—A Christian."

Some of these tributes dated from the Civil War and Reconstruction period. Former slaves were poor, but they invested savings for family tombstones and gravesites. For Afro-Americans (and most whites) the cleaning of graves was a personal task. A Saturday was set aside and members of a particular church where kin and friends were buried gathered early, brought lunches, and spent the day cleaning graves and the cemetery and sharing reminiscences of family members now departed. The entire affair served to strengthen the sense of family and community. A homecoming, or reunion, generally followed at the church within the week after graves were cleaned, and relatives who had moved some distance away came home to visit. Even today blacks (and whites) take time to clean graves of their family members, a tradition which testifies to the reverence for family in the rural South.[35]

Mobility Patterns and Family Ties

Close ties between the generations can be deduced from mobility patterns. Students of the family find a correlation in spatial mobility and family breakdown; parental control is weaker as offspring move further away. The mobility of slaves was strictly controlled by whites; indeed slavery often split families. After the war Edgefield freedmen were as rooted to place as were whites. From 1870 to 1880 the persistence rate for white heads of households was 43 percent, compared to 45 percent for black household heads. Younger married male and female Afro-Americans who died in 1879 had generally lived in Edgefield longer than whites. Similarly, as Frank Huffman notes in his study of Clarke County, Georgia, "family responsibilities" were a key factor in male persistence, and this "is even more true for blacks than for whites, contrary to the stereotype that family ties were lightly regarded by the freedmen."[36]

When Edgefield blacks did move, they often moved as a family. Their response to organized migrations, for example, reveal much about the community and indicate a strong sense of family. All letters to the American Colonization Society referred to families. Two compilations of persons ready to emigrate to Liberia from Edgefield were listed by family (with male heads), as were the passengers on the ship *Azor*, which carried three Edgefield families with other blacks to Liberia. The 1881–82 Arkansas migration, the largest single mass exodus from South Carolina, was also organized and executed by Edgefield County male-headed families.[37]

These migrations, undertaken by a geographically stable population, resulted from the political and economic repressions of Redemption and not from any wanderlust. These people left Edgefield County not out of despair but out of a faith that somewhere in America they could find a home where they could realize the hopes of equality and prosperity they had conceived during Reconstruction.

Edgefield's largest emigration society voted in November 1881 to move to Arkansas where government land was available for 12.5 cents per acre, where there were no fence laws and where wages ran twelve to twenty dollars per month. The Edgefield County correspondent of the Charleston *News and Courier* exclaimed that "there has been nothing like it since the days of Pharaoh."[38]

There is confusion as to exactly how many blacks left Edgefield County. George Brown Tindall, historian of South Carolina blacks during this period, recorded that "an estimated five thousand Negroes left their homes with Arkansas as their goal" between 24 and 31 December 1881.[39] This is consistent with most sources which generally report that one-fifth of the black population left. The local newspaper, however, maintained that the number of blacks actually migrating had been exaggerated. One state representative remarked that "like a great many other highly colored stories, [this one] grows in magnitude and importance the farther [it] goes."[40] The local newspaper estimated the number at about 2,000 on 4 January, but suggested that others were still moving.[41] But even as local whites were trying to deny the scope and impact of the exodus, they could not help but marvel at how the blacks seemed to be conducting the move as a social unit and comment on their intent "to migrate in a body and settle all in a community."[42] The émigrés were willing to leave Edgefield, but only if family and community went together.

Another indication of family closeness and control of other family members was the relationship of subfamilies to household heads (subfamilies were families not headed by the household head; see Table 6-1). Whites tended to have members of the immediate family (parents and children) as subfamily heads. Afro-American households, however, were more likely than white households to take in grandparents, sisters and brothers, aunts and uncles, nieces and nephews, cousins, and stepchildren as family heads. The proportion of extended and augmented households was similar for blacks and whites, but the black household was slightly more likely to include more distant kin subfamilies.

Table 6-1. Relationship of Head of Subfamily to Household Head, 1880
(percentages)

Relationship	Black (N = 280)	White (N = 180)
Sons and daughters-in-law Daughters and sons-in-law Step children	25.4	36.7
Sisters and brothers and spouses	15.0	14.4
Mothers, fathers, grandparents	14.6	17.8
Grandchildren	7.5	6.7
Aunts, uncles, nieces, nephews, cousins, 2nd cousins, other relatives	12.9	5.6
Servants, boarders, indigents, laborers	9.6	2.2
No relation	15.0	16.7
Total	100	100

Missing observations = 7.
Source: Edgefield Data Base.

Family Ties through Correspondence and Visits

Letters and visits between family members and friends reveal a high level of cohesion, although correspondence between nineteenth-century Edgefield Afro-Americans, who were generally illiterate, was rare. Yet the writers of these letters talked of kin and friends in much the same way that whites did. Having missed former governor Milledge Bonham when he visited Augusta in the summer of 1889, George Burt, his former slave and carriage driver, apologized that he had not received Bonham's message about the trip. Burt returned Bonham's affectionate greeting and added that "my-self and family are all in good health except my oldest daughter who has been sick for several months now but is some better recently." The Hammond family maintained contact with a number of their former slaves, and some of the letters revealed black family ties as well as affection between the correspondents. India Gill wrote to Julia Hammond in the 1880s, "Tell uncle William and aunt mealia tell them howdy for me and tell them I would be glad to see them and my dear old home and tell them that I often think of them and my dear old home."[43]

Most of the letters to the Hammonds were from Sidney Dewalt, son of the Hammond's longtime slave gardener. When Julia Hammond was in New York, he wrote her about the white and black families at home. At the time of his marriage in 1900 his future in-laws mailed the following handwritten formal invitation to the Hammond family: "Mr. and Mrs. Hanable Evans acquest you pressen on the third of October at 8 o'clock p.m. at their resident to witness the marriage their daughter Mary to Sidney Dewalt." While on an extended vacation in 1898, Dewalt wrote to his white employer at Beech Island: "I am with my parrens and is having a nice time. . . . I found all well at home Sister Mattie is not so well in Atlanta She been very sick but is better. . . . I went to see one of my uncles found him and famely well and were glad to hear about you all and were glad to hear of Judge Hand. . . . Came back to Prosperity and there stayed with one of my uncles all night all is glad to see me there Said I am at a good place."[44]

Another former Edgefield slave, Henry Morse, whose wife had recently left Edgefield to join him in Florida, wrote to his former master Col. William H. Moss: "Master, please tell me how Uncle George, Aunt Lucy, Maria and Georgiana, Aunt Elsey, Uncle Jake, my sister Maria, and Stephan and Elvira are? Georgiana's husband (Griffin) is in middle Florida. Tell me how Uncle Steven is, and all my acquaintances." Georgiana, like Henry Morse's wife, had remained behind in Edgefield while her husband found a permanent job. Because both Georgiana and Griffin were illiterate, they depended on Morse, who, using his former owner as intermediary, maintained links with the community after he left Edgefield.[45]

The narratives of former slaves also demonstrated that Afro-American family and community ties were maintained over distance much as were white ties (chapter 2). Former Edgefield slaves who migrated to Arkansas returned for visits with relatives and friends in Edgefield. Some stayed an extended time and even married in Edgefield before going back to Arkansas. Warren McKinney and his mother and brothers and sisters migrated to Arkansas when he was sixteen or seventeen. When his mother wanted to return to Edgefield, they all came back. McKinney married in Edgefield, but after the death of his mother he and his wife returned to Arkansas and remained there. Molly Brown's explanation of why she and her husband migrated to Arkansas was similar to those given by whites who migrated to western states: "The reason I come to Arkansas was cause brother Albert and Caroline come here and kept writin' for us to come." Nearly one hundred years old at the time of the interview, she added, "Four years ago I went to South Carolina to see my auntie. Her name Julia."[46]

Reconstruction leader Prince Rivers's youngest son, born in 1883, had "three half brudders, who I never know much 'cause they all go to West Pennsylvania, when I was a small boy. . . . I see some niggers from there one time, and they say they know them and that they was powerful well to do, workin' in de steel mills." Afro-Americans who journeyed from one place to another sometimes acted as messengers.[47]

Kinship Alliances and the Transmittal of Political Values

The political values of white families and their strong family connections shaped and fostered political aspirations. Black kinship alliances during Reconstruction also reflected the strength of family ties. Common surnames indicated kinship ties in communities. Edgefield blacks had a high frequency of repetitive surnames, suggesting stability and indicating interlocking families. These kinship ties were often important in the transmittal of political power and governmental influence. Kinship alliances encouraged civic activism within families into the twentieth century.[48]

Legislator David Harris's son Augustus was a constable; state legislator Paris Simkins and school commissioner Andrew Simkins were half-brothers. The two most powerful black political leaders, who sometimes headed rival factions, were Paris Simkins and Lawrence Cain. One of Cain's daughters married a son of Paris Simkins and named one son Lawrence Cain Simkins. The Simkinses remained active in political and social battles for many generations, both in the South and in the North. Family members, men and women, worked with the NAACP. Grandson C. B. Bailey, denied admission to the University of South Carolina Law School in the 1930s, unsuccessfully sued the university. In the 1940s, Bailey spearheaded the integration of the post office letter carriers in Columbia. Bailey's parents were from Edgefield. He wrote, "My mother's home was in Edgefield, South Carolina, where my grandparents proudly reigned over a brood of sixteen wonderful noisy children." He described Paris Simkins's family as a "close-knit tribe."

Every year Mrs. Bailey returned with her five children to Edgefield "to spend the summer," which gave Bailey a chance to visit with both sets of grandparents. Bailey remembered that grandfather Paris Simkins was often visited by South Carolina's leading white Republican, Tieless Joe Tolbert from nearby Ninety Six. The two men sometimes shared a meal and always sat together at a table and discussed politics. Tolbert would ask Simkins his opinion of white men before he recommended them for political appointments.[49]

These political values were transmitted to other family members. Prominent civil rights activist Modjeska Monteith Simkins was cofounder and first secretary of the South Carolina Conference of the NAACP. This woman, who, in the words of a group of black South Carolinians, "raised more hell in South Carolina" than anyone else, married a son of Reconstruction leader Andrew Simkins.[50]

More typically, however, black women regarded politics as the exclusive domain of men. In retreat before the patriarchal role of males, Molly Brown reflected the more common attitude, "I don't study votin'. I don't vote (disgusted). I reckon my husband and pa did vote. I ain't voted."[51]

The Church

Both as an institution and as a carrier of religious ideals, the church reinforced family values. In the South churches played a dominant role in shaping the society and values of whites and Afro-Americans. Black churches were religious, social, community, and political centers. Dr. Benjamin E. Mays made the following observation, which was just as true for the late nineteenth century as it was for the early twentieth century that Mays remembered. "Old Mount Zion was an important institution in my community. Negroes had nowhere to go but to church. They went there to worship, to hear the choir sing, to listen to the preacher, and to hear and see the people shout. The young people went to Mount Zion to socialize, or simply to stand around and talk. It was a place of worship and a social center as well. There was no other place to go."[52]

Independent black rural churches offered an opportunity to meet together away from the constant scrutiny of whites. Afro-American communities grew up in rural neighborhoods identified with specific churches. Rural churches housed such Afro-American institutions as Masonic lodges, benevolent societies, burial organizations, and educational unions and sponsored schools, fairs, and social gatherings.[53]

The Arkansas "exodusters" held their emigrant society meetings in rural churches. The leader was a black Baptist preacher, John Hammond, and other ministers participated. This Edgefield family exodus carried such religious overtones that a New York newspaper, the *Daily Tribune*, proclaimed they were "all bound for the promised land."[54]

The importance of the church as a symbol of respectability and status for blacks was revealed in the 1877 lists of Edgefield Afro-Americans who applied to emigrate to Liberia. Along with each name and the names of members of the family, occupation, skill, and literacy of those wanting to leave, the denomination of every family member was listed.[55]

As a symbol of the church, the Bible occupied a prominent position within the Afro-American household. Numerous former slaves testified that they had Bibles; some were disgusted that such a question would even be asked. Both white and black families kept important documents tucked away in the Bible. According to one narrative "Liza brought an old Bible from the other room in which she said she kept the history of the old church. There were also pictures from some of her 'white folks' who had moved to North Carolina." Another former slave reported, "I believe in the Bible. . . . This little book—Gospel of

St. John—has been carried in my pocket every day for years and years. And I never miss a day reading it. I don't see how some people can be so unjust. I guess they never read their Bible. The reason I been able to make my three years and ten is because I obeys what the Good Book says."[56]

The delivery of religious texts was also important and could even endanger or save the lives of black leaders. Thomas Sease was murdered in 1865 after he preached in one of Alexander Bettis's churches on the text "The Lord has delivered his sheep out of the hands of the enemy and placed them in the care of Moses." (Coincident to the biblical Moses, Franklin J. Moses, Jr., was a white radical Republican.) Alexander Bettis and Paris Simkins used religion to escape harm from white mobs. When the Ku Klux Klan came to Bettis's house to kill him, he invited them to dinner and said to them, "Gentlemen, you ought never to do anything upon which you cannot ask God's blessing. And while supper is being prepared, let us all bow and pray with me that God will bless whatever we may do tonight." After they had prayed and eaten together, the Klan left peacefully. Simkins also faced down the Ku Klux Klan. Holding his infant son in his arms, he preached a sermon to the mob that had come to kill him, and they left him unharmed. Prayer was not a fool-proof answer; black legislator Simon Coker was shot dead while kneeling in prayer.[57]

Religious Commitment and Discipline

Former slaves affirmed the importance of religion in their lives again and again. They remembered when they had joined the church and why. Most, like Henry Ryan, "joined church to turn from evil ways and to live a better life." Many felt like the former slave who "jined de church when I was 31 years old, because I was seeking salvation. I wanted God to release me from my sins and dat was de way I had to do it. We can't git along widout Jesus." This theme of forgiveness ran through former slave Ryan's favorite song:

> Show pity, O Lord, forgive,
> Let e'er repentant sinner live;
> Are not they mercies large and free,
> May not a sinner trust in thee.[58]

The Edgefield Afro-American community took its faith seriously. The importance of the directives of the Bible in their lives can be seen in their actions. In 1890 the Afro-American Cedar Grove Methodist Church wanted to purchase a copy of the Ten Commandments large enough to be read at fifty feet. They had already paid up a note of $150 to Harry Hammond for their new church building and now wanted to use their scarce capital on this huge testament of righteousness. Writing his daughter Katharine to request a New York catalog, Hammond said that if what they wanted "can be had at what they can afford to pay, I will take measurement of the walls, consult the elders and look after the transaction for them."[59]

The religious community helped its members lead good lives through support and prayer, as well as through committees on discipline which would "cite" members for wrong-doing. White and black church histories and minutes from postbellum black church associations showed that discipline was often family related, to correct a misunderstanding between spouses or to impress members, as the Little River Baptist Association proclaimed, that "intemperance is an evil that has rendered so many families unhappy and without homes."[60]

The rationale for discipline committees was found in the constitutions of the Afro-American Baptist associations of which Edgefield churches were members. The members of the Bethlehem Baptist Association pledged that they would "exercise a Christian care and watchfulness over each other and faithfully warn, exhort, and admonish each other, as occasion may require. . . . We believe . . . that discipline is intended for purity of the Church and for the reclaiming of those members who may be disorderly in either principle or practice and should be faithfully held up for the glory of God."[61]

Whether postbellum white discipline committees cared for church members or were simply unsympathetic agencies of social control, committee members felt they helped people live virtuously. When freedom came, many Afro-American church members wanted more independence and asked to handle their own discipline matters. This was often a step toward setting up an independent black church.

Minutes and histories from black and white postbellum churches in Edgefield were so similar in tone that it is often impossible to distinguish between them, but the worship services differed substantially from church to church and between black and white. A surviving son of George Ouzts (chapter 2), James T. Ouzts, a white yeoman, former overseer, and devout Methodist, attended a black church service in 1874 and was appalled at some of the differences:

Aug 12, 1874 At knigt I went to willow Spring the coloured church to meeting. Wm Brooks preached his Sermon was scattering and not connected at all and upon the whole was sorry, I think he did the best he could. The singing was tolerable good. After the doxolygy was sung and the congregation dismissed. the congregation then commenced their anticks singing shakeing sorter rocking around about half dance fashion, marched around the house and about in the yard at a terrible rate men and women mixed up together, I don't call it nothing more nor less than a species of dancing with no relegeion about it. I saw one woman jumping up and down, and three women holing her to keep her from falling, they carried her to one side like they was going to lay her out, I think the most of these negroes go to these meetings for the frolick of the thing. I do not think much good is done, they seem to be going into heathanism.[62]

Freed from the restraints of planter scrutiny of religious texts, black preachers were more open in their elevation of the status of the newly freed people. At the 1871 funeral of former Edgefield slave beloved "Uncle Burton," the preacher, also a former slave, related how Uncle Burton had told an interpretation of Genesis that featured a black Adam and Eve's turning white from fear of God. This idea that blacks had been created in God's image and whites came about when sin occurred disturbed the editor of the *Advertiser*, who had attended the funeral as a tribute to the former slave.[63]

Independent black churches reinforced their members' concepts of self-worth. Benjamin E. Mays was "encouraged by the Reverend Marshall, and motivated by people in the church who made me believe that I could become something worthwhile in the world." Christian unity was also important. Songs and sermons preached from the early 1870s and recorded in black Baptist associations' minutes often mentioned this goal. Of course, goals were not always met, and black churches had conflicts to resolve. The history of the Mt. Calvary Baptist Church so testified: "A few years passed by, and unfortunately the church was destroyed by fire. It was believed that the destruction of the church came about because of misunderstanding and differences of opinions between the members. . . . Immediately after this vision, and the hearing of this strange dream, the divided members came together and rebuilt the church on this spot."[64]

Churches and Education

Churches took an interest in secular and religious education, which they saw as steps to social, political, and economic betterment. Most considered education to be a parental responsibility, and parents took an active part in setting up schools for their children. Churches, however, had a large role. Literacy among religious leaders was slightly greater than among the former slave population as a whole; it had been forbidden, of course, to teach slaves to read. In the first years after the war churches were often the only buildings available for schools, and even church structures were rare in some areas. In 1870 there were thirty-one more black churches than church buildings in Edgefield. In many cases a brush arbor served as both school and church.

In 1871, Dr. Luther Broadus, pastor of the Edgefield Village Baptist Church, presented his committee's report to the white Edgefield Baptist Association on the religious instruction of blacks. Within the association's boundaries the committee had found only ten black churches and seven ordained Afro-American ministers. He reported "seventeen colored Sunday Schools . . . all of which are managed by colored persons, except one at Ridge Spring under the direction of Brother Watson." Having visited some of the schools, Broadus reported that the committee had "been surprised and gratified to see the good order and thorough system which prevailed."[65]

Edgefield churches belonged to several Baptist associations, and a major concern of each of these associations was education, particularly religious education. The Bethlehem Baptist Sunday School Association stated: "If it was possible to keep the children from Sunday School and any religious training, then there would be no difference between them and a barbarian. . . . Religion is the fundamental principle upon which society, prosperity, happiness and independence is founded. . . . If you then neglect this training . . . look for a speedy . . . depravity for which the parents shall be held responsible." The Little River Baptist Association in 1877 reported, "We are gratified to say that we find good schools in nearly all of our churches, and some outside of any church. The number of schools is 25, with 25 superintendents, 77 teachers, 1230 pupils, 383 books in library."[66]

According to Figures 6-2 and 6-3, in 1870, 6.5 percent of Afro-American households with children of school age sent 4.1 percent of those children to school. These figures compare with the 26.5 percent of white households with children of school age which sent 18.5 percent of those children to school. The 1880 figures were higher for both groups: 9.5 percent of Afro-American households with children of school age sent 6.2 percent of those children to school, and 30.8 percent of white households with children of school age sent 22 percent of them to school. Figures 6-2 and 6-3 also show differences between black and mulatto Afro-Americans and between various wealth levels. The mulattoes' proportion was generally higher. Neither Afro-American nor white parents sent a high proportion of their children to school.

Black church associations such as the Little River Association had a difficult time gathering data on school attendance.

> Dear Brethren: Owing to the inconveniences of finding out the educational condition of our people throughout our Association, we are unable to tell you the exact progress that may be going on in the Association. . . . In the future, we recommend that each church in this Association appoint a committee of two or three brethren, who shall find out the number of children belonging to Baptist families that attend school during our Association year. . . . We made strenuous efforts in that direction this year, but were unsuccessful in obtaining reports from any of our churches—with the exception of Liberty and Springfield.[67]

By the 1880s several associations were more optimistic about the Sunday school programs than about the public schools. Macedonia Baptist Associa-

Figure 6–2. Households with School Age Children Attending School, 1870 and 1880

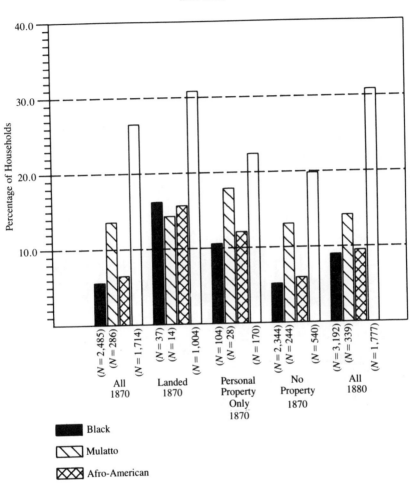

Source: Edgefield Data Base.

tion reported: "We have considered the progress of education among the mass of our people and we find it to be good. We find it to be the most necessary effort that we could put forth. We know that the Public School System is doing little good for the education of our people."[68]

Illiteracy was a major problem. In 1870, 84.1 percent of white household heads were literate (could both read and write), compared to 4.4 percent of

Figure 6–3. School Age Children Attending School, 1870 and 1880

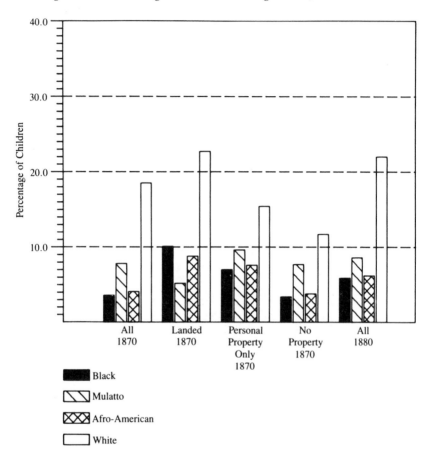

Note: See fig. 6–2 for *N*s and source.

Afro-American household heads (3.9 percent of black and 8.2 percent of mulatto household heads). Although these figures had increased significantly by 1880, they were still far from adequate: 86.7 percent of white and 16.4 percent of Afro-American household heads were literate (15.9 percent of black and 20.6 percent of mulatto household heads). The Little River Baptist Association was especially concerned about illiterate religious leaders. "Therefore, brethren, let us who see the good of Education encourage it, for the time is come that illiterate men are injurious in the pulpit." The association acted on the recommendation; in 1886 they resolved that men aspiring to the ministry were to be licensed only after passing examinations on "Orthography, Writing, English Grammar, Arithmetic, Geography, and the Scriptures."[69]

Former Edgefield slaves believed that preachers had to be able to read the Bible. Because he was illiterate, Squire Harris could not "preach none in de church. . . . I didn't git none o' dat learnin' fum books—dey didn' never let us see inside de Webster." Harris, nevertheless, found a way to contribute to the church community: "I sho' did my part buildin' de church atter freedom. . . . I dug a heap o' dirt for de Lawd. I was smart way back dere."[70]

As exemplified by Benjamin E. Mays, a close relationship existed between the ministry and teaching. Young black men often taught schools in rural areas like Edgefield to earn money to attend college and seminary. Some young Edgefield black teachers were the sons of preachers.[71]

The white churches had interesting reactions to the attempts to educate the former slaves. In 1865 the white Edgefield Baptist Association met to discuss "what arrangements, under existing circumstances, are best for the instruction and discipline of our colored members?" Their answers showed compassion for the newly freed but still politically powerless black population:

1st. It is important that we should not withhold from our colored members kind, earnest, Scriptural instruction, and faithful discipline. So long as they dwell among us, self-interest, as well as benevolence, and regard for the honor of Christ, requires such care, however laborious it may be.

2nd. Great allowances should be made for the exciting circumstances of their new condition of freedom, which they had no agency in producing, but which nevertheless unsettles all their old ideas and relations. So great and sudden a convulsion might well throw from their balance better instructed and more stable minds. Hence, leniency and patience ought to be exercised in regard too such faults as do not absolutely prove the utter absence of piety. . . .

4th. We disapprove of their being organized into separate churches, or assemblages apart from the usual meetings to be under the guidance of ignorant, unqualified, and unauthorized persons.

The whites became less compassionate when the black people they had known as slaves no longer accepted being treated as slaves. An 1868 report of the Committee on Education of the Edgefield Baptist Association stated: "Since your last meeting, a revolution has occurred in South Carolina that is without a parallel in the history of civilization. The government of our state has passed from the hands of the white race into the hands of the Negro race, who were but lately our slaves. Ignorance and cupidity now rule the hour, and gloom and despondency now overcloud the future." As blacks desired more autonomy, more splits occurred. In 1869 black people were excluded from

Callihan's Mill Church and Plum Branch Church. In 1871 the black members took over Pleasant Grove Church; the report to the association stated, "Pleasant Grove has been dissolved and most of the members have joined other churches of our faith. The colored members occupy the place of worship."

In 1871 Christian blacks requested help from their white brethren in order to organize black churches and Sunday school instruction, but with Afro-Americans in political power, the white reaction was less than charitable. Several reports were tabled; then the association adopted the following resolution: "Resolved, That the Association heartily endorse all of the sentiments expressed in the reports of this body relative to the reception of the Messenger from the Colored Association, and highly appreciate the motives which we trust actuated the latter in requesting intercourse with us; yet we deem it inexpedient under the present circumstances, and entirely futile of good results, to open such correspondence."[72]

Violent opposition to some black churches occurred. From the northwest corner of Edgefield the superintendent of Dorn Gold Mine wrote of a group of white terrorists who called themselves "regulators" in 1872. "Last Sunday an attack was made by them on a small building where a Sunday School was held. . . . No one arrested because of fear." The regulators heard of an Afro-American prayer meeting being held with the white property owner's permission and threatened, "There have been meetings of this kind in our community and we find them to terminate politically and not spiritually." Regulators believed it was all right to worship in the daytime, "but not at night at all. We cannot and will not tolerate such in neighboring communities." Despite opposition and without much white local support, Edgefield Afro-American churches persevered.[73]

The 1880s found Afro-American churches still emphasizing education. Little River Association insisted, "Without it we must be slaves to ignorance." The 1890s represented hard times for black people, and their churches reflected the difficult circumstances. The Education Committee of the Friendship Baptist Sunday School Association in July 1892 found "that education is still greatly needed among the people. Since the meeting of the last Convention, the work is dying apparently." In 1894 the Little River Association declared, "In looking at the religious condition of the Baptists of the Little River Association we find, owing to the illiteracy of many of our leaders, that we are not in as prosperous condition as heretofore."[74]

Narratives of the former slaves confirmed the interaction between churches and schools for Afro-Americans. Carrie Fryer, for example, reported, "I would go to school three months when we first gether all the krep [crop]. We had a colored teacher in de Baptist Church were dey taught school. De name was Spring Grove."[75]

Many black children could not benefit from the public school system because qualified, that is, literate, teachers were hard to find. In the District of

Edgefield in 1866, there were only two schools for blacks, both private. One at Edgefield Court House was taught by a black man who was a resident of the district and the other, at Storm Branch near Hamburg, was taught by a white man and his wife. The Freedmen's Bureau agent concluded, "There are no other places at which it would be practicable to open schools at present on account of the unsettled state of the district and it would be unsafe for any teacher from abroad to attempt it." The bureau reported that at "Edgefield Court House . . . a school has been in operation for some time, taught by a mulatto named Lawrence Cain. The number of pupils averages from 30 to 60 and he charges $1.00 for each scholar. He is paid by the colored people, who also pay his house rent. It would not be well I think to interfere in any way with this school as present. The teacher was raised in the district, and I am confident that no one from abroad would be able to teach them unmolested. If anything should be done I should suggest that it be paying the teacher a small salary in addition to what he can collect from the freed people." This teacher, Lawrence Cain, was a founder and trustee of Macedonia Baptist Church, but he kept this school in his home.

In May 1866 freedmen near Aiken built a church and then raised fifty dollars through a community fair to start a school. According to the American Missionary Society representative, W. P. Russell, on one day's notice, "not extensively circulated, fifty scholars assembled in the church on Tuesday morning with quite a number of their parents who looked on with great satisfaction as their children arranged and took their first lessons in the acquirement of knowledge." Despite their poverty these Afro-Americans proposed to supplement the state salary of the two teachers by paying or providing for their room and board.

The school grew fast, but had problems keeping a teacher. In October 1866 the Freedmen's Bureau representative reported that there was one school in Aiken which had 123 pupils. The teacher was a white New Yorker sent south by benevolent societies. On 4 October 1866 the former teacher of this school was driven away by an armed mob, who threatened his life if he did not leave. The next teacher at Aiken lived with the army in the barracks.

The Freedmen's Bureau papers also showed the linkage of churches and schools. "In Storm Branch there are about 175 pupils and there is a church which is well adapted for a school room, and can be had rent free by keeping it in good repair. . . . The local friends [former slaves] of the school will do nearly all that is needed for its maintenance. . . . I cannot consider Edgefield District a promising field for the establishment of schools, there are many bad and dangerous men in it."[76]

In the 1868 constitution of South Carolina there were to be free schools and compulsory education for all children between six and sixteen. It also provided that all schools "supported in whole or in part by public funds shall be free and open to all the children . . . without regard to race or color." A tax on property and also a poll tax, plus all land given by the state or federal government and intestate estates, went to a fund set up for public school education.[77]

Republicans, consisting mostly of former South Carolina slaves, controlled state and local politics and also the schools from 1868 through 1876. They were responsible for the first public school system in South Carolina. Despite a number of problems, evidence suggests that the system was working well for whites and blacks until it was interrupted by the violent restoration of state and local government to the white planter elite.

As in the antebellum years, the implementation of the school system differed from the intent of the law. Compulsory education was not enforced. Moreover, separate schools were established for black and white children even though the Afro-American who headed the educational committee explicitly recommended integrating schools to allow children to associate while young and thereby help to end racial prejudice. But Edgefield's first school commissioner in 1868 was a white Republican who had been a landowner and slaveowner in antebellum Edgefield. Although sympathetic to black freedom and political rights, he, like most southern whites, was against integrated schools. His report to the state superintendant of education (an elected office created by the 1868 constitution) argued that it would be wise to keep the Edgefield whites and blacks in separate schools.[78]

Despite many obstacles one can see the remarkable improvements in public education during Reconstruction in Edgefield. In 1869, eight new public school houses, six of logs and two frame, were constructed at a cost of $3,175. For education in Edgefield County, $2,822.58 was appropriated by the state, and the local poll tax raised another $2,432. That initial year, however, of the 2,880 white boys and 3,041 white girls between the ages of six and sixteen, only 563 boys and 522 girls were in the 49 free schools. The children of the wealthy still employed governesses, although obtaining them from the North was more difficult after the Civil War. In the same year, there were 4,699 Afro-American boys and 4,633 girls between the ages of six and sixteen and only 364 of the boys and 415 of the girls attended school. In 1871, there were thirty-five free white schools, twenty-two taught by men and thirteen by women. This same year there were now sixteen schools for black children, twelve taught by black men and four by black women. The salaries for black and white teachers were identical, $33.54 for men and $24.94 for women.[79]

1872 was a transition year when Edgefield elected an Afro-American former slave and leader of the Baptist Church, Andrew Simkins, as local school commissioner. This signaled even more improvements for Afro-American schools. For 1873–74, white school enrollment rose to 1,286 with an equal number of 27 men and 27 women teachers. There was a rather remarkable increase in the number of black school students; now more black than white students attended the public schools with 1,527 black school children taught by 26 men and 13 women teachers. By 1874, even though the number of white children increased, there were nearly twice the number of black children attending public schools than white children. In 1874, 2,646 black children were taught by 62 teachers. The last session of school under Republican control saw the number of schools becoming more equalized and both black and white school attendance increasing, although the number of black pupils was much higher than the white and hence black teachers had more students per teacher. In 1875–76, the 126 Edgefield schools were nearly equally divided; there were 64 for white children and 62 for black children. The salaries paid black and white teachers were again the same, and the differentials between men and women were less, $33.55 for men and $30.38 for women. Indeed, teacher salaries were quite good during Reconstruction. Republican Governor Robert K. Scott even suggested in 1871 in his message to the state that teachers were paid too much. But the Republican government put a high emphasis on education and was willing to pay to develop a public school system. Moreover, they knew that most of their voters were Afro-American and that they wanted an education for their children. Besides the other taxes and methods of raising money in 1870, cities, towns, and incorporated villages were allowed to collect special taxes to support common schools.[80]

Even after the establishment of a public school system, many black schools were still connected with churches; sometimes the church building was the school, and sometimes the church owned the school building. The Manuscript Teachers Reports for Edgefield for 1869 and 1870 reveal that many black churches and congregations maintained their support of the public school system. "Gad S. Johnson for 88 colored children, southern male colored teacher, Primary school no. 1, Beech Island Nov 1, 1869–Nov 31, 1870. Church owns school, wood, bad condition. Paul Hammond owns land, no rent"; "Rev. FH. W. Tarrants Granitesville, col, 1 sn col male teacher. 39 black students. AME Church owns Nov 21, 1869–Jan 10, 1870."[81]

The connection between churches and schools in the black community, even after the start of public education, was not found between white churches and schools. According to the Manuscript Teachers Reports for Edgefield, no public white school was church related. In the Graniteville Mills or the Langley Mills, school buildings were provided by the company. White schools enjoyed the support of individual benefactors. Black schools represented a community effort, often organized through the churches.

Although the former slaves and their white allies established in South Carolina the basis for a public school system in a very short time, the southern planter aristocracy quickly restored the educational system to one where they were again in control after the 1876 election of Wade Hampton. During that campaign, the Republican platform contained an important message about schools: "In as much as the system of free schools was created in the State by the Republican party, and should be especially fostered and protected by it, we pledge ourselves to the support of the amendment to the State Constitution,

. . . establishing a permanent tax for the support of free schools, and preventing the removal of school funds from the counties where raised."[82]

Although Hampton endorsed this resolution and it became law in 1878, other actions of Hampton and the white Democrats toward education in South Carolina belied Hampton's endorsement of public education. It was also in 1878 that the state legislature passed "an act to alter and amend the School Law of South Carolina." State centralization of control of local school boards was insured by changing the State Board of Education, which under the Republicans had been composed of all the local county commissioners of education and the elected state superintendent of education, to a board of four appointed by the governor to serve with the superintendent of education. The state central board could then appoint the county board, who had been appointed by the elected county superintendent of education. Under the Republican administration, "Juries of view" composed of five voters had been appointed by local school trustees, but the new state government believed this gave the trustees too much power over the landowners, and they centralized all powers and took them away from local control. The state board reviewed all decisions of the local board, examined teachers, and issued and enforced the rules. The Reconstruction law providing for books for school children was repealed, as was the act which allowed poll taxes for payment of school claims. It was not until 1889 that, even if a community wanted to do so, local taxation for school was possible.[83]

In the aftermath of the Republican defeats, blacks in rural backcountry areas such as Edgefield immediately felt the impact. Whereas during Reconstruction Afro-Americans had controlled the schools, local courthouse, and town, the freedmen and their schools were driven from towns with the white Redemption. White private elite academies again appeared in town and in the rural countryside. Some were military academies, but most were once again denominational schools. These exclusive and private academies received public school funds just as they had done in the antebellum years. In addition, with the payscale for teachers reduced, more of the public school teachers of white and black children became women while most school principals in schools with more than one teacher were male.[84]

In spite of such reversals, black churches never gave up their commitment to education. Alexander Bettis, postbellum accommodationist and founder of forty Baptist churches, also founded in 1881 the church-related Bettis Academy, the chief Afro-American institution of learning in the county. Due in large part to Bettis's attitudes, the institution was accepted by leading Edgefield whites, who testified that this academy, which became a social and cultural community center, stood for the "highest moral and Christian values." Students at Bettis Academy brought furniture and even unprepared food from home and remained dependent upon their families for support. At the school itself, there was a familial and community atmosphere even in student housekeeping. They cooked and cleaned together and "under the open sky, with kettles suspended over a log fire, by means of a pole, and with tubs set on benches conveniently arranged they [had], under competent supervision, their natural laundry." Not until 1945 did students stop bringing food from home and begin paying board, giving away some family involvement in favor of modernization.

This religious and educational academy fostered family values of cleanliness, self-sufficiency, and hard work. Bettis Academy also continued an African legacy long after it was outlawed for other Afro-Americans. The beating of drums to call assemblies, common to oral cultures, was terrifying to the white community (especially after the Ned Tennant Riot), and after Reconstruction it was forbidden everywhere except Bettis Academy.[85]

The Church and Patriarchal Values

Just as the Afro-American church stressed family responsibilities and values and the importance of education, it also emphasized the male leadership associated with traditional kinship structures in agrarian society. The Bible, with its rural parables, delivered a powerful patriarchal message to the agrarian former slave population. Old Testament theology, as preached and practiced, focused on a father figure and implanted patriarchal values. Preachers and deacons, leaders charged with the welfare of their fellow worshipers as well as their spiritual guidance, were always men. Even under slavery, slave men had been preachers, exhorters, deacons, and sextons in their own brush-arbor groups and in the congregations established by white missionaries and benevolent planters. In the churches that both whites and blacks attended before Reconstruction, bondsmen were elected as special deacons and sextons and cooperated with the white deacons, especially in the disciplining of slave members. Slave exhorters and preachers had presided over slave baptisms, funerals, weddings, as well as discipline matters. Whether in mixed or in segregated black churches, these male leaders were influential.

Postbellum leadership positions in the churches were also male. The Pleasant Hill Baptist Church history listed its pastors and Sunday school superintendents—who were all male. The Church Mothers and Daughters of Zion of many churches were under male leadership. At the all-male Little River Baptist Association in 1877, "a query concerning the Daughters of Zion organization, from Cross Roads Church, was taken up and debated on by various brethren, which caused serious thought to arise concerning it. A motion was made by Rev. Henry Roberson, that we do recommend that Society one twelve months longer. Carried."[86]

Alexander Bettis allowed only family heads of impeccable reputation to serve as deacons in his churches. Refusing to tolerate "sexual laxity" among his parishioners, he not only preached strict morality but also literally took into his own hands punishment for "misconduct." He ordered disrupters seized and "with his buggy whip he would then and there inflict a whipping wholly commensurate with the offense." Among values preached were standards for family civility as directed by Ephesians:

> Wives, submit yourselves unto your own husbands, as unto the Lord. For the husband is the head of the wife, even as Christ is the head of the church: and he is the saviour of the body. . . . Let every one of you in particular so love his wife even as himself; and the wife see that she reverence her husband. Children obey your parents in the Lord: for this is right. Honour thy father and mother; which is the first commandment with promise; That it may be well with thee, and thou mayest live long on the earth. And, ye fathers, provoke not your children to wrath: but bring them up in the nurture and admonition of the Lord.[87]

Similar family values were preached by Afro-American political activists and radicals, former slaves who were not dependent on whites for their leadership roles in the black community. These religious leaders saw family autonomy as an expression of freedom and dignity. Paris Simkins, state legislator and second in command of the black militia, was a licensed preacher who, along with Lawrence Cain, state senator and commander of the black militia, led blacks out of the white Edgefield Village Baptist church against the wishes of the white congregation and helped found the Macedonia Baptist Church, which grew to rival Bettis's Baptist churches. Simkins and Cain lived and preached the same values as Bettis, with the exception that they also asserted black economic and political rights. Methodist minister David Harris, Sr., was another activist political and religious leader. Harris was at the same time preacher, state representative, and major in the militia, where he served as chaplain. Another black Reconstruction state legislator and militia major, David Graham, was deacon in the Rock Hill Baptist Church and gave the land for the church; he emphasized family values and biblical scriptures on family responsibilities. Black church and religious leaders were often political leaders who spread their particular concern for the traditional family structure and morality to the entire community.[88]

The patriarchal nature of the churches was maintained in the all-male church associations. Rule of Decorum Number 12 of the Little River Baptist Association stated, "The appellation of brother shall be used in our addresses to one another." The associations continued to be male, but the annual Sunday school conventions changed over time. Although both men and women taught Sunday school, only men served as delegates to the convention through the 1870s. In 1877 the Macedonia Association Sunday School Convention had only male delegates, but in 1884 it had eighty-seven male delegates and six female delegates. The Friendship Baptist Sunday School Association had only male delegates in 1885 and 1887. In 1892, however, when many churches did not send delegates and no formal roll was taken, it appears that fourteen men and four women were delegates. Three women delivered formal essays to the convention. Elizabeth Moore spoke on "gentle manners": "Boys I am sure that each of you love your mother and sister, and I do not need to tell you to be kind for their sakes to all women." In 1893 the Sunday school convention of the Little River Baptist Association had fifteen female and thirty-one male delegates, and women were also members of the various committees. At this time the convention still used the salutation "Dear Brethren," but by 1897 "Dear Sisters and Brethren" or "Dear Convention" was the prevailing form of address. Women were more active and more visible in their activities. Whether the patriarchal grasp was loosening or churches were going through rough times and needed women to fill the leadership positions cannot be deduced from the minutes. Some black churches had deaconesses, something no white church records indicate. Acknowledging the shared responsibilities and the family nature of the post, the ordination of a man as deacon in some churches automatically bestowed upon his wife the title of deaconess. These deaconesses helped organize functions, provided food for church gatherings, and kept the churches clean.[89]

Near the turn of the century, at about the same time as did the white churches, black churches noted their first women church secretaries and clerks. In the 1870s, however, church values were articulated by blacks in a traditional male-dominated, Christianized religious format closely resembling that of the surrounding white culture.

Other Organizations and Patriarchal Values

Other organizations besides churches reinforced patriarchal values and family life. The black militia during Reconstruction in particular reflected the Afro-American adherence to a patriarchal arrangement of society. Officers like Cain, Harris, Graham, and Simkins were the political, social, and religious leaders of the Afro-American community. Moreover, every black officer headed a family whose members became involved in other areas of leadership. Parades, drills, political rallies, and picnics were all occasions in which women stood in the wings and watched men perform. Describing a Fourth of July parade in 1874, the *Advertiser* wrote that the Edgefield black regiment of more than a thousand armed men commanded by Col. Lawrence Cain and Lt. Col. Paris Simkins, both former Edgefield slaves, marched through the streets of Edgefield, and "over and above this, every negro man and woman in Edgefield" cheered it on.[90]

After emancipation all other Edgefield black voluntary organizations, such as the funeral benevolent societies or the emigration society, were either all male or were headed by men. Fraternal associations, such as the Masons Lodge, the Sons of Zion, the Mutual Aid and Burial Society, and the secret order of the Knights of Pythias, restricted membership to males with reputations of virtue; the officers of such organizations were invariably the Edgefield Afro-American community leaders. These institutions reinforced the institution of the family and the patriarchal nature of rural society.

Within the patriarchal structure, black women were sometimes able to affect decision making within the family just as did white women (chapter 3). The father of Louise Pettis was a Baptist preacher and a recognized leader among former slaves in the southernmost part of Edgefield District. He had a large part in convincing some South Carolina black families to emigrate to Arkansas, but after arriving in Arkansas, he "grieved for South Carolina, so he went back and took us but ma wanted to come back. They stayed back there a yar or two." Then the mother had her way, and they returned to Arkansas to stay.[91]

Up-country South Carolina black folk tradition reflected patriarchal values. For example, families considered it "lucky" when a boy was born, and if a male was the first to enter a home on New Year's Day, then the family believed that it would have a prosperous year. Men generally said grace before meals, and the father sat at the head of the table and was either the first served or served the others. Although slave men were sometimes cooks and quilted or sewed, Edgefield postbellum black males did not help with the tasks. In rural Edgefield one pattern predominated: strong black (and white) patriarchal families.[92]

Summary

Afro-Americans in Edgefield expressed their newfound freedom not so much by discarding the values and institutions they had known under slavery as by setting up independent versions of those social, political, religious, and educational institutions. The complex system of values and beliefs that they developed shared many similarities with the white culture. Blacks adhered to traditional patriarchal households, and family and kin were important. Edgefield postbellum Afro-Americans exhibited community spirit and extended the "plantation community" ethos to focus on religious and political activity. The role of the church in the definition and maintenance of antebellum and postbellum Afro-American values cannot be overemphasized. The values of hard work, education, devotion to family, and righteous living prevailed. Afro-Americans, who had had stable plantation and interplantation communities during slavery, immediately developed a stable independent Afro-American community. At the center of this community were male-headed families.

Despite white opposition that often included violence, Afro-Americans persisted and made progress in educating their children and reducing illiteracy.

Although there were some differences in literacy and education rates between households headed by mulattoes and those headed by blacks, these differences mainly reflected the wealthier position of the former. Mulatto and black patterns in these matters were basically similar.

Despite later reversals, as we shall see, the black family and the demographic stability of the Afro-American community held firm. Indeed, sharecropping and tenancy were themselves bulwarks of the family. Farming was a family affair, and that was part of the compromise of the labor arrangement. Blacks wanted family farms and worked toward that end with tenancy. Most black household heads were not tenants, and tenancy was a move up the social and occupational ladder, a move made possible by a stable family structure.

7. Black and White Postbellum Household and Family Structure

In the decades after the Civil War, the family was the core of Southern society; within its bounds everything worthwhile took place.

F. B. Simkins,
History of the South (2nd ed. revised)

When Francis Butler Simkins noted the importance of the family in southern society after the Civil War, he could have been speaking of both black and white families. This was true despite enormous disparities in wealth: in 1870 only 266 Afro-Americans (5.5 percent of household heads) owned land and personal estate; that same year some 2,245 whites (65.8 percent of household heads) owned 97.8 percent of all real and 96 percent of all personal property. Notwithstanding these differences, blacks and whites in Edgefield had remarkably similar family structures.[1]

Family Structure

In both 1870 and 1880 two-thirds of both black and white households consisted of nuclear families (see Figure 7-1). The strongest evidence of a male-headed family structure during slavery was the post-emancipation similarity of black and white households (see Table 7-1). In 1870 and 1880 households of both races in Edgefield County had the same proportion of male heads. Even in 1850 and 1860, before the Civil War had taken its toll in the district, white males headed about the same percentage of households as did Edgefield black males in 1870 and 1880 (see chapter 2).

Not only did males of both races head households in about the same proportion but the percentages of two-parent households were also nearly identical. The age difference between husband and wife was almost the same, and black and white households had about the same number of people in them with approximately the same percentage of children. Age variations between

Figure 7–1. Household Structure, 1870 and 1880

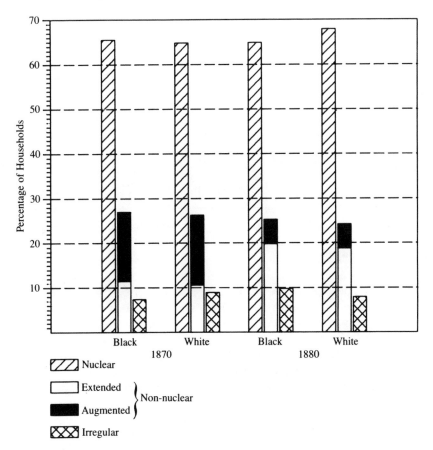

Note: See table 7–1 for *N*s, note, and source.

black and white household heads were minor, with the only significant differences appearing in the youngest and oldest age cohorts. These minor differences were even smaller in 1880, and little variation occurred between 1870 and 1880.

Antebellum poor whites had a smaller proportion of male-headed households than did wealthier white households. Table 7-2 categorizes 1870 postbellum households by wealth. In all three wealth categories Afro-American households (black plus mulatto) were more often male headed and more often had spouses and children present. In every wealth grouping the freedmen more often lived in two-parent families. Black households with wealth, more often

Table 7-1. Selected Characteristics of Households, 1870 and 1880
(percentages shown with selected characteristics)

| | 1870 | | 1880 | |
	Black (N = 4,873)	White (N = 3,419)	Black (N = 5,969)	White (N = 3,301)
Male-headed	83.7	82.0	86.4	86.7
Spouse present	73.8	70.8	75.1	76.2
Children present	76.4	75.1	75.5	76.7
Children and both parents present	59.5	57.7	62.0	64.4

Note: Unless stated otherwise, all tables, figures, and calculations exclude blacks in white households and whites in black households.
Source: Edgefield Data Base.

than white households with wealth, took in other persons. Black and white households with no property are strikingly similar (Figure 7-2). The effects of a slave system that purportedly produced matriarchal families could scarcely have been so quickly reversed.[2]

In 1870 all black farm tenant households in Edgefield were headed by men, and in 1880 almost 97 percent were male headed. These statistics reflected the reluctance of the white landowners to rent to a female household head unless she had sons old enough to help farm. Women, black or white, found it difficult, if not impossible, to run a farm without the help of an adult male or at least a teenage boy. Male household heads predominated on farms because they were capable of heavy, physical work. For the same reason white landowners preferred to hire men for permanent work as farm laborers. Married men with a family were more likely to run farms, since farmers needed wives and children to help. The postbellum Afro-American farm family was male headed to an overwhelming degree.[3]

It has been argued that during the Civil War women took a more active role in the running of plantations and farms. Although they probably did, one would expect that as a result of this experience and the decimation of male landowners and overseers caused by the Civil War, more women would be operating farms in 1870 than before the war in 1860. However, the opposite occurs: both the percentage and actual number of women operating farms in 1870 decrease. While women appear to have taken on more active roles in some areas of community life, farm operation primarily remained a male domain. One reason for this is that as tenantry replaced slavery after the war, a woman was less likely to be able to manage the plantation without the help of an overseer or a trusted driver.[4]

Extended Families

In 1870 and 1880 slightly less than a third of white and black households contained people who were not members of the nuclear family. The percentage of extended families—that is, of households containing the nuclear family and relatives—was also similar for both races. Moreover, controlling for age of household head, the percentages for households of both races which contained married children and their families remained nearly identical for both decades. These statistics on parents and children in black and white households show that the extended family was a cultural phenomenon which transcended barriers of class (see chapter 3), wealth, and race after the Civil War. The similarity of Afro-American and white populations in the same rural county does not disprove, but does cast doubt on, theories that slavery or African origins account for the extended black family. The immediate conditions of the postbellum South seem more important for an explanation of the development of the Afro-American family.[5]

The statistics for extended black and white households raise some interesting points about postbellum southern family structure. Extended white households were smaller after the Civil War than before. Perhaps Civil War deaths caused the decline in white household size. The reverse was true for blacks. The mean number of slaves per slave house (4.2) in 1860 was misleading because many slaves lived in their owners' households or on another farm. Nevertheless, Afro-American households grew while white households decreased in size. As a result, postbellum black and white households were of comparable size (for both 1870 and 1880, blacks 4.9 and whites 4.8).

Postwar economic conditions did, however, cause variations in the family structure of Edgefield blacks and whites. While the percentages of married children heading families who lived in the households of their parents were the same for blacks and whites and constant for age of the parent, white children were more likely to keep living with elderly parents than black children, and the racial differences increased with the household head's age (see Figure 7-3). Young black males set up households while working as farm laborers and tenants, and young black women found employment as domestics. Young white males, however, remained in their parents' households, working on the family farms until they inherited or bought land, and young white women waited to marry.

In 1870 black men who married that census year for the first time did so on an average of two years younger than whites (blacks 23; whites 25), and the one mulatto groom was the same age as the whites (25). Black brides (19) were

Table 7-2. Selected Characteristics of Households by Wealth and Color in 1870 (percentages shown with selected characteristics)

Households	Landed			
	White $(N=1{,}861)$	Afro-American $(N=81)$	Black $(N=55)$	Mulatto $(N=26)$
Male-headed	85.3	93.8	98.2	84.6
Spouse present	73.8	86.4	89.1	80.8
Children present	76.5	81.5	81.8	80.8
Children and both parents present	61.2	75.3	78.2	69.2
Only those households with children that have both parents	80.0	92.4	95.6	85.7

Note: Afro-American includes black and mulatto.
Source: Edgefield Data Base.

on the average a year younger than whites (20) at the age of first marriage, and mulatto women the same age as whites (20). Surprisingly, the ages of whites at marriage were nearly identical before and after the Civil War. And despite losses of men in the marriageable age cohorts, white women married even fewer men younger than themselves in 1870 than in 1860.[6]

Number of Children

Although Afro-American households had fewer children over eighteen both overall and per household, in two-parent households Afro-American fathers had more children of all ages per family than did white households. This situation was the same for all ages and wealth categories except for the oldest white age cohorts in the category of families in 1870 with personal property. For fathers of both races in 1870 and 1880, more children lived at home when the fathers were between the ages of forty and forty-nine. The antebellum pattern of wealthier families having more children than poorer families was also true for the postbellum era.

Afro-American females, like males, had more children of all ages per family than did white women. Afro-American mothers between the ages of thirty and thirty-nine in 1870 and 1880 had the most children at home. The single exception was black mothers in 1870 in landowning families; in this

	Personal Property Only				No Property		
White (N = 388)	Afro-American (N = 187)	Black (N = 147)	Mulatto (N = 40)	White (N = 1,171)	Afro-American (N = 4,607)	Black (N = 4,419)	Mulatto (N = 458)
94.3	98.9	98.6	100.1	72.4	82.9	82.9	82.8
82.0	93.6	92.5	97.5	62.3	72.8	72.6	74.7
74.5	86.6	86.4	87.5	73.5	75.9	76.0	75.3
66.2	81.8	81.0	85.0	49.4	58.4	58.2	59.8
88.9	94.4	93.7	97.1	67.1	76.8	77.1	80.4

group the most children were home for mothers between the ages of forty and forty-nine. These years (forty to forty-nine) were when white mothers had more of their children at home also. Except for children over eighteen, Afro-American women had more children at home in every age cohort than did white women. (When controlled for wealth, in 1870 landed black mothers had more children at home including children over eighteen.) Although few Afro-Americans owned land, these landed mothers and fathers in two-parent households maintained parental control over their children and kept them in the household even more than did landed whites.[7]

The mean number of children under the age of five for women suggests fertility. In 1870 white married women under forty years of age had more children younger than five. For both groups the average number of children under five declined over the decade and was similar in 1880, although whites in the younger age cohorts had slightly more children. For the older age cohorts, the reverse was true: in 1870 and 1880 black women forty years and older had more young children aged five or less at home. These data suggest a higher fertility rate for whites than blacks (less high when controlled for wealth), with declining overall fertility. Moreover, black women were older than white women when children were born. Infant or early childhood mortality was higher for postbellum Afro-Americans, as it was during slavery. These statistics are for married women only; as discussed below, there were significant differences between the number of young children in black and white households in which no man was present. Nevertheless, the fertility rate declined. A comparison of the number of children under five for whites in

Figure 7–2. Household Structure by Wealth and Color, 1870

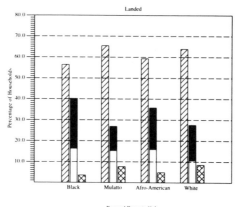

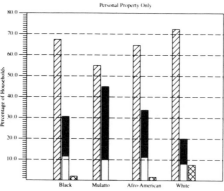

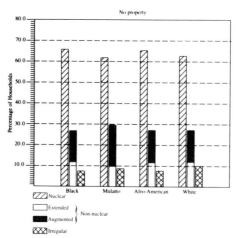

Note: See Table 7–2 for *N*s, note, and source.

Figure 7–3. Households with Children Eighteen Years and Older,
1870 and 1880

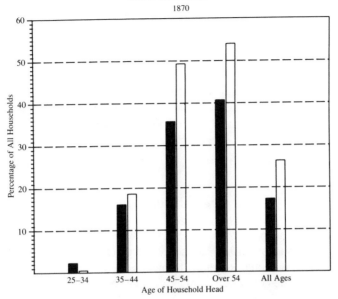

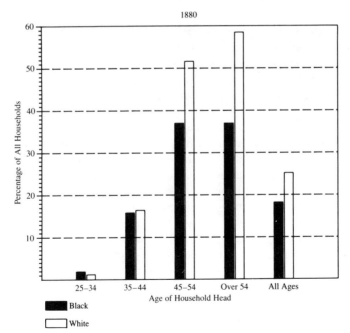

Note: See Table 7–1 for *N*s, note, and source.

1850 and 1860 demonstrates conclusively that married white women were having fewer children after the Civil War than before; this was perhaps because the South was poorer and poorer people had fewer children, because infant mortality rates were higher, or because emotional and psychological stresses affected fertility.

Although the number of black children for two-parent slave families is unavailable, a comparison of the population-based figures of children under five for the number of women of childbearing years for 1850 and 1860 yields a child/mother ratio. This ratio was higher for slaves than for antebellum whites; in the postbellum era the fertility of both races declined. By 1880 the numbers of children under five had become nearly identical for black and white households.[8]

Parental Authority

Despite opposition from some whites, Afro-American families immediately after the Civil War established autonomy and parental authority. The general similarities of household structure by no means eased confusion over the relationship between blacks and whites after the Civil War. In December 1866 the Freedmen's Bureau agent reported from Edgefield Court House that "as the blacks were not considered as having rights while they were slaves there seems to be difficulty in having a recognition of the fact that they have them now." The early contract system supervised by the Freedmen's Bureau was not a form of tenantry, although laborers were paid with a share of the crop. The first years of contracting saw attempts by white landowners, often inadvertently supported by bureau agents and U.S. troops, to maintain their plantations with some form of forced labor.[9]

Planters outlined the behavior they expected from former slaves in labor contracts. In Edgefield Freedmen's Bureau agent Lt. William Stone drew the line at planters' demands that they have disciplinary powers over the freedmen's children. When a planter wrote that he or his agent "must have control of the children on the plantation and make them behave either by constraining them themselves or requiring their parents to do so," the bureau officials changed the wording to read "behave by requiring their parents to correct them." To another Edgefield contract which read, "We the freedmen agree that the youth of our connexion are to be in every respect subject to the discipline of the said Ransom Timmerman or his agent John Parkman; and in the case of obstinancy or disobedience they shall be subject to corporal punishment," Stone added, "by their proper guardians." In another contract, Lieutenant Stone struck the phrase "allow the said Bell employer to correct and control the children." One former slave's distinction between freedom and slavery depended on this shift toward parental autonomy. Whites did not whip him, but "my own folk whooped me. We was free then."[10]

Stone did not interfere when contracts demanded that all laborers, including children, exhibit deferential behavior toward whites. He upheld a clause in one contract that required blacks to "obey and behave ourselves as persons of color in our situation and also that our children are to obey" the employer. The planters did not voluntarily give up their control over Afro-American family matters.[11]

Afro-American Farming Households

The shift in the status of farm laborers from slave to tenant, reflected in the shift in occupational categories from farm laborer to farmer from 1870 to 1880 (Table 7-3), was a major gain for Afro-Americans. White landowners wanted to continue their planting operations with the gang labor system used under slavery, while Afro-Americans wanted their own farms and control over their own families and households. The tenant system was a compromise solution. In 1870, 85 percent of all black household heads identified themselves as farm laborers to the census enumerator, while only 2.2 percent called themselves farmers. By 1880, 44.2 percent of all Afro-American household heads were farmers; the vast majority, renters (57.4 percent) or sharecroppers (29.0 percent), settled on land with their families. This was even truer for male-headed households. On these dispersed family farms, Afro-Americans were not under the close scrutiny of white landowners and their hired supervisors.

Nearly a third of the Afro-American farm operators in 1880 took other blacks into their households. Most blacks worked as farmers and farm laborers. The households of these black agriculturalists were more likely to consist of extended families than were the households of white farmers and farm laborers (Figure 7-4). The household of the farmer both supported and demanded the labor of more people. Whites hired laborers; Afro-Americans relied on kin and friends who moved into the household.

The larger household of the black farmer merits special mention. All freedmen did not become tenants and farmers. Even in 1880 farmers headed fewer than half of the Edgefield Afro-American households. For blacks, even more than for whites, farming was a high-status occupation in postbellum Edgefield. Black farmers had a significantly larger proportion of extended families than did any of the other employed occupational groups, regardless of race. For blacks and whites, because occupational status correlated positively with literacy, age, land tenure, wealth, gender of household head, and household size, black farmer families were even more likely to be extended when controlling for these variables. It is impossible to generalize from the patterns of

*Figure 7–4. Household Structure by Occupation of Household Head,
1870 and 1880*

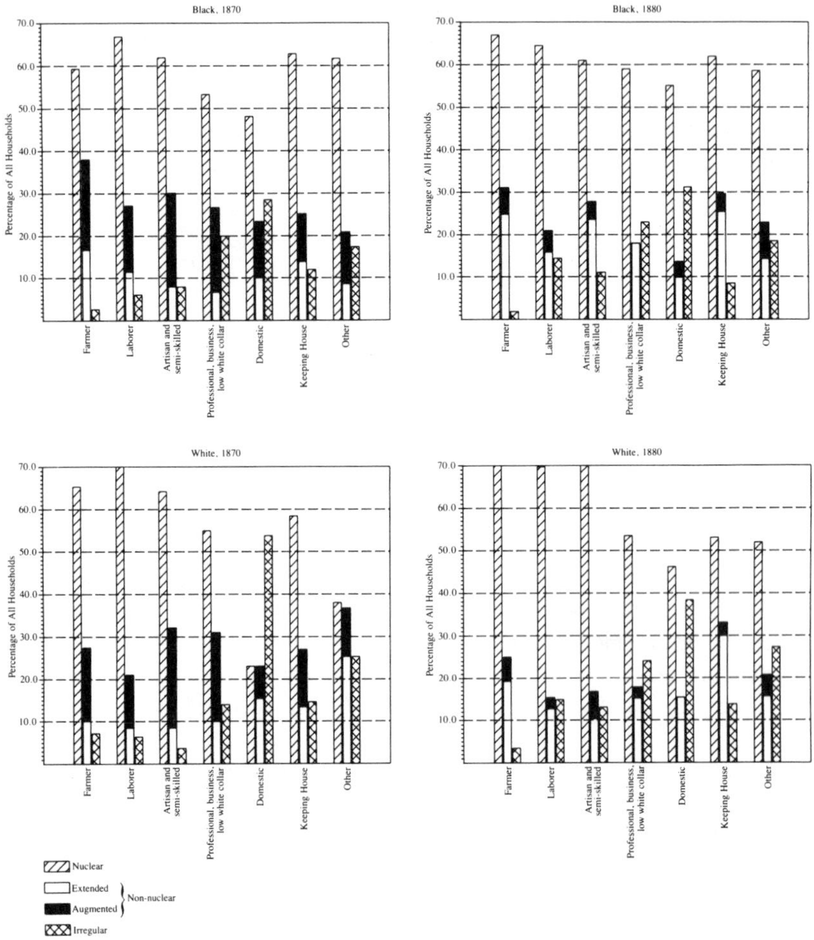

Note: See Table 7–3 for *N*s, note, and source.

Table 7-3. Occupations of Household Heads, 1870 and 1880 (percentages)

	1870				1880			
	White		Black		White		Black	
Occupation	Male (N=2,801)	Female (N=619)	Male (N=4,080)	Female (N=794)	Male (N=2,862)	Female (N=441)	Male (N=5,158)	Female (N=811)
Farmer	57.7	11.0	2.6	0.1	77.5	23.0	49.9	8.0
Laborer	30.2	3.4	92.4	50.4	9.6	6.2	45.0	46.8
Artisan and Semi-skilled	3.8	0	2.8	0	3.7	0	1.4	0
Professional, business, low white collar	7.0	0.4	0.4	0	7.8	0.5	0.4	0
Domestic	0	2.2	0.4	17.7	0.1	3.1	2.3	18.1
Keeping House	0	75.9	0	28.2	0	58.3	0	14.5
Other	1.3	7.1	0	3.5	1.3	8.9	1.0	2.6

Note: Percentages subject to rounding. For occupational groupings see appendix 2.
Source: Edgefield Data Base.

farmers alone to the rest of the Afro-American population; one must look at the other occupational groups.[12]

Care of Young and Old

Although the black farmer was most conspicuous, blacks in every occupational category opened their homes to relative and nonrelative alike. Nonrelatives were sometimes "boarders," but more often they were unofficial members of the family. Afro-Americans lived together for several reasons. Limited housing led families to "double up," to live in one house until a second could be built. Families grouped for safety's sake during Reconstruction violence. Poverty and disability had the same effect as violence. Older persons, children, and others who could not adequately provide for themselves were taken into the homes of others.

Particularly vulnerable were those older former slaves, the legendary "good and faithful servants." Catherine Hammond wrote to her brother-in-law Marcellus in the aftermath of the Civil War: "We have not lost many negroes . . . [but] I wish we could get clear of many of the useless ones." Her son Harry, however, provided for the old and young. He wrote in April 1866, "I am planting this year with 65 full hands; 20 supernumerances or nonworkers, who can be engaged a pinch, and allowed to live on the plantation." Not all planters were as benevolent as Hammond. In 1867, from Edgefield District near Ninety Six, James W. Fouche sent a letter to Dr. E. R. Calhoun, a state agent for distributing relief, concerning "two very old freedmen who are in actual want. Entirely dependent on others for food. Both of them have been faithful servants and I have every reason to believe that both are Christians. Their names are John and Daphne." Fouche added that there were other elderly blacks and whites in adverse circumstances.[13]

Afro-American households, like white households, welcomed the elderly into their homes. In 1880 the percentages of older adults (over fifty years) who were not nuclear family members were nearly identical in black and white households. A difference appeared in the percentages of young people (under twenty years) taken into others' households. In almost every age cohort in 1870 and 1880, Afro-American households had proportionately more young non-nuclear members than did white ones. This pattern was even more pronounced when only male-headed households were considered (23.3 and 15.9 percent black and 18.4 and 8.8 percent white in 1870 and 1880, respectively). Emancipation left a number of orphaned and separated black children, who were brought into the households of other blacks. Some orphaned Afro-American sibling families were apprenticed to whites immediately after the Civil War. In March 1867, Dr. Thomas J. McKie, a large landowner in Edgefield County, had written to Freedmen's Bureau agent William Stone:

I have on my place in Edgefield District five negro children whose ages are respectively about 5, 7, 9, 11 & 13 yrs. Their parents were among my best and most faithful servants, but both are now dead, leaving the said children upon my hands. They have been permitted to stay on the place and have been provided with food and clothing at my expense since the surrender. My object in intruding this letter upon you, is to know if you will apprentice these children to me, and upon what terms, until they become of age. . . . Thus far they have been a tax and care upon me without compensation, and I am unwilling to bear it longer unless there can be some assurance of reward at some future day.[14]

Stone, a conscientious bureau officer, wanted to make sure the orphans received an education and some compensation for their years of labor, but he apprenticed the five children to McKie whom he termed "the master," the legal term in cases of apprenticeship, "until of age he desire them. The form of the indenture is that laid down in the Law of Magistrate." In the 1870 manuscript census, these children appeared as a black family headed by a female, the oldest sibling, in the household of white farmer McKie.

Before blacks assumed political power, children such as these were "apprenticed" to white planters through the Freedmen's Bureau. They could not be released from this apprenticeship and were supposed to be learning a trade, which usually meant that they served as domestics or farm laborers for the white family. When Republicans assumed power, they ended some of this exploitation of black children. White Republican O. H. Hart asked Governor R. K. Scott to end the indenture of Butler Griffin, an Afro-American boy, to a white planter. The governor interceded, and Griffin was released from his indenture on grounds that he was bound against his will. By 1880 this practice of apprenticing black children was less common, which accounts for some of the decrease in the number of blacks living in white households. In 1870 there were twenty and in 1880 only five such black sibling families in white households; the vast majority (75.5 percent) lived in black households. In 1880, 86.5 percent of all young orphaned and sibling black families lived in black households.[15]

Postbellum Housing

The housing patterns that had characterized the antebellum era did not change for most Edgefield whites after the war; they continued to live in houses they owned or rented before the Civil War. Most former slaves, who had lived in concentrated slave quarters on large plantations, in houses close to that of the white owner on smaller farms, or even in the white household, wanted to move away from this form of social control. Yet some of these prewar household patterns persisted into the postbellum era. According to census data on mixed households the antebellum traditions of wealthy whites with black household servants and of small white farmers with black household servants and live-in black laborers continued into the postbellum era.

Although the landed wealthy had more, both rich and poor whites had blacks in their households after the war; few blacks had whites in their households. In 1870, 13.8 percent (471) of all white households had blacks listed in them, and these blacks constituted 4.5 percent (1,126) of the total black population. By 1880 this had dropped to 8.8 percent (291) of white households with 1.8 percent (533) of the black population listed in their households. The percentages of whites in Afro-American households was negligible, 0.8 and 0.4 percent of all whites (141 and 66), respectively, in 1870 and 1880.[16]

In 1870 and 1880 there were a few cases of real mixed families, where blacks and whites were either married to one another or were related in some other way (see Table 7-4). Some of these were continuations of the mixed households that had existed before the war. But mixed households were only a tiny proportion of the total number; of more significance was the postwar intermarriage of black and mulatto. Although a substantial proportion of mulattoes married mulattoes, even more married blacks. This was a dramatic shift from the antebellum free Afro-American patterns and indicated the forging of an Afro-American community.

Development for the Former Slaves

The scarcity of housing following emancipation encouraged the trend for Afro-Americans to take additional people into their households. The immediate shortage of homes may have had a greater influence on this trend than did any enduring African heritage. To some extent the housing situation also explains why some white households had black members after the war.

A former Edgefield slave remembered that immediately after the Civil War there was "not much house room. Several families had to live in one house." Existing housing and funds for new housing were too limited to ensure adequate single-family housing for the newly freed slaves. Under bondage housing belonged to slaveowners, and after 1865 some freedmen lost even these shelters. A sample of 1867 farm labor contracts supervised by the Freedmen's Bureau showed that in the three counties of Edgefield, Abbeville, and Anderson, only 35 percent of the contracts stipulated that employers were to provide housing for the former slaves. Employers also had the right to evict black tenants.[17]

Freedmen's Bureau agent William Stone believed that landowners violated nearly a third of the 646 contracts that existed between Edgefield landowners and former slaves in 1865–66. Violations often meant that blacks were driven

Table 7-4. Color of Spouses of Afro-Americans, 1870 and 1880
(percentages)

| | Spouse's Color | | | | |
| | 1870 | | | 1880 | |
Color of Family Head	Black	Mulatto	White	Black	Mulatto
Black	93.8	6.1	0.1	92.9	7.1
Mulatto	54.8	42.6	2.6	59.8	40.2

Note: For 1870, $N = 3,407$ black, 432 mulatto; for 1880, $N = 4,126$ black, 453 mulatto. This table excludes Indians.
Source: Edgefield Data Base.

from their homes. Stone believed that the landowners broke the contracts because of their "antipathy to the colored race," their desire to see free labor prove a failure, and their "feeling that the stronger race has a cultural right to oppress the weaker." In a neighboring district, a bureau officer reported that when fewer laborers were needed, white employers drove "freedmen having large families" from the plantation.[18]

The diminished need for labor may have motivated the attack on Wade Adams and his family in Edgefield. In 1866, Adams's former owner came into the fields where all his hands were toiling. Adams testified that he singled out Adams's family, tying up him and three of his children, and then "stripping our clothes off and whipped us severely." The former owner threatened that if Adams went to the "dam'ed Yankees he would blow my dam'ed head off." Black families driven off by white landowners had to find a place to live and sometimes it was with another black family. Francis Butler Simkins observed that the poor in Edgefield County would share their homes, but before homes could be shared, former slaves had to get houses, and that too was part of the developing tenantry system.[19]

The testimony of astute agricultural observer Harry Hammond outlined the development of black family housing. By 1900 freedmen's houses were larger and "more comfortable than they had been since slavery times. Immediately after the war any sort of house was put up." Hammond revealed the desire of Afro-American men to place their families in their own homes: "In fact, a hand would come to you and would be willing to build his house if you would let him have a certain piece of land. He would build on the land and live in his house." Hammond, who could only see a black's house as a "miserable cabin," entirely missed the former slave's perspective. During Reconstruction it was the black man who either with his own hands or the aid of kin and friends built the dwelling where his family resided. Hammond also missed the implication of the post-Reconstruction development of housing for blacks. He proudly explained that the housing situation had improved for blacks because the housing was provided by white landowners for whom Afro-Americans worked instead of being constructed by the black laborer. "But recently he has done better than that. The building has been undertaken by the employers themselves, and they build substantial houses. Of course, they are not places of style; it is not necessary that they should be."[20]

Although whites helped to build housing after they resumed control during the era of Redemption, they destroyed black homes during the Reconstruction period, when blacks had political control. This violence affected postbellum housing patterns. The tenant farm system established during Reconstruction dispersed Afro-American and poorer white families on plots of from forty to sixty acres, making them vulnerable to organized violence. In 1866 the Washington, D.C., *Chronicle* printed an accusation that bushwhackers were burning Edgefield Afro-American homes. The local newspaper responded obliquely that "as to the burning of negroes' dwellings . . . it is well known that negroes have no dwellings. Nineteen out of twenty live in outhouses belonging to white people."[21]

Throughout Reconstruction white planters evicted Edgefield blacks from homes and punished nonconforming whites. Col. Lawrence Cain confirmed to Governor Chamberlain that "it is true that many of our men are refused employment and thrown out of house, but the men are not confined to the Militia Companies. Any man who took a prominent part in the last political contest is proscribed." An executive report of the 1875 investigation in Edgefield County noted "that most of the white men whose buildings have been burned were those who refused to unite with others in the recent proscription against the colored people." Benjamin R. Tillman bragged that two hundred black militia were unemployed and homeless in the southwestern section of the county where he lived because landowners committed themselves "not to rent land to any member of the negro militia or give them employment. . . . Those who did not sign rendered themselves very obnoxious and were almost ostracised by their fellows." Tillman particularly regretted the fate of Joshua McKie, "a refined and hightoned gentleman" who, "against the wishes of his neighbors," after the first Tennant riot in 1874, gave Ned Tennant "a home." After McKie "rented the land and signed the lease he found himself shunned and ostracised by his friends, and even by kinsmen." Soon afterward, he committed suicide. State Representative Paris Simkins, a former Edgefield slave, demanded the state protect all black laborers who, "because of having exercised their political rights and privileges," had been discharged by white landowners in Edgefield County.[22]

Postwar violence altered the housing situation; there was safety in numbers and many blacks, as well as whites, lived together as much for protection as for necessity. In 1870 the number of solitary black and white households was small. By the late 1870s violence had decreased considerably and the housing shortage had lessened. As a result the number of single-member households, mostly male, increased tremendously among blacks and whites during the decade.[23]

Afro-American Home Sharing

Black families often moved in with each other for reasons other than lack of housing or safety. Families took in others to care for the elderly, to shelter the poor or disabled, and to augment the family income. Whatever the reasons, the persons who shared a house were frequently related. When they were not related, the mixed households exemplified the sense of responsibility that blacks felt for others in the Afro-American community.

In 1870 black town marshal Cary Harris, his wife, and their four children shared their home with his younger brother Allen's family of seven. The 1870 manuscript census did not usually report the relationship of other persons in the home to the household head, but it contained numerous examples of households that included persons who could have been brothers- or sisters-in-law, nieces, or nephews. Peter Ross, a thirty-six-year-old farm laborer in 1870, lived with thirty-seven-year-old wife Mary and three young children. In addition, Charles, Erasmus, Angeline, and Mark Scott, farm laborers ranging in age from ten to eighteen years, lived in the Ross household. Robert Thomas headed a household of seven individuals. The census listed Thomas, a forty-five-year-old farm laborer, his forty-year-old wife, Eliza, twenty-one-year-old Rebecca, and nineteen-year-old Liddleton, all farm laborers. Listed next were seventy-five-year-old Matt Thomas, also a farm laborer, and Polly Thomas, "without occupation." The last member of the household was a ten-year-old farm laborer, Mary Lee. Although the ages are suggestive, the census did not reveal the relationship of these laborers to the household head.

The 1880 manuscript census recorded the relationship of all persons in a household to the head; this census showed many varieties of extended families. Oliver Holloway, a twenty-six-year-old farmer, was married to twenty-eight-year-old Lila, who kept house and worked as a laborer. They had six children: Alonzo, eight; Whitfield, seven; Sarah, six; Delila, five; Andrew, three; and Lula, one. A nephew and a niece, Augustus Hill and Mary Lou Cochran, fifteen-year-old laborers, lived in the household. Dinah Brown, Holloway's sixty-seven-year-old "dependent" mother-in-law also belonged to the household.

Afro-American households cared for the young, old, and needy. It was not just the older, more established blacks who felt this responsibility. Twenty-five-year-old Fortune Calhoun and his young wife and child also had two sisters, a young brother, and a nephew living in their household. Although much poorer, Afro-American household heads in all age groups brought other people into their homes at the same rate as did their white counterparts.[24]

Black and white families felt obligation and deference toward the old and feeble, a responsibility to care for the young and helpless, and a sense of dignity that forged a feeling of community in Edgefield. An interesting difference between blacks and whites in their willingness to care for the helpless is suggested by the poorhouse figures. From 1870 through 1910, white paupers and indigents in the poorhouse outnumbered blacks in the same circumstances, although blacks made up two-thirds of the population and were much poorer than the white population. In 1870 Afro-Americans controlled the political machinery, and government agencies, such as poorhouses, were open to their use; underrepresentation could not be explained by lack of opportunity.[25]

Afro-American families had kinship patterns similar to those for whites. The black Caless family was an example. Ezekiel Caless was forty-eight years old; his wife Kittie was thirty-three. They had four children; the eldest was eighteen-year-old Anthony, and the youngest, seven-year-old Ezekiel, Jr. Rebecca Griffin, Kittie's sixty-year-old mother, also lived with the family, as did nieces and nephews July and Milledge Bonham (aged sixteen and six), Ned Hutchinson (aged sixteen), and Winston Day (aged sixteen). His older brother Winston rented the farm next to Ezekiel's. In addition to his wife and two children, Winston's household included his and Ezekiel's seventy-year-old mother, their hundred-year-old grandmother, Winston's widowed sister-in-law, three nephews, and a niece. Patterns such as these suggest that separate families sometimes lived next door to households of aunts, uncles, grandmothers to make up a larger extended family, a "kinship colony."

Immediately after the war, augmented and extended black households often included children, elderly relatives, and heads of two entire families. After Reconstruction, while extended households continued to include children and elderly relatives, they usually contained only one male-headed family. By 1880 there was a decline in the number of separate male-headed families living together in a single household, even among relatives. In 1880, Cary Harris and his younger brother still lived near each other in Edgefield, but in separate homes. Afro-American males with families seemed gradually to have freed themselves from situations in which they were dependent on others. In 1870 some black males who had families elsewhere were living in the households of whites (usually as servants) or of nonrelated blacks. By 1880 black males with wives and children seldom lived in the household of someone else. Most black males were listed with their families in 1880, and more families lived in their own households. In 1870, 783 Afro-Americans (14.8 percent of all black family heads) headed families in households headed by another person; by 1880 there were only 320 (5.6 percent of family heads; this excludes irregular, solitary, and institutional arrangements). In 1870 the number of whites who headed families in the household of someone else was 394, which taken as a percentage of white families was 11.2 percent; in 1880 the white proportion was almost identical to the black, 175 (5.4 percent).

Taking in boarders was a necessity for poorer Afro-American families who faced high rents in urban areas. Edgefield whites who owned land and homes in towns took in boarders more often than blacks, few of whom owned town homes. In November 1873 a white boarder wrote, "The price of board at Edgefield Court House is from $20 to at $25 per month . . . at Johnston's Depot about $30 per month. It is sixty dollars a month in private families at Aiken—but little chance for accommodation in the neighborhood." Moreover, whites in Edgefield had hotels and boarding houses, but there were none for Afro-Americans. Therefore, blacks who lived in unrelated households were generally listed only as laborers in rural Afro-American households. Sometimes male or female adult blacks lived in the household of an unrelated black family and were identified as "boarders" by the census. This generally occurred in the households of community leaders and wealthier blacks who owned homes in the town. In 1880 Reconstruction black legislators David Harris and Lawrence Cain had extended families of brothers-in-law and other family members and took in boarders as well. In Harris's twelve-person household one boarder was a twenty-two-year-old laborer; another, a thirty-year-old preacher from Rhode Island; and yet another, a twenty-year-old schoolteacher. All three were single. In Lawrence Cain's household of eleven blacks were an eighteen-year-old laborer and a sixty-year-old laborer; unrelated to any member of the household, they were single. No white boarder in 1880 headed a family, but eighteen blacks who headed families were boarders.[26]

Most of the non-nuclear family members living in either black or white households were not boarders. Although some of these nonfamily household members were employed and provided income for the households, many were dependent on the household unit. For blacks, just as they had been for antebellum poor whites, households and families were the main welfare support system in the county, and they were open to new members. Extra laborers were brought in when needed; extra people were taken in if they were in need.

Black and White Households

Basic similarities and important differences existed between black and white living patterns. Although there were convergent tendencies between black and white families from 1870 to 1880, Afro-Americans in the postemancipation years, as they had in slavery, faced obstacles that whites did not. Variations between black and white family patterns and household structures were evident after the Civil War.

The 1870 and 1880 occupational structure of Edgefield County reflected the postwar economy and racial discrimination (Table 7–3). In 1870, 86.2 percent of all black and 69.8 percent of all white household heads were farmers or farm laborers. In 1880 the respective percentages were 89.1 and 78.2. Only a few black household heads owned and operated farms (2.4 percent in 1870; 2.3 percent in 1880).

In occupational groupings with a significant number of both black and white household heads, variations in age and gender of the household head, in the household size, and even in the type of family were insignificant (refer to Figure 7–4). The Afro-American artisan during Reconstruction was successful and had much the same status as his white counterpart. Differences between black and white household structures existed in family types across the occupational categories, however. These differences can best be seen if one separates households into those headed by males and those headed by females.

Male-headed Households

Male-headed households of the two races became more similar during the Reconstruction decade in every respect except that of the *age* of the household head. Both absolutely and relatively there were more elderly white than elderly black household heads and, conversely, more younger black than younger white male household heads.

These age differences cannot be explained by race alone; one must look to the social and economic conditions of postwar South Carolina. First, South Carolina suffered the highest percentage of men killed of any state during the war. This loss was reflected in the white age group of 25–34 in 1870. Second, because Afro-Americans did not have any economic opportunities during slavery, older blacks had no head start over younger blacks in the accumulation of wealth. In fact, because their labor was of less value, the eldest group of Afro-Americans was at a real disadvantage, especially in the immediate postwar years.

In 1870 and 1880 the difference between white and black male-headed household structures was best explained by differences in the economic life cycles of the two groups. As shown above, few former slaves had personal wealth other than what they earned through physical labor. While younger blacks had as much or more wealth than most older blacks, most younger whites had much less than did older whites. Older whites who were household heads could hire black or white laborers to work their land or maintain younger family members. By contrast, sometimes older blacks, with no money, land, or other means of support, could not keep up their own households, and they, along with the very young, were taken into other homes. If not dependent themselves, they were less likely than whites to be able to maintain dependents in their households. Thus, elderly blacks were often taken in by their children.[27]

By 1880 the differences in age distribution between black and white men who headed households had somewhat lessened. Fifteen years after the Civil War, there was much less difference between the percentages of older whites and blacks who headed households and an increase of white household heads aged 25–34 years.

One major difference in male-headed households was the proportion of wives who were gainfully employed. This had repercussions for the position of women in black and white families and for the matriarchy myth and female independence in the Afro-American family.

Contracts recorded by the Freedmen's Bureau in the first few years after the war revealed that significantly fewer women than men made contracts with white landowners. Of the 140 contracts made between January and September 1868, 85.2 percent of the full hands contracted were males. In 1868 the Freedmen's Bureau agent wrote that Edgefield freedmen worked "for a portion of the crop" and that they did not make very much. The agent was particularly concerned: "The women are generally adverse to working as field hands and few of them have been trained for anything else. Instead, therefore, of being producers they are of little assistance to their families and consume in the way of food a large portion of their husbands wages. As far as possible the office endeavors to discourage the idea that freedom and work are incompatible and that wives should not assist in supporting their families. The men are generally willing to work."[28]

From the Civil War to 1869, James Talbert kept careful records of the work of his former slaves and the time they took off from work. Their ability to accomplish their own goals is revealing of the new economic and social order as tenantry became more established. In 1867 the records for former slave Phil, now known as Phil Freedman, his wife Susan, and their son Pierce, show that on 15 April Susan lost one half-hour of pay because she had stayed at her own home to clean it up before coming to work. Between 16 August and 16 September, Susan quit at noon so she could go home to prepare the meal and do housework. Records for Jacob show that his wife Amanda lost six weeks because she stayed home in bed after the birth of her child. Jacob lost an hour because he went to see about his wife and child. On 22 March, Jeff Freedmen lost one hour "hauling manure for himself." Many of the former slaves took days off to visit relatives; Will went away to visit his father, and Tandy visited his sister. Freedom for the former slaves gave them the opportunity, although at times a costly one (for example, Sibley lost his job), to visit friends and relatives, do work at their own homes, rest after childbirth, or, as in the case of Sibley, who "persisted in refusing to work," just relax.[29]

The Edgefield black community's family orientation conflicted with the economic and social interests of whites. Native white observers also complained about the refusal of black women to work for white households after slavery. One complained that it "necessitates radical change in the management of our households as well as plantations." In 1871 the Edgefield *Advertiser* claimed that black women's refusal to work "was so unreasonable" that it was for the whites "nothing short of absolute torment." Landowners in Edgefield lamented that black women no longer worked in the fields as they had in slavery, but withdrew to their homes and left their husbands to work alone. In 1874 a letter to South Carolina's most influential agricultural publication proclaimed "the impertinence and unreliability of female servants is the greatest annoyance in the country, to our wives and daughters."[30]

Afro-Americans wanted their wives to manage the homes and their husbands to be breadwinners. Black Edgefield society's commitment to the stable family continued to displease whites. In 1901, Harry Hammond testified before a congressional committee that black women would "only work during certain seasons of the year at cotton picking and cotton hoeing." He also complained that "I lost my cook. She just went off to a place she never had known or heard of before, on account of no fault with us, but to follow her husband."[31]

During slavery, black men and women had had little choice when the white master ordered a wife to work in a white household or wanted to separate a family. Edgefield whites believed that Afro-American family ties were not as important as the economic needs and physical comfort of whites; this belief persisted from the antebellum period through the late nineteenth century. Freedmen chose to maintain their families by having wives stay at home. Emancipation resulted in a massive withdrawal of black married women from employment but still a much higher proportion of black than white women worked outside the home. Although many white women were employed in the antebellum labor force, only two wives (both from the poorest 1860 quartile) had jobs. In 1870, 34.5 percent of black wives, compared to 1.2 percent of white wives, worked. In 1880 the percentages rose to 62.2 for black and 3.2 percent for white wives.

There was a possibility that both before and after the war the occupations of wives of farmers were undercounted. Nuclear families had slightly more working spouses than did extended and augmented families, suggesting that when other people were incorporated into the household unit, the wife-mother was too busy at home to look for outside employment. Wealth equalized the proportions of black and white working wives somewhat; neither Afro-American nor white wives in landed families worked outside the home. A high percentage of male domestics had working wives, sometimes with jobs in the same household. Even when controlled for the number of farmers' wives who were not counted as having occupations and for the number of farm laborers and tenants whose wives worked, considerably more black than white wives were employed in postbellum Edgefield County.[32]

The postbellum agricultural system involved the entire black family as a working unit. Early Edgefield contracts, such as that of "D. Walker and A. Washington and wife and two daughters" in 1867, were evidence that wives and children worked. Sometimes the laborer's family was specifically mentioned in a contract. Bureau agent Stone revoked the following clause in a contract: "If at any time said parties Bob and wife fail to perform duties plantation or domestic or disobey any commands reasonable, shall forfeit their wages and will be liable to discharge at any time." The contract between Francis Pickens and his former slave Alfred, whom Pickens hired in a supervisory capacity in 1866, stipulated that "Alfred's wife Nancy is to help milk as she does now and have a general care over poultry to feed and watch after them for F. W. Pickens." Only Alfred and Pickens, however, signed the contract. Black women were expected by planters to work as part of a family team in the immediate postwar years, but the husband was responsible for the family's work.[33]

Black women in rural areas worked alongside their husbands and children, but maintained traditional roles: rearing the children and caring for their husbands. On plantations husbands and wives could work together, and on the tenant farms they worked as a cooperative family enterprise. Husbands expressed great pride in their wives' abilities as workers. One former slave boasted, "I marry Kate at de close of dat revival. De day after de weddin', . . . after gettin' breakfas' she went to de field, poke 'round her neck, basket on her head and picked two hundred pounds of cotton. Dats de kind of woman she is."[34]

The partnership between husband and wife was often commented on by former slaves; as one said, "All the time my wife was my best helper." Another former slave from Edgefield explained that "way me and my husband paid for the house, he farmed for Jim Black and Mr. Gunn. I cooked for Jim Woodfin. Then I run a roomin' house till four years ago." In addition to helping their husbands farm, many black wives sewed and washed and ironed clothes for as little as twenty-five cents a basket.[35]

This theme of partnership appeared in accounts given by Matilda Evans and Ben Tillman of the murder of black state representative Simon Coker. Upon being informed by Nat Butler, captain of a white paramilitary unit, that he had only a few minutes to live, Coker replied, "Here is my cotton house key; I wish you would please send it to my wife and tell her to have our cotton ginned and pay our landlord rent just as soon as she can."[36]

Nearly all black women had worked since childhood as house servants or agricultural laborers under slavery. They had a greater sense of autonomy after the war and were more inclined to go to work than women who had not worked all their lives. This ethic of hard work was discussed in chapter 6 for black men and women.

One of Francis Pickens's former slaves, Carrie Nancy Fryer, insightfully described the attitude of some black men and women who worked. "He didn' 'low me to work. Dat was a good husband! I had six chullun. He say: 'Honey, no! I workin' makin' enough to support you. All I want you to do is keep dis house clean and me and my chillun, and I will pay you de five dollars every week de white lady would pay you.' And he done dat, gimme five dollars every week for myself!" While Mrs. Fryer was devoted to her husband, she also took pride in her endeavors. Her behavior illustrates how women in a patriarchal society often found ways to do what they wanted even when it went against the wishes of their husbands. "A white lady was crazy about my work, jus' her and her husband. I got up soon one morning, time he [Mr. Fryer] left, and runned up dere and washed her clothes and ironed dem." Defiance of her husband plagued Mrs. Fryer. She was convinced that she had been punished for her insubordination by his early death. By choosing to work against her husband's wishes she opposed the dominant Afro-American patriarchal pattern.[37]

Although there were far more black than white wives in the Edgefield work force, both lived in a patriarchal society. Edgefield black people lived in a community organized into families in which the father provided food and shelter. Black men even headed families in greater proportion than white men of equal wealth. Edgefield men of both races assumed the roles of husband, father, and provider.

Female-headed Households

Since scholars have paid so much attention to the proportion of households headed by women, one must compare the small percentage of black and white females who headed households and families.

Control of wealth is an indication of power distribution. Figure 7-5 displays the proportion of wealth owned by women in 1870. White women slightly increased their share of the wealth after the Civil War. Black women controlled a much smaller proportion of Afro-American wealth than Caucasian women did white wealth. Control of wealth is not a key to the black matriarchy myth. In fact, postbellum blacks reversed the antebellum free black pattern (chapter 5), in which a high proportion of the wealth was controlled by women, while white women gained a little more control of the wealth after the Civil War.

White female household heads owned proportionately more wealth than Afro-American women, but black female household heads were much more likely to be employed. Even the inclusion of white female farmers who hired others to work their farms in the proportions of employed female household

Figure 7–5. Female Wealth by Color in 1870

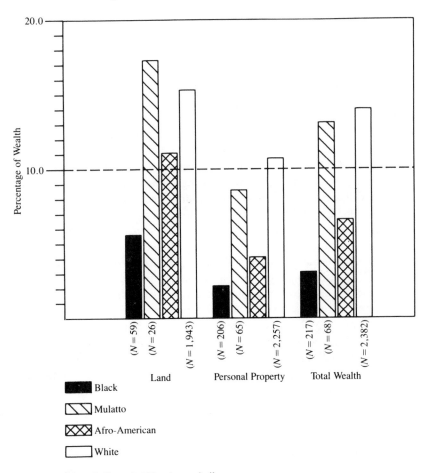

Note: Percentages for household heads are similar.

Source: Edgefield Data Base.

heads in 1870 yields a figure of only 16.8 percent of white female household heads (refer to table 7-3). In 1880 those figures were one-third for whites and four-fifths for blacks. Afro-American women who headed households had to work, since they did not own land as did some white women. In 1870, 68 percent and in 1880, 74.7 percent of black, as compared to only 4 percent and 8.7 percent of white women household heads in those years, were farm laborers or domestics. After the war, however, more white female household heads participated in the labor force. This probably resulted from the increasing poverty of the South and the Panic of 1873, as well as a legacy of female involvement during the Civil War. Although black female household heads were involved in the postwar economy, the most prestigious black occupations were still wholly male dominated, in keeping with the patriarchal nature of Edgefield's black community.[38]

A comparison of general characteristics of black and white and male and female households in 1870 and 1880 highlights basic patterns. Black and white male-headed households were similar in structure and became more so during the decade. The black female household head was as much like her black male counterpart as she was like the white female household head. But black and white female-headed households differed even more after the Reconstruction era.

Female-headed households contained fewer members than those with male heads because the husband-father was missing. A man was seldom listed as the sole parent of a household containing children under four years old. Black men, white men, and white women who were single parents all had fewer young children than black women, suggesting that remarriage was more difficult for black and white widows with children than for widowers, and especially difficult for black women with young children. Although whites and blacks had about the same proportion of children in both male- and female-headed households, Afro-American women were more likely to have children, particularly children aged five to seventeen, in their households. White female household heads had the next highest proportion of children in their households, but had far fewer children under age five than all other groups and were more likely than all other groups to have children eighteen and older. This, combined with the fact that the white female household head was significantly older than the other groups, suggests that a greater proportion of white female household heads were widows. The marital status of household heads in 1880 corroborates the inference that the vast majority of white female household heads were widows in 1870 and 1880.

White female heads of households were strikingly older than black female household heads. Moreover, in 1880, although black and white male-headed households were becoming more alike, black and white female-headed households were even more divergent than in 1870. The average white female household head was older in 1880 than ten years earlier, whereas the average black female household head was slightly younger in 1880 than in 1870.

In 1870 non-nuclear household types were similar for black and white female households. In a reversal of the trend for black and white households, however, the white female-headed household was more likely to be extended than the black female-headed household. In 1880, when the recording of the relationship of the head of the household to each household member made the percentage of extended households explicit, there were significantly more extended families among white female-headed households (27.6 percent) than among black (16.8 percent). The 1880 non-nuclear households were different as well for white (31.0 percent) and black (20.9 percent) female-headed households. Although the percentages of extended and augmented households for all blacks and whites were almost identical, the distribution between male and female household heads differed significantly.[39]

By 1880 the typical white female household head was likely to be relatively old, a widow, rarely with very small children, more often with children over seventeen in the household. By contrast, the typical black female household head was young, less likely to be a widow, and much more likely to be an unwed mother; in any case she had more younger children and fewer older children.[40]

A prominent difference between blacks and whites was the far higher rate of illegitimacy[41] among black female household heads in 1880; 20 percent of black women who headed households were unwed mothers, as contrasted with 3.6 percent of white female household heads (Table 7-5). Fewer of the Afro-American women were widows: 52.5 percent of all black female household heads, contrasted with 77.1 percent of white female household heads. If all female heads of families, not just female household heads, were included, then mothers with illegitimate children became even more numerous among Afro-American women: 22.6 percent of black female family heads were unwed mothers and 48.9 percent of them were widows; by contrast, 5.3 percent of white female family heads were unwed mothers and 73.9 percent were widows. The differences in the rates of widowhood and illegitimacy resulted primarily from differences in cultural background and from the exigencies of postbellum life.

The conditions of postbellum life, particularly the social dislocations that prevented the fulfillment of black family ideals, deeply affected blacks in certain situations and resulted in pockets of black family groups that developed a non-nuclear, non-male-headed family pattern. These families were the result of a helpless, or in some cases defensive, reaction to circumstances, not a positive fulfillment of Afro-American ideals.

The values and ideals of black family life in rural Edgefield were the same as those of whites—a commitment to the patriarchal values of the nineteenth century. These cultural factors originated in an Afro-American tradition that had existed in slavery and that was reinforced by religious values and contemporary circumstances. It was a culture that stressed accommodation in order to survive and a community that accepted what had happened in the past.

Violence toward Black Men

The majority of black women who headed households in 1880 were widows, although the percentage of widows was not as high as it was for white female household heads. The Civil War of course took the husbands of many white

Table 7-5. *Female Household and Family Heads by Marital Status, 1880 (percentages)*

	Female Household Heads[a]				Female Family Heads[b]			
	White (N=441)	Afro-American (N=811)	Black (N=726)	Mulatto (N=85)	White (N=529)	Afro-American (N=1,007)	Black (N=903)	Mulatto (N=104)
Married	4.8	10.1	10.1	10.6	4.9	9.4	9.3	10.6
Single	9.1	11.2	11.4	9.4	9.6	12.3	12.3	12.5
Divorced	3.9	1.6	1.7	1.2	3.6	1.6	1.7	1.0
Widowed	77.1	52.5	52.3	54.1	73.9	48.9	48.8	49.0
Single with Children	3.6	20.0	19.7	22.4	5.3	22.6	22.5	24.0
Unknown	1.6	4.6	4.8	2.4	2.6	5.2	5.4	2.9

a. Households headed by females but with a spouse present have been excluded.
b. Includes household heads and family heads in a household of another.
Note: Afro-American includes black and mulatto.
Source: Edgefield Data Base.

women. Reconstruction in Edgefield was a second civil war, an often bitter encounter between blacks and whites that left many Afro-American widows.[42]

During the first years of Reconstruction murders of former slaves were documented in the Freedmen's Bureau "Reports of Outrages," in which the numbers of black men killed in each district were reported monthly. For example, soon after the war Elbert MacAdams went "to see his wife who lived on Basil Callaham's plantation." At about 10 P.M. on Saturday 12 May 1866, MacAdams was taken from his house, shot three times and his throat cut, and dragged from his house a hundred yards into the woods. Callaham and two other men were arrested for the murder; it was charged that Callaham wanted to prevent MacAdams from taking his wife to live off the plantation. They were released because nothing could be proved.[43]

In a sworn statement before the Freedmen's Bureau, a former Edgefield slave testified "that it is dangerous for a black man to live in Edgefield District, S.C. That almost daily they are hunted down and shot. Knows of several freedmen being found dead in the woods & swamps. His former master Marsh Frazier told him that he could get his brains blown out for $20 at anytime. The soldiers stationed at Edgefield are drinking with the citizens and aiding them in their cruelty toward the freedmen." The Freedmen's Bureau reported two gangs of outlaws operating in Edgefield who immediately after the war committed "with impunity the most fiendish outrages." The gangs "murdered a number of negroes & one white man, without provocation." The leader of one gang, a Confederate Major Coleman, was a native of Edgefield. Freedmen's Bureau officer Maj. H. W. Smith reported that "I saw 8 ears cut from colored persons. He [Coleman] carries them in an envelope & carries them as trophies." Freedmen's Bureau agents were convinced that only the stationing of Federal troops could end violence against Afro-Americans, and troops did help.[44]

Despite the presence of troops, though, at election times violence increased. In the fall of 1869 the newly elected white Republican sheriff of Edgefield, who had lived in Edgefield all his life, testified, "Every day colored men would come in and report the death, also whipping and abusing of persons. . . . I have heard of fully twenty such cases, and have seen the wounds on the parties." White Republican D. L. Turner, also a lifetime Edgefield resident, added, "There has been bushwacking and murdering going on, and several colored people killed." Former slave Jesse William reported that "William Stone and his son William were killed and Alex Rountree was wounded." Hampton Mims testified that he had seen white Elbert Ryans shoot a black man. Jerry Oliphant added that he found fellow former slave Spencer Holmes dead.[45]

Sporadic violence and murder continued throughout Reconstruction. Augustus Harris, a constable with a wife and six children, defied the whites of Edgefield and was murdered while serving a warrant on a white man. In 1875 the governor sent a special agent to Edgefield to investigate the causes of the intense violence. One of his conclusions was that a small group of whites in Edgefield violently opposed "any assertions of equality as a citizen when coming from a colored man" and these whites held "human life at little value being as reckless in risking their own, as they are heartless in taking the lives of others." Years before this report, though, the situation had already turned violent. In 1871 Edgefield black state senator Lawrence Cain introduced a bill to tax the five square miles surrounding any neighborhood "in which a man shall be murdered on account of politics, race, or color to support the widows and orphans of such martyrs."[46]

Ben Tillman, whose memoirs described the murder of Coker mentioned above, explained why whites felt compelled to murder black men in such a cold-blooded manner. "Asked again by the white commander if there were anything else after leaving instructions for his wife, Coker replied he 'would like to pray,' and dropped to his knees in prayer. After a few moments Butler said, 'you are too long'. . . . The order 'aim, fire,' was given with the negro still kneeling. . . . It will appear a ruthless and cruel thing to those unacquainted with the environments. . . . The struggle in which we were engaged meant more than life or death. It involved everything we held dear, Anglo-Saxon civilization included." The sixteenth point of Democratic leader Martin Witherspoon Gary's "Edgefield Plan" to redeem the state read: "Never threaten a man individually if he deserves to be threatened the necessities of the times require that he should die. A dead Radical is very harmless—a threatened Radical or one driven off by threats from the scene of his operation is often very troublesome, sometimes dangerous, always vindictive."[47]

Martha Evans revealed something of the impact of these calculated murders on the black community when she described the execution of five unarmed black militiamen at Hamburg by the white Edgefield Rifle and Sabre Club. Evans had grown up and gone to school near this area, and her retelling years after the incident emphasized that the freedmen "were taken out in the streets, before the eyes of their wives and children and shot to death."[48]

Violence after Reconstruction, such as that described in the following account here by black Edgefield attorney John Mardenborough in April 1877, continued to leave families without fathers: "Colored men are daily being hung, shot and otherwise murdered and ill treated because of their complexion and politics. While I write a colored woman comes and tells me her husband was killed last night in her presence by white men and her children burned to death in the house. . . . Such things as these are common occurrences." This violence reached an apex, but did not end, in the bloodbath of the Redemption of 1876, when traditional white Democrats violently regained control of state and local government from Republicans. The superintendent and the surgeon general of the state penitentiary discovered that of the 285 male black convicts contracted out to build the Greenwood and Augusta Railroad in Edgefield from September 1877 to August 1879, 114 had died. A northern newspaper commented: "Edgefield County, South Carolina, the home of the Butlers, and of Gen. Gary, has a bad name, and these revelations will make it worse."[49]

The toll taken on black families by racial violence during the years of Reconstruction and Redemption has not been properly emphasized, for accounts of violence and murder of Afro-Americans have too often been treated as exaggerations. Yet while these murders were of great symbolic importance, they did not totally explain the number of widows heading Afro-American households. Most black, and white, people died from natural causes. Indeed, from 1850 through 1880, the cause of death was recorded in the manuscript mortality censuses, and in every decade deaths from diseases and other causes greatly outnumbered violent deaths, including those recorded as accidents.

In the antebellum period plantation owners tried to care for their slave investments, but the mortality rates were still frightening. Slaves of every age group in Edgefield were more likely to die than were whites. After the war the black mortality rate continued to be higher than the white. Throughout the decades black men in the younger age cohorts, particularly in the marriageable age groups, died at a higher rate than did white males. Murder and natural deaths reduced the number of Afro-American men of marriageable age compared to the number of women.

From the mortality manuscript censuses, one finds that after white or black men reached the age of twenty-five, they were more likely to be married than to be widowed or single. Younger blacks who died were more likely to be married than were whites (supporting the earlier conclusion that blacks set up independent housekeeping at a younger age than whites). Moreover, the average age of death for black males over twenty years of age was lower than for whites. In 1870 there was an eight-year difference between black (43.9) and white (52.5) mean age at death. The lower mean age of adult male death left fewer men of marriageable age and more Afro-American widows.

Unmarried Women with Children

Of the unmarried women who headed households in 1880, 38 white and 87 black had no children at home (refer to Table 7–5). Only 14 unmarried white women had children in their households, whereas 166 single black women had children (according to the census, their illegitimate offspring) in their households. These households accounted for slightly more than a fifth of all female-headed black households but less than 2.8 percent of all black households. A majority of unmarried black and white women who were household heads with children had more than one child; in this group black women predominated.

Among unmarried women with children who were not household heads, but lived in the household of someone else, more white women than black women had more than one child.[50]

In 1880 eighteen black women with illegitimate children resided in white households. The total percentage (28.1) of unmarried black women with children working in black or white households headed by someone else was similar to the percentage (25.0) for unmarried white women with illegitimate children working in other white households. Here absolute numbers are more important. Only eight unmarried white female family heads with illegitimate children lived in someone else's household in the county in 1880 and only two were working in the households of other people, compared to twenty-eight blacks working of sixty-four family heads who lived in the households of other people.[51]

A different pattern emerged for unmarried black and white mothers in their relationships with their relatives: Three of eight white women lived with sisters, whereas only ten of the forty-six black women did so. A larger proportion of black women lived with their parents: Only one white woman with an illegitimate child lived with her parents, compared to nearly a third of the black women with illegitimate children. This indicates a greater acceptance and forgiveness of illegitimacy by the black culture.

Some Afro-American illegitimate children may have even claimed their paternal heritage. Whereas an unmarried white woman gave her children her own surname, the pattern of names among the children of some unmarried black women suggests that the children were given their fathers' surnames. Perhaps this showed that the black community, which was denied legal marriage before emancipation, acknowledged a certain legitimacy to these unions. Certainly this evidence underscores the patriarchal orientation of the Afro-American community.

After the Civil War, as during slavery, some children were born of white-black sexual liaisons. How such arrangements might affect the census returns can be illustrated with the following example. Two single Afro-American women heading households were listed next to Lucy Pickens in the manuscript census returns. Francis Pickens's third and last wife, the beautiful Lucy Petway Holcombe, had a cousin, Confederate Brigadier General Beverly Holcombe Robertson, and a brother, John T. H. Holcombe, who drifted into Edgefield after the Civil War and lived with the wealthy widow. The brother never married, but black and white oral traditions acknowledged that he and a Major Kirkland, "who came for tea and stayed thirty years," took former slaves as lifelong partners, who bore their children. The children were reared in the Pickens family mansion and played with white children in the neighborhood. There are other similar stories in the area even today.[52]

Like whites, Edgefield blacks preferred the traditional male-headed family with a husband-wife team. Unlike whites, however, blacks tolerated other arrangements. Illegitimacy was no impediment when the community accepted the children of unmarried women, thereby lessening the stigma that was usually attached to the situation.

Afro-American women heading households with children were not all widowed or unmarried. Although the majority of absent husbands in Table 7-5 were dead, some might have been in prison, like the two black inmates in the local jail who recorded their civil status as married and whose families lived in the county. Some husbands, such as that of Harry Hammond's cook and Henry Morse and his friend Griffin, left to find work elsewhere before sending for their families.

Desertion was another possibility, but even if it accounted for all the female-headed households headed by married women, these cases still would have constituted only 10.1 percent of black female-headed households, which was only 1.2 percent of all Afro-American households. Comparable white female-headed households made up 0.4 per cent of all white households.

It was not always the black husband who left the wife. There are indications that even in the patriarchal Edgefield Afro-American society black women had more autonomy than white women did in theirs. Before emancipation the church had to sanction the remarriages of slave couples whom white owners had separated. Some slaves used this precedent to have the church sanction their discarding of mates. Other slaves accepted punishment from white owners in order to break up a marriage and wed someone else. After the war a former Edgefield slave ran away from her soldier husband and returned to her parents' home. According to the daughter of this former slave, her mother "had three husbands and fifteen children." The woman's third husband was a Baptist preacher and a community leader, and they lived together the rest of their lives as a respected, devoted couple.[53]

A devout widowed member of the Silver Bluff Baptist Church spoke of the tradition among Afro-Americans that if a marriage was not working out, one could end the compact. "When asked if people in the old days got married by jumping over a broom she made a chuckling sound and replied: 'No, us had de preacher but us didn't have to buy no license and I can't see no sense in buyin' a license nohow, 'cause when dey gits ready to quit, dey just quits.'" Afro-Americans had more alternatives than whites to a bad marriage because Afro-Americans could opt for ending the arrangement without being rejected by the black community.[54]

In 1872 the black-controlled Republican legislature legalized divorce in South Carolina for the first time, more evidence of black culture's acceptance of divorce. In 1878, as soon as the Redeemers regained firm control of the state, they repealed the divorce legislation. In a strict legal sense, but not in actuality, proportionately more white women heading households than blacks had obtained divorces by 1878. The above cases suggest that Afro-Americans used not the Edgefield courts but a community-acknowledged system for marriage and divorce.[55]

Black women who chose to leave husbands could more easily obtain jobs. Postbellum whites preferred Afro-American domestic workers, especially as nurses for their children. Discussing the problems of finding a suitable nurse for her grandchildren, Emily Cumming wrote from Augusta to her daughter in Edgefield about this preference.[56]

Women who left a marriage could report their marital status as married or single. This raises the possibility that some children of single women, especially black, were not necessarily illegitimate. Some slave narratives mention slaves who were separated from wives and families and married others. After the Civil War those situations had to be straightened out. One instance identified in the manuscript census returns concerned Ida McKinney and her four children. According to her son Warren, "When de war come on my papa went to build forts. He quit ma and took another woman." Ida McKinney was recorded in the 1880 manuscript census returns as an unmarried household head with children. Warren, however, did not perpetuate the female-headed pattern in his own marriage. He and his wife, also from Edgefield, lived together for fifty-seven years and took care of his mother as long as she lived. Even talking about the death of his one and only spouse made him sad.[57]

Former slave Harry Hopkins explained his parents' handling the dislocation of the Civil War period when an earlier estate settlement among relatives had separated his mother from his father:

> They told me that was my father. Then he had another wife and a lot of children. My mother brought me up and my father taken charge of me after she died. I was about ten when my mother died. . . . I was taken from South Carolina when I was about four years old and carried into Georgia and stayed there until emancipation. My mother didn't tarry long in Georgia after she was emancipated. She went back into South Carolina; but she died in a short time.

Married in 1885, Hopkins, too, was devoted to his spouse, who died in 1901. "I never had but the one wife," he said.[58]

In the postwar upheaval many women, like Ida McKinney, claimed that they were single when in fact they were either divorced or had lost their slave husbands to another after they had been separated. The black family and black community learned to deal with these situations, just as they had learned to deal with the circumstances of slavery. The black community did not condemn but, secure in its religion, accepted and absolved its members of their past sins and looked toward the future. An "illegitimate" former slave explained his personal predicament and how he had satisfactorily resolved the situation.

"Some colored churches 'sinuate a child born out of wedlock can't enter de kingdom of heaven. Our church say he can if he ain't a drunkard, and is de husband of one wife and to believe on, and trust in de Lord as your Savior, and live a right kind of life dat he proves of. Dat seem reason to me, and I jine and find peace as long as I done right."[59]

While the majority of slaves listed by slaveowners for Edgefield plantations were listed in male-headed nuclear families, a minority of female slaves were listed only with children. Despite the wishes of the owner, slave women married off the plantation, but some of the women were also not married. Sometimes the children of these women could be identified as having had white fathers. Slaves accepted, socially and personally, sexual intercourse by young unmarried women, even when children resulted. Later, the women married without apparent prejudice and had normal, stable, two-parent families. It is not surprising that a minority of black women after the war also fell into this pattern and that, compared with whites, black women were significantly more likely to have illegitimate children.[60]

One could ask why did this slave pattern of premarital intercourse and children not disappear with industrialization and modernization, as it did with other preindustrial populations? Besides the more obvious economic reasons, the answer is again at least partly cultural. Originally adapted to slavery, the religion that was so central to the black community preached forgiveness of all of one's previous sins and the commencement of a new life when one entered into the church. Black religion, and thus black culture, was less condemnatory than white Christianity.[61]

Combining all "disrupting" black female-headed households in Edgefield District (those families headed by females who had illegitimate children, divorced women, and those households where a husband might have deserted), they constitute only 4.6 percent of all black households—hardly enough to warrant the term "matriarchy."[62] The female-headed black families were concentrated in the towns, although these places, like the courthouse town of Edgefield (see Table 7-6) had at most populations of less than 1,000 people or about 200 families.

Town and Country

Before the end of the Civil War, towns had been off-limits for slaves. Planters seldom rented their slaves to factories or leased them for other kinds of urban employment. They feared that the freer life of the towns would destroy the submissiveness of their slaves, for they felt that town blacks tended to be more independent and presumptuous. Whites feared that the social controls of slavery would not extend into cities, where blacks would be insulated from

Table 7-6. Population of Edgefield Village, 1860–1880

	1860	1870	1880
White	514	324	331
(Male)	(249)	(153)	(161)
(Female)	(265)	(171)	(170)
Black	4[a]	522	475
(Male)	(1)	(245)	(200)
(Female)	(3)	(277)	(275)
Total	518	846	806
Percentage Black	0.7	59.6	58.9

a. The census enumerator did not specify the number of slaves within the corporate limits.
Source: Edgefield Data Base.

immediate contact with the white community. Although occupations in the city required subordination to whites, blacks would have a chance to make more money and to obtain more status in the Afro-American community.[63]

This changed with freedom. During the Reconstruction era, beginning in 1865 and peaking about 1872–76, Afro-Americans suddenly had free access to towns; they could live, work, attend school, hold office, and be born, marry, and die there. Traditionally the town was the focus of the white community, but in postwar times it was a center for the Afro-American community as well. This role was again reversed when the Reconstruction era ended in 1876; the freedom and autonomy of blacks declined everywhere as whites began to assert both subtle and blatant forms of social control during Redemption. Their efforts were particularly vicious in the towns, where whites unleashed the pent-up resentment they had felt at blacks' presence there during Reconstruction. Accordingly, the black community's center shifted to the countryside or to larger urban centers.[64]

Edgefield whites had long (at least since 1819) feared the influence of towns on Afro-Americans. In that year, Coco or Coot, an Augusta slave, conspired to involve Edgefield slaves in an insurrection. At his trial and execution, Coco appeared "bold and impudent" when testimony revealed he had intended to take over Augusta and, if that failed, lead Edgefield and Augusta slaves to Florida, which was still the property of Spain. In the 1839 "Petition of the Inhabitants of the Village of Edgefield for a Charter of Incorporation," town dwellers charged, in seeking "protection against evils," that "the penal laws of the State are violated extensively . . . particularly by the laws against gaming and trading with negroes . . . [with much] injury created by these violations. . . . It is common at night and on Sunday to see crowds of noisy and intoxicated negroes in our streets." The editor of the Edgefield *Advertiser* fumed in 1849 that a most "lamentable spirit of insubordination prevails among our slaves. . . . I know of no place where reform is more needed than in our village and its vicinity. A few privileged negroes will instill corruption and disobedience into all the slaves within their reach." In 1858 a letter to the editor complained of the "irregularities in the administration of our town affairs. . . . [On] Saturday nights gangs of negroes can be seen congregated together conducting themselves in a most boisterous and disorderly manner, evidently too under the influence of liquor." In 1851, when founding a local agricultural and police society in the lower southwestern area of the district, Edgefield planters ascribed "the irregularities of our Negroes" to "the free and unrestricted intercourse they have with the cities," and these landowners committed themselves to "a united and systematic plan with respect to the regulation of our colored population." An Edgefield planter wrote and spoke of the "abolition city of Augusta," which was near his section of Edgefield District. Typically, large planters restricted the visits of slaves to a town to one time a year.[65]

With emancipation, Afro-Americans expressed their desire for independence in their newfound freedom to move about. Bill Arp wrote in November 1865: "Why, the whole of Africy has come to town, women and children, and babies and baboons and all. A man can tell how far it is to the city by the smell better than the mile post." Later the same month this popular racist southern humorist complained, "Jest when the corn needed plowin' the worst, the buro rang the bell and tolled all the niggers to town, and the farmers lost the crops." Whites in Edgefield County noted the same migration. An Edgefield County farmer wrote, "As this year the slaves was emancipated and could run anywhere they pleased many of them quit their former homes, and went to towns and villages." Almost all recorded moves by Afro-Americans in Edgefield from 1865 to 1876 were into or toward towns.[66]

Safety in Towns

For some time after the war the countryside was dangerous for Afro-Americans; even Edgefield Court House resembled a frontier town where Afro-Americans were sometimes at the mercy of desperadoes. After mentioning atrocities committed by bushwhacker gangs in the countryside, a federal commander at Edgefield noted: "The City . . . is inhabited by thieves, murderers, and disloyal men, who promenade the street with six shooters in their belts and Bowie knives thrust in their boots, and do not hesitate to handle freely the weapons thus displayed. [They terrorize] the loyal population [and] the Civil law is powerless to protect against such desperadoes." His command was ridiculed for coming "with 14 or 15 Yanks to rule the District" and warned to leave. Within a few days one trooper was killed on the street. The officer concluded his report: "During the whole of my Military Experience . . . I never travelled so wild and lawless a country."[67]

The Freedmen's Bureau, backed by federal troops, provided some protection, mostly in town, against these "unreconstructed rebels." As early as October 1866 the subassistant commissioner of Edgefield District's Freedmen's Bureau reported: "The condition of the freed people in the immediate vicinity of Edgefield Court House is, I learn, good. The citizens in that village as well as the civil authorities evince a desire to have them treated justly under the laws. Away from there is much uneasiness and terror because of the presence of 'bushwackers' who kill and beat freedpeople and burn their dwellings with impunity." In his next report, on 31 December 1866, the commissioner stated that the presence of federal troops in the area had reduced the incidence of atrocities. Whites from all social stations were arrested for crimes ranging from disturbing the peace to murder; finally they learned that they could no longer simply go out and shoot people. For the first time, the rights of Afro-Americans to assembly and freedom of speech were guaranteed. Whites learned the limits of their power, but, from the white perspective, the "lesson" had meant reducing Edgefield to an occupied territory.[68]

The countryside, on the other hand, continued to be unsafe, particularly for black women working on farms without husbands at hand. On 9 November 1865, Caroline Rogers and her "dependent daughter" Mary were in the field alongside their former master, Luke Rogers. Yelling that "since she became free she would not do anything," he threatened the child and struck Mary several times with a stick. Caroline told Mary to get her things and leave the plantation. Luke told Caroline to "hush up" and struck her across the face with a board, cutting her face badly. Caroline took her daughter and left, but when she returned for her belongings, Luke refused to let her have them.[69]

In another case, Mark Etheridge broke a contract with his former slave Anna Moore and on 17 October 1865 "drove her off" his plantation, but would not let her take her children. He had severely beaten two of her children only two months earlier and threatened to go to Edgefield Court House and get a Yankee soldier to help him whip her children again. Four days later, Anna Moore saw Etheridge riding home from Edgefield Court House with a Union soldier.[70]

Rose Bussey, who lived some ten miles from Hamburg, testified that before the 1868 election about fifteen whites came to her home searching for her husband. When she informed them her husband was out, they forced their way in, guns in hands, "searched the house, broke the lock off the trunk, and took the gun. They then kicked me and my daughter, and told us to tell my husband that they were Ku Klux . . . who had come to kill him." The respect these vigilantes professed for white women was not extended to black.[71]

Employment Opportunities for Men

Reconstruction political success begat economic and social success for Afro-Americans. By 1870 blacks were assuming local administrative positions. In 1874 former Edgefield County slaves held positions as state legislators, wardens, intendants, census marshals, and solicitors. In Edgefield Village former slaves also became sheriffs, marshals, magistrates, militiamen, trial justices, county clerks, school commissioners, probate judges, coroners, and postmasters. Benefiting from political patronage, they held positions at every level of county and town government.

Blacks entered other nonagricultural occupations as well. They became attorneys, clerks, business partners with whites, bakers, and shopkeepers. A professional and white-collar group of black leaders emerged during this period. Afro-Americans moved out of roles assigned as slaves and into nonagricultural occupations centered in towns. Before the end of Reconstruction even Republicans living outside the town complained about the black-dominated political "ring at Edgefield Court House."[72]

After 1876 whites resumed control, and towns again became places of oppression and limited economic opportunity for black men. Occupational choices were again restricted to stereotyped agricultural roles that were vestiges of slavery. As early as 1873 one Edgefield observer who called himself "Facts and Figures" saw in the tenantry system the beginnings of an economically segregated society. As plantation owners rented more and more of their lands to former slaves, "Facts and Figures" predicted a drastic reduction in white control of agriculture. Accompanying this reduction would be a desire among white landowners to move to the towns and villages and establish themselves eventually in promoting the South's manufacturing interests. Thus, in time, whites would attend to industrial concerns almost exclusively, while blacks as a group would devote themselves to the agricultural interests of the South. In fact, by 1880, except for a few who had acquired town property during Reconstruction, the black town population had become residentially segregated and increasingly dependent on whites. Consequently some freedmen chose the anonymity of cities like Augusta and Columbia or moved to the countryside.[73]

These trends can be traced in population shifts and family patterns. During Reconstruction, when more opportunities for black males opened up in the towns, the manuscript census returns for 1870 reported that 73.3 percent of black households in Edgefield Court House were headed by males. After Redemption, however, when black men could find little permanent employment in town, the 1880 manuscript census returns reported that only 60.7 percent of black households were headed by males. The concentration of male-headed black households increased with distance from a town.

In 1870 Hamburg was not defined in the manuscript census returns as a town, but in the township of the same name, in which the town was located, Afro-Americans outnumbered whites. Moreover, the percentage of male-headed households was higher for blacks than for whites. More jobs were available because blacks politically controlled the town of Hamburg in 1870; politics influenced family arrangements. In 1870 the percentage of black male-headed households in Edgefield Village was smaller than the percentage outside of the town, but did not differ significantly from the white pattern. The percentage of black male-headed households in Edgefield Court House and other towns in 1880, however, was significantly lower than the percentage in totally rural areas. The share of black male household heads in towns in 1880 was also lower than the percentage in 1870 and, more significantly, lower than the 1880 percentage for white households, whether in town or country. (Table 7-10, p. 312, is a compilation of this and several other characteristics of the postwar population of Edgefield.)

Differences in family structure between town and country increased between 1870 and 1880. The proportion of nuclear families was smaller and the proportion of solitary-irregular households was greater in the town than in the country. For Afro-Americans in the new, thriving railroad towns of Johnston, Ward, Trenton, and Ridge Spring, fewer than half of the households were nuclear families (see Figure 7-6).

Female-headed Households in Towns

The movement of black men to the country after Redemption left more female-headed households in towns. Although the total proportion of black and white female-headed households in Edgefield County was only about 15 percent, in the towns black female-headed households rose to 40 to 50 percent of black households in 1880. In the rural townships in 1880 that either contained or bordered on towns, the shares of Afro-American male-headed households were lower, while in the townships most distant from incorporated towns or built-up villages, over 90 percent of all black households were headed by men.[74]

Antebellum free blacks also followed this pattern (chapter 5). It is difficult to generalize about free blacks because slaveowners sometimes emancipated their mistresses and their slave children, resulting in sexually skewed rates of manumission. Still, in 1860 all 11 of Edgefield District's 173 free blacks who resided in the incorporated towns of Edgefield or Hamburg lived in female-headed households. No free black male headed a household in either town; in fact, the oldest male in town was a teenage mechanic dwelling in his mother's household.

The decline in the number of nuclear families and male-headed households was accompanied by changes in the status of Afro-American women. Al-

Figure 7–6. Household Structure by Town and Hinterland, 1870 and 1880

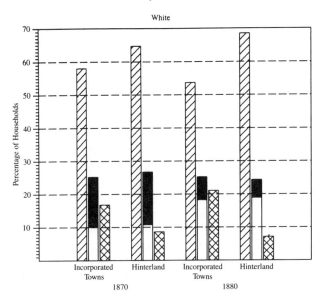

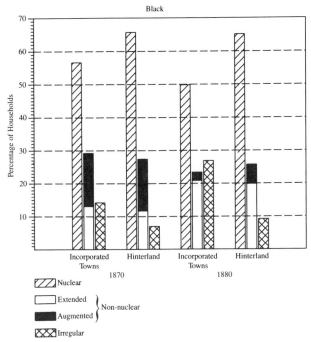

Note: See Table 7–10 for *N*s, notes, and source.

though more than 90 percent of female household heads lived in the country, black women who headed households in the towns saw great shifts in their economic roles (see Table 7-7). During Reconstruction whites constantly complained about the refusal of black women to work as either domestics or laborers. As shown in Figure 7-7, in 1870 women "keeping house" (that is, not gainfully employed) accounted for nearly two-thirds of all town-dwelling black female household heads, and women working as domestics accounted for only one-third (a quarter in Edgefield Village).

After Reconstruction these occupational patterns were reversed. By 1880 domestics accounted for nearly two-thirds of town-dwelling black female household heads, and laborers for another 15 percent. Less than one-fifth of the female household heads were keeping house. The Reconstruction political system had encouraged black women as well as black men to break away from the slave pattern of occupations. By 1880, however, the percentage of black female household heads who were domestics had increased in both the town and country, reflecting the reestablishment of traditional racial relationships. Because whites were begging for servants throughout Reconstruction, this shift from keeping house to domestic service cannot be interpreted as an indication that more opportunities were actually opening for women to work; black women who headed households found it necessary to work because the white-dominated community power structure did not provide for their welfare in the towns, as the Reconstruction leadership had.

Black wives also worked, mainly with family members on a family farm, an expression of their freedom and independence from white control and also an indication of Afro-Americans' strong interest in the family. In the 1880 census most black wives recorded keeping house or laborer as their occupation, but there was a significant increase in the percentage of black working wives—a 28 percent increase, compared to an increase of 2 percent for white wives. This was even more true in the towns. As black men were excluded from town jobs, their wives had to find employment as domestics for whites. Whereas in 1870 and 1880 no white wives worked in towns, the percentage of black working wives rose dramatically from a small number to a majority of all Afro-American wives. The proportion of working Afro-American wives was even higher for the new railroad towns of Johnston, Ward, Trenton, and Ridge Spring than it was for the older and more economically depressed Edgefield Court House.

Whereas unmarried black women with children tended especially to live in town rather than in the country, widows showed the opposite tendency (see Table 7-8). The percentage of black female household heads who were widows increased as one moved away from the towns or villages, probably because they had originally lived there with their husbands. Widows could keep farming because they often had older children to help. Female-headed households in the extreme rural townships more often had older children. The percentage

*Table 7-7. Proportion of Occupations of Female Household Heads in
Incorporated Towns, 1870 and 1880 (percentages)*

	1870		1880	
	Black (N=794)	White (N=619)	Black (N=811)	White (N=441)
Farmer	—	1.5	1.5	—
Laborer	1.3	16.7	2.9	—
Domestic	14.9	30.8	21.1	18.2
Keeping House	13.4	4.0	11.0	9.3
Other	17.9	9.3	4.8	10.3
Total	7.7	4.9	9.1	6.8

Note: Includes in 1870 the township of Hamburg (partly rural) and Edgefield Court House. For occupational groupings see appendix 2.

Source: Edgefield Data Base.

of women with children aged five to seventeen, some of whom were old enough to work, was highest for widows in rural areas.[75]

The importance of older children's labor for rural black female-headed households is confirmed by the fact that their families contained a greater number of people gainfully employed than other types of families. Women who were household heads in the towns, on the other hand, were usually the main source of income for their families. Several Afro-American widows in towns in 1880 who headed households with young children worked as laundresses. The number of black female-headed town households with young children under five years old was greater than that for those with children over eighteen years old.

Like Afro-American widows, white widows preferred life in the countryside. Careful examination of the figures for 1880 urban female-headed families, however, shows that widows comprised three-fourths of the number of white female-headed town households and that no white unwed mothers lived in the towns. On the other hand, slightly larger proportions of unwed Afro-American mothers lived in towns than lived in rural areas. Since mulattoes in the town adhered more closely to the white pattern than to the black pattern of widowhood and illegitimacy, excluding mulattoes makes black unwed mothers an even higher proportion of black town female-headed households. Finally, in the towns the share of married women whose husbands were absent increased for both Afro-American and white women.

Black male occupational patterns in 1880 reflected post-Reconstruction changes as whites regained control of towns and blacks in higher-status occu-

Figure 7–7. Occupations of Female Household Heads in Incorporated Towns, 1870 and 1880

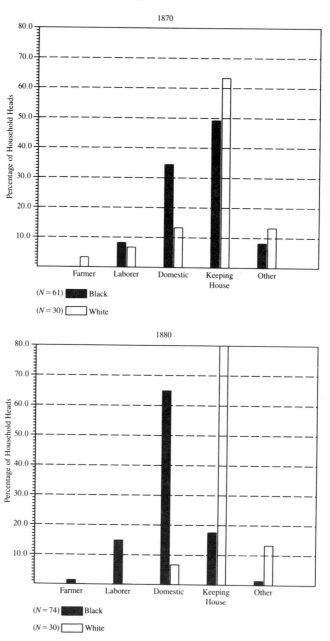

Note: See Table 7–7 for note and source.

Table 7-8. Female Household and Family Heads by Marital Status and Town and Hinterland, 1880 (percentages)

	Incorporated Towns				Hinterlands			
	White	Afro-American	Black	Mulatto	White	Afro-American	Black	Mulatto
Female Household Heads[a]								
Widowed	76.7	41.9	36.1	69.2	77.1	53.6	53.8	51.4
Single	13.3	18.9	21.3	7.7	8.8	10.4	10.5	9.7
Married	10.0	13.5	13.1	15.4	4.4	9.8	9.8	9.7
Divorced					4.1	1.8	1.8	1.4
Single with children		21.6	24.6	7.7	3.9	19.8	19.2	25.0
Unknown		4.1	4.9		1.7	4.6	4.8	2.8
N =	(30)	(74)	(61)	(13)	(411)	(737)	(655)	(72)
Female Family Heads[a]								
Widowed	77.1	39.2	33.8	64.4	73.7	49.7	50.0	46.7
Single	11.5	20.3	23.1	7.1	9.5	11.6	11.5	13.3
Married	11.4	13.9	12.3	21.4	4.5	9.1	9.1	8.9
Divorced					3.8	1.7	1.8	1.1
Single with children		22.8	26.2	7.1	5.7	22.6	22.2	26.7
Unknown		3.8	4.6		2.8	5.3	5.5	3.3
N =	(35)	(79)	(65)	(14)	(494)	(928)	(838)	(90)

Note: Afro-American includes blacks and mulattoes.
a. Includes households listed above.
Source: Edgefield Data Base.

pations moved out. By 1880 few black professionals, ministers, lawyers, teachers, or public officials resided in town. None of the schoolteachers who were household heads in 1870 remained in Edgefield Court House in 1880. In 1880 there was no longer a black law firm in the town, and even the single token government employee, an illiterate black mail carrier, lived outside the town limits. Those black male household heads still in town were no longer able to hold clerical jobs or government appointments such as postmaster, as they had during Reconstruction. Whites replaced even skilled blacks.[76]

Gang Laborers

Outside the towns many black men (more than half of those identified in both the 1870 and 1880 censuses) who were laborers in 1870 had become farmers (renters and sharecroppers) by 1880. This change meant more autonomy; the geographical dispersal of freedmen as tenants allowed them more personal and family freedom than did working under the old slavery system of gang supervision. Tenantry was a move up the economic and social ladder for former slaves, and not every black family could obtain a tenant farm. After Reconstruction the majority of unskilled Afro-Americans, who were not fortunate enough to obtain a tenant farm from a landowner, had few options. A black laborer might find a specific landowner to live with and work for regularly or he might move from farm to farm seeking employment.

Meanwhile, although only 5 percent of black household heads ever lived in a town, blacks in lower-status occupations, particularly laborers, who could not get a tenant farm, either remained in town or moved there (see Table 7-9). Although the 1880 proportion of all "laborer" household heads was less than the 1870 proportion for the county, town laborers did not decline in the same proportion (see Figure 7-8 and Table 7-3). The proportion of all black laborers who lived in Edgefield Court House even slightly increased. To contemporary observers it appeared that the town was becoming a haven for black laborers. Whereas some Afro-Americans residing in households headed by others during Reconstruction were sometimes militiamen or skilled craftsmen, in 1880 they were more likely to be laborers. These laborers were able to find work because landowners began to use the town as a source of cheap temporary labor. Discussing the growth of small towns on South Carolina railroads, the 1883 state handbook stated, "The crossroads store has become an important factor in the organization of labor and distribution of wealth."[77]

Larger hinterland cities, such as Augusta, also provided seasonal agricultural laborers. These males returned home when the hiring season was concluded or may have gone to the countryside during the week to work as wage laborers on farms and only stayed in the town on weekends. Julia Henderson and her husband Frank were a childless, elderly couple, two former Edgefield

Table 7-9. *Proportion of Occupations of Male Household Heads in Incorporated Towns, 1870 and 1880 (percentages)*

	1870		1880	
Occupation	Black (N = 4,081)	White (N = 2,801)	Black (N = 5,156)	White (N = 2,862)
Farmer	6.5	1.1	1.0	1.2
Laborer	4.0	1.1	2.7	2.2
Artisan and Semi-skilled	25.4	13.2	31.9	19.0
Professional, business, low white collar	66.7	24.3	14.3	42.1
Domestic	27.8	0	11.1	0
Other	11.5	0	0	0
Total	5.0	3.2	2.5	5.1

Note: Includes in 1870 the township of Hamburg (partly rural) and Edgefield Court House. For occupational groupings see appendix 2.
Source: Edgefield Data Base.

slaves who moved to Augusta. Julia was alone in Augusta because "Frank gone to the country to pick cotton, and his po' hands all twis' up wid rheumatism too. I don't see how he kin pick, but he said he had to go to make some money for us to pay de rent man." Other ex-slaves' narratives also reported black male seasonal migration from towns and cities to employment on farms. Significantly, these times, June through September, when demand from cotton cultivation on plantations peaked and growers particularly needed men for the demanding jobs, were when the census enumeration was taken. Thus, in 1870 five black women who had been married within the year did not have their husbands in the household. In 1870 all white women married within the year had their husbands at home, but in 1860 three had husbands missing.[78]

After Reconstruction some planters recognized the possibility of using the towns to restore antebellum race relations. They understood that towns could be used to resurrect the gang form of labor that existed on pre–Civil War plantations. In late 1879 in Charleston, Harry Hammond expressed this idea in an agricultural address. In 1880, Charles Jones Jenkins of Summerville wrote a commentary on Hammond's thesis that the plantation system could survive "under existing circumstances, that is, the aggregation of laborers in considerable numbers in village life and with them planting on a large scale." Jenkins claimed that reinstitution of control over Afro-Americans "may perhaps not

Figure 7–8. Occupations of Male Household Heads in Incorporated Towns, 1870 and 1880

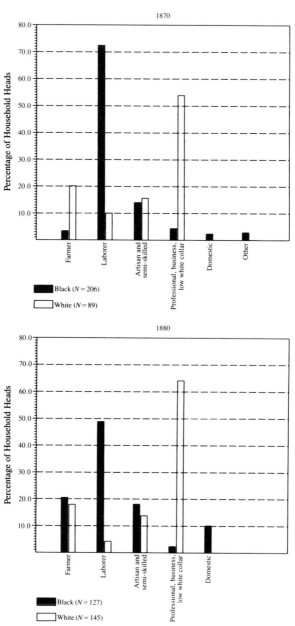

Note: See Table 7–9 for note and source.

have been entirely practicable immediately after emancipation." Reconstruction, however, was an aberration. "The farther we are from emancipation day the more ready they will be to come voluntarily and for a consideration offered and accepted under the control of the white man and for the reason, that this more surely than any other mode of Life open to them issues a livelihood and a kind protectorate." As in Reconstruction, there would be exceptions to white control, but exceptions had existed even under slavery, as evidenced by runaways (and free blacks). Jenkins assured Harry Hammond, "Our people made no greater mistake, after the war, than the assumption that the abolition of Slavery annihilated entirely the white man's control over the negro."[79]

Harry Hammond told a congressional committee of the availability of transient laborers in 1910: "There is none except in the vicinity of towns. There it is esteemed a great advantage to farmers and they always have a full supply of day labor to draw on without any charges for its keep. You often see teams in the cotton-picking season driving to town daily and back to transport cotton pickers." Afro-Americans who remained in towns were segregated and under white domination. Hammond explained: "The negro quarter around the towns now is as marked a feature in a Southern town as a Jew's ghetto anywhere in Europe; they have spread all around the towns, and they get along tolerably well there, but they have a police to keep the peace with them." Rural blacks escaped some of this social control. As Hammond told Congress, tenants were "distributed as much as possible." He assured the congressmen that "the colored laborer likes to be by himself." When challenged by a congressman who asked whether building "laborers' cottages somewhere near together, perhaps in little villages, in farming neighborhoods, would tend to make country life more attractive to them," Hammond answered, "Well I suppose it would if they could be properly policed. It would have to be done on such a scale that they would be policed, something like they were under the old plantation system." Thus, by the end of the nineteenth century, blacks could choose between closely regulated town life and a relatively isolated but comparatively independent rural existence for their families.[80]

Afro-American Churches and Schools

Churches and schools, Afro-American community- and family-oriented institutions that shaped cultural values, reflected the changed conditions of the town and countryside for Edgefield blacks. During Reconstruction schools thrived, and a Columbia Freedmen's Bureau agent wrote: "Urgent calls for the establishment of schools are received from all parts of the district more especially from the Court House Towns, and other important places where the Freedpeople are most centered." After Reconstruction Edgefield town school suffered a marked drop in the mean number of children and rural schools, a corresponding increase in the mean number of Afro-American children attending school (see Table 7-10). In 1877, Harrison N. Bouey, a black schoolteacher and former probate judge of Edgefield, explained this new lack of educational opportunities: "In a few of the Southern states they have fine schools, but only in the cities, towns, and villages, where they can be seen by visitors. But my God, the masses of our people just behind the veil are piteous. You know education makes unprofitable labor in the South. Hence our people must and will, be kept ignorant."[81]

Since religion was so important in the black community, the degree of freedom Afro-Americans enjoyed directly related to the number and location of black churches. Only one black church was founded in the town of Edgefield during the nineteenth century and that one during Reconstruction, when blacks controlled the town. Afro-American political leaders Lawrence Cain and Paris Simkins were the chief organizers of Macedonia Baptist Church, located across a field from the white Edgefield Village Baptist Church, to which most of the black members had previously belonged. After Redemption those blacks who remained in the town of Edgefield concentrated their homes at the far side of Macedonia Baptist Church. This church came to signify the physical barrier between the black and white communities within the town. Most of this area was later carefully gerrymandered outside the corporate limits. Black political leader David Harris, who had moved to Edgefield Village in 1863, was the only town-dwelling household head who was a preacher in 1880. The other ministers lived outside towns and established their churches in rural areas. Accommodationist leader Alexander Bettis founded his forty churches, in the words of Bettis's biographer and successor, "out in the open country." Bettis Academy, founded after Reconstruction, advertised itself as a "school that has gone to the rural people instead of waiting for the rural people to come to the school."[82]

Dynamics of Town and Country

In the town of Edgefield an elite class of Afro-Americans emerged as Reconstruction changed the society. In 1870 and 1880 Afro-Americans who headed households were more likely than their rural counterparts to be mulatto and literate and to have fewer people in their households (see Table 7-10). In 1870 black household heads living in town were also richer and more likely to have children attending school. By 1880 these and other differences between town and country had lessened. In 1870 and 1880 there was a larger percentage of women heading households in towns, and that proportion increased dramatically between 1870 and 1880. In 1870 the proportions of two-parent homes among both blacks and whites were similar in town and country. For the countryside in 1880 they remained so; in the towns blacks had fewer two-parent households than whites and the proportion of working black wives increased dramatically. The share of nuclear families was less and that of solitary-irregular families was higher for blacks and whites in the towns than in the country (refer to Figure 7-6).

With the end of Reconstruction in 1877 the Edgefield black community suffered reversals in almost every area in which progress had been made (except for the rural family) since emancipation—in material wealth and in the political, occupational, and social spheres as well. In the small towns it became more difficult for black men to find work and support their families after Reconstruction. Therefore, the small towns reflected the post-Reconstruction changes more clearly than did the countryside. The black community withdrew into itself. Under post-Reconstruction conditions more blacks chose to leave Edgefield. A few went to Liberia in 1877–78, and many families migrated as a community to Arkansas in 1881–82.[83]

A few Reconstruction leaders, such as David Harris and Paris Simkins, continued to live in elegant cottages in Edgefield and remained symbols of Reconstruction aspirations, but the blacks with whom most whites came in contact were the poorest people, generally women who headed families in which males were absent. As Hammond observed, laborers who had moved into the towns since the Civil War and who were still there in the 1880s were mainly relatively poor day laborers. These laborers concentrated in the towns gave a distorted image of family structure because their families were less frequently male headed than the majority of the Afro-American population in the country. The high percentage of female-headed households, the rise in the numbers of domestic servants, and the decline in the importance of black town artisans all pointed to the town's changing role in race relations after Reconstruction. Towns increasingly were places where whites exercised the closest social control over blacks. In contrast, in rural areas, where black men could find agricultural work and Afro-American churches could meet in comparative freedom, it was easier for black men to rear and support families and for all Afro-Americans to preserve some of the freedom and autonomy that they achieved during Reconstruction. People moved toward or away from towns in specific patterns, and the interactions of person and place explain the dynamics of town and country in the postbellum South.

Table 7-10. *Selected Characteristics of Households by Town and Hinterland, 1870 and 1880 (percentages shown with selected characteristics except for average number in household and average age household head)*

	Incorporated Towns[a]			
	1870		1880	
	Afro-American (N = 267)	White (N = 119)	Afro-American (N = 201)	White (N = 75)
Male-headed	83.9	82.0	63.2	82.9
With school age children attending school	21.3	53.4	12.6	45.3
Children attending school (percentage of school age children)	13.0	37.6	5.9	24.5
Mean number	4.7	4.5	3.6	4.1
Mean age of household head	40.0	44.7	36.8	41.1
Mulatto[b]	22.1	—	21.4	—
Literacy of household head	8.6	86.6	16.4	97.7
Children and both parents present	50.9	48.7	37.8	51.4
Single-parent families[c]	44.1	57.8	70.1	33.1
Single-parent households as a percent of two-parent households	28.7	41.4	65.8	30.0
Working wives	13.0	2.8	55.2	0

Notes: Table excludes seven families headed by Indians. Percentages subject to rounding
a. Includes in 1870 the township of Hamburg (partly rural) and Edgefield Court House.
b. Mulattoes included in all Afro-American percentages and totals.
c. Includes households.
Source: Edgefield Data Base.

Hinterland			
1870		1880	
Afro-American N = 4,608)	White (N = 3,301)	Afro-American (N = 5,766)	White (N = 3,128)
84.1	82.2	87.2	86.9
5.7	25.5	9.4	30.2
3.7	17.4	6.2	21.9
4.9	4.8	4.9	4.8
38.5	42.2	37.8	41.6
10.1	—	9.6	—
4.1	84.0	16.4	86.1
60.0	58.0	63.2	65.3
39.3	39.7	24.2	22.0
27.3	29.9	20.1	18.5
36.2	1.1	62.4	3.4

Conclusion

The general seemed to conclude that free labor has less chance of a fair trial in Edgefield. . . . To me, however, it seems not different from other parts of South Carolina.

John Richard Dennett,
The South as It Is, 1865–1866

Edgefield was a complex society that defied easy categorization. The culture was not dictated by planters, nor was it determined by a harmonious community of yeomen. Unlike New England settlements, southern locales never had a formal ideology that defined community. The meaning of community developed from everyday behavior, social rituals, and experiences as members of families and society. Edgefield's families illustrate intriguing similarities and differences between rich and poor whites, blacks and mulattoes, free Afro-Americans and slaves. Without exception, groups in Edgefield demonstrated reverence for their families by maintaining kinship networks even when relatives moved away and by promoting solid religious values that hallowed domestic life.

Wealth influenced the household and family structure for all groups. The affluent always had more male-headed and larger households. Yet both rich and poor whites connected family values with a sense of personal and regional honor. Little evidence exists to support the unflattering stereotype of degraded, apathetic "poor whites." Antebellum free black families and households were often female headed. Whites and free blacks were sufficiently integrated that interracial marriages occurred even during the 1850s, a time of much hostility toward the free black.

White slaveowners made control of the slaves a central theme for the antebellum white community, and this control restricted the autonomy of the slave family. Still, family and religion were the two institutions that most shielded slaves from the dehumanizing aspects of bondage. The slave community learned to adjust to circumstances beyond its immediate control. Ironically, Christianity, which was for whites a means of control, became for blacks a buffer against oppression and in some cases fostered Afro-American autonomy.

The family, too, provided Edgefield blacks with the strength and confidence to cope successfully with slave conditions and to emerge from bondage after the Civil War eager to influence the course of Reconstruction. After emancipation, blacks went to great lengths to solidify their families in large households and to form kinship communities of closely knit families.

After emancipation whites did not willingly give up their control over black families. Reconstruction was a period of transition when Afro-Americans established their rights to an independent family life. Cultural values and family values, bolstered by life on the land and religious institutions, persisted through slavery into Reconstruction. The postbellum agricultural system, based on tenancy rather than gang labor, was crucial to the development of black and white rural family structure and values. As in antebellum times, wealth, even more than class or race, was the most important variable in the differences in household and family structure between whites and Afro-Americans or between blacks and mulattoes. In the antebellum period free black women controlled a majority of free black wealth, but in 1870 Afro-American women owned an insignificant portion of black wealth. Although postbellum white women controlled twice the proportion of white wealth as black women did black wealth and increased this proportion over time, their wealth remained minimal, and most southern women continued their dependence on husbands and other males. The economic position of women underscored the patriarchal nature of the South. Although the South cast women in a subservient role, both black and white women remained the foremost perpetuators of the companionate family. In their efforts to impart learning and piety to their children and to be the guardians of domestic moral virtue, women impressed their powerful personalities upon the psyche of the South.

The Myth of Black Matriarchy

This study has discovered so much evidence of a patriarchal community, one wonders how the notion of a black matriarchy ever developed. The myth of the disorganized Afro-American family and the black matriarchy was not of scholarly origins; created by reformers, it goes back at least to abolitionist literature. Abolitionists such as Theodore Dwight Weld and Harriet Beecher Stowe argued that the cause of matriarchy lay in the impact of slavery, not race. In postbellum years, however, race was confused with slavery. Southern and northern whites unsympathetic to black equality transmuted this abolitionist attack on slavery into an argument about black people's inability to function as full participants in a modern society. Disparaging views of the Afro-American family had deep roots in southern white cultural beliefs. Whatever the reasons, scholars and the public, until the late 1960s, generally accepted the notion of the "weak" black home, and this in turn has influenced society's attitudes toward black people in general. In the agrarian society of the South, however, there was no matriarchy.

The previous chapter examined economic and cultural conditions explaining the small percentage of unmarried black women with children, but an examination of the ecology of this population is necessary to understanding the origins of the myth of the black matriarchy. Given the acceptance by the slave culture of children with unmarried parents, Afro-American culture in the postbellum South was more tolerant of unmarried women with children. (This was not approval, but was acceptance of the past.) Black female family heads, particularly unwed black women with children, concentrated in the hamlets, small towns, and urban areas because that was where they found jobs and safety. Since these Afro-American women were domestics or laundresses working for whites and in continuous contact with them, these exceptional cases loomed large. Furthermore, they were more visible to those whites and blacks most likely to write about them. Rural economics and slave culture explain the existence of town-centered female-headed households, which some mistook for a "matriarchal" social system. One suspects that this served to "verify" the black matriarchy myth for many well-intentioned whites.[1] In the years after slavery, however, black and white family structures were remarkable more for their similarities than for their differences. Male-headed, two-parent households predominated for both groups, and they shared similarities in the size, occurrence, and structure of nuclear, extended, and augmented families.

Moreover, black and white families shared religious and cultural tenets about the meaning and importance of family life. Black and white religious cultures were at variance over the extent to which they absolved sins and accepted deviations from usual living patterns: Afro-Americans, for example, were more tolerant of divorce. Thus, some evidence suggests that distinctive cultural features survived as a legacy of the remote African or the recent slave past. Yet, in Edgefield the culture of the black family was shaped much more by accumulated generations of survival under white domination. The black emphasis on family values in a patriarchal society—stable marriage, nuclear family, male dominance—was institutionalized in their own Afro-American Christian cultural traditions and preserved by the nature of rural southern economics and society (as formed by both blacks and whites).

Black and white families did show some intriguing differences, especially with regard to aspects of the role of women in families. For example, black families had a far higher proportion of working wives (43 percent as against 2 percent for white families in 1880). A higher proportion of white women were widows, although both groups had many widows. Finally, the Afro-American community had a higher proportion of unwed mothers.

Yet these female-centered differences varied between town and country. Black and white households in towns were more likely to be headed by women than those in the countryside, but white families did not vary as much as did Afro-American families. These differences between black and white female-headed households intensified over time. In 1870 white and black women headed households in about the same proportion; in 1880, however, Afro-American families in towns were much more likely to be female headed than their black country counterparts (40 to 50 percent female headed in towns, as opposed to a rural norm of around 15 percent in 1880).

This meant that a town-dwelling black family with a working female head who had children in the home was much more common in 1880 than in 1870. It also meant that such a family, though nowhere in the majority, was closer to representing the typical Afro-American town family in 1880 than in 1870. On the other hand, it was further removed from the typical white family, in town or country, and also from the typical Afro-American family, which was less likely to have a working wife, a female household head, a gainfully employed female household head, or illegitimate children.

Towns and urban centers attracted white and black women, especially after Reconstruction.[2] Female-headed families were more secure there and had better opportunities for work. Since black men were excluded from occupations other than stereotyped agricultural roles, they gravitated toward the country. Small-town black families took on a distinct female-headed image. The culture of racism may be unmeasurable, but it produced measurable results in towns and cities: significantly more black women headed families and households after Reconstruction.

Popular belief since the beginnings of factory industry has held that a wife's working leads to the weakening of the patriarchal family, and that working wives have more power, including an economic independence that allows for divorce.[3] On the tenant farm black women worked full-time caring for husband and children, as well as laboring in the fields with the family when necessary. In the towns after Reconstruction few black men could find regular employment, but black women could obtain jobs as domestics, cooks, washwomen, and nursemaids in the towns. As black men were excluded from town jobs, their wives had to find employment.

This situation engendered a different sort of patriarchal system from that which prevailed in the countryside. The regularly employed working town wife was in the home of someone else for most of the day. She had to give up some of her traditional roles as caretaker of child and husband and, of course, gained greater autonomy from the family. Whereas black families on the plantations and tenant farms worked together, those in the towns and cities might be together only after the workday was over. The low esteem attached to jobs held by women in a patriarchal society did not detract from the potential negative impact of those jobs on family solidarity. Even in rural Edgefield significantly more black than white wives were gainfully employed.

If any divergence in family types is to be deduced from the data, the line should be drawn not between the typical Afro-American family and the typical white family but between the town-dwelling black family and all the rest, black and white. Such a distinction would not do justice to the similarities underlying the majority of all families in Edgefield County, but it would come closer to representing the true situation than the distinctions that have prevailed in the literature to date.

Origins of the Afro-American Family

This study disputes the theory that distinctive slave or African traditions shaped the development of the Afro-American family in the postemancipation era, while at the same time acknowledging that some slave patterns persisted. For example, the continued pattern of more black than white female involvement in the work force outside the home illustrated the complexity and ambiguity of this and other cultural issues. For at the same time that more black than white women worked, a substantial number of Afro-American women withdrew from the labor force with emancipation. Moreover, this book questions factors such as industrialization, urban city life, illiteracy, mortality, sterility, and the development of the ghetto that recent scholars have put forth (in place of Africa or slavery) as decisive for shaping the Afro-American family.[4] If the impact of slavery was not all-important, neither was the anomie created by urban-industrial life. Edgefield towns and villages, with their populations measured in no more than hundreds and their relatively slow-changing, nonindustrial economic base, could hardly be classified with the massive industrial cities of the North, yet traces of the same destructive impact on black families found in northern city life were present in small nineteenth-century Edgefield towns and villages. The beginning of the decline of the male-headed black family occurred much closer to the traditional homeland of slavery. By 1880 black families in the small towns and villages of Edgefield County were showing the first signs of the disruption that became characteristic of their counterparts in the great cities of industrial America. That this disintegration is not directly traceable to the heritage of slavery is shown, first, by the earlier steady strengthening of the black family in the immediate postemancipation period and, second, by the continuing strength of former slave families in the Edgefield countryside.

For 1870 and 1880 there was a selective migration of white and Afro-American women to the small towns for employment and safety. But this selective migration does not explain what helped produce a female-headed, generally interpreted as "matriarchal," image of the black family. It was not the fact of being black that caused problems for Afro-American families in towns. It was the discriminatory system existing even in small rural villages and towns which excluded Afro-American men from nonagricultural occupations while providing job opportunities for women.[5]

The character of race relations in Edgefield changed because of social and political struggles. Race relations under slavery had been for the most part favorable for the fostering of strong Afro-American families—families were useful as means of social control and population reproduction. With the advent of emancipation, however, Edgefield blacks quickly emerged as a threat to white supremacy. The political rise of Edgefield Afro-Americans paralleled their development of a stable postwar community and challenged the wealthier white-dominated society in all areas of social, political, and economic life.

This confrontation was felt most strongly in the towns. Courthouse towns like Edgefield were places where Afro-Americans, supported in their economic and social advance by Republican political control, had professional, managerial, and skilled jobs during Reconstruction. White reaction to the competition of the freed black population was most virulent in the towns where that threat was strongest. Increasingly, white actions closed the towns, and the mobility associated with them, to Afro-American men and reasserted the idea that lower-level farm occupations were the allowable limits of black male ambitions. Consequently, Afro-American men, who most threatened white society, were systematically driven out of the towns. This was not just the result of the general economic depression of the 1870s, since black men were not excluded from higher-status nonagricultural positions until after the 1876 white political Redemption.

The living patterns for whites in town and country did not change. Conversely, without the political backing of Reconstruction, most black men (except for the very few members of the elite who had purchased land in the towns during Reconstruction) were forced to move, with their families, to the countryside. Dispersed on tenant farms, they were difficult to mobilize politically, and they became less of a threat than when they controlled the political networks in the towns. Racism resulted in the exclusion of black men from town-urban economies, and the fact that the Afro-American male-headed family survived slavery, Reconstruction, and post-Reconstruction in the rural South escaped those intellectuals who counted numbers in the cities, not the countryside.

For Afro-American males, Reconstruction political control mitigated the effects of racism in 1870. But the reinstitution of the system of racial discrimination after Reconstruction, along with the job opportunities that attracted Afro-American women, brought a tremendous decrease in the proportion of black male-headed households in the towns. Politics changed family patterns.

Tenancy did not foster a matriarchal family organization. On the contrary, most tenants were male household heads, simply because working the land was a man's job. Rural agricultural regions were populated overwhelmingly by male-headed households, characterized by the allocation of precedence and power to the males in the family. There was no black matriarchy in rural Edgefield, nor was there a trend toward families without husbands and fathers. An agrarian society and the predominance of the Christian religion among Afro-Americans fostered strong family ties. Far from contributing to the breakdown of the black family, tenantry actually helped preserve it.

These complex patterns of race relations can best be studied on a local level, where processes and changes over time can be closely analyzed. Each local area is also part of the larger society. It is meaningless to dwell on the uniqueness of a community; its role must be seen in relationship to the larger system of which it is a part. Local history becomes a means of seeing and isolating historical problems. More than a testing ground for traditional historical hypotheses, it is a means of ascertaining what forces really influenced the individual in his decision-making and life-style.

Thus, it is possible to see not only how the Afro-American family functioned in Edgefield County, South Carolina, but also how racial discrimination influenced the development of the Afro-American family. When placed with the findings of studies of the black family in other areas, broader conclusions can be drawn. Although there have been no other studies which distinguish small southern towns from the hinterlands, other studies of nineteenth- and twentieth-century urban and rural areas confirm the Edgefield patterns: in northern and southern cities sex ratios were higher for women, and more females and mothers headed households than they did in rural areas.[6]

Noted family historian Tamara K. Hareven has stated that "most recent studies of nineteenth-century American family structures, which are based primarily on the analysis of the census manuscript schedules, have revealed a surprisingly uniform set of patterns: rural/urban differences in family structure appear to be minimal; ethnicity, race, occupation and residential arrangements seem to have no dramatic impact on the varieties of family and household organization."[7] However, the evidence shows otherwise for black families and households. As an example, John Blassingame's careful study of Reconstruction New Orleans noted that "geographical propinquity to the center of the city was one of the most important causal factors in the stability or instability of the Negro family." The Crescent City's outlying areas, in some places rural farmland, had 84.3 percent male-headed households, compared to 74.5 percent for center-city households.[8] Herbert Gutman's statistics on male-present households also indicate a significant difference between rural and urban black families.[9] Whereas in rural Louisa County, Virginia, Crandall Shifflett found few black or white male-absent households, Peter Kolchin discovered that Alabama urban areas had the highest incidence of black and white unmarried adults.[10] These findings suggest the city had places for single or female household heads which rural areas lacked.

After studying seven cities in the Ohio Valley, Paul Lammermeier suggested reappraising E. Franklin Frazier's studies of the black family in northern cities "in light not of a cultural holdover from slavery . . . but as the results of urban life caused by poverty and discrimination."[11] Female-headed households, as Elizabeth Pleck showed in her studies of Boston, were a product of the urban economic structure rather than a "breakdown" resulting from a rural-urban move.[12] Thomas Dublin speculated that the structure of job opportunities accounted for the high proportion of female-headed households among nineteenth-century Irish millhands at Lowell, Massachusetts.[13] However, urban life did not necessarily cause an unusually high incidence of female-headed households or family instability, as Virginia Yan-McLaughlin showed for Buffalo's Italians.[14] Theodore Hershberg and the Philadelphia Social History Project believe that Gutman's statistics support their contention that the "female-headed family . . . emerged, not as a legacy of slavery, but as a result of the destructive conditions of northern urban life."[15] The large cities of the South, however, had proportionately more female-headed households than did northern cities.[16] There are differences in the structures of urban and rural families. The problem of adaptation to a lower-class urban existence cannot be ignored, and the process of alienation and the destruction of rural norms and folkways in an urban industrial economy is a well-documented modern phenomenon.[17]

But these disruptive forces were not operative in Edgefield in 1880, when the town had a population of only 808. Moreover, the community and church and family ties that regulated Afro-American rural society also existed in the small towns of Edgefield County. Yet the same patterns of family disintegration were found in the rural villages as in the large cities, where the absence of such social control mechanisms have been used by scholars to explain family instability, a higher proportion of female-headed households, and illegitimacy. The "destructive conditions" in Edgefield were as sinister as those in cities; there was an unmeasurable cultural component—racism. Moreover, it was not simply racism but racial discrimination in jobs that mattered. Although in rural settings black men were economically disadvantaged compared to whites, there was more racial discrimination against black men in cities and small towns than in rural settings.

Rural Afro-Americans established strong family ties in the years following the Civil War, and racism prevented black men from integrating the town and city economies. Racism exacerbated the problems of urban and rural families. Current studies show that the virtual exclusion of Afro-American men from all but agricultural jobs, as seen in post-Reconstruction Edgefield, continues to this day in urban economies, but in another form. In the southern towns and villages the contradictions had already appeared that would plague American cities one hundred years later.[18]

After Appomattox, the shocks of military defeat, slave emancipation, military occupation, and black political, economic, and social successes battered the Edgefield white community. These traumas undoubtedly altered Edgefieldians' views of themselves and their region; nevertheless, they struggled to maintain their community identity by drawing strength from their families and neighbors.

Despite the ravages of the Civil War, the patriarchal, male-headed household continued to reign supreme in the postbellum white community. With relations between whites and blacks so unpredictable, the male-centered family was a source of strength and certainty for whites and blacks alike. Moreover, like blacks, white males needed an institution in which to assert their autonomy and independence. The family often fulfilled this need.

Although cousin marriages had never been a common practice in Edgefield, unions between siblings in one family and brothers and sisters of another family were prevalent among all wealth groups, blacks and whites. These multiple marriages between the members of different families strengthened community ties and enhanced communal feelings. In some parts of Edgefield, entire neighborhoods were joined by some familial connection. The closeness this engendered also provided solace during the turbulent years of Reconstruction.

It is likely that the solidarity of Edgefield's white community was also derived from its opposition to a common enemy: the freedmen. Newspaper accounts and other literary sources attest to the fact that heaping scorn on the former slave was a favorite activity of the white community. White attacks on the freedmen's difficulties in adjusting to liberation not only provided an outlet for white frustrations but also gave the white community still another common ground around which they could rally their forces.

This study of Edgefield County, South Carolina, has investigated the relationships among all people in one rural locality during the nineteenth century. By comprehensive consideration of nearly every aspect of life in Edgefield, this total history of the county reveals how individuals felt and acted and how families and communities changed over time. Edgefieldians were bonded by economic necessity, a consensus of values, and by a sometimes uneasy accommodation between the forces of domination, subordination, and resistance.

Historian Thomas Bender's observation that conflict can enhance community identification is borne out in the case of Edgefield.[19] The specific circumstances of the sharp divisions between planters and yeomen, masters and slaves, free blacks and poor whites contributed to Edgefield's distinctiveness as a community. During most of the nineteenth century the schisms were contained by the demands of day-to-day existence and the commitment of all contending groups to the principles of evangelical Protestantism. As with so many other American communities, Protestantism was a powerful unifying force in Edgefield. Religion tended to oppress and keep down whites as well as blacks, while paradoxically affording both races the impetus for change and reform and a buffer from exploitation.

This comprehensive study of life in nineteenth-century Edgefield is a story of the continuing interplay between tradition and change. Only by viewing these relationships in a total historical context has the subtlety and significance of this dynamic been able to emerge.

Appendix 1. Methodology

Family Records

My experience has contradicted the notion that Southerners kept few records. Like most agricultural people, black and white Southerners saved everything. Historical records are just hard to find, and have often been preserved in unusual ways. I discovered several volumes of tax records being used to support boards as shelves in a country store.

With a feeling of reverence for the past and family, black and white Southerners have preserved personal documents that link the past to their own recollections and stories. I have examined manuscript collections; plantation, church, and masonic records; letters; diaries; newspapers; and family Bibles. No doubt these are all biased, but as Francis Butler Simkins stated,

> during my childhood here at Edgefield the family history was preserved in a few relics, in the tales of the elders, and in a fat scrapbook. We read this book as often as we did our Shakespeare and our Bible. Some would say that this volume should not have been believed; that it was filled with Victorian fustian gleaned from the reminiscences with which the fifty-odd newspapers of South Carolina were loaded during the fifty years following the fall of the Confederacy. A thousand other families in the state possessed similar books. But such critical disillusionment never entered my mind until, as a young man, I had the experience of being contaminated by the skepticism of Columbia University. Since then the sentimentality or the wisdom of mature years has prompted me to recover faith in the ancestors.[1]

After having enjoyed many of these scrapbooks, I see why Simkins and the elite exalted their forebears. But the records of other black and white Southerners are no less valuable and no more suspect than the records of the elite, which have generally determined the outlines of history books. Southern common folk who persevered left a proud history. Some left scrapbooks, most passed on family Bibles, and all created oral family traditions. Especially useful were such sources as the letters to the American Colonization Society from Edgefield blacks who wanted to emigrate and the letters from poor, yeomen, and middle-class whites and blacks in Edgefield to governors of South Carolina. Often intimate and urgent, these records counterbalance elite versions of particular events, such as Reconstruction. The same is true of investigative reports, depositions, and reports of local commissioners.

I have learned much from those who have opened their homes and shared their lives and their memories with me. I hope I have in no way done a disservice to their hospitality.

The Former Slave Narratives

Primary sources for black family history are rare, and thus many of my arguments depend on a limited number of sources. Records, diaries, and other white-dominated sources, along with the few black sources, have been supplemented by census data and considerably enriched by the WPA interviews with former slaves who were still alive in the 1930s. These narratives were published in a number of volumes edited by George Rawick. Although these often tantalizingly brief accounts must be used with caution, they are still an indispensable source of information on nineteenth-century black life.[2] The abundant detail in the narratives enables one to have a "thick description" of events and institutions. As much material as possible has been quoted in the words of the former slaves since, although this material was originally transcribed and edited by southern whites, the former slaves said it so much better than anyone else could. The dialect used is not meant to be insulting but is copied from the material just as the white interviewers wrote it. The narratives documented the actual experiences of Afro-Americans living in Edgefield on farms and plantations of varying sizes.

In the few instances that a former slave was cited who was not from Edgefield, I indicated so in the text or in the notes. There were no autobiographies from former Edgefield slaves. However, I have read more than a score of autobiographies of former slaves to compare with the slave narratives. A biography of the famed Bishop Henry M. Turner was originally published in 1917 by an admirer and acquaintance of the former free black from neighboring Abbeville District. (See Ponton, *Life and Times of Henry M. Turner*.)

The Manuscript Census Returns

The history of ordinary Southerners before the twentieth century has generally been thought to belong to the history of all inarticulate peoples—slaves, peasants, youth, mobs—shadowy figures who surge onto the historical stage during slave revolts, Reconstruction, or agrarian protest movements, provide a colorful background, wreck the scenery, and then retire to the wings, leaving no tracks for the historian to follow. Sources are biased in favor of various elite groups; consequently history is usually seen through their eyes.

Given the scarcity of records for nineteenth-century common folk, the federal census remains the best source from which to reconstruct a picture of their community. The basic aggregate data can be gathered from the printed volumes. The unpublished manuscript census returns for population, agriculture, slave, mortality, industry, and social statistics can be used to recover information about individuals and their families, households, and neighborhoods.[3]

For this study, the manuscript census returns for 1850, 1860, 1870, and 1880 have been the most useful. The 1850 and 1860 census reports named only free blacks and some of the slaves who died in those census years. The slave manuscript census returns report only the slaveowner's name and the age, sex, and color of the individual slave. Other information concerning whether a slave was a fugitive or disabled, and in 1860 the number of slave houses, was also recorded. The 1850 and 1860 mortality censuses added information on slaves who died in those years. Although these mortality schedules gave the marital status of whites, the marital column was left blank for slaves. Slave names were listed in 1850 and 1860 and usually with those of their owners. In 1860, slave occupations were also given.

Under the name of the farm operator in the agricultural manuscript census returns were lists of the various crops produced, the value of the farm, and so forth. By matching the name of the farm operator in the agricultural manuscript census returns with the same name in the population manuscript census returns, one can determine if the farm operator was Afro-American or white, whether he could read or write, owned land or not, had children in school, and so forth.

The census does not tell us everything we want to know and one has to be sensitive to the nuances of the census manuscripts and the locale worked with. Ten years is a long time in the lives of people, and much of significance can occur between decennial enumerations. Unless the scholar working with the census materials is aware of the political, economic, and social changes that occurred throughout the decade, it would be easy to miss alterations in the social structure. For example, the federal census of 1870 was taken just as effective black resistance to white dominance began and therefore did not reflect all the progress made by Edgefield black people. No black attorneys or businessmen appeared in the census, but they were documented in other records between 1870 and 1880. The census of 1880 was taken after the reassertion of white political and social hegemony in 1876, and only vestiges of Afro-American advancement were to be found. Although the federal manuscript census returns do not include all the details we would like to have, systematic analysis of the returns combined with literary evidence and other records provide abundant information. Statistical data drawn from the census can tell what people did for a living, the property they owned, the size of family, and a number of other things that can assist in the creation of a valuable mosaic of their families and their society. In this study the numbers tell us what *all* the people did because the *total* census returns have been coded and analyzed. Thus, it comes as close as possible to a completely representative study.

Moreover, a systematic merged data record, the Edgefield Data Base, has been assembled for the county. Separate computer files exist for the population, slave, mortality, agricultural, and manufacturing censuses and some tax, marriage, church, and probate records between 1850 and 1880, along with some scattered records for earlier periods. Because the study uses data embracing the entire county, the separate files yield a composite, multifaceted image over time, involving social, political, cultural, and economic information for every household and family in the county. Information put together amounted to 9,877 cases and 47 variables for the 1880 population census alone; more important, it is integrated and cross-connected at the household as well as the township and county levels. Voluminous documentation on community life in Edgefield County fills in details not derived from census data. This data set is the basis for most tables and numbers given in the text.

Since the entire population of Edgefield County is included in this study, errors are inevitable. Yet because I use so many sources, I am confident that any errors are small in number and limited in scope and have no influence on the conclusions of this study.

Since I have coded every household head, every family head, and every spouse and child present, I can compare my results for Edgefield County with the results of other scholars who use different schemes. For this study I addressed issues concerning household heads, family heads, and proportions of one-parent to two-parent families. I welcome inquiries concerning other comparative statistics and specific comparisons to other works.

Coding of Family Types in the Census

Originally I attempted to use the family coding scheme developed by Peter Laslett.[4] I also tried to follow the coding patterns outlined by the Philadelphia Social History Project as described by Theodore Hershberg.[5] I also consulted with Daniel Scott Smith and Mark Friedberger at the Newberry Library Family and Community Studies Program. Finally, with all the other information that I recorded (age of spouse, total number of children, total number of blacks and total number of whites in the household or family for whom the head was being coded), I devised codes for family types in Edgefield which maintained the consistent delineations I needed. For the period prior to 1880 this coding of family types was difficult and involved guesswork. The speculations were conservative so that extended households would be undercounted and augmented households would be overcounted.

Thus, an artifact of census procedures makes it appear that there was a large growth in the number of extended households for whites and blacks in 1880. However, this is a result of a problem in the interpretation of the censuses, in which the relationship to the family head was not given. If an individual in a household had a different name from the head of household and failed to meet various age criteria, I coded the 1850, 1860, and 1870 household as augmented (strangers or nonrelated individuals living with members of a nuclear family) instead of as extended (relatives living with a nuclear family, usually representing three generations). Therefore, a number of households with relatives who could not be identified as such were placed in the augmented category. Unlike earlier manuscript census returns, the 1880 manuscript census returns recorded the relationship of all persons in a household to the head; therefore, households could be accurately coded by family makeup. Decisions as to the relationship of individuals to their family or household head were determined prior to 1880 by the surnames, the sex, the ages, and the order of listing of individuals in households and families within households. Sometimes the occupation and birthplace of individuals could be used as well. These criteria were not completely reliable. Where there was doubt about the existence of blood ties between household members and the household head, the household was coded as augmented. To reiterate, this inevitably resulted in an underestimate of the number of extended families in 1850, 1860, and 1870.

The following explains the household and family grouping for this study:

Nuclear family
   a) husband and wife (and/or children)
   b) single parent and children (including stepchildren)
   c) siblings under the age of 18

Extended family—household head (and/or spouse)
  a) plus parents of household head or spouse
  b) plus married children with their spouses
  c) plus grandchildren
  d) sibling family where head is 18 years or older
  e) nonparent relatives of household head or spouse present—siblings, cousins,
      aunts, uncles, nieces, nephews
Augmented—nuclear family plus
  a) boarders present
  b) servants (of same color as household head) attached to household
  c) strangers present in household not related to other family members
Solitary or Institutional, Irregular
  a) single person household
  b) no indication of family ties between household head and anyone else listed in
      household
  c) institution: hotel, county jail, state guard quarters, rock quarry, poor house

Special codes were given to black and white mixed households in which the races were related or married to one another. It is also possible to regroup the distinct codes in various ways (for example, codes are so precise that one exists for a stranger in the household along with the parents of the household head and the household head's spouse's sister) to fit other coding schemes. In addition, one can recode black servants in white households as being part of an augmented household.

Total Population

This book employs contingency analysis. I am concerned with the total population and have not employed significance testing. For example, although only eight white women who had children and who lived in households headed by other people were listed as single in the population census of 1880, those eight were not a sample, but were every person recorded in the population census. When percentages do not total to 100, it is due to computer roundings. Also, various codes had missing values. Thus, sometimes the number of total households varied slightly. In addition, the exclusion of Indians sometimes affected percentages and total Ns.

There are only two instances in this study where I have used estimates because I did not have an age-specific population base for 1870 and 1880. The United States census published age- and race-specific totals only for the state, not for each county, in those years. Although I have coded onto sheets the name, occupation, age, race, and gender for every person in 1870 and 1880, which will give me the needed age base, most are not yet machine readable.

To estimate the 1870 and 1880 mortality ratios, I took the Edgefield percentages of the state's age bases and computed an age base to determine Edgefield's 1870 and 1880 mortality rates. I also entered four Edgefield sample townships for 1870 and 1880 into the computer and then figured the exact mortality ratios for those townships from the manuscript mortality censuses. My estimates were conservative, and I chose to underestimate mortality ratios. Underestimates strengthened my assertions, since I was comparing blacks and whites in each case, and black male mortality was higher than white.

I had no population base figures for 1870 and 1880 as I had for 1850 and 1860, so my figures for child-mother ratios are not quite comparable for the years in question. However, for 1870 and 1880, I counted every mother and the number of children living with her for those years, as well as the total number of black and white children under the age of five for the entire county. Therefore, I calculated fertility for postbellum decades in two ways. First, as I did for 1850 and 1860, I used the actual number of mothers with children (less than five years of age) for 1870 and 1880 estimates of fertility. Second, I took the total number of children 0–4 years of age from my 1870 and 1880 data sets and selected female household heads or female spouses who were of childbearing years to calculate fertility (this excluded any women who were neither household nor family heads, nor spouses, nor mothers). I also used the number of children 0–4 from these data sets as the numerator and the number of women of childbearing age as the denominator. The number of women came from the estimated population bases that I used to calculate mortality for women. This procedure reaffirmed the assertion that fertility for both black and white women appeared to decline after the Civil War. My postbellum estimate overestimated rather than underestimated fertility, since not all women were used as the base but all children were counted.

Accuracy of Census Records

After an initial burst of enthusiasm for the use of manuscript census returns and quantitative techniques to study anonymous Americans, there has been a reaction in the form of challenges to their accuracy and in the realization that numbers alone yield limited insights. All historical sources have shortcomings, but if the scholar is aware of these flaws, the data can still be useful. Indeed, the manuscript census returns remain the single best and most accurate source of information for a locale, and if used with tax lists and other local sources, they can yield invaluable information. The manuscript census returns have been used extensively enough now that scholars should be familiar with their advantages and disadvantages. The reader is referred to detailed methodological discussions of these sources except for those areas where a discussion of the materials is necessary for understanding this particular study.[6]

1870 Census

Recent censuses have systematically undercounted Afro-Americans by a factor of from 10 to 12 percent.[7] Ransom and Sutch have made the most careful study of the error-filled tallies of the nineteenth-century southern black population and they have estimated a 6.6 percent undercount for 1870, the census most criticized.[8] Probably the worst undercounts of Afro-Americans were in cities and not in rural areas like Edgefield. For Boston whites before and after the Civil War, the most careful historian of the manuscript censuses, Peter R. Knights, conservatively estimated the Boston undercount of whites at about 8 percent. Elizabeth Pleck used methods similar to those used by Knights to estimate that in 1880 the census underenumerated Afro-Americans in Boston by 33 percent.[9]

No city directories are available for similar tests of Edgefield. Tax assessments are available for 1870 and 1879 and all Afro-Americans listed in the county tax assessments were present in the censuses. Also checked were other sources which listed Afro-Americans—state censuses of 1868 and 1875, church records, tombstones, militia records, lien records, Freedmen's Bureau, the newspaper. I could locate in the census almost all the Afro-Americans listed in other sources.

An argument can be made for the accuracy of the 1870 census for Edgefield Afro-Americans. I have carefully studied the habits and the lives of the 1870 census enumerators. All were conscientious. They reported a most accurate and detailed perception of the population. Despite shortcomings, it is unlikely that any more complete source is available than the 1870 population manuscript census returns for either the post–Civil War black or the white population in the locale. Edgefield's three 1870 census enumerators were Republicans. These men held their jobs because they knew and were supported by the Afro-American population. They had lived all their lives in the areas that they enumerated. The enumerator who completed the greatest portion of the census was Edgefield former slave Lawrence Cain. Church leader, schoolteacher, and state legislator, Cain knew the other Edgefield Afro-Americans. He was an extremely careful enumerator for both agriculture and population. Cain, as well as the two white Republican enumerators, was sensitive to the Afro-American community, and I would venture that the 1870 census made the most accurate color distinctions within the Afro-American community. In 1880 the white census enumerator wrote on the side of his schedule that he had consulted with Cain on the Afro-Americans enumerated.

Agricultural Census

Ransom and Sutch rejected the 1870 agricultural manuscript census primarily because it did not include the tenure of the farm operator and because for some farm operators the value of the farm or other items was not enumerated.[10] I matched every farm in the agricultural manuscript census return with an individual in the population returns for 1870 to ascertain the tenure of the farm operator. I was also able to link these people to the county tax returns for 1870 and the state censuses for 1868 and 1875 to check on land ownership, personal estate, and some crop production.[11] When farm values or crops were not reported on an Edgefield farm, a comparison with the population census return, the county tax return, and state census showed that the individual was indeed a tenant on the farm. Cain even scratched out a number of farms where he recorded information because the farm was still managed as part of the plantation by the white owner.

According to Ransom and Sutch, in 1870, where the "assistant marshals who undertook the enumeration performed their job with diligence and care . . . the censuses of population and agriculture appeared to be reasonably complete."[12] In 1870 Edgefield was one of those places.

Mortality Census

The census of mortality must be used with an awareness of its limitations. The death may not have occurred in the census year, and people were often asked to remember when a family member died. Also deaths in childbirth and other causes of death can skew results. But if used with caution and especially when used for internal comparative purposes, the mortality census yields valuable insights. For the purposes of this study, the mortality censuses are sufficiently accurate to allow black/white comparisons for one locale.[13]

Accuracy for Edgefield Black-White Comparisons

An "age-heaping index" test, which detects abnormal clustering of ages, was done for black and white household heads for the 1850, 1860, 1870, and 1880 population and mortality censuses in each five-year age bracket. For Edgefield, in 1870 and 1880 the reporting of ages for black males was more accurate than for white males. The reporting of the ages of black and white women was slightly less accurate than male reporting, but still comparable.[14] Checking those household heads who were linked from 1870 to 1880 confirmed the above analysis of black-white age comparison. I feel confident in my use of the 1870 and 1880 censuses for the comparison of blacks and whites because I included every household and family for 1870 and 1880. Omissions did not occur due to any sampling error. Moreover, the study compares blacks and whites in the same community across time and uses other records which give a sense of the accuracy of the census records. By having every farm and every family or household head or person who died, or who was in jail or in the poor house, one has a total population to compare, thus minimizing the effect of any undercount.

Appendix 2. Occupational Groupings

Farmer: Farmer, Farmer and Carpenter, Farmer and Clerk, Farmer and Mechanic, Farmer and Merchant, Farmer and Miller, Farmer and Physician, Farmer and Ret. D.G.M., Farmer and Retailman, Farming, Planter.

Laborer: Brick Burner, Burning Coal, Coachman, Coach Painter, Common Laborer, Cutting Wood, Day Laborer, Depot Hand, Ditcher, Drayman, Factory Operative, Farm Hand, Farm Laborer, Farm Manager, Farmer Supervisor, Ferryman, Gardener, Guard at Factory, Hack Driver, Hauling, Hostler, House Painter, Huckster, Jobbing, Keeps Railroad Bridge, Laborer, Mill Worker, Night Watchman, Operative, Overseer, Painter, Porter, Pressman, Pump Hand, Railroad Employee, Railroad Hand, Railroad Watchman, Sawyer, Shingle Getter, Shop Worker, Stage Driver, Stock Cutter, Tank Minder, Teamster, Timber Cutting, Timber Hauler, Turner, Wagoner, Wagoning, Watching Papermill, Watchman, Watchman in Paper Mill, Watchman on Canal, Well Digger, White Washer, Wood Cutter, Works at Water Tank, Works in Chalk, Works in Chalk Bed, Works in Clay, Works in Claybed, Works in Cotton Mill, Works in Flour & Grist Mill, Works in Flour Mill, Works in Grist Mill, Works in Jug Factory, Works in Kalmia Mill, Works in Paper Mill, Works in Pottery, Works on Railroad, Works in Saw & Grist Mill, Works in Sawmill, Works on Ship, Works in Shop, Works in Steam, Saw & Grist Mill, Works in Steam Saw Mill, Works in Tan Yard, Works in Warehouse, Apprenticed to Farmer.

Artisan and Semiskilled: Apprenticed to Blacksmith, Apprenticed to Carpenter, Apprenticed to Machinist, Apprenticed to Saddler, Artist, Artist or Painter, Barber, Basket Maker, Basket and Collar Maker, Blacksmith, Brickmaker, Butcher, Cabinetmaker, Carpenter, Carpenter Apprentice, Carriage Maker, Chair Maker, Cooper, Harness Maker, Hatter, Hemp Maker, House Carpenter, Hydrolist, Machinist, Making Shingles, Mason, Mattress Maker, Mechanic, Mill Wright, Miller, Painter or Glazier, Potter, Printer, Saddler, Shingle Maker, Shoe or Bootmaker, Silversmith, Sparksman, Stone Mason, Stoneware Maker, Stoneware Turner, Tailor, Tanner, Telegraph Operator, Tinner, Wagon Maker, Watchmaker, Wheel Wright, Wood Workman, Works in Blacksmith Shop, Works in Carriage Shop, Works in Harness Shop, Works in Printing Office, Works in Saddle Shop, Works in Shoe Shop, Works in Wood Shop.

Professional, Business, Low White Collar: Agent, Agent at Steam Mill, Attends Grist Mill, Bank Teller, Bartender (owns bar room), Bookkeeper, Bridge Builder, Building Contractor, Carriage Manufacturer, Cashier, Civil Engineer, Clerk, Clerk in County Treasury, Clerk in Government Position, Commissioner, Constable, Contractor, Coroner, County Commissioner, County Jailer, Court Clerk, Dentist, Deputy Sheriff, Doctor, Druggist, Dry Goods Merchant, Dry Goods Retailer, Editor, Engineer, Engineer in Mill, Factory Agent, Factory Overseer, Grocer, Hotel Keeper, Insurance Agent, Judge, Keeping Bar, Keeps Bar Room (owns the bar), Keeps Flour and Grist Mill, Landlord, Law Student, Lawyer, Lumber Manager, Mail Carrier, Manager, Manager of Graniteville Factory, Manager Over Cotton Factory, Manufacturer, Manufacturing Man, Marshal, Merchandizing, Merchant, Merchant Agent, Merchant Tailor, Milliner, Miner, Minister, Music Teacher, Musician, Negro Trader, Peddler, Physician, Physician Farquer (?), Postmaster, Preacher, Publisher, Railroad Agent, Railroad Clerk, Railroad Section Master, Real Estate Agent, Retailor, Retired Druggist, Retired Lawyer, Retired Merchant, Retired Physician, Sawmill Business, School Commissioner, Secretary, Secretary of Graniteville Company, Sheriff, Speculator, State Constabulary, State Guard, Superintendent on Railroad, Superintendent at Clayworks, Superintending Mill, Superintends Sawmill, Superintends Steam Mill, Surveyor, Tax Collector, Teacher, Trader, Treasurer, Trial Justice, Tutor, U.S. IR Assessor.

Domestic: Apprenticed to Bakery, Baker, Cook, Domestic, Domestic Servant, Dressmaking, Governess, House Servant, Housekeeper (employed), Keeping House (only in 1860), Keeping House at Depot, Laundress, Mantua Maker, Midwife, Nurse, Seamstress, Servant, Sewing, Washer Woman, Weaver.

Keeping House (only in 1870 and 1880).

Other: Afflicted, At Home, At School, Boarder, Dependent, In Penitentiary, In Poor House, Indigent, Inmate in Jail, Nitton, None, Pauper, No Occupation Reported in Census, Student, Without Occupation.

Notes

Abbreviations

ABHS   American Baptist Historical Society, Colgate Rochester Theological Seminary
ARC   Amistad Research Center, Dillon University
BA   Bettis Academy, Edgefield County, S.C.
BHC   Baptist Historical Collection, Furman University
BL   Baker Library, Harvard University Graduate School of Business Administration
BRFAL Records of the Bureau of Refugees, Freedmen, and Abandoned Lands, RG 105, National Archives
CWVQ   Civil War Veterans Questionnaires, TSLA
Col   Columbia University
CU   Clemson University
DAT   Daniel Augustus Tompkins Library, Edgefield, S.C.
DU   Duke University
ECH   Edgefield Court House
ECHS   Edgefield County Historical Society, Edgefield County, S.C.
FP   Family Possession
GMC   Graniteville Manufacturing Company
GSA   Georgia State Archives
LC   Library of Congress
NA   National Archives
PM   Pottersville Museum, Edgefield, S.C.
SCDAH South Carolina Department of Archives and History
SCHS   South Carolina Historical Society
SCL   South Caroliniana Library, University of South Carolina
SHC   Southern Historical Collection, University of North Carolina Library
SMC   St. Mary's Church, Edgefield, S.C.
TSLA   Tennessee State Library and Archives
UT   University of Texas Library
UV   University of Virginia Library
VU   Vanderbilt University Library
WC   Wofford College, Sandor Teszler Library, archive of the South Carolina Conference of the United Methodist Church

Introduction

1. Typical of paeans to the southern family are the following: "It is easy to see why the emphasis on community, and on the complex social fabric embodied therein, would be conducive to an intensified awareness of the past. The tightly-knit sense of clan and family, which is the woof and warp of the South's complex social fabric, would tend naturally to embrace the past, the ancestral. Family history is traceable in the South, since the region has existed in much the same shape and size for so long a period of time with comparatively little flux and change. And family history can be so clearly tied in with political and social history, that a sense of one involves a sense of the other" (Rubin and Kilpatrick, *Lasting South*, p. 5). "The family has transcended all other interests and affections in the South. It acts as a bridge linking the Southerner to his past" (White, "View from Window," p. 169). See also, Eaton, *Mind of Old South*, p. 241; Thorpe, *Eros and Freedom*, pp. 28-31; Vance, "Regional Family Patterns"; Wyatt-Brown, "Ideal Typology."

2. I use *Redemption* to mean the return of the southern state governments to the control of orthodox and conservative whites. In Edgefield County this meant the return of the local government to the white landowning elite who had ruled before the Civil War.

3. Katz, *People of Hamilton*, p. 310.

4. Robert P. Swierenga has led the crusade for rural history. See Swierenga, "Agriculture and Rural Life," "Rural History," and "Towards 'New Rural History.'"

5. Swierenga, "Rural History," pp. 8–9, and "Agriculture and Rural Life," p. 104.

6. Tang, *Economic Development*; Smith, *Economic Readjustment*; Stokes, *Savannah*.

7. Statistical tests of Edgefield averages of these variables showed them to be less than one standard deviation from the state averages for other rural counties.

8. Ball, *State That Forgot*, p. 22.

9. Eaton, *Mind of Old South*, p. 223, and "Class Differences," pp. 359–60.

10. Hofstadter, Miller, and Aaron, *American Republic*, p. 517.

11. Williams, *Vogues in Villainy*, pp. 2–5. "Edgefield's reputation for excessive crime was undeserved" (p. 3). The other area associated with lawlessness and crime in South Carolina was Charleston; Columbia, Newberry, Greenville, and Chester were also mentioned. Whereas the proportion of murders to all indictments for South Carolina was about 4 percent, for Edgefield it was 8 percent.

12. Brown, *Strain of Violence*, pp. 76–90. Never mentioning Edgefield, John William de Forest devoted a few pages to a discussion of the county of Greenville where he was stationed during Reconstruction. He observed that Greenville was a rough county, but wrote it was a "haven compared to Abbeville, Newberry and half a dozen other districts." He recounted: "There was once a famous 'gentleman of the old school' in Abbeville who ruled his district with the pistol, who during the course of his long and high-toned life killed several other high-toned creatures, and consequently had himself elected to office whenever he pleased." De Forest added, "Abbeville was renowned for its hundreds of shooting men" (de Forest, *Union Officer*, pp. 182–83). The violence so celebrated as distinctively Edgefieldian was in reality much more typically up-country South Carolinian.

13. King, *Louis Wigfall*, p. 9; B. R. Tillman to F. T. Walton, 13 Feb. 1893, Till-

man Papers (SCDAH); Simkins, *Pitchfork Ben*, p. 189; see also Guess, *South Carolina*, pp. 228–29; Schulz, *Nationalism and Sectionalism*, p. 21; Johnston, *Mentor*, March 1929, p. 41; Chapman, *History of Edgefield*, p. 195.

14. Edmunds, "Francis Pickens," is being expanded into a full-scale biography entitled "Politics of Destruction"; Bonham, "Life and Times of Milledge Bonham."

15. On Edgefield and Reconstruction, see Burton, "Race and Reconstruction"; Mims, "Radical Reconstruction."

16. Simkins, *Tillman Movement* and *Pitchfork Ben*; Banks, "Strom Thurmond."

17. The phrase is from Degler, *Other South*; Mays, *Born to Rebel*. On Marion Wright's influence see Randolph, "James McBride Dabbs," pp. 254–55, 259–60; see also Wright Papers (SHC).

18. Farmers Club (SCL); Mims, "Editors Edgefield *Advertiser*."

19. Several are noted above. See especially the preface for acknowledgments.

20. Woodward, *Gift of Life*, esp. pp. 1–116, 298, and *Way Our People Lived*, esp. pp. 160–97, 319–58; Mays, *Born to Rebel*, esp. pp. 1–38, 45–46, 48–49, 100; Wright, *Barefoot in Arcadia*. The latter two are primarily twentieth-century memoirs.

21. See chapter 1 for a description of Edgefield. In 1880 Edgefield County had a population of 45,018 people. In the same year Atlanta had a population of only 37,409. The point is that although Edgefield was rural, the population of this non-urban political unit was greater than that of most southern cities. In the Deep South, only Charleston (and not by much) and New Orleans had larger populations than Edgefield County. In 1870 Charleston had 48,922 people and in 1880, 49,975. New Orleans had more than 200,000 people by 1880.

22. For elaboration see Burton, "Local History"; Swierenga, "Agriculture and Rural Life," p. 104, and "Rural History," p. 8.

23. To paraphrase Katz, *People of Hamilton*, p. 10, it may be that Edgefield was not typical of rural southern counties and that hypotheses presented herein are not borne out. Nevertheless, one of my goals is to stimulate further research and study. When I began this study, there were none of this sort. As more are completed, comparisons can be made. See bibliographies of Burton and McMath, *Class, Conflict, and Consensus*, pp. 291–98, and *Toward a New South*, pp. 301–8.

24. Welty, *Eye of Story*, pp. 128–29.

25. See note 1 above. See also the work by Barney, "Patterns of Crisis," and Censer, "Family Relationships and Power." A growing literature on southern womanhood has been stimulated by Scott, *Southern Lady*. A number of scholars are currently completing books and dissertations dealing with aspects of the southern white family.

26. Woodman, "Sequel to Slavery"; Wiener, "Class Structure and Economic Development," along with comments by Higgs and Woodman, and Wiener's reply; Dew, "Critical Essay on Recent Works"; Hackney, "Origins of the New South in Retrospect."

27. Gray, *History of Agriculture*; Stampp, *Peculiar Institution*; Fogel and Engerman, *Time on Cross*.

28. Genovese, *Political Economy of Slavery*, *In Red and Black*, *World Slaveholders Made*, esp. p. 96, and *Roll, Jordan, Roll*. For Phillips see *American Negro Slavery* and *Life and Labor*.

29. Escott, *Slavery Remembered*, p. 19.

30. Owsley, *Plain Folk*; Owsley and Owsley, "Economic Basis of Society"; Clark,

Tennessee Yeomen; Weaver, *Mississippi Farmers*; Bonner, "Plantation and Farm," pp.
153–60, discussed the work of Owsley and his students. Critical of Owsley's method-
ology were Linden, "Economic Democracy in Slave South"; Wright, " 'Economic
Democracy' and Concentration of Agricultural Wealth" and *Political Economy*; Wiener, *Social Origins*; Campbell, "Planters and Plain Folk." For other portraits of nonplanters see essays in Magdol and Wakelyn, eds., *Southern Common People*, and in
Burton and McMath, eds., *Toward a New South* and *Class, Conflict, and Consensus*;
in the latter see esp. Hahn, "Yeomanry of Nonplantation South" and also his dissertation, "Roots of Southern Populism." See also Bonner, "Profile of Late Antebellum
Community."

31. See for example, Shugg, *Origins of Class Struggle*; Owsley, review of *Origins
of Class Struggle* and letter to editor. The most popular view of dissenting Southerners is Degler, *Other South*. Recent studies of the Civil War question the consensus
view of the antebellum South. Thomas, *Confederacy as Revolutionary Experience*,
pp. 100–105, and *Confederate Nation*, pp. 233–35; Escott, *After Secession*, pp. 94–
135; Paludan, *Victims*. Fred Bailey's forthcoming insightful study, "Class and Tennessee's Confederate Generation," effectively challenges the dominant view. See also
Bailey, "Caste and Classroom" and "Tennessee's Antebellum Society."

32. Eaton, "Class Differences," pp. 357–58, 364–66, 370, *Growth Southern Civilization*, pp. 151–52, and *History Southern Confederacy*, p. 31; Simkins, *History of
South*, pp. 137–38; Cash, *Mind of South*, pp. 22, 70.

33. McDonald and McWhiney, "Antebellum Southern Herdsman," p. 166, and
"South from Self-Sufficiency," p. 1095.

34. Genovese, "Yeomen Farmers in Slaveholders' Democracy," pp. 341–42, and
Political Economy of Slavery, pp. 20, 25–26, 107–10, 141, 246, 250, 265–66, and
Roll, Jordan, Roll, pp. 91–93. Wyatt-Brown, "Community, Class, and Snopesian
Crime," showed that nonplanter whites had remarkable power in shaping community
relations. Thus, in *Southern Honor*, which appeared too late for inclusion in this
work, Wyatt-Brown may be bridging the gap between Owsley's plain folks and
Genovese's paternalistic planters.

35. Potter, "Enigma of the South." In some respects, Potter's cultural perspective
anticipated current work on American communities that draws on the ideas of anthropologists like Robert Redfield. See Redfield, *Little Community* and "Civilizations as
Societal Structures?" See Bender, *Community and Social Change*, pp. 15–43, for social theory and pp. 45–120 for historians' approaches to American communities from
the seventeenth to the nineteenth centuries.

36. Wyatt-Brown, "Ideal Typology," quotation from p. 4.

37. Ibid., pp. 3, 28.

38. The contribution especially of black scholars George W. Williams and Carter
G. Woodson to the African origins argument are highlighted in Fogel and Engerman,
Time on Cross, 2:170–71, 200. See also pp. 169, 175–76, 179–81, 189, 200–207,
210, 215, 222, 225, 231, 233, 235, 239, 243–44, 246–47, for a good discussion on
the slave family literature. Fogel and Engerman insightfully link what they term the
"Negro school" of historians to Herskovits in pp. 192–211. Herskovits, *Myth of Negro Past*; Mintz, "Melville Herskovits."

39. Shimkin, Shimkin, and Frate, eds., *Extended Family in Black Societies*.

40. Odum, *Social and Mental Traits*; Du Bois, *Negro Family*; Frazier, *Negro Family*; Moynihan, *Negro Family*.

41. Fogel and Engerman, *Time on Cross*; Blassingame, *Slave Community*; Genovese, *Roll, Jordan, Roll*.

42. Furstenberg, Hershberg, and Modell, "Origins of Female Headed Black Family." See also, Hershberg, "Free Blacks in Antebellum Philadelphia" and "Free-Born and Slave-Born Blacks." See also Lammermeier, "Urban Black Family."

43. Pleck, *Black Migration*, quotation from p. 11. The radical shift of responsibility for black problems to the destructiveness of the northern urban environment, and away from the acquired and accustomed mores of the rural South can be seen in Pleck's quotation from page 207: "The pattern of contemporary black poverty derives not from the handicaps of slavery or of southern life, but from the disabilities that flow from the employment opportunities available to black men and women in northern cities. Contemporary programs necessary to uproot these inequalities also must be centered there, rather than in the rural South."

44. Shifflett, "Household Composition" and *Patronage and Poverty*; Ransom and Sutch, *One Kind of Freedom*.

45. Becker, *Treatise on Family*; Schultz, ed., *Economics of Family*, esp. pp. 229–344.

46. Sanderson, "Herbert Gutman's *The Black Family*."

47. Goldin, "Female Labor Force Participation."

48. Gutman, "Persistent Myths" and *Black Family*.

49. Despite Gutman's significant contributions, his persistent concern for working-class self-actualization blurred the sharp theoretical questions of the old sociological school. His position on the black family reflects the thesis he posited in earlier articles on other working-class immigrant groups. Gutman saw self-actualization as a process by which a cultural subgroup sets up its own system of values and standards to preserve and/or create an internal identity and status, and to foster an internalized schema of self-worth and self-respect, regardless of the norms and pressures of the dominant society around it. Indeed, Gutman criticized other scholars for having made it appear that Afro-Americans only imitated the cultural norms of whites. See Gutman, *Work, Culture and Society*.

50. Gutman, *Black Family*, esp. pp. 88–91, 93–97, 114, 185–201 for the brilliant analysis of cousin marriage and naming patterns among Afro-Americans.

51. I greatly appreciate the efforts of Stanley Engerman, John Modell, and Dan Scott Smith in making me aware of the statistics for the 1960–80 period.

52. Swierenga, "Agriculture and Rural Life," pp. 92–93, discusses the urban orientation of modern scholars and emphasizes in particular the role of Richard Hofstadter in denigrating rural America. See Hofstadter, *Age of Reform*, esp. pp. 7–8, 60–93, 121–30, and *Anti-Intellectualism in American Life*, esp. pp. 272–82.

Chapter 1

1. Counties did not emerge in South Carolina until Reconstruction. Prior to 1868 Edgefield was designated as a district. The terms *county* and *district* are used inter-

changeably throughout this book and reflect the historical usage.

2. S.C., *Statutes* (1871) 14:695; (1897) 23:604; (1916) 29:717; (1898) 22:896; (1917) 30:573; (1921) 32:6, 35. S.C., *Constitutional Convention, Constitution, 1895,* Art. 7, Sect. 12. U.S., Works Project Administration, p. 3.

3. Ball, *State That Forgot,* p. 18; Pope, *History of Newberry,* p. 189; Rawick, ed., *American Slave,* vol. 10: *Arkansas,* pt. 6, p. 103. Edgefieldians formed law partnerships with attorneys in neighboring counties, each courthouse town having an office (Edgefield *Advertiser,* 30 Dec. 1830, 6 June 1855). Churches from every neighboring county and even churches in Georgia belonged to the Edgefield Baptist Association; in turn, Edgefield churches belonged to neighboring counties' associations as well as to those in Georgia.

4. Meriwether, *Expansion of South Carolina,* pp. 1, 260–61; Wallace, *South Carolina,* p. 23; Petty, *Growth and Distribution of Population,* pp. 3–12; S.C., State Board of Agriculture, *South Carolina,* p. 4; Julien, *Beneath Kind Sky,* p. 1; Freehling, *Prelude to Civil War,* pp. 7–24, esp. pp. 7, 17–19; S.C., Dept. of Agriculture, Commerce, and Immigration, *Handbook of South Carolina,* pp. 66–74, esp. p. 68, and pp. 77–139, esp. pp. 138–39, 176.

5. The fall line is the first major topographical obstacle to river navigation. Petty, *Growth and Distribution of Population,* pp. 35, 40; S.C., Dept. of Agriculture, Commerce, and Immigration, *Handbook of South Carolina,* pp. 78, 147, 150; Cashin, *Story of Augusta,* pp. 5, 10–13. The above and the following descriptions of Edgefield and the surrounding area draw upon a number of sources. None has been more helpful than local historians noted in the preface. See also S.C., State Board of Agriculture, *South Carolina,* esp. pp. 71–182; Chapman, *History of Edgefield*; Simkins, *Pitchfork Ben,* pp. 23–56; Werner, "Hegemony and Conflict," pp. 19–49; Lanham, "Agricultural, Economic, and Social Study"; U.S., Bureau of Chemistry and Soils, *Soil Survey.*

6. Ramsay, *History of South Carolina,* p. 308. See also pp. 6–14, 118–24.

7. Meriwether, *Expansion of South Carolina,* pp. 66–72, 117–35, 160–62, 251–57, 260–61. Petty, *Growth and Distribution of Population,* pp. 35, 40; S.C., Dept. of Agriculture, Commerce, and Immigration, *Handbook of South Carolina,* pp. 511, 513; Chapman, *History of Edgefield,* pp. 11–17; Cook, *Hard Labor Section,* pp. 8–11; Woodson, "German Palatines." In addition to the above-mentioned ethnic groups, small groups of Scottish, Welsh, and Dutch settlers arrived as early as 1764.

8. Meriwether, *Expansion of South Carolina,* pp. 70, 122, 128, 133, 195, 224, 229; Cashin, *Story of Augusta,* p. 10; S.C., Dept. of Agriculture, Commerce, and Immigration, *Handbook of South Carolina,* p. 513; King, *Louis Wigfall,* p. 9.

9. Brooks, "Priority of Silver Bluff"; Smith "Development and History of Negro Churches," pp. 11–12; Raboteau, *Slave Religion,* pp. 139–43; Nicholson, *Brief Sketch*; Mays, *Born to Rebel.*

10. On Rivers see Higginson, *Army Life,* pp. 56–59, 62, 261, 265; Williamson, *After Slavery,* pp. 16–17, 27. For others see Burton, "Race and Reconstruction" and "Ungrateful Servants," esp. pp. 76–90; Coulter, *Negro Legislators,* p. 37, described former Edgefield slave Aaron Alpeoria Bradley as "one of the most amazing minor characters in the annals of American politics." See also pp. 38–120.

11. Mills, *Statistics of South Carolina,* p. 527.

12. Schaper, *Sectionalism and Representation,* pp. 325, 400–401, 406; Klein, *Rise*

of the Planters, pp. 84–86, 106, 293, and esp. 306–7; S.C., Dept. of Agriculture, Commerce, and Immigration, *Handbook of South Carolina*, p. 176; King, *Louis Wigfall*, pp. 9–10; Simkins, *Pitchfork Ben*, p. 25; Freehling, *Prelude to Civil War*, pp. 18–24; S.C., State Board of Agriculture, *South Carolina*, pp. 550–52, 556.

13. See references in note 12 above and Brown, *South Carolina Regulators* and *Strain of Violence*, pp. 67–90.

14. Edgefield citizens proudly display the names of the governors and lieutenant governors on the side of a building that one sees on entering Edgefield from either Augusta or Columbia. Another Edgefieldian, J. Strom Thurmond, is now chairman of the Senate Judiciary Committee.

15. O'Neall, *Biographical Sketches*, Quotations from 2:223 and 279; see also pp. 211–12, 222–32, 276–80, 463–68, 473–75 and 1:198–205; Green, *George McDuffie*, pp. 17–18; Edmunds, "Francis Pickens"; Marshall, "Gentlemen without Country," pp. 182–99; Ramey, *Trial of Booth*, p. 9; Schultz, *Nationalism and Sectionalism*, p. 7; William C. Preston to George Ticknor, 2 Mar. 1824, Preston Papers (SCL). James Henry Hammond read law with Preston.

16. Pope, *History of Newberry*, pp. 177–78, 181, 185, 189.

17. Johnston Baptist Church, Minutes, 16 Jan. 1876 (BHC); for a native Edgefieldian's emphasis upon the centrality of religion for black and white Southerners see Simkins, "Rising Tide of Faith," esp. pp. 84, 102. U.S., Bureau of the Census, *8th (1860) Census*, vol. 4, *Statistics*, pp. 462–64, and *11th (1890) Census*, vol. 9, *Report on Statistics of Churches*, pp. 38, 79, 164, 175, 204, 245, 445, 549, 565, 588, 609, 694, 717; (In 1871, the southernmost section of Edgefield had gone to form part of Aiken County and therefore 1860 and 1890 statistics are not directly comparable). In 1850 the churches would accommodate 26,400 people. While there were only 16,252 whites in Edgefield District, if Afro-Americans were also expected to attend, theoretically 12,862 people would have no seat on a given Sunday (U.S., Bureau of the Census, *7th (1850) Census*, p. 344). Of course, slaves did attend churches with whites, sometimes sitting in balconies; as a former slave of Francis Pickens recalled, "Master want us to go cha'ch. We sit on one side—so—and dey sit over dere" (Rawick, ed., *American Slave*, vol. 13; *Georgia*, pt. 4, p. 228); Harris, "Slaveholding Republic," pp. 298–301.

It was not until 1861 that Sweetwater Baptist Church relegated blacks to the gallery (Sweetwater Baptist Church Records, May 1861 [BHC]). The following discussion of religion in Edgefield draws upon a number of sources including King, *History of South Carolina Baptists*, pp. 69–72, 79–80, 83–84, 87–88, 92–93, 95–98, 101–2, 107–8, 112–13, 115, 119, 127–29, 137–38, 142–43; Owens, *Saints of Clay*, pp. 42–44, 63, 65, 73, 77–79, 91, 93, 110; Jones and Mills, *History of the Presbyterian Church*, esp. pp. 13–14, 56–57, 628–29, 639–42, 655–57, 659–60, 675–76, 1007–9, 1034–39; Betts, *History of South Carolina Methodism*, pp. 49–50, 64–65, 91, 97, 101–5, 107–8, 113–14, 125, 120, 132, 134–35, 142–43, 147, 174, 178, 183, 187, 189, 197, 200–201, 204, 208, 209, 234, 236, 242, 418; Chapman, *History of Edgefield*, pp. 290–329; Saluda County Tricentennial Commission, *Saluda County*, pp. 25–92; S.C., State Board of Agriculture, *South Carolina*, pp. 550–56.

18. Edgefield *Advertiser*, 22 June 1854 and 25 Sept. 1851; Sophia Chapin to Moses Chapin, 31 Jan. 1853 and 21 Jan. 1854, Chapin-Tunnel Papers (SHC). Lutheran minister Godfrey Drehr preached regularly in Edgefield District and left an account of

daily travel from congregation to congregation (Drehr Journal; see especially summaries of May 1819, p. 145, and Apr. 1849, p. 172, Drehr Papers [SCL]).

19. Edgefield *Advertiser*, 6 June 1855; Cornish Diary, 19 Apr. 1848, 26 July 1846, 9 and 23 Mar. 1856, Cornish Papers (SHC). Sweetwater Baptist Church Records, 8 Nov. 1851, Feb. 1861, Mar. 1861; Horn's Creek Baptist Church Records, Jan. 1853 and Aug. 1856; Edgefield Village Baptist Church Records, 29 July 1859 and 22 Jan. 1860; Johnston Baptist Church, Minutes, regularly throughout mentions the "Union" and Fifth Sunday meetings, all four church records at BHC, Bethany Baptist Church Records, May 1830 (SCDAH). Woodson et al., *History of Edgefield Baptist Association*, p. 325; Betts, *History of South Carolina Methodism*, p. 161.

20. Rainsford Diary, 27 Aug. 1833, p. 21, Rainsford Papers (FP).

21. Woodward, *Gift of Life*, pp. 41–43, and *Way Our People Lived*, pp. 338–40.

22. Bermingham Diary, 3 Nov. 1860, Bermingham Papers (SM); Edgefield *Advertiser*, 14 Nov. 1860; Edmunds, "Francis Pickens," p. 250; Thomas, *Historical Account of Episcopal Church*, pp. 550–51.

23. Asbury, *Journal and Letters*, 1:670, 709n, and 2:687, 796; Betts, *History of South Carolina Methodism*, p. 120; Mills, *Statistics of South Carolina*, p. 529. The Reverend Samuel L. Morris exaggerated his work somewhat. As Fig. 1–1 shows, there had always been at least one Presbyterian church in Edgefield and in 1870 besides the regular church there were three congregations that did not have church buildings. However, there was not a Presbyterian church at the village (Morris, *Autobiography* [not paginated] [FP]; Henderson, *Edgefield Presbyterian Church*, p. 2; see also Jones and Mills, *History of the Presbyterian Church*, pp. 159–60, 220, 655–56; Chapman, *History of Edgefield*, pp. 299–302; Cook, *Hard Labor Section*, pp. 27–28).

24. Henderson, *Edgefield Presbyterian Church*, p. 1; Chapman, *History of Edgefield*, pp. 299–302. Jones and Mills, *History of the Presbyterian Church*, p. 656, give a slightly different version: "The one man was elected as elder and Mrs. Hill automatically became the board of deacons, the board of trustees, church and Sunday School treasurer and Sunday School superintendent. These offices she filled most efficiently and only relinquished them as she found someone to fill them." Cook, *Hard Labor Section*, p. 28; Bethany Baptist Church Records, 1809 (SCDAH); all the church records for Edgefield Baptist churches substantiate the role of women, most in BHC. See also the McKendree Methodist Church Records and "History of Harmony Methodist Church" in Harmony Methodist Church Records, Corinth Lutheran Church Records and St. Mark's Lutheran Church Records, St. Thaddeus Protestant Episcopal Church Records and Upper Diocese of South Carolina Protestant Episcopal Church Records, all in SCL; Graniteville Methodist Church Records (WC); "Prayer Book" of Isabella Morrison Blocker, 17 Nov. [?], 23 June 1859, Blocker Papers (FP).

25. Edgefield *Advertiser*, 22 Sept. 1851. The Jones family intermarried with Edgefield's Joseph Abney family.

26. Quotation is cited in Owens, *Saints of Clay*, p. 43; see also pp. 43–45, 71. The quotation also appears in King, *History of South Carolina Baptists*, p. 71; see also pp. 69–70.

27. The quotation is from Edwards, *Materials towards History of Baptists*, pp. 46–52; Woodson et al., *History of Edgefield Baptist Association*, pp. 12–13, 30–31; Klein, "Rise of the Planters," pp. 42–51. Also see the early records of Baptist

churches and early association records, most at BHC. New Light Baptists emphasized "personal experience." Condemnations of these white up-country Baptists foreshadowed later criticisms of black religion. Critics argued that Separate Baptists threatened the family. Such rituals as the "love feast" suggested sexual immorality. Separate Baptist ministers were accused of sexual immorality, of having great influence over the women, and of abusing that influence (this is very similar to the stereotype of the nineteenth- and twentieth-century black preacher).

28. Bethel Baptist Association Minutes, Annual Reports for 1793, 1795, 1797, 1799 (BHC).

29. Bethel Baptist Association Minutes, Annual Report for 1845 (SCDAH); Woodson, *Giant in Land*, pp. 66–72, 120–45; Owens, *Saints of Clay*, pp. 41–42; King, *History of South Carolina Baptists*, pp. 69–72, 79–80, 83–84, 87–88, 92–93, 95–98, 101–2, 107–8, 112–13, 115, 119, 127–29, 137–38, 142–43, 182, 216–19.

30. Petitions of Benjamin Busbee and subsequent petitions of his wife, 1810, 1 Jan. 1815, 29 Nov. 1815, and 5 Dec. 1815; Petitions of Benjamin and John Ryan, 12 Dec. 1816, 1820, 15 Nov. and Dec. 1823, 1824; all in Petitions to the General Assembly, Legislative Papers (SCDAH); S.C., House, *Journal*, 1824, p. 72 (SCDAH). Bradley, "Slave Manumission," pp. 20–21, 50–51; Woodson et al., *History of Edgefield Baptist Association*, pp. 11–16; King, *History of South Carolina Baptists*, pp. 83–85.

31. Manly, *On the Emancipation of Slaves*, 1821, Manly Papers (BHC); Owens, *Saints of Clay*, p. 71; King, *History of South Carolina Baptists*, p. 341; Woodson et al., *History of Edgefield Baptist Association*, p. 211; Mims, *History of Edgefield Baptist Church*. On the Methodists and slavery see Betts, *History of South Carolina Methodism*, pp. 187–88. According to Dr. A. V. Huff, an ordained Methodist minister and historian of antebellum South Carolina who chairs the Furman University history department, the Methodists became so confused on slavery that they published two rule books, one for distribution in the North which prohibited preachers from owning slaves and another for Methodist ministers in South Carolina which allowed them to own slaves.

32. S.C., House, *Journal*, 1835, p. 6. Brookes, *Defence of South*, p. i. James Henry Hammond in 1858 proclaimed: "God created Negroes for no other purpose than to be the 'hewers of wood and drawers of water'—that is to be the slaves of the white race" (in Hammond, *Selections from Letters and Speeches*, p. 338).

33. Klein, "Rise of Planters," pp. 42–51; Owens, *Saints of Clay*, pp. 41–42, and *Banners in Wind*; Woodson et al., *History of Edgefield Baptist Association*, pp. 172, 181; Mims, *History of Women's Missionary Union*. See discussion in chap. 2 and note 24 above.

34. Eighmy, *Churches in Cultural Captivity*; quotation from Julien, *Beneath Kind Sky*, pp. 17–18. See the various Baptist association records and individual Baptist church records in BHC. See also other denominations' records cited in n. 24 above.

35. Jno. Bauskett to Iveson L. Brookes, 19 Apr. 1851; see also Brookes to Rev. William Heath, 20 Mar. 1849, both in Brookes Papers (SHC).

36. Gregg saw churches and schools as necessary for a community of industrial workers. Quotation from Olmsted, *Journey in the Back Country*, 2:63; D. A. Tompkins to Grace Tompkins, 31 Aug. 1907, Tompkins Papers (SHC).

37. After studying the extant records of Edgefield black churches, the ex-slave nar-

ratives, and especially the Negro Baptist Association Records (ABHS), I have concluded that one reason that blacks during Reconstruction did not demand more from their former oppressors was that they were a forgiving Christian community that tried to live out those New Testament ideals. Unfortunately, they expected the same charity from the white Christians. For a similar conclusion about Afro-American religion and Reconstruction in Georgia see Drago, *Black Politicians*. Escott, *Slavery Remembered*, pp. 95–96, 110–16, 149, 158, 179–80, assesses former slaves' statements about religion. For a black perspective see Thomas, *Biblical Faith and the Black American*. The cultural persistence of this idea can be seen in Edgefield native Benjamin E. Mays. See Mays, *Seeking to Be Christian*, pp. 17–18, 26–34, 38–39, 44, 80–103, 108, 112, 118, 122–33. Martin Luther King, Jr., Mays's student at Morehouse College, follows in this tradition. Consider his words following the bombing of his home in Montgomery: "We want to love our enemies. We must love our white brothers no matter what they do to us" (quotation from Lewis, *King*, p. 70).

38. Lingerman, *Small Town America*, esp. pp. 15, 327–28. The quotation is from Hundley, *Social Relations*, p. 26, also cited in Huffman, "Town and Country," p. 366, see also pp. 367–81. For government in antebellum South Carolina see Wooster, *People in Power*, esp. pp. 4–9, 26–27, 49, 53, 64–65, 70–71, 83, 88–90, 92, 94, 105, 108–9, 115–16; Wallace, *History of South Carolina*, 1:343–51; Schaper, *Sectionalism and Representation*, pp. 377–80, 382–83; S.C., *Statutes at Large*, 5:569, 6:12, 9:558–60; Two books that explain South Carolina's county base of government are Coleman, *State Administration*, and Andrews, *Administrative County Government*. See especially the latter for local government before and after the Civil War.

39. Woodman, *King Cotton*, quotation from p. 326 on the postbellum South. I believe this applies to the antebellum period as well. See also pp. 87–95, 181, 328–29.

40. Mills, *Statistics of South Carolina*, p. 522; Edgefield *Advertiser*, 13 Mar. 1851. An excellent description of the town of Edgefield, past and present, is in Bland and Rainsford, *Revitalization Study*.

41. Rhys Isaac has demonstrated a courthouse's symbolic function in the culture of revolutionary-era Virginia in "Dramatizing the Ideology" and *Transformation of Virginia*, pp. 30, 88–92, 135–36; Edgefield *Advertiser*, 24 Feb. and 4 Apr. 1839, 22 Mar. 1854.

42. Derrick, *Centennial History*, esp. pp. 9, 27–28, 32–33; Taylor, "Hamburg"; Cordle, "Henry Shultz"; Phillips, *History of Transportation*, pp. 77–81, 211–27, 238. See also debates and bills on Hamburg and Shultz in S.C., House, *Journal* 1835–36. Also Shultz Papers (SCL). In 1842 Columbia, the state capital, was connected to the railroad line.

43. Chapman, *History of Edgefield*, pp. 103–4; Jones and Dutcher, *Memorial History*; Cashin, *Story of Augusta*; Werner, "Hegemony and Conflict"; Harris, "Slaveholding Republic." The papers of Edgefield planters and farmers contain numerous references to visits to Hamburg and Augusta. For example, see the J. C. and Orlando Sheppard Papers, Ouzts Papers, J. H. Hammond Papers, Bones Family Papers, all in SCL; McKie Papers and Hollingsworth Papers (DU).

44. The Augusta Canal entered the Savannah River well above the fall line. At the fall line, there were rapids and falls formed by the granite formations common to the states of Georgia and South Carolina. As noted earlier, both Hamburg and Augusta grew up at this fall line. For about thirty miles above the fall line navigation was easy

owing to the large number of tributary streams that fed into the Savannah from both Georgia and South Carolina. Pole boats chose to enter the canal above the fall line instead of risking the rapids to get down to Hamburg. The Edgefield *Advertiser*, 10 Mar. 1858, proclaimed Hamburg and Augusta to be economically "one and the same city." Rosson, *North Augusta*; Werner, "Hegemony and Conflict," pp. 22–54; Phillips, *History of Transportation*, pp. 336–46; Derrick, *Centennial History*, p. 212.

45. Stover, *Railroads of the South*, pp. 11, 17, 113–14; Derrick, *Centennial History*, pp. 8–9, 12, 97–98, 200–202, 211–12, 235, 271–72; Phillips, *History of Transportation*, pp. 7, 17, 19, 30–33, 68, 76–77, 99, 102, 106–7, 122–23, 136, 139, 156–59, 207–8, 216, 222–24, 238, 254, 265, 283, 289, 327, 361, 364, 382, 384–85, 391; German "Queen City"; Corley, *Confederate City*, pp. 4–26; Cashin, *Story of Augusta*; Sala, *America Revisited*, pp. 249–57; Somers, *Southern States since War*, pp. 62–63; Woodward, *Way Our People Lived*, pp. 160–97; Werner, "Hegemony and Conflict," pp. 22–54, is especially excellent.

46. Mitchell, *William Gregg*, esp. pp. 41–90; Terrill, "Eager Hands" and "Murder in Graniteville"; Sala, *America Revisited*, p. 239; Woodward, *Way Our People Lived*, pp. 319–58, and *Gift of Life*, pp. 22, 27–86, 92–95, 97, 298; Campbell, *Southern Business Directory*, pp. 311–12; Edgefield County, South Carolina, Records of the Post Office Department, RG28 (NA); Dun and Bradstreet, *Mercantile Agency Reference Book*. Newspapers and the papers of farmers and planters identified Edgefield neighborhoods. For example, see n. 43 above and almost any issue of the Edgefield *Advertiser* or Augusta *Chronicle and Constitutionalist* or Hamburg *Republic*.

47. Edgefield County Military Record, Colonel John Hill Papers (SHC); Louis T. Wigfall to Landon Cheves, Jr., 12 Sept. 1836, Cheves Papers (SCL); Edmunds, "Politics of Destruction," n. 144 in chap. 2; Rainsford Diary, 11 May and 22 Oct. 1835, pp. 20, 22, Rainsford Papers (FP). At a typical Edgefield regimental review, Rainsford, a "1st Sergeant," estimated "there were from 7 to 800 privates and officers" involved. On newspapers see Ellen, "Political Newspapers," esp. chaps 2 and 3, and pp. 18, 66, 75, 92–94, 328–29, 347–48. According to the Edgefield *Advertiser*, 8 May 1873, the *Augusta Chronicle* was disseminated widely on both sides of the Savannah, being as popular in Edgefield as in Richmond County.

48. Former Edgefield slaves identified specific communities. See, for example, Rawick, *American Slave*, vol. 12: *Georgia*, pt. 1, pp. 335–36, 338, and vol. 13: *Georgia*, pt. 4, pp. 226–27; Thompson, "African Influence," p. 134.

49. The best description of these various towns is S.C., State Board of Agriculture, *South Carolina*, esp. pp. 659–60, 692–94, 697–98, 707. See also, Phillips, *History of Transportation*, pp. 158–59, 209–11, 215; Derrick, *Centennial History*, pp. 32–33, 202–3; Carlton, "Mill and Town." Werner, "Hegemony and Conflict," chap. 2, pp. 22–54, has an excellent discussion. Because retailers in these growing towns sought goods from Augusta merchants, Edgefield was made even more dependent on the Georgia city. Edgefield *Advertiser*, 25 Jan. and 11 Mar. 1872; Smith, *Life and Sport*, esp. pp. 1–11; Hall, *Things and Incidents*, pp. 199–205; Sala, *America Revisited*, p. 237; Stirling, *Letters from Slave States*, pp. 284–301.

50. Watson, *Greenwood County*, esp. pp. 1–73; Aull and Aull, *Johnston Family History Book*; Werner, "Hegemony and Conflict," pp. 22–54; Bland and Rainsford, *Revitalization Study*; Watson and Calvin, *History of Ridge Spring*.

51. Mitchell, *William Gregg*; Terrill, "Eager Hands" and "Murder in Graniteville";

U.S., Bureau of the Census, *8th* (1860) *Census*, vol. 3, *Manufactures*, pp. 552–59.
Edgefield Federal Manuscript Industrial Census, *7th* (1850) and *8th* (1860) (SCDAH).

52. Before the days of glass jars and plastic, pottery was essential for transporting liquids. Mills, *Statistics of South Carolina*, pp. 523–24; U.S., Bureau of the Census, Edgefield Federal Manuscript Industrial Census, *6th* (1840), *7th* (1850), and *8th* (1860) (SCDAH); Thompson, "African Influence," pp. 130–43; Vlach, *Afro-American Tradition*, pp. 76–92; Pottersville *Hive*, Apr. and Aug. 1981. Abner Landrum bought the paper and changed the name to the *Hive*, but continued the Unionist editorials until 1831, when he sold his pottery works, including his slaves, to his son-in-law, Lewis Miles, and moved his paper to the state capital. Davies was the brother-in-law of Marcellus Hammond and a close friend of James Henry Hammond. The records of his enterprise are in Davies Papers (SCL). Francis Pickens also owned a pottery works. Carlee McClendon has established a pottery museum in Edgefield at one of the old pottery mills. He has most of the originals and some copies of the sales of the Pottersville Mills and slave potters. See McClendon, "History of Pottersville."

53. U.S., Bureau of the Census, *8th* (1860) *Census*, vol. 3, *Manufactures*, pp. 552–59.

54. Gray, *History of Agriculture*, 1:146–51, 440–44, 2:843; Schaper, *Sectionalism and Representation*, pp. 294, 318, 456. Conflict between the early planters and the nonplanters is a major theme of Klein, "Rise of the Planters." As early as 1848 Edgefield planters debated the need for a fence law (Farmers Club, 1 Jan. 1848 [SCL]). Not all large planters agreed that stock should be fenced. Edgefield blacks gave the newly enacted fence laws as a reason they migrated from Edgefield en masse to Arkansas in 1881–82 (see chap. 6). Edgefield *Chronicle*, 4, 12, 18, 25 Jan. 1882; Charleston *News and Courier*, 2 Jan. 1882; *Appleton's Cyclopedia*, 1882, p. 812; New York *Daily Tribune*, 5 Jan. 1882, p. 5; Tindall, *South Carolina Negroes*, pp. 170–71.

55. U.S., Bureau of the Census, *7th* (1850) *Census*, pp. 345–48 and *8th* (1860) *Census*, vol. 2, *Agriculture*, pp. 128–31. See also, Ramsay, *History of South Carolina*, p. 305; Smith, *Economic Readjustment*, pp. 77–84; Lander, "Antebellum Milling"; Mills, *Statistics of South Carolina*, pp. 363–64, 512–22; Edgefield *Advertiser*, 15 Dec. 1852, 12 Jan. and 9 Nov. 1853, 10 Sept. 1856; Simkins, *Address before State Agricultural Society*. However, districts in the more up-country parts of the state also drove hogs into Edgefield.

56. The occupational and economic structure of Edgefield is discussed in detail in chaps. 2, 5, and 7. See also Burton, "Ungrateful Servants," chap. 5, pp. 194–293. Gray, *History of Agriculture*, 1:550–56, discusses task and gang system. Fogel and Engerman, *Time on Cross*, 1:38–42 and 95, estimate that adult slaves engaged in agriculture made up 80 percent of slave laborers. Ransom and Sutch, *One Kind of Freedom*, pp. 15–16, estimate that male slaves engaged in agriculture composed 88.7 percent of the rural slave population. My estimates are similar to the above, and Table 4–1 lists the occupations of those slaves who died in 1860. Quotation from Hammond, *Address before South Carolina Institute . . . 1849*, pp. 32–33.

57. The description of cotton cultivation draws on S.C., State Board of Agriculture, *South Carolina* pp. 89–92. The notes Harry Hammond took for this handbook are in the Harry Hammond Papers (SCL). See also, Mendenhall, "History of Agriculture"; Hammond, *Cotton Industry*; Battalio and Kagel, "Structure of Antebellum

Southern Agriculture"; Gray, *History of Agriculture*, pp. 689–90, 700–706; U.S., Bureau of the Census, *10th* (1880) *Census*, vols. 5 and 6, *Cotton Production*; U.S., Office of Experiment Stations, *Cotton Plant*; Dickson, *Practical Treatise*, pp. 57–62, 89–90, 124–26, 158–59, 178–79.

58. Simkins, *Address·before State Agriculture Society*, p. 8.

59. Tucker, "James Hammond," p. 31. Oration delivered 4 July 1829, Hammond Papers (LC). Hammond, *Address Delivered before South Carolina Institute . . . 1849*, pp. 12, 15–16. He also referred to the "manly spirit" and "high and virtuous sentiments" that were part of the agrarian life (p. 38).

60. Hammond, *Anniversary Oration State Agricultural Society. . . 1841*, p. 17; also p. 14, and Brookes, *Defence of South*, p. 46. The Edgefield minister also defended agriculture and slavery as the basis of a white man's republic and on the "good feeling amounting to even strong attachment" between master and slave. Thomas Green Clemson to John C. Calhoun, 12 Aug. 1845, Calhoun Papers (CU); Lander, *Calhoun Family*, p. 94. Pickens, *Speech of Pickens 1851*, p. 17. Edgefield *Advertiser*, 26 Aug. 1857. See also Simkins, *Address before State Agricultural Society*, p. 7, where he argues that the southern farmer's growing of cotton has done more than anything to "hasten the civilization of the universal human family. . . . [Slavery is] one of the Almighty's arrangements for the greatest good to the greatest number of his creatures." McDuffie proclaimed, "slavery . . is the corner stone of our republican edifice." S.C., General Assembly, *Journal*, 1835, p. 8.

61. Thomas Jefferson Howard, Civil War Veterans Questionnaire, 1915, p. 1, and 1922, p. 1 (TSLA). Some of these common houses, modified over the years, still stand in Edgefield, a few dating back to the eighteenth century. Rainsford, "Oldest House in Edgefield"; Glassie, *Folk Housing*.

62. Rawick, *American Slave*, sup. ser., 1, vol. 3: *Georgia*, pt. 1, p. 233; sup. ser. 1, vol. 4: *Georgia*, pt. 2, pp. 662–63; vol. 13: *Georgia*, pt. 4, pp. 227–28. For Edgefield planters' different theories on slave housing see Farmers Club, 6 Nov. 1847 (SCL).

63. Flossie Lamb Crouch surveyed Edgefield homes for the WPA, Crouch Papers (SCL). Available at both SCL and DAT are pamphlets with pictures: Guide Books: "Welcome Edgefield," "ECHS Presents," "Stop-Look-and Listen," and "Oakley Park"; see also Julien, *Ninety-Six*; Saluda Standard Sentinel and History Book Committee, *Family History of Saluda*.

64. The Southern elite tried hard to retain their stately homes, which symbolized the family and functioned as more than dwelling places. Despite his being in severe financial straits in 1867, Francis Pickens assured his wife that while they might have to sell land, and even one of the plantations, they would never sell the house (Francis W. Pickens to Lucy Pickens, 17 Sept. 1867, F. W. Pickens Papers [SHC]). James Henry Hammond purchased Dr. Milledge Galphin's house in Feb. 1855. He named it Redcliffe and began to build a new house and requested that he be buried on that land. He wanted to "leave it for a family mansion" (Hammond, Secret Diary, 12 May 1855, J. H. Hammond Papers [SCL]; Tucker, "James Hammond," p. 465). One can better understand Catherine Hammond's delight in her son and daughter-in-law's fondness for Redcliffe: "I have felt gratified at the preference which Harry and Emmie seemed to have for this place" (C.E. Hammond to Julia B. Cumming [1873], Hammond, Bryan, Cumming Papers [SCL]). The death notice of Dr. Alfred Grantam

Howard, who had served as Charleston's port physician, reflected this attachment. "At the time of his death [he] resided upon the patrimonial estate, which had descended regularly through his family for over a hundred years" (Edgefield *Advertiser*, 26 Feb. 1860). For histories of Redcliffe see Billings, "History of Hammond"; Tucker, "James Hammond," p. 86; Bleser, *Hammonds of Redcliffe*, pp. 14–15; Faust, *James Hammond*, pp. 1–2, 335–37.

65. Harry Hammond to Emily Cumming Hammond, 5 Aug. 1864, Hammond, Bryan, Cumming Papers (SCL); Plantation Record Book, Jan. 1851, p. 246, Pickens Papers (DU). Reflecting what Glassie, *Folk Housing*, calls a need for "control," southern monumental architecture imposed itself upon its neighbors. The manor house dominated the slave houses, which were built in small clusters across from each other. The manor house symbolized control and acted as a constant reminder to the slaves of their bondage and the power of the white master. The common houses of whites and the small sheds of the slaves were diminished by comparison.

The importance of the manor house as the symbol of control was not lost on slaves. Willie Lee Rose found that when freedom came to the slaves on the Sea Islands, they often burned the big house but did not harm the whites. In Edgefield, at least one house, that of Walter Allen, was burned during Reconstruction, supposedly by "Negro Radicals." It was rumored that black radical Capt. Edward Tennant hired an arsonist to set the fire that burned Gen. M. C. Butler's home to the ground, supposedly precipitating the "Second Ned Tennant Riot." See Burton, "Race and Reconstruction"; Rose, *Rehearsal for Reconstruction*, pp. 16, 106–7. Perhaps burning the symbol of the southern aristocracy was an even more powerful statement by blacks than physical violence toward the white families themselves would have been.

66. In the early nineteenth century, a historian wrote that there existed a "reciprocal dependence" that cemented "the union of all members of the great family of Carolina" because those who did not grow cotton could sell their produce to the planters (Ramsay, *History of South Carolina*, p. 305). In 1839, James Henry Hammond tallied the thirty-eight members of his Beech Island militia. Hammond worked seventy-five slave hands and thirty-seven plows to cultivate 825 acres of cotton and 730 acres of corn. Jacob Foreman, the second largest "planter," cultivated 120 acres in cotton and 340 acres in corn with seventeen slave hands and ten plows. Only two other farmers in the locale planted any cotton—one planted twenty acres and the other two acres (Plantation Journal, Hammond Papers [LC]; Tucker, "James Hammond," p. 311). Some areas of Beech Island and the rich river bottoms were more suited for corn than cotton. In 1859, "Cambridge" wrote about farmers from Edgefield selling corn to the Augusta and Savannah markets (Edgefield *Advertiser*, 22 June 1859; Plantation Journal, 8 Nov. 1853, J. H. Hammond Papers [SCL], and Day Book, 8 Apr. 1858, Edward Spann Hammond Papers [SCL]; Harris, "Slaveholding Republic," p. 40).

67. After 1819, cotton prices never reached their previous highs. 1823 saw a brief recovery, followed by a low through 1832. Then cotton prices again rose until 1837, when they hit a crisis low. Although prices rose for the next two years, they remained at low levels until 1848. Prices rose sharply in 1849 and 1850; they dropped in 1851, but not as low as previously. Throughout the remainder of the 1850s prices rose. Smith, *Economic Readjustment*, esp. pp. 4, 45–111, 117–30; U.S., Bureau of the Census, *8th* (1860) *Census*, vol. 2, *Agriculture*, p. 129, and vol 4, *Statistics*, p. 312;

Fogel and Engerman, *Time on Cross*, 1:89–94; Hall, "Soil Erosion"; Wright, *Political Economy*. Wright pointed out that the decline was relative. Some in Edgefield openly opposed reforms to farming. Edgefield planters were active in state and local agricultural clubs that promoted reforms. The writings and farming experiments of James Henry Hammond are well known. See Faust, *James Hammond*, p. 396. Col. Whitfield Brooks presented a number of papers to his own local agricultural society, the Ninety Six Agricultural Club in northeast Edgefield District; he was also invited to lecture at other local clubs. In 1844 Brooks's Edgefield plantation won the State Agricultural Society of South Carolina's award, a large engraved silver trophy, still prized by the family, for having the state's best-managed farm. Brooks's remarks and experiments on his agriculture are contained in his diaries, Whitfield Brooks Papers (FP); see also, Farmers Club (SCL).

68. As a standard of measurement and consistency with other studies, I have generally used household heads as my base. In 1850 there were also 67 non–household heads who owned real estate, but they owned only 2.4 percent of the real estate. In 1860, 140 persons who were not household heads owned 3.7 percent of the real estate. Another 445 persons in other persons' households (including those in hotels) claimed personal estate in 1860 which accounted for 6.2 percent of all personalty in the county. In both realty and personalty in 1860, non–household heads owned about 5 percent of the wealth. For precise real and personal property distributions see Burton, "Ungrateful Servants?" pp. 203–4. An overall measure of wealth, like the Gini index of .777 in 1850 and .784 in 1860, shows that ownership of real property was distributed less equally than in the settled rural areas of the old Northwest. This inequality of property ownership, however, was only slightly greater than in the frontier state of Wisconsin in the 1850s, and it was less than in northern cities like Milwaukee or, for that matter, in the major regional city of Augusta itself. A value of 0 indicates a perfectly equal distribution, with all households having the same wealth; the maximum value of 1 indicates a situation in which a single household owned all the wealth. Gini indexes from Soltow, *Patterns of Wealthholding*; see also Soltow, *Men and Wealth*; Wright, *Political Economy*, pp. 25–33; Atack and Bateman, "Egalitarianism, Inequality, and Age," pp. 90, 92, and " 'Egalitarian Ideal,' " p. 125. J. William Harris, "Transformation of a Social Order," p. 3, generously supplied me with the Gini index for a sample from Augusta, Georgia.

69. Edgefield *Advertiser*, 29 Apr. 1852; also Farmers Club, 5 Apr. 1851 (SCL); Hammond, *Address before South Carolina Institute, 1849*, p. 6; Deal, "Preliminary Examination of Edgefield." Whites who stayed accumulated land, even adjusting for inflation.

Persistence rates were calculated on the basis of whether a head of household was listed in the population manuscript census returns for 1850, 1860, 1870, and 1880. For example, if someone was listed in 1850 but not in 1860, I assumed that individual had either died or left. If that person then appeared in the 1870 population census, the individual still was not considered to be a persister for the decade from 1850 to 1860 but was considered a persister from 1850 to 1870. Persistence rates for household heads were determined by taking the total number of households for the base year as the denominator and the number of household heads located in the next census as the numerator. Thus, persistence rates for 1850 to 1860 were as follows:

$$\frac{N \text{ household heads found in both } 1850 \text{ and } 1860}{N \text{ all } 1850 \text{ household heads.}}$$

For an alternative method, known as "priority rates," in which the denominator in the above example would have been all 1860 household heads, see Burton, "Ungrateful Servants?" chap. 4. No attempt was made to control for age or mortality or to exclude the female household heads, who were more difficult to trace. The areas of 1870 Edgefield County that were taken to form the new county of Aiken were excluded from the households used to calculate persistence for 1870 to 1880 except for tracing household heads for the study of Graniteville.

70. Changes in the occupational classifications for the 1860 census resulted in a third of farmers being recorded as nonslaveowners and a quarter of the farmers as landless. About a third of the 1850 nonslaveowning farmers (less than the overall persistence rate) and about a fifth of those who owned neither land nor slaves were still in Edgefield in 1860. Although three-fourths of these yeomen acquired no slaves over the decade, a quarter of the nonslaveowning farmers who stayed did acquire slaves; the average acquisition numbered three. Nearly all the landless farmers who acquired slaves also acquired land. Another third of the nonslaveowning farmers who did not acquire slaves did increase their landholdings. About 40 percent of the yeomen who persisted from 1850 to 1860 remained nonslaveowners and did not gain any additional land. Two-fifths of all 1850 household heads had no land to lose.

71. The linkage of age and wealth can be seen when the Gini index for real property is measured for various age groups. For antebellum white household heads the index fell proportionately from the youngest (those under 30) to the oldest (those over 50). Wealth was more evenly distributed among the old, and the greatest inequality existed among the young; older household heads with little property had little hope for advancement.

72. Edgefield *Advertiser*, 1 July 1857; Aptheker, "Poll Tax"; Salley, "Methods of Raising Taxes," pp. 7–12. By 1864, free blacks paid ten dollars each. In 1857, the district collected $15,715.70 on slaves, $146 on free blacks, $863.445 on sales (at 15¢), $217.70 on professions (at 50¢), $259.762 on lots in towns (at 12½¢), $1,250.00 on bank stock (at 25¢), and $2,491.23 for land. See also, Edgefield *Advertiser*, 11 July 1860; S.C., General Assembly, *Reports and Resolutions, 1845*, p. 343; Bradley, "Slave Manumission," p. 96.

73. Some sense of the different number of Edgefield families owning slaves can be gained from the number of different surnames recorded on the slave manuscript census. From 1850 to 1860 the number decreased from 695 to 615. U.S., Bureau of the Census, *8th* (1860) *Census*, vol. 2, *Agriculture*, p. clxxii; Johnson, *Toward Patriarchal Republic*, p. xxii (n.).

Chapter 2

1. Eaton, *Mind of the Old South*, p. 241. In the 10 Jan. 1838 Senate debate, Calhoun is recorded as saying: "The Southern States are an aggregate, in fact, of communities, not of individuals. Every plantation is a little community, with the master at its head, who concentrates in himself the united interests of capital and labor, of

which he is the common representative. These small communities aggregated make the State in all, whose action, labor, and capital is equally represented and perfectly harmonized" (Wilson, ed., *Papers of John C. Calhoun*, 14:84). Wyatt-Brown, "Ideal Typology," p. 5.

2. Throughout the book I use three categories of wealth: landed gentry, smallholders, and landless families who sometimes, however, possessed personal property. For 1860, the first year personal property information was available, I added personalty and realty values and divided all whites into wealth quartiles. In 1860 the wealthiest quartile of white households contained heads with combined real and personal wealth of $12,000 or more. This did not necessarily mean great riches; most personal estate was invested in slaves, and a prime field hand was valued at about $1,000. At a minimum, persons in this category held some land and slaves and were yeoman middle class. Most yeomen middle class, however, were in the two middling wealth quartiles. The dividing line in the second wealthiest grouping was $2,200. If a household had less than that but more than $270, it was in the third wealth quartile. The poorest quartile of whites owned at most $270 in combined real and personal property. Unless a slave was elderly or crippled, he or she would not have been valued as cheaply as $270 in 1860. Therefore, this poorest quartile of white household heads consisted almost exclusively of nonslaveowners. Because in 1850 only real estate is given in the census and since 40 percent of the household heads were landless, quartiles proved impossible. I divided the bottom group as the landless. The next quartile break came at $500 real estate, but this included only 11 percent of all household heads. The third quartile separation mark was $2,000. The small percentage of household heads who had that amount were included in the third quartile, which broke at 78 percent. The richest "quartile" (really 21 percent), then, had more than $2,000 in real estate in 1850.

In 1860 the richest quartile included mostly farmers by occupation (85.8 percent including those "farming" and the planters). Others were doctors, lawyers, preachers, proprietors, and businessmen. The next wealthiest quartile was similar to the richest, made up of 80 percent farmers with professionals (including teachers) and some artisans and overseers. The third wealthiest had only 67 percent who were farmers (only 56 if those "farming" are not considered). Besides more overseers and artisans than in the wealthier groups, there were preachers, teachers, and factory operatives. The poorest quartile had the smallest proportion of farmers, only about a third of all households (only 19 percent if those "farming" are not included). The poorest quartile had only one preacher, but as many teachers as any other quartile. The poorest had more artisans, laborers, and factory workers than the other quartiles.

In 1850 the structure of occupations was similar to that of 1860. The richest, however, had only 71 percent who were farmers (17 percent of these were planters). The second wealthiest quartile had 73 percent who were farmers. The third wealthiest group had 61 percent, and the landless had 47 percent who were farmers. Also, most of the artisans were in the landless group in 1850, as well as four preachers. More than half the teachers were in the poorest quartile.

3. Taylor, *Cavalier and Yankee*; Osterweis, *Romanticism and Nationalism*. A perceptive account of early antebellum southern social structure is presented in the short stories by an Edgefield intimate in Longstreet, *Georgia Scenes*. Flynt, *Dixie's Forgotten People*, pp. 167–96, has a superb annotated bibliography on the poor white in the

South. Because the sociologist was born in Greenwood County in 1890, was reared there, and taught social studies at Lander College in Greenwood, Coleman, "Poverty and Poor Relief," presents a unique perspective.

4. Especially during the Civil War bartering became prevalent. See Plantation Journal, 27 Jan., 5 Feb., 1 Dec. 1864, 23 Feb. 1865, Talbert Papers (SCL); Ledger, Ramey and Hughes Papers (PM); Ledger, Mitchell Papers (PM); Store Account Book, 1819–29, William Daniel Papers (SCL).

5. Plantation Record Book, Dec. 1850, p. 245, Pickens Papers (DU).

6. Mills, *Statistics of South Carolina*, pp. 527–29; S.C., *Statutes*, 2:594, 595, 597, 5:410–13, 310–12, 41–44; Klein, "Rise of the Planters," pp. 53–59; Edgefield Village Bible Society, 20 and 26 Mar., 30 Apr. 1830 (SCL); Peter J. Lelande and Pressley Bland, Petition, 1 Jan. 1835, Legislative papers (SCDAH); Chapman, *History of Edgefield*, p. 77. See also Coleman, "Poverty and Poor Relief," pp. 127–31.

7. Edgefield *Advertiser*, 3 Apr. 1851, 29 Apr. 1852, 14 Nov. 1860. In addition, Edgefield supported seven "lunatic paupers" confined in the state asylum in Columbia. Coleman, "Poverty and Poor Relief," pp. 158–62.

8. Cook, *Hard Labor Section*, p. 42; Edgefield *Advertiser*, 23 July 1856 and 13 Mar. 1860; Simkins, *Pitchfork Ben*, pp. 32–33; Tillman, "Childhood Days," pp. 3–4; Mims, "Life and Politics of George Tillman," pp. 11–13; Bonham, "Life and Times of Milledge Bonham," pp. 29–30.

9. Augusta *Daily Constitutionalist*, 26 Aug. 1860; Cornish Diary, 18 Feb. 1850, Cornish Papers (SHC); Sorkin, "Occupational Status"; U.S., Bureau of the Census, *8th* (1860) *Census*, Population, Manuscript, Richmond County, Georgia (NA).

10. Petitions for Revolutionary War Pensions: Rachel Temple, 9 Oct. 1830, Esther McGraw, 6 Dec. 1831, Mary Robertson, Oct. 1839, all in Legislative Papers (SCDAH).

11. Dreher Journal, Dreher Papers (SCL); Cartledge Autobiography, Cartledge Papers (SCL); quotation from Cornish Diary, 9 Mar. 1847; see also 2 June 1848, 13 Jan. 1849, 18 Feb. 1850, 9 and 21 Feb., 23 Apr., 20–25 May 1853, 12 Dec. 1858, Cornish Papers (SCH). For a Presbyterian minister's careful records in nearby Abbeville County and esp. in Greenwood, see "Journal of Events," 1838–1864, McLees Papers (SCL).

12. Cornish Diary, 9 Jan. 1847, Cornish Papers (SHC). Those 675 whites "farming" in 1860 have been grouped with the "farmers" in Table 2–1. In 1850 no one listed his occupation as "farming." Harris, "Slaveholding Republic," p. 210, found a tenth of all farms were operated by tenants in his Edgefield sample for 1860. For the Georgia hinterlands he found the proportion higher and nearly one-fourth of all farms in Hart County.

13. In 1850 there were 130 white "laborers" or "farm laborers" but only 9 were household heads. Probably some were recorded as "farmers," which inflated the number of "farmers" in 1850 (Table 2–1). In 1860 more than 300 whites were listed as "laborers" and "farm laborers"; some probably would have been called "farmers" in 1850. Cook, *Hard Labor Section*, p. 42.

14. For the unflattering stereotype of overseers see Harris, "Slaveholding Republic," pp. 155–57; Gray, *History of Agriculture*, 1:501–3, 545–47; Woodward, *Way Our People Lived*, p. 196. Lander, *Calhoun Family*, pp. 84–86, 100–101; Francis W. Pickens to John C. Calhoun, 30 Mar., 4 and 23 May 1845, Thomas Green Clemson

to John C. Calhoun, 29 May, 15 July, and 19 Aug. 1846, John C. Calhoun to Thomas Green Clemson, 26 June 1844, 23 Mar. 1845, 20 Sept., 6 Nov., and 9 Dec. 1846, 19 Mar. and 11 Apr. 1847, all in Calhoun Papers (CU); George Onie to Iveson L. Brookes, 28 Sept. 1847, Brookes Papers (SHC); John C. Calhoun to Francis W. Pickens, 6 May 1845, Calhoun Papers (SCL). See also agreement between A. Ramsay and F. W. Pickens, 18 Feb. 1864, Pickens Papers (SCL). Andrew Ramsey, Jr., was only fifteen years old, and his father signed the agreement for him. Andrew, Sr., had emigrated from Scotland and in 1860 was a postmaster with $1,000 in realty and $1,000 in personalty. See also "Agreement between D. F. Hollingsworth and M. L. Palmer," 13 Jan. 1857, Hollingsworth Papers (DU). In 1850 "overseers" were listed as "farmers," but in 1860, 140 men listed their occupations as "overseer." These represented 3.9 percent of all employed males in 1860. Although they were supervisors, overseers were placed in the category with laborers in Table 2–1.

15. In 1907 Daniel Tompkins complained that the mill hands felt like strangers in the town of Edgefield because "no one except the mill itself took an interest in their welfare." D. A. Tompkins to Grace Tompkins, 31 Aug. 1907, and Grace Tompkins to D. A. Tompkins, 1 Dec. 1907, Tompkins Papers (SHC); Terrill, "Eager Hands" and "Murder in Graniteville"; Kohn, *Cotton Mills*, pp. 26–31, 67–74. U.S., Congress, Senate, Committee on Education and Labor, *Labor and Capital*, 4:737; Woodward, *Way Our People Lived*, pp. 340–41, and *Gift of Life*, pp. 21–22, 27, 68–70, 73, 92, 107; see esp. Carlton, "Mill and Town."

16. Gregg, *Domestic Industry*, p. 48, and "Domestic Industry," esp. pp. 138–39; Taylor, "Manufactures in South Carolina," esp. pp. 26–29; Edgefield *Advertiser*, 25 Oct. 1865; Augusta *Daily Chronicle and Sentinel*, 1 June 1851. Gregg also quoted in Olmsted, *Journey in Back Country*, 2:63. Discussions of Graniteville and of textile mills generally draw upon the above and Mitchell, *William Gregg*; Martin, "Notes and Documents"; Woodward, *Way Our People Lived*, pp. 319–58, and *Gift of Life*, pp. 21–22, 27, 32–86, 92–95, 107, 298; Wallace, "Hundred Years"; see also Whatley, "Textile Development"; Williamson, "Cotton Manufacturing"; Griffin, "Poor White"; Lander, *Textile Industry*; Elijah Webb to Rosa Webb, n.d., Webb papers (SCL); Carlton, "Mill and Town"; Graniteville Manufacturing Company Papers (in two locations, SCL and GMC).

17. Winnsboro *Register*, reprinted in Edgefield *Advertiser*, 16 July 1856.

18. Edgefield *Advertiser*, 21 Nov. 1850.

19. Quotation from Woodward, *Way Our People Lived*, p. 328, see also pp. 319, 322–23, 327–30, 342–43; *Gift of Life*, pp. 41, 55. Church records indicate that about half the residents of Graniteville were on the church membership roles (Terrill, "Murder in Graniteville," p. 206; Graniteville Methodist Church Records [WC]).

20. Cornish Diary, 19 Apr. 1848, Cornish Papers (SHC); Taylor "Manufactures in South Carolina," p. 28; U.S., Congress, Senate, Committee on Education and Labor, *Labor and Capital*, 4:738; Woodward, *Gift of Life*, p. 56, see also pp. 41–43, 54, and *Way Our People Lived*, pp. 332, 338–40.

21. Graniteville Methodist Church Records (WC); Saint George's Episcopal Church, Kaolin, Aiken County, petition for incorporation, in the Minutes of the Directors, Graniteville Manufacturing Co., Graniteville Manufacturing Company Papers (GMC); Terrill, "Murder in Graniteville," pp. 194, 206, 220; Mitchell, *William Gregg*, pp. 51, 54, 218. Examples from the twentieth century show that strict moral

codes were not necessarily imposed from above. When more fundamentalist church sects, the Church of God and Pentecostal Holiness, drew members from the established mill churches, worker-imposed moral codes and rules were much more strict and rigid than those of the Baptist and Methodist churches. Respectability was important for these transplanted rural people, and they guarded their reputations with their church laws. They not only carefully regulated sexual conduct but prohibited drinking, smoking, swearing, and even wearing makeup, jewelry, or provocative clothing. These mill folks thought of themselves as respectable people, and they, more than the mill owners, were determined to keep their communities respectable.

22. Augusta *Chronicle*, 19 Apr. 1878; Terrill, "Murder in Graniteville," p. 214.

23. Woodward, *Gift of Life*, pp. 38–39, 116, and *Way Our People Lived*, pp. 333–34, 350–51; Wallace, "Hundred Years," p. 210; Terrill, "Murder in Graniteville," p. 204.

24. William Gregg to Amos Lawrence, 2 Sept. 1850, cited in Martin, "Notes and Documents," pp. 421–22; *Report of the President of the Graniteville Manufacturing Co. . . . 1877 . . . 1878* (Augusta: Jowitt and Shaver, 1878), p. 8, and *Report of the President of the Graniteville Manufacturing Co.*, 1850–88, in Graniteville Manufacturing Company Papers (both SCL and GMC); Terrill, "Murder in Graniteville," pp. 195–199; Woodward, *Way Our People Lived*, p. 341. The Edgefield *Advertiser*, 25 Oct. 1848, reported that a recently opened textile plant in Augusta had "more applications than the company can employ." Augusta *Daily Chronicle and Sentinel*, 1 June 1851, reported that an Augusta plant's management announced, "We have in the South plenty of poor white people to work in the cotton mills and glad to do it." The term "Eastern men" used by Gregg in his letter to Lawrence referred to experienced textile bosses from the North. U.S., Congress, Senate, Committee on Education and Labor, *Labor and Capital*, 4:737–38. Wright, "Cheap Labor," takes issue with the theory that white labor was abundant.

25. Taylor, "Manufactures in South Carolina," pp. 28–29; Mitchell, *William Gregg*, pp. 55–56; Treasurer's Report, 1851, *Charter and By-Laws of the Graniteville Manufacturing Company* (Charleston: J. B. Nixon, 1851), pp. 12–14, Graniteville Manufacturing Company Papers (GMC); Terrill, "Murder in Graniteville," p. 194.

26. "*Three Hundred Additional White Operatives* principally girls, above the age of fourteen; and also Thirty Matrons to take charge of their boarding Houses," and Gregg, "Rule Book," both in Graniteville Manufacturing Company Papers (GMC); Taylor, "Manufactures in South Carolina," p. 28; Terrill, "Murder in Graniteville," p. 194. In 1883 the president of the company estimated that two-thirds of the employees were women. U.S., Congress, Senate, Committee on Education and Labor, *Labor and Capital*, 4:737.

27. Taylor, "Manufacturing in South Carolina," p. 28; Arthur S. Tompkins to D. A. Tompkins, 14, 16, 17, 30 Feb. 1907, J. B. Boyd to D. A. Tompkins, 28 Aug. 1906, C. H. Fisher to D. A. Tompkins, 23 Feb. 1907, all in Tompkins Papers (SHC). See Carlton, "Mill and Town," for how mills used social control.

28. Hammond, "Address before South Carolina Institute, 1849," pp. 32–34; Wallace, *South Carolina*, 3:103.

29. Gregg, *Domestic Industry*, p. 106, and "Domestic Industry," p. 138; Olmsted, *Journey in Back Country*, 2:127–28, 152; Yale, "Travelers," maintains that a group

descended from wandering Irish tinkers, known in Ireland as the "travelers," has wintered for as long as anyone remembers near North Augusta (old Hamburg). These people would be classified as southern poor whites, and according to local lore they have traveled through South Carolina doing odd jobs since before the Civil War. They were characterized by their "close-knit extended family, sometimes encompassing as many as five generations" (p. 70). See also *New York Times*, 14 Oct. 1970.

30. Quotation from Cook, *Hard Labor Section*, p. 31; Owsley, *Plain Folk*; Wright, *Barefoot in Arcadia*, p. 6. Many artisans to whom the Vanderbilt School ascribed middle-class status did not have $270 property value. Local lore claims that when the Clem boys went off to the Civil War, the squirrels from Edgefield and Abbeville sent a delegation to follow them and make certain that their bullets were being used for other purposes than hunting local game.

31. See Taylor, "Manufactures in South Carolina," p. 28. On temperance, in 1840 the Edgefield grand jury noted that drinking was ruining families. Note that concern about drinking was centered not on the individual but on the effect on the families (Grand Jury Presentation, fall term, 20 Oct. 1841, Legislative Papers [SCDAH]).The problem of liquor also affected the wealthy; for example, alcohol brought out the violent nature of George Tillman. See Tillman, "Childhood Days"; Simkins, *Pitchfork Ben*, pp. 32–33. Julien Cumming, the brother-in-law of Harry Hammond, constantly battled the bottle. Upset over his behavior, Julien's mother wrote her daughter in Edgefield on the eve of the 1860 presidential election about her son. "For some days he was walking about the streets, in his stocking feet and sitting in front of the United States Hotel, noisily shouting out for Douglas" (Julia A. Cumming to Emily C. Hammond, 12 July 1860, Hammond, Bryan, Cumming Papers [SCL]). For a discussion of the class elements involved in the antebellum temperance movement see below and n. 91.

32. Cornish Diaries, antebellum and postbellum, throughout, Cornish Papers (SHC); Cartledge Autobiography, esp. pp. 15–155, Cartledge Papers (SCL); McKendree Methodist Church Records, 15 May 1880 (SCL).

33. Bethany Baptist Church Records, 24 Mar. 1833, 23 May 1840 (SCDAH); Johnston Baptist Church Records, Constitution, 1875, p. 30 (BHC).

34. Examples are typical of those in Edgefield Baptist Church Records. The quotation is from Big Stevens Creek Baptist Church Records, Feb. 1839 (all in BHC). See also McKendree Methodist Church Records (SCL). Farber, *Guardians of Virtue*, argues that in Salem, Massachusetts, middle-class artisans tended to be more religious because of their drive for upward mobility. Greven, *Protestant Temperament*, and Smith, *Inside the Great House*, on colonial Virginians pursue the theme of a growing secularism.

35. Quotations from Horn's Creek Baptist Church Records, June 1838, Apr. 1852; Sweetwater Baptist Church Records, Nov. 1863 and Jan. 1864 (all in BHC).

36. Big Stevens Creek Baptist Church Records, Nov. 1826, May 1810. These are typical from the Edgefield Baptist Church Records (BHC), as well as McKendree Methodist Church Records (SCL).

37. Bethany Baptist Church Records, 24 Aug. 1833, Aug. 1834, Sept. 1836, 26 Sept. 1840 (SCDAH); quotation from McKendree Methodist Church Records, 7 Jan. 1869, see also 20 Apr. 1872, 18 June 1870, Apr. 1872, 17 Apr. 1879 (SCL); see also

Johnston Baptist Church Records, 9 Apr. 1876, p. 17 (BHC); Edgefield Village Bible Society Records, 26 Mar., 30 Apr., and 5 Aug., 1830, 30 Mar. and 29 Sept. 1832, May 1835 and 6 June 1835 (SCL).

38. Francis W. Pickens to Maria Simkins, 21 Aug. 1834, Francis Pickens Papers (SCL): Thomas, *Historical Account of Episcopal Church*, pp. 550–51; Edmunds, "Francis Pickens," p. 250, and esp. "Politics of Destruction," pp. 27–28, for Pickens and religion. On Pickens's mother and father see Hooker, "Diary of Edward Hooker," 27 and 28 Sept. 1806, pp. 901–2.

39. Francis W. Pickens to Maria Simkins, 28 Apr. 1839, Pickens Papers (SCL); Lander, *Calhoun Family*, p. 17.

40. Clay-Clopton, *Belle of the Fifties*, pp. 217–19. The culture of the South was not simply dictated by the planter class. Indeed, as shown below, many of the values were shared equally by rich and poor. They may have originated with the poor as much as with the rich. See McDonald and Shapiro, "Ethnic Origins"; McDonald and McWhiney, "South Self-Sufficiency" and "Antebellum Southern Herdsmen"; McWhiney, "Revolution in Nineteenth-Century Alabama Agriculture"; Wyatt-Brown, "Community, Class, and Snopesian Crime"; Hahn, "Roots of Southern Populism and "Yeomanry of Nonplantation South."

41. Ouzts Diary, Ouzts Papers (SCL); McKendree Methodist Church Records (SCL).

42. I worked on the farm of Curtis Ouzts, a descendant of this family, and he located most of the above information. Last Will and Testament of George Ouzts, 11 Feb. 1878; Will of Peter Ouzts, 30 Oct. 1828, probated 4 May 1829; George Ouzts, Deed of Trust to Jolly James Still, 30 March 1867 and 5 Apr. 1867, Deed Book NNN, p. 19 (ECH); Edgefield *Advertiser*, 6 July 1864; Woodson, *Peter Ouzts*; McClendon, *Edgefield Marriage Records*, pp. 119, 138, and *Edgefield Death Notices*, pp. 161, 176; Chapman, *History of Edgefield*, pp. 287–88.

43. Howard, Civil War Veterans Questionnaire (hereinafter cited as CWVQ), 1915 and 1922, p. 2 (TSLA). Howard maintained that his father owned about thirteen slaves on one questionnaire and about eighteen on the other questionnaire. He also claimed his father owned about 5,000 acres. I have taken the number of slaves and acreage from the manuscript census returns. Howard clearly identified himself in both questionnaires as a yeoman as distinct from the planter class.

44. John Kreps to William Gilliland, Aug. 1849, Gilliland Papers (SCL). Biographies of less affluent whites are provided by local published histories of Edgefield, church records and histories, private genealogies, family Bibles, and more than two hundred interviews with descendants of middle-class or poorer whites. See especially, Broadwater, "David Rush"; Crouch, "Genealogy"; Edgefield County Historical Society, "Data on Norris," "Bonham, Griffin," "Hammond Family," "Martins," "Mims Families," and "Genealogy of Nicholson"; Etheridge, "Etheridge Family Circles" and "Harrison Family Circles"; Harmon, "Plantation Marshes"; Simpson, *Cokers*; Steadman, "Historical Sketch"; Woodson, *Charles May*.

45. Elisha Hammond to James Henry Hammond, 5 and 24 Nov, 1828, J. H. Hammond Papers (SCL).

46. King, *History of South Carolina Baptists*. Owens, *Saints of Clay*; Betts, *History of South Carolina Methodism*. McLees, "Journal of Events," McLees Papers; Cartledge Autobiography, esp. pp. 5, 8, Cartledge Papers; Dreher Journal, Dreher Pa-

pers (all in SCL). Owing $900 to his church in advanced wages, a Baptist preacher asked the wealthy Iveson Brookes for a loan since his friends were "among the Baptists who are like myself poor" (E. H. Evans to Iveson L. Brookes, 20 Sept. 1858, Brookes Papers [SHC]). In 1860, Brookes reported fifty thousand dollars in personalty and $104,850 in realty. Actually, the Edgefield Village Baptist Church had the largest endowment of any church in the district in 1850 and 1860. In addition, William B. Johnson, pastor in 1850, was wealthy with $30,000 in land.

47. Contract of Elijah Timmerman with Peter Dorn, Jacob Timmerman, John Glausier, Henry Ouzts, and William Timmerman, n.d., Timmerman Papers (SCL); Free School Reports, Department of Education Papers (SCDAH); McKendree Methodist Church Records (SCL); Chapman, *History of Edgefield*, p. 479.

48. Edgefield *Advertiser*, 25 Nov. and 3 Dec. 1856; Mims, "Editors of Edgefield *Advertiser*," pp. 79–83; Free School Reports, Department of Education Papers (SCDAH); S.C., General Assembly, *Reports and Resolutions, 1870–71*, p. 204.

49. Andrew Pickens II, Francis's father, married Susan Wilkinson from the coast. This same Andrew Pickens was elected in 1814 as the first South Carolina governor born in the backcountry. On the Regulators, Brown, *South Carolina Regulators*, is the indispensable source. Brown established that an up-country elite existed prior to the great cotton boom. Klein, "Rise of the Planters," esp. pp. 6, 306–7, is the basis of much of my discussion. She has referred to " 'planter' rather than 'leadership' or 'elite' . . . because it became clear from the outset that inland political figures were committed to slave acquisition, landownership, and planting. This fundamental interest tied them to the coastal elite and provided the basis for an evolving class unit" (p. 6). See also SCHS, *South Carolina Genealogies*, 1:267, 285; Meriwether, *Expansion of South Carolina*, pp. 138–39, 314; Chapman, *History of Edgefield*, pp. 130–33; Ferguson, "General Andrew Pickens."

50. Banner, "Problem of South Carolina"; King, *Louis Wigfall*, pp. 8–10; Freehling, *Prelude to Civil War*, pp. 17–24; Main, *Antifederalists*, p. 28; Schaper, *Sectionalism and Representation*; Jaher, *Urban Establishment*, pp. 317–451; Germany, "South Carolina Governing Elite"; Olsberg, "Government of Class and Race"; Norton, "Methodological Study." Wigfall changed the spelling of his name to Louis when he migrated to Texas.

51. Chapman, *History of Edgefield*; Bonham, "Life and Times of Milledge Bonham"; Edmunds, "Francis Pickens" and esp. "Politics of Destruction"; Davidson, *Last Foray*; Simkins, "Simkins Family"; Coit, *John Calhoun*, pp. 184, 334, 392, 417; O'Neall, *Biographical Sketches*, 2:277; Lander, *Calhoun Family*, pp. vii, 13–14; Wiltse, *John Calhoun*. In addition to Pickens and Bonham, another Edgefield relative, John Calhoun Sheppard, was governor.

52. John C. Calhoun to Maria Calhoun, 16 Dec. 1837, Calhoun Papers (CU); Lander, *Calhoun Family*, pp. 13–14; O'Neall, *Biographical Sketches*, 2:277; Edmunds, "Politics of Destruction," pp. 4, 8; Meriwether, *Papers of John Calhoun*, 1:4, 431–34.

53. Butler, "Memoirs of General William Butler"; Jervey, "Butlers of South Carolina"; O'Neall, *Biographical Sketches*, 1:198–208, 2:473–75; Chapman, *History of Edgefield*, pp. 30–47, 50, 74, 96, 265; Bonham, "Life and Times of Milledge Bonham," pp. 29–34; McBee, "Butler Family"; Mathis, "Preston Smith Brooks," pp. 296–98; Hooker, "Diary of Edward Hooker," 4 July 1806, p. 890.

54. On doctors see Waring, *History of Medicine*; Chapman, *History of Edgefield*, pp. 343–64. In 1850 quite a significant number of men were listed as "planters," enough to constitute 11.4 percent of all male household heads, the largest single grouping after "farmers," who constituted 63.8 percent of all male household heads. In 1860 there were only twenty-one "planters" according to the occupational category listings and only nineteen (0.6 percent) of those were household heads. "Planters" are included in the occupational group with "farmer" in Table 2–1. In both decades "planter" signified wealth in slaves and land and implied esteem, but much more so in 1860 when it also included at least two "semi-retired" but wealthy individuals. The 136 wealthiest were an amalgamation of the top hundred persons owning real estate and the top hundred owning personal estate in 1860; these categories overlapped considerably. This is about 4.5 percent of all white families in 1860.

55. Benjamin Nicholson, notebook, p. 41, Hughes Papers (SHC). In 1860, Nicholson at nineteen was the oldest son of his widowed mother, who owned $20,000 in real and $60,000 in personal property. He became an eminent lawyer.

56. O'Neall, *Biographical Sketches*, 2:463–68; Meriwether, *History of Higher Education*, pp. 44–50, Green, *George McDuffie*; Merritt, *James Hammond*; Tucker, "James Hammond"; Faust, *James Hammond*; Bleser, *Hammonds of Redcliff*; Mims, "Editors of Edgefield *Advertiser*," pp. 38–44; Woodson, "Life of Joseph Abney"; Chapman, *History of Edgefield*, pp. 12–14, 246–49, 274.

57. Pottersville *Hive*, 12 Mar. 1830; Edgefield *Advertiser*, 4 Apr. 1839, 20 May 1841, 26 Nov. 1856, 1 Feb. 1865, and 2 Dec. 1868; Mims, "Editors of Edgefield *Advertiser*," pp. 31–77; Chapman, *History of Edgefield*, p. 417.

58. The Hamburg *Republic*, 2 June 1842; Edgefield *Advertiser*, 4 Mar. 1852, 19 June 1861, 6 Sept. 1868; O'Neall, *Biographical Sketches*, 2:224–25, 227; Simkins, *Pitchfork Ben*, p. 24.

59. Graydon, *Francis Simkins*, pp. 39–48; Edgefield *Advertiser*, 3 Sept. 1851; Clark, *Southern Country Editor*; Werner, "Hegemony and Conflict," pp. 19–20; Ellen, "Political Newspapers."

60. Edgefield Village Baptist Church Records, Jan. 1831 through Jan. 1853 (BHC); Woodson, *Giant in Land* and Woodson et al., *History of Edgefield Baptist Association*, pp. 32–34, 214–17; Genealogy (handwritten), Brookes Papers (SCL).

61. Mims, "Editors of Edgefield *Advertiser*," pp. 9, 21; Chapman, *History of Edgefield*, p. 328; Thomas, *Historical Account of Episcopal Church*, p. 550. Before an Episcopal Church was built in Edgefield, a number of Edgefield elite belonged to, or at least associated with, the Episcopal church in Augusta. Bailie, "St. Paul's Episcopal Church."

62. Edward Reed to D. R. Strother, 31 Oct. 1850, Strother Papers (FP).

63. Francis W. Pickens to Lucy Holcombe, 6 Dec. 1857, F. W. Pickens Papers (SCL); Steadman, *History of Spann Family*, pp. 58–59.

64. Francis W. Pickens to Milledge Luke Bonham, 14 Oct. 1859 and 4 Apr. 1860, Luke Bonham Papers (SCL); Edmunds, "Francis Pickens," pp. 70, 186–89.

65. Louis Wigfall to Richard Manning, 7 Sept. and 22 Feb. 1839, 15 Dec. 1843, 3 Jan. 1844, 25 June 1845, Williams-Chesnut-Manning Papers (SCL); Louis Wigfall to William Yancey, 20 June 1864, Yancey Papers (SHC); Wigfall to Armistead Burt, 8 Dec. 1845, Burt Papers (DU); Edgefield *Advertiser*, 7 July–7 Oct. 1846; Sale Book T., pp. 159, 161–68, 10 Apr. and 6 June 1846; Deed book EEE, p. 62 (ECH); "Sale

of L. T. Wigfall's property to pay debts, June 3, 4, 5, 6, 1846," copy Wigfall Papers (UT); King, *Louis Wigfall*, pp. 39, 46–47, 18; Edmunds, "Politics of Destruction," p. 161. Wigfall was aware of the importance of education, and not just from the standpoint of preparing for a profession. As the chairman of a committee to establish a state university for Texas, he argued that college was important for the associations one made while a student (Marshall *Texas Republican*, 30 July 1859).

66. Pottersville *Republic*, 22 Oct. 1825; Land Deeds, Bk. 43, p. 502, Bk. 45, pp. 61–63, Bk. C, p. 153 (ECH).

67. Bk. C, p. 153, Circuit Court, Leon County Courthouse, Florida; Bartlett, *Haley Blocker*, pp. 3–4.

68. Estate and Will of John Blocker, apt. 3, pk, 56, bk. 37, pp. 318–19 (ECH); tombstones at Blocker's Cross Roads, Florida. See also S.C., State Grants, 53:53 (SCDAH); Bartlett, *Haley Blocker*.

69. Edmunds, "Politics of Destruction," captures the essence of the late antebellum political scene in his forthcoming biography of Francis Pickens.

70. G. D. Tillman to J. H. Hammond, 9 Oct. 1860, Hammond Papers (LC).

71. Louis T. Wigfall to Richard Manning, 13, 17, and 27 Feb., 4 and 19 March, and n.d., 1840, Williams-Chesnut-Manning Papers (SCL); Edgefield *Advertiser*, 21 Nov. 1839, 21 Feb. and 30 June 1840; King, "Emergence of Fire-eater," pp. 73–82, and *Louis Wigfall*, pp. 25–29; Lord, "Young Wigfall," p. 101.

72. Edmunds, "Francis Pickens," pp. 57–62; relatives involved were A. P. Butler, Maximilian LaBorde, and Pierce Mason Butler. Louis T. Wigfall to William Manning, 11 and 17 Feb., 4, 10, 19 Mar. 1840, Williams-Chesnut-Manning Papers (SCL); Maximilian LaBorde to James Henry Hammond, 8 July 1840, and Pierce M. Butler to James Henry Hammond, 2, 6, 8 July 1840, both in Hammond Papers (LC); LaBorde, *History of South Carolina College*, pp. v, x, xi; King, *Louis Wigfall*, pp. 28–29.

73. Nearly all Edgefield participants in the disputes described above were members of Trinity Episcopal. The best discussion of the Preston Brooks and Francis Pickens campaign is Edmunds, "Politics of Destruction," chap. 7; see also, "Circular," 6 Feb. 1853, Preston Brooks Papers (SCL); Edgefield *Advertiser*, 29 Dec. 1852, 12, 19, 26 Jan. and 2, 9 Feb., 9 Mar. 1853.

74. Simkins, *Pitchfork Ben*, pp. 34, 293–94, 376–77; Faust, *James Hammond*, pp. 362–63, 374; "Reed Lienage," Strother Papers (FP).

75. S.C., General Assembly, Committee of Investigation, *Evidence by Committee of Investigation*, pp. 678, 683–88, 690–91, 696, 702–3, 705–6, 712. In 1860 Root claimed realty of $1,500 and personalty of $8,000 and owned one slave.

76. Ibid., pp. 677–79.

77. Ball, *State That Forgot*, p. 22.

78. Edgefield *Advertiser*, 26 June 1861; Louis T. Wigfall to Langdon Cheves, Jr., 12 Sept. 1836, Cheves Papers (SCL); Edmunds, "Politics of Destruction," n.p., n. 144 to chap. 2.

79. Bender, *Community and Social Change*, p. 100.

80. Farmers Club, 6 Nov. 1841 (SCL); Edgefield *Advertiser*, 7 May 1856.

81. Edgefield *Advertiser*, 23 Oct. and 20 Nov. 1851.

82. Simkins, *Pitchfork Ben*, esp. pp. 23–37; Mims, "Life and Politics of George Tillman," p. 15. Marshall, "Gentlemen without Country," p. 183, claims Gary was

from an Edgefield "respectable" (Marshall divided South Carolina society into aristocrats, respectables, white laborers, and blacks) family. Gary was from Abbeville. In 1860 his widowed mother owned realty valued at $10,000 and headed a household who together owned $52,000 personalty. Martin C. Gary lived near and owned $5,000 realty and $25,000 personalty. The Garys were the wealthiest people around Cokesbury in Abbeville District (U.S., Bureau of the Census, *8th* (1860) *Census,* Abbeville Manuscript Population, pp. 169, 179 [NA]). Gary's father had represented Abbeville in the state legislature. See Ramey, *Trial of Booth,* p. 9; Edgefield *Advertiser,* 9 and 16 Jan. 1856, 21 Sept. 1853, 1 Mar. 1854, 28 Nov. 1855; S.C., General Assembly, *Legislative Times,* 33rd Legis., 2nd Sess., 1856, pp. 97–101. See the reply by Moragne, *Electoral Question.*

83. Edgefield *Advertiser,* 15 May 1860, 13 and 25 Oct., 1 Nov. 1865; Mims, "Life and Politics of George Tillman," p. 15.

84. Charleston *News and Courier,* 21 and 28 June 1894; Simkins, *Pitchfork Ben,* p. 265.

85. Dolores Janiewski discovered this same phenomenon among mill workers in North Carolina. According to one woman who worked in the mills, until the union became involved, the newspapers never put a "Mrs." before their names ("Sisters under the Skin").

86. Farmers Club, 3 Dec. 1859 (SCL).

87. Spann Hammond Diary, 22 Feb. 1857, E. Spann Hammond papers (SCL).

88. Farmers Club, Oct. 1858, pp. 105–7 (SCL); Wooster, *People in Power,* pp. 8–9. In Edgefield elections for the state legislature nearly 95 percent of eligible voters voted. The election returns were reported by precinct in the October issues of the Edgefield *Advertiser.* This high percentage of voting raises questions about recent interpretations that have stressed the limited popular participation of South Carolina whites in politics (Banner, "Problem of South Carolina," and Greenberg, "Second American Revolution" and "Representation and Isolation"). See the excellent analysis by Harris, "Slaveholding Republic," pp. 309–17, 411.

89. Charleston *News and Courier,* 22 Aug. 1878; Marshall, "Gentlemen without Country," p. 183; Edgefield *Advertiser,* 15 Sept. 1858. Gary owned one slave in 1860. See the interesting exchanges between Gary and W. C. Moragne on the accusation. A duel was avoided since the two came to an understanding. The persecuted Gary also answered charges that he was an atheist. For another instance of a mechanic taking offense, see Edgefield *Advertiser,* 1 July 1857, "For the Advertiser," and the accompanying article, "She Wouldn't Marry a Mechanic." Horatio Alger stories like this one in a southern setting were rather common in the local papers.

90. F. W. Pickens to John C. Calhoun, 18 Oct. 1844, Calhoun Papers (CU); Edmunds, "Francis Pickens," p. 119.

91. Edgefield *Advertiser,* 17 July 1851, 16 July 1856, 5 July 1850, 17 Nov. 1852. The prohibition movement also reflected something of a rural-town division. See discussion in n. 31 above and Sons of Temperance Circular, 1844 (SCL).

92. Edgefield *Advertiser,* 1 July 1857, 20 May 1852; Hamburg *Journal,* 2 June 1842; Howard, CWVQ (1922), p. 3. To the same question on a questionnaire given seven years earlier, he answered, "Generally they did. Of course the standing of the family socially had much to do with their recognition" (CWVQ [1915], p. 3). The question read, "[Did] slaveholders and nonslaveholders mingle on equal footing at

church, school, and public gatherings?"

93. Brutus, *Address to Citizens*, p. 4. The Spartanburg *Spartan* attributed the pamphlet to William H. Brisbane, a Baptist minister who had left South Carolina for the North. A copy of the pamphlet is among J. H. Hammond Papers (SCL). Edgefield *Advertiser*, 6 and 27 June, 8 Aug. 1849; see also the discussion by Harris, "Slaveholding Republic," p. 203. Local tradition holds that in the lower southeast corner, where Edgefield District joined Lexington District and the town of Batesburg grew, Elijah Hall and his sons, all gunsmiths and mechanics, opposed slavery. Supposedly, the Halls and the family of one of the largest slaveowners in that settlement, Paul Quattlebaum, argued vociferously over the issue. Lemuel Hall, studying to be a Baptist preacher, was an especially outspoken opponent of slavery. Interestingly, when former slaves desired to establish their own church during Reconstruction, the sympathetic Lemuel Hall supported their actions. The church asked Hall to recant his support, but instead the white church split as well in 1869–70 (Hall, *Things and Incidents*, pp. 104, 179–83).

94. J. H. Hammond to J. L. Orr, 11 Dec. 1863, Hammond Papers (LC); J. H. Hammond to Marcus C. M. Hammond, 11 Oct. 1858, J. H. Hammond Papers (SCL); Howard, CWVQ (1922), p. 3.

95. Ong, *Presence of the Word* and "Tribal Drum." Cook, *Hard Labor Section*, p. 42; Wright, *Barefoot in Arcadia*, pp. 20–21.

96. B. R. Tillman to Rev. I. L. Brookes, 27 Sept. 1843, Brookes Papers (SCL).

97. Edgefield *Advertiser*, 20 May 1852.

98. Petition from Edgefield District (and Barnwell), 25 Jan. 1811, Legislative Papers (SCDAH).

99. "Report on Free School System," 26 Nov. 1846, Legislative Papers (SCDAH); S.C., General Assembly, *Statutes* (1811) 5:639, 641, 738; S.C., State Board of Agriculture, *South Carolina*, pp. 446–54; Thomason, *Foundations of Public Schools*, pp. 127–31; Meriwether, *History of Higher Education*, pp. 111–12.

100. Petition Praying Repeal Free School, Edgefield, 28 Oct. 1812, and "Report on Free School System," 26 Nov. 1846, both in Legislative Papers (SCDAH); Mills, *Statistics of South Carolina*, p. 529; Meriwether, *History of Higher Education*, pp. 112–17.

101. Howard, CWVQ (1915), p. 4 and (1922), p. 4 (TSLA); Tillman, "Childhood Days," Simkins, *Pitchfork Ben*, pp. 40–44.

102. Howard, CWVQ (1915), p. 4, and (1922), p. 4 (TSLA).

103. Cartledge Autobiography, pp. 3–5, Cartledge Papers (SCL). W. E. Woodward, *Gift of Life*, pp. 37, 82–85, and *Way Our People Lived*, pp. 355–56, celebrated William Marchant, his postbellum schoolteacher at Graniteville. Woodward claimed Marchant had never had schooling himself, but had learned while a prisoner during the Civil War.

104. Contract of Elijah Timmerman with Peter Dorn, Jacob Timmerman, John Glausier, Henry Ouzts, and William Timmerman, n.d., Timmerman Papers (SCL); see also S. N. Kennedy to Sallie, 16 Oct. 1864, Kennedy Papers (SCL); and Cartledge Autobiography, esp. pp. 5–8, Cartledge Papers (SCL).

105. Peter J. Lelande and Pressley Bland, Petition, 1 Jan. 1835, Legislative Papers (SCDAH).

106. Edgefield *Advertiser*, 17 Feb. 1847 and 10 Nov. 1857; Meriwether, *History of*

Higher Education, pp. 115–16.

107. Lott, "Development of Education," pp. 9–10; LaBorde, *History of South Carolina College*, pp. viii–ix; "School Days," Payne Papers (FP); Winston, "Builder of New South," pp. 19–21.

108. Edgefield *Advertiser*, 1 Aug. 1839 and 25 Nov. 1841.

109. Circular Edgefield Female Institute, 1850 (SCL); Isaac William Hayne to James Parsons Carroll, 21 Apr. 1866, Carol Papers (SCL); Ellis, "Educating Daughters of Patriarchy," argues female academies served social purposes, not intellectual. They were institutional proof of the excellence of southern womanhood. Education, like chivalry, partially compensated wives and daughters of the patriarchy while simultaneously subordinating the women. Moreover, academies were vehicles for transmitting southern values to southern girls in an increasingly self-conscious South.

110. B. R. Tillman to Rev. I. L. Brookes, 30 Jan. 1844, 27 Sept. 1843, Brookes Papers (SCL); Cohen, *Barhamville Miscellany*, p. 41; Bleser, *Hammonds of Redcliffe*, pp. 141–42.

111. Quotation from Circular, Edgefield Male Academy, 5 Jan. 1861 (SCL); Hooker, "Diary of Edward Hooker," 27 Feb. to 6 Sept. 1806, pp. 884–93, 903; Meriwether, *History of Higher Education*, pp. 28–30, 37–44; Watson, *Greenwood County*, pp. 22–27; Marshall, "Gentlemen without Country," p. 5. Lott, "Development of Education," pp. 9–32, and Burnett, "History of Education," pp. 14–15, glorify the academies in Edgefield, but have useful descriptions. A letter to John Rennie Blake in 1855 inviting him to become the head teacher of the Edgefield Male Academy guaranteed "a salary of one thousand dollars and give you four hundred dollars additional for an assistant." According to the letter, the institution was well endowed "so that your salary will not depend wholly upon the number of pupils." Blake declined the position. William Caine Moragne to Mr. Raney Blake, 3 Jan. 1855, Moragne Papers (SCL). See also S. N. Kennedy to Sallie, 16 Oct. 1864, Kennedy Papers (SCL).

112. Waddell, "Address to Graduating Class" (1825), Waddell Papers (SCL); Circular, Edgefield Male Academy, 5 Jan. 1861 (SCL), *Catalogue of Edgefield Female Institute*, p. 16 (SCL); Green, *McDuffie*, pp. 152–53; Thomason, *Foundations of Public Schools*, pp. 78–79; Eaton, *Mind of Old South*, rev. ed., pp. 47–48.

113. Quotation is from Cartledge Autobiography, p. 8, Cartledge Papers (SCL). See Meriwether, *History of Higher Education*, pp. 87–108; Lott, "History of Education," pp. 16–18; Woodson, *Giant in the Land*, esp. pp. 66–79, 146–51.

114. B. R. Tillman to Rev. I. L. Brookes, 27 Sept. 1843, 30 Jan. and 6 Aug. 1844, Brookes Papers (SCL).

115. LaBorde, *History of South Carolina College*, pp. viii–ix. See W. E. Woodward, *Gift of Life*, pp. 19–20 for the account of the severity of his father's teacher.

116. "School Days," Payne Papers (FP); Lott, "Development of Education," pp. 10–13; Arthur S. Tompkins to George T. Winston, 25 Oct. 1915, Tompkins Papers (SHC); Winston, "Builder of New South," pp. 19–21; Clay, "Daniel Tompkins," p. 3.

117. Edgefield *Advertiser*, 12 Dec. 1839.

118. Ibid., 22 Dec. 1841 and 3 Jan. 1857; Tillman, "Childhood Days," pp. 13–16; Wiltse, *John Calhoun*, 1:31–32, 165–68, and 2:306–7; Lander, *Calhoun Family*, pp. 4, 11; John C. Calhoun to Anna Calhoun, 16 Dec. 1837, John C. Calhoun Papers

(CU); John C. Calhoun to James Edward Calhoun, 24 Dec. 1826 and 26 Aug. 1827 in Jameson, *Correspondence of John Calhoun*, pp. 238, 240, 248; T. J. McKie, Jr., to T. J. McKie, 23 Jan. 1875, McKie Papers (DU).

119. Edgefield *Advertiser*, 3 Feb. 1838 and 15 Apr. 1857; B. R. Tillman to Rev. I. L. Brookes, 27 Sept. 1843, Brookes Papers (SCL).

120. Edgefield *Advertiser*, 1 Aug. 1839 and 12 May 1857.

121. *Catalogue of Edgefield Female Institute*, pp. 23–25, 32 (SCL).

122. On cultural elite see Wallace, *South Carolina*, pp. 352–53; Mills, *Statistics of South Carolina*, pp. 529–30. See also the notices of speeches and lyceums in Edgefield *Advertiser*, 7 and 17 Mar., 17 May, and 17 Oct. 1839; O'Neall, *Biographical Sketches*, 2:279.

123. "Rules of Graniteville," Graniteville Manufacturing Company Papers (SCL). When Hamilton H. Hickman became president of the company after the Civil War, he repealed the law requiring workers to send their children to the Graniteville school. U.S., Congress, Senate, *Labor and Capital*, p. 745. Report of the President and Treasurer, 1867, p. 12, typescript in Graniteville Manufacturing Company Papers (GMC); Mitchell, *William Gregg*, pp. 250–51; Terrill, "Murder in Graniteville," pp. 200–201; Free School Reports, Records, Department of Education (SCDAH).

124. Mitchell, *William Gregg*, pp. 48–54; Terrill, "Murder in Graniteville," pp. 200–201; Report of the President and Treasurer, 1867, p. 12, typescript; Wallace, "Hundred Years," pp. 28–50, 98, Graniteville Manufacturing Company Papers (GMC); Reports of Presidents and Treasurers, 1849–84, Graniteville Manufacturing Company Papers (GMC or SCL); see for example, *Report of the President of the Graniteville Manufacturing Company. . . 1877 . . . 1878* (Augusta, Ga.: Jowitt and Shaver, 1878), p. 8. A favorable view of the Graniteville schools during the Reconstruction years and 1880s is given by Woodward, *Gift of Life*, pp. 35–37, and *Way Our People Lived*, pp. 354–56.

125. U.S., Congress, Senate, *Labor and Capital*, p. 746.

126. Ibid., p. 745.

127. D. A. Tompkins to Grace Tompkins, 14 Jan. 1908, Grace to D. A., Dec. 1907 and 2 Feb. 1908, Tompkins Papers (SHC); Clay, "Daniel Tompkins," p. 120. Grace was unsuccessful, and D. A. did not act further to help her.

128. Oliphant, *Simms History*, p. 260; "less than ten out of every 100 of the soldiers from South Carolina were unable to read and write."

129. The *Advertiser* and the Hamburg *Republic* sold for two dollars a year in advance and for three dollars otherwise. Cornish Diary, 9 Mar. 1847 and 13 Jan. 1849, Cornish Papers (SHC).

130. Only those families who had children of school age at home were used for the calculations.

131. Women with education could work as governesses and also might become companions to wealthy women. With enough education, one could perhaps get a tutoring job. See discussion in Chap. 3 under "Southern Womanhood" on the suggestion that the feminization of teaching began about 1856 in Edgefield and was accelerated by the Civil War. It does not appear that women were paid less for public teaching until Redemption; see the ads for tutoresses in the McKie Papers (DU). Of course, more rich girls were in school than poor girls.

132. Eaton, *Mind of Old South*, rev. ed., p. 289, and "Class Differences,"

pp. 359–60; King, *Louis Wigfall*, pp. 11–12.

133. Edgefield *Advertiser*, 4 Mar. 1857 and 10 Oct. 1860; King, *Louis Wigfall*, p. 38; Wright, *Southern Girl*, p. 33; Louis T. Wigfall to Armistead Burt, 7 Apr. 1844, Burt Papers (DU); Benjamin Ryan Tillman to Iveson L. Brookes, 6 Aug. 1844, Brookes Papers (SCL); Simkins, *Pitchfork Ben*, p. 11; Eaton, *Mind of Old South*, rev. ed., p. 48; Stokes, *Savannah*, p. 263; Faust, *James Hammond*, pp. 50–54.

134. Seibels Family Papers (SCL). The dueling pistols are displayed at the McKissick Library, University of South Carolina.

135. There are a number of reports of the events. Most interesting is Brooks Diary, Whitfield Brooks Papers (FP); King, *Louis Wigfall*, pp. 32–34.

136. Wilson, *Code of Honor*; Cardwell, "Duel in Old South"; Williams, "Code of Honor in Ante-Bellum South Carolina." An interesting perspective on the "masculinity" of dueling in 1828 is suggested in a letter to Harry Hammond's future mother-in-law from her sister (Maria Bryan to Mrs. Julia A. B. Cumming, 2 June 1828, Hammond, Bryan, Cumming Papers [SCL]).

137. Edgefield District Coroners Inquest Book (SCL); Williams, *Vogues in Villainy*, pp. 35–38; Wigfall, *Sermon upon Duelling*, p. 9 (SCL); Buckingham, *Slave States*, 1:552, 2:3–4.

138. U.S., Congress, *Congressional Globe*, 25th Cong., 3rd Sess., 1 Mar. 1839, appendix, p. 298, and 7:231; J. E. Holmes to James Henry Hammond, 23 July 1849, Hammond Papers (LC); F. W. Pickens to John C. Calhoun, 13 Dec. 1846, Calhoun Papers (CU); Edgefield *Advertiser*, 24 Jan. 1849, 8 May and 19 June 1850, 24 Apr. 1851, 30 July 1856, 28 Nov. 1860, 12 Feb. 1936; Edmunds, "Francis Pickens," pp. 152–53. An Alabama state official reared in Edgefield wrote to the local paper: "I could not be indifferent to anything that concerns S. Carolina, and particularly Edgefield. Her honor will always be dear to me."

139. F. W. Pickens to J. L. Manning, 28 Jan. 1857, Williams-Manning-Chesnut Papers (SCL); F. W. Pickens to Lucy Holcombe, 8 Oct. 1857, Pickens Papers (DU).

140. Preston S. Brooks to M. L. Bonham, 2 Aug. 1849, M. Luke Bonham Papers (SCL). Brooks to Dr. Davis, 25 Sept. 1847; Resolution of officers of the Palmetto Regiment, 6 Dec. 1847; Whitfield Brooks to Hon. James Augustus Black, 12 Jan. 1848, all in P. S. Brooks Papers (SCL).

141. Chester *Standard*, 4 Sept. 1856, typically cheered Brooks, "who so manfully struck for South Carolina and her honor." Edgefield *Advertiser*, 30 July 1856; Donald, *Charles Sumner*, pp. 285–311, 341; Senator A. P. Butler defended Brooks as "acting under the dictates of manhood and honor." U.S., Congress, *Congressional Globe*, 34th Cong., 1st Sess., appendix, pp. 630–31. See Brooks's emotional appeal in court where he declared he would remain "true to the home of my maturity and to the mother that bore me. . . . Public opinion distinguishes between crime and honorable resentment" (*Southern Quarterly Review*, Feb. 1857, p. 358).

142. Preston Brooks to James Hampden Brooks, 23 May 1856 and 21 June 1856, and ms., 28 May 1856, all in P.S. Brooks Papers (SCL). I wish to thank Professor Robert W. Johannsen for directing my attention to the letter of 23 May. The letter was also published as a footnote in slightly altered form in Craven, *Coming of Civil War*, p. 115, and has been compiled by Meriwether, "Preston Brooks on Caning," pp. 1–4.

143. Edgefield *Advertiser*, 18 July 1856, 6 Aug. 1857, quoting *Carolina Spartan*. A reporter covered the testimonial dinner given in support of Brooks at Ninety Six,

reputed to be the largest gathering ever in the up-country. *New York Times*, 8 Oct. 1856, p. 1; Watson, *Greenwood County*, pp. 116–18.

144. Augusta *Constitutionalist*, 28 Jan. 1857; Brooks-Dunovant Square, Willowbrook Cemetery.

145. Edgefield *Advertiser*, 27 May and 25 Nov. 1846, and Centennial Edition, 12 Feb. 1936; Hamburg *Journal*, fragment, n.d.; P. M. Butler to P. S. Brooks, 6 Dec. 1846, P. S. Brooks Papers (SCL); Joseph Abney to A. Burt, 5 June 1846, Thos. G. Key to A. Burt, 15 June, 16 and 23 July 1846, Burt Papers (DU); Edgefield County Historical Society, *Minutes*, 30 July 1948 (ECHS). Comparative studies need to determine in what ways southern nationalism differed from northern, if at all.

146. Edgefield *Advertiser*, 17 May and 16 Oct. 1848, 14 Nov. 1850, Edgefield County Historical Society, *Minutes*, 30 July 1948 (ECHS); Manuscript, United Daughters of the Confederacy Relic Room.

147. Tombstone inscription, Brooks-Dunovant Square, Willowbrook Cemetery; Bartley N. Blocker to W. F. Durisoe, n.d., Strother Papers (FP).

148. Whitfield Brooks Diary, Whitfield Brooks Papers (FP). Whitfield Brooks to Hon. James Augustus Black, 20 Dec. 1847, P. S. Brooks Papers (SCL). Simkins, "Simkins Family," p. 1; Capers, *Confederate History*, 5:240; Tillman, "Childhood Days," p. 17; Simkins, *Pitchfork Ben*, p. 36.

149. U.S., Congress, *Congressional Globe*, 36th Cong., 1st Sess., p. 166; Edgefield *Advertiser*, 5 July 1850; King, *Louis Wigfall*, pp. 6–7.

150. An eyewitness spoke of the courage of the young Adams: "We never witnessed nor read of more deliberate courage" (Edgefield *Advertiser*, Centennial Edition, 12 Feb. 1936; Edgefield County Historical Society, *Minutes*, 30 July 1948 [ECHS]). In 1850, Adams's father had six slaves and reported that he owned land valued at $5,000.

151. Edgefield *Advertiser*, 31 Oct. 1860, and Saluda Minutemen Records (SCL).

152. Revolutionary War Pension Petitions: Rachel Temple, 9 Oct. 1830; Esther McGraw, 6 Dec. 1831; Mary Robertson, Oct. 1839; all in Legislative Papers (SCDAH). The estimate of fourteen hundred is from Ramsay, *History of South Carolina*, 1:258. Landrum, *Colonial and Revolutionary*, pp. 363–64, cited Ramsay's estimation for the Ninety Six District as that for the up-country. An even higher estimate was made by Francisco De Miranda, the "Liberator of Venezuela," who claimed the Revolution left eighteen hundred widows and orphans in Ninety Six District (Bass, *Ninety Six*, p. 9). T. J. Howard recalled that his father regularly received a pension from his service in the War of 1812 (Howard, CWVQ, 1915 and 1922 [TSLA]).

153. Plantation Record Book, 18 Dec. 1846, p. 246, Pickens Papers (DU); Preston S. Brooks to Roger Jones, 2 July 1847, P. S. Brooks Papers (SCL); Julia B. Cumming to Emily C. Hammond, 12 Apr. and 26 May 1861, Hammond, Bryan, Cumming Papers (SCL); George D. Tillman to B. R. Tillman, n.d., Tillman Papers (CU); Tillman, "Childhood Days," p. 2 and unnumbered half page following p. 5; Simkins, *Pitchfork Ben*, p. 35; Mims, "Life and Politics of George Tillman," p. 14.

154. James Henry Hammond to William Gilmore Simms, 12 Dec. 1861 and 2 Nov. 1862, Paul Fitzsimons Hammond to James Henry Hammond, 2 May 1862, Hammond Papers (LC); Thomas Davies to Dear Brother (Marcellus Hammond), n.d., Redcliffe Journal, 6 Mar. and 2 May 1862, J. H. Hammond Papers (SCL); J. H. Hammond to Harry Hammond, 17 Nov. 1861, Hammond, Bryan, Cumming Papers

(SCL); Spann edited a newspaper during the later years of the war. Spann Hammond Scrapbook, Spann Hammond Papers (SCL); Steadman, *Spann Family*, p. 79; Bleser, *Hammonds of Redcliffe*, p. 100; Faust, *James Hammond*, pp. 371–75.

155. Seabrook, *Essay on Management of Slaves*, p. 15; S.C., "Governor's Message," *Journal of the General Assembly, of the State of South Carolina, for the year 1835*, p. 7; Charleston *News and Courier*, 22 Aug. 1878; Marshall, "Gentlemen without Country," p. 183.

156. Deed Bk. 21, p. 517 (ECH). The reaction to Tillman's actions led to the repeal of the statute, S.C., General Assembly, *Acts*, 1910, pp. 704–5. Lucy Francis Tillman ultimately won custody. Simkins, *Pitchfork Ben*, pp. 418–84; Senese, "Legal Thought"; Millar, "Changes of Divorce." A scrapbook about the custody fight is in DAT. Anna Clemson Calhoun to Maria Calhoun, 14 June 1842, John C. Calhoun Papers (SCL); Lander, *Calhoun Family*, p. 42.

157. In 1860, his appeals to South Carolina's maternity helped propel Pickens to the governorship. "I come as a son to lay my head upon the bosom of my mother—to hear her heart beat—beat with glorious and noble accents worthy of her past and glorious future." Charleston *Courier*, 3 Dec. 1860; Charleston *Mercury*, 4 Dec. 1860; see also Edgefield *Advertiser*, 28 Nov. 1860, for an earlier version of the speech Pickens delivered in Edgefield. See Edmunds, "Politics of Destruction," pp. 229–31, for an excellent discussion of the speeches and their settings. F. W. Pickens to M. L. Bonham, 31 Jan. 1857, M. Luke Bonham Papers (SCL); Edgefield *Advertiser*, 28 Nov. 1860; Edmunds, "Francis Pickens," pp. 89, 111.

158. Joseph Abney to Armistead Burt, 23 July 1841, Burt Papers (DU); According to Marshall, "Gentlemen without Country," p. 5, "In the antebellum South ideology and institutions worked hand in hand, with ideology flowing harmoniously through key institutions like family, plantation slavery, South Carolina College, state government, military establishment and patriarchy."

159. Marshall, "Gentlemen without Country," pp. 11, 253–60; Charleston *News and Courier*, 28 June 1894; Simkins, *Pitchfork Ben*, p. 265.

160. Wallace, *History South Carolina*, 3:356–57; Simkins, *Pitchfork Ben*, pp. 185–87.

161. Willowbrook Cemetery, Edgefield.

162. Ibid.

163. "Extracts Beloved Husband's Diary," P. S. Brooks Papers (SCL); Catherine F. Hammond to Marcus C. M. Hammond, 3 Sept. 1865, J. H. Hammond Papers (SCL); Bleser, *Hammonds of Redcliffe*, p. 145.

164. Francis W. Pickens to Lucy Holcombe Pickens, 4 Sept. 1865, Pickens Papers (DU). *Sketch of Life of Francis Pickens*, pp. 2, 20; Charles Martin to Gov. J. L. Orr, 3 Dec. 1866, Orr Papers (SCDAH).

165. Louis T. Wigfall to John Manning, 2 Feb. 1839, Williams-Chesnut-Manning Papers (SCL); King, *Louis Wigfall*, p. 38. Daniel Augustus Tompkins to Harriet Brigham, 14 Oct. 1874, Tompkins Papers (SHC); Clay, "Daniel Tompkins," p. 13.

166. Simkins, *Address before State Agricultural Society, 1855*, pp. 6–8. Because patriarchy refers not only to the gender of household head but also to his extraordinary authority over family members, societies with strong patriarchal values should not be individualistic societies. Yet, as seen in Edgefield, this personal independence did not conflict with the centrality of the family. In the nineteenth century Edgefield-

ians were taught from birth to regard *family* honor in a quasi-aristocratic sense. Edgefield saw every adult male as a patriarch as well as a potential aristocrat. All aristocratic status is based on an assumed hereditary superiority over a subject group; white Southerners had their Afro-American slaves as a negative reference group. This sense of family honor inspired the Southerner's resistance to equality before the law as well. The paradoxical linking of patriarchy and personal independence needs further investigation. Weier, "Writing South Carolina History"; Thornton, *Politics and Power*; Hahn, "Roots of Southern Populism."

Chapter 3

1. *Hamburg Journal*, 2 June 1842; Henry H. Cumming to Julia B. Cumming, n.d., 1832; see also 14 Mar. 1828 and 10 Apr. 1836, Hammond, Bryan, Cumming Papers (SCL); Louis T. Wigfall to Richard Manning, 4 Mar. 1839, Williams-Chestnut-Manning Papers (SCL); King, *Louis Wigfall*, p. 24; Preston S. Brooks to John Hampden Brooks, 21 June 1856, P. S. Brooks Papers (SCL).

2. Harry Hammond to James Henry Hammond, 29 and 30 June 1859, Hammond, Bryan, Cumming Papers (SCL); Bleser, *Hammonds of Redcliffe*, p. 62.

3. M. C. Butler to Maria Butler, 1862, M. C. Butler Papers (SCL).

4. Paul Hammond to William Gilmore Simms, 8 Mar. 1869, Ferris Papers (Col); Bleser, *Hammonds of Redcliffe*, pp. 158, 195; Julia Bryan Hammond to Katherine F. Hammond, 1 May 1881, Hammond, Bryan, Cumming Papers (SCL).

5. Degler, *At Odds*, makes this point from a close reading of Censer, "Family Relationships and Power." Hammond Diary, 12 Apr. 1836, Hammond Papers (LC); Faust, *Sacred Circle*, p. 35; J. H. Hammond to Harry Hammond, 14 Mar. 1851, 20 Dec. 1852, 15 Jan., 23 Aug., 5 Oct., 23 Nov. 1855, 6 May and 7 Aug. 1856, 16 July 1859, Harry Hammond to J. H. Hammond, Oct. 1858, 29 and 30 June 1859. Letters between young Henry H. Cumming and his father Thomas Cumming in Augusta indicated a respectful, dependent relationship. Henry wrote from Europe, where he was studying, to ask his father's permission to change plans and also for his advice. In 1820 when Henry was to return to Augusta, he wrote to his father about his pleasure at returning to family and friends, but also about his apprehensions about finding employment. The future Augusta attorney wrote, "I mention it now under the hope that you will relieve me from it by selecting, yourself, or assisting me in selecting my employment for life" (Henry H. Cumming to Thomas Cumming, 13 April and 19 July 1819, 30 June 1820, Hammond, Bryan, Cumming Papers [SCL]).

6. W. E. Woodward, whose family had sharecropped and then moved to Graniteville and finally Augusta as mill workers, displayed respect for and appreciation of his parents and the values of hard work and education they inculcated in him, just as did the children of elite parents. See Woodward, *Gift of Life*, esp. pp. 21–22, 27, 54–55, 107. Ms., M. C. Butler Papers (SCL); Howard, CWVQ (1915), pp. 3–4 (TSLA). Howard explained that in Edgefield, "among the best business men of the country, the most of whom had commenced poor, labor was considered honorable and commendable. There were a few only who eschewed all kinds of labor and after the war became wanderers and idlers." In one questionnaire he did reveal that of "the sons of those who had many slaves, many were idle while many were studying professions."

7. Francis W. Pickens to Lucy Holcombe Pickens, 4 Sept. 1865, Pickens Papers (DU). Upon the death of his mother-in-law, Mrs. Christopher Fitzsimons, James Henry Hammond wrote in his diary: "She was the most perfect woman I ever knew. She thought only of doing good for others—never of herself" (Diary, 14 Dec. 1841, Hammond papers [LC]; see also Tucker, "James Hammond," p. 404).

8. J. H. Brooks to Preston Brooks, 30 May 1856, and Preston S. Brooks to John Hampden Brooks, 21 June 1856, P. S. Brooks Papers (SCL); Tillman, "Childhood Days," p. 2; Simkins, *Pitchfork Ben*, p. 31; Tucker, "James Hammond," pp. 35, 375–85; King, *Louis Wigfall*; Bonham, "Life and Times of Milledge Bonham."

9. Simkins, "Childhood Days"; Fannie M. Tillman to Ben Tillman, 25 May 1864, Tillman Papers (CU); Simkins, *Pitchfork Ben*, pp. 35–36.

10. Ms., United Daughters of the Confederacy Relic Room, State Capitol, Columbia, S.C.; Edgefield *Advertiser*, 12 Feb. 1936, Centenniel Edition. On another "angel of mercy" see Simkins and Patton, *Women of Confederacy*, p. 22 and Underwood, *Women of Confederacy*, pp. 115–16.

11. Newspaper clipping, n.d., M. C. Butler Papers (SCL).

12. Augusta *Chronicle and Constitutionalist*, 10 Apr. 1881. The editor was James R. Randall, son-in-law of Marcellus Hammond. See also *New York Times*, 10 Apr. 1881; Ramey, *Trial of Booth*, p. 15. Randall celebrated Gary: "We bid farewell then, to the hero, the statesman, the orator, the advocate, the patriot, the good, true son of South Carolina, and the pride of Edgefield."

13. Testament of Levy Lamb, 16 Apr. 1825, box 17, pck. 14, Probate Records (ECH); Mr. L. Cheatham to Mr. Remark Corley, 3 Sept. 1877, Milledge Luke Bonham Papers (SCL); Joseph L. Talbert Will, Talbert Papers (SCL). I drew a sample of a hundred wills as respresentative.

14. Elizabeth Clark Will, 12 Oct. 1827 (probated 3 Nov.), Bk. C, pp. 51–52, Probate Records (ECH).

15. W. B. Johnson to Thomas H. Johnson, 12 July 1862, Johnson Papers (SCL). Within three months both father and son were dead.

16. Sister to B. R. Tillman, 8 May 1862, and Anna Tillman to Tillman, 10 Apr. 1864, also Anna Tillman to Tillman, 16 Sept. 1860, James A. Tillman to Tillman, 8 May 1862, Fannie M. Tillman to Tillman, 10 Apr. 1864, all in Tillman Papers (SCL); Simkins, *Pitchfork Ben*, pp. 42–43; Katharine Hammond to Emily C. Hammond, 16 Aug. 1893, Hammond, Bryan, Cumming Papers (SCL).

17. Harry Hammond to James Henry Hammond, Oct. 1858, Hammond, Bryan, Cumming Papers (SCL); Bleser, *Hammonds of Redcliffe*, pp. 52–53.

18. Tillman, "Childhood Days"; Simkins, *Pitchfork Ben*, p. 44.

19. In 1860, nonnuclear households increased proportionately with the age of poor household heads to 28 percent of those households headed by someone fifty or older and declined with the age of the rich household head to 34 percent of those households headed by someone fifty or older.

20. Coresident siblings when the household head was eighteen years or older marked the family as extended. If only brothers or sisters under the age of eighteen composed a household, I considered the family nuclear. These "double denuded" (in the classification scheme of more detailed family codings) were rare and hardly affected the overall proportions. Some sociologists and historians would have recorded coresident siblings as a nonfamily or irregular household.

21. Mrs. R. E. Morris to Gov. J. L. Orr, 11 Mar. 1867, Orr Papers (SCDAH).

22. Steckel, "Antebellum Southern Fertility," esp. pp. 331, 348–51, believes poor white families in 1860 had fewer children because of greater mortality owing to poorer nutrition. He does not believe family limitation was a factor. However, I suspect the poor may have limited the number of children they had to the number they believed that they could support.

23. There was a difference between rich and poor mothers: the wealthier mothers had slightly more children at home when the mothers were in their thirties; the poor, when they were in their forties. The average number of children for that age grouping was slightly less for affluent than for poor mothers. My conclusions are similar to Katz's and tables were constructed for mother and father cohorts like those in Katz, *People of Hamilton*, pp. 244–48, see esp. p. 248.

24. Helen King to Mary Strother, 23 July 1887, Helen King to Mary and Edgar Strother, n.d., Helen King to Mrs. Strother, 11 May n.d., all in Strother Papers (FP); Mills, *Statistics of South Carolina*, p. 529; Big Stevens Creek Baptist Church Records, Mar. 1853 (BHC).

25. Mills, *Statistics of South Carolina*, p. 529; Edgefield *Advertiser*, 25 Sept. 1838; Cook, *Hard Labor Section*, p. 28; Tillman "Childhood Days," pp. 13–16; Simkins, *Pitchfork Ben*, pp. 38–39; Winston, *Builder of New South*, pp. 6–7; Wright, *Barefoot in Arcadia*, pp. 21–22, Woodward, *Gift of Life*, pp. 41–46, 54, 59–63, 80, and *Way Our People Lived*, pp. 332, 334–40.

26. Louis Wigfall to Mrs. Wigfall, 28 Mar. and Apr. 1861, Wigfall Papers, (LC); Wigfall to Richard Manning, n.d. and 22 Feb. 1839, Williams-Chesnut-Manning Papers (SCL); King, *Louis Wigfall*, pp. 10, 21–22; Tillman, "Childhood Days," pp. 13–16; Simkins, *Pitchfork Ben*, pp. 38–39; Winston, *Builder of New South*, pp. 6–7, 18–19; Woodward, *Gift of Life*, pp. 41, 44, 95, 97, and *Way Our People Lived*, pp. 334, 344–47.

27. Tompkins quoted in Winston, *Builder of New South*, p. 8; ms., M. C. Butler Papers (SCL); B. R. Tillman to Rev. I. L. Brookes, 6 Aug. 1844, Brookes Papers (SCL); Howard, CWVQ (1915), p. 4 (TSLA).

28. Statistics for work covered only households that had children from the ages of 15 to 19 and 20 or above in their families. In 1860, the rich are represented by the wealthiest quartile of white households and the poor by the least wealthy quartile. The general proportions of rich to poorest working is true for 1850 as well.

29. D. A. Tompkins to Harriet Brigham, 7 and 14 June 1874, Tompkins Papers (SHC).

30. Under tremendous parental and cultural pressure to excel, nineteenth-century youths discovered in their love for another person security in what could otherwise be a very unsure world; it provided the lovers with an identity as well as respectability. Christopher Poppenheim to Mary Elinor Bouknight, 26 Sept. 1863, 20 Oct. 1864, 9 July 1865, Poppenheim Papers (SCHS); Matthew C. Butler to Maria Pickens Butler, Mar. 1863, M. C. Butler Papers (SCL); Harry Hammond to Emily Cumming, 7 Apr., 21 May, 5, 11, and 15 July, 8 and 25 Sept. and n.d. Oct. 1859, 23 Dec. 1861, and 7 May 1864, Emily Cumming Hammond to Harry Hammond, 30 Sept. and 4 Oct. 1859, all in Hammond, Bryan, Cumming Papers (SCL); Bleser, *Hammonds of Redcliffe*, pp. 77–83, 118–20; Ball, *State that Forgot*, p. 241. These sentiments were not restricted to youth alone. When her forty-year-old bachelor uncle, James Edward

Calhoun, fell in love with Anna Clemson's best friend, Maria Simkins of Edgefield, Anna wrote of her uncle that he was "more in love than any one you ever saw—can talk of nothing but Maria's perfection and his happiness" (Anna Calhoun Clemson to Patrick Calhoun, 15 Dec. 1838, John C. Calhoun Papers [SCL]; see also Lander, *Calhoun Family*, p. 11). The same is true for Francis Pickens's courting of Lucy Holcombe (see Edmunds, "Politics of Destruction," pp. 207–8, 210–12).

31. Poems, Gary Papers (SCL).

32. Francis W. Pickens to Lucy Holcombe, 27 July 1857, 9 Mar. 1858, Pickens Papers (FP). Lucy may have been using her family as an excuse. She married Pickens only after her true love had been killed filibustering. To memorialize her suitor she wrote "Free Flag Over Cuba" (ms., Pickens Papers [DU]). Lucy was considered both a charmer and a beauty. Her picture appeared on the Confederate hundred-dollar bill. Edmunds, "Francis Pickens," p. 185, and "Politics of Destruction," pp. 208, 262–63; Bull, "Lucy Pickens." Edward Spann Hammond to Annie H. Walker, 14 Aug. 1909, Letter-press Book, Spann Hammond Papers (SCL); Bleser, *Hammonds of Redcliffe*, pp. 21–22, especially notes 10–11. Nearly a half century later, Spann wrote that with the breaking of this engagement, "I have since led a wandering, . . . vagabond life, imbued largely with misanthropy and void of settled purpose or aspiration." For a wealthy merchant's threat to shoot his daughter's suitor see details below and M. Harris to Mr. Christies, 17 May 1856, Hughes Papers (SHC); see also the story in Harris, "Slaveholding Republic," p. 86. Woodward, *Gift of Life*, pp. 20–21, writes that his maternal grandfather opposed his father and mother's marriage. Only after the first child was born from the marriage was there a reconciliation between father and daughter.

33. Liberty Church Records, Bullock County, Alabama (SCHS).

34. Edgefield *Advertiser*, 4 Aug. 1854 (LaBorde still owned slaves in Edgefield in 1860); Emma Blocker Perrin to Isabella Blocker, 4 Apr. 1853, Blocker Papers (FP); Edmunds, "Politics of Destruction," esp. pp. 4–5; S.C. Historical Society, *South Carolina Genealogies*, 1:237–38, 240, 267, 285; Coit, *John Calhoun*, pp. 184, 334, 392, 417; Lander, *Calhoun Family*, pp. vii, 13–14; "Ms," n.d., M. C. Butler Papers (SCL).

35. Rainsford Diary, 13 Dec. 1823 and 1 Apr. 1842, pp. 13, 41, Rainsford Papers (FP); Plantation Record Book, Jan. 1851, Pickens Papers (DU); Maria Bryan Harford to Maria Bryan Cumming, 26 Nov. 1832, Hammond, Bryan, Cumming Papers (SCL).

36. John C. Whitlock to William Whitlock, 12 Jan. 1864, Whitlock Papers (DAT); Cook, *Hard Labor Section*, p. 26; James Thomas Bushell to "Uncle James Bouchelle," 11 Oct. 1867, Sheppard Papers (SCL). Smith and Lewis Papers (FP); Tillman, "Childhood Days"; B. R. Tillman to Mrs. Francis M. Tillman Simpson, 25 Feb. 1918, and to Mrs. Hill, 14 Feb. 1917, Tillman Papers (CU); Simkins, *Pitchfork Ben*, pp. 48–49; Rogers, "Great Population Exodus," pp. 14–21; Mills, *Statistics of South Carolina*, p. 527. Why people selected to migrate to free states instead of slave states needs investigation. Perhaps nonslaveowners and yeomen opted for the northern states. The progressive historian Charles A. Beard suggested this was the case for his North Carolina grandparents, who moved to Indiana (Beard to Frank and Harriet Owsley, 14 May 1940, Owsley Papers [VU]). Until the census of 1850, no information was collected from individuals to show the state of birth. In 1850, the number of

outmigrants from South Carolina was estimated to be equal to two-thirds of all free persons born in South Carolina and still living in the state. The concern for a geographically removed extended family can be seen in the story of James Henry Hammond and his half uncle Sterling Edward Turner. For about thirty years, Turner was involved in trade on the African coast. Not having heard from the elderly uncle in several years, Hammond commissioned an agent to go to Africa to bring his uncle home. He advanced eight hundred dollars and paid all expenses. The partially paralyzed and penurious Turner finally arrived, barely able to walk and his speech and mind impaired. A compassionate Hammond wrote, "Poor fellow! He has not a dollar in the world—but shall not want one while I have." See the excellent account in Tucker, "James Hammond," pp. 163–66; J. H. Hammond to M. C. M. Hammond, 7 Nov. 1833, and Plantation Records, 1831–55, entries for 26 Nov. 1832 and 11 Nov. 1833, all in Hammond Papers (SCL). Tobias Lanham to Margaret Cloud, 12 Oct. 1850, Sheppard Family Papers (SCL).

37. Only thirteen cases were listed in the 1850 census as married within the year. The census enumerator asked every family if anyone had been married that year. I excluded second marriages. Average age for brides was 19.97 and for grooms 25.47 years. Mary E. Bouknight to Christopher Poppenheim, 4 Sept. 1863, Poppenheim Papers (SCHS). Bouknight letter cited in context below on cousin marriage, see n. 45.

38. One is reminded of James Agee's description of both the joys and the problems which marrying a younger woman brought the white Alabama sharecropper Thomas Gallatin (Bud) Woods (Agee and Walker, *Let Us Now*, esp. pp. 293, 337–38).

39. My conclusions on frequency of cousin marriages differ significantly from the findings of other scholars. Davidson, *Last Foray*, pp. 5–6, studied the 440 great planters who are listed in the federal slave manuscript censuses for 1860 South Carolina. He concluded, "They were most amazingly interwed, the marriage of cousins being almost the rule rather than the exception. . . . Nor was this a sectional phenomenon." He believes cousin marriage occurred as much in the up-country as in the coastal region of South Carolina. Citing Davidson's study among others and accepting the received wisdom on white southern cousin intermarriage, Gutman, *Black Family*, pp. 88–91, establishes this as one of his major theses to deny the copying of white marriage rules by Afro-Americans. Gutman, however, did find some endogamous marriages among Afro-Americans, and I too have located a few cases. That the general pattern for whites included a taboo against cousin marriage would not in itself work against Gutman's argument that slaves had well-organized kin groups and carefully avoided first-cousin marriage even though their masters did not. See also Wyatt-Brown, "Ideal Typology," pp. 11–13; in his *Southern Honor*, Wyatt-Brown has apparently found evidence consistent with Gutman's theory. According to C. Vann Woodward's review, "Intermarriage among cousins has never been adequately studied, but its frequency is undeniable" ("Primal Code," p. 27). The popular literature is filled with examples of southern cousin marriage; see for among the aristocrats and merchant classes, respectively, Mitchell, *Gone with Wind*, and Hellman, *Little Foxes*.

There are indications that ruling classes around the world have tended toward endogamy (especially aristocracies), but few well-documented examples existed in Edgefield. Even when cases of cousin-endogamous marriage were found, it was usually not clear if the relatives involved were first, second, third, or even more distant cousins. Yale, "Travelers," p. 69, claims that the Irish-descended families who winter near North Augusta (see chap. 2) intermarry. Although Yale does not discuss cousin marriage, he suggests it; thus, of three hundred families the number of "in-group marriages have narrowed the number of surnames to just seven."

40. Clay, "Daniel Tompkins," pp. 5–6; Mathis, "Preston Brooks," p. 301; SCHS, *South Carolina Genealogies*, 3:110–11, esp. and 107–21; McClendon, *Edgefield Marriage Records*, p. 22; McClendon, *Edgefield Death Notices*, p. 42; Edgefield *Advertiser*, 19 July 1843. The plantation house was Belle Grove and the family the Talbert family.

41. Genealogies in the Reed Papers (FP) and Strother Papers (FP); quotation from Brooks, *Stories of the Confederacy*, p. 58.

42. Rainsford Diary, 13 Dec. 1833, p. 12, Rainsford Papers (FP); Cook, *Hard Labor Section*, pp. 36–37.

43. King, *Louis Wigfall*, pp. 8–9; Trezevant, *Trezevant Family*, pp. 103–4. It should be noted that in 1842 Lyell, *Travels in North America*, 1:154–55, was amazed how sparsely settled the South Country up-country was. I am not the only one to doubt some of Lyell's observations; see Williams, *Vogues in Villainy*, p. 143.

44. James Henry Hammond to Harry Hammond, 17 Nov. 1861, Hammond, Bryan, Cumming Papers (SCL). Bleser, *Hammonds of Redcliffe*, pp. 21–22, 91 (n. 3). James Henry broke his son Spann's engagement to a second cousin. The father claimed that the action resulted from the fiancée's family's refusal to give Spann the cousin's inheritance. See the discussion below. Emily Cumming Hammond's oldest brother, Alfred Cumming, married his first cousin, Sarah Matilda Davis, in 1861 (Cumming, *Northern Daughter*, p. 108). One of South Carolina's most celebrated cousin marriages took place between John C. Calhoun, of neighboring Abbeville District, and his first cousin's daughter, Floride Colhoun, of Charleston in 1811 (SCHS, *South Carolina Genealogies*, 1:249–84). See also Lander, *Calhoun Family*, esp. pp. 160–61. Apparently there were no other later cousin marriages within the Calhoun family, although William Lowndes Calhoun did marry his brother's widow. Another Abbeville family related to the Calhouns and tied intimately with Edgefield and especially Francis Pickens was the Noble family. In 1768, Alexander Noble married his first cousin, Catherine, daughter of Ezekiel and Jean Ewing Calhoun. These early marriages to cousins become much scarcer with the settlement of the up-country. In conversations with one local historian, I asked about cousin marriage and he pointed to some folk I knew from Ninety Six and added knowingly, "But they are salt-water people."

45. M. E. Bouknight to Christopher Poppenheim, 4 Sept. 1863, Poppenheim Papers (SCHS). See above under age of marriage and n. 37. She was two years older. His letters to her, which began in November 1860, never mentioned the problem of the two being cousins. In searches in other archives, I found no more mention of the two being cousins. An interesting excerpt from Mrs. Poppenheim's memoirs on her fleeing the Union troops as they approached Charleston is in Andrews, *Women of the South*, pp. 247–56.

46. T. P. Baily to T. J. McKie, 13 May 1875, McKie Papers (DU). It should be noted that this letter occurs during Reconstruction, twelve years after the above letter by Mary Bouknight of Edgefield.

47. Julia A. Cumming to Emily C. Hammond, 18 Feb. 1873, Hammond, Bryan, Cumming Papers (SCL); Bleser, *Hammonds of Redcliffe*, p. 166.

48. Emma Blocker Perrin to Isabella M. Blocker, 4 Apr. 1853, Blocker Papers (FP).

49. Pottersville *Hive*, 19 Nov. 1830; Scott, *Southern Lady* and "Women's Perspective"; Hagler, "Ideal Woman." Within the patriarchy of Edgefield, women played crucial roles. The images of white women were especially important to the self-concepts of the Southerners. Whereas scholars maintain that the southern character emphasized an organic community and hierarchy, in contrast to the urbanizing and industrializing North's individualism and egalitarianism, it also retained essential features that are often imputed to feminine character (moral consciousness, sentimentality, introspection, benevolence, and hospitality). Thus, women were more readily incorporated into the southern vision of society than into the northern. The archetypal Southerner was not in flight from society but immersed in family; persons were significant less as individuals (as in the North) and more as members of an organic community. Women were identified with the region's civilization and culture and with the honor of the family, home, and community. The antebellum southern woman was portrayed in literature as essentially passive and ornamental, unable to defend herself from the dangers of the world. This upper-class image supported the patriarchal structure of family life and society and lent a certain grace to the patriarchal defense of the slave system. Wives, daughters, and slaves were parts of a supposedly beneficent society ordered for their protection along the traditional lines of white male aristocratic authority. According to this world view, slaves, white women, and white men each had their place and their concommitent rights and obligations. See chap. 6, n. 6 below.

50. Anna Calhoun Clemson to Maria Simkins Calhoun, 28 Jan. 1844, J. C. Calhoun Papers (SCL); Lander, *Calhoun Family*, p. 72.

51. Howard, CWVQ (1915), pp. 2–3.

52. On the feminization of teaching in the Northeast see Mattingly, *Classless Profession*, and Mann, *Republic and School*, pp. 44–52, 54–56; Edgefield Free School Reports, 1835–65, Superintendent of Education Papers, Records of the Department of Education (SCDAH).

53. Jordan, "Education for Community."

54. Hickman quoted in U.S., Congress, Senate, *Labor and Capital*, p. 737; D. A. Tompkins to Grace Tompkins, 14 Jan. 1908, Grace to D. A., 1 Dec. 1907, and 2 Feb. 1908, Tompkins Papers (SHC); Clay, "Daniel Tompkins," p. 120. See "Education" in chap. 2.

55. Corley, *Confederate City*, pp. 46–56; Jones and Dutcher, *Memorial History*, p. 185; Werner, "Hegemony and Conflict," pp. 30–31. Augusta became a major supplier of military goods for the Confederacy. Still, representatives of the upper orders, such as Harry Hammond, were troubled when they learned that their wives were doing menial labor. See Harry Hammond to Emily Cumming Hammond, 22 July 1864, Hammond, Bryan, Cumming Papers (SCL), in which Harry fretted after having learned that Emily was making cartridges.

56. Pottersville *Hive*, 19 Nov. 1830.

57. Louis T. Wigfall to Richard Manning, 22 Feb. 1839 and 19 Apr. 1841, Williams-Chesnut-Manning Papers (SCL); King, *Louis Wigfall*, p. 38; Francis W. Pickens to J. Edward Calhoun, 7 Dec. 1844, F. W. Pickens Papers (SCH); Edmunds, "Francis Pickens," pp. 82–83.

58. Louis T. Wigfall to Richard Manning, n.d. (early 1839), Williams-Chesnut-

Manning Papers (SCL); King, *Louis Wigfall*, p. 24; Elisha Hammond to James Henry Hammond, 21 Dec. 1827, James Henry to Marcellus C. M. Hammond, 1 Apr. 1840, 9 Mar. 1842, and J. H. Hammond to John F. Hammond, 6 and 22 Mar. 1842, all in J. H. Hammond Papers (SCL); Tucker, "James Hammond," pp. 19–20, 377, 383. On tariffs and nullification, see Freehling, *Prelude to Civil War*.

59. Inscriptions from tombstones in Willowbrook Cemetery, Edgefield.

60. Francis W. Pickens to Lucy Pickens, 23 Feb. 1861, Pickens Papers (FP); Francis W. Pickens to Lucy Pickens, 4 Sept. 1865, Pickens Papers (DU); Edmunds, "Francis Pickens," pp. 185–86.

61. Emily C. Hammond to Julia B. Cumming, 21 June 1861, Henry Cumming to Julia B. Cumming, 22 May 1834, Maria B. Harford to Julia B. Cumming, Mar. 1839, 12 May and 8 Oct. 1840, 27 June 1842, all in Hammond, Bryan, Cumming Papers (SCL). Southerners were aware of the weighty responsibilities of the plantation mistress. A relative of Harry Hammond's future in-laws in Augusta in 1834 had remarried, and Henry Cumming wrote to his wife, Julia, of the problems the new wife faced. She "suffers occasionally from being mother to another's children, and mistress of servants who have had none for a long time period." In four letters in four years' time, Maria Bryan Harford wrote to her sister Julia Bryan Cumming about how busy she was in making clothes for the slaves. See also, Sides, "Women and Slaves" and "Southern Women and Slavery."

62. Lebsock, "Radical Reconstruction," has an excellent discussion of southern women's property rights and is particularly good in analyzing the complicated changes in South Carolina's laws. John C. Sheppard, Edgefield representative to the 1895 constitutional convention and future governor, remarked that the "legislature tinkering with the laws relating to the property of married women had caused more litigation and expense to the people of the State than any other one thing. . . . now a Philadelphia lawyer could not tell what the law in this State on the subject was" (Charleston *News and Courier*, 1 Oct. 1895). The notes to Lebsock's article are an excellent guide to sources; Senese, "Legal Thought."

63. A preliminary study of Marengo County, Alabama, found that no daughter of 99 wealthy families inherited substantial landed property in her own name, but sons and wives did. Wiener, *Social Origins*, p. 236. Wyatt-Brown, "Ideal Typology," agrees with Wiener and suggests this reinforced patriarchy. Harris, "Slaveholding Republic," found that sons and daughters shared equally inheritances although daughters did not as often get their share in real property. My reading of wills produced conclusions similar to Harris. See "Family Relations" above, and n. 13.

64. Rainsford Diary, 13 Dec. 1833, Rainsford Papers (FP); Butler, *Memoirs of General Butler*; "Memoirs of Gen. William Butler's Family," Milledge Lipscomb Bonham Papers (SCL); SCHS, *South Carolina Genealogies*, 1:233–36; Chapman, *History of Edgefield*, pp. 43–46, 72; O'Neall, *Biographical Sketches*, pp. 198–99. When James Henry Hammond decided he wanted to live at the Beech Island plantation and manage it himself, he wrote his wife, "I *must* settle there." Hammond's biographer adds that "it was Mrs. Hammond's wish that they should settle there." J. H. Hammond to Catherine Fitzsimmons, 21 July 1831, in letter-press book 1831–33, and Plantation Records, 1856–87, 21 May 1859, J. H. Hammond Papers (SCL); Tucker, "James Hammond," p. 84.

65. Degler, *At Odds*, makes this point.

66. Matthew Calbraith Butler to Maria Calhoun Pickens Butler, n.d., Butler Papers (DU). For the separation of Marcellus Hammond's brother-in-law Tom Davies from his wife, see Catherine Elizabeth Fitzsimmons Hammond to Harry Hammond, 15 July 1855, Hammond, Bryan, Cumming Papers (SCL). See also, Maria Simkins Calhoun to J. Edward Calhoun, 4 Apr. 1841. (Maria, on the other hand, wrote, "I feel quite anxious to get a letter saying how much you miss me.") J. E. Calhoun Papers (SCL).

67. The incident with the Hampton girls is explained below; Hammond Diary, 15 Dec. 1850, 1, 3, 9, and 31 May, 8, 15, and 17 June, 7 Sept., 15, 21, 25 Oct. 1851, 4 Mar., 7 June, 16 Nov. 1852, 7 Jan. and 5 Mar., 1853; Christopher Fitzsimmons to James Henry Hammond, 17 Nov. 1852; Hammond Papers (SCL); Bleser, *Hammonds of Redcliffe*, pp. 10–11; Faust, *James Hammond*, pp. 86–88, 314–17.

68. Lucy Pickens to Mrs. Beverly Holcombe, n.d., and 2 Dec. 1859, Pickens-Dugas Papers (SHC); Francis W. Pickens to Lucy Pickens 23 Feb. 1861, Pickens Papers (FP); Edmunds, "Francis Pickens," pp. 185–86.

69. When Elisha Hammond's grave was removed to the Redcliffe graveyard, a family member reported: "Because of the ring of command in this inscription about where she wished her remains to be forever, she was not dug up . . . to lie beside the husband of her youth . . . and among her offspring" (George Black Hammond quoted in Steadman, *History of Spann Family*, p. 68).

70. Rawick, *American Slave*, vol. 2: *South Carolina*, pt. 2, p. 215.

71. Ibid., supplement series vol. 4: *Georgia*, pt. 2, p. 662.

72. Ibid., vol. 2: *South Carolina*, pt. 1, p. 157. See also Ibid., vol 10: *Arkansas*, pt. 6, pp. 103–14. Casper Rumple had belonged to John Griffin, whose wife, Rebecca, owned four separate plantations. Both of the Griffins were elderly, and John was Rebecca's second husband. Rumple remembered that the white mistress "had some grown girls. He [John] had no children. They called him Pa and I did too." As a slave, Rumple slept in the same room with John Griffin; Griffin's wife slept in a different room with her two girls. The authority in this household was the wife. "Master John didn't want em to work at night but she made em work all the same. They b'long to her. . . . At night after they work in the field Miss Rebecca give em tasks—so many bats to card or so much spinnin' to do."

73. Ibid., vol. 2: *South Carolina*, pt. 2, p. 100.

74. Edgefield *Advertiser*, 22 Sept. 1851; an example of an Edgefield scholar attributing religious instruction to slave mistresses is Simkins and Patton, *Women of Confederacy*, pp. 168–69; interestingly, in a remarkably old school interpretation which presents South Carolina slaves as "uncivilized," Fickling, "Christianization," never mentions the white southern woman; Nicholson, *Brief Sketch*, pp. 8–9, 14; Winston, *Builder of New South*, p. 18; DuBois, *Negro American Family*, p. 47; Frazier, *Negro Family*, pp. 480–82; Rawick, *American Slave*, vol 2: *South Carolina*, pt. 2, p. 174; Brooks, *Stories of the Confederacy*, p. 46. The above mention women teaching slaves, but the manuscript collections of planters do not.

75. Edgefield *Advertiser*, 11 Mar. 1857, 20 Nov. 1851, 15 Dec. 1852, 23 June 1858, 4 July 1860, all contain editorials suggesting the proper role of southern womanhood. Traditional womanhood conformed to the paternalistic, traditional ethos, ignoring religion, and encouraged a flirtatious chastity. Often the editor glided easily between stereotypes of traditional womanhood and evangelical womanhood, but his

advice often was along these lines: "Young sparks who are pleased to think of a wife as an elegant plaything, intended only to dress and dance, visit and spend money, please look at the following picture of a good wife drawn from the pencil of Solomon: Prov. xxxi." See Ruoff, "Southern Womanhood," for good depictions of the evangelical and traditional womanhood of the South.

76. Horn's Creek Baptist Church Records, May, Sept., and Oct. 1851 (BHC). How the extended families of relatives influenced what one felt one could openly talk about in church needs investigation.

77. Big Stevens Creek Baptist Church Records, May 1813. Edgefield Village Baptist Church Records, Oct. 1827, Johnston Baptist Church Records, 9 Apr. 1876, p. 17, Mt. Moriah Baptist Church Records, 1833, Edgefield Baptist Association Records, Minutes for 1829, 1830, 1832, 1833 (BHC); Woodson, et al., *History of Edgefield Baptist Association*, pp. 40–43, 63.

78. U.S., Congress, Senate, *Mission of Women*; see newspaper references to n. 75 above and compare the editor's comments of 20 Nov. 1851 with Tillman: "In a struggle between the 'Lords of Creation' and the weaker but fairer and better sex."

79. Francis W. Pickens to Maria Simkins, 15 Sept. 1833, and Francis W. Pickens to Anna Calhoun, 21 Aug. 1837, F. W. Pickens Papers (SCL); Edmunds, "Politics of Destruction," pp. 28–29, n. 10, chap. 2.

80. Henry H. Cumming to Julia A. Bryan, 4 Aug. 1823, Hammond, Bryan, Cumming Papers (SCL); Christopher Poppenheim to Mary Elinor Bouknight, 20 Oct. 1864, and see 26 Sept. 1863, Poppenheim Papers (SCHS); Maria Simkins Calhoun to Col. J. Edward Calhoun, 4 Apr. 1841, J. Edward Calhoun Papers (SCL).

81. Harry Hammond to Emily C. Hammond, 19 Aug. 1864, Hammond, Bryan, Cumming Papers (SCL); Bleser, *Hammonds of Redcliffe*, p. 124.

82. B. R. Tillman to Rev. I. L. Brookes, 27 Sept. 1842, Brookes Papers (SCL); Daniel Augustus Tompkins to Miss Mai Dozier, 25 Aug. and 22 Nov. 1897, Daniel Augustus Tompkins to Mrs. Emilia C. Holland, 2 Dec. 1898, Daniel Augustus Tompkins to Grace Tompkins, 14 Jan. 1908, Grace to D. A. Tompkins, 2 Mar., 1 and 30 Apr., 2 and 4 June, 1 Nov., 1 Dec. 1907, and 11 Jan., 2 Feb., 1 Mar. 1908, all in Tompkins Papers (SHC); Clay, "Daniel Tompkins," pp. 118–22; Edgefield *Chronicle*, 8 Nov. 1906, Woodward, *Gift of Life*, pp. 35–37, 54–55 and *Way Our People Lived*, pp. 354–56.

83. Mills, *Statistics of South Carolina*, pp. 138–39. (However, some men were members, and this may have inhibited the sharing and bonding of Edgefield women.) Edgefield *Advertiser*, 30 Sept., 12 and 19 Oct., 7 Nov. 1860.

84. Ms., United Daughters of the Confederacy Relic Room; Edgefield *Advertiser*, 12 Feb. 1936, Centenniel Edition.

85. Edgefield *Advertiser*, 3, 17, and 31 July, 7 and 21 Aug., 4 and 11 Sept. 1861, 9, 16, 30 Oct. 1861, 25 June and 19 Nov. 1862.

86. Mims, *History Women's Missionary Union*; Ms., United Daughters of the Confederacy Relic Room.

87. Tillman, "Childhood Days," pp. 1–2, 6; Simkins, *Pitchfork Ben*, pp. 30–31; Will of B. R. Tillman, 15 July 1846, Will Book D, pp. 407–9 (ECH).

88. Edgefield County Historical Society, "Hammond Family" (ECHS); Chapman, *History of Edgefield*, pp. 41–42.

89. "Memoirs of the Nicholson Family," Nicholson Papers (FP); Clay, "Daniel

Tompkins," pp. 4–5; Winston, *Builder of New South*, pp. 14–17; Willowbrook Cemetery, Edgefield.

90. Simkins, *Pitchfork Ben*, p. 33. For other examples of southern business women see Brooks, *Stories of the Confederacy*, p. 44; Woodward, *Gift of Life*, p. 79, and *Way Our People Lived*, pp. 168, 319; O'Neall, *Biographical Sketches*, 1:198.

91. Weems, *Devil in Petticoats*; Trial Records, Martin Posey, 3 Oct. 1849; *S.C.* v. *Martin Posey* (1849) 4:103, 142, General Sessions (SCL and ECH); *Report of the Trial of Martin Posey* (SCL).

92. Big Stevens Creek Baptist Church Records, July and Aug. 1810, May 1839, Aug. 1866, Dry Creek Baptist Church Records, 24 Feb. 1827, 22 Aug. 1840, 24 July 1841, 22 June 1842, quotation from Edgefield Village Baptist Church Records, 4 Feb. 1826, see also Phillipi Baptist Church Records, 8 Jan. 1861, 18 March 1876, Horn's Creek Baptist Church Records, Mar. 1855, Aug. 1866, all in (BHC); McKendrie Methodist Church Records, 16 June 1878 (SCL).

93. Lebsock, "Radical Reconstruction," p. 195; Millar, "Changes of Divorce"; Senese, "Legal Thought." Divorce was legalized in 1872 by the Radicals, a majority of whom were black, and the Redeemers repealed the divorce legislation in 1878. Tillman's constitution made divorce unconstitutional in 1895. See chap. 7 below. Legal Notes, John Smyth Richardson Papers (SCL); Hindus, *Prison and Plantation*, pp. 57, 92; Petition of Elizabeth Hamilton, 1 Dec. 1813, Legislative Papers (SCDAH). Hamilton apparently did not receive the annulment.

94. McKendrie Methodist Church Records, 16 June 1878 (SCL); Cornish Diary, 18 Feb. 1850, Cornish Papers (SHC); Marcellus Hammond to William Gilmore Simms, 24 Jan. 1870, Ferris Collection (Col); Loula Comer Hammond to Virginia C. T. Clay, 11 Aug. 1871, and to Celeste Comer Clay, 1 Sept. 1878, both in Clay Papers (DU); Hammond, *History and Genealogy*, p. 270; Bleser, *Hammonds of Redcliffe*, p. 159 (n. 5); for another prewar Edgefield separation, Tom Davies from his wife, see Catherine Elizabeth Fitzsimmons Hammond to Harry Hammond, 15 July 1855, Hammond, Bryan, Cumming Papers (SCL).

95. Woodmason, *Carolina Backcountry*, pp. 39, 99–100, 225–26; Hindus, *Prison and Plantation*, pp. 54–56; Klein, "Rise of the Planters," pp. 46, 50, 53–55.

96. Grace Tompkins to D. A. Tompkins, 2 Mar., 1 and 30 Apr., 2 and 4 June, 1 Nov., 1 Dec. 1907, 11 Jan., 2 Feb., 1 Mar. 1908, Tompkins Papers (SHC); Clay, "Daniel Tompkins," pp. 120–21.

97. Marcellus C. M. Hammond to Postmaster, Fort Gibson, Arkansas, 18 June 1871, to Rachel Huey, 16 Mar. and 5 Apr. 1874, 16 July 1875, all copies in the Marcellus Hammond Papers (SCL); Bleser, *Hammonds of Redcliffe*, p. 13.

98. R. M. T. Hunter to Mrs. R. M. T. Hunter, 3 Dec. 1839, Hunter Papers (UV); Edmunds, "Politics of Destruction," pp. 65–66.

99. Francis W. Pickens to M. L. Bonham, 14 Oct., 21 and 31 Dec. 1859, Milledge Luke Bonham Papers (SCL); Edmunds, "Francis Pickens," p. 187.

100. Ibid.

101. Elisha Hammond to James Henry Hammond, 5 Nov. 1828, J. H. Hammond Papers (SCL); Tucker, "James Hammond," pp. 23–24.

102. Bleser, *Hammonds of Redcliffe*, p. 4. Hammond "Secret" Diary, 16 and 24 Feb. 1840, J. H. Hammond Papers (SCL); Tucker, "James Hammond," p. 338.

103. On his thirty-sixth birthday, Hammond wrote, apparently after the affair, that

"if spared I hope to amend my life." (Hammond Plantation Records, 15 Nov. 1842, J. H. Hammond Papers [SCL]); Tucker, "James Hammond," p. 425; R. F. W. Allston to Adele Allston, 10 Dec. 1846, Allston Papers (SCL); Francis W. Pickens to Lucy Holcombe, 6 Dec. 1857, F. W. Pickens Papers (SCL); James Henry Hammond to Marcus C. M. Hammond, 6 June 1844, and to William Gilmore Simms, 6 Oct. 1846, 8 July 1848, and 13 Aug. 1857, Diary, 2 July 1844, all in Hammond Papers (LC); J. H. Hammond to John Fox Hammond, 6 Mar. 1842, Hammond, Bryan, Cumming Papers (SCL); Hammond Diary, 16 and 24 Feb. 1842, 2 July 1844, 3 July 1845 and 9 Dec. 1846, all in J. H. Hammond Papers (SCL); Faust, *Sacred Circle*, pp. 41–42, and *James Hammond*, pp. 241–44; Tucker, "James Hammond," pp. 424–27; Bleser, *Hammonds of Redcliffe*, pp. 9–10, 28–33; Eaton, *Mind of Old South*, pp. 54–55.

104. Court Records (ECH); Edgefield Village Baptist Church Records, 4 Feb. 1826, Big Stevens Creek Baptist Church Records, Sept. and Nov. 1836, Phillipi Baptist Church Records, 18 Mar. 1876, all in BHC; Edgefield *Advertiser*, 14 Nov. 1860; Cartledge Autobiography, Cartledge Papers (SCL); Dreher Journal, Dreher Papers (SCL); Diary, 17 Nov. 1854, Cornish Papers (SHC); Harris, "Slaveholding Republic," p. 99; James Henry Hammond to Marcus C. M. Hammond, 25 Aug. 1858, James Henry Hammond to W. G. Simms, 29 July 1860, both in Hammond Papers (LC). Hammond became particularly fond of this daughter-in-law.

105. M. Harris to Mr. Christies, 17 May 1856, Hughes Papers (SHC); Harris, "Slaveholding Republic," p. 86.

106. Lucy Pickens to Mrs. Beverly Holcombe, n.d., 1859, Pickens-Dugas Papers (SHC); John Bacon to Lewis Cass, 26 Sept. 1859, Cass Papers (NA); Edmunds, "Politics of Destruction," pp. 217–18.

107. Hindus, *Prison and Plantation*, pp. 52–53. Hindus proposes an interesting if insufficiently documented theory: up-country men resorted to adultery with whites, while low-country planters had slave mistresses.

108. Jury Presentments to General Assembly, Edgefield, 1805, Barnwell, 1823 and 1830, Orangeburg, 1828, Darlington, 1830, Chesterfield, 1814, Pendleton, 1814, and Union, 1822, Bills, General Assembly, 1822, 1844, 1856, Report of Committee on Religion, 1824 (Benjamin James, Chairman), all in Legislative Papers (SCDAH); Woodmason, *Carolina Backcountry*, pp. 15, 52, 56, 256–57, 281–82; Hindus, *Prison and Plantation*, pp. 50–53; Klein, "Rise of the Planters," pp. 46, 50, 53–55.

109. George Mays had $15,000 personalty, which was mostly invested in his 18 slaves. Neither brother was convicted. Edgefield *Advertiser*, 10 Oct. 1860; Tillman, "Childhood Days," p. 2; Simkins, *Pitchfork Ben*, p. 34; Aiken *Courier Journal*, 11 Dec. 1877; Charleston *News and Courier*, 22, 24, 25, 27 Apr., 5, 6, 8, 9 May, 11 and 20 Oct., and 23 Nov. 1876, 19 Jan. 1877, 8, 15, 18, 23 Feb., 11 and 16 Mar., 10, 15, 18, 19, 20 Apr. 1878; Augusta *Chronicle and Sentinel*, 20 Apr. 1878; *State against Robert McEvoy*, General Sessions Court, Aiken (SCL and Aiken County Courthouse); Statement of McEvoy to Carlyle McKinney, 10 Apr. 1878, Francis W. Dawson to Gov. Wade Hampton, 7 Apr. 1878, both in Hampton Papers (SCDAH); Terrill, "Murder in Graniteville." The attorneys for McEvoy were black, and the jury that convicted him was predominantly black. For another Graniteville resident's defense of his sister's honor, see Woodward, *Gift of Life*, pp. 81–82.

110. Rainsford Diary, 2 Sept. 1833, p. 12; see also 10 Nov. 1839, p. 35, Rainsford Papers (FP).

111. Dreher Journal, 2nd Sunday, 11 and 13 Jan. 1843, Nov. entries 1843, and 10, 13, and 23 Sept. 1851, pp. 58, 61, 85, Dreher Papers (SCL); Autobiography, Cartledge Papers (SCL); "Journal of events," McLees Papers (SCL); Cornish Diary, 2 June 1848, 20 Apr. 1856, 12 Dec. 1858, Cornish Papers (SHC); Andrew Dunbar to Iveson L. Brookes, 8 Mar. 1852, Brookes Papers (SHC). The man died at the age of forty-two.

112. Cornish Diary, 13 Jan. 1849, 9 and 21 Feb., 23 Apr. 1854, 5 Jan. 1857, Cornish Papers (SHC).

113. A. B. Miller to Isabella Morrison Blocker, 23 Dec. 1816, Blocker Papers (FP).

114. Blocker Prayer Book, 10 and 26 June 1860, 23 Apr. 1865, and passim, Blocker Papers (FP).

115. Francis W. Pickens to Maria Calhoun, 25 Sept. 1842, F. W. Pickens Papers (SCL); Edmunds, "Francis Pickens," p. 120; Lander, *Calhoun Family*, p. 53.

116. Judgments and Decrees, Bk. 20, pp. 139–41; Executors and Guardians, apt. 47, pk. 2023, both in Probate Records (ECH); Lord, "Young Louis Wigfall," p. 96; King, *Louis Wigfall*, pp. 10–11.

117. S.C., State Board of Agriculture, *South Carolina,* pp. 473–75; County Wills, Abbeville County, I, pp. 167–75 (SCDAH); (Columbia) *State,* 2 Feb. 1919; interview with John Coleman Shifflet, superintendent of De La Howe School (this 1,800-acre farm school exists today); Will of Alexander Downing, amended 20 Nov. 1820, Records of Probate (ECH), reproduced in Dunbar, "History of Education," pp. 18–23; Thomason, *Foundations of Public Schools,* pp. 71, 76; Coleman, "Poverty and Poor Relief," pp. 152–57; Meriwether, *History of Higher Education,* p. 16. In 1860 one pauper left the Edgefield poorhouse to attend the Downer School (Edgefield *Advertiser,* 14 Nov. 1860).

118. Thomason, *Foundations of Public Schools,* pp. 127–40; Klein, "Rise of the Planters," pp. 282–83.

119. One has to question the stereotype of the black wet-nurse for the babies of the rich. For both the antebellum and postbellum years in Edgefield I have discovered a number of wealthy white women who nursed their children themselves. Even the extremely fashion-conscious Lucy Pickens breast-fed her child. If, however, wealthier women did use slave wet-nurses, these wealthy women would have missed some of the joys and bondings between mothers and infants which slaves and less wealthy white women experienced. Edmunds, "Politics of Destruction," p. 217; Bull, "Lucy Pickens," p. 11. A number of former slaves recalled blacks wet-nursing white children. See, for example, Rawick, *American Slave,* vol. 10: *Arkansas,* pt. 5, p. 334. For the traditional views of southern women see Sides, "Women and Slaves" and "Southern Women and Slavery"; Carrigan, "Nineteenth Century Rural."

120. Edgefield Coroner's Book, 1844–59 (SCL) *S.C.* v. *Martin Posey* (1849), 4:103, 142, General Sessions (SCL and ECH); Williams, *Vogues in Villainy,* pp. 36–37; *Report of Trial of Martin Posey* (SCL and DAT); Petition of Thomas Griffis, 3 Oct. 1828, Legislative Papers (SCDAH). For articles on interracial violence in Edgefield see the *Advertiser,* 2 May 1849, 10 July 1850, and on the murder of the editor's

own favored family servant by a white, 4 and 18 Mar. 1857. Fredrickson, "Masters and Mudsills," emphasizes the racism that pervaded and bound all levels of white South Carolina.

121. Englishman paraphrased in Cashin, *Story of Augusta*, p. 66; Thorpe, *Eros and Freedom*, pp. 3–27; Blassingame, "Planter on the Couch"; Petition of Edward B. Hibbler, 13 Dec. 1826, Legislative Papers (SCDAH).

122. Edgefield *Advertiser*, 12 Dec. 1850, quoting Columbus (Georgia) *Times*; *Advertiser*, 2 Mar. 1864.

123. Edgefield *Advertiser*, 16 Feb. 1859 and 28 Nov. 1860. See also 27 Aug. 1856, in which the paper reported that a Baptist preacher in neighboring Barnwell had to resign and go north when he expressed approval of Senator Sumner's actions. Grier argued that he believed God had punished man with slavery because of original sin (Grier's Broadside [SCL]). Harris, "Slaveholding Republic," pp. 168–99; Open Letter of Committee of Safety, 11 Aug. 1849 (SCL); Edmunds, "Francis Pickens," pp. 146–47. Burch was driven from Edgefield and his description circulated to newspapers.

124. Edgefield *Advertiser*, 28 Nov. 1860. See the Saluda Minuteman Association Records (SCL). Reopening the slave trade was debated throughout the 1850s in the local paper. However, large planters were not of one mind. One planter worried that already slavery worked against the interests of the white mechanics and laborers, and suggested to his fellow slaveowners, "We had better . . . give employment to our poor men." See the debate in Farmers Club, 3 Sept. 1859 (SCL).

125. F. W. Pickens to J. L. Orr, 4 and 9 Feb., 22 Mar. 1866, Orr Papers (SCDAH).

126. Edgefield *Advertiser*, 2 May 1849; Grace Tompkins to D. A. Tompkins, 1 Dec. 1907 and 2 Feb. 1908, D. A. Tompkins to Grace Tompkins, 14 Jan. 1908, A. S. Tompkins to D. A. Tompkins, 6 Apr. 1899, all in Tompkins Papers (SHC); Clay, "Daniel Tompkins," pp. 119–22; Woodward, *Gift of Life*, pp. 38–39, and *Way Our People Lived*, pp. 333–34. See also Burton, "Race and Reconstruction" and "Ungrateful Servants."

Chapter 4

1. It must be remembered that most of the evidence presented in this chapter concerns the late, "mature" period of slavery and may not necessarily be relevant to the earlier periods of plantation agriculture that accompanied the emergence of cotton monoculture. The decade prior to the Civil War was one of cotton prosperity. Other years saw depression and hard times for the cotton-producing areas of the South and might have meant different family experiences for slaves and antebellum free blacks.

2. Foner and Genovese, *Slavery in the New World*; Degler, *Neither Black nor White*; Curtin, *Atlantic Slave Trade*; Fogel and Engerman, "Recent Findings."

3. Important slave family studies include Blassingame, *Slave Community*, pp. 77–103; Genovese, *Roll, Jordan, Roll*, pp. 451–58, 482–523; Levine, *Black Culture*; Gutman, *Black Family*; Owens, *This Species of Property*; Fogel and Engerman, *Time on Cross*, 1:5, 52, 84–85, 126–44, vol 2, notes and reviews of literature; see especially 2:168–247. Gutman, *Slavery and Numbers Game*, pp. 9–10, 88–94, 98, 100–124, 126, 129, 137–40, 162–64, 176; Jones, "Cultural Middle Passage"; Ripley,

"Black Family," pp. 369–80. Blassingame's work, *Black New Orleans*, pp. 79–83, is closer to the DuBois and Frazier interpretations of slavery as "crippling" the black family than his *Slave Community*, in which he emphasizes the strengths of the slave family. An excellent interpretative and suggestive bibliographical essay on the slave family is found in Fogel, "Cliometrics and Culture," pp. 40–47. Springfield, Ohio, *Daily Republic*, 13 Sept. 1883.

4. Examples of abolitionist critiques of slavery are Weld, *American Slavery*; Stowe, *Uncle Tom's Cabin*.

5. Plantation Record Book, 29 Apr. 1839, Pickens Papers (DU); Hammond to Tappan, 6 Sept. 1850, Hammond Papers (LC); Farmers' Club, p. 36 (SCL).

6. Rawick, *American Slave*, sup. series, vol. 4: *Georgia*, p. 660.

7. Plantation Journal, 6 Dec. 1856; Plantation Diary, 7 Dec. 1854, J. H. Hammond to Marcelus Hammond, 12 Dec. 1847 and 3 Mar. 1864, all in J. H. Hammond Papers (SCL); letters are also in Hammond Papers (LC). See also analysis by Faust, "Culture, Conflict, and Community," pp. 90–91, and in Faust, *James Hammond*, pp. 94–97.

8. Plantation Record Book, pp. 3, 5, 7, 9, 11–39, 44, 49, 51, 53, 57, 73–75, 121–44, 171–73, 181, 349–53, Pickens Papers (DU); Plantation Diary, 20 Nov. 1853, 1 Jan. 1843, 6 Feb. 1842, pp. 490, 265, 242, J. H. Hammond Papers (SCL); Faust, *James Hammond*, p. 85; Whitfield Brooks Diaries, inside covers and pp. 1–2 for 1843 and not paginated, 1852 entry, Whitfield Brooks Papers (FP); Plantation Books, 1838, 1844–49, 1854–64, Talbert Papers (SCL); Plantation Records, McKie Papers (DU); Rainsford Diary, 8 Jan. 1834 and 22 Sept. 1844, Rainsford Papers (FP).

9. Rawick, *American Slave*, sup. ser., vol. 4: *Georgia*, pt. 2, p. 442, 554; vol. 13: *Georgia*, pt. 4, p. 229; vol. 8: *Arkansas*, pt. 1, p. 303; sup. ser., vol. 3: *Georgia*, pt. 1, pp. 327–28.

10. Ibid. sup. ser., vol 4: *Georgia*, p. 663; vol. 13: *Georgia*, p. 226.

11. Ibid., sup. ser., vol. 4: *Georgia*, pp. 433–35.

12. Ibid., vol. 8; *Arkansas*, pt. 1, pp. 303–5. Molly Brown was at least ninety, perhaps over a hundred years old, when interviewed. The sentences quoted are in direct response to a white interviewer's questions.

13. Thomas Green Clemson to John C. Calhoun, Sept. 1845 and 27 Mar. 1846, John C. Calhoun to T. G. Clemson, 13 Dec. 1845, Calhoun Papers (CU); Thomas Green Clemson to Francis W. Pickens, 7 Oct. 1850, Pickens Papers (DU); Thomas Green Clemson to Patrick Calhoun, 6 Aug. 1850, John C. Calhoun Papers (SCL); Florida Colhoun Calhoun to Anna Calhoun Clemson, 15 Dec. 1850, and Francis W. Pickens to Thomas Green Clemson, 14 May 1856, Clemson Papers (CU); Edgefield Deeds, GGG, pp. 170–74 (ECH); Lander, *Calhoun Family*, pp. 135–36; Rawick, *American Slave*, vol. 12: *Georgia*, pt. 1, pp. 333–43. (It is possible that the last sentence in the paragraph "got married to" is a dialect meaning "at the plantation.") Apparently the Clemson slaves were all sold together, although they were sold away from the plantation. Francis Pickens's father-in-law, Alfred Dearing, purchased the land and buildings. It is not clear who bought the slaves. On community, see Guthrie, "Catching Sense."

14. Rawick, *American Slave*, vol. 12: *Georgia*, pt. 1, p. 157; vol. 3: *South Carolina*, pt. 4, p. 72. Squire Harris explained about banjos and fiddles: "I never place myself in wid de people play banjers and fiddles. But I had my part in my badness

coming up!" (sup. ser., vol. 3: *Georgia*, p. 309). A former Georgia slave explained that "I tell my grandchildren sometimes that my brother-in-law would carry us to dance and wouldn' allow us to sleep, we'd dance all night long. We had a good time, us girls!" (vol. 13: *Georgia*, pt. 4, p. 335).

15. Farmers Club, 3 Dec. 1854, 7 Mar. 1857 (SCL); Edgefield *Advertiser*, 2 May 1847.

16. Folk tales that pitted black against white revealed this sense of community. One such Edgefield folktale carried a number of messages to the slaves and revealed problems of slave courting practices that were not shared by whites. Asked about "hoodoo," former Edgefield slave Julia Henderson told the following story:

"Hoodoo don't always work," she laughed. "Dis fellow, he wanted to go to see his sweetheart every night instead of jus' on pass nights. He knowed he would get whupped if he got caught, so he went to the old hoodoo man—de root-worker— and asked him to help him. The root man says 'I'll give a piece of root to chew. When you face the boss-man, you be talkin' and jus' a-spittin', and de boss-man can't put his hand on you.' So he went dere de nex' morning. De boss-man in de blacksmith shop jus' a hammerin' down. He say: 'Tom, what you doing so late?' Tom commence a-spitting. 'Tom, what you doin' so late?' Tom kept on a-spittin'. De boss-man light in on him, and mos' beat him to death! Tom thow'ed dat root jus' as far as he could and when he met de old hoodoo man, he give him a good cussin', cause de hoodoo wouldn't work!"

The white interviewer was unaware of some of the message of the Edgefield folktale. The slave, even with the aid of magic, should not have confronted the white owner. There was also, as in many other stories in the slave narratives, evidence of a slave community. A slave owned by one person is in love with a slave owned by another. Overcoming the restrictions on the movement of slaves required ingenuity. The slave went to other slaves within the community for help. The ardent courter, for example, did not go to the master and ask for extra passes. The white man beat the slave, but the slave in turn only cursed his fellow slave, the old hoodoo man (Rawick, *American Slave*, sup. ser., vol. 3: *Georgia*, p. 319). Throughout the slave narratives were similar folktales, beliefs, and superstitions that were shared across regional boundaries. See Levine, *Black Culture*.

17. McClendon, "History of Pottersville"; Pottersville *Hive*, Apr. 1981 and Aug. 1981.

18. Brooks, "Priority of Silver Bluff"; Raboteau, *Slave Religion*, pp. 139–43; Rawick, *American Slave*, vol. 13: *Georgia*, pt. 3, p. 124.

19. Rainsford Diary, between entries of 14 and 29 June 1833, Rainsford Papers (FP); Brookes, *Defence of Slavery*, pp. 17–18.

20. There has been long-standing debate among scholars about the function of religion. Scholars such as E. Franklin Frazier and Benjamin E. Mays emphasized the compensatory function of the black church during slavery and in the post-bellum years. Reflecting Karl Marx's contention that religion was an opiate, these black scholars emphasized the church's other-worldly orientation and its teaching of biblical scriptures that stressed the obedience of the servant to the master. According to these scholars, the church kept the slaves, and after the Civil War the freedmen, humble and submissive. See Frazier, *Negro Church*; Woodson, *History of Negro Church*; Mays, *Negro's God*; Mays and Nicholson, *Negro's Church*.

21. Farmers Club, 4 Sept. 1849 (SCL). On 29 Oct. 1831 prominent Augusta attorney Henry H. Cumming wrote to his wife, Julia, about a slave Rachel, who had run away and been punished. Cumming noted that Rachel had asked permission to join the Methodist church, and he implied that her joining the church would solve the problem of her running away. See also 4 May 1829, both in Hammond, Bryan, Cumming Papers (SCL).

22. Rawick, *American Slave*, sup. ser., vol. 4: *Georgia*, pp. 660 and 551.

23. Ibid. vol. 2: *South Carolina*, pt. 1, p. 185; vol. 11: *Arkansas*, pt. 7, p. 231.

24. Examples throughout the records of the various Edgefield Baptist churches. For example, see Horn's Creek Baptist Church Records, July 1838, Oct. 1841, Apr. and June 1853, Dec. 1862, Big Stevens Creek Church Records, July, Nov., Dec. 1843, Dec. 1847, Jan. 1854, Sept. 1858, Edgefield Village Baptist Church Records, 2 July and 3 Sept. 1825, Mar. and Sept. 1829, Dry Creek Baptist Church Records, 28 Feb. 1827, 28 July 1841 (all in BHC); Woodson et al., *History of Edgefield Baptist Association*, pp. 170, 324.

25. On obtaining his plantation, Hammond got the following advice: "Raise [sic] their church to the ground—keep them from fanaticism for God sake as well as for your own" (James L. Clark to Hammond, 19 Dec. 1831, Hammond Papers [LC] and in Tucker "James Hammond," p. 89). See Faust, "Culture, Conflict, and Community," pp. 84–85, where she describes Hammond's struggles with black religion so well. See also, Hammond, Plantation Diary, 8, 15 and 16 Dec. 1831, 11 May 1832, 3 May 1835, 6 Apr. and 16 Oct. 1845, 14 Jan. 1851, J. H. Hammond Papers (SCL).

26. Farmers Club, 3 Dec. 1854 (SCL).

27. Rawick, *American Slave*, sup. ser., vol. 4: *Georgia*, p. 435.

28. Nicholson, *Brief Sketch*, p. 28.

29. Big Stevens Creek, Oct. 1819 (BHC).

30. Hammond, Plantation Diary, 26 Dec. 1847, J. H. Hammond Papers (SCL); Pickens, Plantation Record Book, pp. 60–61, 1839 Rules; Pickens Papers (DU); Rawick, *American Slave*, vol. 3: *South Carolina*, pt. 4, p. 72, and vol. 3: *South Carolina*, pt. 3, pp. 285–86, and *Georgia*, pt. 4, p. 73; Farmers Club, 3 Dec. 1864. (SCL).

31. Raboteau, *Slave Religion*; Levine, *Black Culture*, esp. pp. 3–80, 136–89; Genovese, *Roll, Jordan, Roll*, pp. 5–7, 148, 161–284, 288–89, 364–65, 608, 625, 659–60.

32. Rawick, *American Slave*, vol. 3: *South Carolina*, pt. 3, pp. 205–7. Moore was from near Edgefield.

33. Plantation Records, Apr. 1854, Apr. 1858, June 1858, M. Luke Bonham Papers (SCL); Plantation Records, Oct. 1853, Hughes Papers (SHC). This occurs throughout the Edgefield Baptist Church Records, for example, see Horn's Creek Baptist Church Records, Oct. 1853 and June 1859 (BHC).

34. Plantation Record Book, slave lists for 1839, 1840, 1841, 1843 ("in families"), 1844, 1847, 1848, 1849, 1850, 1852, 1853, 1857, 1860, 1864, pp. 3, 5, 7, 9, 11–39, 44, 49, 51, 53, 57, 73–75, 121–44, 171–73, 181, 349–53, Pickens Papers (DU); Plantation Diary, 8 Dec. 1831 and the birth and death registers, Plantation Journal, Silver Bluff Plantation Slave Lists, 1843, 1845, 1853, 1863, "Names of Negroes on Silver Bluff Plantation the 1 Jan. 1863, in families" (ms. in Hammond Land and Slave Papers), "Silver Bluff, Cathwood, Cowden, and Redcliffe," birth and death reg-

isters, ms., 1856–87, all in J. H. Hammond Papers (SCL); "List of Negroes 1846" and "The Number of Negroes and Each Family, Jan. 1, 1856," Hammond Papers (LC); Faust, *James Hammond*, pp. 71, 76, 88; Whitfield Brooks Diaries, inside covers and pp. 1–2 for 1843 and not paginated, 1852 entry, Whitfield Brooks Papers (FP); Plantation Records, McKie Papers (DU); Plantation Books, 1838, 1844–49, 1854–64, Talbert Papers (SCL); List of slaves, n.d., 4 pp., P. M. Butler Papers (SCL); Plantation Records, Perrin Family Papers (SHC).

35. Gutman, *Black Family*, described both the predominant two-parent marriage pattern as well as the pattern of children born out of wedlock. Having children prior to marriage is still an accepted means to prove fertility in some peasant cultures. The records of Edgefield's wealthiest slaveowners yielded glimpses of the white master's views of his slaves' living arrangements and insight into how slaves created their family arrangements. Although this information was strictly from the owner's point of view, voluminous slave narratives reaffirm that slaves lived in families that were male headed. Illegitimacy, hard to determine for slaves, was based on one of the following criteria: 1. the father listed for a child is listed as the husband of a slave other than the slave mother; 2. the father was listed as white; 3. no man was listed as the father and the mother was listed in the slaveowner's listing as without a mate.

36. Whitfield Brooks Diaries, inside covers and pp. 1–2 for 1843 and not paginated, 1852 entry, Whitfield Brooks Papers (FP).

37. Plantation Record Book, slave lists for 1839, 1840, 1841, 1843 ("in families"), 1844, 1847, 1848, 1849, 1850, 1852, 1853, 1854, 1857, 1860, 1864, pp. 3, 5, 7, 9, 11–39, 44, 49, 51, 53, 57, 73–75, 121–51, 171–73, 181, 349–53, Pickens Papers (DU).

38. Plantation Diary, 8 Dec. 1831 and the birth and death registers, Plantation Journal, Silver Bluff Plantation Slave Lists, 1843, 1845, 1853, 1863, "Names of Negroes on Silver Bluff Plantation the 1 Jan. 1863, in families" (ms. in Hammond Land and Slave Papers), "Silver Bluff, Cathwood, Cowden, and Redcliffe," birth and death registers, ms., 1856–87, all in J. H. Hammond Papers (SCL); "List of Negroes 1846" and "The Number of Negroes and Each Family, Jan. 1, 1856," Hammond Papers (LC); Faust, *James Hammond*, pp. 71, 76, 88; Faust, *Sacred Circle*, p. 207. Tucker, "James Hammond," pp. 65–68, 79–116, 156–74, 191–218, 298–319, 361–408; Bleser, *Hammonds of Redcliffe*, pp. 3–18.

39. See note above; Faust, *James Hammond*, pp. 83–86. I have looked at the records, but have relied on Faust's careful analysis of Hammond's slaves' marriage patterns. Premarital pregnancy was assumed if the father was not listed or if the father listed did not have a stable relationship with the mother. The high separation rate and its significance is discussed below in chapter 7.

40. Plantation Diary, "Rules," J. H. Hammond Papers (SCL); Rose, *Documentary History*, pp. 345–54; Faust, *James Hammond*, p. 85; Plantation Record Book, "General Directions as to Treatment of Negroes," pp. 60–61 and 20, Pickens Papers (DU).

41. Plantation Record Book, "General Directions as to Treatment of Negroes," pp. 21–23, 60–61, Pickens Papers (DU); Rawick, *American Slave*, vol. 10: *Arkansas*, pt. 6, pp. 103–5, and vol. 12: *Georgia*, pt. 2, p. 61.

42. Rawick, *American Slave*, vol. 3: *South Carolina*, pt. 4, pp. 71–74; vol 2: *South Carolina*, pt. 2, p. 2; vol. 12: *Georgia*, pt. 2, pp. 61–63. Pickens allowed

slaves to raise their own hogs. See Plantation Record Book, pp. 145–51, Pickens Papers (DU); See also Plantation Record, 26 Dec. 1853, "List of Negro crops of cotton and corn," Perrin Family Papers (SHC).

43. Rawick, *American Slave*, vol. 17: *Florida*, pp. 47–52, and vol. 13: *Georgia*, pt. 3, p. 234. See also p. 224 for the following: directly across the Savannah River from Edgefield, a former slave remembered that on her plantation at Augusta, "every slave family had de garden patch, and chickens. Marster buy eggs and chickens fum us at market prices." These slaves could even sell their excess eggs for cash to their owners.

44. Ibid., vol. 13: *Georgia*, pt. 3, pp. 233–35; vol. 3: *South Carolina*, pt. 4, pp. 71–74; vol. 2: *South Carolina*, pt. 2, p. 215; for neighboring slaves in Laurens and Newberry see vol. 2: *South Carolina*, pp. 316 and 14. In neighboring Laurens County, a former slave woman who had a "Mean Master" nevertheless reported that "we had plenty to eat like fat meat, turnip, cabbages, cornbread, milk and pot liquor." Pot liquor is the water and juice that cooks out of greens such as turnips, cabbages, and collards. It has a strong taste usually flavored by the fatmeat that was cooked in the pot with the vegetable. "The men hunted some squirrels, rabbits, possums, and birds." Former slaves who lived in Newberry District, across the Saluda River from Edgefield, before the Civil War testified to the hunting and fishing they did as slaves. Moses Davenport remembered that "all that part of the country was good for hunting. The deer, fox, and wild turkey . . . were abundant. Fishing in the rivers was much done. They fished with hooks on old-time canes. They had fish baskets, made of wooden splits; with an opening at the end like the wire baskets now used. If they were set anytime, day or night, a few hours afterwards would be soon enough time to catch some fish."

45. Ibid., sup. ser., vol 3: *Georgia*, pp. 319–23. See Farmers Club, 13 Apr. 1847 (SCL). Hammond Plantation Diary, 18 Dec. 1833, 9 Jan. 1845, 14 Mar. 1846, Hammond Papers (SCL); Faust, "Culture, Conflict, and Community," p. 88; Rainsford Diary, 9 Aug. 1834, Rainsford Papers (FP).

46. The most elegant and moving account of the strengths and resources of the slave family is, of course, Gutman, *Black Family*. See also, Blassingame, *Slave Community*, pp. 77–103. An excellent survey of what former slaves felt about the family is Escott, *Slavery Remembered*, pp. 46–51, 94, 138–39, 144, 148–49. Genovese, *Roll, Jordan, Roll*, pp. 451–58, 482–523, presents more of a mixed view of the strengths and problems of the slave family.

47. Rawick, *American Slave*, vol. 13: *Georgia*, pp. 315–16; sup. ser., vol. 4: *Georgia*, pt. 2, pp. 439–44 and 665; vol. 10: *Arkansas*, pt. 5, pp. 64–65; vol. 2: *South Carolina*, p. 184.

48. Ibid., sup. ser., vol. 4: *Georgia*, pt. 2, pp. 439–44 and 573; vol. 13: *Georgia*, pt. 3, pp. 233–34. See also vol. 2: *South Carolina*, p. 56, for an ex-slave from Spartanburg who explained that her boyfriend "wanted to marry me then, but father would not let us marry."

49. Whitfield Brooks Diaries, inside covers and pp. 1–2, Whitfield Brooks Papers (FP); Rawick, *American Slave*, vol. 13: *Georgia*, pt. 3, pp. 233–34.

50. Rawick, *American Slave*, vol. 13: *Georgia*, pt. 3, pp. 226–28. Hammond Plantation Diary, "Rules," J. H. Hammond Papers (SCL). See also the published ver-

sion by Rose, *Documentary History*, pp. 345–54; Faust, *James Hammond*, p. 85.

51. Rawick, *American Slave*, vol. 2: *South Carolina*, pt. 2, p. 174. This slave was not from Edgefield.

52. Hammond Plantation Diary, 14 June 1849, J. H. Hammond Papers (SCL).

53. Plantation Diary, "Rules," J. H. Hammond Papers (SCL); Faust, *James Hammond*, pp. 88–89; Rose, *Documentary History*, pp. 345–54; see also Plantation Record Book, "General Directions as to Treatment of Negroes," pp. 60–61, Pickens Papers (DU); and Farmers Club, 9 Oct. 1847 (SCL).

54. Hammond Plantation Diary, 26 Dec. 1840 and 10 May 1844, pp. 217, 295, J. H. Hammond Papers (SCL); Faust, *James Hammond*, p. 89.

55. Rawick, *American Slave*, sup. ser., vol. 4: *Georgia*, pp. 440–41; vol. 10: *Arkansas*, pt. 5, p. 27; sup. ser., vol. 4: *Georgia*, pt. 2, p. 662. See also Farmers Club, 9 Oct. 1847 (SCL).

56. Rawick, *American Slave*, vol. 17: *Florida*, p. 48; vol. 13: *Georgia*, pt. 4, p. 222, and pt. 3, p. 233.

57. Ibid., vol. 3: *South Carolina*, pt. 3, p. 124; vol. 3: *South Carolina*, pt. 4, p. 73.

58. Most of my evidence comes from the slaveowners' lists, and I have only limited independent evidence concerning slave attitudes toward first names and surnames. I was inspired to look for other examples by Drew Faust's discovery, among Hammond's slaves, of a case in which the master had renamed slaves and subsequently the renamed slave's original name reappeared among the children of the renamed slave. F. W. Pickens to M. L. Bonham, 14 Oct. 1859, M. Luke Bonham Papers (SCL); Plantation Record Book, slave lists for 1839, 1840, 1841, 1843 ("in families"), 1844, 1847, 1848, 1849, 1850, 1852, 1853, 1857, 1860, 1864, pp. 3, 5, 7, 9, 11–39, 44, 49, 51, 53, 57, 73–75, 121–44, 171–73, 181, 349–53, Pickens Papers (DU); Faust, *James Hammond*, p. 88, for story of Sam/Wesley.

59. This question of who named slaves and its historic significance is a tricky one, which raises other questions. What choices of names did the slaves have? One can argue that the evidence is against the avoidance of patronyms. Faust analyzed the Hammond slave lists, *James Hammond*, p. 392, Appendix Table 1. She shared an earlier version with me, which motivated me to attempt the same. My 177 names do not include Hammond's slaves.

60. This naming for grandmothers, and in particular maternal grandmothers, may be significant as a minor theme in Afro-American culture. The final chapter of Frazier, *Negro Family*, "In the House of the Mother," was entitled "Granny: The Guardian of the Generations." As part of Frazier's thesis of the matriarchal slave family, he developed the idea that the "Negro grandmother stands . . . as the 'oldest head' in the House of the Mother."

61. In 1850, different surnames totalled 695.

62. Plantation Diary, "Rules," and 26 Dec. 1840, 20 Nov. 1853, J. H. Hammond Papers (SCL); Rose, *Documentary History*, pp. 345–54; Faust, *James Hammond*, p. 85. See also Cornelius, "Slave Marriages."

63. Horn's Creek Baptist Church Records, Oct. 1835 and Aug. 1862 (BHC); Edgefield Village Baptist Church Records, Sept. and Mar. 1829, Apr. 1830, p. 79 (BHC); Woodson et al., *History of Edgefield Baptist Association*, p. 210. On companionate marriage see Degler, *At Odds*.

64. Of the 121 slaveowners who listed no slave houses, 40.5 percent owned only one slave. Only 5 percent owned more than a dozen slaves. Rawick, *American Slave*, vol. 12: *Georgia*, pt. 1, p. 156, and sup. ser., vol. 4: *Georgia*, p. 557.

65. The average was found by dividing the number of slaves owned by the number of slave dwellings of each slaveowner who reported any slave houses. This average is extremely small in demographic terms. Some of the small size is accounted for by the number of slaves who lived in their master's house or who were rented out or married off the plantation. A better test is the average size of slave housing units for the different-sized farms with slave housing. Fogel and Engerman, *Time on Cross*, pp. 114–15 and fig. 35, found an average of "5.2 slaves per house on large plantations." Edgefield was more consistent with their finding when the size of slaveholding was considered.

Number of Slaves	Mean Number of Slaves per House	Standard Deviation	N
1	1.0	0.11	159
2–5	3.0	1.2	363
6–9	4.7	2.0	283
10–14	5.2	2.3	208
15–19	5.4	2.6	127
20–29	5.7	3.4	173
30–49	5.4	2.7	127
50–99	5.2	1.2	76
100+	5.4	1.0	10
Total	4.2	2.5	1,526

Source: Edgefield Data Base.

66. Rawick, *American Slave*, vol. 3: *South Carolina*, pt. 3, p. 167, and vol. 2: *South Carolina*, pt. 2, p. 231. These slaves were not from Edgefield. David Smith to Rev. Iveson L. Brookes, 10 Jan. 1852, Brookes Papers (SCL).

67. Rawick, *American Slave*, vol. 13: *Georgia*, pt. 3, pp. 233–35.

68. Nicholson, *Brief Sketch*. Harris, "Slaveholding Republic," tells much about both the slave and white community. He has generously shared his findings. Escott, *Slavery Remembered*, pp. 50–52, found that 27.5 percent of slaves who reported marriages in the ex-slave narratives had married off the plantation.

69. Edgefield *Advertiser*, 10 Aug. 1854; Plantation Record Book, "General Directions as to Treatment of Negroes," pp. 60–61, Pickens Papers (DU); Plantation Diary, "Rules," J. H. Hammond Papers (SCL); Faust, *James Hammond*, pp. 85–86; Rose, *Documentary History*, pp. 345–54; Farmers Club, 7 Aug 1847, p. 36 (SCL). Faust has suggested to me that Hammond may have made exceptions.

70. Rawick, *American Slave*, vol. 2: *South Carolina*, pp. 251–52; sup. ser., vol. 3: *Georgia*, p. 233. Davis was not from Edgefield.

71. Ibid., vol. 2: *South Carolina*, pt. 1, p. 68. Boulware was not from Edgefield.

72. Ibid., sup. ser., vol. 4: *Georgia*, p. 556.

73. Ibid., vol. 13: *Georgia*, pt. 4, pp. 221, 224–25.

74. Ibid., sup. ser., vol. 3: *Georgia*, pp. 305–7. It could also indicate that the woman never married.

75. F. W. Pickens to M. L. Bonham, 14 Oct. 1859, M. Luke Bonham Papers (SCL); Rawick, *American Slave*, sup. ser., vol. 4: *Georgia*, p. 441. Harry Hammond to Emily C. Hammond, 1 May, 30 June, and 17 July 1864, Hammond, Bryan, Cumming Papers (SCL); Julia B. Cumming to Emily C. Hammond reported that the servant Lucius had been sent to Pensacola to "be an attendant upon all of the Boys." Simkins, "Paris Simkins," reported an Edgefield slave's point of view in being taken off to the Civil War. Maria Bryan to Julia B. Cumming, 15 June 1860, requested she send a slave to help cut out clothes (Hammond, Bryan, Cumming Papers [SCL]). See also Hammond Diary, 16 May 1836, Hammond Papers (LC), and "Instructions from J. H. H. on Leaving for Europe, 1836," Hammond Papers (SCL); Tucker, "James Hammond," p. 262.

76. Maria Bryan Harford to Julia B. Cumming, 1 May 1838, Hammond, Bryan, Cumming Papers (SCL).

77. Rawick, *American Slave*, vol. 10: *Arkansas*, pt. 5, p. 78. See also Maria Bryan Harford to Julia B. Cumming, 18 Jan. 1838 and 29 Dec. 1836, Hammond, Bryan, Cumming Papers (SCL). The 1860 manuscript slave census distinguished those slaves who were hired to someone from those who were owned. James Henry Hammond, 14 and 23 Mar. and 14 Apr. 1830, J. H. Hammond Papers (SCL); Tucker, "James Hammond," p. 37; Edgefield *Advertiser*, 20 Nov. 1851. See also F. W. Pickens to Col. J. Edward Calhoun, 26 Oct. 1851 and 17 Jan. 1852, J. E. Calhoun Papers (SCL). Farmers Club, 2 May 1857 (SCL). The Millers were not from Edgefield.

78. Rawick, *American Slave*, vol. 13: *Georgia*, pt. 4, p. 222; vol. 10: *Arkansas*, pt. 5, p. 335. Anonymous to James H. Hammond, 20 Mar. 1860, James H. Hammond to Alexander H. Stephens, 19 Apr. 1860, Stephens Papers (LC).

79. J. C. Calhoun to T. G. Clemson, 27 Oct. 1845, Calhoun Papers (CU); also in Dew, "Disciplining Slave Ironworkers," p. 393; Thomas H. Pope to N. L. Griffin, 20 Dec. 1845, Griffin Papers (SCL).

80. Rawick, *American Slave*, vol. 10: *Arkansas*, pt. 5, pp. 27–29; sup. ser., vol. 4: *Georgia*, p. 306; vol. 12: *Georgia*, pt. 2, p. 63; vol. 13: *Georgia*, pt. 4, p. 224. "Confederate Conscription of Slaves," L. C. Grant papers (GSA). The slave who accompanied Whitfield Butler Brooks to the Mexican War and returned the young soldier's body was effectively (not legally) made free by Whitfield Brooks upon his return. See also, Simkins, "Paris Simkins"; Tucker, "James Hammond," pp. 479–80; Edgefield *Advertiser*, 3 Apr. 1865.

81. Disputes over the effects of the slave trade on families have focused on long-distance sales in the westward migration. Large numbers of slaves, however, were sold and separated from their families locally. These short-distance sales furthered the negative impacts on the slave family's relationships. Escott, *Slavery Remembered*, p. 46, found about a fifth of former slaves interviewed in the ex-slave narratives had experienced family separations.

82. Brookes, *Defence of Slavery*, p. 10.

83. Rawick, *American Slave*, sup. ser., vol. 4: *Georgia*, p. 440. F. W. Pickens to M. L. Bonham, 14 Apr. 1860, M. Luke Bonham Papers (SCL); Plantation Record Book, slave list for 1839, pp. 3, 5, 7, 9, and Oct. 1843, Pickens Papers (DU); Whit-

field Brooks Diaries, inside covers and pp. 1–2 for 1843 list, Whitfield Brooks Papers (FP).

84. Plantation Record Book, Dec. 1846, Pickens Papers (DU); see also purchase and sale slips of slaves by William Oliphant, 1808–32, Oliphant Papers (SCL).

85. Plantation Record Book, Sept. 1838, Pickens Papers (DU). Estate of Mrs. Mary Carroll, J. P. Carroll, Exec., 23 Aug. 1861, box 59, package 2451, Edgefield County Probate Records (ECH).

86. Petitions of Benjamin Busbee, 1810, 1 Jan. 1815, 29 Nov. 1815, 5 Dec. 1815, Benjamin and John Ryan, 12 Dec. 1816, 1820, 15 Nov. 1823, and Dec. 1823, 1824, Petitions to the General Assembly, Legislative Papers (SCDAH); Columbia *Daily Telegraph*, 6 Dec. 1847, p. 2; S. C., General Assembly, *House Journal*, 1824, p. 72; S. C., General Assembly, *House Journal*, 1847, pp. 118, 169. See also Bradley, "Slave Manumission," pp. 11, 19–28, 40–42, 48, 50–51, 67, 71–73, 96; County Wills, Edgefield County, I, pp. 238–39; Alexander Downer's will, amended 20 Nov. 1820, is reproduced in Dunbar, "History of Education," pp. 18–23.

87. Plantation Record Book, Sept. and Dec. 1838, Pickens Papers (DU); Plantation Diary, 1 July 1834, 8 July 1835, 23 Jan. and 31 May 1845, J. H. Hammond Papers (SCL); Faust, *James Hammond*, p. 85; Whitfield Brooks Diaries, inside covers and pp. 1–2 for 1843, not paginated, 1852 entry, and various receipts of sales for slaves, Whitfield Brooks Papers (FP); Rawick, *American Slave*, vol. 13: *Georgia*, pt. 3, pp. 226–28.

88. Rainsford Diary, 8 Jan. 1834, p. 14, Rainsford Papers (FP).

89. Advertisement, 20 Jan. 1819, Schultz Papers (SCL).

90. Almost any issue of any Edgefield antebellum newspaper carried advertisements for the sale of slaves. See, for example, the administrator's sale for N. I. Griffin or the trustee's sale for Richard Burton, Edgefield *Advertiser*, 28 Nov. 1855 and 27 Jan. 1858. Henry Cumming to Julia B. Cumming, 17 Jan. 1835, Agreement between James Henry Hammond and Pierce Mason Butler in 1835, Thomas N. Gadsen to James Henry Hammond, 14 Apr. 1843, all in Hammond, Bryan, Cumming Papers (SCL).

91. For example, see estate sale of Eliza Simkins (n. 84) and Mr. Coleman (n. 88) above. Also, see C. W. DuBose to Henry H. Cumming, 9 Dec. 1862, where he is advised to "come and receive the negroes bequeathed to you"; if not, the slaves "will be unemployed and unprovided for"; Maria Bryan Harford to Julia B. Cumming, Dec. 1836, on their father shipping slaves to Alabama, both in Hammond, Bryan, Cumming Papers (SCL); Hammond Plantation Diary, 28 Nov. and 10 Dec. 1839, J. H. Hammond Papers (SCL); Tucker "James Hammond," p. 305.

92. Maria Bryan to Julia Bryan Cumming, 8 Feb. 1827, Hammond, Bryan, Cumming Papers (SCL). Rawick, *American Slave*, vol. 12: *Georgia*, pt. 1, pp. 155–59, and sup. ser., vol. 4: *Georgia*, p. 592.

93. Rawick, *American Slave*, sup. ser., vol. 4: *Georgia*, pp. 439–41.

94. "Butler Family Memoirs," in Lipscomb Bonham Papers (SCL); Butler, *Memoirs General William Butler*, pp. 29–30; Chapman, *History of Edgefield*, p. 45.

95. John C. Calhoun to T. G. Clemson, 13 Dec. 1845, Thomas Green Clemson to John C. Calhoun, Sept. 1845 and 27 Mar. 1846, Calhoun Papers (CU); Lander, *Calhoun Family*, pp. 135–36.

96. Henry H. Cumming to Julia B. Cumming, 22 May 1834 and 14 Nov. 1833,

Maria Bryan Harford to Julia B. Cumming, 9 Apr. 1839 and 10 May 1841 (see also 26–27 Dec., in which Maria tells Julia that their father has found his slave George drunk and "said if any one would give what he had paid for him, he would sell him"; Maria added that the slave was scolded by his wife Patsy), Hammond, Bryan, Cumming Papers (SCL).

97. See Bills of Sale in the Hammond, Bryan, Cumming Papers (SCL). Also see Faust, *Sacred Circle*, p. 38, on Hammond's profiting on sales and acquiring property during the depressions of 1840 and 1830. See same in F. W. Pickens Papers (FP). Edmunds, "Politics of Destruction," does a remarkable job in tracing Pickens's land acquisitions.

98. Tillman, "Childhood Days," p. 18; Harry Hammond to James Henry Hammond, 29 and 30 June 1859, Hammond, Bryan, Cumming Papers (SCL); Quotation on Hammond from Faust, "Culture, Class, Conflict," p. 92. The decade of the 1850s was a time when slaveowners were conscious of the "wrong" in selling slaves. Also, slaveowners articulated the belief that the longer they had slaves, the greater their obligation not to sell them. William C. Preston advised James Hammond in the dispute on the settlement of his wife's possessions at their marriage that Hammond should settle upon fifty slaves being given to his wife; that would "make your triumph complete. Being of personal property—the control will always be in your hands. You can sell when you please by substituting others in the place of those sold" (Preston to Hammond, 28 Jan. 1832, and Hammond to John W. Clark, 26 Aug. 1831, both in Letterpress Book, 1831–33). Plantation Records, 13 Dec. 1831, 11, 15, 30 May, 8, 16, 17 June 1833, 14 Mar. 1834; J. H. Hammond Plantation Diary, 19 Feb., 19 Sept., and 5 Nov. 1844, all in J. H. Hammond Papers (SCL); Tucker, "James Hammond," pp. 83, 88, 128, 212; Faust, *James Hammond*, pp. 85, 97.

99. Rawick, *American Slave*, vol. 14: *Georgia*, pt. 2, pp. 598–99; vol. 2: *South Carolina*, p. 62; sup. ser., vol. 11: *North and South Carolina*, p. 317; vol. 2: *South Carolina*, pt. 1, p. 188; vol. 13: *Georgia*, pt. 4, p. 343; sup. ser., vol. 4: *Georgia*, pt. 2, p. 594. Most of the WPA slave narratives were written down by southern white interviewers who gave the best possible picture of the "beneficent institution." But even the most laundered reports told heart-wrenching stories of the separation of families. The last two former slaves cited, Eugene Smith and Laura Stewart, were disputing a newspaper article by a local white lady, which denied slaves had been sold in Augusta. It took a great deal of courage to retort to white interviewers "in spite of what white ladies say in de papers." The slave quarters building was still standing in Hamburg in 1937 when the former slaves were interviewed. One former slave remembered it as "the old brick building . . . all de colored people whut gonner be sold was kept dere."

100. Ibid., vol. 13: *Georgia*, pt. 4, p. 233.

101. Ibid., sup. ser., vol. 4: *Georgia*, pt. 2, p. 373.

102. Butler, *Descendants of Butler*; Rawick, *American Slave*, sup. ser., vol. 4: *Georgia*, pt. 3, p. 434, and vol. 10: *Arkansas*, pt. 6, p. 105.

103. Ibid., vol. 2: *South Carolina*, pt. 1, pp. 187–89; sup. ser., vol. 3: *Georgia*, pt. 1, p. 233.

104. Rainsford Diary, 14 Feb. 1838, Rainsford Papers (FP). For an account given by a former slave from South Carolina who was stolen as a child see Rawick, *American Slave*, vol. 9: *Arkansas*, pt. 3, p. 170.

105. Gutman, *Black Family*, has brilliantly described the adaptive patterns that were in action in antebellum Edgefield, including plantation-based obligations. Some implications of these adaptive patterns are discussed in the remainder of the book.

106. Thomas Green Clemson to John C. Calhoun, Sept. 1845, John C. Calhoun to Thomas Green Clemson, 13 Dec. 1845, both in Calhoun Papers (CU).

107. For Edgefield population breakdown, see Burton, "Ungrateful Servants," pp. 388–89.

108. See discussion in Farmers Club, Aug. 1847 (SCL); Dennett, *South as It Is*, pp. 246–47; see also Rainsford Diary, 11 Sept. and 29 Nov. 1834, 14 and 21 Feb. 1835, pp. 17, 19–20, Rainsford Papers (FP).

109. Plantation Diary, 8 Dec. 1831 and 1 Jan. 1832, J. H. Hammond Papers (SCL); Faust, *James Hammond*, p. 71.

110. Thompson, "African Influence," esp. pp. 133–35; Vlach, *Afro-American Tradition*, pp. 77–85; Pottersville *Hive*, Aug. 1981.

111. J. H. Hammond to William Gilmore Simms, 14 Jan. 1848, Hammond Papers (LC); Rawick, *American Slave*, sup. ser., vol. 3: *Georgia*, pt. 1, p. 232. Soon after taking over the plantation, Hammond recorded that he "had Jane flogged" in support of his slave driver. In 1834 he wrote that he had the slave driver "flogged . . . slightly. Left him unable to walk scarcely." Hammond's biographer reported that "one man died partially as a result of being flogged. . . . He died, ironically, on Independence Day." According to Tucker, Hammond did not do the whipping, and when he saw the slave who had starved and taken cold while running away from the plantation, he ordered the slave to be sent to bed, but too late. Plantation Records, 1831–55, 10 Dec. 1831 and 13, 17 Feb. 1834, J. H. Hammond Papers (SCL); Tucker, "James Hammond," pp. 211–12.

112. Rawick, *American Slave*, vol. 8: *Arkansas*, pt. 1, pp. 303–7.

113. Statistics of different-sized farms from Escott, *Slavery Remembered*, see esp. Tables 2.10 and 2.12, pp. 56–57; Rawick, *American Slave*, vol. 11: *Arkansas*, pt. 7, p. 229, and sup. ser., vol. 4: *Georgia*, pp. 433–38.

114. Ibid., sup. ser., vol. 4: *Georgia*, pt. 2, pp. 349–51.

115. The violence of slavery caused some of the guilt that plagued Southerners. Maria Bryan wrote to Julia Bryan Cumming, 27 Jan. 1827, that the slave Jenny had come in with her face swollen and explained further that she had been beaten for not spinning enough. Maria exclaimed: "Oh! How great an evil is slavery" (Hammond, Bryan, Cumming Papers [SCL]). See the careful instructions that planters wrote out for overseers and others in governing slaves about the number and intensity of lashes. Plantation Record Book, pp. 60–61, Pickens Papers (DU); Agreement between A. Ramsay and F. W. Pickens, 18 Feb. 1864, F. W. Pickens Papers (SCL); Plantation Diary, "Rules," J. H. Hammond Papers (SCL); Rose, *Documentary History*, p. 354; Faust, *James Hammond*, p. 100; "Agreement between D. F. Hollingsworth and M. L. Palmer," 13 Jan. 1857, Hollingsworth Papers (DU); George Onie to Iveson L. Brookes, 28 Sept. 1847, Brookes Papers (SHC). See discussion in Farmers Club, 9 Oct. 1847 (SCL); Edgefield *Advertiser*, 2 May 1849; Rawick, *American Slave*, sup. ser., vol. 4: *Georgia*, p. 422; vol. 13: *Georgia*, pt. 3, p. 235; sup. ser., vol. 4: *Georgia*, p. 435; vol. 10: *Arkansas*, pt. 6, p. 1051; sup. ser., vol. 3: *Georgia*, p. 321; sup. ser., vol. 4: *Georgia*, pt. 2, p. 576, and vol. 3: *Georgia*, p. 307; vol. 2: *South Carolina*, pt. 2, pp. 215, 100.

116. Ibid., vol. 3: *South Carolina*, pt. 4, p. 171; sup. ser., vol. 3: *Georgia*, pp. 319, 321; vol. 10: *Arkansas*, pt. 5, p. 27.

117. I appreciate the use of the family pictures and especially appreciate the many hours that the family of Paris Simkins spent with me. Simkins's grandson, Charles Bailey, Sr., and his wife have been especially helpful. For a written version of the above story see Simkins, "Paris Simkins," which was written by Simkins's children about the time of his death in 1930. The topic of illicit love between master and slave has generally received only sensational attention. There has been little serious work among historians except in the celebrated case of Thomas Jefferson and Sally Hemings. The dallying of slave masters in the quarters is more a comment on the quality of upper-class white family life than an indictment of the Afro-American family. It is ironic that some of the same men who had slave mistresses left letters and diaries that contain drippingly romantic tributes to their wives. On Jefferson and Hemings see Brodie, *Thomas Jefferson*; Beloff, "Sally Hemings Affair," pp. 52–56; Fleming, *Man from Monticello*; Graham, "Thomas Jefferson and Sally Hemings"; Jordan, *White Over Black*, pp. 464–79; Miller, *Wolf by Ears*.

118. Brookes, "Defence of South," p. 18.

119. F. W. Pickens to M. L. Bonham, 14 Oct. 1859, M. Luke Bonham Papers (SCL); Coulter, *Negro Legislators*, pp. 37, 185.

120. Slave Bill of Sales in Hammond, Bryan, Cumming Papers (SCL); James Henry Hammond to Harry Hammond, 19 Feb. 1856, J. H. Hammond Papers (SCL).

121. Chesnut, *Diary from Dixie*, pp. 21–22. Chesnut was cousin to Edgefield's Joseph Abney's wife.

122. Mays, *Born to Rebel*, pp. 30–32.

123. Taken from an index of probability presented by Steckel, "Miscegenation."

124. Big Stevens Creek Church Records, Apr. 1834 and June 1835 (BHC).

125. Plantation Record Book, slave lists for 1839, 1840, 1841, 1843 ("in families"), 1844, 1847, 1848, 1849, 1850, 1852, 1853, 1857, 1860, 1864, pp. 3, 5, 7, 9, 11–39, 44, 49, 51, 53, 57, 73–75, 121–44, 171–73, 181, 349–53, Pickens Papers (DU); Plantation Diary, 8 Dec. 1831 and the birth and death registers, Plantation Journal, Silver Bluff Plantation Slave Lists, 1843, 1845, 1853, 1863, "Names of Negroes on Silver Bluff Plantation the 1 Jan. 1863, in families" (ms. in Hammond Land and Slave Papers); "Silver Bluff, Cathwood, Cowden, and Redcliffe," birth and death registers, ms., 1856–87, all in J. H. Hammond Papers (SCL); "List of Negroes 1846" and "The Number of Negroes and Each Family, Jan. 1, 1856," Hammond Papers (LC). Some of these whites are identifiable as whites hired as farm laborers by the planters. See Faust, *James Hammond*, pp. 86–87; Whitfield Brooks Diaries, inside covers and pp. 1–2 for 1843 and not paginated, 1852 entry, Whitfield Brooks Papers (FP); Plantation Records, McKie Papers (DU); Plantation Books, 1838, 1844–49, 1854–64, Talbert Papers (SCL); List of slaves, n.d., 4 pp., P. M. Butler Papers (SCL); Plantation Records, Perrin Family Papers (SHC); Rawick, *American Slave*, vol. 13: *Georgia*, pt. 4, p. 227; sup. ser., vol. 4: *Georgia*, pp. 436–37.

126. Rawick, *American Slave*, vol. 8: *Arkansas*, pt. 1, pp. 303–7.

127. Ibid., vol. 10: *Arkansas*, pt. 6, p. 103.

128. Woodson et al., *History of Edgefield Baptist Association*, p. 221.

129. Edgefield District, Grand Jury Presentment, 5 Oct., 1 Nov. 1859, Legislative Papers (SCDAH); James Henry Hammond to William Gilmore Simms, 15 Apr. 1862,

Hammond Papers (SCL) and Simms to Hammond, 15 Dec. 1852, Hammond Papers (LC); Maria Bryan to Julia B. Cumming, 11 Mar. 1831, Hammond, Bryan, Cumming Papers (SCL).

Chapter 5

1. Berlin, *Slaves without Masters*, pp. 35–36; Wallace, *South Carolina*, p. 442; Wikramanayake, *World in Shadow*, pp. 10–13, 34–36, 43–44, 114–15, 168, 176. Scholars have argued that the preponderance of mulattoes in the free population is reason to believe that most of the free black population came from the freeing of mulatto children by their white fathers. In Edgefield District in 1850, 55.1 percent of all free blacks were listed in the manuscript census population returns as mulatto. By 1860, 72.6 percent of all free blacks were mulatto, but only 7.5 percent of the slaves. The overwhelming percentage of mulattoes in the free black population is prima facie evidence of close association, at the very least of past sexual relationships, between whites and blacks in antebellum Edgefield District (Sydnor, "Free Negro in Mississippi"; Franklin, *Slavery to Freedom*, pp. 215–17). Part of the explanation for the small percentage of mulattoes in the slave population was the manner in which the census enumerator solicited data. He visited all the households that had free blacks in them, just as he did every household that had only whites. At plantations, however, he never saw the slaves and only asked an overseer or slaveowner for a description of the slaves.

Manumission was prohibited in 1820. In Edgefield District in 1850, 209 free blacks, 73.3 percent of the free black population, were under 30 years of age, and in 1860, 143 free blacks, 83.2 percent of the free black population, were under 40 years of age and thus second generation —presumably the natural increase of those blacks freed before the prohibition.

2. Columbia *Daily Telegraph*, 6 Dec. 1847, p. 2; S.C., General Assembly (House), *Journal*, 1847, pp. 118, 169. David L. Adams owned only six slaves in 1850 and had $5,000 in land. Between 1820 and 1840 manumission could be granted only by the state legislature. Very few blacks were freed by the state legislature in this twenty-year span. A statute of 1841 forbade the sending of slaves abroad to be freed. After 1840, although manumission was impossible, some masters continued to appeal to the state legislature to free slaves. Even before 1820, records suggest that manumission was difficult. Between 1815 and 1823, six separate petitions were presented to the General Assembly on the behalf of certain slaves by two Edgefield slaveowners and later by their executors. All petitions were denied. See, for example, the petitions on behalf of a slave of Benjamin Busbee dated 1 Jan. 1815, 29 Nov. 1815, and 5 Dec. 1815 and for the slaves of Benjamin Ryan dated 12 Dec. 1816, 15 Nov. 1823, and Dec. 1823. One slave from the Ninety Six District was freed because of his service to the cause of American independence. In petitions to the General Assembly a number of free blacks (although none were located in Edgefield) petitioned to free their relatives. All in petitions to the General Assembly, Legislative Papers (SCDAH); see also Bradley, "Slave Manumission," pp. 3, 5–6, 11, 19–28, 40–42, 50, 67–68, 71–73, 96.

3. Berlin, *Slaves without Masters*, pp. 105, 195–96, 343–80, has an excellent dis-

cussion of why antebellum free blacks remained in the South and on South Carolina's comparatively lenient laws governing free blacks. See Edgefield *Advertiser*, 7 May 1856, for a free black in the North who supposedly wanted to be a slave again in Edgefield. In 1850 free blacks made up 1.2 percent of the district's Afro-American population; in 1860, 0.7 percent. In 1850 they were 0.7 and in 1860, 0.4 percent of the district's aggregate population. E. Franklin Frazier argued that antebellum free blacks transmitted to the masses of emancipated Afro-Americans the idea of the traditional male-headed, two-parent family. Ira Berlin suggested that southern whites developed ideas of how to treat the former slave from their experiences with antebellum free blacks. Frazier, *Free Negro Family* and *Negro Family*, pp. viii, ix, 102, 118, 151–52, 201–2, 362; Berlin, *Slaves without Masters*, especially pp. 246, 302, and n. 31.

4. U.S., Bureau of the Census, *7th (1850) Census*, pp. 340, 338, 339; *8th (1860) Census*, vol. 1., *Population*, p. 452. See table in note 6 for the Edgefield free black population from 1790 to 1860. Edgefield *Advertiser*, 11 July 1860. The tax collector reported three free black deaths and two births in 1859.

5. The mood of the decade was set by Governor Seabrook in his annual message to the state legislature. The message was printed in the Edgefield *Advertiser*, 5 Dec. 1850: "In every community, where the institution of slavery is interwoven with its social system, the public tranquility and safety demands the toleration of only two classes, white men and colored slaves." S.C., General Assembly (House), *Journal*, 1850, p. 23; Brown, *Strain of Violence*, pp. 67–90; Berlin, *Slaves without Masters*.

6. A ferry and a bridge between Hamburg in Edgefield District and Augusta, Georgia, facilitated emigration in both directions. The following table gives some indication of migration patterns between Edgefield and Augusta, as well as of the changes in the free black population in the South Carolina districts that bordered Edgefield.

Free Afro-American Population

	1790	1800	1810	1820	1830	1840	1850	1860
Edgefield District (Hamburg, S.C.)	65	61	151	57	203	294	285 (21)	173 (7)
Richmond County, Ga. (Augusta, Ga.)	39	54	72	110	235	186 (148)	281 (243)	490 (386)
Adjacent S.C. districts	216	362	428	622	769	1376	1056	1569

7. The remarkable free black population of Charleston has received quite a bit of attention. The basis of the most recent scholarly references to free blacks in Charleston is Fitchett, "Free Negro in Charleston," and his earlier articles, "Traditions of Free Negroes," "Origin of Free Negro Population," and "Status of Free Negro." The disproportionate influence of the free black in Charleston on the history of the free black in antebellum South Carolina can be seen in Wikramanayake, *World in Shadow*, and in her dissertation, on which her book is based, "Free Negro." For New Orleans see Berlin, *Slaves without Masters*, pp. 108–32, 172, 174, 231, 262, 376, and Sterkx, *Free Negro in Louisiana*. Michael P. Johnson and James L. Roark are mining the rich collection of free black manuscripts of the wealthy free black Ellison family of Sumter District.

8. Hammond, Plantation Diary, 29 Oct. 1845, Hammond Papers (SCL).

9. Bermingham, "Baptism and Execution of a negro man who killed his wife and thru force of compunction—became his own accuser," Bermingham Diary, 21 May 1852 (SMC).

10. Barnwell, Grand Jury Presentments, 1830, and also in 1860; also see "Report of the Committee on Colored Population," 29 Nov. 1860, in the General Assembly Papers, Legislative Papers (SCDAH); Hindus, *Prison and Plantation*, p. 63 (n. 67), and p. 51 (n. 61); Berlin, *Slaves without Masters*, p. 268 (n. 300). The 1830 petition reads: "Edward Ramsey and Nancy Grubs, Thomas Wodson & Polly Grubs, and Bolan Grubs, and a free negro woman are living in a state of lewdness and fornification [sic] to the great annoyance of the good people of the upperpart of the said District. . . . We believe that the process of this Court ought to issue against the said parties for the very corrupt and abandoned conduct." In 1860 in the same district the jury petitioned against whites "frequently found living in open connection with negro and mulatto women." The General Assembly as usual did nothing about up-country complaints against adultery. The bill was dropped with the comment, "The evil complained of cannot be prevented by legislation."

11. Brookes, *Defence of South* and *Defence of Slavery*.

12. More on towns in chapter 7; see nn. 63–65. See especially "Journal of the Proceedings of the Beech Island Agricultural and Police Society Organized June 28th 1851," pp. 157–62, and 3 Dec. 1854, Farmers Club (SCL). Joel Williamson, *New People*, p. 66, has suggested that this vigilante committee's tightened surveillance probably induced some of the free black outmigration from Edgefield between 1850 and 1860. However, Barnwell District planters were also members of the same Agricultural and Police Society, and the number of free blacks in neighboring Barnwell had doubled in number to 640 by 1860.

13. Woodson, *Free Negro Heads of Families*, found this same pattern of fewer male-headed households in urban than rural areas. Stanley Engerman brought Woodson's findings to my attention.

14. 64.5 percent of all black-headed households and 72.0 percent of all households with blacks in any capacity lived in neighborhoods dominated by the landless. The balance was fairly evenly split between yeoman neighborhoods and wealthy neighborhoods, where $1,000 of real property is taken as the dividing line between these two categories.

15. The pattern of all households with blacks in any capacity is similar to that of household heads in 1860.

16. In 1850 less than four of every ten black-headed households did not live near another household with free blacks. By 1860 this number had increased to three out of every five who did not live near other blacks.

17. Historians generally agree with sociologists that occupation is the best indicator of social status in nineteenth-century American society. See Katz, "Occupational Classification"; Griffin, "Occupational Mobility."

Occupations were originally grouped according to color, literacy, age, family type, wealth, tenure, and other variables. Table 5–2 should guide the reader throughout the essay, but the table is limited in what it can tell about the social structure of antebellum free blacks, since few women, black or white, recorded occupations in 1850 and since some male household heads had no occupation in 1850 or 1860. Although occupation was important, it was only one of several factors that must be investigated to understand the antebellum free black social structure in antebellum Edgefield. For example, the three 1850 landowners were listed as having no occupation.

18. In 1860 the most frequent occupation listed for landowners was "farmer" (four), then two "farming," and one each for "mechanic," "laborer," "governess," "laundress." Three 1860 landowners had no occupation.

19. As late as 1850 some of the least fertile land in Edgefield had still not been granted by the state to anyone, presumably because the sandy, sparsely vegetated land was so poor no one wanted it. Two of the 1850 free black landowners had five hundred dollars real estate (as much or more than half of Edgefield white household heads) and one had property valued at a thousand dollars (as much as two-thirds of Edgefield white household heads). In 1860, their land ranged in value from a meager $40 (as much as or more than 38.3 percent of white household heads) to a mechanic's $1,740 (as much as or more than the 64th percentile of all white household heads).

My earlier conclusions showed a decline in white landowners between 1850 and 1860; this was in error. Eliminating errors from the data set proved that an increase of landownership was shared by black and white alike. Burton, "Anatomy of a Free Black Community," p. 301 and Table 2.

20. Documents signed by the Citizens of Augusta, 23 Feb. 1819, in the Hammond, Bryan, Cumming Papers (SCL).

21. Paten Kerwin, another "farmer" by occupation, owned land but was not a household head and is not included in the discussion above.

22. Three "farmers"—one of those "farming," the "mechanic," and one who had no occupation—cultivated a farm. Paten Kerwin was not listed as a farm operator. Probably this "farmer" worked the land that he and Druscilla Kerwin owned jointly. See discussion below.

A person whose occupation was recorded as "farmer" or "farming" in the population manuscript census is distinct from a farm operator in the agricultural manuscript census. In 1860 only twelve free blacks (eleven household heads) were farm operators in Edgefield District, but twenty free blacks were listed either as "farmer" or "farming" in the population manuscript census returns.

23. The tenants' occupations were one "farmer," three "farming," and two without any gainful occupation.

24. Actually, one tenant, William Quarles, had *no* personal estate. Neither did this twenty-five year old list an occupation, but his father, George Quarles, was one of the most successful free black farmers. George lent the farming animals and implements to his son William in 1859 (the Quarles family was not among the Edgefield free population in 1850). The range of the other tenants' personal property was $50 (compares to as much or more than the 13th percentile of Edgefield 1860 white household heads) to $400 (compares to the 39th percentile of 1860 white household heads). The landowning farm operators ranged from a low range of $317 to $600 (as much as the 46th percentile of Edgefield white household heads) to Martha Ardis's $2,200 (as much as the 58th percentile of Edgefield 1860 white household heads) in personal wealth.

25. John Hope Franklin noted that in North Carolina antebellum free blacks made very good tenants; the white landowners were responsible for the taxes levied on free blacks living on their land, and yet, despite these financial risks, "free Negro tenants

were still living on the land of white landowners" (Franklin, "Free Negro," p. 362; see also his *Free Negro in North Carolina*). Luther Porter Jackson, in studying free blacks from 1830 to 1860, found that tenantry was a means by which they were able to obtain land of their own (Jackson, "Virginia Free Negro," pp. 398, 401). I suspect that this was also the case for free blacks in Edgefield. In North Carolina, Franklin found that the "free Negro farmer, living in the inarticulate and relatively sparsely settled countryside, steadily rose in economic independence and consequently in the respect—somewhat disquieted perhaps, of his fellows" ("Free Negro," p. 363). Jackson, "Virginia Free Negro," p. 437, in finding that 35 percent of the free black heads of families in Virginia owned or rented land in 1860, caused Carter G. Woodson to remark that this economic progress in a rural area was unusual (Woodson, review of *Free Negro Labor* by Jackson, p. 812). But in 1860 nearly half of the free black heads of households in Edgefield District owned or rented land.

Frank Owsley described "tenant farmers whose agricultural production . . . indicated thrift, energy, and self-respect," in *Plain Folk*, p. 8. The only difference in these "plain folks" was that these Edgefield tenants were Afro-Americans.

26. So there would be no confusion, the census enumerator penned the letters FMC beside Martin Wilson's name to indicate for all that the operator of this 89-acre farm was a "free man of color."

27. For the landowners who farmed, only a third of their households were nuclear, half were augmented and one was extended. In contrast, two-thirds of the tenants lived in nuclear households and the others in augmented households.

28. Only the three tenants whose occupations were "farming" lived near other free blacks.

29. Luther Porter Jackson found that in Virginia the "outstanding fact in free Negro rural labor was the preponderance of the farm hand" ("Virginia Free Negro," pp. 395, 437).

30. Perhaps these whites were also the legal guardians of the free blacks, as required by the statute of 1820. According to Wikramanayake, "Free Negro," p. 82, this guardian was less a protector of the black than a guarantor of the free black's good behavior. Only in one instance in 1860 Edgefield District was there a wealthy white household which contained free blacks.

31. These poorer free blacks had a higher proportion of two-parent households than did their poor white neighbors. The high proportion of two-parent families among Edgefield's propertyless laborers also suggests a revision of Frazier's contention that it was the landed antebellum free black who brought the cultural idea of two-parent families into the postbellum South (Frazier, *Negro Family*, pp. viii, ix, 102, 113, 151–52, 201–2, 362).

32. Proportionately, only about a third as many free black households in 1850 had individuals in them with different surnames as did white households.

33. As noted above, the occupation of women was not reported in the 1850 census. In addition, two women who had no occupations listed in the population census were listed in the agricultural census in 1860.

34. In 1850 white women represented 12 percent of all white owners of land, but they controlled only 9 percent of the total value of real property. In 1860 white women represented 15 percent of landowners, but controlled only 11 percent of the property.

35. In 1860 white women were 17 percent of whites with personal property, but their share of that property (which included slaves) was only 12 percent.

36. In the 1830 enumeration of free blacks who owned slaves, a Marey Moore headed a household of seven and owned three slaves (Woodson, *Free Negro Owners*, p. 37). In 1850, she had eight slaves, and in 1860 Susan Moore (probably the same person) owned twenty-four slave houses.

37. The question of why free black women owned such a large proportion of the wealth of free blacks (in contrast to the white situation) needs more study. One might guess that some of the women were consorts of white men who gave them money. This did happen with an Augusta ancestor of noted Afro-American educator John Hope. Indeed, the population manuscript census returns sometimes made teasing suggestions. For example, next to the name of one free Afro-American family in 1850 Hamburg was scribbled "Jim Mathew's Negress family." Then again perhaps some free black women who worked as domestics had endeared themselves to their white families, who provided financial rewards. Of course, one contributing factor to the black-white female wealth differential was the higher proportion of free black female-headed households. But that begs the question rather than answers it.

38. Petition of Elizabeth Bug, 1859, and Petition of Lucy Dennis, 1860, both in Legislative Papers (SCDAH); Bradley, "Slave Manumission," pp. 104–5. A good idea of the pressures to reenslave free blacks at this time is found in Pope, *History of Newberry County*, pp. 116–17. Summarizing petitions to the General Assembly, he writes that the "mischievous influence . . . on slaves rendered them [free blacks] a nuisance to any community."

39. Johnson, "Wealth and Class," p. 71.

40. Ten of the thirty-seven household heads in 1860 were nonmulatto.

41. Rawick, *American Slave*, vol. 8: *Arkansas*, pt. 1, p. 329. The white interviewer probably misunderstood; Bryan said that her grandfather "made" (not "molded") his own money to differentiate her grandfather from slaves.

42. Ibid., sup. ser., vol. 4: *Georgia*, pp. 433–34. Presumably, if twenty-one children is a correct transcription, they refer to the children that Annette's mother had. The interviewer did not say otherwise. Annette, herself, during and after the Civil War, had twelve children.

43. In 1860 it was impossible to manumit slaves in Edgefield District, even by sending them out of the state, and blacks may have purchased slaves, even relatives, to make conditions easier for them. Franklin, *Free Negro in North Carolina*, concluded that the greater portion of free black owners of slaves possessed them for benevolent reasons.

44. Rawick, *American Slave*, vol. 2: *South Carolina*, pt. 2, p. 1.

45. Petition from Priscilla Jessup, 1845, and Report of the Committee on the Colored Population on the Petition of Priscilla Jessup, 1845, both in Legislative Papers (SCDAH); Bradley, "Slave Manumission," pp. 70–71. The petition was denied; although the committee claimed to be sympathetic, it reported that the "true policy of the state is vigilantly to guard against what might become an abuse of sympathy on behalf of the petitioner."

46. The two whites who interviewed Annette Milledge interviewed a number of ex-slaves. Where appropriate, they noted if the former slave was mulatto, light-skinned,

or appeared to have Indian blood. There was no mention of any color characterization for Annette Milledge, which would suggest that she was not mulatto and that her parents were not mulatto as well. The white interviewer for Ida Bryant was explicit, placing after her name the following description: "very very black Negro woman." Rawick, *American Slave*, vol. 8: *Arkansas*, pt. 1, p. 329; sup. ser., vol. 4: *Georgia*, pp. 433–34.

47. Drayton was not found among the 1850 free blacks. At thirty, he was one of the oldest free blacks in this mixed household type, and the only one who owned any personal property.

48. Bethany Baptist Church Records, 29 July 1837 ("Reuben Strauther and his wife Moriah"), Mar. and 10 Oct. 1840 (SCDAH); Woodson, et al., *History of Edgefield Baptist Association*, p. 168.

49. S.C., General Assembly, *Journal*, 1935, George McDuffie, "Governor's Message," p. 7.

50. S.C., General Assembly (House), *Journal*, 1850, p. 23; Bradley, "Slave Manumission," pp. 95, 102; Wikramanayake, *World in Shadow*, p. 169.

51. Edgefield District Grand Jury Presentment, 5 Oct. 1859, Legislative Papers (SCDAH).

52. "List of Negroes Hired and Impressed," Grant papers (GSA). I am grateful to Jerry Thornbery for bringing this list to my attention and to Clarence Mohr for sharing a copy.

53. Big Stevens Creek Baptist Church Records, 1809 and 1811 membership list (BHC).

54. Although whites could not legally free their slaves in South Carolina after 1820, some found ways to do so. Even during the heightened proslavery feelings of the decade of the 1850s, Alfred Cuthbert, a Georgia planter near Augusta, freed his slaves by shipping them to Liberia. Julia Cumming wrote to her daughter, Emily C. Hammond, in Edgefield District, that Cuthbert "knew his friends at the South condemned his course, but he was the best judge in his own affairs." Subsequently, Julia reported to Emily that Mrs. Tillman learned of Cuthbert's intended move to Patterson, New Jersey, where he would live on a small farm, and she asked Annie Cuthbert what her husband, "a Southern planter, was going to do in New Jersey." Such actions were rare, but they illustrate that, even when the South was most opposed to abolition, some wanted to free their slaves. Others may have found ways to skirt the law prohibiting manumission (Julia B. Cumming to Emily Cumming Hammond, 14 and 17 May 1860, Hammond, Bryan, Cumming Papers [SCL]). Berlin, *Slaves without Masters*, pp. 32–33, 144–49, discusses illegal manumission practices and slaves who lived as free blacks in the antebellum period. See also Bradley, "Slave Manumission," pp. 59–66, 112.

The proportion of antebellum free blacks who were mulatto was probably even higher than the manuscript census suggested. For example, see below and n. 1. Franklin, *Slavery to Freedom*, pp. 215–17, and Sydnor, "Free Negro in Mississippi"; Edgefield District Grand Jury Presentment, 5 Oct. 1859, Legislative Papers (SCDAH); Maria Bryan to Julia B. Cumming, 11 Mar. 1831, Hammond, Bryan, Cumming Papers (SCL).

55. In the 1950s, persons in this area talked of black children who were reared in

white homes because they were the children of the white father (but not children of the father's white wife) and were reared with the white children. See also Mays, *Born to Rebel*, p. 18.

56. Cornish Diary, 22 Feb. 1856, Cornish Papers (SHC).

57. Up-country petitions against adultery seldom mentioned interracial liaisons. I did find references from Barnwell (near the border of Edgefield) in 1830 and 1860. See n. 10. Hindus, *Prison and Plantation*, p. 53.

58. For age cohorts by race and gender see my "Ungrateful Servants," pp. 388–89.

59. Davenport, "Population Persistence," discovered the same phenomenon of a mixture of black and white children in mixed and in free black households in upstate New York. Since the 1855 New York state census recorded the relationship of household members, the children listed as white could be positively determined to be the descendants of free Afro-Americans.

60. In 1850, 72.4 percent of those household heads twenty years and older were literate; 65 percent were literate in 1860 (79.6 percent of the poorest quartile of 1860 white household heads were literate). Thus, most could read and write if those skills were needed in urban or in a more industrial society. The high literacy rates, despite education being illegal, support Franklin's contention that a surprising number were able to get the rudiments of learning. His evidence came from the city areas, where schools did exist; in Edgefield District there were no schools for free blacks, yet they somehow learned to read and write. The decline in the percentage of literate adult free blacks over the decade may have resulted from the tightening of restrictions on free blacks in the decade (Franklin, *Slavery to Freedom*, p. 229).

61. J. Morgan Kousser generously shared his research on the relatives of John Hope and other antebellum free black descendants who passed for white.

62. Edgefield examples support the thesis of Woodward, *Strange Career*. Judge Chancellor William Harper set a precedent in 1835 when he ruled that "the condition is not to be determined solely by . . . visible mixture . . . but by reputation . . . and it may be proper, that a man of worth . . . should have the rank of a white man, while a vagabond of the same degree of blood should be confined to the inferior caste." Wikramanayake, *World in Shadow*, pp. 14, 51–52, 81–83, 92, concluded that it was "color, rather than the degree of admixture, which prevailed" in the question of citizenship.

63. Edgefield Co. (S.C.) Military Record, 4 Dec. 1840 (not paginated), Hill Papers (SHC). One line of inquiry not explored is the thesis, which dates back to E. Horace Fitchett's studies of Charleston's free blacks, that the free black served to safeguard the master class. In the words of Fitchett, "Upper caste free Negro served as a custodian of the system" in Charleston ("Free Negro in Charleston").

64. Edgefield *Advertiser*, 18 Mar. 1863.

65. Columbia *Daily Register*, 17 Oct. 1895. See also Tindall, *South Carolina Negroes*, p. 299. I have located one elderly white lady in Augusta who in tracing her Edgefield genealogy has found a free black ancestor. This Augusta lady is a member of both the Daughters of the American Revolution and the United Daughters of the Confederacy. Her family, the Harrises, predates the American Revolution in Edgefield, and her family at one time lived in the first house built in the town of Edgefield. One of the white Harris boys lived with a free black wife by the name of Rachel Oli-

ver Chaney. This antebellum interracial couple had two sons, who with their descendants were assimilated into the white world.

66. Wikramanayake, *World in Shadow*, p. 98, after a survey of rural free antebellum Afro-Americans, concluded that white yeomen's farms "were essentially the same as the blacks." In her dissertation, "Free Negro," p. 129, she concluded from a survey of Abbeville District, which bordered Edgefield on the north and east, that "on the whole rural free Negroes maintained the same economic standards as the yeoman farmers who made up the majority of South Carolina's white population."

67. Craven, "Poor Whites and Negroes," p. 15, in his discussion of slaves and poor whites in the South, waxed eloquent in explaining the conditions that produced unique relationships such as those discussed in antebellum Edgefield District. "Life was so individualized by rural and frontier forces that each relationship was a thing unique in itself; that the human element ever looms large in rural worlds and that the accidents of health, wealth, and personal qualities rise in proportion."

Of course, there is firm evidence of only a few mixed households, and it appears that many of these antebellum free blacks were almost white. Perhaps because there were so few free blacks, white society was not threatened by their presence. Because unacceptable behavior was confined to a few marginal cases, antebellum white society tended to be tolerant of free blacks; they had little numerical, but perhaps great symbolic, significance. In this view there was a rather loose and easy relationship between antebellum free blacks (some of whom were mostly white) and the white community. What is surprising then is that some whites overreacted to this association of some free blacks and whites in the 1850s.

Chapter 6

1. Historiography on the transitional South has begun to bloom. See Huffman, "Old South, New South"; Wiener, *Social Origins*; Cooper, *Conservative Regime*; Shifflett, *Patronage and Poverty*; Woodman, "Sequel to Slavery"; Davis, *Good and Faithful Labor*; Wayne, *Reshaping of Plantation Society*; Ransom and Sutch, *One Kind of Freedom*.

2. Minute Men, Saluda Association, Minutes, 24 Nov., 1, 8, 15, and 22 Dec. 1860 (SCL); Edgefield *Advertiser*, 31 Oct. 1860.

3. Edgefield *Advertiser*, 31 Oct. 1860 and 20 May 1846.

4. Simkins, *Pitchfork Ben*, p. 25. Thomas, *Confederate Nation*, p. 155, has estimated that 75 percent of the eighteen to forty-five age group enlisted for at least some period of time. Edgefield companies included soldiers from other areas but not those from Edgefield who joined other companies.

5. Edgefield *Advertiser*, 13 Sept. and 11 Oct. 1865, 2 May 1866; Hill, "Confederate Exodus." After the war some Southerners considered leaving the South for South America. One of the more active emigration societies was formed at Edgefield with Joseph Abney as president, but very few whites actually left Edgefield for South America. Some young single Confederate veterans traveled to Brazil, stayed a year or two, and returned. One prominent wealthy antebellum planter who migrated to Brazil and stayed was Robert Meriwether. However, his move was as much motivated by

his debts as by an ideological commitment to establishing another slave society. A great-great uncle of former first lady Rosalynn Carter also migrated from Edgefield to Brazil. On wealth distributions and comparative standard deviations before and after the Civil War, see Burton, "Ungrateful Servants," pp. 197–208.

6. David Potter argued that American women have not participated in the national character ("American Women"). But the southern character has also differed from the American national character, which emphasized individualism, self-reliance, and egalitarianism. William R. Taylor claims that the South adopted essentially feminine characteristics because the region failed in the masculine world of the marketplace (Taylor, *Cavalier and Yankee*, pp. 147–48). See also Gaines, *Southern Plantation*; Osterweis, *Romanticism and Nationalism*. Most recent studies demonstrate that the South had not failed in the chase after wealth, but had simply taken a different and perhaps more lucrative path. The classic argument is Fogel and Engerman, *Time on Cross*. Both adherents of the Old South after the Civil War, such as Charles Colcock Jones, Jr., and advocates of the New South, such as Daniel A. Tompkins, acquiesced in a sentimental portrayal of the plantation South which justified the existing social order. Paul Gaston best explained "the vital nexus" between the views of the Old South and the Cult of the Lost Cause (Gaston, *New South Creed*, pp. 151–86, see especially 154–58). For images in the literature of "Southern Womanhood" see Ruoff, "Frivolity to Consumption" and "Southern Womanhood"; Hogeland, "Female Appendage," p. 103; Scott, "Women's Perspective"; Eaton, *Waning Old South*, pp. 108, 149, 151; Woodward, *Origins of New South*, pp. 173–74, and *Burden of Southern History*, p. 110; Underwood, *Women of Confederacy*; Simkins and Patton, *Women of Confederacy*; Massey, *Ersatz in Confederacy*, *Refugee Life in Confederacy*, and *Bonnet Brigades*; Wiley, *Confederate Women*; Sterkx, *Partners in Rebellion*; Wolff, "South and American Imagination"; Wood, *Black Scare*; Mullins, "Lynching in South Carolina," esp. pp. 4–11 on Ben Tillman.

7. Simkins, "Ben Tillman's View," p. 161 and *Pitchfork Ben*, pp. 224–25, 396–97; U.S., Congress, *Congressional Record*, 57th Cong., 1st Sess., 1902, vol. 35, pt. 5, p. 5102, and 59th Cong., 2d Sess., 1907, vol. 41, pt. 2, pp. 1440–41; *New York Times*, 5 Aug. 1901, p. 1; Mullins, "Lynching in South Carolina," pp. 4–11.

8. See Burton, "Race and Reconstruction" and "Ungrateful Servants."

9. Burton, "Ungrateful Servants," pp. 294–317; chap. 6 applies the frontier thesis to Edgefield Afro-Americans forging a community identity.

10. Tillman, "Struggles of 1876," pp. 25, 33; Edgefield *Advertiser*, 17 July 1867; Edgefield County, Teachers Reports, 1868–76, Superintendent of Education Papers, Records of the Department of Education (SCDAH); S.C., General Assembly, *Journal*, 1870–71, p. 204.

11. Harrison N. Bouey to William Coppinger, 23 May 1877, and to H. M. Turner, 23 May 1877, American Colonization Papers (LC); Edgefield *Advertiser*, 14 Feb. 1866.

12. Edgefield *Advertiser*, 11 July 1866, 2 Dec. 1868, 15 Dec. 1870, 12 and 19 Jan. 1871, 25 Jan., 29 Feb., and 21 March 1872, 16 Jan. and 3 Feb. 1873; Reynolds, *Reconstruction in South Carolina*, p. 365; U.S., Congress, *Congressional Record*, 57th Congress, 2d Sess., pp. 2562–64; B. R. Tillman to Benjamin R. Tillman, Jr., 17 Nov. 1913, Tillman Papers (CU); Simkins, *Pitchfork Ben*, p. 399; Howard, Civil War Veterans Questionnaires, 1915, p. 4 (TSLA).

13. Rawick, *American Slave*, vol. 3: *South Carolina*, pp. 283, 285.

14. See Burton, "Race and Reconstruction" and "Ungrateful Servants." I am revising the latter to be published as a monograph. I have also written an unpublished paper, "The Civil War in the Confederate Interior: From Community to the Nation—The Transformation of Local Values in Edgefield, South Carolina."

15. F. W. Pickens to J. L. Orr, 9 Feb. 1866, Orr Papers (SCDAH); William N. Yeldell to F. W. Pickens, 13 June 1868, Pickens Papers (DU); "Petition of Sundry Citizens of Edgefield," May 1870, M. C. Butler to C. P. Leslie, Jan. 1870, Loose Papers, Land Transfer File, 1866–77, Questionnaire, both in Land Commission Papers, 1869–73 (SCDAH); Bleser, *Promised Land*, pp. 35–36. Burton, "Race and Reconstruction," pp. 38–39.

16. John Devereux, General Order no. 1, newspaper clipping, microfilm series 869, roll 1, p. 177 (printed) and p. 263 (handwritten) and Circular no. 3, 5 Feb. 1866, MS 1869, vol. 26, General Orders and Circulars, 15 Jan. 1866 to 3 May 1869, BRFAL, RG 105 (NA). Following an interview with President Andrew Johnson, Provisional Gov. Benjamin Perry announced that the president had proclaimed that "freedmen must learn that their freedom consists in working for themselves and their families" (Abbeville *Press and Banner*, 17 Aug. 1865, and Edgefield *Advertiser*, 23 Aug. 1865). E. R. Calhoun to J. L. Orr, 1 June 1867, J. W. Coleman to J. L. Orr, 6 May 1867, Orr Papers (SCDAH). Scott believed the examples made of bigamists and polygamists by the law in Charleston would end the problem.

17. Edgefield *Advertiser*, 3 Apr. 1865; see also 3 Jan. 1866, 24 May, 12 July 1865. The above references indicate that whites thought of the black family as a means of social control and manipulation even after slavery.

18. Mrs. R. E. Morris to Gov. J. L. Orr, 11 Mar. 1867, Orr Papers (SCDAH).

19. Rawick, *American Slave*, sup. ser. vol. 3: *Georgia*, pt. 1, p. 233.

20. "Family album and scrapbook," Simkins and Bailey Papers (FP); Simkins, "Paris Simkins"; Roston, *Major Perry*; Nicholson, *Brief Sketch*; Mays, *Born to Rebel*, pp. 1–2. See also below and the excellent discussion of naming patterns by Gutman, *Black Family*, chap. 6; the ex-slave narratives are filled with examples of naming patterns.

21. Harrison, *Know Your Roots*, p. 3.

22. Harrison N. Bouey to William Coppinger, 31 May 1877, and John Mardenborough to Coppinger, 15 May 1877, American Colonization Papers, vol. 227, p. 161 (LC).

23. Rawick, *American Slave*, vol. 10: *Arkansas*, pt. 5, p. 29; sup. ser., vol. 3: *Georgia*, p. 305.

24. Ibid., vol. 13: *Georgia*, pt. 3, p. 123; sup. ser., vol. 3: *Georgia*, pt. 1, p. 232; vol. 10: *Arkansas*, pt. 5, p. 334.

25. Ibid., sup. ser., vol. 4: *Georgia*, p. 436; vol. 3: *South Carolina*, pt. 4, p. 73; vol. 13: *Georgia*, pt. 3, p. 123. Bailey, "Memoirs," Simkins and Bailey Papers (FP).

26. Mays, *Born to Rebel*, p. 20.

27. Rawick, *American Slave*, vol. 2: *South Carolina*, pt. 2, p. 101; vol. 8: *Arkansas*, pt. 1, p. 309; sup. ser., vol. 4: *Georgia*, p. 433; vol. 2: *South Carolina*, pt. 1, p. 28.

28. Ibid., sup. ser., vol. 4: *Georgia*, p. 433; vol. 10: *Arkansas*, pt. 6, p. 107. See also, vol. 8: *Arkansas*, pt. 1, p. 303.

29. Ibid., vol. 8: *Arkansas*, pt. 1, p. 310; vol. 13: *Georgia*, pt. 3, p. 125.

30. Ibid., sup. ser., vol. 4: *Georgia*, p. 444.

31. Ibid., vol. 10: *Arkansas*, pt. 5, p. 336. "In Africa, elders were the most respected members of society. They maintained this position into the era of slaves" (Davis, *Black Aged*, pp. xiv–xvii).

32. Simkins died in 1930, and I have interviewed people who attended both his wake and his funeral. See also Simkins, "Paris Simkins"; Act of the General Assembly of Georgia, 23 Dec. 1843, cited in Rawick, *American Slave*, vol. 13: *Georgia*, pt. 4, p. 319. Other examples of the importance of funeral rituals that accompanied slave deaths: Harry Hammond to Emily Bryan Hammond, 30 Mar. 1860, Maria Bryan Harford to Mrs. Julia A. Cumming, 12 Jan. 1834, Hammond, Bryan, Cumming Papers (SCL); Rawick, *American Slave*, sup. ser., vol. 3: *Georgia*, pt. 1, p. 38; vol. 2: *South Carolina*, pt. 1, p. 231; vol. 3: *South Carolina*, pt. 4, p. 179. Pleck, *Black Migration*, p. 69, referred to the funeral as "the most important ritual of slave life."

33. Evans, *Martha Schofield*, pp. 47, 56; Tillman, "Struggles of 1876" and "Childhood Days." See also Shimkin, et al., *Extended Family*, pp. 24, 30–31, 54, 67–69, 114, 119, 187, 189, 195, 217–18, 262, 291, 361, 393.

34. Edgefield *Advertiser*, 1 Nov. 1870.

35. Inscriptions found in Afro-American cemeteries are also found in white graveyards. On blacks cleaning white graves see the five-dollar receipt from Orlando Sheppard to George Simkins, 2 Mar. 1877, Sheppard Papers (SCL).

36. Quotation from Huffman, "Old South, New South," p. 48. On the manuscript mortality censuses see Methodological Appendix.

37. John Mardenborough to William Coppinger, 25 May and 6 June 1877, American Colonization Papers, vol. 227 (LC). Colonization Papers listed 356 names, all of which were in family units headed by males. Edgefield *Chronicle*, 25 Jan. 1882; Williams, *Liberian Exodus*, pp. 31–32; Tindall, *South Carolina Negroes*, pp. 153–68, 170–73. Burton, "Ungrateful Servants," pp. 157–78, details descriptions of organized efforts to leave Edgefield for both Liberia and Arkansas. Both movements were discussed by blacks in the religious terms of Exodus.

38. Quoted in both Charleston *News and Courier*, 2 Jan. 1882, and New York *Daily Tribune*, 5 Jan. 1882, p. 2. For what black and white tenants were having to pay for fertilizer and fences, and how much they cleared in 1880, see Burton, "Ungrateful Servants," pp. 170–75. Two former slaves, neither from Edgefield, explained about fence laws. "I have been farming and working all my life. . . . I married and long time after come to Arkansas. They said you could raise stock here—no fence law." Another former slave complained after the fence laws were also enacted in Arkansas. "This here new fence law was one of the lowest things they ever did. . . . If they would let the old people raise meat, they wouldn't have to get so much help from the government. God don't like that, God wants the people to raise things." Rawick, *American Slave*, vol. 10: *Arkansas*, pt. 5, pp. 57–63, 103.

39. Tindall, *South Carolina Negroes*, p. 170.

40. T. R. Denny quoted in Edgefield *Chronicle*, 25 Jan. 1882.

41. Edgefield *Chronicle*, 4 Jan. 1882.

42. Edgefield *Chronicle*, 4, 12, 18, 25 Jan. 1882; quotation from T. R. Denny.

43. George Burt to M. L. Bonham, 8 July 1889, M. Luke Bonham Papers (SCL); India Gill to Julia Hammond, 26 Mar. 1887, Emma Franklin to Harry Hammond, 29 Sept. 1900, Hammond, Bryan, Cumming Papers (SCL).

44. Sidney Dewalt to Miss Julia (in New York), n.d., Mr. and Mrs. Hanable Evans to the Hammond family, 3 Oct. 1900, Robert Perry to Mrs. Emily Hammond, 22 Nov. 1904, Sidney Dewalt to Mrs. Hammond, 31 Dec. 1908, all in the Hammond, Bryan, Cumming Papers (SCL).

45. Edgefield *Advertiser*, 7 Aug. 1867; letter reprinted by Moss in *Advertiser*.

46. Rawick, *American Slave*, vol. 8: *Arkansas*, pt. 1, p. 310; vol. 10: *Arkansas*, pt. 5, p. 27.

47. Ibid., sup. ser., vol. 11: *North Carolina and South Carolina*, pp. 274–77.

48. Johnston, "Resistance to Migration," reported that for an English rural area people whose surnames occurred five or more times among household heads were significantly more likely to persist than were individuals with less common surnames. As to the frequency of occurrence of surnames, I am unaware of other comparative community studies, but I suspect that Edgefield had a higher frequency of surnames that were common for at least ten household heads. One would expect a higher discrepancy between white and black surname recurrence if slaves had taken their masters' names after freedom. In 1870 Afro-Americans had 142 surnames repeated more than ten times compared to 78 surnames for whites. In 1880 the recurrence for black surnames ten or more times was 153 and for whites 80.

49. Bailey, "Memoirs" and memorabilia, Simkins and Bailey Papers (FP).

50. Aba-Mecha, "Black Woman Activist." For discussion of the transmission of activism from one black Boston generation to the next see Horton, "Generations of Protest."

51. Rawick, *American Slave*, vol. 8: *Arkansas*, pt. 1, p. 310.

52. Mays, *Born to Rebel*, p. 13. On significance of the black church to the rural Afro-American community, see Frazier, *Negro Church*, pp. 41–42, 33 (on social control until 1940); Rose, *Negro in America*, pp. 277, 297; Ashmore, "African Methodist Episcopal Church," pp. 1–2, 36–37, 43, 54–55 (a number of examples are from neighboring Abbeville County).

53. Tindall, *South Carolina Negroes*, pp. 170–73. See also the ex-slave narratives, which are filled with examples of church-related activities and country patterns. See, for example, Frank Adams of Winslow in Rawick, *American Slave*, vol. 2: *South Carolina*, p. 214.

54. On the Arkansas migration see above, and Burton, "Ungrateful Servants," pp. 166–89. Quotation from Charleston *News and Courier*, 2 Jan. 1882, also given in New York *Daily Tribune*, 5 Jan. 1882, p. 2.

55. The two lists are John Mardenborough to William J. Coppinger, 15 May and 6 June 1877, American Colonization Papers, vol. 227, microfilm reel 16 A (LC).

56. Rawick, *American Slave*, vol. 13: *Georgia*, pt. 3, p. 125; vol. 10: *Arkansas*, p. 83 (the second former slave was not from Edgefield).

57. Edgefield *Advertiser*, 15 Nov. 1865; Nicholson, *Brief Sketch*, pp. 45–46; Simkins, "Paris Simkins"; Tillman, "Struggles of 76"; Evans, *Martha Schofield*, pp. 57–58, 68–70. For more detail see Burton, "Ungrateful Servants," pp. 116–17. Moses was Gov. Francis Pickens's secretary during the Civil War.

58. Rawick, *American Slave*, vol. 3: *South Carolina*, pt. 3, pp. 73, 124.

59. Harry Hammond to Katharine Hammond, 18 Nov. 1890, Hammond, Bryan, Cumming Papers (SCL).

60. Woodson et al., *History of Edgefield Baptist Association*, p. 170; Little River Baptist Association Minutes, Sept. 1886, p. 12 (ABHS). According to Ashmore, "African Methodist Episcopal Church," pp. 35, 63–64, the church in South Carolina denounced liquor, cards, checkers, dominoes, dancing, illegitimacy, and temporary marriages.

61. Bethlehem Baptist Association Covenant, 9 Nov. 1877, p. 11, Macedonia Baptist Association Minutes, 9 Oct. 1895, p. 7 (ABHS).

62. Ouzts Farm Journal, 12 Aug. 1874. Ouzts Papers (SCL). White and black commentators before and after the Civil War remarked on the lack of organization and order of black religion. See for example, Ashmore, "African Methodist Episcopal Church," pp. 26–27, 54. Black people generally preferred the loose organization of the Baptist church.

63. Edgefield *Advertiser*, 28 Dec. 1871. For more details see Burton, "Ungrateful Servants," p. 116 (see chap. 4 for the Charity Moore version).

64. Mays, *Born to Rebel*, p. 21. Association minutes show songs such as "Blest Be the Tie That Binds" and sermons such as Romans 13 on loving one another. These can be found in nearly all the records of the Negro Baptist associations for Georgia and South Carolina. See, for example, Little River Baptist Association, 24 Aug. 1898, p. 7, "evening session" (ABHS); *History of Mt. Calvary Baptist Church*, p. 1.

65. Edgefield Baptist Association Records, Sept. 1871 (BHC); Woodson et al., *History of Edgefield Baptist Association*, pp. 57–59.

66. Bethlehem Baptist Sunday School Convention, Nov. 1877, p. 45; Little River Baptist Association Minutes, Aug. 1877, p. 2 (ABHS).

67. Little River Baptist Association Minutes, Sept. 1886, pp. 10–11 (ABHS). Liberty had a total of 197 Baptist children, of whom 113 went to school. Springfield reported 55 children in school and 20 who did not attend.

68. Macedonia Baptist Association Minutes, 9 Oct. 1885, p. 5 (ABHS).

69. Little River Baptist Association Minutes, 23–25 Aug. 1877, p. 4, Sept. 1886, p. 7 (ABHS). On the concern of black Methodists for education and the development of Payne Institute at Cokesbury in Abbeville District near Edgefield, see Ashmore, "African Methodist Episcopal Church," p. 34. A black Methodist church in Abbeville sponsored a literary society, an agricultural society, a singing society, and held meetings for the Colored Alliance (pp. 36–37, 43, 54–55).

70. Rawick, *American Slave*, sup. ser., vol. 3: *Georgia*, p. 305. Peter Randolph, not from South Carolina but Virginia, was converted at the age of ten. "After receiving this revelation from the Lord, I became impressed that I was called of God to preach to the other slaves . . . but then I could not read the Bible, and I thought I could never preach unless I learned to read the Bible" (Randolph, *Sketches of Slave Life*, pp. 10–11; Cornelius, "We Slipped and Learned to Read," p. 17). See also Rawick, *American Slave*, vol. 10: *Arkansas*, pt. 6, pp. 187, 190, and vol. 17: *Florida*, p. 98; Boothe, *Cyclopedia of Colored Baptists*, pp. 69–70.

71. Pegues and Witherspoon, *Baptist Ministers*, pp. 81, 145–57, 373, 457–59. For details see Burton, "Ungrateful Servants," chap. 5.

72. Edgefield Baptist Association Minutes, July 1865, Nov. 1868, July 1869, July,

Sept. and Nov. 1871, Sept. 1873, Edgefield Village Baptist Church Records, Sept. 1873, all church records in BHC. See Woodson et al., *History of Edgefield Baptist Association*, pp. 55–60.

73. Charles Wright to R. K. Scott, 13 Feb. 1872, Scott Papers (SCDAH).

74. Little River Baptist Association Minutes, 1888, p. 10, Friendship Baptist Sunday School Association, July 1892, p. 8, Little River Baptist Association Minutes, 1894, p. 14 (ABHS).

75. Rawick, *American Slave*, vol. 12: *Georgia*, pt. 1, pp. 335–36.

76. W. P. Russell to M. E. Strieby, May 1866. American Missionary Association Records (ARC). Russell was the minister in Augusta, Georgia. S. Walker to Brvt. Brig. Gen. Ben. P. Hunkle, Oct. 1866, and Annual Report of the Bureau District of Anderson, pp. 771, 883–84. "Brave actions then on part of school teachers to teach in these circumstances" (Annual Report, Walker, Bureau District of Anderson). Soon "a native colored man," Robert Greene, joined Albert Dugspring and his wife to teach at Storm Branch. (Dugspring was from Ohio and had served in the army nine years.) All in BRFAL, RG 105 (NA).

77. S.C., Constitutional Convention, *Constitution of South Carolina*, 1868, Art. 10, Sec. 3–4; S.C., General Assembly, *Acts*, 1870, pt. 1, p. 339.

78. *Annual Report of the State Superintendent of Education*, 1869, p. 101, in Superintendent of Education Papers, Records of the Department of Education, and in Legislative Papers (both SCDAH).

79. S.C., General Assembly, *Reports and Resolutions*, 1869, pp. 53, 78, 1871, pp. 88, 90.

80. S.C., General Assembly, *Reports and Resolutions*, 1873–74, pp. 46, 426; Governor's Message of 28 Nov. 1871 in S.C., House, *Journal*, 1872, p. 37; *Annual Report of the State Superintendent of Education*, 1870, pp. 26–29, in Superintendent of Education Papers, Records of the Department of Education, and in Legislative Papers (both SCDAH); S.C., *Statutes at Large* (1878) 14:339–48; Thomason, *Foundations of Public Schools*, pp. 207–9; Lott, "Development of Education," pp. 33–36; Burnett, "History of Education," pp. 17–20, 59–60.

81. Teachers Reports, Edgefield, 1868–70, five folders, Superintendent of Education Papers, Records of the Department of Education (SCDAH).

82. Reynolds, *Reconstruction*, p. 369.

83. S.C., House, *Journal*, 1877–78, pp. 18, 249; S.C., *Statutes at Large* (1878) 14:511–86, 453, 565; Thomason, *Foundations of Public Schools*, pp. 221–26, 229; Tindall, *South Carolina Negroes*, pp. 209–32.

84. On town and country shifts during Reconstruction, see below in chap. 7 and Burton, "Rise and Fall"; Burnett, "History of Education," pp. 23–64; Lott, "Development of Education," pp. 36–60.

85. Nicholson, *Brief Sketch*, p. 29.

86. Little River Baptist Association Minutes, 1877 (ABHS).

87. Nicholson, *Brief Sketch*, pp. 30–31, 36–37; *Bettis Academy Bulletin*, 1930 (BA); McMillan, *Negro Higher Education*, pp. 36–41; Col. E. H. Aull in Newberry *Herald and News*, 2 articles, n.d., in scrapbook in possession of Hortense Woodson. See also the Saluda County Tricentennial Commission, *Saluda County*, pp. 25–96. Although I have not located the WPA Church Record Survey for Edgefield County, I have researched those for the following counties, all or at least partly formed from

Edgefield: Saluda, McCormick, Greenwood, Aiken (originals in SCL). Among published volumes on locally famous Edgefield Afro-American ministers, Nicholson, *Brief Sketch*, and Roston, *Major Perry*, are both indispensable for understanding how the ideals of a society were to be put into practice for blacks in the rural South. See also Tindall, *South Carolina Negroes*, pp. 187–89. In addition, for a later period, see Evans, *Martha Schofield*, and Mays, *Born to Rebel*, pp. 1–34; the latter is peppered with information relating family relations to religion. I also find it suggestive that Samuel DuBois Cook's introduction to Dr. Mays's autobiography mentions, "Because of a divine moral restlessness implanted in his *Puritan* (my emphasis) conscience" ("Reflections on a Rebel," in Mays, *Born to Rebel*, p. xviii). Indeed, all these records point to very strict moral standards while displaying a forgiveness of sins.

88. Rock Hill Baptist Church Records, Edgefield County, and Special Order 72, 18 Nov. 1873 (ABHS); *South Carolina Military Records*, p. 114 (SCDAH); Simkins, "Paris Simkins"; interviews with Simkins's descendents; Bailey, Sr., "Childhood Remembrances"; Mays, *Born to Rebel*; Pegues and Witherspoon, *Baptist Ministers*, pp. 31, 145–47, 373, 457–59.

89. Little River Baptist Association Minutes, 1 Aug. 1872, p. 18, Macedonia Association Sunday School Conventions, 1877 and 1884, Friendship Baptist Sunday School Association, 1892, p. 11, Little River Baptist Sunday School Conventions, 1893, 1897, throughout (ABHS).

90. Singletary, *Negro Militia*; *South Carolina Military Records*, for example, pp. 58–82, 83, 84, 85 (SCDAH); Edgefield *Advertiser*, 2 June, 5 May, 14 Sept., 18 Aug., 8 Dec. 1870, 17 Aug. 1876; H. W. Purvis to D. H. Chamberlain, 30 Jan. 1875, Chamberlain Papers (SCDAH); *South Carolina Military Records*, List of Commissions Issued, 1870–99, 1:58, 82–85, 114, and Militia Enrollments, 1869, vol. 12 (SCDAH).

91. Rawick, *American Slave*, vol. 10: *Arkansas*, pt. 5, p. 336.

92. These folk traditions persist today. See also Nichols, "Black Women."

Chapter 7

1. Simkins, *History of the South*, 2d ed., rev. (1959), pp. 388–89. The Civil War reversed the antebellum trend of white wealth concentration. The 1870 gini index for land ownership for white household heads was .767. See chaps. 1 and 2.

2. It should be noted that Blassingame, *Black New Orleans*, does argue for a rapid shift from slavery to freedom. However, I believe that the idea of the male-headed nuclear family had to exist already in order for such a pattern to be so prevalent in 1870.

3. Females may have preferred not to have farms. E. Franklin Frazier's wrong, but persistent, assertion that tenancy, which he considered the predominant form of rural labor arrangement, was the natural extension of slavery, and so was the cause of the maternal family organization, supported the idea of rural matriarchy. He asserted that at emancipation "the masses of illiterate and propertyless Negroes were forced to become croppers and tenants under a modified plantation system. . . . Within the world of the black folk, social relations have developed out of intimate and sympathetic contact. Consequently, the maternal-family organization, a heritage from slavery, has

continued on a fairly large scale" (Frazier, *Negro Family*, pp. viii, ix, 102, 113, 151–52, 201–2, 362).

4. Scott, *Southern Lady*, pp. 81, 96, 106–7, has been the basis of the view that women became more actively involved in farming in the postbellum South. Although they probably did during the Civil War, the evidence suggests that they were less so after the war. My findings for all women who operated farms in Edgefield are consistent with Wiener, "Female Planters," on elite women planters from five Alabama counties.

5. On slavery see chap. 4 above. Shimkin, reviving Herskovits's pioneering arguments concerning the African-American connection, contended that "detailed comparisons with African extended families . . . strongly indicate deep historical roots for the black extended family in the United States, a presumption which is compatible with a number of important facts in the history of the Southern plantation." However much this argument may appeal to the historian's search for historical continuity, it is inevitably weakened, in the Edgefield County case at least, by the black family's close approximation of white family structure in the decade of the 1870s. While the structural similarities do not entirely rule out the possibility of an African legacy, it is far harder to pinpoint the residue of that legacy than Shimkin's arguments suggest. Quotation from Shimkin et al., "abstract," *Extended Family*, p. 25. Gutman, of course, is too good a historian to make the unqualified leap from Africa to the southern United States, but in *Black Family*, pp. 213–29, where he outlines extended and fictive kin obligation, he is clearly in sympathy with Shimkin's work. So much time has elapsed that we now know too little about the varieties and components of the many West African traditions accurately to identify African influences even if they were there.

Laslett, *World We Lost*, found that it was uncommon for children to live at home after marriage in seventeenth-century England. In a village atmosphere characterized by youthfulness, agricultural innovation could take place easily without parental interference. Perhaps part of the South's slow development and agricultural backwardness may be explained by the prevalence of an extended-family patriarchal society among the whites and blacks who owned and worked the land.

6. The fall in average age for white males was 0.47 years. One would have expected more of a demographic shift with the war casualties. But within five years, marriage ages had stabilized at their prewar levels; see chap. 3.

7. Calculations based upon tables constructed similar to Katz, *People of Hamilton*, pp. 247–48.

8. In most places in the world poverty seems to lead to a higher rather than a lower birthrate. Deaths in the first year of life might have counterbalanced a high rate of fertility among the poor. There may also have been periodic malnutrition among women, which resulted in temporary sterilization, causing seasonal fluctuations in conception rates (reflecting seasonal scarcities of food). There is a need for more study on fertility, and particularly with population-based figures for the postbellum period.

9. G. Walker, Monthly Report, filed 5 Dec. 1866, Summary for Edgefield, from report of Lt. W. Walsh, BRFAL, RG 105 (NA). See also Chartock, "History and Analysis"; Shlomowitz, "Transition from Slave to Freedman" and "Squad System"; Burton, "Race and Reconstruction." Litwack, *Been in Storm*, pp. 335–499, is espe-

cially good on the development of postbellum labor arrangements.

10. B. Williams and 8 hands, H. W. LeLand and freedmen, R. Timmerman and 5 hands, James Bell and freedmen, 1867, all in BRFAL, RG 105 (NA); Rawick, *American Slave*, vol. 9: *Arkansas*, pt. 3, p. 139.

11. D. R. Strother and 28 hands, J. P. Padgett and 16 freedmen, H. Strom and 9 hands, 1867, in BRFAL, RG 105 (NA). Stone's concern was not shared by agents in other counties.

12. The occupational classification "keeping house" was not considered employed. Neither was the group of "other" considered employed. If Edgefield County's occupational structure was at all typical, as most evidence indicates, there would be a danger should one study only the farmers in a rural community. Such a study would not yield a true profile of the community. Edgefield County blacks who listed "farmer" for their occupation in the population manuscript census returns were higher on social and wealth ladders than most blacks in the county. The occupation of "farmer" in the 1870 and 1880 population census schedules correlates almost perfectly with blacks who listed "farm operator" in the agricultural census schedules. See Shifflett, "Household Composition" and *Patronage and Poverty*, pp. 84–98.

13. Catherine Hammond to M. C. M. Hammond, 3 Sept. 1865, and Harry Hammond in Plantation Diary, 1 Apr. 1866, p. 135, both in J. H. Hammond Papers (SCL); James W. Fouche to Dr. E. R. Calhoun, 8 May 1867, and to J. L. Orr, 10 May 1867, both in Orr Papers (SCDAH).

14. Thomas J. McKie to Agt. Freedman's Bureau, 1 Mar. 1867, and reply of William Stone, 1st Lieut., 45th Infantry, Agent for the Bureau of Refugees, Freedman and Abandoned Land (BRFAL), 7 May 1867, McKie Papers (DU). See also papers of the BRFAL in South Carolina, microfilm roll 42, RG 105 (NA).

15. O. H. Hart to Governor R. K. Scott, 8 Sept. 1869, Scott Papers (SCDAH). Hart was a Freedmen's Bureau agent in neighboring Abbeville. For a pathetic case of a woman, not from Edgefield, desperately pleading for her children see the letter from Kattie Collins to Gov. D. H. Chamberlain, 5 June 1876, Chamberlain Papers (SCDAH).

16. For calculations of household size and family type, this study disregards the person who is of a different color than the household head unless otherwise stated. These black family groups in white households can be analyzed in more detail. Of the blacks living in white households in 1870, 250 (22.2 percent) were the sole Afro-Americans in individual white households. In 1880 the corresponding percentage, 36.9, was higher but the absolute number, 197, was lower. In 1870, 179 groups and in 1880, 58 groups of more than one Afro-American in white households were family groups. Of these, males headed 24 percent in 1870 and 41.4 percent ten years later. In 1870, 17.9 percent of these families included the spouse of the household head. In 1880, 24.1 percent were married (one married person's spouse was absent). Another 12.1 percent were widowed, and 51.7 percent were single. In 1870 and 1880 about one-fifth of these family heads were eighteen or younger and some were black sibling families like those discussed above.

17. Rawick, *American Slave*, vol. 10: *Arkansas*, pt. 5, p. 336; Chartock, "History and Analysis," pp. 45–46, 130. Since Abbeville had the highest proportion, Edgefield's percentage was even less.

18. L. Walker to R. K. Scott, Annual Report for 1865–66, citing Brvt. Major Wm.

Stone, Oct. 1866, and Lt. Col. Lancaster to R. K. Scott, Annual Report for 1865–66, both vol. 8, microfilm series 869, roll 34, p. 889 BRFAL, RG 105 (NA). See also ms., 1848–49, 1854–69, Talbert Papers (SCL).

19. Statement of Wade Adams, 18 Sept. 1865, microfilm roll 42, p. 677, BRFAL, RG 105 (NA); Simkins, "Problems of South Carolina Agriculture," esp. p. 48, "Solution of Post-Bellum Agricultural Problems," and "Race Legislation."

20. Harry Hammond in Report of the U.S., Congress, House, *Report of Industrial Commission*, p. 821.

21. Edgefield *Advertiser*, 19 Dec. 1866.

22. Edgefield *Advertiser*, 19 Jan. 1871, and 27 June 1872; Col. Lawrence Cain to D. H. Chamberlain, 9 Jan. 1875, and Col. Theodore W. Parmele to Gov. D. H. Chamberlain, 23 Feb. 1875, Chamberlain Papers (SCDAH); Tillman, "Struggles of 1876," pp. 45–46, and "Childhood Days," second p. 7; Reynolds, *Reconstruction in South Carolina*, pp. 304–5; Allen, *Chamberlain's Administration*, pp. 74–76. McKie owned forty-five slaves in 1860.

23. Three-fourths of the single-member householders were male. The percent of single-person households in 1870 for blacks was 1.2 and for whites 5.6.

24. This discussion is limited to blacks purely to save space. The white pattern, as demonstrated by the statistics, was almost identical to that of the blacks (see chap. 3). Although not enough to be statistically significant, black household heads (who were generally younger) in all age groups brought other people into their homes more uniformly across the age cohorts than did whites.

25. Pleck, *Black Migration*, pp. 190–91, has a similar observation and discussion on Boston blacks and Irish. The poor in these homes were not just elderly people.

26. E. Keese to D. A. Tompkins, 10 Nov. 1873, and D. A. Tompkins to Dr. M. C. Beaumont, 9 Dec. 1871 and 7 Mar. 1873, Tompkins Papers (SHC). On urban Afro-American boarding see Katzman, *Before the Ghetto*, pp. 75–77; Osofsky, *Harlem*, pp. 138–39 (26 percent of one neighborhood surveyed in 1920 had commercialized their homes by taking in lodgers); Spear, *Black Chicago*, pp. 24, 149–50 (in a 1911–12 survey of Federal Street in Southside Chicago 31 percent of those queried were lodgers; after World War I another survey found 35 percent to be boarders).

27. My conclusions on black extended and augmented families differ from the findings of Pleck, "Mother's Wages"; Smith, "Life Course"; Smith, Dahlin, and Friedberger, "Family Structure"; Reiff, Dahlin, and Smith, "Rural Push." They have argued that, for blacks more than whites, welfare flowed from older to younger generations. My evidence suggests the contrary: that younger blacks supported older blacks more than younger whites supported older whites. This issue needs more investigation.

28. R. K. Scott to Maj. Gen. O. O. Howard, 22 Apr. 1868, citing Maj. L. Walker on Edgefield District, microfilm series 869, roll 1, BRFAL, RG 105 (NA).

29. MS vol. bd, 1844–49, 1854–69, Talbert Papers (SCL).

30. Edgefield *Advertiser*, 30 Aug. 1865, 12 Jan. 1871, 21 Feb. 1866; Howard, "Thoughts on Labor Question," p. 5; J. S. McKie to Mrs. T. J. McKie, 20 May 1874, McKie Papers (DU).

31. Harry Hammond to Katherine Hammond, 21 July 1889, Hammond, Bryan, Cumming Papers (SCL): Hammond, in U.S., Congress, House, *Report of Industrial Commission*, pp. 816, 820; Edgefield's problem was typical for the South. See

Somers, *Southern States*, p. 59. The Freedmen's Bureau agent for Greenville made the same observation in de Forrest, *Union Officer*, p. 94. Wilson, *Black Codes*, pp. 53–54, states, "The greatest loss to the labor force resulted from the decision of growing numbers of Negro women to devote their time to their homes and children. This decision had the blessing of their husbands." Loring and Atkinson, *Cotton Culture*, pp. 4–5, 13–16, 20, 22, 24, 72–75, 103, 109, 137; Rosengarten, *All God's Dangers*, p. 128; Abzug, "Black Family," pp. 26–41; Ruoff, "Southern Womanhood," tables on pp. 141–42. This is the same theme found in the recent econometric study by Ransom and Sutch, *One Kind of Freedom*. For differing views see Goldin, "Female Labor Force," see esp. Table 4, p. 95, and Pleck, *Black Migration*, pp. 177–78 and 26. For an interpretation different from the one in *Black Migration*, see Pleck, "Mother's Wages," pp. 490–510.

32. The point needed to be made that black men wanted their wives to withdraw from work and keep house and that the women so desired. However, this point has now become so well made that it has been misinterpreted by other scholars so as to suggest there were no differences in white and black attitudes and numbers of women working during Reconstruction.

33. D. Walker and A. Washington and wife and two daughters, David Miner and 2 hands, both Edgefield contracts, 1867, BRFAL, RG 105 (NA); Chartock, "History and Analysis," pp. 157, 172; Contract between Alfred and Francis W. Pickens, 1 Jan. 1866, Pickens Papers (SHC).

34. Rawick, *American Slave*, vol. 2: *South Carolina*, p. 15. Proverbs 31 provided religious and scriptural sanction for the arrangement of working wives. For example, in describing a good wife, verse 16 states, "With the fruit of her hands she plants a vineyard." Verse 24 says, "She makes linen garments and sells them." This former slave was not from Edgefield proper, but from near there.

35. Ibid., vol. 10: *Arkansas*, pt. 5, p. 83; vol. 2: *South Carolina*, pt. 3, p. 90. The former slave also discussed the farming partnership between her and her husband. Another former slave was married to a man who wanted to be a preacher, and she asked him if he had enough education to be a leader. She plowed three years while he went to Benedict College (vol. 2: *South Carolina*, pt. 2, pp. 259–60). This slave was from near Edgefield.

36. Evans, *Martha Schofield*, pp. 57–58; Tillman, "Struggles of 76."

37. Rawick, *American Slave*, vol. 12: *Georgia*, pt. 1, pp. 333–43. This tradition of the working wife helps to explain modern survey polls which reveal that black more than white men respond favorably to the idea of working wives.

38. The effect of the depression on female participation in the work force needs more study. Also, the single-person households need more study. Assuming that this was not a census artifact, the increasing number of young workers living in single-person households could indicate the initiation of a postwar pattern.

39. In 1870 black female-headed households had proportionately more non-nuclear members of all ages than did white female-headed ones; in 1880 the percentages were reversed, and white female households had more. Breaking the figures down into percentages for older and younger non-nuclear household members, in 1870 white and black female-headed households (with non-nuclear household members older than fifty) were similar, with whites having a few more residents. The comparative figures for 1880 were more dramatic, 8.0 white to 2.5 percent black, the reverse of the male-

headed pattern. In 1880 the percentages for female-headed households for whites and blacks (with non-nuclear household members younger than twenty years of age) were almost identical. These differences between male and female household heads balanced the overall percentages for extended, augmented, and households with younger and older non-nuclear members, and therefore obscured differences developing between the black and white family structure.

40. There was a small percentage of female-headed households (in 1870, 3.1 and 2.2 percent for black and white, respectively, and in 1880, 2.2 and 2.6 percent, respectively) that were really nuclear families with the male present. For some reason the male was not listed as the head of household. These have been left out of the tables for female-headed households.

41. The 1880 census listed "civil condition" in three separate categories: "single," "married," and "widowed/divorced," the last distinguished between the two. I used the 1880 census listing of civil condition to determine legitimacy. If a woman gave her marital status as single and had children, I recorded that information so that the two pieces of information together gave the designation of illegitimate children. (Illegitimacy is difficult to recognize in the 1850, 1860, and 1870 census data, since the relationship of household members to the household head was not specified. Because of the difficulty in determining the structure of single-parent families in 1870, I did not attempt to differentiate widows from unwed mothers.) Some individuals probably said they were either married or widowed, but I am convinced this would have been more likely for white than for black women with illegitimate children. The number of black women who did report that they had illegitimate children is one indication of the accuracy of the information. Moreover, black society in 1870 and 1880 was basically an oral culture, and great value was placed on veracity. The norm was reinforced in this rural community by people's knowing one another and each other's secrets.

42. The point is not to minimize the number of white men killed. But by 1880 the number of white females heading households who had been widowed during the Civil War was dwarfed by the number of women who had been left widows in the intervening fifteen years by their husbands' deaths of natural causes.

43. "Monthly Report of Outrages for Edgefield District," microfilm series 869, roll 34, throughout, BRFAL, RG 105 (NA). For example, see the case of MacAdams and Callaham.

44. Capt. C. R. Becker to John Devereux, May 1866, John Picksley, Deposition, 1866, microfilm roll 42, p. 670, and Maj. William Stone to Maj. H. W. Smith, 28 Feb. 1866, Records of the Subordinate Field Commanders, Bureau District of Aiken, Subassistant Commissioner for the District of Edgefield, Series 3056, Narrative Reports of Operations, BRFAL, RG 105 (NA).

45. S.C., Committee of Investigation, *Evidence by Committee of Investigation*, pp. 681, 692, 697, 699, 700.

46. Edgefield *Advertiser*, 7 Aug. 1867, 19 Jan. 1871, 11 Oct. 1872; Col. Theodore W. Parmele to Gov. D. H. Chamberlain, Feb. 1875, Chamberlain Papers (SCDAH). Burton, "Race and Reconstruction."

47. Tillman, "Struggles of 76," estimated that 150 to 200 black men were killed during the Hamburg and Ellington riots in those areas. Gary, "Plan of the Campaign of 1876," Gary Papers (SCL); Evans, *Martha Schofield*, pp. 57–58.

48. Evans, *Martha Schofield*, p. 47.

49. John Mardenborough to William J. Coppinger, 11 Apr. 1877, American Colonization Papers, vol. 197 (LC); Cincinnati *Daily Gazette*, 8 Jan. 1880. It was a culture of violence such as this that produced a local white worthy, Bob Burnett, who lived until the 1930s. Burnett's fame rested on his favorite sport, riding through the countryside shooting at black men with a rifle. People still remember Burnett stating that his goal was to shoot a man as he plowed in the fields so that the black would fall dead over the plow traces.

50. The proportion of white female household heads with illegitimate children to all female-headed households was 3.3; for blacks it was 21.8. A possible measure of difference in values between white and black women with illegitimate children was the number of children that the woman had. Unless there was more than one illegitimate child, illegitimacy did not by itself indicate a repeated pattern of premarital sex for the woman. Moreover, qualification should be made before using the number of children which unmarried women had as any basis for values; more than one child did not necessarily indicate promiscuity, as the children could be fathered by one or by different sex partners. Of household heads, 71 percent of the black and 52.9 percent of the white women who had illegitimate children had more than one child. For black women living in black households, the percentage was 46.8, for black women in white households 44.4 percent, and for white women in white households the percentage was 57.1. However, whereas a significant proportion of both black and white women household heads had more than two illegitimate children (47 and 29.4 percent, respectively), and 27.6 percent black family heads living in other households had more than two illegitimate children, no white in the household of another person had more than two illegitimate children. Of course, children could have left home. Records for both blacks and whites suggest children often lived with or visited relatives for extended periods of time.

51. Some female heads of households in 1880 apparently lived with another Afro-American family in the same dwelling; no whites were listed as living in similar situations. For example, Lizzie Blocker was married, twenty-four years old, and had a three-year-old son, George Washington. She was recorded as a head of household although she lived with her sister and brother in the dwelling house of forty-seven-year-old Aaron Gray and his family. But even if all those cases that were census enumeration differences are deleted from analysis, the difference between black and white unmarried mothers who had children is significant. I have not altered the status of any of the households or families from the way they were set down by the census enumerator.

52. Capt. Taggart of McCormick County figured in another celebrated incident. Taggart built a separate house for his black "consort" directly beside his own. He acknowledged all the black children as his own. He never married. Modjeska Simkins relates similar stories for other areas.

53. Rawick, *American Slave*, vol. 10: *Arkansas*, pt. 5, p. 334.

54. Rawick, *American Slave*, vol. 13: *Georgia*, pt. 3, p. 122.

55. Lebsock, "Radical Reconstruction," p. 195; Millar, "Changes of Divorce"; Senese, "Legal Thought." Ben Tillman's 1895 constitution made divorce unconstitutional, and not until 1948 was divorce again legalized in South Carolina. Pleck, *Black Migration*, pp. 85–87; S.C., Constitutional Convention, *Constitution, 1895*. S.C.,

Dept. of Agriculture, Commerce, and Immigration, *Handbook of South Carolina*, p. 351.

56. Emily B. Cumming to Julia C. Hammond, 28 June 1870, 14 Sept. 1873, 2 May 1876, Hammond, Bryan, Cumming Papers (SCL).

57. Rawick, *American Slave*, vol. 10: *Arkansas*, pt. 5, p. 27. See also sup. ser. vol. 4: *Georgia*, p. 639: "My mammy's fus' husban' was taken by de spec'lators, she say she wait seven years 'fore she marry my father, thinkin' he come back, but freedom declared, and he never come back from dat Nigger Drove."

58. Ibid., vol. 9: *Arkansas*, pt. 3, p. 308.

59. Ibid., vol. 3: *South Carolina*, pt. 3, p. 41 (not from Edgefield, but near).

60. Gutman, *Black Family*, pp. 73–79, 114–15, 117–18, 388–89, 556–57, explained the acceptance of slave illegitimacy. The following example from Gaffney, South Carolina, illustrates illegitimacy, acceptance by the community and family, including the naming of children after the grandfather, and, most important, religion as forgiveness.

> I is what is known as a outside child. . . . My mother had three outside chilluns, and we each had a different father. After she married Ned; den he jest come to be our Pa, dat is he let her give us his name. She and Ned had four chillun. My first wife is dead and my second wife is named Alice Jefferies. I got one child by my first wife, and I ain't got no outside chilluns. Dat work out bad, at best. . . . Firt thing I had to do as a child was to mind my Ma's other chilluns as I was de first outside one dat she had. Dis I did until I was about twelve years old. . . . My grandpa never called me dat (nickname 'Uncle Zer'), kaise I was named atter him, and he too proud of dat fact to call me any nickname. . . . When I was a big boy, my Ma got religion at de camp meeting. She went around to all de people dat she had done wrong and begged dere forgiveness. Sent for those wronged her and told them she was born again and a new woman and dat she would forgive them. (Rawick, *American Slave*, vol. 3: *South Carolina*, pt. 3, p. 17).

61. See Genovese, "Solidarity and Servitude," in which he raises the question of why this pattern continued. Part of the answer was the emphasis the Catholic church placed on abstinence.

62. The values and living arrangements of Afro-Americans in the United States need to be studied in a comparative context. For example, scholars suggest that blacks in the Caribbean and the West Indies, particularly Barbados, were much more matriarchal and tended to have significantly more illegitimate children than in the United States. Anthropologists conclude that in Jamaica, Barbados, and other West Indian societies illegitimacy, matrifocal families, concubinage, and cohabitation are socially approved. Thus, the comparative relative disapproval of these by black Americans suggests how much whites and Afro-Americans in the United States share values. Clarke, *My Mother Who Fathered Me*, has an excellent bibliographical guide. The comparison is confused by the argument in Osofsky, *Harlem*, p. 134, that whereas the native-born United States black family in New York City was matriarchal and unstable, the black family of West Indian immigrants to New York was stable and decidedly patriarchal. It could be that immigration restrictions allowed only the wealthiest of West Indians to emigrate and hence, as in Edgefield, the wealthiest were most often male headed.

63. Wade, *Slavery in Cities*, argues that the social control of slavery did not work in the city. It is safer to say that it did not work as well in the city. Goldin, *Urban Slavery*; Coulter, "Slavery and Freedom," pp. 264–93; Seip, "Slaves and Free Negroes"; Richter, "Slavery in Baton Rouge"; Reinders, "Slavery in New Orleans"; Berlin, *Slaves without Masters*; Hammond, *Address Delivered before South Carolina Institute, 1849*, pp. 31–32.

64. The nonfamily themes of the "town and country" and the historiographical literature are covered in more detail in Burton, "Rise and Fall."

65. Arthur Simkins, et al., "Petition of the Inhabitants of the Village of Edgefield for a Charter of Incorporation," 1839, Legislative Papers (SCDAH); Edgefield *Advertiser*, 2 May 1849 and 27 Jan. 1858; "Journal of the Proceedings of the Beech Island Agricultural and Police Society Organized June 28th 1851," pp. 157–62, and 3 Dec. 1859, Farmers Club (SCL); J. H. Hammond to W. G. Simms, 13 Nov. 1860, and Plantation Diary, J. H. Hammond Papers (SCL); Burton "Ungrateful Servants," pp. 30–31. Story of Coco's rebellion from Cashin, *Story of Augusta*, p. 67.

66. Edgefield *Advertiser*, 6 and 24 Nov. 1865; Ouzts Diary, n.d., follows 30 Nov. 1865 entry, Ouzts Papers (SCL); S.C., Committee of Investigation, *Evidence by Committee of Investigation*, pp. 677–718; Assistant Adjutant Gen. W. L. M. Burger to Brig. Maj. Gen. Charles Devans, 13 Dec. 1865, and reply, 16 Dec. 1865, Records of the Subordinate Field Commanders, Bureau District of Charleston, BRFAL, RG 105 (NA).

67. John Tuialy to Br. Major S. Walker, 9 Mar. 1866, Record Group 393, part 1, series 4112, "Letters and Reports Received Relating to Freedmen and Civil Affairs, 1865–67," Dept. of the South, and South Carolina, and 2nd Military District, BRFAL, RG 105 (NA).

68. Major William Stone to Major T. Walker, 31 Oct. and 31 Dec. 1866, and William Stone to Major H. W. Smith, 28 Feb. 1866, Entry 3051, Records of the Subordinate Field Commanders, Bureau District of Aiken, Subassistant Commissioner for the District of Edgefield, series 3056, Narrative Reports of Operations, all in BRFAL, RG 105 (NA); Lt. Charles Snyder for Brvt. Maj. Gen. R. K. Scott to Brvt. Lt. Col. H. W. Smith, 16 July 1866, Orr Papers (SCDAH); *New York Times*, 9 April 1866; Williamson, *After Slavery*, p. 97; Simkins and Woody, *South Carolina During Reconstruction*, p. 57; Edgefield *Advertiser*, 12 July 1865, 19 Dec. 1866, 5 June 1867, 12 Feb. 1936; Mims, "Editors of Edgefield *Advertiser*," pp. 72–75; Abbott, *Freedmen's Bureau*; Chartock, "History and Analysis."

69. Caroline Rogers, 9 Nov. 1865, Edgefield Affidavits, p. 671, microfilm roll 42, and Gen. Rufus Saxton to Gen. O. O. Howard, 19 Dec. 1865, Registers and Letters Received by the Commissioner of the Bureau of Refugees, Freedmen, and Abandoned Lands, 1865–72, microfilm roll 24, both in BRFAL, RG 105 (NA).

70. *U.S.* vs. *Mark Ethridge*, 13 Oct. 1865, p. 665 (Anna Moore got her children back.); Statement of Mrs. Butler (colored) in regard to U.S. soldiers whipping a colored woman, 15 Sept. 1868, microfilm roll 42, both in BRFAL RG 105 (NA).

71. S.C., Committee of Investigation, *Evidence by Committee of Investigation*, p. 710 (see chap. 3, stories of Root and Eichelberger); Chartock, "History and Analysis," p. 40.

72. Dr. John A. Barker to Gov. D. H. Chamberlain, 1 Jan. 1876, Chamberlain Papers (SCDAH). The occupations and political offices were gathered from a wide vari-

ety of sources, newspapers, manuscript collections, and state documents from 1868 to 1876. For documentation and details see Burton, "Ungrateful Servants," chap. 5.

73. Edgefield *Advertiser*, 19 June 1873. This theme is developed more fully in Burton, "Ungrateful Servants" and "Race and Reconstruction."

74. In order to define and examine these ecological patterns more closely, an effort was made to separate out those town and village centers in Edgefield County in 1880 that were not distinguished in the census returns from the rural hinterlands. This was accomplished by selecting from the 1880 population census returns those occupations one might find in towns or more built-up "urbanized" areas. Since the occupations of every household head in the county have been placed in a computer file, I was able to select all the managerial, clerical, professional, and artisanal occupations and then check to see if there were any areas in which the census taker recorded several such occupations. These areas were then blocked out and recorded as "urbanized" areas. I also checked names of individuals on maps and in Dun and Bradstreet, *Mercantile Reference Books* (LC), and Campbell, *Southern Business Directory*, and searched the computer files for the names of businessmen to see if these might give a clue to crossroad towns. So strong is this demographic correlation that when one groups out 1880 population nodes that contain small concentrations of nonagricultural occupations, one finds that the number of black female-headed households increases in the vicinity of these "villages," following the same pattern as the incorporated towns.

75. An Edgefield example, Warren McKinney and his mother, can be found in Rawick, *American Slave*, vol. 10: *Arkansas*, pt. 5, pp. 27, 28, 30.

76. This occurred both in the town and on the plantation. The replacement of former slave artisans by whites is seen in a letter from the son of Thomas J. McKie to his father, who had hired an immigrant from Scotland to replace the former slave shoemaker on the plantation. The son wrote of the scene when the Scotsman arrived: "It would have been better for the Scotch if Harry had taken himself out of the way before they got there" (T. J. McKie, Jr., to Thomas Jefferson McKie, 5 June 1873, McKie Papers [DU]). An organizer for black migration to Liberia after Redemption aptly remarked, when the ship *Azor* on which three Edgefield black families sailed reached Africa in 1878, "The white men took care that no more negroes should learn trades and mechanics, but, thank God, they couldn't take them away from those who had already acquired them" (Williams, *Liberian Exodus*, p. 36). See also Burton, "Rise and Fall," pp. 179–80.

77. Burton, "Development of Tenantry"; S.C., State Board of Agriculture, *South Carolina*, p. 559, is referring to towns in Edgefield such as Johnston, Ridge Spring, Parksville, Trenton, Ward.

78. Rawick, *American Slave*, sup. ser. vol. 3: *Georgia*, p. 319. See chap. 3 and also my review of *Black Migration*.

79. C. J. Jenkins to H. Hammond, 28 Feb. 1880, in the Hammond, Bryan, Cumming Papers (SCL).

80. Hammond in U.S., Congress, House, *Report of Industrial Commission*, pp. 821, 822, 819.

81. J. D. Greene to Gen. E. L. Deane, 30 Apr. 1867. Records of the Subordinate Field Commanders, Bureau District of Columbia, series 3153, Letters Sent, BRFAL, RG 105 (NA); Harrison N. Bouey to Rev. H. M. Turner, 23 May 1877, American Colonization Papers, 227:142 (LC).

82. Simkins and Bailey Papers; Edgefield Sanborne Insurance Maps (LC); Edgefield Village Baptist Church Records, Oct., 20 Nov. 1867, and 13 July 1869 (BHC); Mims, *History of Edgefield Baptist Church*; Woodson et al., *History of Edgefield Baptist Association*, pp. 55–60; S.C., Committee of Investigation, *Evidence by Committee of Investigation*, pp. 702–3; Edgefield *Advertiser*, 6 Oct. 1870; Nicholson, *Brief Sketch*, p. 70; Bettis Academy, *Academy Bulletin*, 1930 (BA); Chapman, *History of Edgefield*, p. 316. No Federal Works Project Administration survey was done for Edgefield County. The original WPA Church Record Surveys are in SCL. For Saluda, McCormick, and Greenwood, all counties formed at least partly from Edgefield, the above pattern holds. The Edgefield pattern also holds for Abbeville, Allendale, and Anderson counties. See also the Negro Baptist Association Records at ABHS.

83. Gill, "Economics and Black Exodus"; Vickery, "Economics of Negro Migration"; Woodson, *Century of Negro Migration*; Pleck, *Black Migration*, pp. 44–75; Kiser, *Sea Island to City*; Jones, "Black Migration."

Conclusion

1. For nonscholarly views of the quality of black home life see Page, "Southern Bully"; Winter, "Letters," p. 845; Page, *The Negro*; Watson, *Bethany*; Logan, *Betrayal of the Negro*, p. 25. For views of a "moderate" South Carolinian see Hampton, "Negro Supremacy," p. 389. See also Ruoff, "Southern Womanhood," chap. 5. Early influential scholarly views are represented by DuBois, *Negro Family*; Odum, *Social and Mental Traits*; Frazier, *Negro Family*.

2. This is consistent with economist Claudia Goldin's findings for cities (Goldin, "Female Labor Force").

3. For a thorough bibliography of sociological literature and theories, see Mindel and Habenstein, *Ethnic Families*, pp. 243–47.

4. Willie Lee Rose has suggested that modern writers have "blithely attributed" the fragmentation of the ghetto family to the "heritage of slavery." On the other hand, Eugene D. Genovese wrote: "If it is true that the black family has disintegrated in the ghettos . . . then the source will have to be found in the conditions of economic and social oppression imposed upon blacks during recent decades. The slave experience . . . pointed toward a stable postslavery family life, and recent scholarship demonstrates conclusively that the Reconstruction and post-Reconstruction black experience carried forward acceptance of nuclear family norm." Both statements are right, yet both are misleading, as explained below. Rose, review of *First Freedom*, 608–9; Genovese, *Red and Black*, n. 3, p. 113.

5. Regression analysis demonstrated this racial discrimination which the above observation of data in chapter 7 suggested. The percentage of black households headed by a female in each of the twenty-eight townships was regressed on the percentage of employed white male household heads who were in professional, managerial, clerical, and business occupations. This regression explained a remarkably high percentage of the variation in black female-headed households, 71 percent of the variation in black female household heads—an extremely high r^2 for a bivariate regression. The identical regression equation of the percentage of white women heading households

with the same occupations in each township produced an insignificnt r^2 of .0095. Widowed white female household heads often owned farms in the countryside, and white female household heads in 1880 were not so concentrated in town areas as were black women household heads. Adding the percentage of white female household heads to the regression of nonfarming occupations and percentage of black female household heads raises the r^2 to only .76006. Thus, one can even measure the impact of the small clusters of townlike places on the general rural landscape.

6. Pleck, *Black Migration*, pp. 183–84, placed studies according to northern cities, southern cities, and southern rural in tabular format (Table 6-8). My own study is confused in the table with the work of Crandall Shifflett.

7. Hareven, "Family as Process," p. 322.

8. Blassingame, *Black New Orleans*, pp. 100, 102.

9. Gutman, "Persistent Myths," Table 1, p. 195, and *Black Family*, esp. pp. 442–50, 485–530, 624–25.

10. Shifflett, "Household Composition" and *Patronage and Poverty*, p. 236; Kolchin, *First Freedom*, p. 69.

11. Lammermeier, "Urban Black Family," p. 505.

12. Elizabeth Pleck has shown this in two works. In "Two-Parent Household," tables 4, 5, pp. 5–6, 18–19, and in *Black Migration*, Pleck argues convincingly that southern migrants maintained their families better than northern born. In the latter work she says, "City life in some way also seemed to foster separation and desertion" (p. 175). See my review of *Black Migration*.

13. Dublin, *Women at Work*, pp. 170–71.

14. Yans-McLaughlin, *Family and Community*.

15. Furstenberg, Hershberg, and Modell, "Origins of Female Headed Black Family," p. 232.

16. Pleck, *Black Migration*, pp. 182, 183–84, Table 6-8.

17. On matriarchal families among the urban poor in twentieth-century Latin America, see Lewis, *Children of Sanchez* and *La Vida*; Fernandes, *Negro in Brazilian Society*.

18. Fusfeld, *Basic Economics*; Liebow, *Talley's Corner*; Osofsky, *Harlem*; Katzman, *Before the Ghetto*; Spear, *Black Chicago*; Thernstrom, *Other Bostonians*, pp. 176–219. Gerber, "Politics of Limited Options," pp. 235–55, reviews the literature on blacks in the northen cities. A powerful "conservative" southern intellectual's statement of the relegation of blacks to agrarian roles from the 1930s is Warren, "Briar Patch." For example, p. 262: "Rural life provides the most satisfactory relationship between races."

19. Bender, *Community and Social Change*, p. 100.

Methodological Appendix

(A more detailed methodological appendix and additional tables are available from the author for the costs of copying and mailing.)

1. Simkins, *Simkins Family*, p. 2 (SCL).

2. Problems with the slave narratives are discussed by several scholars. Rawick, *American Slave*, sup. ser., for example, vol. 11: *North and South Carolina*, pp. ix–

lvi, "General Introduction" and "Appendix," has excellent discussions concerning use of the narratives. See also Woodward, "History from Slave Sources"; Davidson and Lytle, *After the Fact*, 1:169–204; Blassingame, "Using Testimony of Ex-Slaves" and *Slave Testimony*, pp. xxxii–lxii; Yetman, "Background of Slave Narrative Collection"; Escott, *Slavery Remembered*; Van Deburg, *Slave Drivers*, pp. 77–94; Bailey, "Divided Prism."

3. The instructions to the census enumerators are conveniently reprinted in Soltow, *Men and Wealth*, p. 1. See also on the manuscript censuses, Ransom and Sutch, *One Kind of Freedom*, pp. 220, 283–89; Fogel and Engerman, *Time on Cross*, 2:21; Burton, "Using the Computer."

4. Laslett, *Household and Family*, pp. 23–39, 41–42.

5. Hershberg, "Method of Computerized Study."

6. Berkner, "Use and Misuse of Census Data"; Furstenberg et al., "What Happened." Pioneering work with the manuscript census returns and quantitative techniques was done by Frank L. Owsley and his graduate students. See Owsley, *Plain Folk*; Lathrop, *Migration into East Texas* and "History from Census Returns"; Bonner, "Profile of Late Antebellum Community"; Curti, *Making of American Community*; Sellers, *Slavery in Alabama*; Wright, "Note on the Manuscript Census Samples"; Ransom and Sutch, "Impact of Civil War" and *One Kind of Freedom*, pp. 273–305; Wiener, *Social Origins*, pp. 229–39; Pleck, *Black Migration*, pp. 214–20.

7. Pleck, *Black Migration*, p. 214 (n. 1).

8. Ransom and Sutch, "Impact of Civil War," pp. 8–10, and *One Kind of Freedom*, pp. 53–54, 224.

9. Knights, *Plain People of Boston*, appendix C, pp. 144–47, and "City Directories as Aids"; Pleck, *Black Migration*, p. 215.

10. Ransom and Sutch, "Impact of Civil War," pp. 6–11, and *One Kind of Freedom*, pp. 54, 284, 294–95, 369 (n. 19), 371 (nn. 26 and 27).

11. Burton, "Development of Tenantry."

12. Ransom and Sutch, *One Kind of Freedom*, p. 295.

13. Ibid., pp. 220–23; Fogel and Engerman, *Time on Cross*, 2:27, 100; Crimmins, "Completeness of 1900 Mortality Data."

14. Based on technique used by Pleck, *Black Migration*, pp. 215–16.

Bibliography

Manuscript and Archival Materials

American Baptist Historical Society, Colgate-Rochester Seminary, Rochester, N.Y.
  Records of Negro Baptist Associations, South Carolina and Georgia Groups
  Atlanta University Records
  Payne College Records
Amistad Research Center, Dillon University, New Orleans, La.
  American Missionary Association Records, South Carolina and Georgia
    (microfilm).
Baker Library, Harvard University Graduate School of Business Administration,
  Boston, Mass.
    R. G. Dun & Co. Collection
Baptist Historical Collection, Furman University, Greenville, S.C.
  Association Minutes (all had Edgefield churches as members.)
    Abbeville
    Aiken
    Bethel
    Edgefield
    Edisto
    Lexington
    Ridge
    Savannah River
  Edgefield Church Records
    Big Stevens Creek
    Dean Swamp
    Dry Creek
    Edgefield Village (First Edgefield) Church
    Horn's Creek
    Johnston
    Little Stevens Creek (Steven's Creek)
    Red Bank
    Sweetwater
  Basil Manly, Sr., Papers
Bettis Academy, rural Edgefield County
  Miscellaneous papers (includes Academy Bulletins)
Clemson University Library, Clemson, S.C.
  James F. Byrnes Papers

John C. Calhoun Papers
Thomas Green Clemson Papers
Benjamin Ryan Tillman Papers
Columbia University, Rare Book and Manuscript Library, New York
William Hawkins Ferris Manuscripts
Daniel Augustus Tompkins Library, Edgefield, S.C.
Miscellaneous Collection
William Whitlock Papers
Duke University, Perkins Library, Durham, N.C.
Iveson L. Brookes Papers
Armistead Burt Papers
Compiled Service Records of Confederate Soldiers Who Served in Organizations
    from the State of South Carolina
Matthew Calbraith Butler Papers
John C. Calhoun Papers
William Patrick Calhoun Papers
Daniel Henry Chamberlain Papers
Clement Clairborne Papers
Thomas Green Clemson Papers
Francis Warrington Dawson Papers (collection includes papers of Matthew
    Calbraith Butler, Francis Wilkinson Pickens, Arthur Simkins)
Frederick A. Dugas Papers
Martin Witherspoon Gary Papers
Wade Hampton Papers
John Hollingsworth Papers
Matthias Jones Papers
Thomas Jefferson McKie Papers
James L. Orr Papers
Abner M. Perrin Papers
Benjamin Franklin Perry Papers
Francis Wilkinson Pickens Papers
Louisa Bouknight and Mary Barnett Poppenheim Papers
Joseph H. Rainey Papers
Richard Realf Papers
Jesse Roundtree Papers
Sheppard Brothers Papers
Arthur Simkins Papers
Frederick C. Smith Papers
South Carolina Militia Papers
South Carolina Reconstruction Papers
Benjamin R. Tillman Papers
Daniel Augustus Tompkins Papers
William Henry Trescott Papers
United Daughters of the Confederacy Papers
Milten and Oliphant S. Walker Papers
Josephus Woodruff Diary
Agatha (Abney) Woodson Papers

Edgefield Court House, Edgefield, S.C.
  Bethany Baptist Church Records
  County Tax Books
  Court Records
    Civil Court Records—Bills and Petitions
    Commissioner's Minute Book of Civil Records
    Common Pleas and General Sessions Records
    Coroner's Book of Inquisitions
    Deeds
    Equity Court Records
    Pension Records
    Probate Court Records
    Records of Proceeding in Cases of Summons in Partition (Court of Ordinary)
Family Papers in Private Possession of the Families:
  Blocker Family Papers
  Bones Family Papers
  Whitfield Brooks Papers and Diaries
  Butler Papers (Simon and Easter)
  Lewis and Smith Family Papers
  Morgan Papers
  David Parker Papers
  Johanna Payne Papers
  Francis and Lucy Holcombe Pickens Papers
  James Beale Rainsford Papers
  Reed Family Papers
  Simkins Family Papers (Arthur Simkins)
  Simkins and Bailey Papers (Paris Simkins)
  Strother Family Papers
  Hortense Woodson Papers
Georgia State Archives, Atlanta
  L. C. Grant Papers
Graniteville Manufacturing Company, Graniteville, S.C.
  Graniteville Manufacturing Company Papers
Library of Congress, Washington, D.C.
  American Colonization Society Papers
  Milledge Luke Bonham Papers
  R. G. Dun and Company and Dun and Bradstreet *Mercantile Reference Books*
  Ulysses S. Grant Papers
  James Henry Hammond Papers
  Francis Wilkinson Pickens Papers
  Alexander Hamilton Stephens Papers
  Louis Trezevant Wigfall Papers (and Wigfall Family Papers)
  Geography and Map Division (Sanborne Insurance Maps of Edgefield and
    Johnston)
Methodist Archives, Wofford College, Spartanburg, S.C.
  Graniteville Methodist Church Records
National Archives, Washington, D.C.

Records of the Office of the Adjutant General (RG 94)
Records of the Bureau of the Census
Cartographic Division—Maps
Civil War Pension Files, Records of the Veterans Administration (RG 15)
General Records, Department of Justice (RG 60)
Lewis Cass Papers
Official Records of the War of the Rebellion
Records of the Post Office Department
Records of the Bureau of Refugees, Freedmen, and Abandoned Lands (RG 105)
Records of United States Army Continental Commands: Departments of the South
    and South Carolina and 2d Military District, 1862–83; Department of the South,
    1866; Division of the South, 1869–76
Records of the Work Projects Administration
Pottersville Museum, Edgefield, S.C.
Mitchell Account Books
Hughes and Ramey Merchant Ledgers
St. Mary's Church, Edgefield, S.C.
Diary, Fr. Bermingham Papers
Marriage Records
Death Records
South Carolina Department of Archives and History, Columbia, S.C. (Readers should
be aware that the South Carolina Archives was reorganizing collections referred to in
my notes when I researched the material. An index of holdings is being prepared and
this index will make it much easier to locate specific records.)
Church Records
    Records of Bethany Baptist Church
    Records of Bethel Baptist Church
    Records of the Edgefield Baptist Church
    Miscellaneous Records, Life of the Reverend Abraham Marshall and the
        Reverend Daniel Marshall
Records of the Governor
    Milledge Luke Bonham Papers
    Daniel H. Chamberlain Papers
    John Gary Evans Papers
    Wade Hampton Papers
    Franklin J. Moses, Jr., Papers
    James L. Orr Papers
    Benjamin F. Perry Papers
    Francis Wilkinson Pickens Papers
    Robert K. Scott Papers
    John C. Sheppard Papers
    Benjamin Ryan Tillman Papers
    Office of the Governor as Chief Executive
Green Files
Convention of 1832
Convention of 1852
Convention of 1860

Convention of 1868
Convention of 1895
Records of the Secretary of State
State Census Schedules, 1829–69
State Grants
Documents of the Palmetto Regiment
Voter Registrations, 1867–68, 1898
Minutes of the Palmetto Regiment Association, 1869–81
Correspondence Relating to Mexican War Medals, 1852–55
State Plats, 1840–90
Direct Tax, 1862–66, 1892
Schedules of Taxes Paid, 1862–66
Military Records: S.C. Military Department; Military Affairs
Maps
Correspondence and Other Material Relating to Confederate Money Rolls and
    Histories
General Assembly Records and Petitions; in Legislative Papers
Grand Jury Presentments; in Legislative Papers
Joint Investigating Committee on Public Frauds
House of Representatives Records; in Legislative Papers
Clerk of the House, List of Claims against the State, 1870–77
Committee on Ways and Means; Register of Bills, 1872–76
Senate Records, in Legislative Papers
Records of the Attorney General
Records of the State Treasurer
Office of Public Treasurers
Office of the Treasurer of the Upper Division
Records of the Comptroller General
Commissioners of Forfeited Estates, Papers Relating to Claims, 1840–50
Office of the State Auditor
Records of the University of South Carolina, Correspondence of the Secretary,
    1869–76
Records of the Court of Appeals, 1859–68
Records of the Court of Appeals in Equity, 1840–59
Records of the Department of Education: Free School Reports, Superintendent of
    Education Papers
State Board of Canvassers
    Election Returns, 1868–1900
    Minutes, 1868–1900
Records of the Supreme Court
Records of the Department of Agriculture
Records of the Chief Constable
Records of the Court of Claims, 1878
Sinking Fund Commission
Public Land Division
Land Commission Records
Historic Marker Survey

Confederate Home
Board of Equalization, Minutes, 1873–1900
City of Aiken
The South Carolina Historical Records Survey Project Inventory of the County
    Archives of South Carolina, No. 19, Edgefield County (April 1946)
Records of Aiken County
Records of Edgefield County
Records of Greenwood County
Records of McCormick County
Records of Saluda County
South Carolina Historical Society, Charleston, S.C.
David T. Corbin Papers
Anne King Gregorie Papers
List of Emigrants for Liberia, 17 November 1867
Liberty Church Records, Bullock County, Ala.
Maps and Muniments
Palmetto Regiment, Charleston
Christopher Pritchard Poppenheim Papers
Porcher Family Papers
Jacob Frederick Schirmer Diary of Travels
South Carolina Agricultural Society
South Carolina File
Survivors Association Records
David Duncan Wallace Papers
South Caroliniana Library, University of South Carolina, Columbia, S.C.
Benjamin Lindsay Abney Papers
David Wyatt Aiken Papers
Thomas Aiton Papers
Robert Francis Withers Allston Papers
Mrs. Charles G. Anderson Papers
Anthenaeum Fire Insurance Company, Charleston
John Asbill Papers
John Edmund Bacon Papers
Baptist Church, Edgefield County, Horn's Creek
Baptist Church, Edgefield County, Mountain Creek
Baptist Church, Saluda County, Bethel
Elise Lake Chase (Mrs. John Shaw) Billings Papers
John Shaw Billings Papers
John Shaw Billings and Frederica Wade Papers
Katharine Hammond Billings Papers
Jesse Blocker Papers
Bones Family Papers
Milledge Lipscomb Bonham Papers
Milledge Luke Bonham Papers
Benjamin Booth Papers
Mary Bouknight Papers
Iveson L. Brookes Papers

Preston Smith Brooks Papers
Andrew Pickens Butler Papers
Butler Family Papers
Matthew Calbraith Butler Papers
[Matthew Calbraith] Butler and [Leroy] Youmans Papers
Pierce Butler Papers
Pierce Mason Butler Papers
James Edward Calhoun (Colhoun) Papers
John Caldwell Calhoun Papers
Carolina, Cumberland Gap and Chicago Railroad Papers
James Parsons Carroll Papers
Abiah Morgan Cartledge Papers
Langdon Cheves Papers
Addison Clinkscales Papers
William Coleman Papers
Confederate States Army, Department of South Carolina and Georgia
Coroner's Inquest Book, Edgefield, 1844–59
Mrs. Flossie Lamb Crouch Papers
Daniel Family Papers
William Daniel Papers
Thomas Jones Davies Papers
Godfrey Dreher Papers
Dugas-Kerblay Families Papers
Isaac H. Dyches Papers
Edgefield Committee, 1851
Edgefield County Papers
Edgefield County Court of General Sessions Records
Edgefield Female Institute Circular
Edgefield Female Institute Catalogue, 1850
Edgefield Male Academy Papers
Edgefield Village Bible Society
John Gary Evans Papers
Farmers Club, Beech Island. Records of the ABC Farmers Club
Finley-Henderson Family Papers
Martin Witherspoon Gary Papers
William H. Gilliland Papers
Graniteville Manufacturing Company Papers
James R. Gregg Papers
Kittie [Catherine W.] Gregg Papers
William Gregg Papers
Robert C. Grier, 1850 Broadside
Nathan Lipscomb Griffin Papers
Hammond, Bryan, Cumming Families Papers
Edward Spann Hammond Papers
Emily Cumming Hammond Papers
Hammond Family Papers
Harry Hammond Papers

Henry Cumming Hammond Papers
James Henry Hammond Papers
Hammond and Lark, Hamburg Papers
Marcellus Claudius Hammond Papers
Paul Fitzsimons Hammond Papers
Hampton Family Papers
John S. Hard Papers
William Henry Hare Papers
Harris Family Papers
Robert Young Haynes Papers
Mrs. Susan B. Hill Papers
P. S. Jacobs Papers
William Jeter Papers
Johnson Female University
Francis Cleveland Johnson Papers
William Bullein Johnson Papers
S. N. Kennedy Papers
Knights of Honor, Edgefield Lodge Papers
Maximilian LaBorde Papers
Ladies Memorial Association Broadside "To the Patriotic Women of Edgefield"
    (c. 1890)
G. W. Landrum Papers
Joshua Lockwood Papers
Augustus Baldwin Longstreet Papers
Lutheran Church, Saluda County, Corinth
Lutheran Church, Saluda County, St. Mark's
John Charles McClenaghan Papers
Dorothy K. MacDowell Papers
George McDuffie Papers
Thomas Jefferson McKie Papers
William Dickinson Martin Journal
Methodist Church, Harmony, Edgefield County
Methodist Church, McKendree, Edgefield
Hugh Graves Middleton Papers
Minutemen, Saluda Association
Mary Elizabeth Moragne Papers
William Caine Moragne Papers
Nicholson, Hughes, and Bones Families Papers
Ninth Regiment, S.C., Militia
Noble Family Papers
William Oliphant Papers
John Belton O'Neall Papers
Open Letter of the Committee of Safety, 11 August 1849
James Lawrence Orr Papers
James Talbert Ouzts Papers (plantation books include diary)
James Louis Pettigru Papers
Andrew Pickens Papers

Andrew Pickens, Jr., Papers
Douschka Pickens Papers
Pickens Family Papers
Francis Wilkinson Pickens Papers
Octavius Theodore Porcher Papers
William Campbell Preston Papers
Mrs. J. M. Prioleau Papers
Protestant Episcopal Church, Aiken, St. Thaddeus
Protestant Episcopal Church, Upper Diocese of South Carolina Records
J. Quattlebaum Papers
A. Ramsay 1861 Broadside Letter
Richard Realf Papers
Daniel Richardson Papers
John Smyth Richardson Papers
Thomas Rodgers Papers
Rodgers and Latimer, Hamburg, 1825 Account
Sams Family Papers
Seibels Family Papers
Sheppard Brothers (J. C. and Orlando), Edgefield Papers
Sheppard Family Papers
J. C. and Orlando Sheppard Papers
John Calhoun Sheppard Papers
Henry Shultz Papers
Arthur Simkins Papers
Eldred Simkins Papers
Simkins Family Papers
William Gilmore Simms Papers
Yates Snowden Collection
Sons of Temperance in South Carolina Circular
South Carolina Militia, Seventh Regiment
South Carolina Railroad Company
James Spann Papers
Swearingen Family Papers
John Eldred Swearingen Papers
John Forsythe Talbert Papers
Benjamin Ryan Tillman Papers
George Dionysius Tillman Papers
Elijah Timmerman Papers
David Tobin Papers
John Etienne Tobin Papers
Daniel Augustus Tompkins Papers
Tompkins Family Papers
Henrietta Tompkins Papers
Trezevant Family Papers
United Confederate Veterans, Abner Perrin Camp, Edgefield
Moses Waddel Papers
William I. Walker Papers

Philemon Berry Waters, Notebooks "Historical Notes on Edgefield County" and "Miscellaneous Historical Notes of Edgefield"
Beaufort T. Watts Papers
Elijah Webb Papers
Belle Williams Papers
Williams-Chesnut-Manning Families Papers
LeRoy Franklin Youmans Papers
Southern Historical Collection, University of North Carolina, Chapel Hill, N.C.
Iveson Lewis Brookes Papers
Chapin and Tunnel Family Papers
John Hamilton Cornish Papers
James Henry Hammond Papers
John Hill Papers (includes Col. John Hill Military Record)
Hughes Family Papers
Edward Lipscomb Papers
N. A. Nicholson Papers
Orr-Patterson Papers and Books
Perrin Family Papers
Benjamin F. Perry Papers
Pickens-Dugas Papers
Francis Wilkinson Pickens Papers
Martha Schofield Diary
John McKee Sharpe Papers
William Henry Trescot Letters
Marion Wright Papers
William Lowndes Yancey Papers
Tennessee State Library and Archives, Nashville, Tenn.
Tennessee Civil War Veterans' Questionnaires
United Daughters of the Confederacy Relic Room, State Capitol, Columbia, S.C.
Edgefield Records
University of Texas at Austin, Eugene C. Barker History Center
Louis T. Wigfall Papers
University of Virginia Library, Charlottesville, Va.
R. M. T. Hunter Papers
Vanderbilt University Library, Nashville, Tenn.
Frank L. Owsley Papers

Government Publications

South Carolina. Committee of Investigation. *Evidence Taken by the Committee of Investigation of the 3rd Congressional District*. Columbia, 1870.
———. Constitutional Convention. *The Constitution of South Carolina, Adopted 16 April 1868*. Columbia: John W. Denny, 1868.
———. Constitutional Convention. *Constitution of the State of South Carolina, Ratified in Convention December 4, 1895*. Columbia: R. L. Bryan, 1909.

_____. Dept. of Agriculture, Commerce, and Immigration. *Handbook of South Carolina: Resources, Institutions and Industries of the State: A Summary of the Statistics of Agriculture, Climate, Geology and Physiography, Minerals and Mining, Education, Transportation, Commerce, Government, Etc.* 2nd ed. Columbia: State Company, 1908.

_____. General Assembly. [Journal.] *Reports and Joint Resolutions of the General Assembly of the State of South Carolina. Journals of the House* and *Journals of the Senate.* The *Journals* of the House and Senate were not printed until the 1831 session. The unpublished journals are in the South Carolina Department of Archives and History. From 1831 until 1841 they are included in abbreviated form with the published volumes of the *Acts of the General Assembly.* Since 1842 the journals have been printed separately.

_____. General Assembly. *Code of Laws of South Carolina.* Clinton: Jacobs Press, 1942.

_____. General Assembly. *South Carolina Legislative Times*, 33rd Legis., 2nd Sess. Columbia: E. H. Britton & Co., 1856.

_____. General Assembly. *Statutes at Large of South Carolina.* Thomas Cooper and David J. McCord, eds. vols. 1–10. Columbia: A. S. Johnston, 1840.

_____. State Board of Agriculture. *South Carolina: Resources and Population. Institutions and Industries.* Compiled by Harry Hammond. Charleston: Walker, Evans and Cogswell, 1883.

U.S. Bureau of the Census. *Census*, 1830, 5th, 1840, 6th, 1850, 7th, 1860, 8th, 1870, 9th, 1880, 10th, 1890, 11th, 1900, 12th. Washington: Government Printing Office.

U.S. Bureau of Chemistry and Soils (Department of Agriculture). *Soil Survey of Edgefield County, South Carolina.* Prepared by F. R. Lesh. Series 1935, no. 1. Washington, Government Printing Office, 1938.

U.S. Congress. *Congressional Globe*, 1834–73. 46 vols. Washington: Government Printing Office.

_____. *Congressional Record*, 1873–1920. Washington: Government Printing Office.

_____. House. *Journal*, 1830–80. Washington: Government Printing Office.

_____. House. *Report of the Industrial Commission on Agriculture and Agriculture Labor.* Document no. 179, 57th Cong., 2d Sess. Washington: Government Printing Office, 1901.

_____. Senate. Committee on Education and Labor, *Labor and Capital.* 48th Cong. Washington: Government Printing Office, 1885.

_____. Senate. *Journal*, 1830–90. Washington: Government Printing Office.

_____. Senate. *The Mission of Women: An Article Printed in the Southern Review, October, 1871*, by Albert Taylor Bledsoe. Document 174, 63rd Cong., 1st Sess., 1913. Washington: Government Printing Office, 1913 (presented by Sen. Tillman of South Carolina).

U.S. Office of Experiment Stations. *The Cotton Plant: Its History, Botany, Chemistry, Culture, Enemies, and Uses.* Bulletin No. 33. Washington: Government Printing Office, 1896.

U.S. Works Project Administration. The South Carolina Historical Records Survey

Project, Division of Professional and Service Projects, *Inventory of the County Archives of South Carolina, No. 19, Edgefield County (Edgefield)*. Columbia: South Carolina Historical Records Survey Project, April 1940 (available in SCDAH).

Newspapers and Periodicals

Abbeville *Banner and Press*
Aiken *Courier Journal*
Appleton's Annual Cyclopaedia and Register of Important Events of the Year
Augusta *Chronicle and Constitutionalist*
Augusta *Daily Chronicle and Sentinel*
Augusta *Daily Constitutionalist*
Campbells Business Directory
Charleston *Chronicle*
Charleston *Mercury*
Charleston *News and Courier* (also cited as the *Courier*)
Chester *Standard*
Cincinnati *Daily Gazette*
Columbia *Daily Register*
Columbia *Daily Telegraph*
Columbus *Daily Gazette*
DeBow's Review
Edgefield *Advertiser*
Edgefield *Chronicle*
(Edgefield) *Plow Boy*
Hamburg *Courier*
Hamburg *Journal*
Hamburg *Republic*
Hamburg *Valley Pioneer*
Johnston *Mentor*
Marshall *Texas Republican*
Newberry *Herald and News*
New York *Daily Tribune*
New York Times
Pottersville *Hive*
Pottersville *Republic*
Rural Carolinian
Southern Agriculturalist
Southern Quarterly Review
Springfield Ohio *Daily Republic*
Tribune Almanac and Political Register, published annually by the New York *Tribune*

Three periodicals that were not contemporary to the research for this volume contained such important information that they are listed for their publication period.

Many important articles on specific subjects have not been included in the bibliography.

Bulletins of the Historical Commission of South Carolina

Proceedings of the South Carolina Historical Association

The South Carolina Historical and Genealogical Magazine, renamed in 1941 *South Carolina Historical Magazine*. Articles from the former have been reprinted in four volumes with a fifth volume index compiled by Margaret H. Cannon.

South Carolina Genealogies: Articles from the South Carolina Historical (and Genealogical) Magazine. 5 vols. Published in association with the South Carolina Historical Society, Spartanburg, S.C.: Reprint Company, 1983.

Books, Articles, Genealogies, Dissertations, Theses, and Unpublished Papers (Secondary sources are limited to works that are mentioned in the notes.)

Aba-Mecha, Barbara W. "Black Woman Activist in Twentieth Century South Carolina: Modjeska Monteith Simkins," Ph.D. dissertation, Emory University, 1978.

Abbott, Martin. *The Freedmen's Bureau in South Carolina, 1865-1872*. Chapel Hill: University of North Carolina Press, 1967.

Abzug, Robert. "The Black Family during Reconstruction." In *Key Issues in the Afro-American Experience*, edited by Nathan J. Huggins, Martin Kilson, and Daniel M. Fox. Pp. 26–41. New York: Harcourt Brace Jovanovich, 1971.

Agee, James, and Evans, Walker. *Let Us Now Praise Famous Men*. Boston: Houghton Mifflin, 1941.

Allen, Walter. *Governor Chamberlain's Administration in South Carolina*. New York: Putnam, 1888.

Andrews, Columbus. *Administrative County Government in South Carolina*. Chapel Hill: University of North Carolina Press, 1933.

Andrews, Mathew Page, comp. *The Women of the South in War Times*. Baltimore: Norman, Remington Co., 1920.

Aptheker, Herbert. "South Carolina Poll Tax, 1737–1895." *Journal of Negro History* 31 (Apr. 1946): 131–39.

Asbury, Francis. *The Journal and Letters of Francis Asbury, Bishop of the Methodist Episcopal Church, from August 7, 1771, to December 7, 1815*. 3 vols. New York, 1821. Reprint edited by Elmer T. Clark. London: Epworth and Abingdon Press, 1958.

Ashmore, Nancy V. "The Development of the African Methodist Episcopal Church in South Carolina, 1865–1965." M.A. thesis, University of South Carolina, 1969.

Atack, Jeremy, and Bateman, Fred. " 'The Egalitarian Ideal' and the Distribution of Wealth in the Northern Agricultural Community: A Backward Look." *Review of Economics and Statistics* 63 (Feb. 1981): 124–29.

———. "Egalitarianism, Inequality, and Age: The Rural North in 1860." *Journal of Economic History* 41 (Mar. 1981): 85–93.

Aull, J. Luther, and Aull, Peggy Hite, eds. *The Johnston Area Family History Book*.

Johnston, S.C.: *Ridge Citizen*, 1981.

Bailey, C. Bruce, Sr. "Childhood Remembrances." N.p., n.d. (in possession of author).

Bailey, Fred A. "Caste and the Classroom in Antebellum Tennessee." *Maryland Historian* 13 (Spring/Summer 1982): 40–54.

————. "Class and Tennessee's Confederate Generation." Unpublished manuscript in possession of the author.

————. "Tennessee's Antebellum Society from the Bottom Up." *Journal of Southern Studies: Interdisciplinary Journal of the South.* 22 (Fall 1983): 260–73.

Bailey, Thomas David. "A Divided Prism: Two Sources of Black Testimony on Slavery," *Journal of Southern History* 46 (August 1980): 381–404.

Bailie, Glover R., Jr. "St. Paul's Episcopal Church: Marriages Solemnized between 1820–1868 at Augusta's Oldest Church." *Ancestoring: A Publication of the Augusta Genealogical Society, Inc.*, 3 (1981): 19–27.

Ball, William Watts. *The State that Forgot: South Carolina's Surrender to Democracy.* Indianapolis: Bobbs-Merrill, 1932.

Banister, Eme O'Dell. *The Family of Rogers of the Piedmont Section, South Carolina and Allied Families.* Anderson, S.C.: n.p., 1965.

Banks, James G. "Strom Thurmond and the Revolt against Modernity." Ph.D. dissertation, Kent State University, 1970.

Banner, James, Jr. "The Problem of South Carolina." In *The Hofstadter Aegis: A Memorial*, edited by Stanley Elkins and Eric McKitrick. New York: Knopf, 1974.

Bartlett, Marguerite Blocker. *Haley Talbot Blocker: His Background and Life.* St. Petersburg, Fla.; Galaher's Letter Shop, 1970.

Barton, Josef J. *Peasants and Strangers: Italians, Rumanians, and Slovaks in an American City, 1890–1950.* Cambridge: Harvard University Press, 1975.

Barney, William L. "Patterns of Crisis: Alabama White Families and Social Change, 1850-1870." *Sociology and Social Research: An International Journal* 63 (Apr. 1979): 524–43.

Bass, Robert D. *Ninety Six: The Struggle for the South Carolina Backcountry.* Lexington, S.C.: Sandlapper Store, 1978.

Battalio, Raymond C., and Kagel, John. "The Structure of Antebellum Southern Agriculture: South Carolina, a Case Study." *Agricultural History* 44 (Oct. 1970): 25–37.

Becker, Gary S. *A Treatise on the Family.* Cambridge: Harvard University Press, 1981.

Beloff, Max. "The Sally Hemings Affair." *Encounter* 43 (Sept. 1974): 52–56.

Bender, Thomas. *Community and Social Change in America.* New Brunswick: Rutgers University Press, 1978.

Berkner, Lutz K. "The Use and Misuse of Census Data for the Historical Analysis of Family Structure." *Journal of Interdisciplinary History* 4 (Spring 1975): 721–38.

Berlin, Ira. *Slaves without Masters: The Free Negro in the Antebellum South.* New York: Pantheon, 1976.

Betts, Albert Deems. *History of South Carolina Methodism.* Columbia: Advocate Press, 1952.

Billings, John Shaw. "History of the Hammond, Fox and Spann Families, with special attention to James Henry Hammond and Information on Silver Bluff, Cow-

den, and Redcliffe Plantations." N.p.., n.d. (in Billings Papers, South Caroliniana Library).

Bland, Hugh M., and Rainsford, Bettis C. *Revitalization Study: Edgefield Central
Business District, Edgefield, South Carolina*. Edgefield: privately published,
May 1978.

Blassingame, John W. *Black New Orleans, 1860–1880*. Chicago: University of Chicago Press, 1973.

_____. "The Planter on the Couch: Earl Thorpe and the Psychodynamics of Slav-
ery." *Journal of Negro History* 60 (April 1975): 320–31.

_____. *The Slave Community*. New York: Oxford University Press, 1972.

_____. *Slave Testimony: Two Centuries of Letters, Speeches, Interviews, and Auto-
biographies*. Baton Rouge: Louisiana State University Press, 1977.

_____. "Using the Testimony of Ex-slaves: Approaches and Problems." *Journal of
Southern History* 41 (1975): 473–92.

Bleser, Carol K. Rothrock, ed. *The Hammonds of Redcliffe*. New York: Oxford University Press, 1981.

_____. *The Promised Land: The History of the South Carolina Land Commission,
1869–1890*. Columbia: University of South Carolina Press, 1964.

Bonham, Milledge Louis. "The Life and Times of Milledge Luke Bonham." Typescript, 1938, in Milledge Luke Bonham Papers, South Caroliniana Library.

Bonner, James C. "Plantation and Farm: The Agricultural South." In *Writing Southern History: Essays in Historiography in Honor of Fletcher M. Green*, edited
by Arthur S. Link and Rembert W. Patrick. Pp. 147–74. Baton Rouge: Louisiana
State University Press, 1965.

Bonner, James C. "Profile of a Late Ante-Bellum Community." *American Historical
Review* 19 (Jan. 1944): 663–80.

Boothe, Charles Octavius. *The Cyclopedia of the Colored Baptists of Alabama: Their
Leaders and Their Work*. Birmingham: Alabama Publishing Co., 1895.

Bradley, John Livingston. "Slave Manumission in South Carolina, 1820–1860."
M.A. thesis, University of South Carolina, 1964.

Broadwater, Mary Jane Rush. *David Rush and His Descendants and Stories of the
Community*. N.p., n.d. (Daniel Augustus Tomkins Library and South Caroliniana Library).

Brodie, Fawn. *Thomas Jefferson: An Intimate History*. New York: Norton, 1974.

Brookes, Iveson L. *A Defence of Southern Slavery. Against the Attacks of Henry Clay
and Alex'r Campbell.: In Which Much of the False Philanthropy and Mawkish
Sentimentalism of the Abolitionists Is Met and Refuted. In Which it is Moreover
Shown that the Association of the White And Black Races in the Relation of Mas-
ter and Slave is the Appointed Order of God, As Set Forth in the Bible and Con-
stitutes the Best Social Condition of Both Races, and the Only True Principle of
Republicanism*. Hamburg, S.C.: Robinson and Carlisle, 1851 (pamphlet in
South Caroliniana Library).

_____. *A Defence of the South Against the Reproaches of the North; in which Slav-
ery Is Shown to Be an Institution of God Intended to Form the Basis of the Best
Social State and the only Safeguard to the Permanence of a Republican Government*. Hamburg, S.C.: Republican Office, 1850 (pamphlet in South Caroliniana
Library).

Brooks, U. R., ed. *Stories of the Confederacy*. Columbia: *State* Company, 1912.

Brooks, Walter H. "The Priority of the Silver Bluff Church and Its Promoters." *Journal of Negro History* 7 (Apr. 1922): 172–218.

Brown, Richard Maxwell. *The South Carolina Regulators*. Cambridge: Harvard University Press, Belknap Press, 1963.

———. *Strain of Violence: Historical Studies of American Violence and Vigilantism.* New York: Oxford University Press, 1977.

Brutus. *An Address to the Citizens of South Carolina*. N.p., n.d. [circa 1849] (pamphlet in South Caroliniana Library).

Buckingham, James S. *The Slave States of America*. 2 vols. London: Fisher, 1842.

Bull, Emily L. "Lucy Pickens: First Lady of the South Carolina Confederacy." *Proceedings of the South Carolina Historical Association* 52 (1982): 5–18.

Burnett, Hoyt Cromwell. "A History of Education in Saluda County." M.A. thesis, University of South Carolina, 1935.

Burton, Orville Vernon. "Anatomy of an Antebellum Rural Free Black Community: Social Structure and Social Interraction in Edgefield District, South Carolina, 1850–1860." *Southern Studies: An Interdisciplinary Journal of the South* 21 (Fall 1982): 294–325.

———. "The Development of Tenantry and the Post-Bellum Afro-American Social Structure in Edgefield County, South Carolina." In *Presentations Paysannes, Dimes, Rente foncière et Mouvement de la Production Agricole à l'époque Préindustrielle: Actes du Colloque préparatoire (30 juin–2 juillet 1977) au VIIe Congrès international d'Histoire économique Section A3. Édimbourg 13–19 août 1978*, edited by E. LeRoy Ladurie and J. Goy. Vol. 2, pp. 762–78. Paris: Mouton Editions de l'École des Hautes Études en Sciences Sociales, 1982.

———. "Local History and Social Science History." Paper presented at American Historical Association's Annual Meeting, 1976. Revised copy in possession of author.

———. "Race and Reconstruction: Edgefield County, South Carolina." *Journal of Social History* 12 (Fall 1978): 31–56.

———. Review of *Black Migration and Poverty*, by Elizabeth Hafkin Pleck. *Social Science History* 5 (Fall 1981): 483–88.

———. "The Rise and Fall of Afro-American Town Life: Town and Country in Reconstruction Edgefield County, South Carolina." In *Toward a New South? Studies in Post–Civil War Southern Communities*, edited by Orville Vernon Burton and Robert C. McMath, Jr. Pp. 152–92. Westport: Greenwood Press, 1982.

———. "Ungrateful Servants? Edgefield's Black Reconstruction: Part 1 of the Total History of Edgefield County, South Carolina." Ph.D. dissertation, Princeton University, 1976.

———. "Using the Computer and Manuscript Census Returns to Teach American Social History." *History Teacher* 13 (Nov. 1979): 71–88.

———, and McMath, Robert C., Jr., eds., *Class, Conflict, and Consensus: Antebellum Southern Community Studies*. Westport: Greenwood Press, 1982.

———. *Toward a New South? Studies in Post–Civil War Southern Communities.* Westport: Greenwood Press, 1982.

Butler, Ruth Ann. *Descendants of Simon and Easter Butler*. Greenville, S.C.: privately published, 1982 (Family Possession).

Butler, William. *Memoirs of General William Butler, Including a Brief Sketch of his Father and Brother . . . Together with Incidents, Anecdotes and Stirring Events Connected with his Life.* Edited by T. P. Slider (from a manuscript left by Andrew Pickens Butler). Atlanta: Jas. P. Harrison, 1885.

Campbell, John P. *The Southern Business Directory and General Commercial Advertiser.* Charleston: Steam Power Press of Walker and James, 1854.

Campbell, Randolph H. "Planters and Plain Folk: Harrison County, Texas, as a Test Case." *Journal of Southern History* 40 (Aug. 1974): 369–98.

Capers, Ellison. *Confederate Military History.* Vol. 5. Atlanta: Confederate Publishing Company, 1899.

Cardwell, Guy. "The Duel in the Old South: Crux of a Concept." *South Atlantic Quarterly* 66 (Winter 1967): 50–69.

Carlton, David Lee. "Mill and Town: The Cotton Mill Workers and the Middle Class in South Carolina, 1880–1920." Ph.D. dissertation, Yale University, 1977.

Carrigan, Jo Ann. "Nineteenth-Century Rural Self-Sufficiency: A Planter's and Housewife's 'Do-It-Yourself' Encyclopedia." *Arkansas Historical Quarterly* 21 (Summer 1962): 132–45.

Cash, Wilbur J. *The Mind of the South.* New York: Knopf, 1941.

Cashin, Edward J. *The Story of Augusta.* Augusta: Richmond County Board of Education, 1981.

Cass, Michael M. "Charles C. Jones, Jr. and the 'Lost Cause.'" *Georgia Historical Quarterly* 55 (Summer 1971): 222–33.

Censer, Jane Turner. "Family Relationships and Power in Nineteenth Century North Carolina." Ph.D. dissertation, Johns Hopkins University, 1980.

Chapman, John A. *History of Edgefield County from the Earliest Settlements to 1897.* Newberry, S.C.: Elbert H. Aull, 1897.

Charter and By-Laws of the Graniteville Manufacturing Co. Charleston: J. B. Nixon, Printer, 1851 (in South Caroliniana Library and Graniteville Manufacturing Company).

Chartock, Lewis C. "A History and Analysis of Labor Contracts Administered by the Bureau of Refugees, Freedmen, and Abandoned Lands in Edgefield, Abbeville and Anderson Counties in South Carolina, 1865–1868." Ph.D. dissertation, Bryn Mawr College, 1974.

Chesnut, Mary Boykin. *A Diary from Dixie.* Edited by Ben Ames Williams. Boston: Houghton Mifflin, 1949.

Clark, Blanche H. *The Tennessee Yeomen, 1840–1860.* Nashville: Vanderbilt University Press, 1942.

Clarke, Edith. *My Mother Who Fathered Me.* London: Allen and Unwin, 1957.

Clark, Thomas Dionysius. *The Southern Country Editor.* Indianapolis: Bobbs-Merrill, 1948.

Clay, Howard Bunyan. "Daniel Augustus Tompkins: An American Bourbon." Ph.D. dissertation, University of North Carolina, 1951.

———. *Daniel Augustus Tompkins: The Role of a New South Industrialist in Politics.* Studies in the History of the South, no. 3. Greenville, N.C.: East Carolina College Publications in History, 1966.

Clay-Clopton, Virginia. *A Belle of the Fifties: Memoirs of Mrs. Clay, of Alabama, Covering Social and Political Life in Washington and the South, 1853–66.* Put into narrative form by Ada Sterling. New York: Doubleday, 1905.

Cohen, Hennig, ed. *A Barhamville Miscellany: Notes and Documents Concerning the South Carolina Female Collegiate Institute, 1826–1865, Chiefly from the Collection of the Late Henry Campbell Davis*. Columbia: University of South Carolina Press, 1956.

Coit, Margaret L. *John C. Calhoun: American Portrait*. Boston: Houghton Mifflin, 1950.

Coleman, James Karl. *State Administration in South Carolina*. New York: Columbia University Press, 1935.

Coleman, Maybelle. "Poverty and Poor Relief in the Plantation Society of South Carolina: A Study in the Sociology of a Social Problem." Ph.D. dissertation, Duke University, 1943.

Coles, Robert. *The South Goes North*. Vol. 3 of *The Children of Crisis*. Boston: Little, Brown, 1967.

Cook, Harvey T. *The Hard Labor Section*. Greenwood, S.C.: Attic Press, 1979.

Cooper, William J., Jr. *The Conservative Regime: South Carolina, 1877–1890*. Baltimore: Johns Hopkins University Press, 1968.

Cordle, Charles. "Henry Shultz and the Founding of Hamburg, South Carolina." In *Studies in Georgia History and Government*, edited by James Boner and Lucien Robert. Pp. 79–92. Athens: University of Georgia Press, 1940.

Corley, Florence. *Confederate City: Augusta, Georgia, 1860–1865*. Columbia: University of South Carolina Press, 1960.

Cornelius, Janet. "Slave Marriages in a Georgia Congregation." In *Class, Conflict, and Consensus: Antebellum Southern Communities*, edited by Orville Vernon Burton and Robert C. McMath, Jr. Pp. 128–45. Westport: Greenwood Press, 1982.

———. "We Slipped and Learned to Read: Slaves and the Literacy Process, 1830–1865." Unpublished paper, in possession of author.

Coulter, E. Merton. *Negro Legislators in Georgia during the Reconstruction Period*. Athens: University of Georgia Press, 1968.

———. "Slavery and Freedom in Athens, Georgia, 1860–66." *Georgia Historical Quarterly* 49 (Sept. 1965): 264–93.

Craven, Avery O. *The Coming of the Civil War*. New York: Scribner, 1942.

———. "Poor Whites and Negroes in the Antebellum South." *Journal of Negro History* 15 (Jan. 1930): 14–25.

Crimmins, Eileen M. "The Completeness of 1900 Mortality Data Collected by Registration and Enumeration for Rural and Urban Parts of States: Estimates Using the Chandra Sekar-Deming Technique." *Historical Methods* 13 (Summer 1980): 163–69.

Crouch, Flossie Lamb. *Genealogy of Mrs. Flossie Lamb Crouch and Allied Lines*. N.p., n.d. (copy in South Caroliniana Library).

Cumming, Katharine H. *A Northern Daughter and a Southern Wife: The Civil War Reminiscences and Letters of Katharine H. Cumming, 1860–1865*. Edited by W. Kirk Wood. Augusta: Richmond County Historical Society, 1976.

Curti, Merle, et al. *The Making of an American Community: A Case Study in Democracy in a Frontier County*. Stanford: Stanford University Press, 1959.

Curtin, Philip. *The Atlantic Slave Trade: A Census*. Madison: University of Wisconsin Press, 1969.

_____. "Epidemiology and the Slave Trade." *Political Science Quarterly* 83 (1968): 190–216.

Davenport, David Paul. "Population Persistence and Migration in Rural New York, 1855–1860." Ph.D. thesis, University of Illinois, Urbana-Champaign, 1983.

Davidson, Chalmers Gaston. *The Last Foray: South Carolina Planters of 1860: A Sociological Study*. Columbia: University of South Carolina Press, 1971.

Davidson, James West, and Lytle, Mark Hamilton. *After the Fact: The Art of Historical Detection*. Vol. 1, New York: Knopf, 1982.

Davis, Lenwood G. *The Black Aged in the U.S.: An Annotated Bibliography*. Westport: Greenwood Press, 1980.

Davis, Ronald L. F. *Good and Faithful Labor: From Slavery to Sharecropping in the Natchez District, 1860–1890*. Westport: Greenwood Press, 1982.

Deal, Douglas. "A Preliminary Examination of Edgefield District, South Carolina in the Late Ante-Bellum Period." Unpublished paper, 14 Dec. 1973, in possession of the author.

de Forrest, John William. *A Union Officer in the Reconstruction*. Edited by James H. Croushore and David M. Potter. New Haven: Yale University Press, 1948.

Degler, Carl N. *At Odds: Women and the Family in America from the Revolution to the Present*. New York: Oxford University Press, 1980.

_____. *Neither Black Nor White: Slavery and Race Relations in Brazil and the United States*. New York: Macmillan, 1971.

_____. *The Other South: Southern Dissenters in the Nineteenth Century*. New York: Harper and Row, 1974.

Dennett, John Richard. *The South as It Is: 1865–1866*. Edited by Henry M. Chrisman. New York: Viking, 1965.

Derrick, Samuel. *Centennial History of the South Carolina Railroad*. Columbia: University of South Carolina Press, 1930.

Dew, Charles B. "Disciplining Slave Ironworkers in the Antebellum South: Coercion, Conciliation, and Accommodation." *American Historical Review* 79 (Apr. 1974): 393–418.

_____. "Critical Essay on Recent Works." In C. Vann Woodward, *Origins of the New South, 1877–1913*. Baton Rouge: Louisiana State University Press, 1971 ed. Pp. 591–96.

Dew, Thomas Roderick. "Dissertation on the Characteristic Differences between the Sexes, and on the Position and Influence of Woman in Society." *Southern Literacy Messenger* 1 (May–Aug. 1835): 493–512, 621–32, 672–91.

Dickson, David. *A Practical Treatise on Agriculture; to which is added the Author's Published Letters*. Edited by J. Dickson Smith. Macon: J. W. Burke and Company, 1870.

Donald, David. *Charles Sumner and the Coming of the Civil War*. New York: Knopf, 1960.

Drago, Edmund L. *Black Politicians and Reconstruction in Georgia: A Splendid Failure*. Baton Rouge: Louisiana State University Press, 1982.

Dublin, Thomas. *Women at Work: The Transformation of Work and Community in*

Lowell, Massachusetts, 1826–1860. New York: Columbia University Press, 1979.

DuBois, William Edmund Burghardt. *The Negro American Family.* Atlanta University Publications, no. 13. Atlanta: Atlanta University Press, 1908.

Dun and Bradstreet (originally R. G. Dun and Co.). *The Mercantile Agency Reference Books.* New York: R. G. Dun, for each year 1866–1900 (bound volumes in Library of Congress).

Dunbar, Arabella Sumter. "The History of the Development of Education in Beech Island, South Carolina." M.A. thesis, University of South Carolina, 1929.

Eaton, Clement. "Class Differences in the Old South." *Virginia Quarterly Review* 33 (Summer 1957): 357–70.

―――. *The Growth of Southern Civilization.* New York: Harper and Row, 1961.

―――. *History of the Southern Confederacy.* New York: Harper, 1954.

―――. *The Mind of the Old South.* Rev. ed. Baton Rouge: Louisiana State University Press, 1967.

―――. *The Waning of the Old South Civilization.* Athens: University of Georgia Press, 1968.

Edgefield County Historical Society. *Data on Norris and Kindred Families.* Edgefield: privately published, 1956.

―――. *Bonham, Griffin, Lipscomb, Smith Families as Featured at the Mid-summer Meeting of the Edgefield County Historical Society, July 18, 1941.* Edgefield: Edgefield *Advertiser* Print, 1941.

―――. *The Hammond Family of Edgefield District.* Edgefield: *Advertiser* Press, 1954.

―――. *The Martins of Martintown.* N.p., 1953.

―――. *The Mims Families of Edgefield.* N.p., 1951.

―――. *Genealogy of Nicholson and Allied Families.* Edgefield: Edgefield *Advertiser* Print, 1944.

Edmunds, John Boyd, Jr. "Francis W. Pickens: A Political Biography." Ph.D. dissertation, University of South Carolina, 1967.

Edwards, Morgan. "Materials Towards a History of the Baptists in the Provinces of Maryland, Virginia, North Carolina, South Carolina, Georgia." 1772 (available in the Baptist Historical Collection, Furman University).

Eighmy, John Lee. *Churches in Cultural Captivity: A History of the Social Attitudes of Southern Baptists.* Introduction and epilogue by Sam S. Hill, Jr. Knoxville: University of Tennessee Press, 1972.

Ellen, John Calhoun, Jr. "Political Newspapers of the Piedmont Carolinas in the 1850's." Ph.D. dissertation, University of South Carolina, 1958.

Ellis, Elizabeth. "Educating Daughters of the Patriarchy: Female Academies in the American South, 1830–1860." Senior thesis, Harvard University, 1982.

Escott, Paul D. *After Secession: Jefferson Davis and the Failure of Confederate Nationalism.* Baton Rouge: Louisiana State University Press, 1978.

―――. *Slavery Remembered: A Record of Twentieth-Century Slave Narratives.* Chapel Hill: University of North Carolina Press, 1979.

Etheredge, Hamlin Walpole. *Our Etheredge Family Circles from 1753 to 1953.* Johnston, S.C.: Ridge Citizen, 1953.

―――. *Our Harrison Family Circles: Benjamin and Mary Walpole Harrison and*

Their Descendants. Anderson, S.C.: Alvin M. Wright, 1947.

Evans, Matilda A. *Martha Schofield: Pioneer Negro Educator.* Columbia: Dupre Printing Co., 1916.

Family History of Saluda County, 1895–1980: Saluda, South Carolina. Clinton, S.C.: Intercollegiate Press, 1980.

Farber, Bernard. *Guardians of Virtue: Salem Families in 1800.* New York: Basic Books, 1972.

Faust, Drew. "Culture, Conflict, and Community: The Meaning of Power on an Ante-Bellum Plantation." *Journal of Social History* 14 (Fall 1980): 83–97.

————. *James Henry Hammond and the Old South: A Design for Mastery.* Baton Rouge: Louisiana State University Press, 1982.

————. *A Sacred Circle: The Dilemma of the Intellectual in the Old South, 1840–1860.* Baltimore: Johns Hopkins University Press, 1977.

Ferguson, Clyde R. "General Andrew Pickens." Ph.D. dissertation, Duke University, 1960.

Fernandes, Floresten. *The Negro in Brazilian Society.* New York: Columbia University Press, 1969.

Fickling, Susan M. "The Christianization of the Negro in South Carolina, 1830–1860." M.A. thesis, University of South Carolina, 1923.

Fitchett, G. Horace. "The Free Negro in Charleston, South Carolina." Ph.D. dissertation, University of Chicago, 1950.

————. "The Origin and Growth of the Free Negro Population of Charleston, South Carolina." *Journal of Negro History* 26 (Oct. 1941): 421–37.

————. "The Status of the Free Negro in Charleston, South Carolina, and His Descendants in Modern Society." *Journal of Negro History* 32 (Oct. 1947): 350–51.

————. "Traditions of the Free Negroes in Charleston, South Carolina." *Journal of Negro History* 25 (Apr. 1940): 421–37.

Fleming, Thomas. *The Man from Monticello: The Intimate Life of Thomas Jefferson.* New York: Morrow, 1969.

Flynt, J. Wayne. *Dixie's Forgotten People: The South's Poor Whites.* Bloomington: Indiana University Press, 1979.

Fogel, Robert. "Cliometrics and Culture: Some Recent Developments in the Historiography of Slavery." *Journal of Social History* 2 (Fall 1977): 40–47.

————, and Engerman, Stanley L. "Recent Findings in the Study of Slave Demography and Family Structure." *Sociology and Social Research* 63 (Apr. 1979): 566–89.

————. *Time on the Cross: The Economics of American Negro Slavery.* Boston: Little, Brown, 1974.

Foner, Laura, and Genovese, Eugene D., eds. *Slavery in the New World: A Reader in Comparative History.* Englewood Cliffs, N.J.: Prentice-Hall, 1969.

Franklin, John Hope. "The Free Negro in the Economic Life of Antebellum North Carolina, Part 2." *North Carolina Historical Review* 19 (Oct. 1942): 359–75.

————. *The Free Negro in North Carolina.* Chapel Hill: University of North Carolina Press, 1943.

————. *From Slavery to Freedom: A History of Negro Americans.* 3d ed. New York: Knopf, 1967.

————. *The Militant South, 1800–1861*. Cambridge: Harvard University Press, 1956.

Frazier, E. Franklin. *The Free Negro Family*. Nashville: Fisk University Press, 1932.

————. *The Negro Church*. New York: Schocken, 1963.

————. *The Negro Family in the United States*. Chicago: University of Chicago Press, 1939. Revised and abridged editions, 1940, 1960.

Fredrickson, George M. "Masters and Mudsills: The Role of Race in the Planter Ideology of South Carolina." *South Atlantic Urban Studies* 2 (1978): 34–48.

Freehling, William W. *Prelude to Civil War: The Nullification Controversy in South Carolina, 1816–1836*. New York: Harper and Row, 1965.

Furstenberg, Frank F., Jr.; Hershberg, Theodore; and Modell, John. "The Origins of the Female Headed Black Family: The Impact of the Urban Experience." *Journal of Interdisciplinary History* 6 (Autumn 1975): 211–34.

Furstenberg, Frank F., Jr.; Strong, Douglas; and Crawford, Albert C. "What Happened When the Census Was Redone: An Analysis of the Recount of 1870 in Philadelphia." *Sociology and Social Research* 63 (Apr. 1979): 475–505.

Fusfeld, Daniel Roland. *The Basic Economics of the Urban Racial Crisis*. New York: Holt, 1973.

Gaines, Francis Pendleton. *The Southern Plantation: A Study in the Development and Accuracy of a Tradition*. New York: Columbia University Press, 1925.

Gaston, Paul M. *The New South Creed: A Study in Southern Mythmaking*. New York: Knopf, 1970.

Genovese, Eugene D. *The Political Economy of Slavery: Studies in the Economy and Society of the Slave South*. New York: Random House, Vintage, 1965.

————. *In Red and Black: Marxian Explorations in Southern and Afro-American History*. New York: Pantheon, 1974.

————. *Roll, Jordan, Roll: The World the Slaves Made*. New York: Pantheon, 1974.

————. "Solidarity and Servitude." In *Times Literary Supplement* (25 Feb. 1977): 198–200.

————. "Yeomen Farmers in a Slaveholders' Democracy." *Agricultural History* 49 (Apr. 1975): 331–42.

————. *The Slave Economics*. 2 vols. New York: Wiley, 1973.

————. *The World the Slaveholders Made: Two Essays in Interpretation*. New York: Pantheon, 1969.

Gerber, David. "A Politics of Limited Options: Northern Black Politics and the Problem of Change and Continuity in Race Relations Historiography." *Journal of Social History* 14 (Winter 1980): 235–55.

German, Richard. "Queen City of the Savannah: Augusta, Georgia, during the Urban Progressive Era, 1890–1917." Ph.D. dissertation, University of Florida, 1971.

Germany, George. "The South Carolina Governing Elite, 1820–1860." Ph.D. dissertation, University of California, Berkeley, 1972.

Gill, Flora Davidov. "Economics and the Black Exodus: An Analysis of Negro Emancipation from the Southern United States, 1910–1970." Ph.D. dissertation, Stanford University, 1975.

Glassie, Henry H. *Folk Housing in Middle Virginia: A Structural Analysis of Historic Artifacts*. Knoxville: University of Tennessee Press, 1975.

Goldin, Claudia. "Female Labor Force Participation: The Origin of Black and White

Differences, 1870 and 1880." *Journal of Economic History* 37 (Mar. 1977): 87–108.

―――. *Urban Slavery in the American South*. Chicago: University of Chicago Press, 1976.

Goldstein, Mark L. "Southern Emigrants to Brazil." Senior thesis, Harvard University, 1983.

Graham, Pearl. "Thomas Jefferson and Sally Hemings." *Journal of Negro History* 45 (Apr. 1961): 89–104.

Gray, Lewis Cecil. *History of Agriculture in the Southern United States to 1860*. 2 vols. Washington: Carnegie Institution, 1933.

Graydon, Augustus T., ed. *Francis Butler Simkins, 1897–1966: Historian of the South: A Pamphlet Published by His Family in Memory of the Edgefield Native Who Spent His Teaching Career at Longwood College in Farmville, Virginia*. Columbia: *State* Printing, 1966.

Green, Edwin Luther. *George McDuffie*. Columbia: *State* Company, 1936.

Greenberg, Kenneth S. "Representation and the Isolation of South Carolina, 1776–1860." *Journal of American History* 64 (Dec. 1977): 723–43.

―――. "The Second American Revolution: South Carolina Politics, Society, and Secession, 1776–1860." Ph.D. dissertation, University of Wisconsin–Madison, 1976.

Gregg, William. "Domestic Industry," *DeBow's Review*, new series, 2 (Feb. 1850): 134–46.

―――. *Essays on Domestic Industry: Or, An Inquiry into the Expediency of Establishing Cotton Manufactures in South Carolina*. Charleston: Burges and James, Publishers, 1845.

Greven, Phillip. *The Protestant Temperament: Patterns of Child-Rearing, Religious Experience, and the Self in Early America*. New York: Knopf, 1977.

Griffen, Clyde. "Occupational Mobility in Nineteenth-Century America: Problems and Possibilities." *Journal of Social History* 5 (Spring 1972): 312–30.

Griffin, Richard W. "Poor White Laborers in Southern Cotton Factories, 1789–1865." *South Carolina Historical Magazine* 61 (1960): 26–40.

Guess, William Francis. *South Carolina: Annals of Pride and Protest*. New York: Harper and Row, 1957.

Guthrie, Patricia. "Catching Sense: The Meaning of Plantation Membership among Blacks on St. Helena Island, South Carolina." Ph.D. dissertation, University of Rochester, 1977.

Gutman, Herbert G. *The Black Family in Slavery and Freedom, 1750–1925*. New York: Pantheon, 1976.

―――. "Persistent Myths about the Afro-American Family." *Journal of Interdisciplinary History* 6 (Autumn 1975): 181–210.

―――. *Slavery and the Numbers Game: A Critique of "Time on the Cross."* Urbana: University of Illinois Press, 1975.

―――. *Work, Culture and Society in Industrializing America: Essays in American Working Class and Social History*. New York: Random House, 1976.

Hackney, Sheldon. "Origins of the New South in Retrospect." *Journal of Southern History* 38 (May 1972): 191–216.

Hagler, D. Harlan. "The Ideal Woman in the Antebellum South: Lady or Farmwife?"

Journal of Southern History 46 (Aug. 1980): 405–18.

Hahn, Steven Howard. "The Roots of Southern Populism: Yeoman Farmers and the Transformation of Georgia's Upper Piedmont, 1850–1890." Ph.D. dissertation, Yale University, 1979.

———. "The Yeomanry of the Nonplantation South: Upper Piedmont Georgia, 1850–1860." In *Class, Conflict, and Consensus: Antebellum Southern Community Studies*, edited by Orville Vernon Burton and Robert C. McMath, Jr. Pp. 29–56. Westport: Greenwood Press, 1982.

Haley, Alex. *Roots.* Garden City, N.Y.: Doubleday, 1976.

Hall, Arthur R. "Soil Erosion and Agriculture in the Southern Piedmont: A History." Ph.D. dissertation, Duke University, 1948.

Hall, Lindsey G. *Things and Incidents of Long Ago.* Columbia: *State* Printing, 1970.

Hammond, James Henry. *An Address Delivered before the South Carolina Institute, at Its First Annual Fair, on the 20th November, 1849.* Charleston: Walker and James, 1849.

———. *Anniversary Oration of the State Agricultural Society of South Carolina; by Gen. James H. Hammond. Read Before the Society on the 25th November, 1841, at Their Annual Meeting. . . .* Columbia: A. S. Johnston, 1841

———. "Gov. Hammond's Address before the South Carolina Institute, 1850." *DeBow's Review,* new series, 2 (June 1850): 501–22.

———. "Gov. Hammond's Letters on Slavery—No. 4." *DeBow's Review,* new series, 2 (Mar. 1850): 252–64.

———, "Gov. Hammond's Letters on Slavery—No. 4." *DeBow's Review,* new series, 2 (Mar. 1850): 252–64.

———. *Selections from the Letters and Speeches of the Hon. James H. Hammond, of South Carolina.* New York: John F. Trow, 1866.

Hammond, M. C. M. *Anniversary Oration Delivered before the Burke County Central Agricultural Society, 13 January 1846.* Pamphlet in South Caroliniana Library.

Hammond, Matthew B. *The Cotton Industry: An Essay in American Economic History. Part I, the Cotton Culture and the Cotton Trade.* New York: Macmillan Company for the American Economic Association (Ithaca, N.Y.: Press of Andrus and Church), 1897.

Hammond, Roland. *A History and Genealogy of the Descendants of William Hammond of London, England, and His Wife Elizabeth Penn; Through Their Son Benjamin of Sandwich and Rochester, Mass., 1600–1894.* Boston: D. Clapp and Son, 1894.

Hampton, Wade. "What Negro Supremacy Means." *Forum* 5 (June 1888): 383–95.

Hareven, Tamara K. "The Family as Process: The Historical Study of the Family Cycle." *Journal of Social History* 7 (Spring 1974): 322–29.

Harmon, Lillian Marsh. *The Plantation Marshes: The Colony of Edgefield County Marshes and the Account of Their Lineage.* Edgefield: Edgefield *Advertiser*, 1964.

Harris, J. William. "A Slaveholding Republic: Augusta's Hinterlands before the Civil War." Ph.D. dissertation, Johns Hopkins University, 1982.

———. "The Transformation of a Social Order: Augusta's Hinterlands, 1850–1880."

Paper presented at the annual meeting of the Organization of American Historians, 1980. Available from the author.

Harrison, Jannie Ruth Goodwin. *Know Your Roots: Morgan Family History (Genealogy)*. Edgefield: privately published by the family, 1975. Copy in the Morgan family papers in the possession of the family.

Hellman, Lillian. *The Little Foxes and Another Part of the Forest: Two Plays*. New York: Penguin, 1976.

Henderson, June Rainsford. *Edgefield Presbyterian Church*. Typescript, in possession of the author and in Daniel Augustus Tompkins Library.

Hendricks, Carlanna. "John Gary Evans: A Political Biography." Ph.D. dissertation, University of South Carolina, 1966.

Hershberg, Theodore. "Free Blacks in Ante Bellum Philadelphia: A Study of Ex-Slaves, Free-Born and Socio-Economic Decline." *Journal of Social History* 5 (Dec. 1971): 183–209.

_____. "Free-Born and Slave-Born Blacks in Antebellum Philadelphia." In *Race and Slavery in the Western Hemisphere: Quantitative Studies*, edited by Stanley L. Engerman and Eugene D. Genovese. Pp. 395–426. Princeton: Princeton University Press, 1975.

_____. "A Method of the Computerized Study of Family and Household Structure Using the Manuscript Schedules of the U.S. Census of Population, 1850–1880." *Family in Historical Perspective: An International Newsletter* 3 (Spring 1973): 6–19.

Herskovits, Melville J. *The Myth of the Negro Past*. New York: Harper and Row, 1941.

Higginson, Thomas Wentworth. *Army Life in a Black Regiment*. Boston: Field, Osgood, and Co., 1870.

Hill, Lawrence F. "The Confederate Exodus to Latin America." *Southwestern Historical Quarterly* 39 (Oct. 1935, Jan. and Apr. 1936): 100–34, 161–99, 309–26.

Hindus, Michael S. *Prison and Plantation: Crime, Justice, and Authority in Massachusetts and South Carolina, 1767-1878*. Chapel Hill: University of North Carolina Press, 1980.

History of Mt. Calvary Baptist Church. Johnston, S.C.: Centennial Committee, 1979.

Hofstadter, Richard. *The Age of Reform: From Bryan to F.D.R.* New York: Random House, Vintage, 1955.

_____. *Anti-intellectualism in American Life*. New York: Vintage, 1962.

_____; Miller, William; and Aaron, Daniel. *The American Republic*. Vol. 1. Englewood Cliffs, N.J.: Prentice-Hall, 1959.

Hogeland, Ronald W. " 'The Female Appendage': Feminine Life-Styles in America, 1820–1860." *Civil War History* 17 (June 1971): 101–14.

Holmes, Alester G., and Sherrill, George R. *Thomas Green Clemson: His Life and His Work*. Richmond: Garrett and Massie, 1937.

Hooker, Edward. "Diary of Edward Hooker." Edited by J. Franklin Jameson. In *Annual Report of the American Historical Association for the Year 1896*. Vol. 1, pp. 842–929. Washington: Government Printing Office, 1897.

Horton, James. "Generations of Protest: Black Families and Social Reform in Antebellum Boston." *New England Quarterly* 44 (June 1976): 242–56.

Howard, C. W. "Some Thoughts on the Labor Question." *Rural Carolinian* 6 (Oct. 1874): 5.

Huffman, Frank Jackson, Jr. "Old South, New South: Continuity and Change in a Georgia County, 1850–1880." Ph.D. dissertation, Yale University, 1974.

———. "Town and Country in the South, 1850–1880: A Comparison of Urban and Rural Social Structures." *South Atlantic Quarterly* 76 (Summer 1977): 366–81.

Hundley, Daniel R. *Social Relations in Our Southern States.* New York: H. D. Price, 1860.

Isaac, Rhys. "Dramatizing the Ideology of the Revolution: Popular Mobilization in Virginia, 1774–1776." *William and Mary Quarterly* 33, no. 3 (1976): 357–85.

———. *The Transformation of Virginia, 1740–1790.* Chapel Hill: University of North Carolina Press, 1982.

Jackson, Luther Porter. *Free Negro Labor and Property Holding in Virginia, 1830–1860.* New York: Appleton, 1942.

———. "The Virginia Free Negro Farmer and Property Owner, 1830-1860." *Journal of Negro History* 24 (Oct. 1939): 390–439.

Jaher, Frederic Cople. *The Urban Establishment: Upper Strata in Boston, New York, Charleston, Chicago, and Los Angeles.* Urbana: University of Illinois Press, 1982.

Jameson, J. Franklin, ed. *Correspondence of John C. Calhoun.* In *Annual Report of the American Historical Association for the Year 1899.* Vol. 2. Washington: Government Printing Office, 1900.

Janiewski, Dolores. "Sisters under the Skin: Working Women in the South." Paper presented at the University of Mississippi, Chancellor's Symposium on Southern History, 1982.

Jervey, T. D. "The Butlers of South Carolina." *South Carolina Historical and Genealogical Magazine* 4 (Oct. 1903): 296–314.

Johnson, Michael P. *Toward a Patriarchal Republic: The Secession of Georgia.* Baton Rouge: Louisiana State University Press, 1977.

———. "Wealth and Class in Charleston in 1860." In *From the Old South to the New: Essays on the Transitional South,* edited by Walter J. Fraser, Jr., and Winfred B. Moore, Jr. Pp. 65–80. Westport: Greenwood Press, 1981.

Johnston, R. J. "Resistance to Migration and the Mover/Stayer Dichotomy: Aspects of Kinship and Population Stability in an English Rural Area." *Geografiska Annaler* 53 (1971): 16–27.

Jones, Bobby Frank. "A Cultural Middle Passage: Slave Marriage and Family in the Ante-Bellum South." Ph.D. dissertation, University of North Carolina, 1965.

Jones, Charles C., and Dutcher, Salem. *Memorial History of Augusta, Georgia.* Syracuse: D. Mason, 1890.

Jones, Frank Dudley, and Mills, W. H., eds. *History of the Presbyterian Church in South Carolina since 1850.* Columbia: R. L. Bryan, 1926.

Jones, Marcus E. "Black Migration in the United States with Emphasis on Selected Central Cities." Ph.D. dissertation, Southern Illinois University, 1978.

Jordan, Laylon Wayne. "Education for Community: C. G. Memminger and the Origination of Common Schools in Antebellum Charleston." *South Carolina Historical Magazine* 82 (Apr. 1982): 99–115.

Jordan, Winthrop D. *White Over Black: American Attitudes toward the Negro, 1550–*

1812. Chapel Hill: University of North Carolina Press, 1968.

Julien, Carl. *Beneath So Kind a Sky: The Scenic and Architectural Beauty of South Carolina*. With introduction by Chapman J. Milling. Columbia: University of South Carolina Press, 1948.

_____. *Ninety-Six: Landmarks of South Carolina's Last Frontier Region*. Columbia: University of South Carolina Press, 1950. Rev. ed. with introduction by H. L. Watson, 1968.

Katz, Michael B. "Occupational Classification in History." *Journal of Interdisciplinary History* 3 (Summer 1972): 63–88.

_____. *The People of Hamilton Canada West: Family and Class in a Mid-Nineteenth-Century City*. Cambridge: Harvard University Press, 1975.

Katzman, David M. *Before the Ghetto: Black Detroit in the Nineteenth Century*. Urbana: University of Illinois Press, 1973.

King, Alvy L. "Emergence of a Fire-eater: Louis T. Wigfall." *Louisiana Studies* 7 (Spring 1968): 73–82.

_____. *Louis T. Wigfall: Southern Fireater*. Baton Rouge: Louisiana State University Press, 1970.

King, Joe Madison. *A History of South Carolina Baptists*. Columbia: General Board of the South Carolina Baptist Convention, 1964.

Kiser, Clyde V. *Sea Island to City: A Study of St. Helena Islanders in Harlem and Other Urban Centers*. New York: Columbia University Press, 1932.

Klein, Rachel. "The Rise of the Planters in the South Carolina Backcountry, 1767–1808." Ph.D. dissertation, Yale University, 1979.

Knights, Peter R. "City Directories as Aids to Antebellum Urban Studies: A Research Note." *Historical Methods Newsletter* 2 (Sept. 1969): 1–10.

_____. *The Plain People of Boston, 1830–1860: A Study in City Growth*. New York: Oxford University Press, 1971.

Kohn, August. *The Cotton Mills of South Carolina*. Columbia: South Carolina Department of Agriculture, Commerce, and Immigration, 1907.

Kolchin, Peter. *First Freedom: The Response of Alabama's Blacks to Emancipation and Reconstruction*. Westport: Greenwood Press, 1972.

LaBorde, Maximilian. *History of the South Carolina College, from its Incorporation, Dec. 19, 1801, to Dec. 19, 1865, Including Sketches of its Presidents and Professors. With an Appendix. Prefaced with a Life of the Author, by J. L. Reynolds, D.D.* 2d ed. Charleston: Walker, Evans and Cogswell, 1874.

Lammermeier, Paul J. "The Urban Black Family of the Nineteenth Century: A Study of Black Family Structure in the Ohio Valley, 1850–1880." *Journal of Marriage and the Family* 35 (Autumn 1975): 440–56.

Lander, Ernest McPherson, Jr. "Antebellum Milling in South Carolina." *South Carolina Historical and Genealogical Magazine* 52 (July 1951): 125–32.

_____. *The Calhoun Family and Thomas Green Clemson: The Decline of a Southern Patriarchy*. Columbia: University of South Carolina Press, 1983.

_____. *The Textile Industry in Ante-bellum South Carolina*. Baton Rouge: Louisiana State University Press, 1969.

Landrum, J. B. *Colonial and Revolutionary History of Upper South Carolina*. Greenville, S.C.: Sharmon, 1897.

Lanham, Ben T. "An Agricultural, Economic, and Social Study of Edgefield County."

Thesis for B.S. in Agricultural Economics, Clemson College, 1937.

Laslett, Peter, ed. (with the assistance of Richard Wall). *Household and Family in Past Time: Comparative Studies in the Size and Structure of the Domestic Group over the Last Three Centuries in England, France, Serbia, Japan, and Colonial North America, with Further Materials from Western Europe.* Cambridge: Cambridge University Press, 1972.

_____. *The World We Have Lost: England before the Industrial Age.* New York: Scribner's, 1965.

Lathrop, Barnes F. "History from the Census Returns." In *Sociology and History: Methods,* edited by Seymour Martin Lipset and Richard Hofstadter. Pp. 70–101. New York: Basic Books, 1968.

_____. *Migration into East Texas, 1835–1860: A Study from the United States Census.* Austin: University of Texas Press, 1949.

Lebsock, Suzanne D. "Radical Reconstruction and the Property Rights of Southern Women." *Journal of Southern History* 43 (May 1977): 195–216.

Levine, Lawrence W. *Black Culture and Black Consciousness: Afro-American Folk Thought from Slavery to Freedom.* Oxford: Oxford University Press, 1977.

Lewis, David Levering. *King: A Biography.* 2nd ed. Urbana: University of Illinois Press, 1978.

Lewis, Oscar. *Children of Sanchez.* New York: Random House, 1961.

_____. *La Vida.* New York: Random House, 1966.

Liebow, Elliot. *Talley's Corner: A Study of Negro Streetcorner Men.* Boston: Little, Brown, 1967.

Linden, Fabian. "Economic Democracy in the Slave South: An Appraisal of Some Recent Views." *Journal of Negro History* 31 (Apr. 1946): 140–89.

Lingerman, Richard R. *Small Town America: A Narrative History 1620 to the Present.* New York: Random House, 1980.

Litwack, Leon F. *Been in the Storm So Long: The Aftermath of Slavery.* New York: Knopf, 1979.

Logan, Rayford W. *The Betrayal of the Negro: From Rutherford B. Hayes to Woodrow Wilson.* New, enl. ed. London: Collier, 1965 (originally published as *The Negro in American Life and Thought: The Nadir, 1877–1901.* New York: Dial Press, 1954).

Longstreet, Augustus Baldwin. *Georgia Scenes.* New York: Harper, 1840.

Lord, Clyde W. "Louis T. Wigfall." M.A. thesis, University of Texas, 1925.

_____. "Young Louis Wigfall: South Carolina Politician and Duelist." *South Carolina Historical Magazine* 59 (Apr. 1958): 96–112.

Loring, Francis W., and Atkinson, C. F. *Cotton Culture and the South Considered with Reference to Emigration.* Boston: A. William, 1869.

Lott, Stanton Norris. "The Development of Education in Edgefield County, South Carolina, 1748–1930." M.A. thesis, University of South Carolina, 1930.

Lyell, Sir Charles. *Travels in North America, in the Years 1841–2; with Geological Observations on the United States, Canada, and Nova Scotia.* 2 vols. London: John Murray, 1845.

McBee, Mrs. Harriet Butler. "The Butler Family." Manuscript, 1895. In possession of the family.

McClendon, Carlee T. *Edgefield Death Notices and Cemetery Records.* Columbia: Hive Press, 1977.

————. *Edgefield Marriage Records, Edgefield, South Carolina: From the Late Eighteenth Century up through 1870.* Columbia: R. L. Bryan, 1970.

————. "The History of Pottersville." Unpublished paper in possession of author and Pottersville Museum.

McDonald, Forrest, and McWhiney, Grady. "The Antebellum Southern Herdsmen: A Reinterpretation." *Journal of Southern History* 41 (May 1975): 147–66.

————. "The South from Self-Sufficiency to Peonage: An Interpretation." *American Historical Review* 85 (Dec. 1980): 1095–1118.

McDonald, Forrest, and Shapiro, Ellen. "The Ethnic Origins of the American People, 1790." *William and Mary Quarterly* 37 (1980): 179–99.

McMillan, Lewis K. *Negro Higher Education in the State of South Carolina.* Orangeburg: privately printed by the author at South Carolina State A&M College, 1952.

McWhiney, Grady. "The Revolution in Nineteenth-Century Alabama Agriculture." *Alabama Review* 31 (Jan. 1978): 3–32.

Magdol, Edward, and Wakelyn, Jon L., eds. *The Southern Common People: Studies in Nineteenth-Century Social History.* Westport: Greenwood Press, 1980.

Main, Jackson Turner. *The Antifederalists: Critics of the Constitution, 1781–1788.* Chapel Hill: University of North Carolina Press, 1961.

Mann, Horace. *The Republic and the School.* Lawrence Cremin, ed. New York: Teachers College Press, 1961.

Marshall, Howard J. "Gentlemen without a Country: A Social and Intellectual History of South Carolina, 1860–1900." Ph.D. dissertation, University of North Carolina, 1979.

Martin, Thomas P., ed. "Notes and Documents: The Advent of William Gregg and the Graniteville Company." *Journal of Southern History* 11 (Aug. 1945): 389–423.

Massey, Mary Elizabeth. *Bonnet Brigades.* New York: Knopf, 1966.

————. *Ersatz in the Confederacy.* Columbia: University of South Carolina Press, 1952.

————. *Refugee Life in the Confederacy.* Baton Rouge: Louisiana State University Press, 1964.

Mathis, Robert Neil. "Preston Smith Brooks: The Man and His Image." *South Carolina Historical Magazine* 79 (Oct. 1978): 296–310.

Mattingly, Paul. *Classless Profession.* New York: New York University Press, 1980.

Mays, Benjamin Elijah. *Seeking to Be Christian in Race Relations.* New York: Friendship Press, 1957, rev. ed., 1964.

————. *Born to Rebel: An Autobiography.* New York: Scribner's, 1971.

————. *The Negro's God as Reflected in His Literature.* New York: Russell and Russell, 1938.

————, and Nicholson, Joseph Williamson. *The Negro's Church.* New York: Institute of Social and Religious Research, 1933.

Mendenhall, Marjorie S. "A History of Agriculture in South Carolina, 1790 to 1860." Ph.D. dissertation, University of North Carolina, 1940.

Meriwether, Coyler. *History of Higher Education in South Carolina with a Sketch of the Free School System* (originally published in 1889). Spartanburg, S.C.: The Reprint Company, 1972

Meriwether, Robert L. *The Expansion of South Carolina, 1729–1765.* Kingsport, Tenn.: Southern Publishers, 1940.

————. *The Papers of John C. Calhoun.* Vol. 1. Columbia: University of South Carolina Press, 1959.

————, ed. "Preston S. Brooks on the Caning of Charles Sumner." *South Carolina Historical and Genealogical Magazine* 52 (Jan. 1951): 1–4.

Merritt, Elizabeth. *James Henry Hammond, 1807–1864.* Baltimore: Johns Hopkins University Press, 1923.

Millar, John R., Jr. "A Study of the Changes of Divorce Legislation in the State of South Carolina." Ph.D. dissertation, Florida State University, 1954.

Miller, John Chester. *The Wolf by the Ears: Thomas Jefferson and Slavery.* New York: Free Press, 1977.

Miller, Nora. *The Girl in the Rural Family.* Chapel Hill: University of North Carolina Press, 1935.

Mills, Robert. *Statistics of South Carolina, Including a View of Its Natural, Civil, and Military History, General and Particular.* Charleston, S.C.: Hurlbut and Lloyd, 1826.

Mims, Eleanor Elizabeth. "The Editors of the Edgefield *Advertiser*, Oldest Newspaper in South Carolina, 1863–1930." M.A. thesis, University of South Carolina, 1930.

Mims, Julian Landrum, Jr. "The Life and Politics of George Dionysius Tillman, 1826–1902." Unpublished manuscript, 1972, in possession of the author.

————. "Radical Reconstruction in Edgefield County, 1868–1877." M.A. thesis, University of South Carolina, 1969.

Mims, Mrs. Julian Landrum. *A History of the Edgefield Village Baptist Church.* N.p., n.d. (copies in Daniel Augustus Tompkins Library and South Carolina Department of Archives and History).

————. *History of the Women's Missionary Union, Edgefield Association, 1873–1914.* Edgefield: Edgefield *Advertiser*, n.d.

Mindel, Charles H., and Habenstein, Robert W. *Ethnic Families in America.* New York: Elsevier Press, 1976.

Mintz, Sidney W. "Melville J. Herskovits and Caribbean Studies: A Retrospective Tribute." *Carribbean Studies* 4 (July 1964): 42-51.

Mitchell, Broadus. *William Gregg: Factory Master of the Old South.* Chapel Hill: University of North Carolina Press, 1928.

Mitchell, Margaret. *Gone with the Wind.* New York: Macmillan, 1936.

Moragne, William C. *The Electoral Question: To the Citizens of Edgefield District.* Edgefield, S.C., 1859 (pamphlet in South Caroliniana Library).

Morgan, Edmund S. *American Slavery, American Freedom: The Ordeal of Colonial Virginia.* New York: Norton, 1975.

Morris, Samuel L. *The Autobiography of Reverend S. L. Morris.* N.p., n.d., in possession of the family.

Moynihan, Daniel Patrick. *The Negro Family: The Case for National Action.* Washington, D.C.: Office of Policy Planning and Research, United States Department of Labor, March 1965.

Mullins, Jack Simpson. "Lynching in South Carolina, 1890–1914." M.A. thesis, University of South Carolina, 1961.

Neale, Diane. "Benjamin Ryan Tillman: The South Carolina Years, 1847–1894." Ph.D. dissertation, Kent State University, 1976.

Nichols, Patricia C. "Black Women in the Rural South: Conservative and Innovative." *International Journal of the Sociology of Language* 17 (1978): 45–54.

Nicholson, Alfred W. *Brief Sketch of the Life and Labors of Rev. Alexander Bettis: Also an Account of the Founding and Development of the Bettis Academy.* Trenton, S.C.: published by the author, 1913.

Norton, Diane Cook. "A Methodological Study of the South Carolina Political Elite of the 1830s." Ph.D. dissertation, University of Pennsylvania, 1972.

Odum, Howard Washington. *Social and Mental Traits of the Negro.* New York: Columbia University Press, 1910.

Oliphant, Mary C. Simms. *The Simms History of South Carolina.* Columbia: *State* Company, 1932.

Olmsted, Frederick Law. *A Journey in the Back Country, 1853–1854.* Originally printed in 1860. Reprint, New York: G. P. Putnam & Sons, 1907.

Olsberg, Robert Nicholas. "A Government of Class and Race: William Henry Trescot and the South Carolina Chivalry, 1860–1865." Ph.D. dissertation, University of South Carolina, 1972.

O'Neall, John Belton. *Biographical Sketches of the Bench and Bar of South Carolina.* 2 vols. Charleston: S. G. Courtenay, 1859.

Ong, Walter J. *The Presence of the Word: Some Prolegomena for Cultural and Religious History.* New Haven: Yale University Press, 1967.

———. "Tribal Drum as Quintessence of Oral Culture." Unpublished paper, in possession of author.

Osofsky, Gilbert. *Harlem—The Making of a Ghetto: Negro New York, 1890–1930.* New York: Harper and Row, 1966.

Osterweis, Rollin G. *Romanticism and Nationalism in the Old South.* New Haven: Yale University Press, 1949.

Owens, Leslie. *This Species of Property: Slave Life and Culture in the Old South.* New York: Oxford University Press, 1976.

Owens, Loulie Latimer. *Banners in the Wind.* Columbia: Women's Missionary Union of South Carolina, 1950.

———. *Saints of Clay: The Shaping of South Carolina Baptists.* Columbia: R. L. Bryan, 1971.

Owsley, Frank L. Letter to Editor. *American Historical Review* 52 (July 1947): 845–49.

———. *Plain Folk of the Old South.* Baton Rouge: Louisiana State University Press, 1950.

———. Review of *Origins of Class Struggle in Louisiana* by Roger W. Shugg. *Journal of Southern History* 6 (Feb. 1940): 116–17.

———, and Owsley, Harriet C. "The Economic Basis of Society in the Late Ante-Bellum South." *Journal of Southern History* 6 (Jan. 1940): 26–40.

Page, Thomas Nelson. *The Negro: The Southerner's Problem*. New York: Scribner, 1904.

Page, Walter Hines. "The Last Hold of the Southern Bully." *Forum* 16 (Nov. 1893): 303–14.

Paludan, Phillip S. *Victims: A True Story of the Civil War*. Knoxville: University of Tennessee Press, 1981.

Pegues, A. W., and Witherspoon, Albert. *Our Baptist Ministers and Schools*. Springfield, Mass.: Wiley, 1982.

Petty, Julian J. *The Growth and Distribution of Population in South Carolina*. Bulletin no. 11, prepared for South Carolina State Planning Board. Columbia: State Council for Defense, Industrial Development Committee, July, 1943.

Phillips, Ulrich Bonnell. *American Negro Slavery: A Survey of the Supply, Employment and Control of Negro Labor as Determined by the Plantation Regime*. New York: Appleton, 1918.

———. *A History of Transportation in the Eastern Cotton Belt to 1860*. New York: Macmillan, 1913.

———. *Life and Labor in the Old South*. Boston: Little, Brown and Company, 1929.

Pickens, Francis W. *Speech of Hon. F. W. Pickens, Delivered before a Public Meeting of the People of the District, Held at Edgefield C.H., S.C., July 7, 1851*. Edgefield, S.C., 1851 (pamphlet in South Caroliniana Library).

Pleck, Elizabeth Hafkin. *Black Migration and Poverty: Boston 1865–1900*. New York: Academic Press, 1979.

———. "A Mother's Wages: Income Earning among Married Italian and Black Women, 1898–1911." In *The American Family in Socio-Historical Perspective*, 2d ed., edited by Michael Gordon. Pp. 490–510. New York: St. Martin's Press, 1978.

———. "The Two-Parent Household: Black Family Structure in Late Nineteenth-Century Boston." *Journal of Social History* 6 (Fall 1972): 1–31.

Ponton, Mungo Melanchton. *Life and Times of Henry M. Turner: The Antecedent and Preliminary History of the Life and Times of Bishop H. M. Turner. His Boyhood, Education and Public Career, and His Relation to His Associates, Colleagues and Contemporaries* (originally published in 1917). New York: Negro Universities Press, 1970.

Pope, Thomas H. *The History of Newberry County South Carolina*, vol. 1, *1749–1860*. Columbia: University of South Carolina Press, 1973.

Potter, David M. "American Women and the American Character." *Stetson University Bulletin* 62 (Jan. 1961): 1–22.

———. "The Enigma of the South." *Yale Review* 51 (Autumn 1961): 142–51.

Raboteau, Albert J. *Slave Religion: The "Invisible Institution" in the Ante-Bellum South*. Oxford: Oxford University Press, 1978.

Rainsford, Bettis Cantolou. "The Oldest House in Edgefield." N.p., n.d. (in possession of author).

Ramey, William. *Trial of the Booth and Toney Homicide in the Court of sessions for the County of Edgefield, at Edgefield Court House, S.C., Before the Hon. Thomas J. Mackey Containing the Testimony, the Argument, the Counsel, and the Charge of the Court . . . and Biographies of the Counsel engaged*. Edgefield, S.C.: N.p., 1880 (available in the Daniel Augustus Tompkins Library).

Ramsay, David. *Ramsay's History of South Carolina, from its First Settlement in 1670 to the Year 1808.* Newberry, S.C.: W. J. Duffie, printed by Walker, Evans, 1858.

Randolph, Peter. *Sketches of Slave Life: Or, Illustrations of the "Peculiar Institution"* (1855). Reprint, Philadelphia: Rhistoric Publications, 1969.

Randolph, Robert M. "James McBride Dabbs: Spokesman for Racial Liberalism." In *From the Old to the New South: Essays on the Transitional South,* edited by Walter J. Fraser, Jr., and Winfred B. Moore, Jr., pp. 253–64. Westport: Greenwood Press, 1981.

Ransom, Roger, and Sutch, Richard. "The Impact of the Civil War and of Emancipation on Southern Agriculture." *Explorations in Economic History* 12 (Jan. 1975): 1–28.

_____. *One Kind of Freedom: The Economic Consequences of Emancipation.* Cambridge: Cambridge University Press, 1977.

Rawick, George P., ed. *The American Slave: A Composite Autobiography.* 19 vols. and supplement series 1, 12 vols. Westport: Greenwood Press, 1972 and 1977.

Redfield, Robert. "Civilizations as Societal Structures? The Development of Community Studies." In *Human Nature and the Study of Society: The Papers of Robert Redfield,* edited by Margaret Park Redfield. Vol. 1, pp. 375–91. Chicago: University of Chicago Press, 1962.

_____. *The Little Community: Viewpoints of the Study of a Human Whole.* Chicago: University of Chicago Press, 1955.

Reiff, Janice L.; Dahlin, Michel R.; and Smith, Daniel Scott. "Rural Push and Urban Pull: Work and Family Experiences of Older Black Women in Southern Cities, 1880–1900." In *The Urban Experience of Afro-American Women: A Social History,* edited by Sharon Hurley. Boston: G. H. Hall, forthcoming.

Reinders, Robert C. "Slavery in New Orleans in the Decade before the Civil War." *Mid-America* 44 (Oct. 1962): 211–21.

Report of the Trial of Martin Posey for the Murder of His Wife. N.p., 1850 (pamphlet in the South Caroliniana Library).

Reports of the President of the Graniteville Manufacturing Co. Augusta, Ga.: M. Hill, various years (available in the South Caroliniana Library and at the Graniteville Manufacturing Company).

Reynolds, John Schreiner. *Reconstruction in South Carolina, 1865–1877.* Columbia: State Printing, 1905.

Richter, William L. "Slavery in Baton Rouge, 1820–60." *Louisiana History* 10 (Spring 1969): 125–45.

Ripley, C. Peter. "The Black Family in Transition: Louisiana, 1860–1865." *Journal of Southern History* 41 (Aug. 1975): 369–80.

Robertson, Ben. *Red Hills and Cotton: An Upcountry Memory.* First published 1942. Reprint, Columbia: University of South Carolina Press, 1960.

Rogers, Tommy W. "The Great Population Exodus from South Carolina, 1850–1860." *South Carolina Historical Magazine* 68 (Jan. 1968): 14–21.

Rose, Arnold. *The Negro in America* (condensed version of Gunnar Myrdal, *An American Dilemma*). New York: Harper and Row, 1944.

Rose, Willie Lee, ed. *A Documentary History of Slavery in North America.* New York: Oxford University Press, 1976.

_____. Review of *First Freedom*, by Peter Kolchin. *Journal of Southern History* 39 (Nov. 1973): 608–9.

_____. *Rehearsal for Reconstruction: The Port Royal Experiment*. New York: Oxford University Press, 1964.

Rosengarten, Theodore. *All God's Dangers: The Life of Nate Shaw*. New York: Random House, 1974.

Rosson, Elizabeth Murphy, ed. *History of North Augusta, South Carolina*. North Augusta: North Augusta Historical Society, 1981.

Roston, R. D. *Major Perry: The Sleeping Preacher, 1831–1925*. Trenton, S.C.: privately printed, 1925.

Rubin, Louis D., Jr., and Kilpatrick, James Jackson, eds. *The Lasting South: Fourteen Southerners Look at Their Home*. Chicago: Regnery, 1957.

Ruoff, John Carl. "Southern Womanhood, 1865–1920: An Intellectual and Cultural Study." Ph.D. dissertation, University of Illinois at Urbana-Champaign, 1976.

_____. "Frivolity to Consumption: Or, Southern Womanhood in Antebellum Literature." *Civil War History* 18 (Sept. 1972): 213–29.

Sala, George. *America Revisted*. . . . 6th ed., 2 vols. London: Vizetelly, 1886.

Salley, A. S., Jr. "The Methods of Raising Taxes in South Carolina Prior to 1868." Bulletins of the Historical Commission of South Carolina, no. F, pp. 1–13. Columbia: *State* Company, 1925.

Saluda County Tricentennial Commission. *Saluda County in Scene and Story*. Columbia: R. L. Bryan, 1970.

Saluda Standard Sentinel and History Book Committee. *The Family History of Saluda County, 1895–1980: Saluda, South Carolina*. Clinton, S.C.: Intercollegiate Press, 1980.

Sanderson, Warren C. "Herbert Gutman's *The Black Family in Slavery and Freedom, 1750–1925*: A Cliometric Reconsideration." *Social Science History* 3 (Oct. 1979): 66–85.

Schaper, William A. *Sectionalism and Representation in South Carolina*. In *Annual Report of the American Historical Association for the Year 1900*. 2 vols., 1: 237–463. Washington, D.C., 1901.

Schultz, Harold S. *Nationalism and Sectionalism in South Carolina, 1852–1860*. Durham: Duke University Press, 1950.

Schultz, Theodore W., ed. *Economics of the Family*. Chicago: University of Chicago Press, 1974.

Scott, Anne Firor. *The Southern Lady: From Pedestal to Politics, 1830–1939*. Chicago: University of Chicago Press, 1970.

_____. "Women's Perspective on the Patriarchy in the 1850s." *Journal of American History* 61 (June 1974): 52–64.

Seabrook, Whitemarsh B. *Essay on the Management of Slaves*. Charleston: Miller and Brown, 1844.

Seip, Terry L. "Slaves and Free Negroes in Alexandria, 1850–60." *Louisiana History* 10 (Spring 1969): 147–65.

Sellers, James Benson. *Slavery in Alabama*. University: University of Alabama Press, 1950.

Senese, Donald Joseph. "Legal Thought in South Carolina, 1800–1860." Ph.D. dissertation, University of South Carolina, 1970.

Shifflett, Crandall A. "The Household Composition of Rural Black Families: Louisa County, Virginia, 1880." *Journal of Interdisciplinary History* 6 (Autumn 1975): 235–60.
_____. *Patronage and Poverty in the Tobacco South: Louisa County, Virginia, 1860–1900*. Knoxville: University of Tennessee Press, 1982.
Shimkin, Demitri B.; Shimkin, Edith M.; and Frate, Dennis A., eds. *The Extended Family in Black Societies*. The Hague: Mouton, 1978.
Shlomowitz, Ralph. "The Squad System on Postbellum Cotton Plantations." In *Towards a New South? Studies in Post–Civil War Southern Communities*, edited by Orville Vernon Burton and Robert C. McMath, Jr. Pp. 265–80. Westport: Greenwood Press, 1980.
_____. "The Transition from Slave to Freedman: Labor Arrangements in Southern Agriculture, 1865–1870." Ph.D. dissertation, University of Chicago, 1978.
Shugg, Roger W. *Origins of Class Struggle in Louisiana: A Social History of White Farmers and Laborers during Slavery and After, 1840–1875*. Baton Rouge: Louisiana State University Press, 1939.
Sides, Sudie Duncan. "Women and Slaves: An Interpretation Based on the Writings of Southern Women." Ph.D. dissertation, University of North Carolina at Chapel Hill, 1969.
_____. "Southern Women and Slavery." *History Today* 20 (Jan. 1970): 54–60.
Simkins, Arthur. *An Address Before the State Agricultural Society of South Carolina at its First Anniversay Meeting, held during the Month of November, 1855, at Columbia, S.C.* Edgefield, S.C.: printed at the *Advertiser* office, 1855 (pamphlet in the South Caroliniana Library).
Simkins, Boothe, et al. "The Life of Paris Simkins." Unpublished paper, 1931 (copy in possession of family).
Simkins, Francis Butler. "Ben Tillman's View of the Negro." *Journal of Southern History* 3 (May 1937): 161–74.
_____. *A History of the South*. 3d ed. New York: Knopf, 1963.
_____. *Pitchfork Ben Tillman: South Carolinian*. Baton Rouge: Louisiana State University Press, 1944.
_____. "The Problems of South Carolina Agriculture after the Civil War." *North Carolina Historical Review* 7 (Jan. 1930): 46–57.
_____. "Race Legislation in South Carolina since 1865." *South Atlantic Quarterly* 20 (Jan.–Apr. 1921): 61–71, 165–77.
_____. "The Rising Tide of Faith." In *The Lasting South: Fourteen Southerners Look at Their Home*, edited by Louis D. Rubin, Jr., and James Jackson Kilpatrick. Pp. 84–103. Chicago: Regnery, 1957.
_____. "The Simkins Family." N.d. (typescript in the South Caroliniana Library).
_____. "The Solution of the Post-Bellum Agricultural Problems in South Carolina." *North Carolina Historical Review* 7 (Apr. 1930): 192–219.
_____. *The Tillman Movement in South Carolina*. Durham: Duke University Press, 1926.
_____, and Patton, James Welch. *The Women of the Confederacy*. Richmond: Garrett and Massie, 1930.
_____, and Woody, Robert Hilliard. *South Carolina during Reconstruction*. Chapel Hill: University of North Carolina Press, 1932.

Simpson, George Lee. *The Cokers of Carolina*. Chapel Hill: University of North Carolina Press, 1956

Singletary, Otis A. *Negro Militia and Reconstruction*. Austin: University of Texas Press, 1957.

A Sketch of the Life and Services of Francis W. Pickens of South Carolina. N.p., n.d. (copy in library of Bruce Ezell, Ninety Six, S.C.).

Smith, Alfred Glaze, Jr. *Economic Readjustment of an Old Cotton State: South Carolina, 1820–1860*. Columbia: University of South Carolina Press, 1958.

Smith, Daniel Blake. *Inside the Great House: Planter Family Life in Eighteenth-Century Chesapeake Society*. Ithaca: Cornell University Press, 1980.

Smith, Daniel Scott. "Life Course, Norms, and the Family System of Older Americans in 1900." *Journal of Family History* 3 (Fall 1979): 285–98.

―――; Dahlin, Michel; and Friedberger, Mark. "The Family Structure of the Older Black Population in the American South in 1880 and 1900." *Sociology and Social Research* 63 (Apr. 1979): 544–65.

Smith, Harry Worcester. *Life and Sport in Aiken and Those Who Made It*. New York: Derrydale Press, 1935.

Smith, Septima Chappell. "The Development and History of Some Negro Churches in South Carolina." M.A. thesis, University of South Carolina, 1942.

Smith, Thomas. "Reconstructing Occupational Structures: The Case of the Ambiguous Artisans." *Historical Methods Newsletter* 8 (June 1975): 134–46.

Soltow, Lee. *Men and Wealth in the United States, 1850–1870*. New Haven: Yale University Press, 1975.

―――. *Patterns of Wealthholding in Wisconsin since 1850*. Madison: University of Wisconsin Press, 1971.

Somers, Robert. *The Southern States since the War, 1870–1*. New York: Macmillan, 1871.

Sorkin, Alan L. "On the Occupational Status of Women, 1870–1970." *American Journal of Economics and Sociology* 32 (July 1973): 235–43.

Spear, Allan H. *Black Chicago: The Making of a Negro Ghetto, 1890–1920*. Chicago: University of Chicago Press, 1967.

Stampp, Kenneth. *The Peculiar Institution: Slavery in the Antebellum South*. New York: Knopf, 1956.

Staples, Robert. "Towards a Sociology of the Black Family: A Theoretical and Methological Assessment." *Journal of Marriage and the Family* 33 (Feb. 1971): 119–38.

Steadman, Joseph Earle, Sr. *A Historical Sketch of the Emory Methodist Church in Saluda County, S.C.* Edgefield: Edgefield *Advertiser*, 1965.

―――. *A History of the Spann Family*. N.p., n.d.

Steckel, Richard H. "Antebellum Southern White Fertility: A Demographic and Economic Analysis." *Journal of Economic History* 40 (June 1980): 331–50.

―――. "Miscegenation and the American Slave Schedules." *Journal of Interdisciplinary History* 11 (Autumn 1980): 251–64.

Sterkx, Herbert E. *The Free Negro in Antebellum Louisiana*. Rutherford, N.J.: Fairleigh Dickinson University Press, 1972.

―――. *Partners in Rebellion: Alabama Women in the Civil War*. Rutherford, N.J.:

Fairleigh Dickinson University Press, 1970.

Stirling, James. *Letters from the Slave States*. London: Parker, 1857.

Stokes, Thomas L. *The Savannah*. New York: Rinehart, 1951.

Stover, John. *The Railroads of the South, 1865–1900: A Study in Finance and Control*. Chapel Hill: University of North Carolina Press, 1955.

Stowe, Harriet Beecher. *Uncle Tom's Cabin: or Life Among the Lowly*. First published as a serial in *National Era*, 1851–52. New York: Washington Square Press, 1963.

Swierenga, Robert P. "Agriculture and Rural Life: The New Rural History." In *Ordinary People and Everyday Life: Perspectives on the New Social History*, edited by James B. Gardner and George Rollie Adams. Pp. 91–113. Nashville: Association for State and Local History, 1983.

_____. "Rural History: A Complement to Urban History." *Minnesota Social History Project Newsletter* 1 (Jan. 1979): 1–14.

_____. "Towards the 'New Rural History': A Review Essay." *Historical Methods Newsletter* 6 (June 1973): 111–22.

Sydnor, Charles. "The Free Negro in Mississippi before the Civil War." *American Historical Review* 32 (July 1927): 769–88.

Takaki, Ronald. "The Movement to Reopen the Slave Trade in South Carolina." *South Carolina Historical Magazine* 66 (Jan. 1965): 38–54.

Tang, Anthony M. *Economic Development in the Southern Piedmont, 1860–1950: Its Impact on Agriculture*. Chapel Hill: University of North Carolina Press, 1958.

Taylor, J. H. "Manufactures in South Carolina." *DeBow's Review*, new series, 2 (Jan. 1850): 24–29.

Taylor, Rosser H. "Hamburg: An Experiment in Town Promotion." *North Carolina Historical Review* 11 (Jan. 1934): 20–38.

Taylor, William R. *Cavalier and Yankee: The Old South and American National Character*. New York: George Braziller, 1961.

Terrill, Tom. "Eager Hands: Labor for Southern Textiles, 1850–1860." *Journal of Economic History* 36 (Mar. 1976): 84–99.

_____. "Murder in Graniteville." In *Class, Conflict, and Consensus: Antebellum Southern Communities*, edited by Orville Vernon Burton and Robert C. McMath, Jr. Pp. 193–222. Westport: Greenwood Press, 1982.

Thernstrom, Stephen. *The Other Bostonians and Progress in the American Metropolis: 1880–1970*. Cambridge: Harvard University Press, 1973.

Thomas, Albert S. *A Historical Account of the Episcopal Church in South Carolina, 1820–1957: Being a Continuation of Dalcho's Account, 1670–1820*. Columbia: R. C. Bryan, 1957.

Thomas, Emory M. *The Confederacy as a Revolutionary Experience*. Englewood Cliffs: Prentice-Hall, 1971.

_____. *The Confederate Nation, 1861–1865*. New York: Harper and Row, 1979.

Thomas, Latta R. *Biblical Faith and the Black American*. Valley Forge: Judson Press, 1976.

Thomason, John Furman. *The Foundations of the Public Schools of South Carolina*. Columbia: *State* Company, 1925.

Thompson, Robert Farris. "African Influence on the Art of the United States." In

Black Studies in the University: A Symposium, edited by Armstead L. Robinson, Craig C. Foster, Donald H. Ogilvie. Pp. 122–70. New Haven: Yale University Press, 1969.

Thornton, J. Mills, III. *Politics and Power in a Slave Society: Alabama, 1800–1860*. Baton Rouge: Louisiana State University Press, 1978.

Thorpe, Earl E. *Eros and Freedom in Southern Life and Thought*. Durham: published by author, 1967.

Tillman, Benjamin R. "The Struggles of 1876: How South Carolina Was Delivered from Carpet-Bag and Negro Rule." Speech at the Red-Shirt Reunion at Anderson, S.C., 1909 (copy in South Caroliniana Library).

———. "Childhood Days." N.p., n.d. (copy in South Caroliniana Library).

Tindall, George B. "The South Carolina Constitutional Convention of 1895." M.A. thesis, University of North Carolina, 1948.

———. *South Carolina Negroes, 1877–1900*. Columbia: University of South Carolina Press, 1952.

Tompkins, Daniel Augustus, and Tompkins, Arthur Smyly. *Company K, The Fourteenth South Carolina Volunteers*. Charlotte: published by the authors, 1897.

Trezevant, John Timothee. *The Trezevant Family in the United States*. . . . Columbia: *State* Company, 1914.

Tucker, Robert Cinnamond. "James Henry Hammond: South Carolinian." Ph.D. dissertation, University of North Carolina, 1958.

Underwood, Rev. J. L. *The Women of the Confederacy*. . . . New York: Neale Publishing, 1905.

Vance, Rupert B. "Regional Family Patterns: The Southern Family." *American Journal of Sociology* 53 (May 1948): 426–29.

Van Deburg, William L. *The Slave Drivers: Black Agricultural Labor Supervisors in the Antebellum South*. Westport: Greenwood Press, 1979.

Vickery, William Edward. "The Economics of the Negro Migration, 1900–1960." Ph.D. dissertation, University of Chicago, 1969.

Vlach, Michael John. *The Afro-American Tradition in Decorative Arts*. Cleveland: Cleveland Museum of Art, 1978.

Wade, John Donald. "Old Wine in a New Bottle." *Virginia Quarterly Review* 11 (Apr. 1935): 239–52.

Wade, Richard. *Slavery in the Cities: The South, 1820–1860*. New York: Oxford University Press, 1964.

Wallace, David D. *The History of South Carolina*. 4 vols. New York: American Historical Society, 1934.

———. "A Hundred Years of William Gregg and Graniteville." Unpublished manuscript, Spartanburg, S.C., 1946 (copy at Graniteville Manufacturing Company).

———. *South Carolina: A Short History, 1520–1948*. Chapel Hill: University of North Carolina Press, 1951.

Waring, Joseph Ioor. *A History of Medicine in South Carolina, 1670–1825*. Columbia: R. L. Bryan, 1964.

———. *A History of Medicine in South Carolina, 1825–1900*. Columbia: R. L. Bryan, 1967.

Warren, Robert Penn. "The Briar Patch." In *Twelve Southerners: I'll Take My Stand:*

The South and the Agrarian Tradition, edited by John Crowe Ransom. Pp. 246–64. New York: Harper, 1930.

Watson, Margaret. *Greenwood County Sketches: Old Roads and Early Families.* Greenwood, S.C.: Attic Press, 1970.

Watson, Mrs. Magnard Spigener, and Calvin, Mrs. Fred. *History of Ridge Spring.* Ridge Spring: privately published, 1982.

Watson, Thomas Edward. *Bethany: A Story of the Old South.* New York: Appleton, 1904.

Wayne, Michael. *The Reshaping of Plantation Society: The Natchez District, 1860–1880.* Baton Rouge: Louisiana State University Press, 1983.

Weaver, Herbert. *Mississippi Farmers, 1850–1860.* Nashville: Vanderbilt University Press, 1945.

Weems, Mason Locke. *The Devil in Petticoats, or God's Revenge Against Husband Killing.* Edgefield, S.C.: Edgefield *Advertiser* Press, 1878.

Weier, Robert M. "The Writing of South Carolina History: The Early National Period." Unpublished paper in possession of author.

Weld, Theodore D. *American Slavery, As It Is: Testimony of a Thousand Witnesses.* New York: American Anti-Slavery Society, 1839.

_____. *Slavery and the Internal Slave Trade in the United States* (1841). Reprint, New York: Arno Press, 1969.

Welty, Eudora. *The Eye of the Story: Selected Essays and Reviews.* New York: Random House, 1978.

Werner, Randolph Dennis. "Hegemony and Conflict: The Political Economy of a Southern Region, Augusta, Georgia, 1865–1895." Ph.D. dissertation, University of Virginia, 1977.

Whatley, William. "A History of the Textile Development of Augusta, Georgia, 1865–1883." M.A. thesis, University of South Carolina, 1964.

White, Ellington. "The View from the Window." In *The Lasting South: Fourteen Southerners Look at Their Home*, edited by Louis D. Rubin, Jr., and James Jackson Kilpatrick. Pp. 163–71. Chicago: Regnery, 1957.

Wiener, Jonathan M. "Class Structure and Economic Development in the American South, 1865–1955." Including "Comments" by Robert Higgs and Harold D. Woodman and Wiener's "Reply," all in "*AHR* Forum." *American Historical Review* 84 (Oct. 1979): 970–1006.

_____. "Female Planters and Planters' Wives in Civil War and Reconstruction: Alabama, 1850–1870." *Alabama Review* 30 (Apr. 1977): 135–49.

_____. *Social Origins of the New South: Alabama, 1860–1885.* Baton Rouge: Louisiana State University Press, 1978.

Wigfall, Arthur. *A Sermon upon Duelling.* Charleston, 1856 (available in the South Caroliniana Library).

Wikramanayake, Ivy Marina. "The Free Negro in Antebellum South Carolina." Ph.D. dissertation, University of Wisconsin, 1966.

_____. *A World in Shadow: The Free Black in Antebellum South Carolina.* Columbia: University of South Carolina Press, 1973.

Wiley, Bell Irvin. *Confederate Women.* Westport: Greenwood Press, 1975.

Williams, Alfred B. *The Liberian Exodus: An Account of Voyage of the First Emi-*

grants in the Bark "Azor," and their Reception at Monrovia: With a Description of Liberia—Its Customs and Civilization, Romances and Prospects. Charleston: *News and Courier*, 1878 (in the South Caroliniana Library).

Williams, Jack Kenny. "The Code of Honor in Ante-Bellum South Carolina." *South Carolina Historical Magazine* 54 (1953): 113–28.

————. *Vogues in Villainy: Crime and Retribution in Antebellum South Carolina.* Columbia: University of South Carolina Press, 1959.

Williamson, Gustavus. "Cotton Manufacturing in South Carolina, 1865–1892." Ph.D. dissertation, Johns Hopkins University, 1954.

Williamson, Joel R. *New People: Miscegenation and Mulattoes in the United States.* New York: Free Press, 1980.

————. *After Slavery: The Negro in South Carolina during Reconstruction, 1861–1877.* Chapel Hill: University of North Carolina Press, 1965.

Wilson, Clyde N., ed. *The Papers of John C. Calhoun.* Vol. 14. Columbia: University of South Carolina Press, 1981.

Wilson, John Lyde. *The Code of Honor.* Charleston, 1838 (in the South Caroliniana Library).

Wilson, Theodore Brantner. *The Black Codes of the South.* University: University of Alabama Press, 1965.

Wiltse, Charles Maurice. *John C. Calhoun.* 3 vols. Indianapolis: Bobbs-Merrill, 1944, 1951.

Winston, George Tayloe. *A Builder of the New South: Being the Story of the Life Work of Daniel Augustus Tompkins.* Garden City, N.Y.: Doubleday, 1920.

Winter, Lovick P. "Letters to *The Outlook*: The Negro Question Again, III." *Outlook* 84 (1 Dec. 1906): 845.

Wolff, Alfred Young, Jr. "The South and the American Imagination: Mythical Views of the Old South, 1865–1900" Ph.D. dissertation, University of Virginia, 1971.

Wood, Forrest G. *Black Scare: The Racist Response to Emancipation and Reconstruction.* Berkeley: University of California Press, 1968.

Woodman, Harold D. *King Cotton and His Retainers: Financing and Marketing the Cotton Crop of the South, 1800–1925.* Lexington: University of Kentucky Press, 1968.

————. "Sequel to Slavery: The New History Views the Postbellum South." *Journal of Southern History* 43 (Nov. 1977): 523–54.

Woodmason, Charles. *The Carolina Backcountry on the Eve of the Revolution.* Edited by Richard J. Hooker. Chapel Hill: University of North Carolina Press, 1953.

Woodson, Agatha Abney. *Life of Joseph Abney.* Typescript, 1914 (copy in Daniel Augustus Tompkins Library).

Woodson, Carter Goodwin. *A Century of Negro Migration.* Washington: Association for the Study of Negro Life and History, 1918.

————. *Free Negro Heads of Families in the United States in 1830.* Washington, D.C.: Association for the Study of Negro Life and History, 1925.

————. Review of *Free Negro Labor and Property Holding in Virginia* by Luther Porter Jackson. *American Historical Review* 48 (July 1943): 812.

————. *Free Negro Owners of Slaves in the United States in 1830, Together with Absentee Ownership of Slaves in the United States in 1830.* Washington, D.C.: Association for the Study of Negro Life and History, 1924.

————. *The History of the Negro Church*. Washington, D.C.: Associated Publishers, 1921 (2d ed., 1945).

Woodson, Hortense. *Charles Mays and His Descendants Who Settled at Mays Cross Roads in Old Edgefield County*. Edgefield: Edgefield Advertiser, 1956.

————. "Edgefield's German Palatines," in possession of the author.

————. *Giant in the Land: A Biography of William Bullein Johnson, First President of the Southern Baptist Convention*. Nashville: Broadman Press, 1950.

————. *Peter Ouzts I and His Descendants*. Edgefield: Edgefield *Advertiser*, 1949.

————, and Church Historians. *History of Edgefield Baptist Association, 1807–1957*. Edgefield: Edgefield *Advertiser*, 1957.

Woodward, C. Vann. *The Burden of Southern History*. 2d ed., rev. Baton Rouge: Louisiana State University Press, 1968.

————. "History from Slave Sources: A Review Article." *American Historical Review* 79 (Apr. 1974): 470–81.

————. *Origins of the New South, 1877–1913*. Baton Rouge: Louisiana State University Press, 1959.

————. "The Primal Code." *New York Review of Books*, 18 Nov. 1982, pp. 26–28.

————. *The Strange Career of Jim Crow*. 2d ed., rev. New York: Oxford University Press, 1966.

Woodward, William E. *The Gift of Life: An Autobiography*. New York: Dutton, 1947.

————. *The Way Our People Lived: An Intimate American History*. New York: Dutton, 1944.

Wooster, Ralph. *The People in Power: Courthouse and Statehouse in the Lower South, 1850–1860*. Knoxville: University of Tennessee Press, 1969.

Wright, Mrs. D. Giraud [Louise Wigfall Wright]. *A Southern Girl in '61: The War-Time Memories of a Confederate Senator's Daughter*. New York: Doubleday, 1905.

Wright, Gavin. "Cheap Labor and Southern Textiles before 1880." Unpublished paper, 1978, in possession of the author.

————. " 'Economic Democracy' and the Concentration of Agricultural Wealth in the Cotton South, 1850–1860." *Agricultural History* 44 (Jan. 1970): 63–94.

————. "Note on the Manuscript Census Samples Used in These Studies." *Agricultural History* 44 (Jan. 1970): 95–99.

————. *The Political Economy of the Cotton South: Households, Markets, and Wealth in the Nineteenth Century*. New York: Norton, 1978.

Wright, Louis B. *Barefoot in Arcadia: Memories of a More Innocent Era*. Columbia: University of South Carolina Press, 1972.

Wyatt-Brown, Bertram. "Community, Class, and Snopesian Crime: Local Justice in the Old South." In *Class, Conflict and Consensus: Antebellum Southern Community Studies*, edited by Orville Vernon Burton and Robert C. McMath, Jr. Pp. 173–207. Westport: Greenwood Press, 1982.

————. "The Ideal Typology and Antebellum Southern History: A Testing of a New Approach." *Societas* 5 (Winter 1975): 1–29.

————. *Southern Honor: Ethics and Behavior in the Old South*. New York: Oxford University Press, 1982.

Yale, Andrew. "The Travelers: From Ireland to South Carolina" *Southern Exposure* 10 (July–Aug. 1982): 67–71.

Yans-McLaughlin, Virginia. *Family and Community: Italian Immigrants in Buffalo, 1880–1930.* Ithaca: Cornell University Press, 1977.

Yetman, Norman R. "The Background of the Slave Narrative Collection." *American Quarterly* 19, no. 3 (Fall 1967): 534–53.

Index